THE WORLD'S GREATE

26TH ANNUAL

# KNIVES 2006

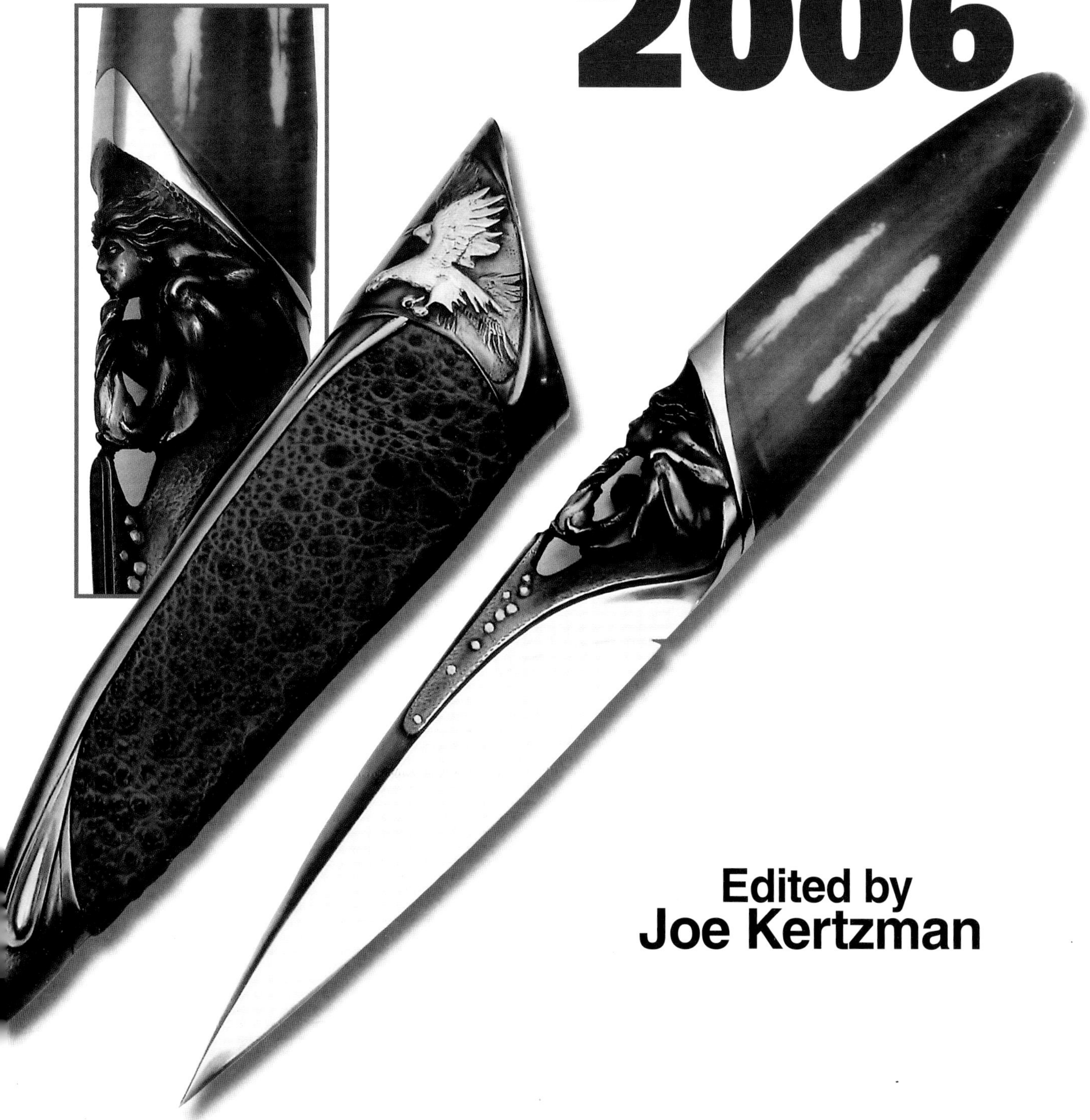

Edited by
Joe Kertzman

## The Cover Knives

A book could be written about the Searles bowie reproduction at the far left of the front cover. Knifemaker T.R. Overeynder fashioned the handsome piece, which features a checkered African blackwood handle, a BG-42 blade, a blued O-1 guard and pommel, and a stainless steel sheath lined with stingray skin. The guard, pommel and sheath feature engraving and gold inlay by Tim George. The only folder of the group is Steve Dunn's work and showcases more gold inlay and engraving, a 4-inch damascus blade and a gold-lip-pearl handle. There is a long-stemmed rose engraved on the escutcheon plate, just in case you need something to impress your girl. Get a load of the star in the center—Ron Newton's Sheriff's Knife—wearing a steel-and-meteorite damascus blade, and an ebony handle parading a pattern of silver pins and a mother-of-pearl star inlay. At right is a Gene Baskett fixed blade in the Tlingit Indian style, complete with a carved raven-head pommel, a walrus-ivory handle and a 5-inch blade. The knife features some of the coolest scrimshaw, done by Gary "Garbo" Williams, this side of Anchorage, including a northern Indian in traditional Alaskan garb, and a raven peeking over his shoulder. The whole piece is stunning, as are all the knives on the cover and inside the pages of KNIVES 2006.



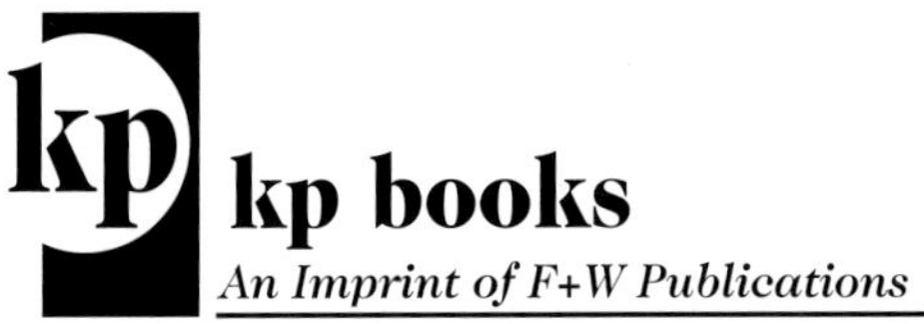


**700 East State Street • Iola, WI 54990-0001**
**715-445-2214 • 888-457-2873**

Our toll-free number to place an order or obtain a free catalog is (800) 258-0929.



Library of Congress Catalog Number: 2005906838

ISBN: 0-89689-149-6

Designed by Kara Grundman and Patsy Howell

Edited by Ken Ramage

Printed in the United States of America

# Introduction

There are a lot worse kinds of junkies to be. Let's start with junk-food junkies, television junkies, radio-talk-show junkies, Internet junkies and sports junkies. In all likelihood, there's a bit of at least one of those groups in all of us. Then there are those whose stories are varied and sad—the junkies everyone thinks about when discussing "junkies." Such folks have fallen victim to the worst kinds of habits and addictions.

Being a shop junkie doesn't seem so bad, does it?

Shop junkies—now there's an interesting group of people. Lazy? No. Unmotivated? Not hardly. Dull? They're definitely not dull. Shop junkies, and especially knife-shop junkies, are tempted by irresistible urges to be in cold, damp, dust-choked workshops, pole buildings, garages and basements, feverishly grinding, cutting, buffing and honing steel. They break out in cold sweats upon completion of month-long projects. Their teeth chatter, they talk incessantly (to themselves), drink Coca-Cola and coffee, twitch from long days and longer nights of perpetually going through the motions, filing the spines of blades, hand-rubbing steel, profiling, pounding, heating and cooling. Periods of heavy weight loss and equally damaging weight gain are followed by physical exhaustion and eventual deep slumber, and even then, rest eludes them. They dream of bold bolsters, upswept blades, gargantuan guards, tricked-out locking mechanisms, daring designs, fresh patterns and hot steel. There's always hot steel. They can't get enough of it. They wake with red eyes and immediately reach for a forge hammer. Another day of prettying up cold, hard, rust-resistant and bulletproof knife materials awaits them.

The thing about shop junkies, though, is that a vast majority of them eventually succeed in bringing beauty into the world. They sacrifice their own well being for the good of mankind (or at least for the good of knife enthusiasts who make up a minute percentage of the human race).

And that's where Knives 2006 comes into the picture. It is time to shine a bright spotlight on the knives some of the most skilled shop junkies—those in the throes of steel addiction—output daily for the consumption of equally hooked collectors, dealers and fans. Ah, the fans. We need more knife fans in the world. Vast distribution of this book should help bring knives to the forefront, or at least the back door, of society. If we could just get a handful of "knife unawares" to pick up the book and open it to any page—it doesn't even matter which page—they'd be instant converts. The knives are that gosh-darn beautiful. Years of perspiration, sleeplessness and physical debilitation have paid off handsomely.

In the "Trends" section of this book, you'll see "Black-Lip and Abalone Blades," those outfitted with pink, green, black, blue, red, orange and yellow handles that only nature, and a few knifemakers, could produce. There will be knives donned in "Full Frontier Fashion," looking as though they just leaped off the big screen of a Western movie. Other edged pieces have "Burl-esque" handles, including wood grains even Paul Bunyan wouldn't have fathomed. There are "True Tacticals" "Bird, Trout and Bambi Blades," "Fast-Track Folders," "Customary Pocketknives" and "Hordes of Swords."

The "State of the Art" and "Factory Trends" chapters uncover hundreds of edged *objets d'art*, just waiting for eager readers to look at, admire and pore over. Feature articles penned by some of the world's most renowned knife writers and an extensive directory of every custom knifemaker in the world, including complete contact information, specialties, technical information, prices and remarks, round out the Knives 2006 offerings. Be warned, knife collecting, and even coveting, can be as addictive as being a knife-shop junkie, and it can be just as hard to kick the habit. Try to show some self-restraint.

*Joe Kertzman*

# Contents

## FACTORY TRENDS



## DIRECTORY



# 2006 WOODEN SWORD AWARD

It's an amazing feat for a man who's been making knives on a part-time basis since 1990. Count them up—that's only 15 years, folks, and Takeshi Matsusaki has progressed to the level of building this remarkable 24-blade office knife. Measuring 3-1/4 inches closed, it sports no less than seven file-worked liners between which two dozen implements, most of them edged, slide silently when the multi-blade folder is closed. The white pearl is carved in a classic, shapely style exhibiting smooth lines and rounded corners. The pin pattern around the escutcheon plate is exquisite and the overall workmanship is spotless. Matsusaki specializes in working and collector-grade front-lock and slip-joint folders, including Sheffield-style pieces. His prices are $250-$1,000, some up to $8,000, for each knife and, understandably, this 24-blade beauty would be in the upper end. For one eye-opening folder with many moving parts, Takeshi Matsusaki lands the coveted 2006 Wooden Sword Award.

# Knives and "A Century Of Progress"

## *Check out the world-class folding knives that commemorated the 1933 Chicago World's Fair*

*By Richard D. White*

With lavishness unknown even today, the 1933 Chicago World's Fair managed to capture the hearts and imaginations of throngs of people across our great nation. With fairgrounds spread along its Lake Michigan shoreline, the city of Chicago hosted the extravaganza, adopting as its motto "A Century of Progress"—a theme appropriately chosen to celebrate Chicago's 100th anniversary of being incorporated as a town.

Fair organizers chose "light" and "color" as overall artistic elements, specifically using art deco architectural style to tie the major exhibits together. The commemorative knives resulting from the fair illustrate the stylized, art deco theme. World's Fair knives featuring engraving do not depict foreign buildings that were part of the fair, but only showcase domestic buildings and exhibits built by the federal government or the city of Chicago.

Hibbard Spencer Bartlett & Co., located in Chicago, unveiled a noteworthy souvenir knife that has become collectible in its own right. Hibbard Spencer Bartlett, a knife company that would later lay the foundation for the giant Tru-Value Hardware conglomerate, made a tip-bolster, celluloid-handle pocketknife advertising the 1933 Chicago World's Fair. On one side of the "cracked-ice"-celluloid-handle knife is engraved "World's Fair Chicago 1933," while on the reverse is the etching "Hib-

**Shown beside a postcard aerial view of the 1933 Chicago World's Fair, the souvenir knife is engraved with a graphic of the Federal Building, one of the special structures constructed for the fair. The art deco styling evident at the World's Fair is clearly evident in the pocketknife engraving. The reverse of the Federal Building souvenir knife shows a graphic of the Hall of Science Building at the World's Fair. This building housed the latest in scientific developments and exhibits. The tang stamp on the master blade reads "N. Shure, Chicago," the maker of the pocketknife.** *(the photo of the postcard courtesy of the Chicago Historical Society)*

*All photos by Richard D. White*

bard Spencer Bartlett & Co."

## A Fair But Oft-Overlooked Knife

Hibbard Spencer Bartlett also produced various celluloid-handle knives engraved with "A Century of Progress." Because the motto was usually engraved on knives with dark celluloid grips, potential collectors often overlook the lettering and, thus, the edged collectibles. Like other brass-handle knives engraved with images of the impressive fair buildings, the celluloid advertising knives are unique and can often be found in remarkable condition. Logically, the engraving also accurately dates the knives to 1933.

With the rare opportunity to showcase their newest technologies to an enormous population gathered together in one location, many domestic corporations jumped on the World's Fair bandwagon. Among the well-known exhibitors were Ford Motor Co.; Chrysler; Otis Elevator Co. (which built the famous sky ride); Crane (bath fixtures); Coca-Cola; Firestone (tires); International Harvester; Greyhound; Kraft Foods; General Motors; Armour and Co. (meats); Maxwell House Coffee; Goodyear; Sears, Roebuck and Co.; Nash (automobiles); Western Union; Owens Glass Co.; Swift & Co. (meats); Texaco (Havoline oil products); Sinclair Oil; and Wilson and Co. (meats).

As a way of enticing visitors into the buildings, the companies built lavish edifices complete with fountains, colored lighting and massive amounts of glass in all forms.

**Lying on a reproduction of the official poster of the 1933 Chicago World's Fair is a Hibbard Spencer Bartlett & Co. souvenir pocketknife handled in light-colored "cracked ice" celluloid, an ideal background material for the etchings "Worlds Fair Chicago 1933" and "Hibbard Spencer Bartlett & Co."** *(the poster reproduction courtesy of the Chicago Historical Society)*

## N. Shure Knives Ensure A Fair Collection

The Chicago World's Fair commissioned a local knife manufacturer, the N. Shure Co., headquartered at 200 Madison Avenue in downtown Chicago, to design and produce a series of handsome pocketknives. Each N. Shure knife showcases one of the more impressive fair exhibits.

Founded in 1888, the N. Shure Co. was not considered a major mover in the knife industry, generally importing various cutlery and novelty products. The series of brass penknives the company offered, however, were ornately engraved to depict significant buildings of the Chicago World's Fair.

Each two-blade knife is engraved on both sides of the handle, including the name of the building it commemorates and "1933 Chicago World's Fair" or "1934 Chicago World's Fair." It is unknown just how many scenes were immortalized on the knives, since not many pieces were produced and each knife is quite rare. Collecting the N. Shure knives makes for a rather unique specialty.

Interestingly, the art deco style being a prominent architectural theme throughout the fair is quite

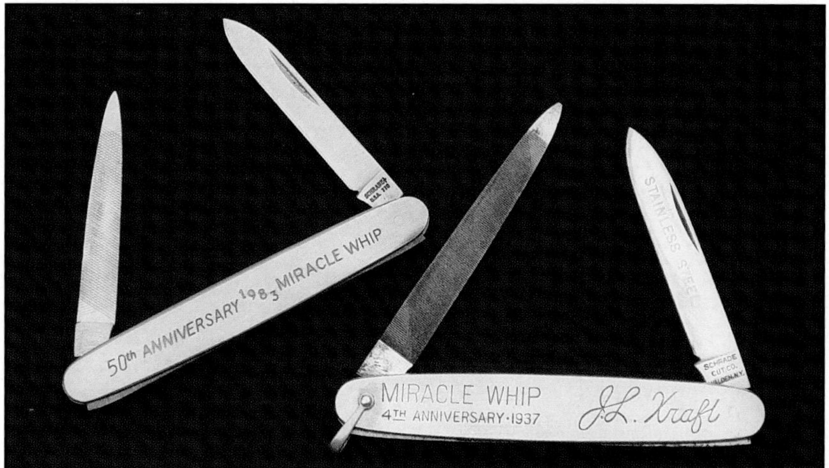


**Two knives released after the 1933 World's Fair celebrate the introduction of Miracle Whip by Kraft Foods at the fair. At top is a Schrade "50th Anniversary 1983 Miracle Whip" pocketknife, and pictured below it is Schrade's "Miracle Whip 4th Anniversary 1937" knife. Both sport a single blade and a nail file.**

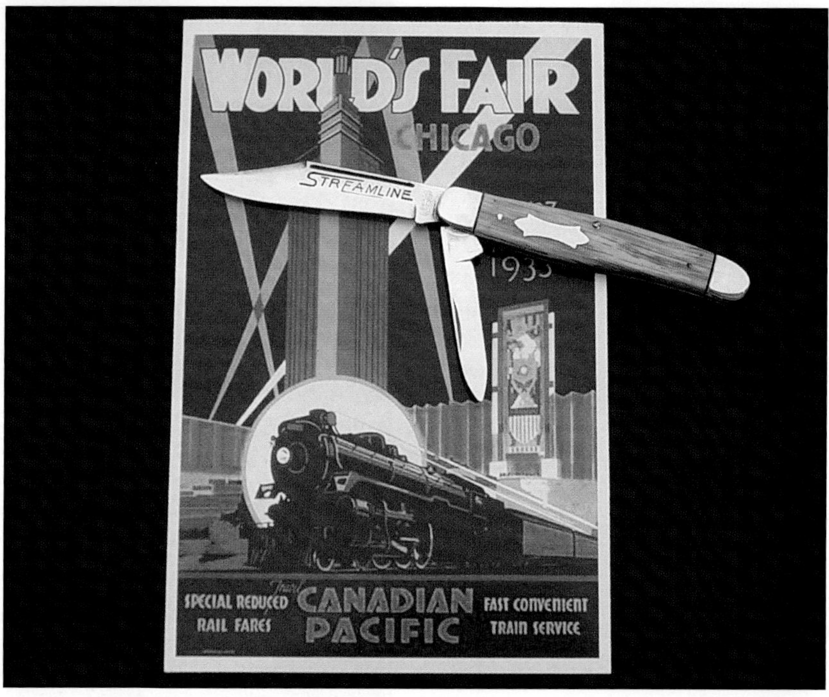


**One of the highlights of the World's Fair was the introduction of several "streamliner" trains by the Burlington Northern, Santa Fe and Union Pacific railroads. Designed by Camillus to commemorate the introduction of the streamliner was a large, two-blade, serpentine jackknife. Handled in celluloid with an elongated shield, it is exceptional because of the engraving of the master blade. With one of the deepest etchings ever produced on a pocketknife, it was designed as a tribute to the newest innovations in rail line technology. Most collectors who have seen the streamline knife have no idea of its connection with the 1933 Chicago World's Fair.**

evident as a design feature on the knives. There are serious World's Fair knife collectors, all of who would certainly be attracted to N. Shure knives. At least one book has been published and is entirely devoted to the various souvenir items, including knives, sold or given away at different world's fairs.

There were a number of general buildings that housed exhibits dedicated to the areas of science and technology. In the Horticultural Building, visitors encountered numerous floral scenes, as well as flowing brooks and towering trees. With hidden skylights to provide light, they roamed through the floral dioramic settings.

The Electrical Building housed exhibits honoring some of the most famous inventors up to that time, including Samuel Morse, Guglielmo Marconi, Blaise Pascal and Antonio Franconi. The General Exhibits Group buildings were devoted to various cosmetics, leather products, jewelry, sporting goods, office supplies and graphic arts.

Spectacular sights lying just beyond the four main entrances likely overwhelmed fair visitors. The harbor area featured a real submarine at anchor, and the ship City of New York, made famous by Admiral Byrd's voyage to Antarctica, was moored for tours. Several participants who sailed with Admiral Byrd manned the ship, and numerous scientific instruments and other curiosities were on display. The Sinclair Refining Co. built a prehistoric exhibit filled with giant dinosaurs to demonstrate what the world was like in prehistoric times.

## Streamlined Knives

Although not a World's Fair commemorative or souvenir knife, Camillus Cutlery (Camillus, New York) offered a pocketknife with a fair connection. One of the highlights of the World's Fair was the introduction of several "streamliner" trains by the Burlington Northern, Santa Fe and Union Pacific railroads. Thousands of people flocked to the local rail lines to view the futuristic trains, dubbed "wingless airplanes on tracks," and enthusiasts weren't disappointed by the latest in train design and passenger comfort.

Union Pacific and Burlington made the World's Fair a contest of design and ingenuity by debuting their own versions of streamliners, and it was Burlington Railroad's entry—the Zephyr—that broke records and dazzled the crowds of people who surged forward to touch the train.

The pocketknife designed by Camillus to commemorate the introduction of the streamliner train into American society was a large, two-blade, serpentine jackknife. Handled in celluloid with an elongated shield, it is exceptional because of the engraving of the master blade. With one of the deepest etchings ever produced on a pocketknife—"STREAMLINE" in large, diagonal lettering on the master blade—the knife was designed as a tribute to the newest innovations in rail line innovation. Most collectors who have seen the streamline knife have no idea of its connection with the 1933 Chicago World's Fair.

At the fair, the midway section had a carnival atmosphere, including one of the most popular attractions—alligator wrestlers—and diving acts that were sure to attract huge crowds. The midway included a special section for kids where they could visit a fairy castle, view a play or slide down Magic Mountain.

A "free beer day" attracted many of the adults to the midway area. Ripley's "Believe it or Not" had a special building where such oddities as the "human pin cushion" and the "baby with three arms and four legs" were exhibited. Members of at least four American Indian tribes danced in costume and allowed visitors to tour their teepees.

The Chicago World's Fair was truly an international event. The list of participating countries reads like a "Who's Who" among the nations of the world. In total, 21 nations built buildings and exhibited in Chicago. Among them were Morocco; Japan; Italy; the Dominican Republic; Czechoslovakia; China; Sweden; Canada; Great Britain; Costa Rica; Norway; Egypt; and Germany.

The exhibits set up by the various countries included a Japanese tea garden, complete with Geisha girls, a Bavarian black forest, a Saharan oasis, Spanish village, the golden temple of Jahol, a Paris street with restaurants, and both an English and Belgian village.

Millions of visitors strolled among the exhibits, from the quiet confines of the Japanese tea gardens through the loud and boisterous crowds watching diving horses in the midway. Whether it was a

WORLD'S FAIR CHICAGO
GENERAL MOTORS
THE GENERAL MOTORS BUILDING, AGAINST THE BACKGROUND OF THE AURORA BOREALIS

**The World's Fair sky ride is commemorated on the engraved sides of a two-blade pocketknife made by N. Shure of Chicago. Lying below the knife is a postcard reproduction of the General Motors Building. The reverse side of the knife shows a detailed etching of the Electrical Building Group built for the World's Fair. Behind it is a photograph of the Chrysler Building, a major exhibitor at the fair. The reflection below the building is a water structure that was a part of the Chrysler Building's exhibit.** *(the postcard reproduction and Chrysler Building photograph courtesy of the Chicago Historical Society)*

**The Schrade "50th Anniversary 1983 Miracle Whip" knife is shown lying on a colored drawing of the Kraft Building at the 1933 Chicago World's Fair. This building utilized the fair's required color scheme, which emphasized bright reds, yellows and blues.** *(drawing courtesy of the Chicago Historical Society)*

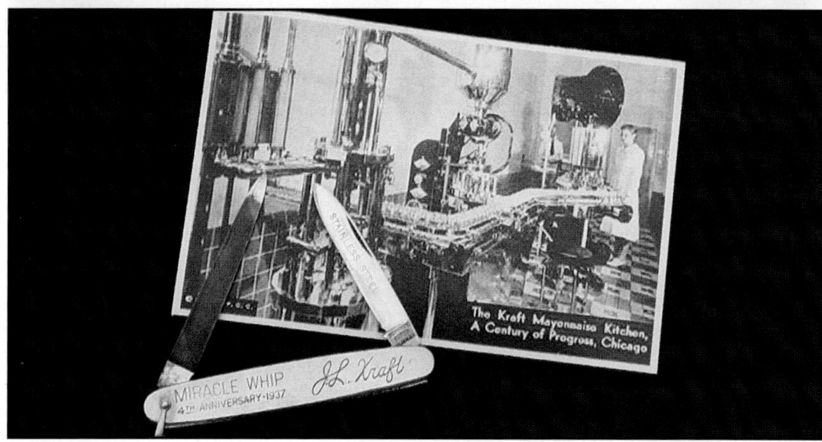


**Schrade's "Miracle Whip 4th Anniversary 1937" knife was commissioned by Kraft to commemorate the sandwich spread introduced at the 1933 Chicago World's Fair. The knife is pictured on a photograph of the Kraft Kitchen where Miracle Whip was produced. Miracle Whip was one of the novel foodstuffs of the fair.** *(photo of the Kraft Kitchen courtesy of the Chicago Historical Society)*

visit to an art deco building or a science exhibit, the World's Fair could only be compared to Disney's EPCOT Center in Orlando, Florida, today.

Foods generally associated with carnivals and midways were available for purchase or given out as samples, including the ethnic foods of various countries.

One of the most interesting foodstuffs introduced at the 1933 World's Fair was developed by Kraft. The then-new product, which today we take for granted, was a sandwich spread known as "Miracle Whip."

You can just imagine crowds of people lining up around the Kraft building to get a free sample of sandwich spread. The Kraft Foods exhibit included a complete kitchen where huge stainless steel beaters whipped water, flour, white vinegar, eggs, vegetable oil, sugar, salt, dried mustard, and smidges of lemon juice and paprika, together to produce a novel dressing. Along with the spread came the slogan, "A sandwich just isn't a sandwich without Miracle Whip."

## Kraft Knife Sandwich Spreader?

Kraft Foods was so proud of its new product, it commissioned Schrade Cutlery Co. of Walden, New York, to build a pocketknife commemorating the introduction of Miracle Whip. In fact, Kraft commissioned Schrade to make several commemorative pocketknives, numbered by year, long after Miracle Whip's 1933 introduction. In 1983, Kraft and Schrade collaborated on a pocketknife marking the 50th anniversary of the introduction of Miracle Whip to the American public.

For knife collectors, amassing a selection of Miracle Whip anniversary knives is a worthwhile endeavor, as these knives appear on the market fairly frequently. More significantly, with the Miracle Whip knives, Schrade once again lived up to its reputation as a manufacturer of quality cutlery.

Knives were only one of a multitude of souvenirs given away or sold at the World's Fair. Some collectors specialize in other World's Fair memorabilia like salt and pepper shakers; postcards; sewing kits; lucky pennies; pictorial folders; tokens; badges; ribbons; coins; Boy Scout collectibles; Stanhope pictures; cast metal banks; and a host of other items.

The 1933 Chicago World's Fair was the stimulus for the production of a variety of different pocketknives. Some commemorated the fair specifically, and others the resulting innovations. Like much of this type of Americana, the knives tell the story of an event held during the darkest days of The Great Depression, a World's Fair that proved to the American public that, although the economy looked dark, the future was as bright and shiny as a sparkling-new pocketknife!

# The Addictive, Rhythmic Beat of Offbeat Folders

## *Exotically designed folding knives are user friendly and collectible*

*By William Hovey Smith*

For the French, a blade, pivot pin and a pair of handle scales isn't enough. South Africans want more in a folder than a grip and a bevel. The German military holds higher standards than simple folding knives. Spaniards set loftier goals than sharpened steel and hollow grips that hold the folding blades when not in use.

The world's diversity of folding knives reaches far beyond the simple construct of blades, pivots and handles to include unique locking mechanisms, purpose-designed blades, exotic styles and folder patterns that cannot be comfortably pocketed.

### Open an Opinel

The French have a flair for design, as witnessed in the Citron automobile and the Darne shotgun. The car and gun, noted for being mechanically fascinating, tend to be overly complicated. In contrast, the French Opinel folder is pure simplicity.

The folding knife pattern consists of a thin, steel blade retained by a barrel lock that folds into a one-piece wooden handle. On all but the smallest Opinel knives, the blades are locked open by rotating steel rings that jam-lock the edged steel in the open and ready position.

Mechanically, the Opinel has

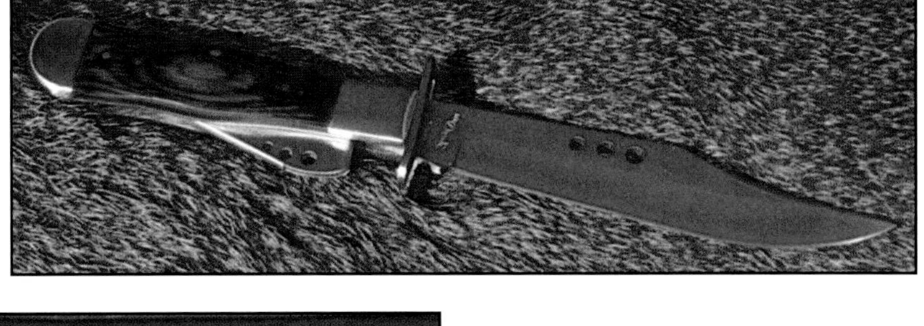

**Fury's version of the Marble's Safety Hunter is shown here on the neck of a 10-point 150-class Missouri whitetail. The knife had no difficulty in skinning and de-boning the large buck.**

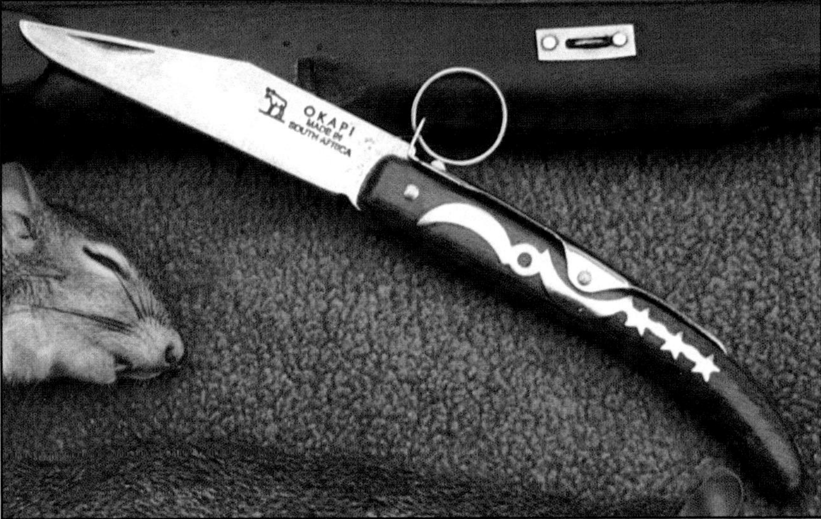


**The Okapi, with its distinctive ring lock and blade stamping, is shown here with an Indian-made musket and a Georgia squirrel taken with the smoothbore. A pattern that dates from the 1600s, it is an effective utility knife and game cleaner.**

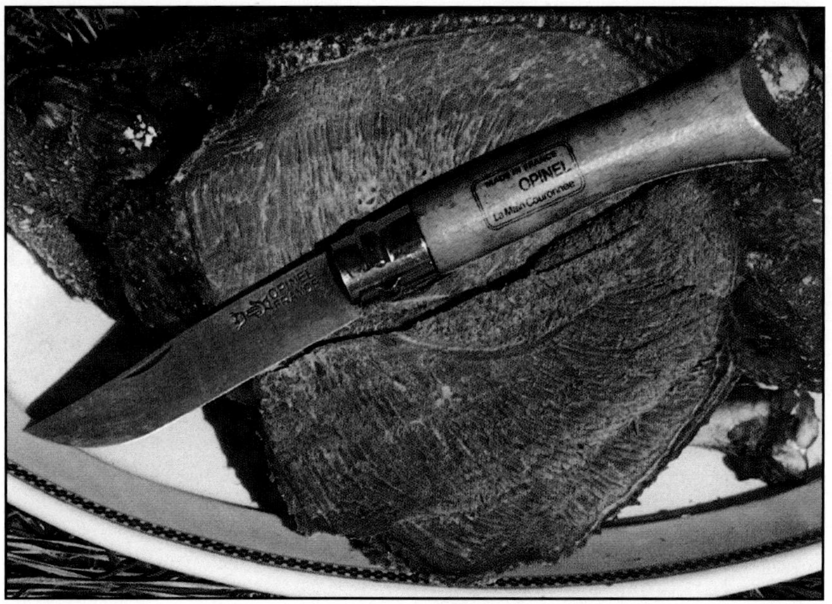


**The French Opinel, with its clever rotating barrel lock, has always featured a sharp, thin blade that is ideal for such tasks as slicing up a Wisconsin goose. Made in a variety of blade lengths, Opinels have always been inexpensive utilitarian folders and long favored by farmers, hunters and tradesmen in Europe.**

only four steel parts, including an open-topped steel collar, a blade, a pivot pin and a rotating barrel lock. With so few metallic parts, Opinel knives are lighter than most folders with blades of comparable lengths. Even an Opinel with a 4-inch blade rides comfortably in the pocket.

Designed by Joseph Opinel in 1890, the knives became extremely popular in the Savoie region of the French Alps. To this day, Opinel blades are stamped with the hand of St. John the Baptist (the town symbol of St. Jean-de-Maurienne) and the crown of the dukedom of Savoie.

The handles of most Opinels are pear wood or ash, but beech, oak, walnut and olivewood grips are known to exist.

In 2004, Smoky Mountain Knife Works advertised a 10-piece set of Opinels, in varying sizes and sold together in a case, for less than $60—a bargain in the knife collecting community.

Opinel knives have always featured thin, hard blades that hold sharp edges. Like others of their type, Opinel blades respond well to fine hones and leather straps. Their razor-sharp edges are equally suited for cutting thin slices of meat and field dressing game.

These knives have been in continuous production for over a century, speaking volumes for Joseph's original, low-priced folder that farmers and shepherds could afford to own and employ.

## Cop a South African Okapi

Combining a ring lock and ratchet mechanisms with an elongated spring-steel back and wooden handle, the Okapi is as distinctive as its namesake antelope. A sturdy 4 1/4-inch locking blade and hand-filling handle permit the South African knife to be used for skinning anything from dik-dik to elephant.

The 1055 carbon steel blade, hardened to 55 RC on the Rockwell hardness scale, is best sharpened with a coarse-toothed file. A piece of soft sandstone is often used to restore a keen cutting edge when the knife is dulled in the field.

Opening the Okapi has a different feel and sound than the single, solid click of a spring-loaded lock-back blade. There are six clicks as each of the rounded ratchets is caught and released by the back spring.

Pulling up on the large ring relieves tension on the back spring, allowing the blade to be folded back into its two-piece wooden handle.

This general style was first developed during the 1600s in Southern Europe and was widely used in Spain and among gypsies.

Similarly styled navajas were generally 10 inches long and designed to be slid behind sashes, their sharply curved, knobby butts helping to hold them in place.

While the Okapi retains something of the hooked end of the navaja, the shape now serves more to fill the palm than retain the knife in a sash. Most commonly, the Okapi is carried in a pocket.

Attesting to the knife's continued use is the fact that many such pieces are still seen in the hands of African hunters. Most Okapi blades have been sharpened so many times they are ground away to practically nothing.

My use of an Okapi is usually during muzzleloader hunting because the style and decoration of the knife complements the antique pattern of the rifle or shotgun. The Okapi does an efficient job of cleaning small game and certainly has more than enough blade length and strength to clean and de-bone a deer.

## Get a German Military Folder

It should not come as a surprise that folding knives issued to members of the world's armed forces are versatile enough to have crossover appeal in civilian life.

One especially useful knife is the West German clasp knife, complete with a spear-point blade, a saw blade with a cap lifter/screwdriver, a corkscrew and an awl. Of the many knives I own, this one frequently finds its way into my pocket during hunting season.

Not only is the blade useful

for tasks like cutting tent ropes and decoy lines, the saw suffices for trimming small branches from trees. With its two rows of sharp teeth, the saw is an effective cutting instrument for severing branches up to 1 inch thick.

The awl has often been employed to punch holes in dog collars or to pierce leather for thongs. The corkscrew removes corks nicely and catches tie-cords that have slipped too far back into their sleeves to grasp with fingernails.

I have owned and given away several West German clasp knives over the years. They originally came with folded-steel, slip-on covers over the saw blades, but they were often lost.

The two clasp knives that I now own are made by Victorinox and feature sharp, stainless steel blades, brass liners and non-slip, checkered-plastic handle scales stamped with German eagles.

## Pluck a Spanish Fruit Knife

One of my personal favorite folders is the Spanish fruit knife and, in particular, a pattern made by J.J. Martinez of Santa Cruz, Spain.

The knife features a sturdy spear-point blade, nearly 4 inches long and 3/8-inch thick, and a brass handle inset with wood panels. The result is a combination of a strong blade and a knife with an extremely slim profile that carries easily and inconspicuously in a pocket.

Besides being particularly useful for slicing fruit, the blade excels at general cutting chores. Longer than most folders, it is particularly useful for cutting boxes and slicing thick-skinned watermelons and cantaloupe.

Other potential uses for the handy folder include cleaning game on backpacking trips and as a veterinarian's knife. Of all the knives outlined herein, this one appeals to most people as a rare and demonstrably useful knife that they would carry every day.

**A gentleman's blade for a gentleman's sport, the Winchester cartridge knife is suitable for low-stress cutting and spreading chores where a larger blade would seem somewhat less than socially acceptable among the tweed-wearing shooting set.**

**Some offbeat folding knives lie on an old shooting coat. From the top are the Fury safety folder, a French Opinel, a South African Okapi, a Spanish fruit knife, and an Italian Winchester-brand cartridge knife flanked by a Dutch Naval knife (left) and a German Army folder (right).**

Its slim profile fits just as well in a suit pocket as in a lady's handbag.

## Cart off a Cartridge Knife

Cartridge knives are generally thought of as being advertising or novelty items rather than having any real utility. Compared to larger knives, 1 3/8 inches of stainless steel blade doesn't sound like much.

Among the tweed-wearing shooting set, where a single shotgun might cost $30,000 (or more) and a set of shooting clothes is $3,000, it is considered ungentlemanly to pull out a 6-inch bowie knife to cut the ribbon from your box lunch.

However, no one feels intimidated if you produce a cartridge knife out of your shell vest and use it to open your lunch and spread your crackers with cheese and pâte.

Winchester chose as its cartridge knife a version with a plastic body and brass-colored head stamped with the Winchester logo. Other versions of cartridge knives have also been made in the shapes of common rifle and pistol cartridges.

Out of curiosity, I dropped the shotshell look-a-like knife into the chamber of an old single-barreled Stevens 12-gauge with a loose chamber. The body of the case was large enough to keep a neophyte from loading his scattergun with the cartridge knife, although I am sure that it has been attempted.

It is generally unappreciated that a steel blade, even a short one, has great value as a game dressing and survival tool. Even a blade as short as this one can dress a deer with considerable efficiency, and it certainly can be used to clean game. I would rather use a larger knife, but even a tiny steel blade will work if needed.

**A Dutch Naval knife, shown here on a piling, showcases a reground main blade, a cap lifter, spear-point can opener and marlinspike. The blade has obviously "seen time in the service," but remains a useful camp knife.**

## Nab a Dutch Naval Knife

Sailors working with ropes need knives, and many of the world's navies have issued folding knives. Typically each knife is distinguished by a main blade, a marlin spike for splicing rope, a cap lifter/screwdriver and a can opener, the latter usually used for opening tinned rations.

The Dutch knife in the accompanying photo also features rustproof, brown, plastic handle scales and brass liners. The 2 1/2-inch high-carbon steel blade on this particular model was apparently snapped off and another point shaped with a rotary grinder.

During the grinding operation, the knife must have slipped in the sailor's hand and the grinding apparatus cut across the flat of the blade, leaving visible scars. The blade still functioned, so there was no need to polish away the cosmetic blemish.

The knife is identified as a KL 66 on the handle and has the manufacturer's name, AMEFA, stamped on the blade. A bail allows it to be snapped onto a sailor's belt for convenient access. The unusual grips, instead of being flat or slightly rounded, are cut away on top to provide easy access to the blade and other implements.

Civilians typically use the strong, 7/8-inch spear-point can openers of such knives to pry open oysters and other shellfish. A Dutch Naval Knife also makes a fine folding camp or Boy Scout knife.

Naval knives are not only useful for sailors and riggers, but are also quite handy for horsemen who employ long marlin spikes to clean horses' hooves. In fact, the British used a version of a Navy knife for dual purposes, issuing it to cavalry units.

The British version featured a main blade shaped like a straight razor, a 2 1/2-inch spike and a can opener. Some badly rusted versions of the knife are available from Atlanta Cutlery.

Some of the British blades are stamped with World War II production dates, but the knives themselves were mostly made in the late 1940s and 1950s. They employed coarsely checkered plastic scales and carbon steel components and liners.

## Make Mine a Marble's Safety Hunter

Webster Marble introduced the Safety Folding Hunter in 1902, basing it on an original design by Milton Rowland. In 1908, the knife was "fancied up" with a decorative handle and bolsters.

The oversized blade backs into the handle, extending beyond the grip, and is protected by a pivoting metal extension. The extension also serves to lock the blade in the open position. The knife has a pivoting cross-guard that lies flush against the handle when the folding blade is closed.

Although the original advertisement stated, "This is a folding knife intended to be carried in the pocket or on the belt," most people found the heavy, 7-inch knife a bit much for a pocket.

The Folding Hunters were originally sold with leather sheaths, and I suspect that most users carried such knives on their belts.

Fury makes a version that, with a 6-inch blade, is approximately the same size as the 1902 model. The Fury knife differs slightly, showcasing all-stainless construction, and a bowie-style hollow-ground stainless blade and laminated-wood handle scales. The Chinese-made knife is not an exact copy of the Marble's Safety Hunter, but is similar in size, shape and functionality.

Interestingly, A.G. Russell Knives offers a truer copy of the Marble's #3 Safety Pocket Knife as a limited edition for collectors. It is made under license from Marble.

Two A.G. Russell versions with different handle materials were

**A West German army knife is pictured on top of a decoy bag. With a main blade and a saw, the small folder performs a variety of sportsmen's tasks. I often use the small yet efficient saw to cut small branches when attempting to open shooting lanes around tree stands and hunting blinds.**

**A Spanish fruit knife is shown here spearing a tub of pears. Besides being particularly useful for cutting such things as melons, the tough spear-point blade has some real penetrating power in performing tasks like killing fish.**

advertised in 2003 and 2004. The 2004 limited edition sold for about $400, while the Chinese-made Fury costs less than $12 and includes a nylon sheath. I have no doubt that the Russell was/is the better knife, but a $12 version of the Folding Hunter is an excellent buy.

Fury knives are noted for their good steel, functionality and flashy looks, and often have some sort of milled indentations in the blades.

The knife I have showcases a 5 3/4-inch blade and red laminated-wood grips. The stainless steel components are brush polished, and though the polishing job is adequate, it is not quite first-rate quality. Some scratches remain on the metal and wood parts.

Given the chance to skin and clean a nice Missouri 10-point whitetail deer, the Fury made short work of it. The blade retained its edge throughout the process and is still sharp enough to process another deer. One of the handle scales has a tiny crack near the two rear pins, but I don't see it as a real problem.

Folding hunting knives of this general style have also been made in Europe since at least the mid-1800s. Shorter than straight knives of the same blade length, they do not catch on quite as much brush when walking through thick undergrowth.

Although slow to bring into action and somewhat small, such a knife could be used for general camp chores and, if nothing else was available, for self-protection.

There is much more to the world of folding knives than everyday pocketknives, however interesting they may be. Necessity and human ingenuity have combined to produce some odd-looking but useful folders.

# Go Ahead, Make My Blade!

## *The author challenges novices to try his rudimentary yet effective knifemaking techniques*

*By Rod Halvorsen*

One of the most basic human pleasures is the making of basic tools. Many of us possess a drive to take something from the world around us and convert it into a useful instrument.

The creative urge runs deep. I have always felt that the changes taking place as steel is hardened and tempered add a mysterious dimension to knifemaking, as opposed to other handcrafts. Having made knives for some years, the mystery has not abated.

Amateur knifemaking needs not demand a large financial investment in materials and tooling. My tooling is rudimentary. Yet, in spite of this, my knives are functional and serve my purposes well.

One area where no skimping should occur is in the provision of safety equipment and safety procedures. Anyone making knives must realize that the endeavor is dangerous. Good eye protection and a proper respirator are must-haves.

Gloves are necessary to prevent cuts and burns. Adequate ventilation is a requirement. The high heat generated in hardening and tempering operations requires proper safety procedures to prevent fire and immediate access to charged and rated fire extinguishers.

I practice the stock-removal method of knifemaking and fashion almost all of my blades from scrap steel that can be hardened. Using a 4-inch angle grinder for cutting out shapes and rough-grinding edges, I have never forged a blade and, as a result, I rely on materials with original thicknesses that are close to that I desire on my finished knives.

Such raw materials are, in my area, quite easy to acquire. Varying nicely from about .06-inch to .20-inch, obsolete machine shop hacksaws, springs, mill saws and chainsaw guide bars are readily converted into superb hunting, kitchen and utility knives. I have used much thicker materials, like plow blades, in the past, but the effort required to grind a nice knife from a piece of 1/2-inch-thick steel is daunting!

Most scrap steel possesses a temper and hardness appropriate to its original purpose. Before annealing, chainsaw guide bars and mill saws generally hover around 42-44 Rc on the Rockwell Hardness scale. This is as hard as many machetes and some older production knives, though it is now considered too soft for hunting and survival knives.

I have cold-ground a few knives from such material without any

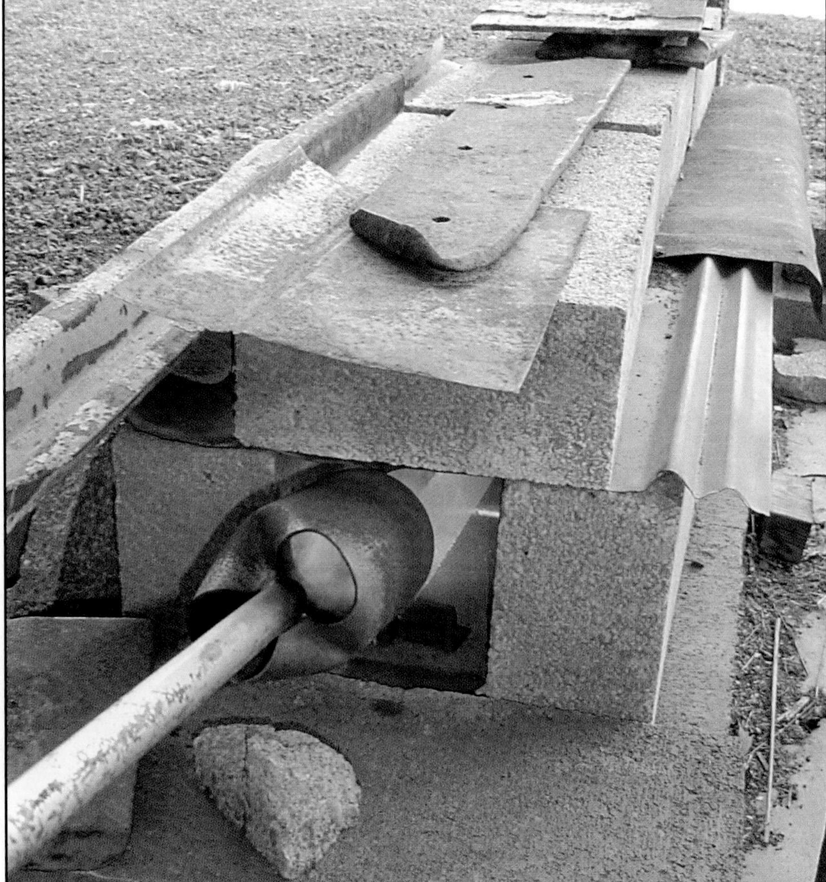

**A forge need not be complex or expensive. This one is made up of an LP gas torch and a simple arrangement of firebrick to contain the flame.**

hardening and they served quite admirably. Today, knife enthusiasts demand Rockwell hardness values in the upper 50s or even low 60s, but the hobby maker will find that many scrap steels perform acceptably even at a much lower levels of hardness.

## Beware of Brittle Blades

The harder a blade is, the more brittle it will be, and since most scrap steel is of unknown alloy, it pays to lean a little to the soft and tough side than to the hard and more brittle side of the Rockwell scale. A somewhat softer blade can always be re-sharpened, but a blade too hard that snaps in normal use is not much good at all!

Past tests on mill saws and chainsaw guide bars have indicated hardness values of 57 Rc produced by a 450 degree Fahrenheit tempering cycle; values of 52-53 Rc when tempered at 500 degrees F; and 50 Rc when subjected to a 600-degree tempering cycle. The values approximate what can be expected from simple 1065 to 1075 high-carbon spring steel.

Part of the reason I have stuck to scrapped-out saws and springs for knifemaking is that this material can be annealed, re-hardened and tempered quite easily. Other scrap steel certainly can be used, but before expending a lot of effort to make a blade, I first heat a small piece until bright red and then I quench it in water or oil and strike it with a file.

If the file skids without biting in, the steel is probably a good candidate for a knife and I use it. If it remains soft and the file bites in, the scrap probably has too little carbon in it to be hardened, or it requires a more sophisticated hardening technique and I avoid it.

I am not a metallurgist, and I readily admit that I work within my own simplistic limitations!

The forge I use to heat-treat my knives is a firebrick-lined tunnel that effectively contains and channels the flame of my torch. While blade stock can be heated in the open, it is difficult to apply the flame evenly, and the result is inevitable warping. In my forge tunnel, the flame can be shifted from side-to-side and the material heated evenly. In addition, when annealing, both ends of the tunnel can be sealed and the material thus cooled slowly, again decreasing the tendency to warp.

**With this fixture and an inexpensive set of stamps, initials or other identifying markings can be stamped on the annealed stock.**

**Blade cutout and rough-edge grinding takes time but is not difficult using the 4-inch grinder.**

I have found an LP gas "weed burner" torch to be a superb heat source for both annealing and hardening. Maximum temperatures generated by my torch are stated by the manual to be in the 2,000 degrees F range. Since the temperature required for annealing and hardening most carbon steels is about 1,550 to 1,650 degrees, the flame produced by the LP gas torch is sufficient when directed into a tunnel forge like mine.

Critical temperature is reached when I see a "bright salmon" color. I hold the blade at that temperature for a couple minutes before I seal up the forge when annealing, or I then quench when hardening. I have never had a blade break in service and always obtain a successful hardening, thus indicating that I am neither burning the steel nor missing critical temperature.

Handles and grip scales require relatively small pieces of wood, so hardwood scraps from a friend's cabinet shop supply most of my needs. In addition, I cut and season mountain vine maple and serviceberry, both available here on my ranch. Though growing no thicker than about 5 inches and possessing plain grain, both are hard and tough when dry, and add another "local" dimension to my knives.

Full-tang blades make for stiff

**After the blade is cut out and before the cutting edge is ground, hand filing dresses down all the high and rough spots on the semi-finished blade.**

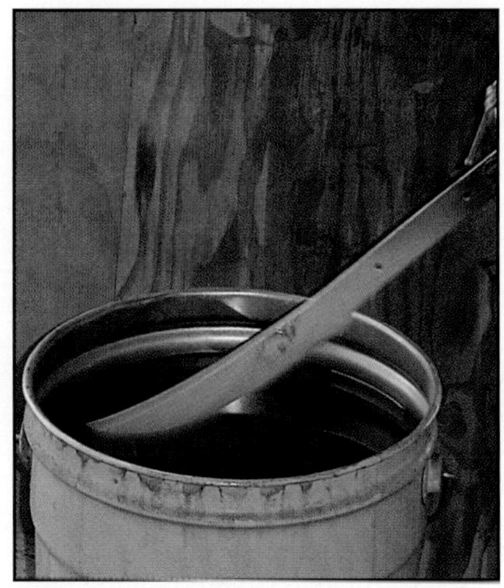

**Ready for the quench, the red-hot steel is plunged into the oil medium.**

and sturdy knives, and fortunately are easily fashioned. Rivets for attachment of the handle scales can be made from a variety of materials.

Certainly, proper "cutlery" rivets can be purchased, but I have found that common 16d and 8d nails with snug-fitting washers work well and add "period flavor" to knives based on older models. For many of my knives, I continue to dip into my supply of 3/16-inch-thick soft-iron rivets I obtained from a retired blacksmith.

## A Whale of a Knife to Replicate

Some years ago, while playing in the dirt on the dike of one of my stock ponds, my son and a friend turned up an interesting blade. Rising as it did from a frost heave, I have no idea where this knife originally came from, but it is clearly of a general "trade knife" known to be popular during the days of early settlement in our area.

Strangely, the closest knives in dimension and shape I can find to it are whaling and sealing knives of the early 1900s. How such a blade meandered its way to the mountains of north Idaho is a mystery yet to be solved!

In totally unusable, relic condition, such a knife just begged to be recreated! Selection of the basic blade material was easy. Similar in thickness to the relic knife, I chose a piece of mill saw that was cut by a friend using an acetylene torch. At .137-inch thick, the end result would be a sturdy utility, butcher and kitchen knife

Before attempting to shape the basic stock, it needed to be annealed, or softened. The procedure I used for annealing was simple. The blade stock was placed in a fixture made from a piece of angle iron into which a slot was cut, thus holding the stock edge down so the flame could be evenly distributed on either side.

The metal was then heated slowly in my crude forge until it looked bright orange to my eye, allowed to maintain this temperature for a couple minutes to make sure that all spots were fully heated, and then the forge was sealed up, allowing the metal to cool somewhat slowly. When cool, the steel was dead soft and easily filed, ground, drilled and stamped.

With the rough stock annealed, the next step was to trace the basic blade shape onto it. Frequently I make patterns out of cardboard, but with my old trade knife, the blade itself was used as a stencil.

A scribe can be used to draw the outline of a blade, but I prefer to use a permanent marker. Mistakes drawn with such a marker can be rectified with acetone on a cotton swab.

With the outline completed, but before cutting out the blade, I stamped my initials and the date on the dead-soft, annealed material. Letters were easily kept in line with a simple jig made from a piece of hardwood clamped to the steel.

Holes were drilled for handle rivets.

Certainly, a drill press is most effective at getting through the annealed steel, but it isn't necessary. An angle grinder used to cut out the blade can also be employed to grind deep grooves in the tang (along the long axis of the tang), and a hand drill or even a heavy center punch could then be used to create the rivet holes.

Fitting of the handle slabs is made much easier if either the tang or grip holes are made slightly oversize, especially if three or more rivet holes are used. After drilling, each hole is then countersunk with a rotary file held in a cordless drill.

## Stay in the Grind Lines!

Following the lines, the rough blade was cut out using a 1/8-inch cutoff wheel fitted to a 4-inch grinder. While I have used larger diameter grinders, I find the smaller 4- and 4 1/2-inch models preferable for following blade curves. They are also much less fatiguing to hold.

Quick release clamps are used whenever possible, though regular C-clamps certainly suffice. Cutoff wheels are thin and allow fairly precise holding, but I have found that it is best to start my approach to the trace line from outside the blade pattern, touching down just when the line is reached.

This method avoids the tendency to bounce when the wheel contacts the rough stock. Somehow such bouncing always seems to result in the wheel skidding over the face of the blade, marring its surface! Holding to the lines as closely as possible will save time with files later.

Cutting out the basic blade was quite simple. However, once the blade was cut out, it was obvious that the edges had to be smoothed. This step is particularly important along the cutting edge, where the curve of the blade must be maintained and all bumps removed before grinding the edge. If these bumps are not removed, the edge, after grinding, will finish with high spots.

After the basic blade was cut out and the rough edges dressed down, I then used the permanent marker to draw a line demarking where to stop grinding the edge. Another line was drawn along the edge itself at half of the thickness of the edge. Just about all material between these lines was then removed by freehand grinding.

Constant sweeping movements of the grinder are required in order to prevent burning the steel and/or leaving an uneven finish. I frequently stop and lift up the blade and "sight" it along the edge, returning it to the grinding board to remove anything that doesn't look like a knife edge. With the simple blade profile of my trade knife, this procedure was quite simple.

In order to create an even flow along the edge, much file work is needed. In fact, I spend more time with files than I do with a grinder. Starting with a fairly coarse mill bastard file, I set the angle of the final cutting edge. Successively finer files are then used until the grinding marks are removed.

An edge is attained, but it is left dull to eliminate the possibility of stress fractures that can occur when quenching a fine edge. A belt grinder can speed all of this work, but it is not necessary.

Using a coarse oilstone followed by successively finer grits of wet/dry sandpaper dipped in 3-In-One or some other light oil, a mirror-polished blade is possible. Only time limits the shine! A brightly gleaming blade is attractive, but it is not a requirement for a working knife.

On my trade knife, I simply started with a coarse stone to remove file marks and then moved to 180-grit wet/dry paper, finishing with 220-grit paper.

## The Motor Oil Quench

After achieving an acceptable finish, the blade is hardened. I have never had much success with a water quench, having cracked a couple knives before I decided upon the less stressful medium of used motor oil. Since using this medium, I have never cracked a blade and have always achieved a good, hard piece of steel after the quench. However, used motor oil is not without its own disadvantages.

The fumes generated are hazardous, and obviously the oil is extremely flammable. This is a job best done outside. A sufficient amount of oil should be used to allow complete submersion of the parts, and it should be in a sturdy, stable metal bucket.

To minimize the possibility of a dangerous fire, it is important that the entire blade and heated portion of the holding fixture are submerged in the oil immediately when quenching. If any portion is exposed to the air, a flare-up will result. Obviously, adequate and appropriate fire extinguishers should be kept close at hand.

Plastic buckets should be avoided. A red-hot knife blade will punch a hole through a plastic bucket. I never allow the oil to heat up. I keep it cool while quenching. Plunging multiple blades will heat the oil, and it can reach a dangerous temperature at which a flare-up occurs.

The actual hardening and tempering process for simple high carbon steel is quite straightforward. First, in preparation for tempering, I preheat my kitchen oven, verifying my chosen temperature with a thermometer placed inside the oven itself. While the oven preheats, I harden the blade at the forge.

For the trade knife, I selected

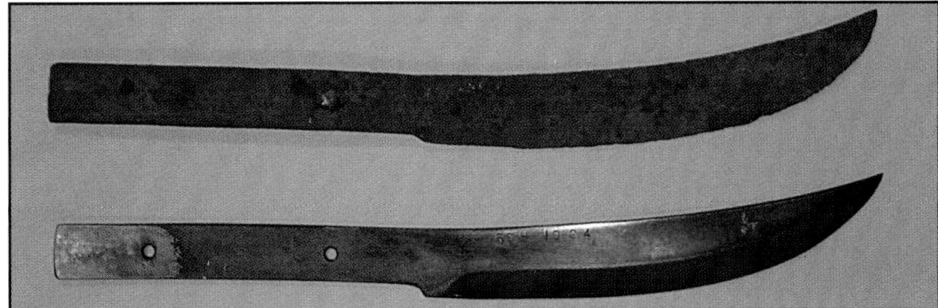

**Starting to look like a knife, the tempered mill saw blade and the old knife it is being replicated from are lined up for comparison.**

**Holes in the blade tang serve as guides for where to drill the correlating holes in the handle scales.**

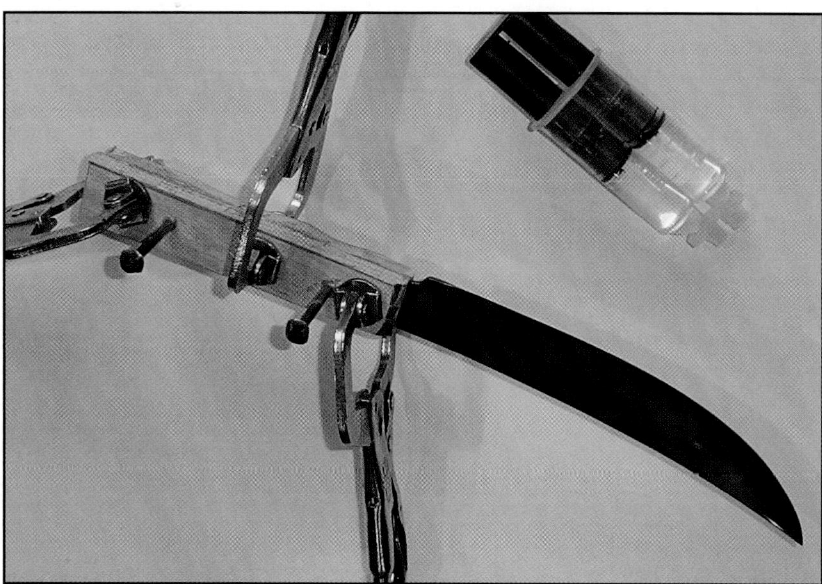

**Like just about every step in the knifemaking process, gluing the handle scales to the tang requires clamps.**

**Setting handle rivets without marring the grips is best done using a purpose-made riveting anvil for the head, and a heavy nail set to peen the ends over the washers.**

a 550-degree tempering cycle, as I wanted a tough blade with a lot of flex that would easily sharpen with a kitchen steel. Based on previous tests, this temperature would produce a Rockwell hardness value of about 50 Rc.

To harden the blade, I placed it in the forge, held edge down with a simple C-clamp. A pair of vise-grips latched onto the C-clamp allowed me to handle the hot parts without getting burned. The blade was then heated slowly, with small increases of gas pressure until it reached a salmon color, where it was allowed to remain for a couple minutes.

The blade and heated jig were then quickly plunged into the oil. A heavy block of steel and a hammer were kept close by in the event that the blade warped either in the forge or after plunging. If the blade were to warp, it could be reheated, tapped lightly to straighten it, and then quenched again.

Once the blade is quenched, it is gently wiped clean and tested with a new file. If the file skids over the blade edge, it is called good. If not, it goes back into the forge. If it fails this hardness test a second time, it is scrapped, as likely it is a piece of low-carbon steel, not suitable for a knife blade. If the blade proves hard, extreme care is taken to prevent cracking it or breaking it.

Dropping it on a concrete floor will send the hobby knifemaker back to the drawing board. Placing an even slightly warped knife in a vise will break it. The blade is nearly glass hard, full of stress and needs to be tempered soon. In preparation for that step, I simply clean off the burnt-on motor oil scale with wet/dry 220-grit paper, degrease the blade with mineral spirits and place the knife in the oven.

## Temper, Temper

I temper my knives at least twice. My trade knife was first left in the oven for one hour, and then it was removed, cooled in the air, polished and sent back into the oven for one-and-a-half hours. This double step insured full tempering of the blade and produced a truly tough tool.

After the second go-round in the oven, the tempering colors were removed using oil-dipped 320-400-grit wet/dry sandpaper. An attractive final finish was achieved using this method. Since the blade was previously polished only to a 220-grit finish, tiny microscopic scale particles were left embedded in its surface. The extra fine paper polished the metal on top of the imperfections, leaving an almost aged "patina" on the blade.

The blade completed, it needed only a pair of handle scales to make a knife out of it. For my trade knife, I chose a piece of oak. Oak is tough, hard, and though some have disparaged its porosity, I have found that trait to be something of an advantage on a knife that will be exposed to moisture, grease and fat. The open pores of the wood readily absorb varnish and other finishes, and thus seal the grip from liquid penetration.

Two pieces of wood were cut out using crosscut and rip saws. Slightly larger in width than the tang itself, they were both clamped onto one side of the tang. Rivet holes in the wood were then drilled using the previously drilled tang holes as a guide.

Either a hand drill or drill press can be used for this step, and the knife itself doesn't even need to be clamped down during the drilling operation, though it is imperative that gloves are worn and the blade is heavily wrapped with paper and cloth to adequately protect the hands in the event that the bit binds and the knife swings free. Even without its final edge, the blade is dangerous!

I bed all my grip scales in five-minute epoxy. I have used more substantial adhesives, but normally they take at least a day to sufficiently harden, and I prefer to be able to keep working on my projects without that delay. Since I rivet grip scales, the purpose of the epoxy is twofold: First it provides a "bed" for the grips, which prevents water from getting underneath them; and second, it allows the grips to be shaped on the tang before the rivets are set.

Both the interior of the grips and the tang itself are scarred up with a file point to assist bonding of the epoxy, and finally, the tang is degreased with acetone before the epoxy is mixed and the grip scales assembled.

I adjust my clamps to fit the assembled handle before I start mixing the adhesive, and I always use properly sized "slave" pins to hold the grip scales in place while the epoxy hardens. With a slight amount of grease applied to the pins, they remove easily. In about an hour, the clamps and pins are removed and the handle can be shaped.

I have found that a common farrier's rasp is the most efficient hand tool available for rapid removal of material in shaping the grips. Such a rasp can be found at equine or farm supply stores. Final shaping is done with 80-grit sandpaper, finishing the grip in successively finer grits down to about a 220-grit paper.

Once an acceptably smooth finish is obtained, I then provide a countersink to receive the rivet heads and washers. This allows them to be seated below the level of the grip surface and makes for a more comfortable handle.

**Many useful and practical blades can be fashioned at little expense from readily available scrap materials. Here, an assortment of blades made by the author includes small fishing and hunting knives, heavy bush knives, bolos and, of course, the trade knife relic and its clone.**

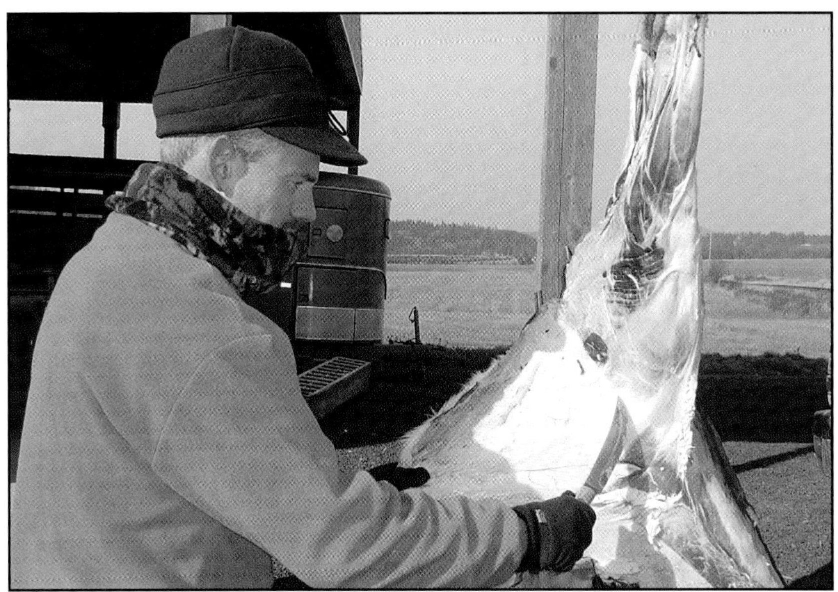

**With many practical uses, the trade knife gets put to work. As a skinner and general kitchen utility knife, it serves just as well as did its predecessor once upon a time!**

## A Riveting Experience

Rivets are slid into the holes, and with washers in place, are marked for where they need to be shortened, leaving a small amount above the washer for final peening. They are then removed from the handle, clipped off with side cutters or a hacksaw, replaced with washers seated and peened into place.

Stained an attractive color and sporting several coats of satin varnish, the knife is ready for final sharpening on a medium stone.

Great satisfaction comes from using a tool I have made myself. With the mysteries reduced to the manageable, many other novice knifemakers should find the experience equally rewarding.

# The Perfect Survival Knife

## *The author managed to survive hard times thanks to a knife of "singing steel" he bought at the House of Aragorn*

*By James Ayres*

I was sitting in a quiet corner of the station with my back against the wall, putting the finishing touches on an already sharp blade, when the train pulled in. The knife was a well-used Randall Model One. I expected to need it where I was going.

I tossed the sheathed knife on top of my other gear in a worn canvas rucksack, slung the comfortable old pack over one shoulder and found a seat on the train out of Mexicali, headed south a few minutes after dawn. It was May of 1969, and I was traveling to meet a friend in Mexico City, and then planned to proceed to the Yucatan. We were going in search of a lost Mayan city.

The train was ancient, circa Pancho Villa, with red brocade seats, worn red carpet and open windows that filled the car with smoke when the locomotive inched up steep grades. I watched the sunrise—purple, grey, and lavender—over the Sonora desert as we "click-clacked" down the tracks, across the flat landscape, chamisos and smoke trees silhouetted against the sky. At the station, I had noticed cages with live chickens being loaded onto the kitchen car, which was the car next to mine. Around noon the chickens started squawking.

The stewed chicken in red chili sauce was tasty, spicy, pungent and tough, much like Mexico. During the next two days and nights, the chuffing old train wheezed up and down mountains, and through jungle so dense the foliage slapped at the side of the cars.

We stopped in small towns where vendors sold Chiclets (chewing gum), tacos, ice cream, fresh mangos, candy, hand-woven baskets, serapes, live iguanas, tortillas ... and more Chiclets. The train terminated in Guadalajara, where I caught a bus for the last leg to Mexico City.

The bus driver thrashed through miles of the semi-contained chaos that is Mexico City traffic, and we pulled into the bus station late in the afternoon. A cab took me to my friend's home. The 12-foot-high, iron-bound timber doors, the only break in the high wall, swung open to reveal a large compound with three separate houses around a lush garden, and the entire Mendoza family gathered to welcome me. The family included my friend Jorge, his parents, brothers, sisters-in-law, cousins, servants and a few people whose relationships I never did catch.

### An Abrazzo, a Barbecue ... and soon ... a Blade

Sr. Mendoza, Jorge's father, gave me an enthusiastic *abrazzo* (hug) and said, "Mi casa es su casa (My house is your house)." This phrase is normally a courteous formality, not meant to be taken literally. But in this case it was heartfelt and

**The author headed to a market in Oaxaca City, Mexico, to do some outfitting for an expedition. He was there in search of mosquito netting, hammocks and a forge where knives of "singing steel" were forged.**

sincere. That evening, the family and friends all gathered in the garden for a barbeque welcoming me to Mexico.

After most of the guests went home, Sr. Mendoza, a professor at the National University, an erudite, cultured man with exquisite Old World manners, introduced me to one of his colleagues. Professor Sanchez was an authority on the pre-Columbian world. Over maps of the Yucatan, professor Sanchez pointed out areas where he suspected there were undiscovered Mayan sites.

The goal of our little expedition, which was to consist of Jorge, myself and whatever local guides we could hire in the Yucatan, was to locate and map any new sites we found in the area set out by professor Mendoza.

We were not accredited by the university or the National Museao de Anthropologico, of which professor Sanchez was a director. I'd taken exactly one course in archeology/anthropology at U.C.L.A., and Jorge was a total playboy who was going for fun. But the professor provided us with a letter of introduction, stating that we were on university business. We planned to wave the letter at whatever authorities we might encounter.

I stayed a week with the Mendoza family, enjoying their hospitality and waiting for Jorge's classes to finish so we could leave. But Jorge flunked a final exam and had to make up work or fail the course. This would be unthinkable in the Mendoza family. We decided that I would go ahead and meet him in Oaxaca, which was on the way, or in Merida, where we were to start our expedition into the bush.

Oaxaca City is near the center of the Valley of Oaxaca, a high, dry valley, home to the Zapotec Indians and the place where corn was first cultivated over 2,000 years ago. The Spanish, under the rule of The Marquis de Valle (Hernan Cortez), built the city. In 1969, Oaxaca still retained its colonial flavor, with buildings of large stone block and inward-turned houses.

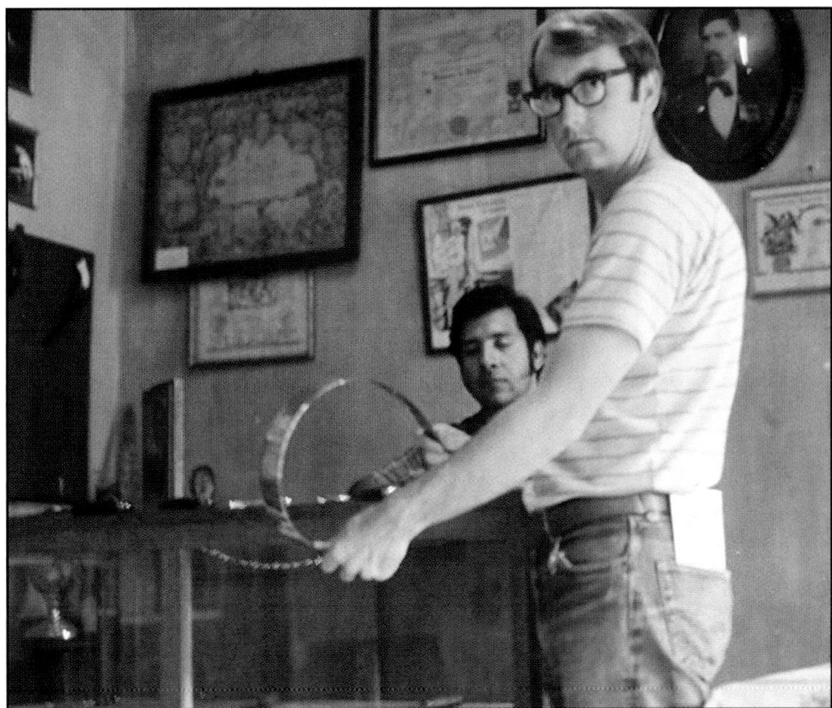

**In a knife showroom in Oaxaca, the proprietor of the shop bent one of his swords to almost a full circle. When he released the blade, it sprang back to true with a ringing sound, like a bell, thus the "singing steel" legend.**

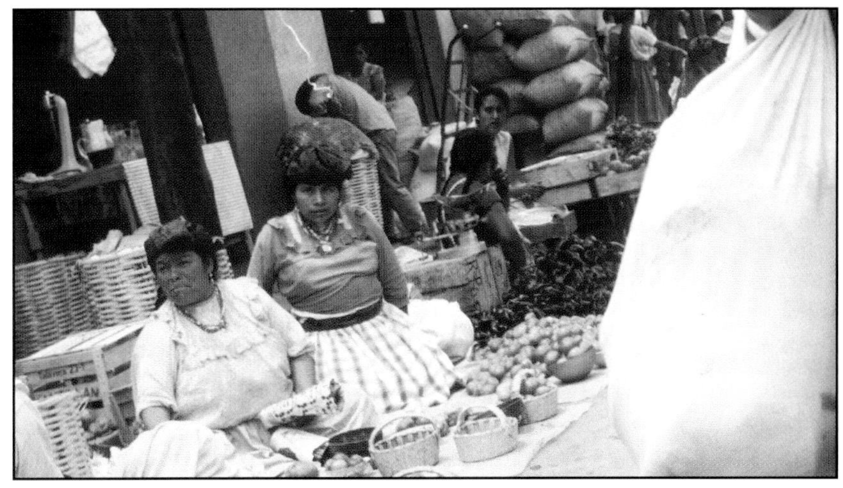

**Though the author had heard about a family from Spain who forged knives of "singing steel," no one at the Oaxaca market knew where to find the family or the knives.**

## In Search of Singing Steel

I headed to the market to do some outfitting. We needed some mosquito netting and hammocks for our jungle expedition. The Indian market, filled with fabulous color from baskets of flowers and fresh fruit, spread out along streets surrounding the *mercado* (market) proper. I was also looking for a forge where knives of "singing steel" were forged.

I had just heard about a family that forged knives of "singing steel" from a mariachi late the previous night in a cafe. The lights were low, the place was about to close and we

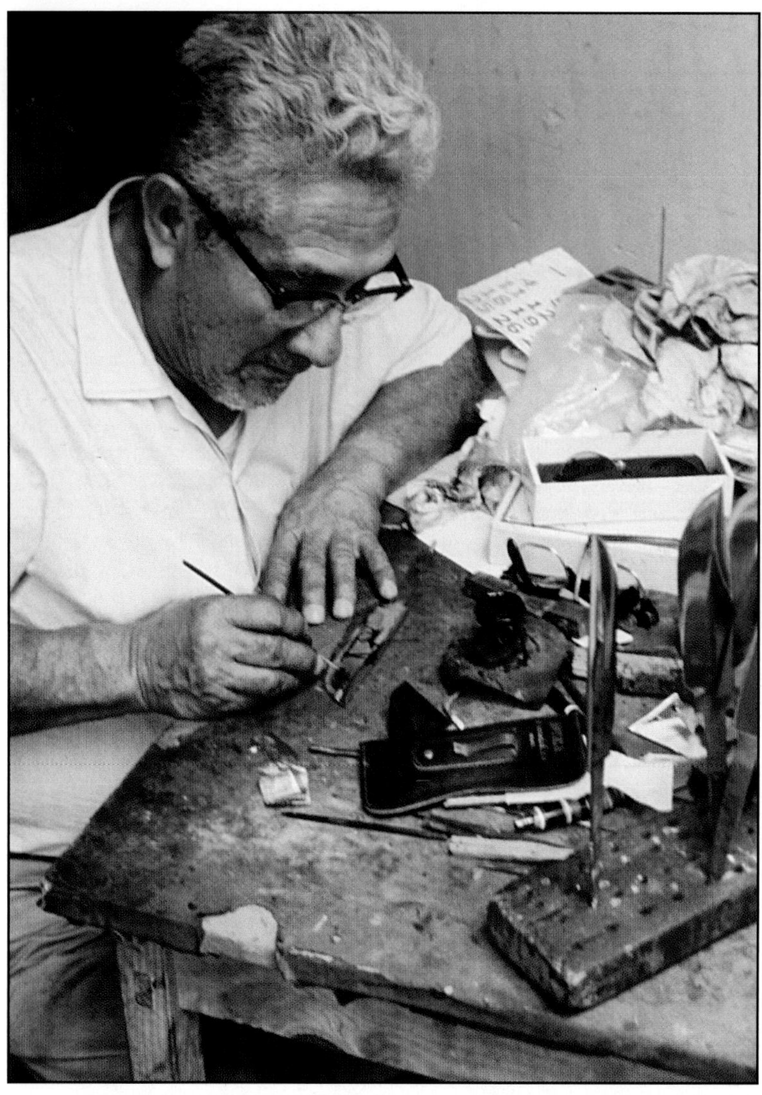

**In The House of Aragorn, an older man sat at a table with a hedge of blades around the perimeter of his work surface. He covered the blades with a resist, and then used a graver to draw scenes and slogans through the resist.**

were having a last drink together. Francisco slipped his knife from under his shirt and laid it on the table. It had a long, slender blade and a horn handle.

He said that the family who had made it came from Spain with the conquistadors, and that they had made swords for Cortez's men, and later for Benito Juarez, a Zapotec Indian who became president of Mexico. Now, he noted, the same family continued to make fine knives and swords. The name of the family was Aragorn, and they were right there in Oaxaca.

Aragorn—that was a portentous and magical name. I had recently read "The Lord Of The Rings" trilogy by J.R.R. Tolkien, and had spent three months in Spain the preceding year. The Aragorn name is famous in Spanish history. There is a city of that name. The association conjured up thoughts of Roland, Charlemagne and the Moorish wars.

My imagination was inflamed. Could this family be connected to those who forged the swords of legend? Tolkien's work might well be fantasy, about a world that never was, but the stories of Roland's sword were part of our world.

"Just go to the market; you will find them," my mariachi friend told me. The next day I searched market streets and questioned passersby in my halting Spanish. I peeked into courtyards and knocked on likely looking doors.

As I progressed, I drew a map of the area, and then crossed off the streets as I covered them. I listened for a hammer on an anvil, but I heard only the sounds of the market—people bargaining in two or three languages, caged birds singing and meat sizzling on open fires.

I asked many people if they knew where I could find anyone making knives or swords. I heard rumors. I received directions that took me nowhere. By late afternoon of the second day, I had covered every street in the entire market and had extended my search to the surrounding neighborhood. I found nothing. Perhaps they didn't really exist anymore. Maybe they died off or moved away, or maybe they were just a story.

It was a child who led me to the House of Aragorn.

I trudged into the cool shade of a stretched canvas roof and ordered a *refresco*, an iced drink made from fruit juice. A small, dirty boy with coal-black hair and eyes had been tagging along behind me for the past few blocks, in the way of small boys everywhere who have nothing to do, and who will fall in with any plan that offers amusement. His name was Paco. I bought him a *refresco* and asked him if he knew anything about a place where they made knives.

"*Si, como no* (Yes, of course)," he said. "I know the place. I will take you there." I followed him to a building a half-dozen blocks away.

"*Esta aqui* (It is here)," he said, pointing at a raspberry-sherbet-colored building. There was no sign at the door, no indication that this was anything other than another retail shop selling dishes, clothing or baskets. I had passed this building at least twice. I asked him if he was sure, wondering if he really had any idea what he was talking about, or if he was just pulling the big gringo's leg.

"*Aqui, aqui*," he said, jumping from foot to foot. "*Entrar*, (Go inside)," he insisted.

## Cases of Knives

Finally I walked through the wide doorway and past the portals. I found myself in a room of glass cases filled with knives. There were framed photos on the walls, pictures of men on horseback with swords at their sides, a photograph of an old man with steel in his eyes, surrounded by knives and swords. This was it: The House of Aragorn.

A stocky, muscular man came from the back and introduced himself. Hector was the manager of the workshop. He said no one from the family was available. I walked with him into the courtyard of the building, where various craftsmen were attending to the tasks required to make a finished knife: filing, polishing, fitting handles, and so on.

At one table sat an older man with a hedge of blades around the edge of his work surface. He covered the blades with a resist, and then used a graver to draw scenes and slogans through the resist. The blades were then washed in acid, which etched them, and the resist was removed.

The forge and the anvil were in the very back of the building. Here was the sound for which I had been listening—the clang of steel on steel reverberated and echoed back from the walls.

Back in the showroom, Hector bent one of his swords to almost a full circle. When he released the blade, it sprang back to true with a ringing sound, like a bell, thus the "singing steel" legend. He then drove the point of a knife I selected through a 20-peso coin, and the edge through a rusty old bolt, tests of a blade from days gone by.

I had to have an Aragorn knife. Yes, they would make one to my own design. They would make whatever I wanted, a sword or a machete, or any style of knife. I showed him my Randall, which I carried in a woven market bag with a camera and a few odds and ends. I wanted to use the Randall as the pattern for a larger knife.

"*Con permisso*? (With your permission?)," Hector asked. I handed

**The author embarked on a journey to the Yucatan, carrying only a worn canvas rucksack of meager supplies, and his Randall Model One survival knife.**

**The blades were washed in acid, which etched them, and then the resist was removed.**

the Randall to him and he touched the blade to his tongue, tasting the carbon in the steel. Then he took it to an anvil and tapped it very lightly with a hammer, listening to the sound it made. Next he put the blade in a vise, and with his weight behind it, bent the blade slightly. It sprang back to true. "Good steel," he said, "good knife."

Hector was as interested in the sheath with the sharpening stone as he was with the Randall knife. He thought it was a good idea to keep the stone with the knife, but that the sheath would be awkward to carry.

After some discussion, we agreed on a 10-inch-bladed bowie styled after the Randall, to be ready in one week. Jorge was due to arrive in Oaxaca the following week and I wanted to take the Aragorn knife with me to the jungles of Yucatan.

Jorge arrived on time, but the knife was not ready. Hector was running a little late. He would have the knife for me in only two more days, or maybe three. But we couldn't wait. We were anxious to start our expedition. The Randall was a good and familiar knife. It would do.

## Sheathed and Ready

Hector did have a new sheath for the Randall ready for me. It was a plain slip sheath with a spring clip that would allow me to carry the Randall more discreetly. Swallowing my disappointment, I slid the Randall into its new sheath and left the unfinished bowie to be picked up on my return.

We departed on my first expedition in search of ancient cities, to find the treasures of the Maya. After some false starts and some adventures, we did find our lost city. Well, maybe not a city, but we did find a 50-foot-high pyramid and some outbuildings, all covered with vines, overgrown with jungle and time. Two Lacandon Indians we met in Merida guided us to our goal. But that's a story for another time.

I picked up the Aragorn bowie on my way back through Oaxaca. It was everything I wanted it to be. It had a horn handle, a graceful blade and sweet balance. I was disappointed that I had not been able to try it in the jungle.

Later, back in Los Angeles, I found that the forged Mexican blade was a perfect survival knife. I was a college student struggling to pay tuition and living off the meager aid of the G.I. Bill, which amounted to the grand sum of $125 a month.

No books were paid for, no classes were financed; nothing else was paid. My young wife and I had to scuffle pretty hard to keep the wolf away from the door, to take care of an ailing parent and to pay school expenses. But we were getting by. Then I lost my job three weeks before Christmas.

Now I was faced with a survival challenge, one that millions of people have had to face, and one that involved no jungles or wild animals, just everyday necessity. I retrieved the Aragorn knife from its place of honor on the wall, and took it to a gun dealer who had a custom knife department. The big knife was still shiny, new, never used. I showed the knife to him, along with some photos and told him my story.

He took the knife on consignment, and I left hoping it would sell before the holidays. The Aragorn bowie sold on December 21. The dealer called me the same day and had a check ready for me when I arrived at the store.

"That knife was a beauty," he said. Too bad you never got to use it as a survival knife."

"But I did," I said. "It worked perfectly."

I sold that knife for 10 times what I paid for it. We all had a nice Christmas and managed to pay the doctor's bill. The next spring I was back on the road to Mexico, to another lost city...and to the House of Aragorn.

# Are Daggers Sporting Knives?

***Is this a dagger which I see before me ... ?***

*William Shakespeare's "Macbeth" (Act II, Scene I)*

*By Evan F. Nappen*

The view that daggers have only one purpose and that purpose is to kill people demonstrates a profound ignorance about the history and use of daggers. Often a dagger can mean the difference between life and death when facing outdoor challenges.

It is well established that daggers are and have been used by outdoorsmen in hunting; fishing; scuba diving; trapping; camping; hiking; backpacking; mountain climbing; skydiving; farming; and ranching. Utilization of daggers is common in any outdoor activity that involves or necessitates a reliable cutting tool.

Your humble writer has personally hunted and killed wild boar in South Carolina using only a Randall Model 2 knife with an 8-inch, double-edge blade. The 350-pound hog dropped faster when downed with the blade than if it had been shot. The Randall was particularly effective because it penetrated the wild boar's thick hide with ease and made for a quick and humane kill. A single-edge knife simply would not have been as effective.

Other personal examples of "sporting" daggers include: (1) my scuba diving knife, a well-worn, double-edge Wenoka that I have had since I was 13 years old; (2) my Tru-Bal double-edge throwing knife called to action when I informally compete in knife throwing contests; (3) a double-edge Gerber Mark II that a good friend of mine never goes camping or hiking without, and that he carried in Vietnam; and (4) my Randall Model 13 "Arkansas Toothpick" with a 12-inch, double-edge blade (it beats flossing every time).

To thoroughly explore this topic, one must first define "dagger." There are various definitions that vary between sources. The *A.G. Russell Online Knife Encyclopedia* defines "dagger" as a "double-edge sheath knife with a symmetrical blade intended for stabbing." (http://www.agrussell.com/knife_information/knife_encyclopedia/index.html) This is a fair and common view of what is generally thought of as a "dagger."

A hidden agenda can often be found in legal and statutory definitions that reflect an anti-knife bias. The problem is that false or unclear definitions of edged tools

**Modern-day daggers that utilize advanced technology give the outdoorsman a special edge in facing sporting challenges. From edge-holding ability to corrosion resistance, to the durability of the steel itself, a wide range of choices for individual application is available to the ordinary person. Bud Nealy's modern rendition of the OSS collar dagger features a high-tech CPM S30V blade and an MCS sheath.**

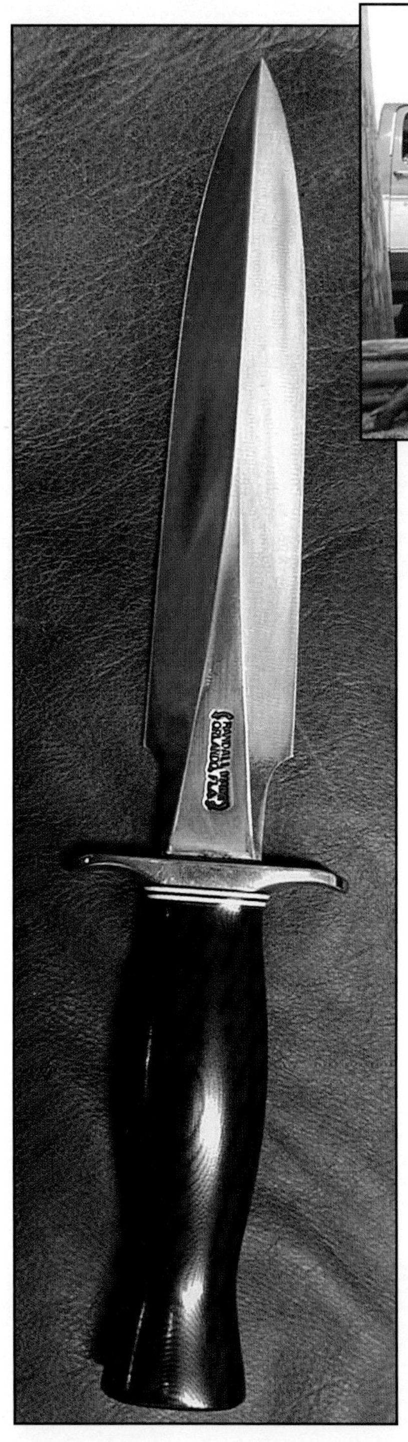

**Furthering his argument that daggers do have sporting uses is the fact that the author downed this wild boar using a Randall Made Model 2 with an 8-inch blade.**

are employed to lump together dissimilar knives into one category. The same technique is used by the anti-gun crowd to exploit a "scary" gun and use it as a "strawman" to ban several firearms falling under one umbrella definition. A great example of this is the state of California's defintion of "dagger":

*(a) Any person in this state who does any of the following is punishable by imprisonment in a county jail not exceeding one year or in the state prison:*

*(a)(4) Carries concealed upon his or her person any dirk or dagger.*

*(c)(24) As used in this section, a "dirk" or "dagger" means a knife or other instrument with or without a handguard that is capable of ready use as a stabbing weapon that may inflict great bodily injury or death.*

*A nonlocking folding knife, a folding knife that is not prohibited by Section 653k [switchblade], or a pocketknife is capable of ready use as a stabbing weapon that may inflict great bodily injury or death only if the blade of the knife is exposed and locked into position.*

Shockingly, under this definition, "dagger" simply means a "knife." What do "hand guards," or a lack thereof, have to do with the price of fish? Then, the intrinsically evil "knife" only has to be "capable of ready use as a stabbing weapon." Gee, that's a rather broad definition, wouldn't you say? Now the courts have to sort it out while the law-abiding knife owner suffers.

## The Garden State Dagger

New Jersey takes another approach that makes the honest dagger owner "guilty until proven innocent." The Garden State's dagger law says:

*Any person who knowingly has in his possession any gravity knife, switchblade knife, dagger, dirk, stiletto, billy, blackjack, metal knuckle, sandclub, slingshot, cestus or similar leather band studded with metal filings or razor blades imbedded in wood, ballistic knife, without any explainable lawful purpose, is guilty of a crime of the fourth degree.*

This contradicts fundamental fairness for the dagger owner by switching the burden of proof from the prosecution to the defendant. The law-abiding knife owner must prove an "explainable lawful purpose" as an affirmative defense to a jury of 12 folks who the prosecution will try to "pump up" about "why anyone would need such a knife." But what would one expect from a state that also prohibits "slingshots" (in the same law cited above), thereby turning Bart Simpson and Dennis the Menace into felons.

Now compare California and New Jersey to Montana, which prohibits a person who *"carries or bears concealed upon his person a dirk, dagger... sword cane... knife having a blade 4 inches long or longer,"* but then has the following exceptions for all persons who are *lawfully engaged in hunting, fishing, trapping, camping, hiking, backpacking, farming, ranching, or other outdoor activity in which weapons are often carried for recreation or protection.*

Montana law specifically recognizes the sporting use of daggers! These exceptions say it loud and clear. Whether it be hunting, fishing, trapping, camping, hiking, backpacking, farming, ranching or other outdoor activity, Montana's legislators know that knives save lives and are an important tool of the outdoorsman.

Oklahoma also prohibits *"any person to carry upon or about his or her person, or in a purse or other container belonging to the person ... any dagger."* However, Okalahoma, like Montana, also recognizes the sporting use of daggers. Okalahoma has important exceptions to this prohibition, even including historical reenactment! Okalahoma's insightful exceptions acknowledge:

*1. The proper use of guns and knives for hunting, fishing, educational or recreational purposes;*

*2. The carrying or use of weapons in a manner otherwise permitted by statute or authorized by the Oklahoma Self-Defense Act;*

*3. The carrying, possession and use of any weapon by a peace officer or other person authorized by law to carry a weapon in the performance of official duties and in compliance with the rules of the employing agency; or*

*4. The carrying and use of firearms and other weapons provided in this subsection when used for the purpose of living history reenactment. For purposes of this paragraph, "living history reenactment" means depiction of historical characters, scenes, historical life or events for entertainment, education or historical documentation through the wearing or use of period, historical, antique or vintage clothing, accessories, firearms, weapons and other implements of the historical period.*

Oklahoma has legislatively declared a "proper use" of knives for recreational purposes. The modern dagger serves an important role as today's man pushes the envelope with greater outdoor and survival challenges. The views expressed by Montana and Oklahoma reflect a practical understanding of the use of daggers and, significantly, the importance of daggers in history.

## The Indomitable Dagger

The dagger as a lineage reaching back to ancient times and has been a constant tool of man. The history of daggers demonstrates an established use of the knives for everything from daily utilitarian tasks to man's survival against nature.

Considered by many to be the preeminent authority on daggers, the legendary Bashford Dean wrote in his classic 332-page book, The Metropolitan of Art Catalogue of European Daggers that, *"during these epochs, the dagger, partly because it could be used as a knife, was worn oftener than any other arm, and as it increased in usefulness, its forms multiplied. In a general way,*

**The Benchmade Model 175 CBK is beveled only on one side of the blade, and flat on the other. A palpable handle design offers an intuitive, fast-response grip, and a molded sheath design provides for secure carry inverted or otherwise.**

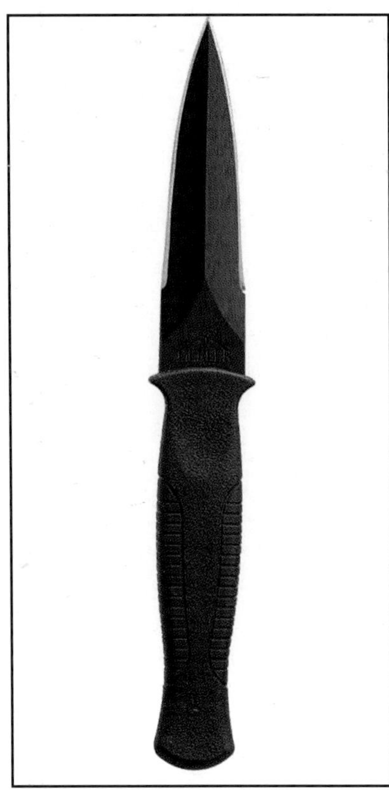

The design of the new Gerber Guardian is based on the 20-year-old classic Mark II dagger. The handle is no longer cat's tongue aluminum, but rather a Santoprene™ rubber coating that provides a strong, non-slip grip.

*it played a role which the swords in their own lines of specialization could not fill. It was par excellence an instrument of convenience and precision."* It is for this fact that the dagger holds a special place in the world of knives, and its sporting uses are undeniable.

Second only to the club as man's earliest weapon, edged instruments have been part of man's existence since the first chipped stone cut the hide of a hunter's kill. The use of two edges by primitive man can be seen in spears, arrow heads and handheld cutting tools, with these being the earliest known "daggers."

The earliest flint daggers had hilts made of wrapped natural material, like animal hide or skins. Such knives have been discovered in Egypt and date back to approximately 3,000 B.C. Similar pieces in Scandinavia date to between 1800 and 1500 B.C.

According to "Daggers & Fighting Knives of the Western World from the Stone Age till 1900," written by Harold L. Peterson, the Scandinavian daggers were so popular and vital during this time that archeologists have actually named the period the *Dolktid* or Dagger Period of Scandinavian prehistory. The daggers were used for a multitude of purposes, including hunting, skinning, butchering and many other tasks when a sharp edge was demanded.

Although flint and stone could take and hold a sharp edge, it was brittle, could break easily and was difficult to repair. The advent of metal made a huge difference in the evolution of daggers. One of the earliest metals to be utilized is believed to be copper. Daggers made of copper have been found in Mesopotamia, Egypt, India and the Great Lakes region of North America.

Copper worked better than stone as a knife blade, but being relatively soft, it would bend easily and not hold an edge as well as desired. It was eventually discovered that if tin was added to copper, a harder alloy could be created.

This then-new alloy, known as bronze, became one of the most significant technological achievements of ancient times. The Bronze Age, as it was known, saw a tremendous growth in the production and use of daggers. As early as 2500 B.C., bronze daggers were being made in Mesopotamia. Bronze allowed the blades to be thinner and longer without the risk of failure.

After the Bronze Age, a new metal was used in the manufacture

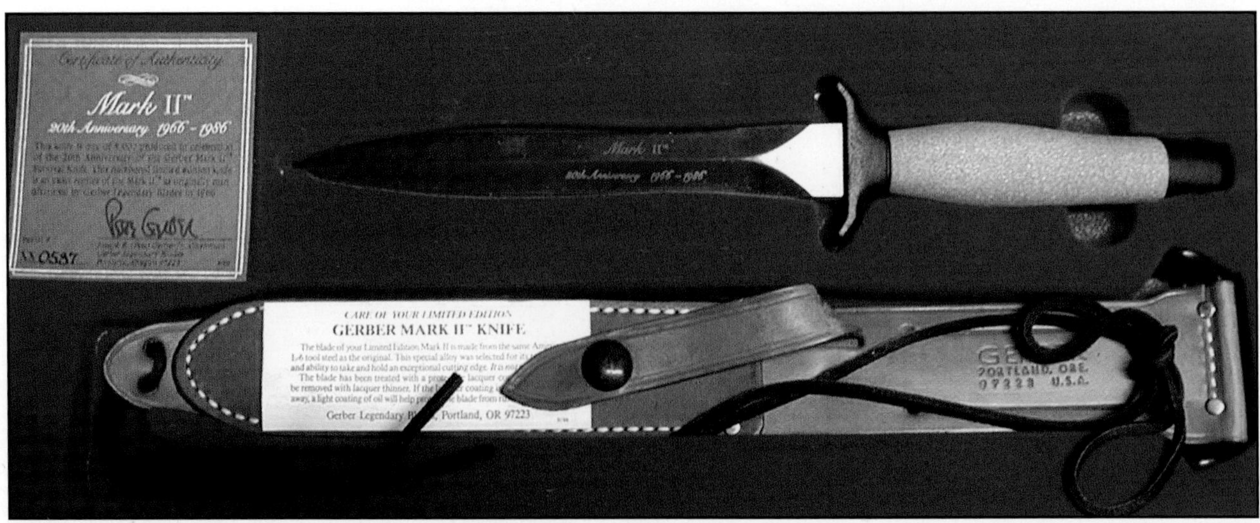


The author has a friend who carried a double-edge Gerber Mark II in Vietnam and never goes camping or hiking without the knife. Pictured is the boxed 20th anniversary Mark II model.

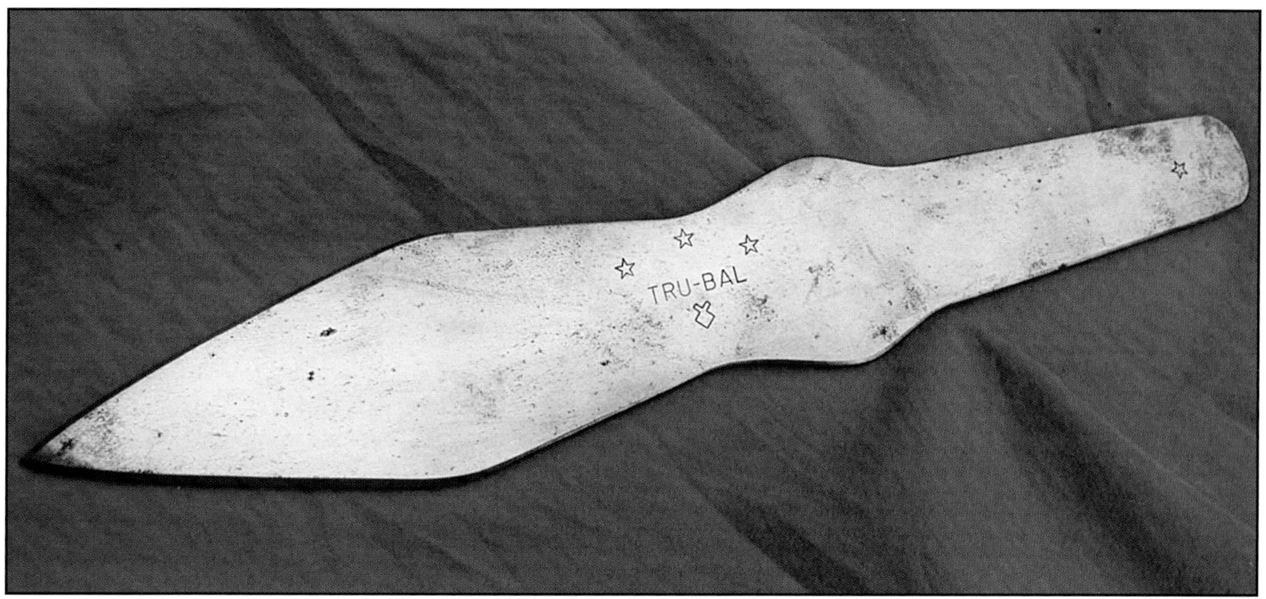


**The author's personal collection of "sporting daggers" includes a Tru-Bal double-edge throwing knife called to action when he informally competes in knife-throwing contests.**

of daggers. Called "iron," it was sometimes left behind by meteors, and the Egyptians even called iron "black copper from the skies." Ancient iron was wrought by heating the metal in a fire and hammering it into a desired shape.

Sometimes the iron picked up carbon from the fire and turned into a type of steel. Steel is technically iron with a percentage of carbon added to it. This technique of "steeling iron" was first learned by bladesmiths of the Hittite Empire around 1500 B.C., and it became a highly protected military and commercial secret.

## Steely-Eyed Ancients

Eventually the secret became known and the popularity of steel in knives lives on to this day. Of course, modern forging techniques can be used to accomplish incredible things with high-tech steels. The ancients would surely marvel in awe at the quality and consistency of high-tech steels.

Modern-day daggers that utilize advanced technology give the outdoorsman a special edge in facing sporting challenges. From edge-holding ability to corrosion resistance, to the durability of the steel itself, a wide range of choices for individual application is available to the ordinary person.

The ability to choose a dagger as one's edged companion is a freedom that should not be taken away from law-abiding knife owners. It is particularly disturbing when the reason for the loss of liberty is pure politics, focused on selling a "bill of goods" to a gullible public by dishonest politicians.

The sporting use of daggers is a historical and provable fact. To defame the dagger as "only designed to kill people" is at best hyperbole, and at worst, an attempt to turn otherwise honest knife owners into criminals. Any politician who promotes banning inanimate objects as a cure for crime fails to address the real problem—the criminals.

Instead, the liberty-sucking politician has made the inanimate object the symbol and the scapegoat for the government's failure to tackle the hard issue.

Whether it is used hunting, fishing, scuba diving, trapping, camping, hiking, backpacking, mountain climbing, skydiving, farming or ranching, the dagger is a useful outdoor tool. The sporting use of daggers has been around for as long as there have been such double-edged knives in the hand of man. Unfortunately, sometimes those daggers have been used to kill other men, but it is not the dagger's fault, but rather the fault of the hand that holds it.

## Bibliography


Cook, Eiler R., *Travels for Daggers.* Historic Edged Weaponry, Hendersonville, North Carolina, 2004.

Dean, Bashford, *Catalogue of European Daggers, 1300-1800.* The Metropolitan Museum of Art, New York, 1929.

Peterson, Harold L., *Daggers & Fighting Knives of the Western World*, The Arms & Armour Series. Walker & Company, New York, 1968.

Thompson, Logan, *Daggers and Bayonets, A History.* Paladin Press, Boulder, Colorado, 1999.

Wilkinson, F., *Swords & Daggers, An Illustrated Reference Guide for Collectors*. Arms and Armour Press, London, 1985.

# Neck Knives—Blades You Can Hang With

## *The lady knife writer looks at knives as more than jewelry but sees the advantages of neck knives*

*By Linda Moll Smith*

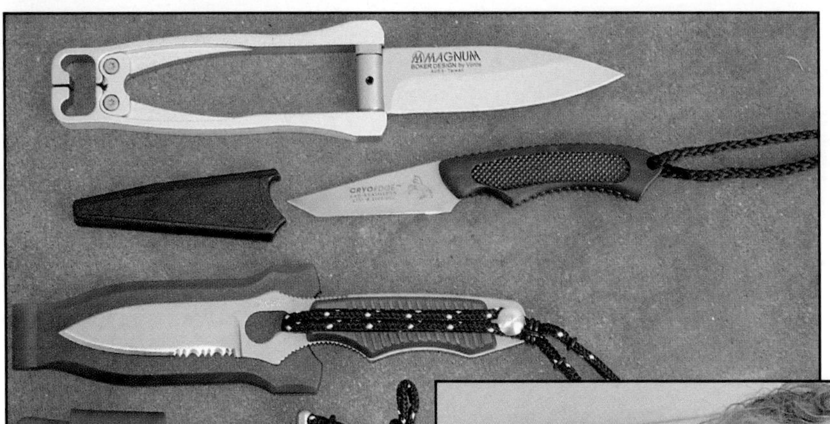


**Three hot neck knives to hang with are (from top) the new Boker Magnum BO450 Neck Knife donning a unique breakaway carrying clip, the Colt Cryo-edge with magnet sheath and the CRKT Hawk K-AT.**

Today, a whole selection of neck, or necklace, knives is available for the choosing and ideally suited as cutting-edge weapons to "hang with."

My own personal neck knife is a favorite piece that I wear suspended from a cord when I run for exercise. It's the A.G. Russell Bird & Trout knife, a sleek, thin-ground, drop-point fixed blade with a molded-Zytel sheath that features a Thumb-bolt® release with snap swivel.

Incorporating a 3-inch blade and measuring less than 7 inches overall, there's no knife simpler and more accessible. I've had to pry it out of the hands of several envious girlfriends! This knife comes in several blade-steel options—D-2, AUS-8 and VG-10—with corresponding price points, none over $50.

The Bird & Trout and a larger version, the Deer Hunter, also come with upside-down sheaths, perfect for around-the-neck wear and flashier than a necktie worn to the office! The knives are available

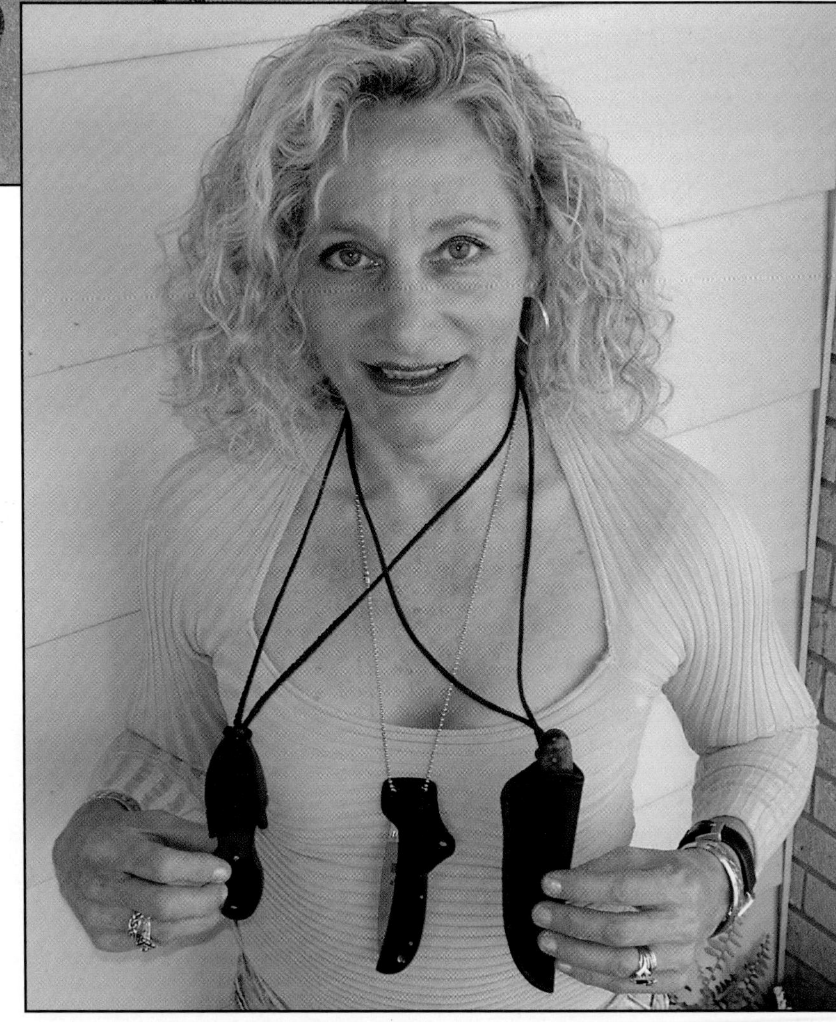

**Author Linda Moll Smith models a trio of wearable neck knives.**



*All photos by Linda Moll Smith and Mac Overto*

online at http://www.agrussell.com.

In researching neck knives, I wore several blades, some made for the purpose and others easily adapted to "neckware." For a fixed blade, a snug-fitting and lightweight protective sheath is essential, and such is almost always crafted from Kydex, Zytel or similar materials. Although most sheaths allow for the blade to be toted tip-up or tip-down, I personally prefer the former over the latter.

A few neck-knife sheaths include magnets within their makeup to further secure the steel blades and prevent them from slipping out of the neck rigs and toward the torsos or limbs of their unwary wearers. Some sheath manufacturers include lanyards, swivel clips or split rings, along with stout cording, with which to hang the knives.

Other personalization options include leather thongs or beaded chains. The one advantage to beaded chains is that most will break away when pulled hard, preventing a choking hazard in emergency circumstances.

Many lightweight folders can also be fitted to perform as neck knives and are handy for hikers, boaters, joggers and ladies, the latter of whom tend not to have, or use, pockets for carrying knives—something most manufacturers seem not to consider!

## Knifemakers Go for the Jugular

Most quality production companies and quite a few custom makers turn out their own versions of neck

**These are tough, durable neck knives from Fallkniven of Sweden. Both feature blades of fine VG-10 edge-holding stainless steel. The single-edge model is the WM, while the dagger is the Garm, named for the dog that, in Norse mythology, guards the entrance to hell.**

**Award-winning custom knifemaker Sidney "Pete" Moon makes neck knives in a variety of useful blade shapes and handle materials. The top piece sports a modified-sheepsfoot blade and a black-Micarta® handle, while the other knife has a drop-point blade and red jigged-bone handle. For more information, email knifeman@aol.com.**

**The fixed blade at left, with a handle of moose antler, is by Silver Stag. At center is an Al Mar Ultralight Eagle with a special, optional friction sheath. At right is an early Al Mar Eagle featuring a synthetic-ivory handle and an aftermarket sheath from Wild Boar Blades. The pendants are of 52100-and-15N20 damascus, and were made by Ray Kirk (Raker Knives). While they are useful as screwdrivers, Kirk originally designed them to be carried by his wife on her key chain as defensive weapons.**

**The A.G. Russell Neck Knives are made of Hitachi Blue high-carbon steel. They are built in the same manner that simple knives have been made in Japan for hundreds of years. A.G. says, "These are the handiest little neck/utility knives you have ever seen." The top knife is a square-end blade style, while the bottom one is a small clip-point caper.**

**This neck knife from American Bladesmith Society master smith Murray Carter has been used quite a bit over the past three years by knife writer Mac Overton, and is still razor sharp! Jigged bone is only one of many handle options. The smaller knife is atypical of Carter's work, and was fashioned from a scrapped kitchen knife. Overton persuaded Carter to sell it to him at the 2004 BLADE Show, and drilled the hole in the Kydex® sheath, adding the cord later. Mac says you'd be amazed how useful it is!**

knives these days. Following is an overview, by no means comprehensive, of neck knives *prêt a porter* (ready to wear). The knives I reviewed were more recreational in nature than tactical, the latter of which presents an entire subcategory of neck-carry knives.

## Benchmade

I have a friend who won't even consider buying a knife unless it's a Benchmade—that's brand loyalty and American-made pride for you. This is for him, and he would love it. He serves in the U.S. armed forces, stationed in the Persian Gulf, and the Benchmade Model 160 TK-1 Tether Knife looks fittingly militaristic.

The one-piece knife showcases a 2-inch, midnight-black, semi-serrated 440C blade, thermoplastic coating on an integral, skeletonized handle and a slick Kydex sheath fitted with a cord tether. It's less a knife than a work of architecture. At a closed length of 5 3/4 inches, it weighs a mere 1.5 ounces—a light but tough traveler for multi-time-zone challenges. It carries a manufacturer's suggested retail price (MSRP) of $80 and might just be the only field knife you need. The Tether Knife is available online at www.benchmade.com.

## Boker

A German knife company, Boker offers what I call a "cutie-patootie." The Magnum Keyring Light in Silver, made in the Orient, measures a mere 2 3/4 inches closed. It features a 2-inch 420 stainless blade anchored by a lightweight aluminum handle. Petite enough to come with a keychain, I would wear it slung from the neck and ready for instant use. At around $10, it makes an edgy but practical little gift for almost anyone.

At the other end of the neck-knife scale, Boker offers the innovative Magnum B0450 Neck Knife with a 3 3/8-inch 8-A blade. It employs a unique breakaway clip attached to a neck cord, rather than a sheath, and the blade flips open sideways!

## Camillus

The Camillus CUDA (Camillus Ultra Design Advantage) line of knives includes a likeable necklace knife. The Arclite #CU120 showcases a curved and skeletonized handle, complete with an integral guard, that is actually comfortable to use. If you prefer a cord-wrapped handle, it's a breeze to customize. The 3.125-inch, plain-edge, modified-bowie-style 420HC blade is sleek and uncomplicated. It includes a slim-silhouetted Kydex sheath and bead chain, and a TekLock buckle system is available separately for wear on a belt or safety harness. Buying and using the versatile utility knife is a no-brainer, especially at an MSRP of less than $35. The Arclite is available online at www.camillusknives.com.

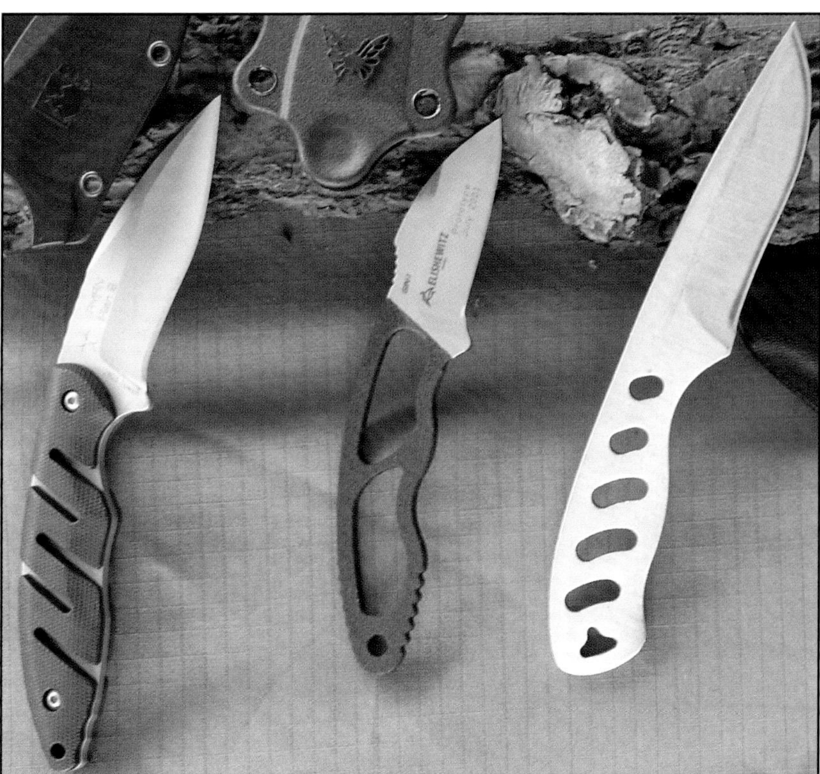

**This trio includes, from left, a Columbia River Knife & Tool Ryan Plan B, a Benchmade Tether knife and a Darrel Ralph-designed ArcLite from Camillus.**

## Cold Steel

I promised I wouldn't talk about tactical knives, but here I am hedging my bets with a couple of neck knives that exhibit distinct bodyguard tendencies. Cold Steel's Spike, designed by custom knifemaker Barry Dawson, looks to be awesome and fearsome as a minimalist weapon. Its 4-inch sub-zero-quenched 420 blade is shaped like a genteel railroad spike, with a thick-yet-narrow blade that merges into a solid-steel, black-cord-wrapped handle. It's scary, even tucked away in a Secure Ex molded sheath, and the steel bead lanyard adds its own no-nonsense aura.

At 8 inches overall, it might be a little long to be worn comfortably as a neck knife—indeed Cold Steel calls it a boot knife—but better to feel awkward than threatened! A male friend of mine has urged me to carry just such a knife while out and about, but I'm not sure I'm that bloodthirsty—yet! It also comes in equally intimidating tanto and talon point blade options. At around $40 retail, it's a steal to conceal.

A pudgy, but equally sharp baby brother to the Spike is Cold Steel's Para Edge. I tried the dagger (double-edged) version, but there is also a tanto blade shown in a recent catalog. The Para Edge's 3-inch AUS-6A stainless blade is ground to a razor edge and tucks lightly into a Concealex™ neck sheath, making it an easy-carry utility or rescue knife for less than $50. It is available online at www.coldsteel.com.

## Columbia River Knife & Tool

Columbia River Knife & Tool carries at least two noteworthy neck knives. The Kit Carson-designed F4, which sounds like it should be a fighter jet, flies jet-high, at least in fixed-blade terms, and is equally as fast in its hardy cutting ability. Though the high-carbon stainless blade is less than 3 inches long, it features a full tang hugged by molded-Zytel grips. The 5 1/2-inch knife slings on handily, head-over-heels, in its custom-molded sheath, featuring a reversible clip and various holes and slots. The F4 is versatile enough to hang with any adventurer rappelling cliffs, running rapids or driving an SUV-load of little leaguers to their next tournament! The knife comes complete with a black-nylon lanyard and a bead chain for an MSRP of $24.99.

The K-AT (Knife—All Terrain) is a full-tang fixed blade designed by knifemaker Grant Hawk to incorporate a 2 1/4-inch spear-point blade. It offers unique looks and flexibility. A cord lanyard can be stowed by wrapping it through the blade and around the handle. You have to see and hold this knife to truly grasp it. The neck knife is worth a look. The K-AT's molded-urethane sheath remains quiet when the blade is extracted from it, and it can be converted to a neck-carry rig with the addition of a bead chain. The MSRP is $39.99. The knives are available online at www.crkt.com.

## Fallkniven

The Swedish company, which has been establishing a following for its specialty fixed blades,

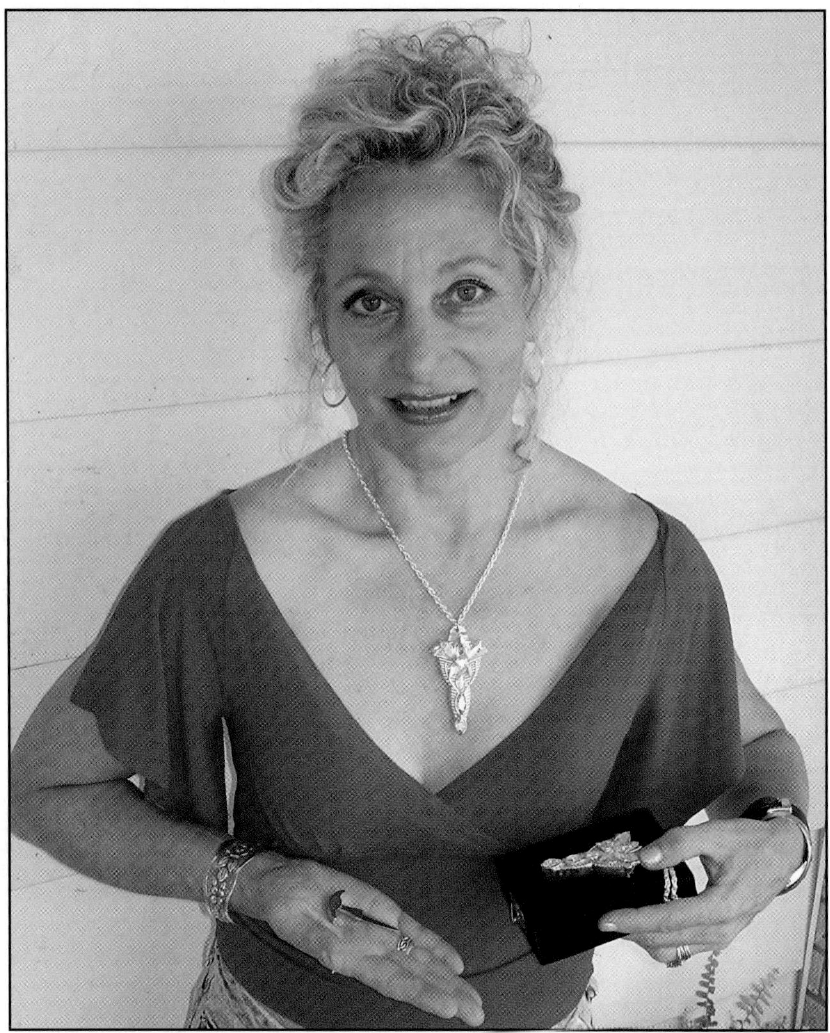

**Linda Moll Smith is shown wearing the jeweled Axtion Bladez Elvenspike Classic neck knife and displaying a second model to show the dagger and jeweled sheath/case.**

is now, unfortunately, on the sale block. But most of its stock is still available, including a couple of desirable neck knives, both of superior VG-10 steel. Grab yourself a dagger-like Garm (named for the Norse guard-dog of the gates of Hell) or a WM1 while you still can! The G1 Garm Fighter is a fierce little contender for neck knife featherweight fighter of the year! The double-edged blade is just over 3 1/2 inches, but black-coated and ground with double edges that won't quit.

The shaped Thermorun™ rubber handle makes for a safe grip while pulling the Garm from its Kydex neck sheath. Take my word for it—it lies easy in the palm, yet is poised for action. The WM1, on the other hand, is designed specifically for a woman's grip, hence the "WM" designation. The blade is chunky and convex ground—it measures 2.8 inches but runs narrow-tang through a shapely synthetic handle, giving users a secure feeling. It also finds a quick-release home in a Kydex neck sheath—a great knife for both men and ladies. The knives retail for under $100 apiece and are available online at www.fallkniven.com.

## Others in Good Company

Only lack of space keeps me from reviewing a slew of other neck knives that hang around with their aforementioned cousins, behaving quite nicely. I cannot fail to mention Timberline's sweet little Mini Pit Bull (a 3-inch-bladed fighting pup of a knife) at around $30. And there's the Al Mar Ultralight Eagle, one of my all-time favorite knives, which can be converted to neck carry. It is as elegant as a string of cultured pearls, and more useable for around $120. Visit www.almarknives.com.

SOG is introducing its new Topo Contour—an awesome collectible—boasting a black-coated beauty of a 2 1/2-inch, upswept AUS-8 blade and a layered-aluminum-and-Zytel handle. The Kydex sheath system allows for multiple carry options. Hang the C47T model in a place it can be seen for under $100. Visit www.sogknives.com.

An itty-bitty neck knife, which I wear as jewelry on a neck chain, comes in the form of the Spyderco Jester. Classified as a keychain knife, it measures only 2 1/2 inches closed and can be carried everywhere (except on board commercial aircraft). Visit www.spyderco.com.

## Accessorize with The Elvenspike

Speaking of jewelry, for years I wondered, with bent-on-beauty feminine logic, "Why doesn't someone craft a necklace knife that really looks like a necklace—one that is as elegant as it is useful?"

What I've had in mind is a sleek little dagger disguised as a wearable, jeweled case, a genteel weapon for milady. I was thinking the Renaissance, the Middle Ages, fantasy kingdoms and courtesans needing to dispatch annoying suitors with discreet class.

Cometh the Elvenspike Classic necklace knife to the rescue! Photos cannot do this collector's piece justice—it is the piece de resistance when worn! This classic silver design, which glimmers hypnotically with genuine Czech Aurora Borealis crystals, and comes complete with heavy neck chain and velvet presentation box, conceals a shapely little dagger. Yes, it's a real knife, so guys, be nice to your lady if you give her one of these! Visit www.axtionbladez.com.

# Save a Blade—Heave a Sheath

## *Check out this selection of sheaths, and you'll never go bare-bladed again!*

*By Durwood Hollis*

We talk a lot about the "dawn of civilization" when discussing knives. We say that the knife is "man's oldest tool," and that "early civilizations" were built, in part, by the knife. Well, sheaths are nothing to sneeze at, either.

As mankind spread across the face of the earth, he would inevitably land in some locations where there were no adequate materials for tool making. Subsequently, the demand for something to carry tools in became necessary. Here's where the sheath comes into the picture.

No doubt, the earliest sheaths were crafted from leaf wrappings, lengths of fibrous vines or hollowed-out pieces of wood. Indeed, similar sheaths are still used in many primitive societies. Once the preservation of animal skin was developed, however, leather emerged as the sheath material of choice, and rightfully so.

Leather can be cut and sewn to fit a wide variety of blade shapes and sizes. Not only does a leather sheath make for adequate containment, it also provides a protective barrier between the sharpened edge and easily lacerated body parts.

Even though leather is a suitable sheath material, it does have some drawbacks. Leather can stretch out of shape, become dry and brittle, stain horribly and will serve as a growth media for mold and fungus. Without adequate care, over time, exposure to the environment will have a detrimental effect on leather. To protect the integrity of this natural material, it must be kept clean and well-maintained.

There are other problems with leather, namely cost and manufacturing time. Quality tanned leather

**The sheaths offered by Buck Knives (left) and Knives of Alaska exhibit the versatility of leather as a knife-slip material.**

of an appropriate grade and weight for sheath construction can be costly. Since the difference between various leathers isn't well understood by the customer, many cutlery manufacturers give little consideration to the caliber of the material used in their knife sheaths. Yet, a knowledgeable knife buyer will not only consider the knife, but also the leather that accompanies it.

In a recent discussion with renowned knifemaker Bob Loveless,

**Press-to-fit leather sheaths include those from (left to right) Rapala, D.H. Russell and Benchmark. Regardless of the tightness of fit, the absence of a safety strap to hold the knives in the sheaths can result in inadvertent knife loss.**

he commented on the importance of a quality leather sheath. He said, "If you're in the market for a new house, you can tell a lot about it just by looking at the outside. A lawn in need of care, fading paint and missing roof tiles are clues to what can be expected on the inside. And the same thing is true when it comes to a knife sheath. A quality knife should be housed in a sheath that reflects its contents. If not, then approach such a purchase with caution. The sheath is the house in which the knife resides. And that says a lot about its resident tenant."

## No Sacrificial Sheaths

When it comes to sheaths, all too often quality is sacrificed on the altar of knife manufacturing, sacrificed, it seems, for the good of lower manufacturer's suggested retail prices. In an effort to undercut the competition, lightweight, poor-quality leather is often used. I've seen some sheath leather that wasn't much better than cardboard. You can be sure that when a manufacturer is guilty of trying to slip cardboard-like leather by the buyer, there will be flaws in the knives, too.

When purchasing a knife, look closely at the sheath. A quality sheath will be made from leather heavy enough to retain its shape when the knife is removed. Sheath edges should be beveled and points of strain reinforced. It's also important that the welt be positioned properly. This prevents the blade edge from cutting through the leather when the knife is inserted into the sheath.

Waxed thread and close stitches are other indicators of superior construction. The sheath should fit the knife like a glove. Some manufacturers are consumed with the "one size fits all" approach to sheath making. Expect a knife to rattle around inside a one-size-fits-all sheath.

Adequate knife containment means that a retention mechanism should be engineered into the sheath. A simple strap-and-snap closure is the most common type of knife retention. In time, however, an unsecured retaining strap, one that is simply slipped through slots in the leather, will go missing. A superior design features a retaining strap that is an integral part of the sheath itself.

Some sheaths eschew a keeper strap and rely solely on handle contact with the interior of the sheath for retention. Since leather can stretch over time, make sure that the sheath design provides an adequate retention surface.

**A.G. Russell provides a pancake sheath, designed to fit in a hip pocket, for the Woodswalker bird and trout knife.**

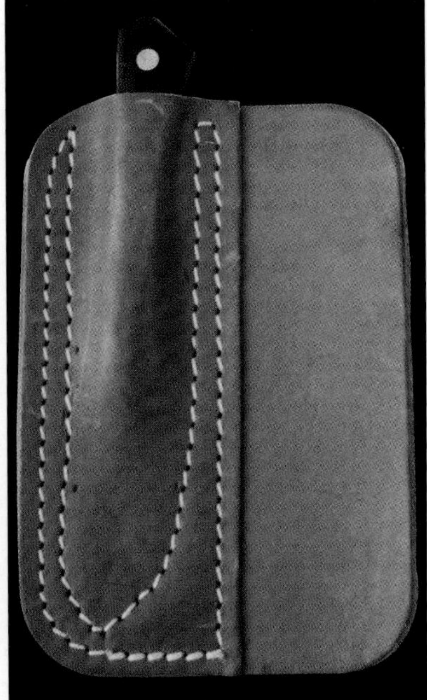

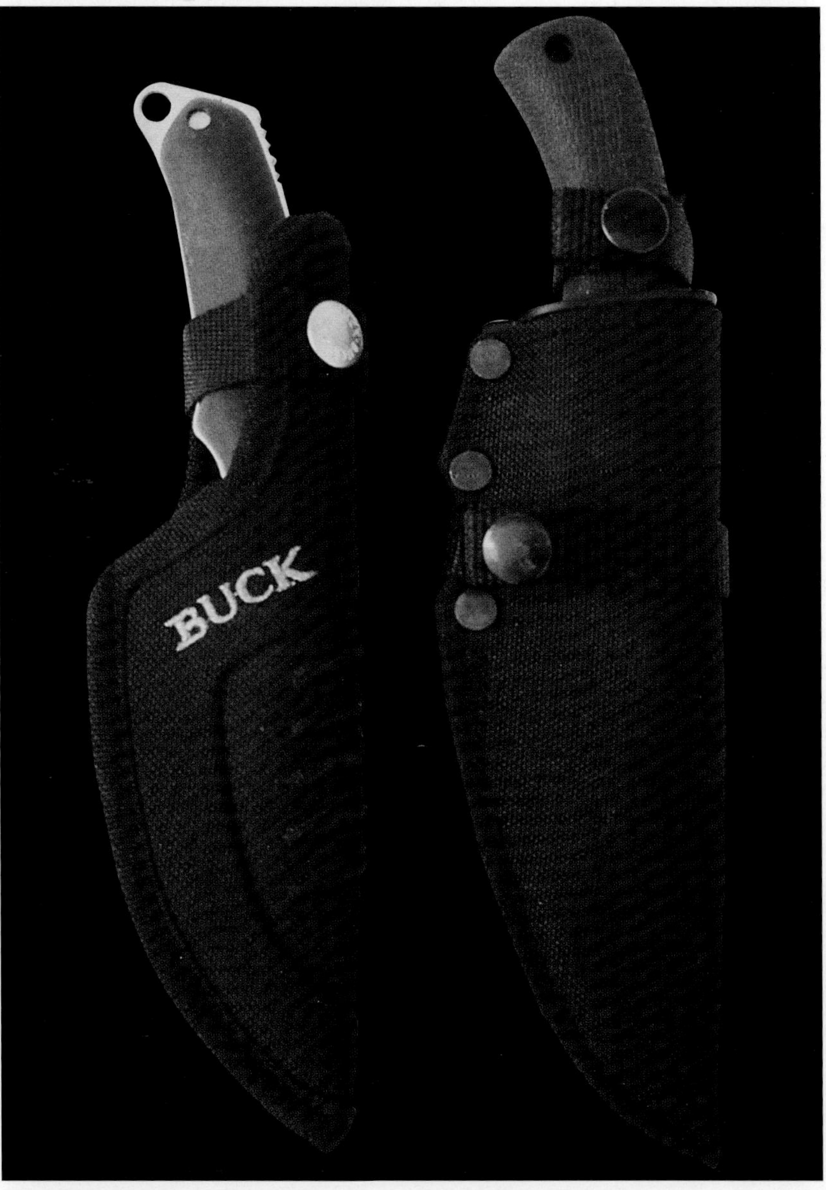


**With hard-plastic inserts, Cordura (nylon) sheaths make sufficient slips for Buck (left) and Gerber knives.**

Buck outfits a camouflage-handle fixed blade with a camouflage Cordura® sheath.

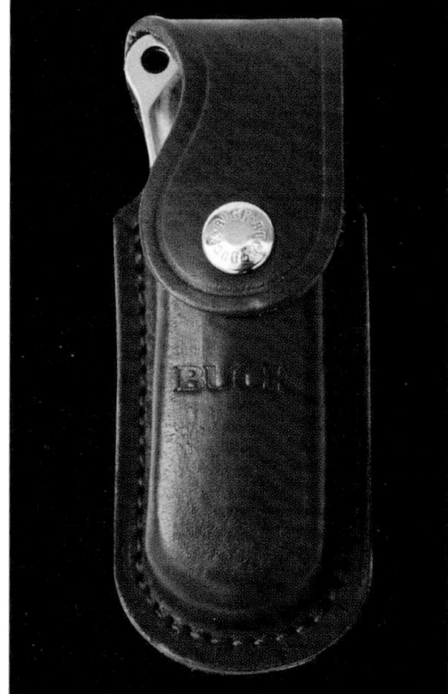


The leather belt case was designed specifically for the Buck folder. The cover flap and snap closure are engineered to prevent accidental knife loss.

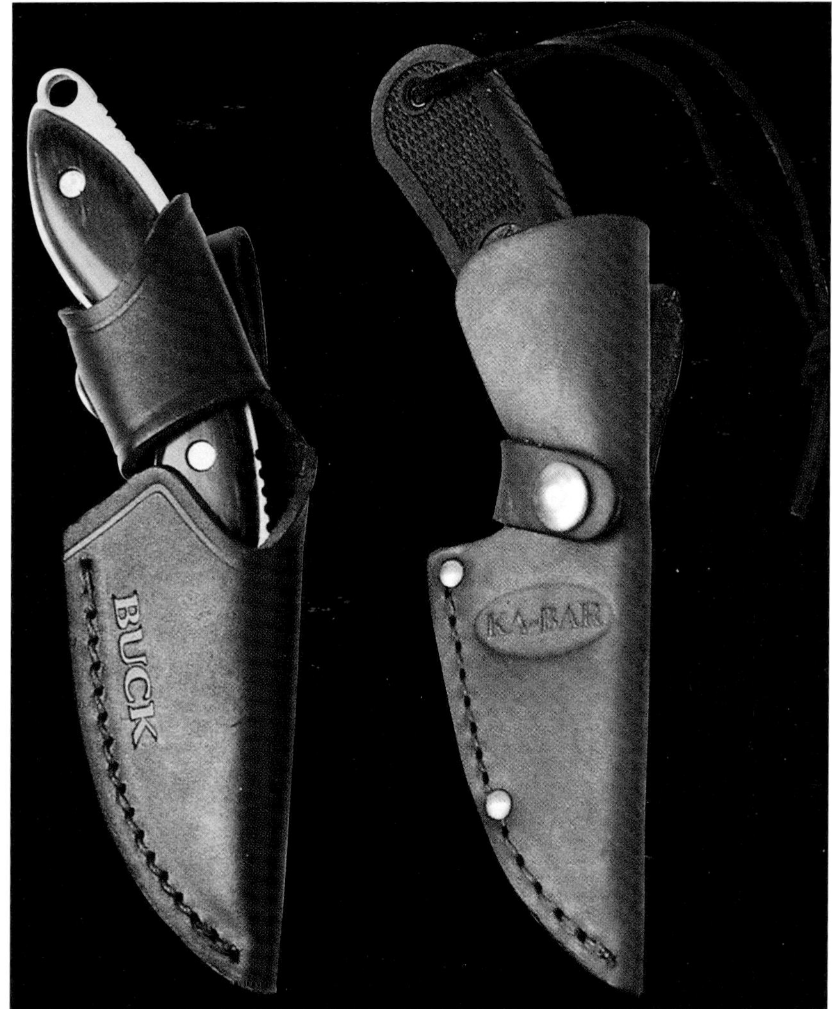


Designed for individual knife models, well-engineered sheaths by Buck (left) and Ka-Bar provide safe blade transport and ready access.

Beyond the basic material and construction, leather also lends itself to adornment. Like engraving on a firearm, design impression or tooling provides a distinctive look to a leather sheath. This work can be as simple or as extensively decorated as the sheath maker desires.

Custom knifemakers are able to take such adornment to a higher level. And a made-to-order sheath can be tooled to meet the customer's wishes.

While leather has the edge when it comes to sheath tradition, many recently developed, high-tech materials have proven their worth in this arena. The various thermoplastics, like Kydex®, Zytel® and ABS plastic, have established a place for themselves as sheath materials. Knife cases made from such fabrics as Cordura®, ballistic cloth and nylon webbing can serve as safe and secure methods of carrying folding knives.

Since synthetics are inert, the materials can withstand inclement weather and nature's other elements with virtually no maintenance. Furthermore, synthetics are easier to mass produce, so plastic or nylon sheaths can be fabricated at lower costs than leather sheaths.

The choice between a tradition-

Cordura® cases for folding knives are widely used in the cutlery industry.

**Regardless of the simplicity of design, the one-piece leather sheath from Case Cutlery secures the knife well, is sturdy and still easy to use.**

al leather sheath and a synthetic blade slip is influenced by many factors. Moisture is easily absorbed by leather and wet leather takes time to dry. Dampness will cause tanning chemicals and oils to leech out of the leather, leaving the sheath dry and stiff. All of this will have a negative impact on any knife housed in a sodden sheath.

## No Sodden Sheaths

Sodden leather sheaths explain why knives designed for diving, fishing and other water sports are most often housed in synthetics. Entry-level knives and those meant to compete at particular price points often come with synthetic sheaths. Since molded sheaths can be manufactured at a fraction of the cost of leather, the use of synthetics in sheath construction doesn't significantly add to the cost of the knife. In an arena where pennies count, this approach to sheath construction makes real sense to both the manufacturer and the consumer.

At the other end of the cost spectrum, there are costly knives that come with synthetic sheaths. Many tactical folders and fixed blades carry hefty price tags. Because these knives can be subjected to rigorous conditions where regular maintenance isn't always possible, synthetic sheaths are the most suitable blade coverings. It is also a lot easier to design synthetic sheaths that can be attached to parachutes, harnesses, backpacks or webbing.

A host of ancillary tools can be engineered into synthetic knife sheaths. For example, some military bayonet sheaths have built-in wire cutters. I've also seen thermoplastic fishing knife sheaths that also house pliers. Often, knife sharpeners are molded directly into synthetic sheaths, a practice that can't be duplicated with leather.

Carrying comfort is another consideration. Since most knives are carried in belt sheaths, the manner in which the sheaths are attached to the belts is of significant importance. The length of a sheath doesn't matter when a person is standing, but once seated, sheath length becomes a factor. To prevent a knife handle from digging into a person's back, the sheath cannot be worn too far above the waist.

While most knives are carried vertically on the belt, some folding knife cases, and even those designed for fixed blades, are designed to be positioned horizontally. And there are sheaths that can be carried with the knife blade point up or down, depending entirely on how and where the sheath is attached. While a sheath may function properly, the manner in which it's carried can become uncomfortable. A properly designed sheath will likely position the knife in the most optimal carrying location. While secure attachment is important, it is not nearly as significant as user comfort.

The final point to consider is secure knife containment. This is important to prevent personal injury or knife loss. A fixed-blade knife should easily slip into and out of its sheath. If the knife encounters more

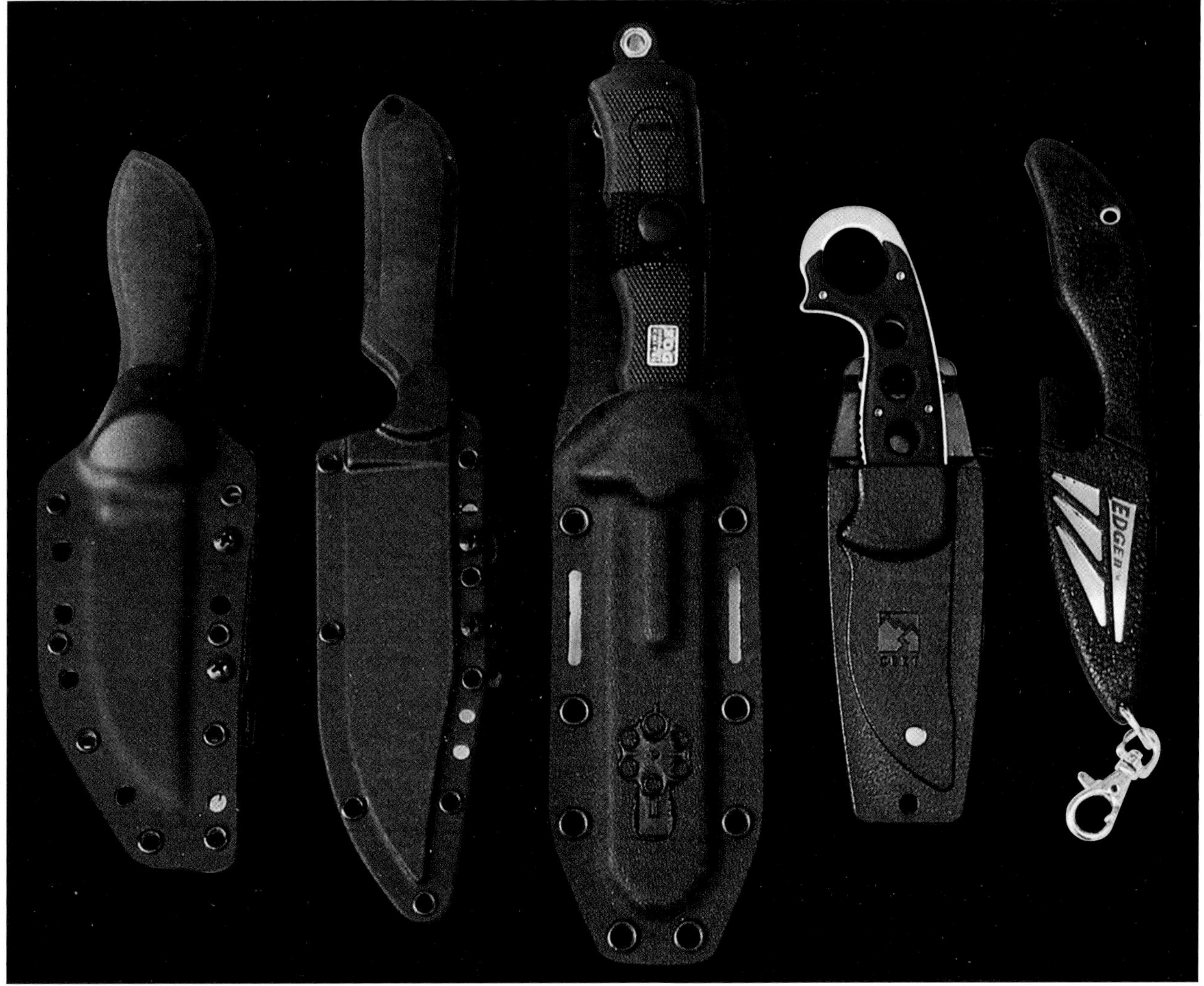


**From left to right, Spyderco (two knives), SOG Specialty Knives, Columbia River Knife & Tool and Outdoor Edge employ thermoplastic knife sheaths.**

resistance than necessary, then the use of overt force may push the blade right through a leather sheath, or across your hand or fingers. Believe me, I've been there and done that. When such an incident occurs, a trip to the hospital emergency room will be in the offing. An accidental fall is something we've all suffered. Should that occur, will the knife sheath provide protection from blade contact? These may seem like minor points, but knife safety is all important.

Like many others, I've lost my share of knives that have fallen out of inferior sheaths. The worst offenders have been press-to-fit sheaths. If you're not careful, the absence of a keeper strap on a knife sheath can result in a lost knife. And should your knife slip out of the sheath, it can be an accident waiting to happen.

On one occasion, I was hunting ducks in a layout blind, which called for a lot of up and down movement. The knife I carried was in a press-to-fit sheath. On my way back to the blind from retrieving a duck, I noticed the knife lying in the bottom of the blind. Apparently, it had somehow slipped out of the sheath. Had I not become aware of the missing knife, an accident could have resulted. And that's not the only time I've had a knife liberate itself from a sheath. Straps come loose, handle lanyards get snagged and gravity can free a knife from its sheath. Such can go unnoticed. Lose your hunting knife and the hunt is over.

The knife, in one form or another, has been with us from the beginning. Once the concept of a blade covering came to fruition, then the sheath became nearly as important as the knife itself. In recent times, sheath significance has been overlooked in favor of keeping manufacturing costs at a minimum. Nonetheless, a quality knife deserves a sheath of similar character. Should that not be the case, then the integrity of the knife is diminished.

Whether the sheath is constructed of top-grade leather or some innovative synthetic material does not matter. Important, however, is quality material, functional design and superior craftsmanship. If you compromise on any of these elements, the result is disastrous. It has worked like that from the beginning ... once upon a time ... since the dawn of civilization.

# Laminated Blades Loom Large

## *Knife companies are making "steel sandwiches," combining hard cutting edges with soft, tough, outer steel layers*

*By Mac Overton*

Knifemakers since the beginning of time have worked to solve the blade hardness versus toughness problem. Hardness increases edge-holding, all other things being equal, especially the heat treatment of the steel, but it also increases brittleness.

Tougher blades stand up better and are less likely to chip, crack or break in normal use, but don't always take or hold an edge as well as harder blades.

One traditional solution to the problem is still being employed today—laminating blades by sandwiching an extremely hard steel core between two softer,

**Two great laminated fixed blades from Scandinavia are the Fallkniven (Swedish) TK2 (top) and the Helle Harding 99 (Norway).**

**With laminated blades, even plain Nordic knives, like these inexpensive examples from Frost, made in Mora, Sweden, are incredibly serviceable. At purchase, the knives came in several versions and many sizes, two of which are shown here. The top model is a great value, but be ready to buy an aftermarket sheath if you plan to carry it much. The bottom example sports a blond-leather sheath to match the arctic-birch handle.**

more ductile steel layers. Think of a sandwich with the "meat" being the core, and the "bread" being the softer, outer layers of steel.

This style of steel-making has been around for more than 1,000 years!

In a mid-1960s catalog of knives made by the late Harry Morseth, it is revealed that the laminated blades of his hunting knives were like those of ancient Japan, Scandinavia and the city of Toledo in old Spain.

The Morseth blades, now produced by A.G. Russell Knives, contain hard, high-carbon-steel cores, each of which measures approximately 64 Rc on the Rockwell hardness scale. The outer layers are of soft iron. Morseth said that if the entire blade was made up of the core steel, it would break or chip easily.

I have held a Viking sword owned by Daniel Watson of Angel Forge. Daniel had it on display at his booth at the Scarborough Faire, a renaissance fair held every spring in Waxahachie, Texas. The sword, which has been appraised at $100,000, was made between about 900 and 1000 A.D., Watson said. He explained that it could be dated because the type of fold (folded steel) used in making the blade was a style incorporated only during that time period. It contained a hard edge folded into softer steel or iron.

In the case of Viking-era swords and knives, high-carbon steel was rare and expensive, and only used when it absolutely had to be welded onto the edges. Less-expensive, softer material was used for the bodies of the blades. Some contemporary Japanese weapons exhibit the same properties and for the same reasons.

An excellent reference that shows many types of pattern welding used by the Vikings is Ian Peirce's great book, *Swords of the Viking Age*, published by Boydell & Brewer Inc.

It takes some skill to be able to forge-weld different types of steel together.

## Natural Knife Flux

According to Jim Schippnich of Ragweed Forge, an importer of a variety of knives from Norway, Finland and Sweden, the wrought iron used by the ancients for most of their welding contained silica impurities, which would act as a natural "flux." Known as Ragnar on the Internet and by the Society for Creative Anachronism, Schippnich is a wealth of information about historical blades. (Visit his Web site at www.ragweedforge.com.)

"The purpose of flux is to protect the hot metal from contact with air, specifically oxygen," he said. "If air gets to the metal at welding heat, an oxide called 'scale' forms, which prevents a good weld.

"Most of the welding done by 'the ancients' was with wrought iron, which has silica impurities. The silica melts at heat and forms a natural flux. In other words, you don't have to flux wrought iron if you are somewhat careful with your heats," he said. Schippnich added that another function of flux is, when the liquid squirts out of the weld, it helps carry away any scale or other impurities that are present between the surfaces.

He explained how people throughout history worked blade steel. "The steel for the edges was originally gotten in a couple of ways," he said.

If you take a piece of wrought iron and repeatedly fold it and weld it in a reducing fire, the surface picks up carbon and the repeated folding and welding blends the carbon into the billet. The core of the old Japanese swords are said to have 10,000 to 100,000-plus layers. As you continue this process, the silica is gradually worked out of the iron/steel billet and it becomes more susceptible to forming scale.

"Flux is used to coat the surfaces to be welded, and preferably the rest

**Murray Carter's neck knives, of laminated steel with a core that reaches 64 Rc on the Rockwell hardness scale, will out-cut most similar patterns.**

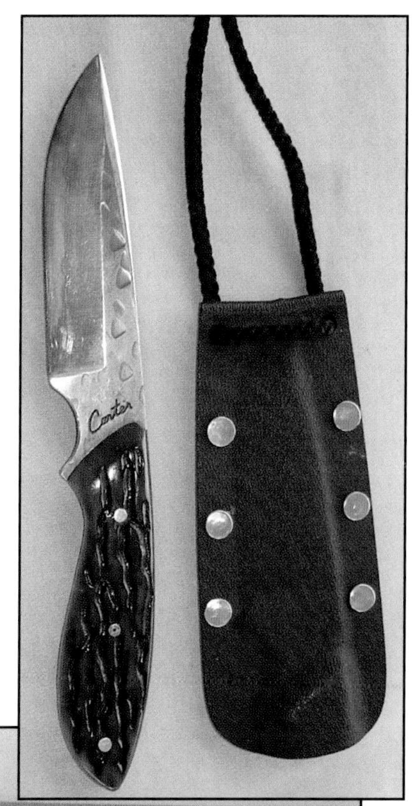


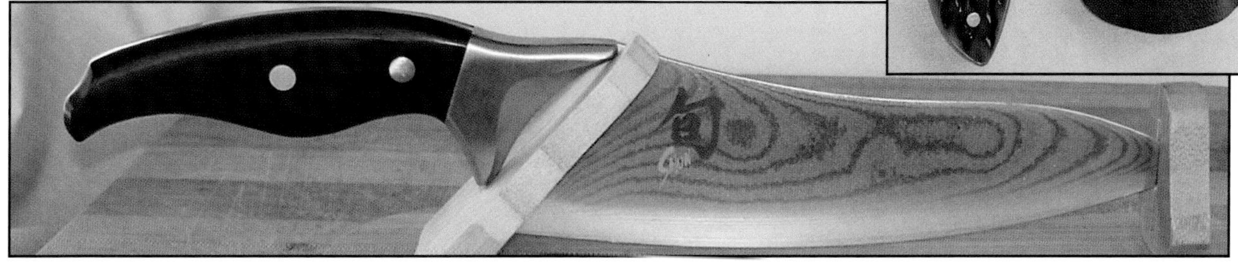

**The Keshaw Kai Shun "Multi-Task" knife may look a little strange, but the curvature of the blade is great for rocking cuts, while the laminated-wood handle provides the beauty of wood and the durability of plastic.**

of the billet, as well," Schippnich noted. "Later, thin strips of iron were packed in charcoal and bone and heated in an airtight container for days at a time. The carbon migrated into the strip of iron, forming steel. Of course, all the carbon was at the surface of the strip, so the strips were folded and welded to blend the carbon more evenly. Such is now called 'blister steel' because of the appearance of the strips after they come out of the bake. Again, flux is used in the welding to keep air away from the billets.

"The traditional flux before borax was sand, which is just powdered silica," he continued. "I expect powdered glass would work well, but I haven't gotten around to trying it. Borax works well, but it's best if you drive off the water first. Laundry borax has a lot of water chemically bonded in it, and if you use it raw, it tends to suck the heat out of the piece when it's applied, and the steam tends to blow it off the surface. You just heat it to drive off the water, and then pulverize it again.

"A number of years ago, I attended a conference on damascus [pattern-welded] steel in Germany," Schippnich said. "A prominent German 'smith was discussing fluxes and felt strongly that the only proper flux for traditional pattern welding was river sand. It works well enough, but is hard to find in clean, consistent grades and it doesn't stick to the piece as well as borax. I expect it has a higher melting temperature.

"The expensive commercial fluxes are usually anhydrous borax with silica and/or iron filings," he said. "I have to confess to a certain lack of curiosity about different fluxes. Bill Moran once

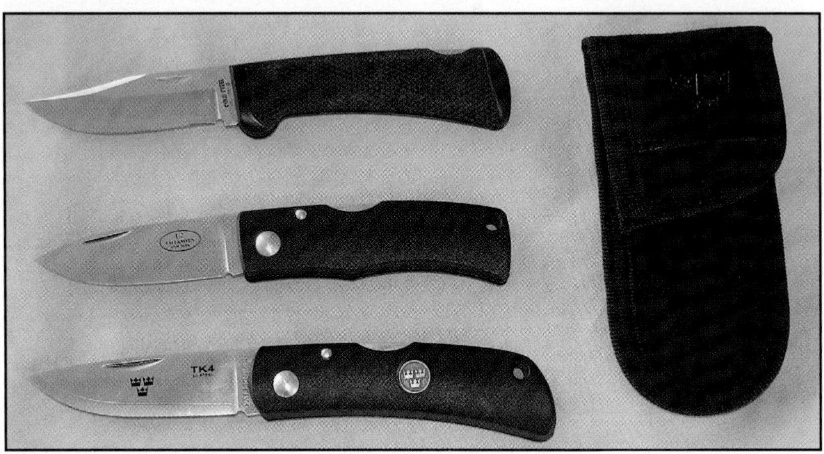


**Folders with laminated blades are rare. At top is a discontinued Cold Steel model featuring a laminated San Mai III stainless steel blade. The middle knife is a Fallkniven U2, considered by several aficionados as the perfect pocketknife, including a blade core of SGPS (Super Gold Powder Steel) sandwiched between layers of soft, tough and stain resistant 420 J2 stainless. At bottom is the Tre Kroner TK4, which contains the same blade core as the U2 (a CPM S30V clone), but with even tougher outside layers of VG-2 steel.**

**Frost Cutlery's Swedish Mora knives are shown at their dressiest, complete with beautiful hardwood handles, and brass bolsters and end caps.**

told me plain borax works best for the welding used in knifemaking and I just took his word for it. He'd already done all the trial and error work, and I was content with that."

Most laminated blades today are of different types of stainless steel. This includes those from Japan, where most laminated steel is known as "San Mai" (three layers), Norway, Sweden and Finland.

## Highly Patterned Laminates

Some damascus is worked into laminated steel. A homogenous, high-carbon steel core is surrounded by pattern-welded steel, giving the edge-holding ability of the hard, center core. The steel surrounding the core is of one of several fascinating patterns of damascus.

Increasingly encountered, especially in kitchen cutlery from a variety of makers, is "clad steel."

The most common example of clad steel, employed by Kershaw, A.G. Russell Knives, Fallkniven, Al Mar and other companies for kitchen knives, involves a hard core of VG-10 "clad" in 16 layers of 416 stainless spring steel. Some ads refer to it as "damascus," while others describe it as having a "damascus look."

Dennis Epstein, sales manager for Kershaw's kitchen knife division, said that after accomplishing the complicated, high-tech process of producing the blade billets, an added benefit to clad steel was discovered.

"Once they (the billets) are ground into blades, food does not tend to stick to them (due to the damascus-like swirls on the outsides of the blades)," he said.

Perhaps the first to popularize San Mai steel in the United States is Cold Steel, a company that incorporates its trademarked San Mai III in a version of the Trailmaster Bowie. Cold Steel says that a stainless, triple-layer San Mai III blade is 25 percent stronger than the company's other favorite blade material—the incredibly tough AUS-8A stainless steel.

Fallkniven, a Swedish company that builds fine blades using Japanese billets, employs VG-10-based laminates for much of its line. Recently, however, the company has gone a step further. Several Fallkniven models sport cores of hard powder steel (with a Rockwell hardness of 62 Rc) and softer stainless steel outer layers.

## It Bends but Won't Break

"It's correct that most of our products are made in laminate blades, since we have found that these provide another 20-plus-percent extra bending strength compared to solid steel," said Peter Hjortberger, president of Fallkniven. "The knife isn't used for pure cutting tasks only, but for quite many other purposes. As some of our products are meant to work as survival knives, we have added this quality as extra life insurance."

The first laminated blade Fallkniven offered in powder steel was the U2 folder. It featured a core of SGPS (Super Gold Powder Steel) sandwiched by outer layers of 420 J2 mild stainless steel. I've seen the specifications of SGPS steel, and it is a virtual clone to CPM S30V.

More recently, Fallkniven has introduced the Tre Kroner (three crowns) series. The TK models integrate 3G-laminated-steel blades. Hjortberger says that the core of each blade is the same SGPS as used in the U2, but that the outer layers of steel are even "stronger and less scratch sensitive compared to the laminate SGPS steels."

The Fallkniven catalog states that the outer layers are of VG-2, a low-carbon version of VG10 that some custom knifemakers use for blades!

A prominent custom maker of laminated blades is Murray Carter, a Canadian who has worked as a 'smith in Japan for several years and who is currently in the process of moving to Oregon.

If you haven't heard of Carter, you will! His sporting and kitchen knives have achieved an enviable following, and if you want to buy one of his knives at one of the major knife shows, such as the annual BLADE Show, where he exhibits, you better get there early!

Carter said that for using knives, he prefers steel laminates to damascus. His damascus is basically reserved for exhibition-grade knives.

"Damascus is beautiful, but no two pieces will be exactly alike," he said. He feels this will give slightly different performance from blade to blade, even from the same maker.

His laminated knives usually contain a core of one of two grades of Hitachi steel—White No. 1 or Blue Super Steel. Both are similar, with about 1.4 percent carbon each. They mainly differ in that the Blue Super Steel also contains traces of chrome, tungsten, molybdenum and vanadium.

Carter offers ZDP 247 for the laminate core when an all-stainless blade is desired. Unfortunately, he does not list the ingredients, and I couldn't find it on the Internet or in steel charts I have.

Carter lists W-1 as a "Western steel" that is comparable to the steels he uses. The Japanese steel contains fewer impurities. W-1, for instance, contains 10 times the sulfur as either of the Hitachi steels.

## Tough and Springy Steel

The outer layers of most of Carter's laminated blades are 410-grade stainless steel. He employs S25C or S35C, each of which is equivalent in makeup to 1025C or 1035C, respectively, for some high-carbon-steel knives. Carter said the steels add toughness and springiness to the blades, with S35C being superior to S25C.

For traditional Japanese-style knives that are laminated on only one side, Carter employs *Gokunan-tetsu*. "It is an extremely pure non-alloy mild steel that is used for laminating with high-carbon steel for Japanese blades," he said. "It enables Japanese blades to be sharpened easily."

As for Carter's knives that feature 410 stainless steel outer layers, only the exposed carbon-steel edges and the exposed carbon steel along the backs of the blades and tangs require extra care.

In his catalog, which is well worth having if you have much interest in knives, he states, "There is no such thing as a 'best' steel for every application. However, there is a best-known steel for a given application. The steels I use are all top quality and each is specialized in one way."

He said that White Steel is his personal favorite because it is an "amazingly pure steel, and therefore the carbides in the steel allow for the keenest edge possible." "So, when a surgically clean cut is required," Carter added, "such as in some types of food preparation (sushi, etc.), or in woodcarving, White Steel reigns as king.

"Blue Super Steel is basically White Steel with chrome, tungsten, molybdenum and vanadium added. This results in oddly shaped carbides in the steel, so keenness is sacrificed somewhat," Carter noted. "However, the new carbides enable this steel to retain its edge longer than any other grade of cutlery steel. Therefore, Blue Super Steel is the king of edge retention."

On knives where Blue Super Steel is an option, Carter is forced to raise the price of each model by 20 percent.

"ZDP 247 is the superior choice when stain-resistant cutlery steel is necessary, as in certain medical applications, or when using [the blades] close to salt water, etc. It doesn't cut as keenly as White Steel and doesn't hold an edge as long as Blue Super Steel, but it is the king as far as stainless cutlery is concerned," Carter said.

Carter makes two lines of forged laminated knives—Muteki ("without rival") and Hand Forged. With the Muteki models, which include a number of sporting and kitchen knives, the blades are laser cut to shape, annealed, cold forged, stamped, coated with clay, and then heat-treated to between 63 and 64 Rc. Finally, they are ground from their original blanked thickness on Japanese rotating water stones, Carter stated. Most have a core of White No. 1, but some are made of Blue Super Steel, and 410 stainless makes up the outer laminates.

## Refining the Grain of Steel

"Our forged blades are not laser cut, but rather forged to shape, a process which refines the grain of the steel, making it strong," he said. "Also, after annealing but before heat-treating, the blades are cold forged, a traditional Japanese process that brings out more of the steel's potential. The forging process, as well as having the choice between steel types, style, size, etc., is what separates forged blades from Muteki blades."

Carter said that his hand-forged knives are heated in a charcoal fire and forged to final thickness. "No metal is removed from the final forged surface except to grind the edge," he noted.

As these makers of Scandinavian, Japanese and Japanese-style Western knives claim, laminated blades provide a way to solve the hardness versus toughness problem that has faced blade makers for thousands of years.

The process by which laminated blades are made might be thousands of years old, but knife companies are increasingly realizing its advantages. Laminated blades loom large. Let's use them to their full potential.

**Kershaw/Kai Cutlery's Shun line continues to astound. Here are only three of many models showcasing laminated blades with VG-10 cores and damascus-looking outer steel layers. From top are an 8-inch chef's knife, a 6-inch utility blade and a 4 1/2-inch vegetable cutter with a 10-degree offset handle.**

**One of Kershaw/Kai's 6-inch Shun utility knives (top) in clad stainless steel is shown with a Murray Carter handmade laminated kitchen knife of about the same length. Both have their own attributes—the Kershaw Shun has a "D-shaped" handle, which is comfortable for right-handers, and a laminated blade with a hard, durable core, while the Carter knife has a super-hard blade core reaching up to 64 Rc on the Rockwell hardness scale.**

# Peruse the Fine Edges of the Philippines

## *Out of necessity, Filipino villagers developed fighting techniques and the edged weapons to go along with them*

*by Greg Bean*

Since 9/11, learning to deal with armed adversaries, whether in a subway, parking lot or airplane—and learning it quick—has moved a lot of citizen soldiers through many martial arts studio doors.

Handling close-quarters encounters with edged-weaponed assailants is one of the key features of *kali*, a weapons-based martial arts form originating in the Philippines. Kali, also known as *eskrima* or *arnis*, depending on who's talking, is one of the most efficient and sophisticated weapons and empty-hands systems in the world. Since 9/11, the interest in the Filipino martial arts, or FMA, has been on a steady ascent.

Practical over esoteric, kali was developed to quickly train villagers to become an effective fighting force, in months rather than years. Unlike most other martial arts that require mastery with the open hands before weapons training begins, kali training starts with the use of weapons. This practicality draws students wanting defense expertise in a hurry.

The demand for the Filipino weapons used in kali has grown as fast as the demand for training, and maybe faster. Traditional Filipino weapons are as exotic, unconventional and beautiful as a South Pacific vacation. This has not been lost on collectors.

Responding to the demand for such island blades, C.A.S. Iberia introduced a line of traditional

**One of the most beguiling of Filipino weapons, the karambit looks like a mounted talon from a steel tiger. With an Indonesian lineage, the weapon is primarily a defensive tool. Shown is a model offered by C.A.S. Iberia.**

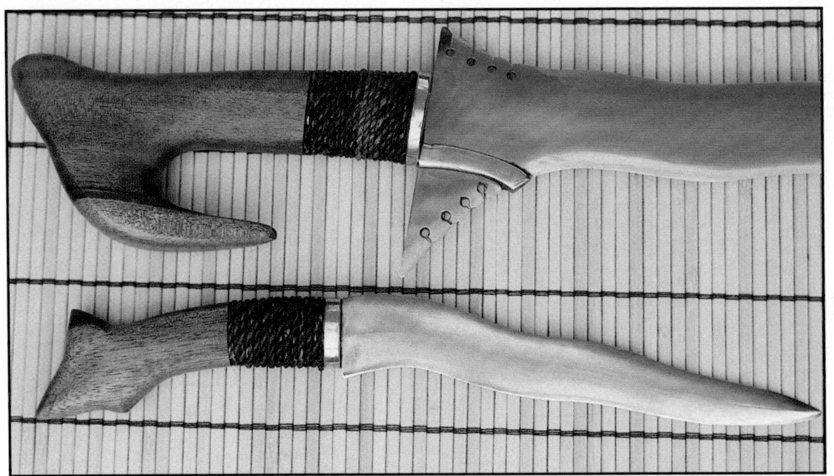

**Spain's occupation and rule of the Philippines ended in 1898, but the country's influence on the Filipino martial arts continues. Spanish fencing made its way into the martial arts tradition, especially with the use of the sword and dagger. Called *espada y daga* (stick and dagger), the techniques were more linear and closer to dueling than guerilla warfare. The Filipino technique uses the dagger as an offensive weapon. Shown is a C.A.S. Iberia keris gunnong and dagger.**

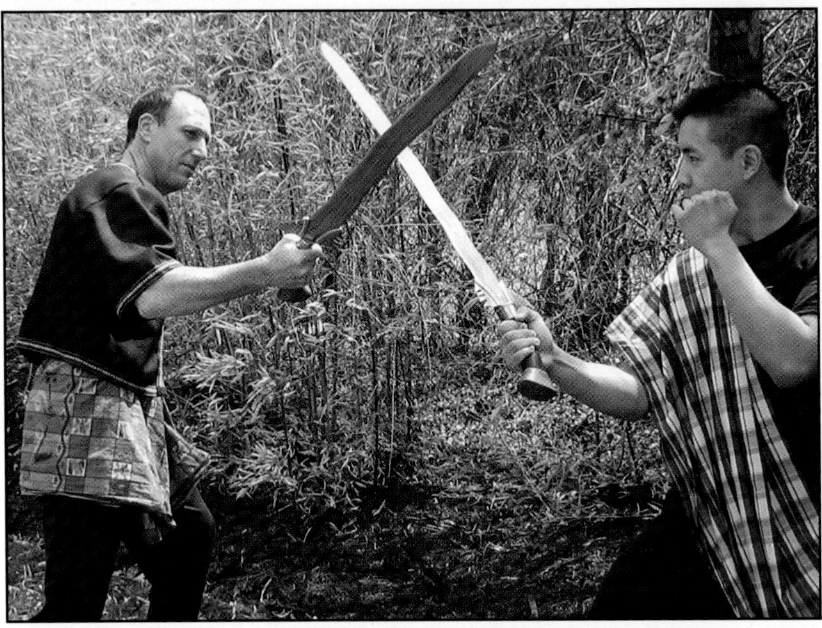

**Keris swords are believed to have originated in the 13th century on the island of Java in the Indonesian archipelago, and migrated to the Philippines, Malaysia and various Southeast Asian countries. The keris sword is distinct in appearance with various shapes and sizes of blades, all widening near the handles and including sharp pointed protrusions. The protrusions act as hand guards against opponents' slashes and thrusts.**

Filipino knives and weapons, appropriately manufactured in the Philippines.

Dale Brown of C.A.S. Iberia, a martial artist in his own right, saw a great deal of interest in the Filipino weapons and arts through various trade shows and tournaments. Dale reports, "No one was catering to that market. People would bring pieces back from the Philippines or have custom makers create them."

Even though C.A.S. Iberia offers about 20 Filipino pieces, Brown reports their popularity often leaves the company's shelves empty.

Through a martial arts convention, Dale met Rick Tucci, a leading practitioner of FMA. Besides running his own school—the Princeton Academy of Martial Arts—Rick is also an in-demand teacher within and outside of the United States. The interview for this article had to be sandwiched between teaching trips to Georgia, London and Belgium.

Sifu Tucci (*Sifu* is a traditional designation for a master) has an impressive pedigree, being a protégé of Dan Insonato, who, in turn, was a protégé of the martial artist made famous through movies, Bruce Lee. Rick's credentials, aside from the too-numerous martial arts notches to be mentioned, include training and experience as a professional bodyguard. If the thought of being a bodyguard brings up notions of protecting

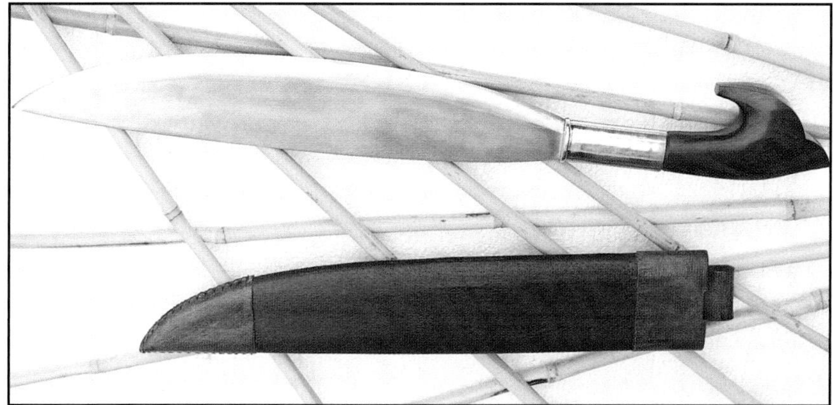

**The barong's unique leaf-shaped blade, like this C.A.S. Iberia model, distinguishes it from other Filipino weaponry. The heavy, single-edged Filipino barong blades range from 12 to 18 inches in length and are without guards.**

the famous from paparazzi, think Kosovo and Iraq.

Preaching what he practices, Rick is devoted to passing on his knowledge and experience and does so with enthusiasm. Part of his mentoring includes advising C.A.S. Iberia on the development of the island weapons. Acknowledging his help, the C.A.S. Web site (www.casiberia.com) also carries a video series developed by Rick for those going it alone in their martial arts development.

**Traditionally, the Barong was an indispensable part of the Moro's attire, specifically the Tausug, Samal, and Yakan warriors of the Sulu Archipelago. So the barong would not slip out of the hand of the wielder during the heat of battle, it was stylized with a "cockatoo beak" (kakatua) handle. Shown is a C.A.S. Iberia model.**

## Bird Beak Blades

The exotic look of the Philippines' weaponry comes from the curved blades, at times leaf shaped, and in other instances with edged steel formed in the shapes of what can best be described as outrigger canoe paddles. The Filipino blades are sinewy and serpentine. The natural aspect of the Filipino culture is evident in the look of the island weapons. The blade features, though decorative and functional, often resemble bird talons and beaks, snakes, open-mouthed crocodiles, bird tails, flowering vines or stingray wings and tails.

The C.A.S. Iberia models feature blades of L-6 tool steel, a hard but flexible, high-carbon steel. The handles are lustrous native woods with foreign-sounding names like *kamagong* (East Indian ebony) and *igim*. Sheaths are crafted from both leather and cord-wrapped wood, and some flaunt an appearance as intriguing as the blades they encase.

The Filipino sword smith's pride at forging weapons representing his own nation shows in the careful crafting of the edged tools and weapons. The quality of the weapons is outstanding, attracting notice wherever they're displayed. According to Rick, at the 2005 Arnold Martial Arts Festival, a martial arts/fighting trade show, the C.A.S. Filipino weapons exhibit was constantly mobbed and more interest was shown for the exotic blades than for anything else at the show.

The history of the intriguing weapons starts with the first wave of migrations from the Malays about 200 B.C. The keris, an often-wavy-bladed knife from the island of Java, was the first foreign weapon to be transplanted into the Filipino fighting arts and the weapon most identified with the Philippines.

The FMA developed out of the need for villagers and farmers to defend their land against other villages and foreign invaders. These were not professional soldiers or trained martial artists, but villagers, farmers and craftsmen. Training had to be brief and effective; years for developing an open-hand technique just weren't available. As a combat-oriented method, in which weapons were a given, FMA weapons training was first priority.

In 1518, Ferdinand Magellan, commissioned by the king of Spain

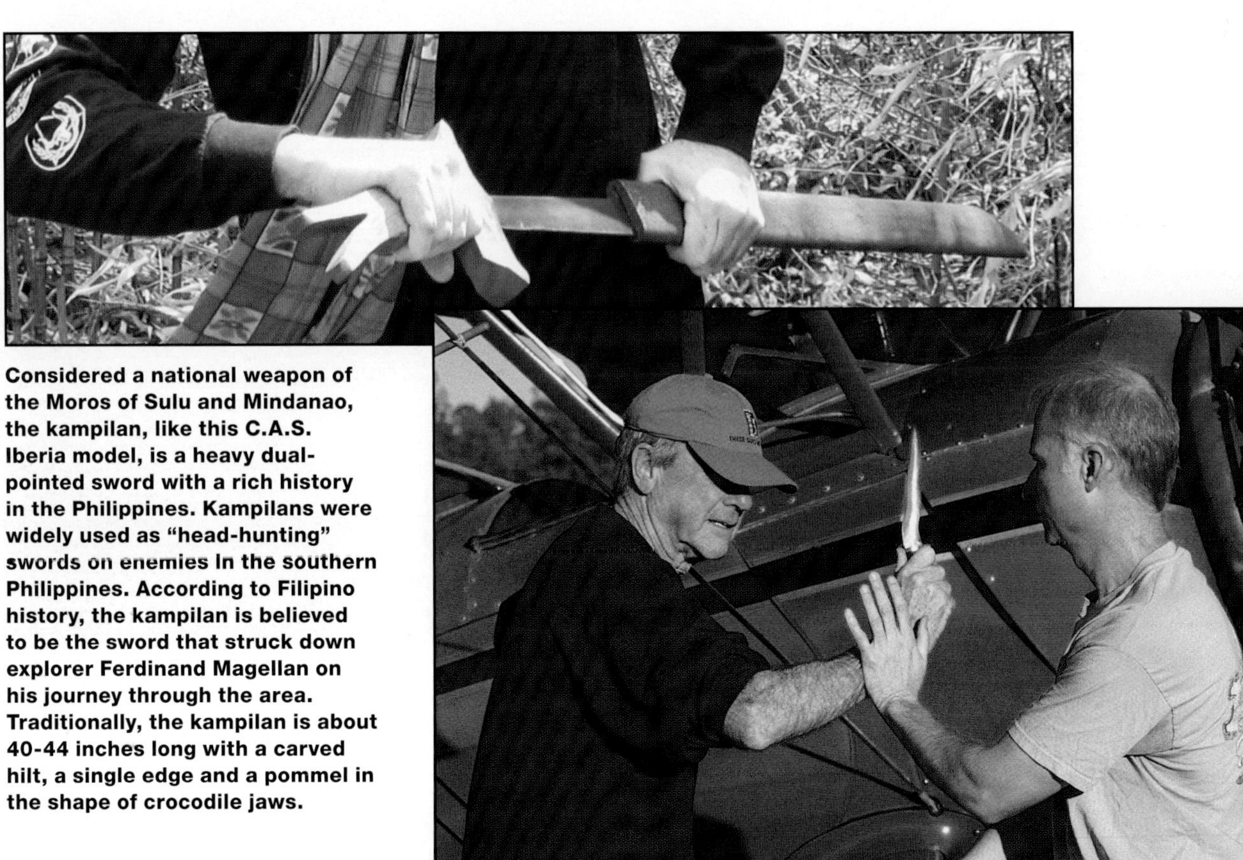

**Considered a national weapon of the Moros of Sulu and Mindanao, the kampilan, like this C.A.S. Iberia model, is a heavy dual-pointed sword with a rich history in the Philippines. Kampilans were widely used as "head-hunting" swords on enemies in the southern Philippines. According to Filipino history, the kampilan is believed to be the sword that struck down explorer Ferdinand Magellan on his journey through the area. Traditionally, the kampilan is about 40-44 inches long with a carved hilt, a single edge and a pommel in the shape of crocodile jaws.**

**Mike Ratty, in 35 years as an airline pilot, has never had to defend against a hostile takeover. Now the pilot of his own biplane, he's prepared to overcome a knife-wielding attacker. Taking his turn as the aggressor, Mike finds his attack blocked and the C.A.S. Iberia karambit shows its value as a thrusting weapon.**

and seeking the spice islands of the Moluccas, led the first expedition to sail around the world.

Magellan did not make it around the world but he became the first European acquainted with the double-pointed sword called the kampilan. In a battle against 20-to-1 odds, the scribe Antonia Pigafetta recorded that Magellan was killed by the islander's leader, Raja Lapu Lapu, with a thrust to the leg followed by another to the neck. While he may not have appreciated it at the time, Magellan set the stage for Spain to dominate the islands for the next 400 years.

The early part of the Spanish occupation occurred during Spain's dominance of Europe, if not the world. Financed by the New World's gold and silver, the Spanish galleon routes and influence went around the globe, including the Philippines.

Filipino fighters began to see the world and the world began to see them during this period. The Spanish pressed natives into their naval service, and other nations hired them as mercenaries. The Filipinos brought their own weapons and fighting techniques, some of which had very specialized uses, such as fighting waist deep in water, on poor footing and in various shipboard conditions.

Their influence arrived in the Americas during this period. Many islanders jumped ship in California, Louisiana and Mexico, where the governance of the islands was located.

Spain's rule in the Philippines ended in 1898 after losing the Spanish-American War but their influence on the FMA continues.

The Spanish imposed a ban on the use of weapons, no doubt to save a few of their own lives. As a result, the Filipinos developed open-hand martial arts styles and fighting with rattan canes. The stick fighting, for which the Philippines are known, incorporated the same system of strikes as the bladed styles, keeping those techniques alive through the occupation.

## Stick and Dagger Dueling

Spanish fencing made its way into the Filipino martial arts tradition with a system of angles of attack and defense, Spain's systematic approach to training and especially the use of the sword and

Taking an opponent's head off is within reason with the barong. While this may seem a quaint and arcane skill, it resonates well to competitive fencer and sword enthusiast Ryan Bean who adopts a wary posture, ready for anything.

The most basic and widely used sword in the Philippines is the agricultural-based bolo. Typically, the bolo blade is rough and unfinished due to its agricultural use. Bolos were utilized extensively during the Philippine Revolution of 1896 against Spain.

dagger. Called *espada y daga* (stick and dagger), the techniques were more linear and closer to dueling than guerilla warfare. The stick fighting, with long and short canes, reflects the sword and dagger practices.

The oft-wavy blade of the keris is the shape most readily identified with the South Pacific island of Archipelago. The keris' double-edged blade can be wavy or straight. The blade widens near the handle and includes sharp, pointed protrusions that act as a guard and create another offensive surface. The sharpened and pointed projections would make a nasty impression at close range with either a thrown blow or a draw cut.

The triangle-shaped protrusions extend further above the blade than below, creating a distinctive look not found in other cultures' edged weapons or tools. In combat, the sword is primarily a slashing weapon but its shape also lends itself to thrusting.

Tucci reports there is no credible documentation on the purpose of the waves in the blade. Contrary to common belief, the curves do not increase its cutting effectiveness but do add to its aesthetics. The early keris swords, believed to be from Indonesia, were fairly short, more like long knives, and may have been used in their religious ceremonies. Such ceremonies could be intense and not to the liking of all of the participants.

The combination of sword and dagger might have preceded the Spanish, but the style and techniques of *espada y daga* are clearly from Spanish dueling.

The keris and the barong were the two weapons most often carried by the islanders, and according to tradition, most islanders carried some kind of edged weapon.

The barong's unique leaf-shaped blade distinguishes it from other Filipino weaponry. The heavy, single-edged blades range from 12 to 18 inches in length and are without guards. The handles have beak-like shapes that wrap around the hand, creating stable grips. Each heavy wood grip creates a balanced feel, but there is no mistaking the power of the barong. Its heft and shape make it ideal for removing heads, arms and legs.

One of the most beguiling weapons, the karambit, looks like a mounted talon from a steel tiger. With an Indonesian lineage, the weapon is primarily a defensive tool. Techniques differ with the hold on the grip. According to Rick, the karambit can be held curve out for defense or cutting, or curve in for a more aggressive use. The karambit is highly effective at limb destruction when an attack comes within the weapon's range.

While this favored kali concept—limb destruction—sounds vicious, it is defensive in nature, a disabling response to an attacker's limb entering the fighter's range. Practitioners of the Filipino martial arts train thus for close quarters attacks, using open hands, edged weapons or "weapons of chance," such as notebook computers or ballpoint pens.

The FMA's appeal lies with such practical training, as evidenced by the practice of wearing shoes while training. You work out in the clothes you'd wear if you had to defend yourself. And of course you want to protect your feet from dropped weapons.

While using clever, curved blades to stop a terrorist on a modern airliner is less likely than finding a terrorist in an anthrax-laden biplane, the training is aimed at either situation.

# Net Those Knives as if They're Big Fish

## *It's nearly as common to buy high-end custom knives off the Internet as it is to purchase books, clothes and DVDs*

*by Roger Combs*

These days, you can buy just about anything over the Internet, from medicines, movies and clothing, to houses, vehicles and power tools. Factory knives have long been available electronically, but only recently have we been able to obtain some of the best custom knives via the Internet.

I must admit that my personal bias was surprise and doubt when I first learned about people sending money—sometimes BIG money—off to unknown individuals to pay for custom knives.

I had always felt that a fine custom knife must be seen, felt and examined in person before it could be purchased. But with more thought into it, I came to the conclusion that if the seller's reputation—a knifemaker, collector or a dealer—is sound, the buyer can be confident in the transaction.

Factory production knives are and have been available via catalogs, mail order and electronically for years. It goes to reason that sending a check to a mail-order address and awaiting the shipment of a new knife takes no less faith and trust than buying knives off the Internet.

A look inside your favorite knife magazine will reveal advertisements from several top-name custom knifemakers that include their Web addresses. The Web sites display information about the knifemakers and their knives, as well as detailed steps necessary to obtain the blades.

The sites usually include pictures or drawings, specifications and prices of the custom knives. In some cases, information is included on whether or not the knives are available and how long the waiting period is before such models can be delivered.

Some custom knifemakers will take special orders through their Web sites, but keep in mind that, especially with the most popular makers, the time from order placement to knife transaction can be considerable.

Consulting one of several knife dealers can solve the wait-

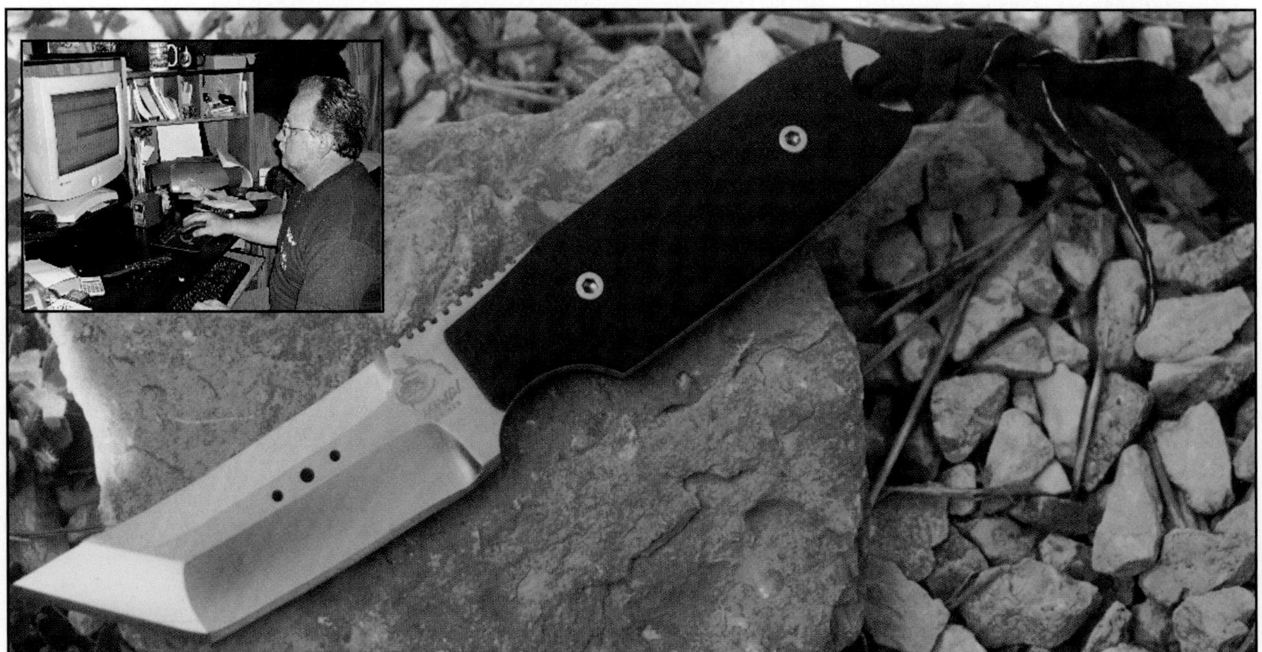

**Increasingly, knifemakers like Mike Franklin of Hawg Knives use the Internet to supplement their knife sales. Franklin's NTSK model features a tanto- or chisel-style, double-hollow-ground, 3 1/4-inch CPM 440V blade, a G-10 handle, a lanyard and a Kydex® sheath.**

ing-time problem. Some who have decades of reliable, trusted service behind them include A. G. Russell Knives (www.agrussell.com), Dan Delavan of Plaza Cutlery (www.plazacutlery.com) or Arizona Custom Knives (www.arizonacustomknives.com). There are many others.

## Knives Now!

Even the most expensive custom knives, as well as plenty of production models, can be purchased with confidence from dealer sites. Site managers often contract with custom knifemakers and collectors who provide the knives listed on the Web pages. Because well-organized online dealers update their sites daily, adding or subtracting knives as they are bought and sold, there is almost no waiting time.

It wasn't so long ago that delivery times of two, three or more years from the most popular custom knifemakers were not uncommon, and it is still the case for some. With the growth of Internet sales, many knife collectors can find what they want, when they want it. Not every maker's knives are found on every knife site at a given time. Knives sell and are placed in the buyers' collections. They may not come before the public again for several years.

A long and reputable involvement with the custom knife movement is an asset to selling over the Internet. Mike Franklin of Aberdeen, Ohio is one of those with more than 35 years of knifemaking behind him. His experience may not be typical of most custom knifemakers who have found success with the Internet, but he has embraced the technology.

Mike built his first knife in 1969 and became a member of The Knifemakers' Guild in 1973. He was a full-time knifemaker within the next year, so he is no newcomer to the business. He views the Internet as another method of presenting his knives to the public, supplementing the practices of attending knife shows, employing the services of knife dealers, advertising and offering his designs to several manufacturers.

**On his Web site (www.plazacutlery.com), knife dealer and retailer Dan Delevan, center, showcases many well-known custom knives and knifemakers, as well as hundreds of popular factory knives.**

Aberdeen is in the southern part of Ohio, in the middle of some of the greatest deer and wild hog hunting country. Franklin is an avid handgun and rifle shooter, and a fanatical bow hunter. He spends time with ATVs while hunting and scouting for game.

His archery hunting experience brought him into the titanium broadhead business, and wild hog hunting influenced the design and production of the "HAWG" line of folding knives.

The HAWG knives started out as supplemental models to his other custom knives but have come to dominate Franklin's edged production. The original HAWG design has received numerous awards and recognition, and the HAWG logo—a tusk-heavy wild boar—has received considerable attention. Mike often refers to himself as the "Hawg man."

## Supplemental Cyber Sales

While the Internet is an increasingly important part of his business, Mike continues to attend guns shows, hunting shows, The Knifemakers' Guild Show and other events to get the word out about his knives.

At the 2001 Guild show, he introduced the Remora knife model. It is a large general-use folder with a main blade and two supplemental, removable blades, one attached to each side of the handle frame.

Each secondary blade is extracted from the handle by raising a titanium lock and swinging the edged steel down off a locater pin. And each of the extra blades complements the main blade by performing a specialized outdoor cutting task.

On Saturday morning of The 2001 Knifemakers' Guild Show, Franklin and his wife, Marsha, experienced a "feeding frenzy" at his table. Old and new customers were grabbing up Remora knives as fast as they could, or having the Franklins take their names and hold knives for them until they could return later to pay for them.

A bit later in the day, noted knife purveyor A. G. Russell came by the table. Russell bought the last Remora knife left. He said that if he were crossing the Serengeti, he would want to have that knife with him.

So the design name changed to "Serengeti" that day. Russell took the knife to the people at Columbia River Knife & Tool (CRKT) in Wilsonville, Oregon. Rod Bremer and Doug Flagg of CRKT collaborate with several well-known custom knifemakers on edged tool designs.

Mike recalls, "They [CRKT] worked on my custom design for

about two years to slightly modify the knife for the public. They changed the locking mechanism on the handle a bit and added an extra safety lock. Their workmanship on the production version of my knife is unbelievable—an exact copy of my prototype."

Mike won the "Most Innovative Folder" award for the Serengeti at the 2001 Guild Show. The knife features three AUS-4 stainless steel blades. The main folding blade is 3-1/4 inches long and locks open solidly, leaving no play between blade and handle.

Latching onto the outside of the handle are two additional blades. One is a 1 3/4-inch skinning blade, and the other is a 1 3/4-inch hawksbill caping blade. Each smaller blade can be removed for detailed game care.

## Hog Wild for the Side Hawg

At the next Knifemakers' Guild Show, Franklin brought along a little knife he designed, without a sheath, for hunting season. Similar to how the extra blades of the Serengeti lock onto the sides of the handle, the integral Side Hawg fixed blade locks onto the side of a knife-shaped plate, or paddle, that is outfitted with a saddle clip, or carabineer. When shown to CRKT, the design was snapped up immediately.

The knife was named Side Hawg and was introduced at the 2005 Shooting Hunting Outdoor Trade (SHOT) Show in Las Vegas. Within two hours of the show opening, orders were being written for the Side Hawg by CRKT, and Franklin was asked for more and similar designs.

As produced by CRKT, the little knife weighs less than 2 ounces and features a 420-J2 stainless steel blade and skeletonized handle. The modified drop-point blade is 1.625 inches long. The sheath plate is made of black Zytel® with a stainless steel post and saddle clip, similar to the Serengeti.

For use, the knife pivots out of the saddle and pushes upward off the post and the sheath plate. A carabineer and nylon strap let you carry the knife clipped to a belt loop or D-ring. Add a simple boot string or bead chain and it becomes a neck knife, as lanyard holes are included in the sheath plate design. Because nothing is enclosed, the Side Hawg is easy to deploy and clean.

CRKT is not selling Mike Franklin custom knives, of course, but the very design is available from the company through its dealers, its catalog or through the Internet, and at a considerably lower cost than the handmade version.

For handmade Franklin knives, take a look at www.franklincustomknives.com or visit the Plaza Cutlery Web site.

Franklin has this to say about his latest designs: "I think we can call 2005 the year of the Tactical Extreme line. Since its introduction, the line has taken over most of my business. The one model that has risen above the others is called the Samurai. This knife features a 6-inch blade with a double-edge grind (both lower and upper edges being sharpened).

## Sly Samurai

"The curved grip, copied from Japanese knives and swords, permits the blade to fold all the way up into the frame when closed," Franklin notes. "The blade stop pin must fit precisely into the frame so that it prevents the lower edge from protruding through the top of the frame.

"The design of the Samurai was the most difficult in my 30 years of knifemaking. I can build knives like that because I make them one at a time, by hand. It has become so popular, though, I could fill orders for only that one model for the rest of the year and keep busy. Other models in my Tactical Extreme group are the Brute, Lightning, El Toro, Tank and the Samurai," he says.

Franklin's son, Jarrod, is a U.S. Marine serving in Iraq.

**Known as "the knifemaker to the stars," Chuck Stapel is pictured holding one of several bowie knives he was commissioned to build for the movie "Alamo." Another of Stapel's bowie-style knives (right), the Conqueror features an 8 3/4-inch damascus blade, a stag and fossil-walrus-ivory handle, and black-Micarta® spacers. The knife is featured on Stapel's Web site, www.stapelknives.com.**

**The Mike Franklin US Hunter sports a 2 1/2-inch, hollow-ground ATS-34 blade, a Diamondwood™ handle and a Kydex® sheath.**

**The Columbia River Knife & Tool Serengeti is a Mike Franklin-designed hunting knife featuring three AUS-4 stainless steel blades. The main folding blade is 3-1/4 inches long and locks open solidly, leaving no play between blade and handle. Latching onto the outside of the handle are two additional blades. One is a 1 3/4-inch skinning blade, and the other is a 1 3/4-inch hawksbill caping blade. Each smaller blade can be removed from the handle for detailed game care.**

As this is written, Jarrod carries a large tactical folder designed and made by Mike, and it is serving him well.

Franklin is not the only custom maker who sells his knives via the Internet. Among the many others is California's Chuck Stapel, also a man with more than three decades of knifemaking experience. In addition, Stapel has been making movie prop knives for more than 20 years at his shop in Los Angeles.

In recent times, Stapel has made knives for such movies as "Kill Bill," "Once Upon A Time In Mexico," "Quigley Down Under," "The Alamo" and many others. The final look of the knives, many of which are not sharpened for safety reasons, is up to the movie prop masters or producers, not the maker. His contributions to the movie industry helped make Stapel known as the "knifemaker to the stars."

Stapel also fashions a number of art and culinary knives for customers. He even builds custom corkscrews and cigar clippers. Stapel's Web site mentions dozens upon dozens of special knives he has donated to various organizations to raise money for deserving groups. But he also has been commissioned several times to make pieces auctioned off at SHOT Shows.

The SHOT Show auctions raise money for the National Shooting Sports Foundation's hunting and shooting sports projects. Stapel can and does build custom knives at a prodigious rate. Many of his knives are sold through retail dealers, and many of the customers are repeat buyers seeking out the latest from Stapel.

There are hundreds of custom knifemakers who market their wares through the Internet. And there are many other jobbers and on-line dealers who handle the same quality knives. On the other hand, plenty of us still need to see, handle, feel and examine the products of a skilled knifemaker before buying.

Plenty of opportunities have arisen to satisfy both camps. For the most part, knife Web sites are easy to navigate, they are updated regularly and are reliable sources of fine handmade knives.

*NOTE: In these days of sophisticated Cyber crooks and rip-off artists, the Internet buyer must use utmost care and be convinced of the integrity of the maker or dealer and his Web site.*

**Similar to how the extra blades of the Serengeti lock onto the sides of the handle, the integral Side Hawg fixed blade locks onto the side of a knife-shaped plate, or paddle, that is outfitted with a saddle clip, or carabineer. The knife is a Mike Franklin design and offered by Columbia River Knife & Tool. It weighs less than 2 ounces and features a 420-J2 stainless steel blade and skeletonized handle. The modified drop-point blade is 1.625 inches long. The sheath plate is made of black Zytel® with a stainless steel post and saddle clip, similar to the Serengeti.**

▼**JOHN FRAPS:** Whether you prefer the subtle hues of the black-lip pearl or the dramatic effects of the heat-colored Timascus bolsters, the damascus blade will still cut the mustard. *(Hoffman photo)*

▲**BILL COFFEY:** Just as the red abalone was born, the sun peeked through the clouds and scorched the land where it rested.

▶**LARRY NEWTON:** Black-lip pearl blossoms on a stainless-damascus dagger as the flowers open their petals along the spine of the knife. *(PointSeven photo)*

▲**JIM MINNICK:** The push button dagger showcases Joyce Minnick's Art Deco relief engraving, Jerry Rados' Turkish damascus and black-lip pearl offered up by the sea. *(PointSeven photo)*

▲**MURRAY STERLING:** Black-lip pearl is framed by Damasteel, Damasteel and more Damasteel.

▲**DARRELL RALPH:** The butterfly knife came out of its damascus cocoon to spread its pearly wings and fly. Mike Norris helped out with the "crazy lace" damascus pattern.

▶ **HOWARD HITCHMOUGH: The black-lip pearl was so strikingly handsome, Julie Warenski decide to just engrave around it rather than asking it to move.**
*(PointSeven photo)*

◀ **HIROYUKI SAKURAI: The black-lip pearl of the top knife is also inset at bottom, and abalone takes center stage on the two knives in the middle.**
*(PointSeven photo)*

▶ **MARK LARAMIE: Is it so far-fetched to believe that, since you can hear the ocean in certain shells, you can see it in others? Bob Eggerling heat-colored some damascus for the occasion.**

◀ **DON HANSON III: Mosaic damascus makes faces and offers up figures, while black-lip pearl shows off its own colorful character.**
*(PointSeven photo)*

▲ **JEFF CLAIBORNE: Abalone makes a splash on a congress-pattern pocket folder.**
*(Hoffman photo)*

# Burl-esque Blades

▶ **KEN ONION:** The S-shaped bolster is married to a curly-koa handle for an altogether contoured coupling. *(Mitch Lum photo)*

▼ **ALEXANDER FELIX:** Maybe African blackwood and desert ironwood share the same roots.

◀ **ALAIN MIVILLE-DESCHENES:** Stabilized snakewood is shined up to a shimmering sheen.

▲ **HARUMI HIRAYAMA:** It's amazing how owls can camouflage themselves against maple that way. *(Hasegawa photo)*

▶ **JOHN OWENS:** The dyed maple handle made its new owner feel like he died and went to heaven. Randy Anderson stitched up the sheath for the colorful cutter.

▶ **JON CHRISTENSEN:** Curly koa wood can't even outdo the mosaic damascus, so it plays along as well as it can.

▶ **DICK FAUST:** Box elder rarely emits such vivid blues and browns, but then again hunters are seldom so handsome.

▲ **PETER MARZITELLI:** Zebrawood and buckeye burl are as hard to tame as the wild damascus blades.

▲ **MACE VITALE:** Birdseye maple perches atop its nickel silver nest overlooking steel city.

▲ **NEIL BLACKWOOD:** When you've got amboyna burl that looks like that, you make a set of hunting knives. *(PointSeven photo)*

▶ **KEVIN HARVEY**: Only engraved bronze could hold up to box elder wood and Turkish-twist damascus.

▶ **BILL LEVENGOOD**: It's got that black, red and brass thing going on, and that can only be good. By the way, he calls it a "palm-handle hunter," probably because it's so palm-able.

▲ **WILLIAM BEHNKE**: It's difficult to decide whether the damascus or snakewood is more striking.

◀ **MARK MCCOUN**: It's not only the leaves of maple trees that leave lasting impressions.

▲ **AL KAJIN**: The juniper handle is deep enough to dive into, and just the right touch on a damascus hunter.

▶ **DAN FARR:** A desert-ironwood grip was appropriately chosen for the "Outdoorsman." *(SharpByCoop.com photo)*

▼ **ROB SPROKHOLT:** Spalted maple was a splendid choice for a 440C "Woodsman" model.

▶ **EDDIE STALCUP:** The old 56-er struck gold under an ironwood tree. *(Hoffman photo)*

◀ **ROBERT BEATY:** Don't tell the knifemaker, but dyed maple burl can't really be stabilized, and neither can such static random-pattern damascus.

▲ **BILL BUXTON:** Damascus bookends redwood burl like wafers sandwich a cream cookie. *(BladeGallery.com photo)*

▼ **MIKE DRAPER:** Dyed and stabilized black ash gives the titanium and damascus folder a debonair demeanor. *(BladeGallery.com photo)*

▶ **RANDY LEE:** The combination of redwood burl, fossil oosic and yellow amber is surprisingly uncommon considering the results. *(BladeGallery.com photo)*

▶ **TONY PAINTER:** The random-pattern damascus blade called for a special section of stabilized tiger maple.

◀ **CHARLIE AND HARRY MATHEWS:** Snakewood snuck up on the steel and almost swallowed it whole before feeling the edge and backing off a bit.

▲ **MARVIN SOLOMON:** It took several forge welds to achieve the pattern in the blade, but only water and sunlight to achieve the swirls in the California buckeye burl. *(Ward photo)*

▲ **WAYNE HENSLEY:** An artist couldn't have chosen better colors than those of the natural, petrified, black palm wood. *(PointSeven photo)*

▶ **TOM WATSON:** Who'd want to cover up the ironwood with their hand . . . well, maybe for a little while?

▶ **COLTEN TIPPETTS:** An engraved green-maple-burl-handled knife like that would stop all hunting activities for the day in my neck of the woods. Guys would just pass the knife around and chew the fat. Bruce Shaw would, of course, be mentioned as the engraver. *(PointSeven photo)*

▲ **LOYD MCCONNELL:** Loyd let the curly oak live a little longer in the form of an S30V folder. *(PointSeven photo)*

▶ **JODY MULLER:** Nature provided the blue buckeye burl and the clay that quenched the blade.

▶ **BILL AMOUREUX:** Tuck the box-elder-handle boot knife in good, or someone is sure to blow your cover. *(BladeGallery.com photo)*

▲ **T.R. OVEREYNDER:** When Terry Drew designed the knife, it's doubtful the layered-like look of the Arizona ironwood was envisioned. *(PointSeven photo)*

**▶ MIKE O'BRIEN:** The knightly figure is cloaked in Macassar ebony and stainless steel armor. *(PointSeven photo)*

**▲ SARAH MCCLURE:** Seven-year-old Sarah McClure fashioned the full-tang damascus darling of a knife and hafted it with a smooth slab of olivewood. *(PointSeven photo)*

**▲ LUDWIG FRUHMANN:** The grains of the stabilized spalted maple actually emulate those of tree bark.

**▼ R. BOYES:** Well, we know the maple handle was dyed the right color, and it looks as though John Vukos engraved the brass guard and butt cap perfectly, so all that's left to evaluate is that stunning twist-pattern-damascus blade.

**▲ DAVE DODDS:** It's cool how the box elder and damascus share the same shades, and the mokumé bolster is highlighted by the circles around the pinheads. *(PointSeven photo)*

**▲ J.D. BARTH:** If tree trunks were the color of green maple burl, there'd be a lot more log houses in the world.

# Real Tacticals

There aren't any locks that will slip. Few of these knives fold at all, and the thumb studs and pocket clips are mysteriously missing. There is no need for safeties, and whether they'll fit into pants pockets doesn't seem to be a consideration. The knives pictured are stripped of pearl, ivory, stone, jewels, gold, fancy filework, engraving or scrimshaw. Full blade tangs abound, and integral guards are the flavor of the day.

Amazingly enough, without all of the embellishment, the blades are still handsome in their own right. It's not that they're clunky or boxy. There's nothing awkward about them, and the knives certainly aren't unfriendly to handle. In fact, most of them are easily maneuvered, lightweight, perfectly balanced and ergonomic. They can be used in emergency situations. They're versatile, well built, reliable, long lasting, tough, strong, sharp and penetrating. They're tactical!

Some of the knives are long, some have hilts and sub-hilts, others are shaped like bird beaks or claws and many share characteristics like double hand guards, saw teeth, lanyards, spikes, choils and thick blade steel.

No one is condemning or disrespecting locking-liner folders with thumb studs and pocket clips. No one is saying all-black folding tantos aren't handy tools and reliable weapons. Heck, locking-liner folders with thumb studs and pocket clips revolutionized the knife industry, brought it back to life, revived it! It's not that a lockback folder can't be a backup self-defense weapon.

It's just that not everyone agrees on the meaning of "tactical," so all doubt was taken out when choosing the following knives. No matter what the definition of "tactical" is, the following knives fit it. They are as "tactical" as tactical gets. They are real tacticals.

*Joe Kertzman*

◀ **BRUCE BUMP:** The 19th Century Tactical Pistol, which was fashioned in the 21st century, is a working 22-caliber black-powder pistol with an ATS-34 knife blade and a G-10 handle. *(Mitch Lum photo)*

▲ **SEAN O'HARE:** If its CPM S30V blade had a mind to, the "Pathfinder" could blaze many a trail.

▲ **RANDY DOUCETTE:** Here's one called the "Hound Dog," and its bite is worse than its bark. The puppy sports a rose-pattern Damasteel blade and a blue-twill G-10 handle.

◀ **COLIN COX:** The best things about a combat-grade D-guard fighter are the spiked brass guard, the spike on the end of the handle, and the way the blade begs to be abused. *(Weyer photo)*.

▼ **RANDALL MADE:** The question, "Why mess with perfection?" takes on a double meaning here. *(PointSeven photo)*

▶ **RICKY FOWLER:** The integral tanto has a camel-bone handle and a hump along its back. I'd take it into the desert.

▼ **TOM MAYO:** Slip the pinkie finger into the hole of steel, silently slip the wooden grip into the palm of your hand and rest your thumb on the ramp before brandishing this bad blade.

▼ **CARLOS ZAKHAROV:** The blackened steel and cord contribute to the stealth look, but the design and execution complete the package. *(PointSeven photo)*

▲ **JENS ANSO:** The steel-and-titanium Tukan Balisong floats like a butterfly and stings like a bee.

▲ **SHIVA KI:** He built the paratrooper chute knife from clay-tempered 1095 steel, and a good guard and grip that won't let the blade get away. *(Beaucant photo)*

▲ **TODD BEGG:** I guess which one you choose depends on the size of the job. *(Mitch Lum photo)*

▲ **ALAIN MIVILLE-DESCHENES:** The neck knife is a claw-shaped cutter with notches, grooves and more than passable palpability.

▲ **PAT AND WES CRAWFORD:** It might look like pruning shears, and that's exactly what it's supposed to look like when sheathed, but it's a self-defense knife that can probably be carried around town. *(PointSeven photo)*

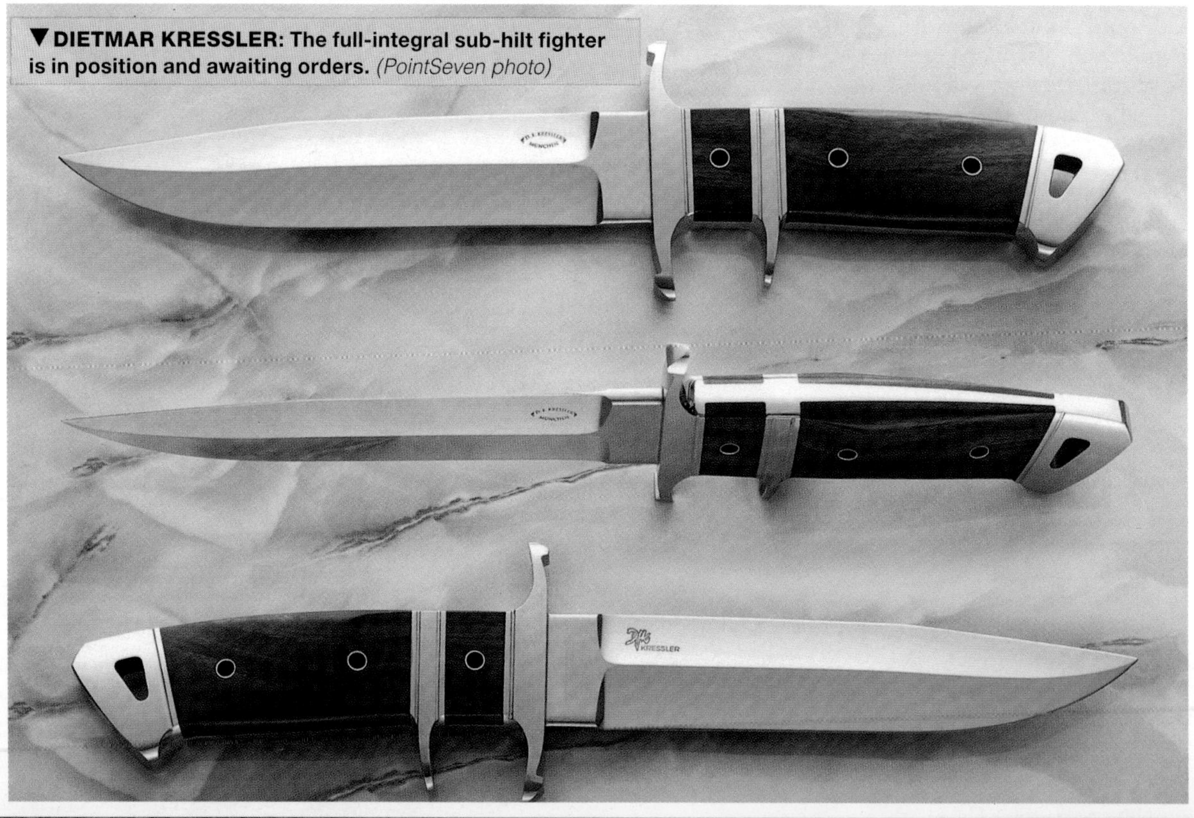

▼ **DIETMAR KRESSLER:** The full-integral sub-hilt fighter is in position and awaiting orders. *(PointSeven photo)*

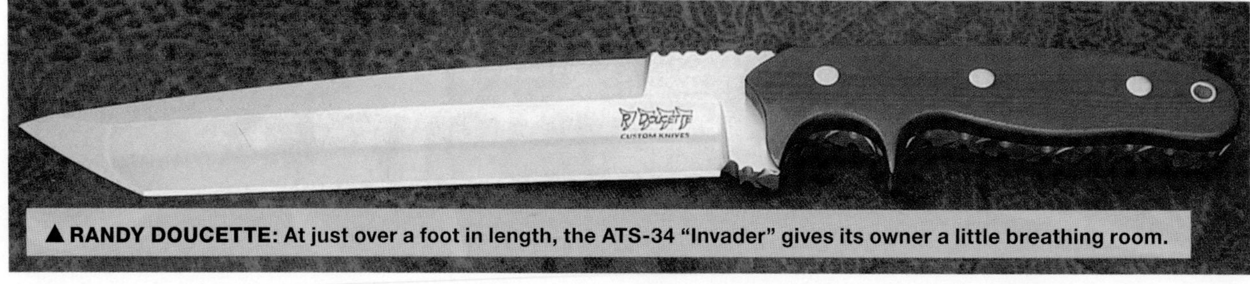

▲ **RANDY DOUCETTE:** At just over a foot in length, the ATS-34 "Invader" gives its owner a little breathing room.

**▼CHARLES OCHS:** Charles likes to be well armed when defending his honor. *(PointSeven photo)*

**▲TODD BEGG:** "Achilles" and "Hector" are D-2 integral push daggers inspired by the mythological fight between Achilles and Hector. *(SharpByCoop.com photo)*

**▲BILL COFFEY:** My bulldog looks like that sometimes, but his teeth aren't nearly as sharp as the Jim Ferguson damascus blade with integral points and protrusions.

**▲REESE WEILAND:** The 2-foot-long Mike Norris damascus sickle is scything mad and ready to rumble. *(Bob Doggett photo)*

**▼PAUL LEBATARD:** It's his standard "Scout" knife for going it alone in the lead.

**▲BRENT BESHARA:** A similar diamond-shaped blade from Brent appeared in "Knives 2005," but without the Kevlar®-scale handle, and this one is photographed to better appreciate the full 18 inches of cold, hard steel. *(PointSeven photo)*

**▲REESE WEILAND:** Let's talk again about how we penetrate the armored battalion. *(Bob Doggett photo)*

# Fast-Track Folders

There's a reason that almost every knifemaker who has ever taken a bastard file to steel started his or her career fashioning fixed blades. It's not the case for every knifemaker, but most embark on building their first blades using uncomplicated patterns. That would mean skipping moving parts, like folding blades. Fixed blades don't have pivots, nail nicks, thumb studs, assisted-opening devices, buttons, bushings, washers or springs. They don't snap to attention; they're already upright and ready.

A fixed blade doesn't require smooth action. It doesn't need to be held to tight tolerances. The liners of a fixed blade can bookend the tang with nary a worry about staying clear of a swinging blade. Nothing rubs the wrong way on a fixed blade. The handle of a straight knife can be shorter than the blade. Try that with a folder and see what happens when it comes time to close the blade. Fixed blades can be any shape or size. They don't have to fit into pockets or clip onto vests. The steel of a fixed blade can be 1/4-inch thick if a knifemaker so desires. The possibilities are limitless.

But a folder, oh a folder, now there's a complicated little gadget. On the one hand, a folding knife is a handy tool because it folds up into a nice, neat little package. When not in use, the blade edge hides inside the handle. Most folders fit in pants pockets. On the other hand, try taking several moving parts, one of which has a sharp edge, put them together, and have them all operate smoothly, with minimal friction and working as one unit. Building such a blade takes a little more time at the drawing board.

The technology of folder-making has come a long way. Folders are dressed up in such fancy handles and blades, that one can't help but wonder if the maker spent any time on operation. Upon picking up a quality, modern folder, one fashioned by a top-notch knifemaker, doubters become believers. Flicking open a folder has become an art, like throwing a curve ball or tossing a horseshoe. More often than not, folding knives have become the chosen ones. They're on the fast track and headed into the final lap.

*Joe Kertzman*

▶ **GORDON CHARD: The blending of so many materials—George Werth damascus, Jim Ferguson damascus, G-10, titanium and mother of pearl—was done classically, without chaos or confusion.** *(Hopkins photo)*

▶ **TODD BEGG: When you're able to "forge texture" titanium, you've got knifemaking down to a science.** *(SharpByCoop.com photo)*

▲ **R.J. MARTIN: This one's got the competition green with envy.** *(SharpByCoop.com photo)*

▶ **BRIAN TIGHE: The gorgeously grooved tantos are tough as nails.** *(PointSeven photo)*

▲ **SALVATORE PUDDU: The all-stainless "PLP" knife is primped, lapped and polished.**

▲ **PHILIP BOOTH: When not in use, the Jim Ferguson damascus blade hides in its tortoise shell.** *(Custom Knife Gallery of Colorado photo)*

◀ **ANDRE THORBURN: The geriatric giraffe bone found a final resting place on a knife handle and had a go-around with a folding Sandvik stainless steel blade.** *(Custom Knife Gallery of Colorado photo)*

▲ **RON CAMERON: Devin Thomas damascus is married to tiger coral in one instance and apple corral in the other. Either way, it's a match made in heaven.** *(BladeGallery.com photo)*

▶ **KEVIN HOFFMAN:** Bubbles floating skyward are less beautiful than this blade.

▲ **CHUCK STEFFEN:** Everyone stares as circles surround squares. *(Hoffman photo)*

▶ **MICHAEL WALKER:** One look and you are star-struck. *(PointSeven photo)*

▲ **GAYLE BRADLEY:** The red bolsters are built from Devin Thomas mokume, accented with gold and anchored by black. *(PointSeven photo)*

◀ **TOM WATSON:** When Jack Busfield gave permission for Tom to use his knife design, he had no idea how serious the maker would take the honor.

◀ **TOM MAYO:** Please pass the Mayo. *(Hoffman photo)*

▶ **DOC HAGEN: He polished everything else so the natural ray skin would be the textured attention grabber.** *(Custom Knife Gallery of Colorado photo)*

▼ **REESE WEILAND: The "Eagle" double-action automatic has a beak of Robert Eggerling damascus and highly figured bark-mammoth-ivory tail feathers.** *(Doggett photo)*

▶ **KEN ONION: Timascus adds some swirl to the pearl.** *(Mitch Lum photo)*

▶ **PETER MARZITELLI: The "Swift Claw" sports a "translucent G-10" handle, complete with carved dinosaur skull, and an anodized pocket clip.**

◀ **FRANK BONASSI AND FLAVIO PORATELLI: The fast-track folder is built with sculpted titanium frames.**

▶ **JOHN BARTLOW:** Voted best-dressed blade, he wore emerald-green titanium, silver steel and beige mastodon ivory. *(PointSeven photo)*

▲ **A.R. MAHOMEDY:** Lady's and gent's folders are fashioned from elephant ivory, giraffe bone, Robert Eggerling damascus, stainless steel and titanium.

▶ **JENS ANSO:** The "Amok" folder, complete with textured-titanium bolsters, carbon-fiber handle and RWL-34 blade, runs anything but amok. The round opening hole on the blade was used under license from Spyderco Knife Co.

▲ **GAYLE BRADLEY:** Devin Thomas Spirograph damascus dizzies up the pearl. *(PointSeven photo)*

◀ **JIM HARRISON:** Apple coral looks red and delicious.

◀ **DARREL RALPH:** Black-lip pearl got the window seat on an airborne folding dagger. *(Hoffman photo)*

▲ **BILL LEVENGOOD:** Mokume and pearl enliven a coffin-handle folder.

▲ **DES HORN:** The little Damasteel dart is styled splendidly.

▶ **DES HORN:** One's coral and the other is hand-carved. *(PointSeven photo)*

# Stone-Cold Slicers

There's no such thing as lackadaisical lapidary work. Someone building a brick wall might be able to get away with a few uneven mortar spaces, and inequity in a field-stone foundation can be made up for with extra cement thrown in here or there. A cobblestone street is worked with heavy machinery to make up for the high and rough spots. But a knife handle has to be smooth. There can be no gaps between handle materials.

Like most aspects of knife-making, lapidary work requires precision methodology. The first thing prospective knife buyers do in showrooms is to inspect the merchandise. They lightly touch the blade edges to fingers or fingernails, they gaze at the grind lines, palm the handles, squeeze them, change grips, feel for rough spots, look for gaps, slice pieces of paper, pocket the knives, sheath them, pull them back out and sight them up as if they're precision rifles. They treat them as if they're tools that might save their bacon someday, or slice it.

Stone grips do more than provide hand purchase. They brighten up the steely demeanor of edged tools. Stones have character. They're colorful entities in their own right. They're hard, barely permeable, resistant to water, oil, dirt, sand, grease, chemicals and other agents. The knives fortunate enough to be ordained with such materials are in another class. They're monumental, set-in-stone, rock-solid, stone-cold slicers.

*Joe Kertzman*

▲ **BERTIE RIETVELD: Carved in art deco style, anodized-titanium ferrules frame an exhibition-grade green Verdite handle, and "dragon-skin" damascus flanks a center blade billet exhibiting distinct lines of nickel.**

▶ **MICK WARDELL: The whale's tooth has a green malachite cap, and the blade reflects the waves.**

▲ **DOC HAGEN: How'd you like to core something with this apple-coral-handle damascus dual-action folder?** *(Custom Knife Gallery of Colorado photo)*

▲ **J. NEILSON:** Between a box-elder-burl handle and an etched 1084 blade is a Charoite throat turned purple from the squeeze put on by the other two. The appropriately purple sheath is Tess Neilson's handiwork.

▲ **JOVAN DEBRAGA:** Jet stone and lapis lazuli make the "Rebirth Dagger" a stone-cold slicer of the most smashing kind.

◀ **MIKE TAMBOLI:** He who offered up the dagger to the king would have been spared from the dungeon. The composite stone guard and Spyrograph damascus blade would have pleased even the most ornery of royalty. *(Engaged Productions photo)*

▼ **BRUCE ALLRED:** Reconstituted stone is the wild card that makes the "Cheetah" a wild cat.

▼ **JAY FISHER:** The African red jasper gemstone handle is the fire that fuels the engraved carbon-steel bolsters.

# Visions of Bowie

He emerges from the mist, or is it the mists of time? It's hazy. His dress is drab—a black overcoat, boots, a hat, chiseled face peeking out from beneath shadowed brow, and nondescript facial features. He walks with a limp and there might be a cane in his left hand. He comes in and out of focus. There is meanness in his eyes, or is it just anger? Anger, yes it's anger. He's been wronged, and revenge is his intent. He must defend himself. He's come for a showdown, laying his life on the line to defend his honor, reputation and righteousness, if for no other reason than to finish what was started. He slides a knife from its sheath. The steel glimmers in the half-light, condensation immediately forming on the edge. The grip fills his hand, and the guard protects his fingers.

There's a secondary edge, but it's impossible to discern its sharpness. Perhaps it's not an edge at all, but more of a sweeping blade, a clipped edge or point. It's not a pretty knife. It's not a pretty scene. There's no action or visual satisfaction. He has purpose in his demeanor, and the knife matches the mood.

Another appears from behind the brush. This one is mean; his intentions aren't honorable. There will be blood today. Neither sizes the other up. It's been done. They barely look at each other, but move around as if acknowledging another presence. A fight is brewing and death permeates the air. Two men, two guns, untold other forms of weaponry, and that knife; it's the most impressive of all. There's something about it that's familiar. How can something so stark be so incredibly beautiful? The steel, the edge that cuts, is actually inviting. The tip, the one that penetrates, evokes emotion. The handle is palpable from a distance and the guard commands respect. This is no ordinary boar-hunting blade.

It's difficult to tell if the knife belongs to the man, or the man to the knife ... or neither. Now it becomes clear. The sun penetrates the fog, but only for a moment. The man and knife fade back into the unknown, resurrected only as fable and fashion allow.

Nothing so pure can be improved upon, no patterns repeated. Hands disconnected from bodies replicate the knife he carried, but each is just an interpretation. No one will ever improve upon perfection, yet each tries to reach knife nirvana, where legends transcend place and time. The knives they fashion do not belong to them. Such bladed visions must be captured before they, too, fade into the mists of time.

*Joe Kertzman*

▶ **STEVEN RAPP:** So regal is the Horsehead Bowie, ivory was fluted to honor it. *(Hoffman photo)*

◀ **STEPHEN LELAND:** The ivory coffin could be a prelude of things to come. *(PointSeven photo)*

◀ **DICK FAUST:** He built his bowie with a hilt and a sub-hilt, flavoring it with a bit of maple.

▶ **GEORGE GARNER:** A Razorback Bowie is ready to go hog wild. *(Hoffman photo)*

▲ **JAMES BATSON:** Silver sleeves bookend the walrus-tusk grip of the Texas Ranger Bowie. *(Ward photo)*

▶ **BRETT GATLIN:** It's all about stag and swagger. *(Ward photo)*

▶ **STEPHEN MACKRILL:** The brass along the blade spine ties the browns of the mammoth ivory, the hues of the Wyoming jade and the silver of the blade together as one thematic unit. *(Mitch Lum photo)*

▶ **BILL BURKE:** So "bowie" is the blade, there's nothing else to say. *(BladeGallery.com photo)*

◀ **GARRETT WHITE:** The scrolls in the S-guard are compliments of Billy Bates, and the mirror-polished "say it will never be demolished" 440C blade is of Garrett White's doing. *(Hoffman photo)*

◀ **MICK WARDELL:** The sea of steel was angry that day, my friends.

◀ **BILL SOWELL:** A gentleman named A. Pradel made a bowie in the 1830s, and our own Bill Sowell revisited it for a spell before giving it up for the greater good. *(Hoffman photo)*

▶ **JAMES SHAVER: This is a pretty cool red, white and blue interpretation of a great American design.** *(Jason Shaver photo)*

▶ **TIM FOSTER: The knifemaker strapped a mustangs-pattern mosaic damascus blade onto a cowboy bowie and gave it a stag saddle horn.** *(BladeGallery.com photo)*

▶ **GARY RODEWALD: The pattern of the 320-layer damascus is as spectacular as the rare popcorn-variety Sambar stag.** *(BladeGallery.com photo)*

▶ **NICK WHEELER: The *hamon* (blade temper line) is clear, and the *oosic* (fossilized walrus penis bone, or *baculum*) is murky.** *(BladeGallery.com photo)*

▶ **MICHAEL WATTELET: Below the skull and bones was the hulking body of the brute.**

▲ **KEVIN CASHEN: Between the twist damascus and the wrapping rope filework, the small bowie/hunter has my head spinning.** *(PointSeven photo)*

▶ **JAMES BATSON:** Fido better keep his jowls off the early American dog-bone bowie. *(Ward photo)*

▶ **JOE CORDOVA:** Cable damascus escapes from the coffin-handle bowie like the dead rising. *(KnifeShop.tv photo)*

▲ **BRUCE BUMP:** Finding its conscience, the outlaw bowie is outfitted with a pre-ban elephant-ivory grip. *(Mitch Lum photo)*

▶ **RICK SMITH:** The balance point is just in front of the D-Guard on the ricasso, right where it should be.

▶ **JIM WALKER:** Curly maple escorts a Southwest bowie to the dance. *(Ward photo)*

▲ **DON FOGG:** The storm raged and he pointed the bowie skyward just as lightning struck, leaving its image on the foot-long blade. The ferrule is carved, and it's for real.

▲ **JAMES COOK:** Damascus dances along the spine, face and edge of the giraffe-leg-bone bowie. *(Ward photo)*

▶ **RAY KIRK:** You've got to like the Lil' Bowie with the sharp damascus blade and clean elephant ivory grip. *(Ward photo)*

▶ **JASON KNIGHT AND RON NEWTON:** Jason chose big and blackwood, and Ron went more toward the small and stag end of things. *(PointSeven photo)*

▲ **HARVEY DEAN:** It has a checkered past but a spotless future. *(PointSeven photo)*

▶ **MICHAEL RUTH:** Michael etched a line where the damascus fades into the bevels of bowie. *(Ward photo)*

◀ **LIN RHEA:** It took two to tangle—ironwood burl and 1084 blade steel. *(Ward photo)*

▶ **BILLY BATES:** This one's got brass—and engraved brass at that. *(Ward photo)*

◀ **BURT FOSTER:** After hand-rubbing the flats and mirror-polishing the spine, the maker added blue giraffe bone using domed-head nickel silver pins.

▲ **DAVID DARBY:** Is that a bowie-cue on the butt of the blade? *(Ward photo)*

▲ **DAVID AND JEROME ANDERS:** The presentation of this one is as it should be, complete with stars and stripes. *(PointSeven photo)*

# Full Frontier Fashion

Would an Apache chief command respect without a headdress or war paint? Could a cowboy mosey up to the bar without boots and spurs? Better yet, could he settle a score without six-shooters and bullets? How would it look if a Mexican bandito came screaming into town wearing his best Sunday trousers and starched dress shirt? The clothes early frontiersmen wore were like badges of honor. They went hand-in-hand with the notches in their gunstocks and skins in their saddlebags. The ceremonial costumes and traditional garb of the Native Americans were like feathers in their caps. Every part of the wardrobe had meaning, from frayed buckskins and bead-worked moccasins to beaver pelts and wolf skins with heads still attached.

Equally out of place would be an early settler carrying an Italian stiletto, or a Cherokee tribal member lugging around a Samurai sword. The tools matched the trades, so to speak. Tomahawks and neck knives were as commonplace in teepee circles as were skinners, bowies and hatchets in Western settlements and homesteads. Blazing new trails could hardly be done with pearl-handle pocketknives.

The knives matched not only the period dress of brave warriors and Western wranglers, but also the tasks to which they were put. If a skinning knife was needed, a double-edged dagger just wouldn't do. Few folks wiled away the hours opening UPS boxes and cutting cucumbers in those days. Times called for wood grips, high-carbon steel blades and brass tacks. Stainless steel assisted-opening folders might have impressed outlaws and young bucks, but they might not have known how to use them.

Preachers didn't wear shotgun-shielding trench coats any more than squaws paraded around in short skirts and high heels. Blacksmiths didn't don ponchos, and fur traders were rarely seen in silk scarves. It would be like a bronc buster wearing a machete or a sheriff packing a poleax.

*Joe Kertzman*

▲ **JAMES BATSON:** The Nesmuck hunter stands arrow stiff, outfitted in damascus and crowned in stag. *(Ward photo)*

◄ **STACY APLET:** The tomahawk head was forged from a railroad spike and the curly maple haft inlaid with the finest silver in honor of the old iron horse. *(Hoffman photo)*

▲ **JOE ZEMITIS:** The mighty oak fell to clear the way for the wagon train, yet a branch was saved and forever preserved in the form of an axe haft.

◀ **JOE SZILASKI:** They sat in a circle, smoking the pipe hawk and admiring the handwork that went into it. Images of cattle skulls and warrior shields came to them as darkness descended. *(PointSeven photo)*

◀ **ED BRANDSEY:** For reasons that may never be known, they called him Four Stones. *(Hoffman photo)*

◀ **DANIEL WINKLER:** Only frontier deer have antlers like that, and only frontiersmen forge such jaw-dropping damascus. The frontier lady, Karen Shook, was up to the task of fashioning the sheath. *(PointSeven photo)*

▶ **ROBERT ROSSDEUTSCHER:** It's the same golden brown as the sun-baked frontier. *(Hoffman photo)*

▲ **BILL SOWELL:** The damascus is dark, as if an antique patina was applied to give it a frontier flavor. *(Hoffman photo)*

▶ **ROBERT BLASINGAME:** The Miller bowie reproduction boasts brass fittings and a curly maple handle.

▶ **LONNIE HANSEN:** In much the same way as tribal representatives met to discuss the future of the Indian nations, carved chevrons bring blackwood and box elder together as one unifying force. *(BladeGallery.com photo)*

▶ **E. JAY HENDRICKSON:** Native colors embedded in curly maple and framed by silver wire put the "wow" in powwow. *(PointSeven photo)*

▶ **ALEXANDER FELIX:** The railroad spike knife was wrapped in copper before being offered as a gift of friendship.

▲ **ALAN TIENSVOLD**: The head of the hawk looks at you as it strikes. *(PointSeven photo)*

◀ **HEATHER HARVEY**: Few original frontier friction folders sported "moth-antennae"-patterned damascus blades, so an old coin was planted nearby to mark the spot where history was made.

◀ **MARK MCCOUN**: The crosscut blade wore out and a friction folder blade was born. Only tiger maple would do for the grip of this one.

▲ **RIK PALM**: With needle files, chisels and ball burs, Rik carved a bear head, feathers and a medicine wheel, attaching the resulting tomahawk head onto an ash haft.

# Steadfast Fighters

◀ **S.R. JOHNSON:** With a single hollow grind on one side of the blade, and a double hollow grind on the other, it's three times the fun. *(PointSeven photo)*

▲ **MICHAEL MCCLURE:** Hold onto that Sambar stag, the 5160 blade is ready for a brawl. *(PointSeven photo)*

▲ **JAMES COOK:** The teardrop-shaped ebony handle nestles in the palm of a hand like a newborn lamb in a bed of hay. The guard accepts the forefinger and thumb as a baby takes to the bottle. *(Ward photo)*

▶ **STEVE LELAND:** Nickel silver and stabilized ebony live together in perfect harmony. *(PointSeven photo)*

▲ **ROBERT NELSON PARKER:** A mother-of-pearl spacer is the mediator between fightin'-mad damascus and equally ornery water buffalo horn.

▼ **SHIVA KI:** The blade and butt will do damage. *(Dominique Beaucant photo)*

▶ **NICK WHEELER:** Like a dog-eared alley cat, the damascus isn't afraid to show off its battle scars. *(PointSeven photo)*

▶ **RICARDO VELARDE:** The full-grown fighter is proud of his little chute knife. *(PointSeven photo)*

▶ **DIETMAR KRESSLER:** He's a little fighter who has big aspirations and a good role model. *(PointSeven photo)*

◀ **DON NORRIS:** When he saw them, Don Norris instantly recognized a standout piece of Jim Ferguson damascus and a highly figured section of sheep horn. *(ScreenSurge photo)*

▲ **BURT FOSTER:** The notches along his spine tell most of the story, and the rest can be read in the depths of the desert ironwood and clay-hardened blade.

▼ **WALLY HAYES:** She's filed, styled and riled. *(SharpByCoop.com photo)*

▶ **JOHN YOUNG:** The mosaic pins, the Julie Warenski engraving and the groovy, well-ground blade play side-by-side with no quarrels among them. *(Hoffman photo)*

◀ **JOHN WHITE:** The wood is warm, the brass and silicone bronze are cold, and the steel is hot. *(Ward photo)*

▼ **VIRGIL ENGLAND:** At last count, the "Wasp" medium fighter had four stingers, including an extremely long one forge welded by Daryl Meier. The body is segmented to better deploy all weaponry.

# Damascus Dynamics

▶ **MARVIN SOLOMON:** Even brass and ram horn couldn't outdo the droopy damascus of the stylish skinner. *(Ward photo)*

▶ **STEVE DUNN:** When pushed out of its nesting place, the feather-damascus fixed blade sings like a bird. Gold inlay and scroll engraving are the goose's golden eggs. *(PointSeven photo)*

▼ **JERRY DURAN:** More than a few wheels were turning when the axe head was forged from tram-track cable.

▲ **A.C. RICHARDS:** Ball bearings were forged into a ballsy damascus blade and butted up against a boxed tang and a giraffe-bone grip. *(Custom Knife Gallery of Colorado photo)*

◀ **ART TYCER:** Robert Eggerling forged the bolsters as a fisherman fashions a net, and the damascus blade was blackened like a pan-seared catfish. *(Ward photo)*

▲ **JASON MAGRUDER:** Twenty-four layers of motorcycle-chain damascus were born to be wild. Only one walrus-ivory handle slab was attached as to further appreciate the wild side of the integral blade/handle.

▲ **LARRY HARLEY:** The W-pattern damascus blade whets your appetite for a bell-shaped laminated-steel guard and a dyed and carved oosic grip.

◀ **DAN WESTLIND:** With a damascus delivery like this, his encore could only have been done in ivory. *(BladeGallery.com photo)*

▲ **J. NEILSON:** He hung some cable damascus on a high-mountain dagger and went for a hike in hopes of finding just the right length of purple tiger maple.

▶ **ROGER BERGH:** After forming 80 layers of damascus and one bar of ancient wrought iron into a suitable axe head, some desert ironwood was chopped down for the occasion. *(BladeGallery.com photo)*

◀ **POUL STRANDE:** Are they eyes, noses and open mouths or tunnels, whirlpools and volcanic craters?

▶ **GEORGE MULLER:** And they say nature can't be duplicated. *(Custom Knife Gallery of Colorado photo)*

▶ **RICHARD VAN DIJK:** Files and saw blades were sacrificed to the forge gods for the good of two tremendous talon-shaped damascus blades. *(PointSeven photo)*

▶ **RUSTY POLK:** Whether it conjures up images of fossils, cave painting or vertebrae, the blade is a powerful example of what can be done in combining steels.

▼ **MARK NEVLING:** Radial and zigzag patterns rarely meet anywhere except perhaps on an artist's palette. Note how his eye chose a tiger-eye thumb stud to complement the mammoth ivory.

◀ **NICK WHEELER:** He's developing a pattern of blade behavior.

▼ **GEORGE BAARTMAN:** The semi-circles of raindrop damascus are perfect blade partners for the pinwheels of the Robert Eggerling bolsters.

▲ **PER BILLGREN:** Those are the rings of the trees it has downed.

▶ **CHARLES GEDRAITIS:** Diamonds, flowers and gold will woo even the most prim and proper ladies.

▶ **MIKE MOONEY:** Snakewood takes root in a Devin Thomas raindrop-pattern damascus blade and drinks up all it has to offer. *(ScreenSurge photo)*

▲ **DON HANSON III:** Don't cross the sea of damascus without a life preserver.

▶ **TOM FERRY**: The "Drifter Bowie" couldn't help but take in the scenic beauty.

▶ **T.R. OVEREYNDER**: Only a Texas tornado could have twisted Damasteel to this extent. *(PointSeven photo)*

◀ **J.W. MCFARLIN**: Devin Thomas lent the Spirograph damascus steel and the maker built a blade that would portray it in the best possible light. *(Weyer photo)*

▲ **MARVIN SOLOMON**: The blade of this skinner is already penetrating before it even touches wild game. *(Ward photo)*

▲ **JAMES SHAVER**: Who knew damascus could be coaxed into the color of giraffe bone? *(Jason Shaver photo)*

▲ **BILL BURKE**: It's an amazing maze of damascus. *(BladeGallery.com photo)*

▶ **ANDREW MCLURKIN:** Blending bars of steel like this, and matching the resulting pattern from blade to bolster, is akin to coming up with a chemical cure for the common cold.

▼ **RON CAMERON:** The "reptilian" and Spirograph blade patterns are credited to Devin Thomas, but the way they're married as if one species can only be a supernatural phenomenon. *(Custom Knife Gallery of Colorado photo)*

▼ **BILL COFFEY:** The blued Robert Eggerling bolster brings out the blues, browns and beiges of the mammoth ivory.

▼ **CHRIS BOOYSEN:** Done up in Odin's Eye Damasteel and "winding river" damascus from Heavin Forge, the "Cheetah folder" got hold of a giraffe bone and wouldn't give it up for anything. *(Custom Knife Gallery of Colorado photo)*

◀ **GAIL LUNN:** "Odin's Eye" Damasteel is looking right at you. *(PointSeven photo)*

▼ **HEATHER HARVEY**: The "Ribbons and Bows" dagger is forged as pretty as a Christmas present and tied together with a bell-metal bow. *(BladeGallery.com photo)*

▼ **RUSS SUTTON**: There's a ladder pattern on the blade, a mosaic pattern on the bolsters, and a wooly mammoth pattern on the handle. Devin Thomas and Robert Eggerling provided the blade and bolster steels, respectively.

▲ **DON MAXWELL**: Equally distinct and attractive are the Robert Eggerling damascus blade and bolsters, all complemented cleverly by a giraffe-bone handle and topaz-inlaid thumb stud.

▲ **PETER MARTIN**: The flame along the edge wasn't inadvertently left there during forging, but appeared purposely because of it. It's a San Mai damascus blade with a 1095 core and a "flame edge." *(Hoffman photo)*

◀ **RICK SMITH**: Like rungs of a ladder, the damascus pattern climbs all the way up the 8 1/2-inch blade.

▲ **CARLTON EVANS**: Like the hair of a supermodel, gold highlights enliven the Devin Thomas damascus blade and bolsters of the "Cowboy" model. Paul Long fashioned the sheath.

# Height-Challenged Knives

There lives this nice, happily married couple—Tom and Gwen Guinn—who collect knives. They're good people, always smiling, never say a bad word about anyone, and they make a nice looking couple, too. Their passion for knives is catchy. They not only collect knives, but also display their high-dollar wares at knife shows. That's right. They travel to knife shows across the country, pay for table space and display their edged collectibles in glass cases. It doesn't take many cases, though. It's not that they don't have many knives to parade before appreciative audiences—they do. The knives don't take up much room. They are miniatures (not Tom and Gwen, but the knives).

The couple once told me that the number of makers who fashion miniature knives is dwindling. The happy couple often asks makers of full-size knives if they'd like to try their hands at fashioning scale model pieces so Tom and Gwen can buy them. That's right—they have to encourage cutlers to make knives, which they'll, in turn, spend hard-earned money to purchase. It's called ordering knives, and no, they're not tall orders! They're small orders, often with big price tags. Here's the catch. Some knifemakers turn down Tom and Gwen's offers. They don't want to make miniature knives. So here is this nice couple offering good money to folks who haven't even made anything yet, and the craftsmen turn them down!

It seems that making tiny knives can be much more difficult than building regular knives. The parts are smaller but most knifemakers' fingers are big. The spaces are tinier, the tolerances are tighter, the material is harder to cut and shape, the screws are microscopic, pivot pins and springs are maddeningly miniature, and blades are burdensomely hard to hone. Everything is so tiny! And, that's exactly what makes fashioning height-challenged knives so challenging. So, Tom and Gwen and all the miniature knifemakers out there (the knives are mini, not the makers) deserve our praise for doing the little jobs no one else wants to do.

*Joe Kertzman*

◀ **SCOTT SLOBODIAN: The miniature gladiator swords have the smallest whalebone handles ever made—we're talking small whale, here, folks. Chris Peterson and Gary House did up the damascus.**

▼ **GARY HOUSE: The integral damascus blade and guard are 4 inches in length and offset by a miniscule amount of mammoth ivory.** *(PointSeven photo)*

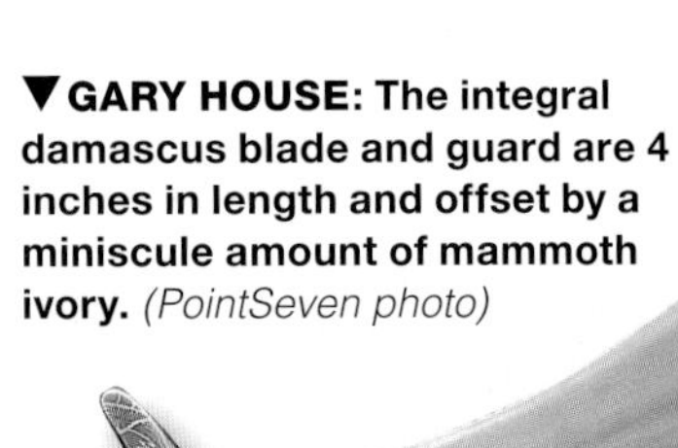

▼ **RICHARD SELF: The handsome height-challenged lopper wears a pinstripe suit coat and herringbone dress pants.** *(Ward photo)*

▶ **DON COWLES:** The "Thorn" would do a little more damage if stepped on than, say, a thorn. *(SharpByCoop.com photo)*

▲ **PHILIP BOOTH:** You can call on this miniature push-button automatic anytime. Delbert Ealy forged the diminutive Persian damascus, and Philip found just the right bite-sized black-lip pearl. *(Hoffman photo)*

▶ **BILL COFFEY:** It's more than a paper clipper in ATS-34, Robert Eggerling Turkish damascus, anodized titanium and blue mammoth ivory.

▲ **WAYNE HENSLEY:** The miniature dagger and Persian-style fixed blades wear ATS-34 blades, mastodon-ivory handles, and stainless bolsters and guards. *(Hoffman photo)*

▼ **RUSTY POLK:** The blade and handle patterns keep going and going and going . . . *(Ward photo)*

▲ **TERRY PRIMOS:** Forging a fine damascus blade in miniature is like giving a manicure to a Barbie doll. Terry would much prefer forging the damascus. *(Ward photo)*

# Bird, Trout & Bambi Blades

When the sun peeks out over the horizon and the mist rises off the pond, when dew drops from tree branches and the loons are calling, when the breeze blows and you can smell the willow trees—that is when you know all is right in the world. Alone in your tree stand, with the cold, winter air penetrating your bones, air so crisp it hurts your lungs, and when your breath creates its own mist, you know you're home. With the fish tugging on your line and the drag sounding on your reel, with the sun throwing spots in your eyes as the rays reflect off the water, a feeling of satisfaction penetrates your very being.

After hours of turkey calls, when a tom finally pokes its head out and emerges with feathers fully fanned, your heart races and you pray you don't scare him before he comes close enough for a clear shot. As the sweat pours off your body and your mouth dries up like the Sahara, when you finally pull the trigger and see the bird drop, a feeling of elation washes over you and your pulse pounds so hard you can feel your temples throb, that's when it all seems worthwhile.

As you perform the final grind on a hunting blade and apply a satin finish to the edged tool, when you rub the finest grit of paper over the now-shiny steel and you can see your reflection in the most perfect drop-point hunter you've ever made, then and only then do the planets align in your favor. When you pull the stag-handle hunting knife from its tanned-leather sheath, and it makes a sound that only steel and leather tugging at each other can make, when you think about the knifemaker you met, the one who fashioned the finest knife you've known, only then you can concentrate on the job at hand.

When you remember saving more than a few dollars from every paycheck, and you feel the semi-skinner you bought start to slide under the deer skin, peeling it away from the flesh of a downed buck, you remember why you love life in the first place. These are the reasons the sun rises, the clouds float by and the moon rises at dusk to say goodnight. Believing in nature and all she has to offer, and take away, that's why knifemakers build bird, trout and Bambi blades. This is why tradition has held true for hundreds—scratch that—thousands of years, and this is the one constant in the world—the way it should be, the way it was intended.

*Joe Kertzman*

◀ **BOB DOGGETT:** The "Resolute Hunter" is determined to win you over with its steely stare and uncommon character.

▲ **MICHAEL KANTER:** Mokumé accents sheep horn like white softens buckskin. *(PointSeven photo)*

▲ **BILL AMOUREUX:** You'll want to wrap this one up with your fingers and put the bow over your shoulder. *(BladeGallery.com photo)*

▶ **JOHN YOUNG:** There's one for each camouflage-pattern shirt in the closet. *(PointSeven photo)*

▶ **ED STALCUP:** Giraffe bone begs not with, but for an open palm. *(Custom Knife Gallery of Colorado photo)*

▲ **YASUTAKA WADA:** You pull the gut-hook hunter out of its sheath, and your buddies stare in disbelief. It's then, and only then, that you tell them the handle is black coral and the spacers are jet. Yes, it's moments like this that we can relish forever.

▲ **DAVE LARSEN:** The head of the skinning axe, the file and pin work, the black haft and the red liners, these are the elements that set it apart from the others. *(SharpByCoop.com photo)*

▲ **JOHN BARTLOW:** Mastodon ivory adds color to the hunt, while a sharpened hook just before the blade gives the hunter an extra edge. *(PointSeven photo)*

▼**R.F. "BOB" DODD:** Inside the ironwood forest, the hunter envisioned the ideal blade shape. *(Hoffman photo)*

▲**GENO DENNING:** He calls it the "Big Boy," and he's hoping to tag one while toting it.

▲**DICK FAUST:** Like the loops that secure a shoulder strap to rifle stock, rivets hold cocobolo to the full tang of a 154CM hunter.

▲**MARVIN SOLOMON:** He dug deep into the recesses of his mind, calling up all his instincts, before arriving at the perfect combination of ram horn, damascus and textured brass. *(Ward photo)*

▶**MICK WARDELL:** He flint-knapped a K6 Stellite blade in his tree stand one day, while contemplating the ways of the wild and considering his own existence.

▲**LOYD THOMSEN:** Stacked leather, stag and ladder-pattern damascus spell successful hunt like nobody's business.

▼**JERRY FISK:** An engraved guard and mosaic pins give a stag-handle hunter some sophistication. *(Ward photo)*

▲**S.R. JOHNSON:** Nature provided the ivory, pipe briarwood and stag, and the maker molded them into a stick-tang hunter that only he could imagine. *(Doggett photo)*

▲**JASON HOWELL:** It's as simple as 5160 steel, some stag and an understanding of how it must perform. *(PointSeven photo)*

▲**MIKE WILLIAMS:** Mike went with tradition in fashioning a stag and damascus Quachita hunter. *(PointSeven photo)*

▲**BILL BURKE:** Black sheep horn and brass clash like ram horns on a mountain pass. *(BladeGallery.com photo)*

▲**GARY RODEWALD:** He was a bitterroot huntsman, but he won over a few admirers along the way. *(BladeGallery.com photo)*

▲**THAD BUCHANAN:** Draped in black-canvas Micarta®, and with a full head of steel, he stalked game as if it was his first nature, and not his second. *(BladeGallery.com photo)*

▶ W.J. "JERRY" MCDONALD: The "Safari Skinner" enters the Serengeti donned in 154CM and desert ironwood.

▲ KEN DAVIS: If it's a three-day hunt, you're in luck. *(PointSeven photo)*

▼ CHARLIE AND HARRY MATTHEWS: Filework along the blade spine gives this one backbone.

▲ STEVE SANDO: The teardrop-shaped stabilized-Masur-burl handle is as sexy as the straightforward, hand-rubbed 154CM blade.

▲ RIK PALM: The stag hunter sports a 1084 steel blade, a mortised tang and some teeth with which to bite.

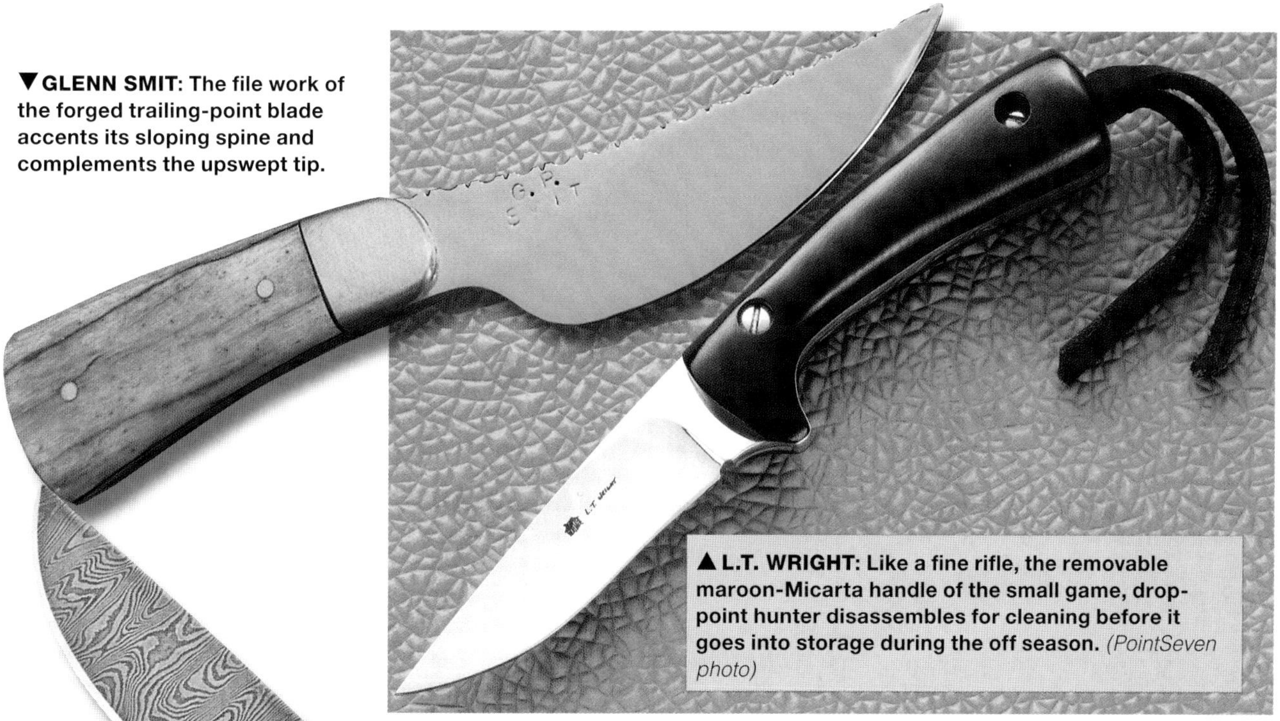

▼**GLENN SMIT**: The file work of the forged trailing-point blade accents its sloping spine and complements the upswept tip.

▲**L.T. WRIGHT**: Like a fine rifle, the removable maroon-Micarta handle of the small game, drop-point hunter disassembles for cleaning before it goes into storage during the off season. *(PointSeven photo)*

◀**ROB HUDSON**: He found the fossil ivory, forged the stainless damascus and delivered a drop-point hunter.

▶**CAL GANSHORN**: Abalone shell was just the thing he needed to gussy up a damascus and black-paper-Micarta® hunting knife.

▶**ART TYCER**: Hey, howdy, this is one swell Haw Creek Skinner. *(Ward photo)*

▲**ALAIN MIVILLE-DESCHENES**: The stabilized moose antler came from his last hunt, and the blade shape was born from ingenuity.

# Chips off the old Block

Have you ever seen a father and son walking down the street, built the same, similar statures and swaggers, identical haircuts, the same mannerisms, and you think to yourself how easy it is to tell they're related? Most of it is just genetics, but some of it is mimicry, whether conscious or unconscious. Everyone has someone they look up to and admire. Knifemakers are no different.

In some cases, it's the knives that inspire replication, and other times, it's the men who originally built the blades that provoke copying the patterns. Sometimes, it's a combination of the two. Great men and women tend to do great things. Like many tools and inventions, great knife designs are timeless and never go out of style. Being a tool, a knife needs to perform a duty, and if it succeeds or excels at the task, then it is copied and tweaked over time. If the lady or gentleman who built the original is likeable or memorable, then it adds fuel to the forge fire.

Take Bob Loveless—now there's a memorable character. He parades around in a multi-colored painter's cap, filter-less cigarette hanging out of his mouth and a smile, or scowl, depending on his mood, plastered on his face. He practically invented the drop-point hunting knife, etched a naked lady on his knife bolsters and guards, and brought ATS-34 blade steel to the United States from Japan. Japanese knife collectors worship the guy, and American knife enthusiasts can't get enough of him. Loveless has inspired many knives; his designs are copied, his fixed blades replicated, his blade styles mimicked.

Honoring someone who is admired is a great tribute, as long as credit is given where credit is due. It doesn't hurt to ask permission, either. With all cordialities out of the way, it's time to replicate what is great. Whether mimicking a knife style, the man behind the steel or a combination of the two, the replicated knives remain chips off the old block.

*Joe Kertzman*

◀ **JAMES BATSON: The Bill Moran-style gentleman's folder basks in the limelight wearing a pearl handle and German silver bolsters engraved by Billy Bates.** *(Ward photo)*

▶ **ROGER "MUDBONE" JONES: A couple William Scagel reproductions were worked up in hand-forged, clay-quenched, triple-drawn W-2 blade steel, antler, leather and brass. The result is a "sticker and skinner" hunting knife set.**

▲ **JIM SORNBERGER: California gold quartz of various colors, including Cinnabar and California jade, were incorporated into the 14k-gold-wrapped handle of a San Francisco-style fixed blade. The piece is fully engraved, and the sheath sports a gold shield in a mining motif on one side, and the California state seal on the other side.** *(Hoffman photo)*

◀ **JAMES LUCIE:** At top is an original William Scagel folder, and at bottom is as close as you can possibly come to it.

▼ **WILLIAM BEHNKE:** When William Scagel fashioned hatchets, he typically forged high-carbon spring steel, complementing the hatchet heads with a little bronze, leather, copper, black fiber and antler crown, kind of like how William Behnke fashions them.

▼ **GARY WHEELER:** Two Marble's-style knives sport cable-damascus and 356-layer, random-pattern-damascus blades.

▼ **JAMES LUCIE:** Now where Dr. Jim found fossilized crown stag, no one but he and William Scagel know, but he did, and he complemented it with a hand-forged 1084 blade and some stacked leather.

▶ **RIK PALM:** The earth trembled once again in California when Michael Price sat up in his grave to get a better look at the clay-hardened 1084 dagger fashioned in his very own style.

**▶ TY MONTELL:** This one opens in the style of Barry Woods and looks like the style of Ty Montell. *(ScreenSurge photo)*

**▼ KEVIN JOHN HARVEY:** If Henry Schively were alive today, his heart would have skipped a beat upon viewing the "heartbeat"-pattern damascus blade, the ball-metal ferrule and butt cup, and especially the checkered-African-blackwood handle prepared just the way he would have done it. *(BladeGallery.com photo)*

**▼ CHARLIE WEISS:** The Will & Finck San Francisco-style dagger is sent to market with a carved-fossil-walrus handle and an engraved nickel-silver sheath.

**▲ EDMUND DAVIDSON:** Many folks build Bob Loveless-style knives, but few can fashion a near-perfect, all-integral Loveless Lama semi-skinner in mastodon ivory and BG-42 blade steel. *(PointSeven photo)*

**▲ LARRY MENSCH:** Going strictly by the numbers, Larry made a #1 Randall style with a #27 handle and an ATS-34 blade. He has it listed for $700, by the way.

# Edged Ethnicity

How dull the world would be without ethnic diversity. How blue-eyed and blonde-haired we'd be, or green-eyed and red-haired, or brown-eyed and brown-haired. The lack of diversity would dilute things to the point of mundane monotony and austere autonomy. If we didn't drive each other insane with our sameness, we'd die of inbred boredom. At least cloning would go away. Who'd want another one of themselves? Well, OK, cloning would be restricted to egotistical maniacs, but you get the point.

There would be no exotic foods, ethnic costume, romantic languages, other worldly vistas, Eastern influence, south-of-the-border flavor, mystical music, Oriental ornament or Polish heritage. Hamburgers and hotdogs would be the fare for the day, the duds would be cotton, the houses ranch-style, the fitness centers without spas or saunas, the sports limited to baseball, basketball and football, and the dances, well, we'd be better off skipping the dances.

Imagine the colors, words, foods, styles, art, culture, music, dance, traditions, people, places ... and knife styles we'd miss. Bowie makers wouldn't mind, but the rest of the knife world would crave an occasional scimitar, *puukko*, *tanto*, saber, dirk, *navaja*, halberd, stiletto or kukri. How can Tom Cruise play a Samurai swordsman without a Japanese culture to fall back on occasionally? Who'd wear dirks and play the bagpipes? What would pirates be without cutlasses, Arabian knights without sabers or sword swallowers without swords? How would we cut the sushi and what would the Minnesota football team be called? How could we challenge each other to duels without rapiers?

That's enough questions. This isn't the Spanish Inquisition. Let's give ethnicity the edge and sheath the cutting humor for awhile.

*Joe Kertzman*

▲ **LARRY LUNN:** Rope file work sets off the San Mai damascus blade, while koi fish and crabs crawl along the sterling silver fittings and ancient-ivory grip. *(Gail Lunn photo)*

◀ **SCOTT SLOBODIAN:** Dyed birch meets engraved bird and tempered blade, all on the island of Japan.

◀ **ANDERS HOGSTROM:** The Swedish bowie showcases a stunning damascus blade and equally mind-boggling musk-ox-horn handle. *(BladeGallery.com photo)*

▼ **JOE ZEMITIS:** The Scottish dirk is a foot-and-a-half worth of carved ebony, sterling silver and W-1 steel. Great Scot!

▶ **A.G. BARNES:** Why are all the Persian fighters such pretty boys? *(Studio One photo)*

▼ **STEVE HILL:** Steve says the handle of his "Cactus Jack" folding Mexican bowie is jalapeno-green mammoth ivory. There are carved Apache arrowheads on the handle spine, a carved eagle in the rocker lock, and anodized-cactus edge protection when the blade, which is longer than the handle, is closed. *(SharpByCoop.com photo)*

▲ **KEVIN CASHEN:** Actually wearing a cup is a good idea when playing with this cup-hilt rapier. The blade, after all, is 160-layers of O-1 and L-6 twist damascus. **Ouch!** *(Weyer photo)*

▲ **GREGER FORSELIUS:** The materials—giraffe bone, whale's tooth, birch and mammoth ivory—are as exotic as the Finnish *puukko* pattern. *(Custom Knife Gallery of Colorado photo)*

▲ **SCOTT SLOBODIAN:** Legend has it that a Japanese piece like this requires about 1,000 layers of Daryl Meier damascus, sterling-silver furniture, a stingray-skin handle with a leather wrap and a buffalo horn scabbard ... well, local legend has it that way.

◀ **ED SCHEMPP:** The Gurkhas carried kukris, but none as nifty as the one-hand-opening, folding piece of fine cutlery, complete with a San Mai style blade and blue-toned fossil-mammoth-ivory handle, that Ed Schempp fashioned just for fun. *(BladeGallery.com photo)*

▶ **GERT VAN DEN ELSEN:** A finely crafted Celtic utility knife is decked out in Sambar stag, Cape buffalo horn and sterling silver.

▲ **DON LOZIER:** The mighty Mike Norris damascus blade branches out like the tail of a Filipino feathered friend. Don Lozier's friend David Morton engraved the guards around the walrus-ivory grip. *(PointSeven photo)*

▲ **ALEXANDER FELIX:** Think about it—the Japanese used stingray skin as a handle material and wrapped it in cord. Is that cool or what?

▶ **NORMAN SANDOW:** Rendition meets tradition within the confines of an ATS-34 *tanto* with an ivory-Micarta® grip.

▲ **DON POLZIEN:** Are you finished looking at the nice knife yet? Good, check out the carved-red-lobster-tail scabbard. I kid you not. *(PointSeven photo)*

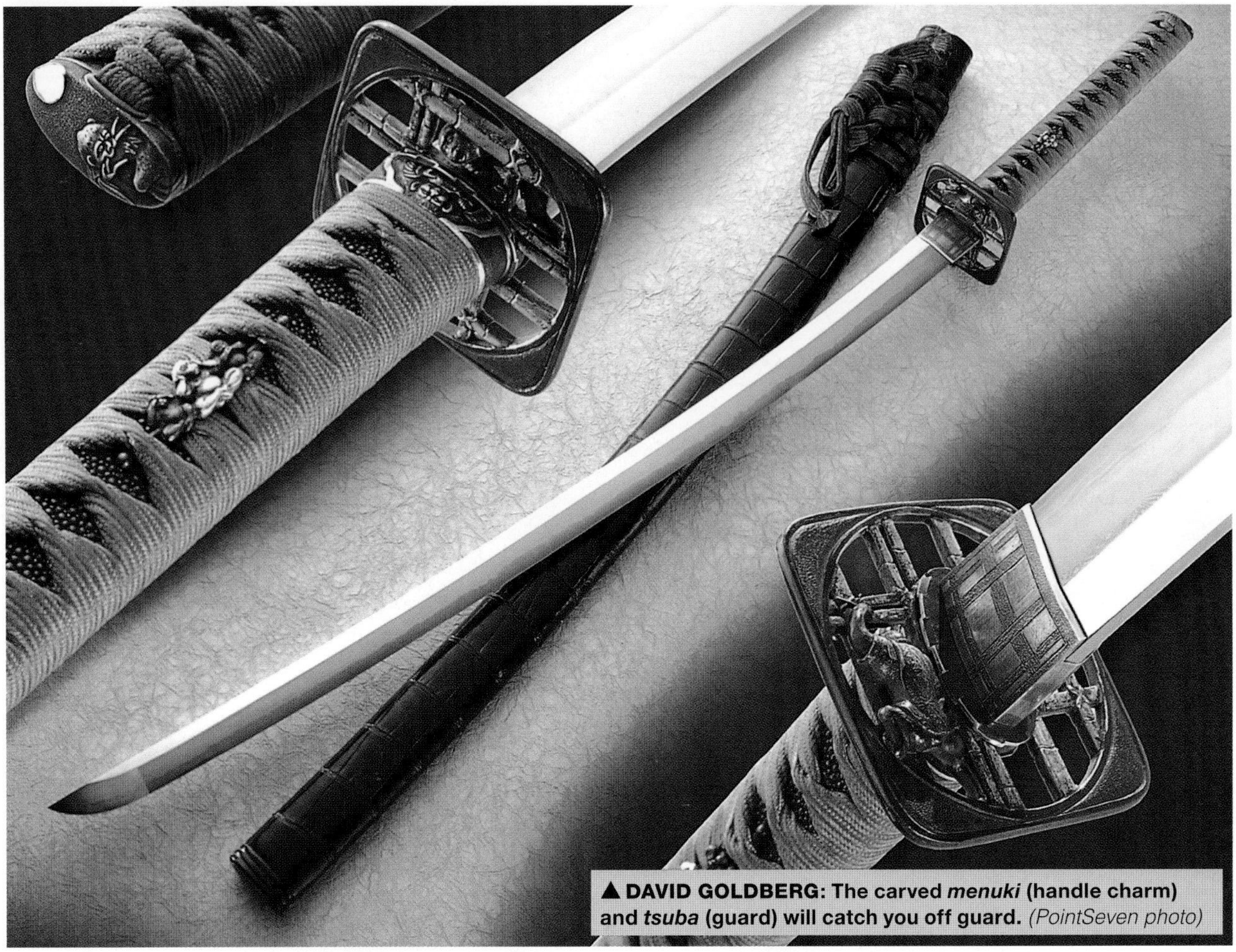

▲ **DAVID GOLDBERG:** The carved *menuki* (handle charm) and *tsuba* (guard) will catch you off guard. *(PointSeven photo)*

▲ **WALLY HAYES:** Four-hundred layers of damascus, as well as stingray skin, teal silk, copper and lacquered wood make the O-Tanto "oh too tough."

▶ **A.G. BARNES:** The silver wire motif was copied from an original Viking sword scabbard, with the Viking's permission, of course. *(Studio One photo)*

▲ **WAYNE HENSLEY:** Scottish is the dirk, and it hasn't "kilt" a soul. *(Hoffman photo)*

▲ **DAVID GOLDBERG:** Fifteen-and-a-half inches start in steel and end in ebony. *(PointSeven photo)*

# Hordes of Swords

Thanks to moviegoers and martial arts enthusiasts, swords have become hot commodities. What could it be about movies and martial arts that have caused such a sword stir? What do the two have in common? Even though most forms of martial arts are based on scientific body movements, kinetics, striking motions, deflections, counter-movements, pressure points, attacking, releasing, breaking free and even fleeing, some teachings are also based on mind over matter. You could even go as far as saying that there are aspects of martial arts that are abstract, metaphysical and transcendental. And then there are the folks who want to believe they are ninja warriors. Maybe they've seen too many movies. With the media constantly reminding us of all that is wrong in the world, perhaps the escapism provided by movies, and the mind and body exercises involved in martial arts, are good things. Swords are a common denominator. Japanese, Chinese and Korean martial artists carry and use swords, and many of the main characters Hollywood has brought to life lug around long blades.

Cutlasses abounded in "Pirates of the Caribbean," Roman swords in "The Gladiator," all kinds of fantasy swords in the "Lord of the Rings" trilogy, and there were plenty of long blades in such movies as "Kingdom of Heaven," "Blade" and "Kill Bill."

Artists working with steel have more room to roam in building big blades. There is more canvas to cover, more steel to forge, more area to differentially heat treat, clay temper and edge quench. There are hilts, pommels, scabbards and guards to decorate. There's more surface to engrave, carve and etch, and plenty of space for inlays, encrustations and indentations. Some make historically accurate pieces, others try new utilitarian shapes and still others open their minds to fantasy pieces.

All swords have long edges, points, protrusions, spikes and curves. With such a wide range of styles, with such a huge fan base, with so many collectors and enthusiasts, the world hungers for more. The real and imagined war lords want loads of loppers, heaps of hard edges, hordes of swords.

*Joe Kertzman*

▲ **JENS ANSO: Wanting to make an impression with his first sword, Jens hand-rubbed the RWL-34 blade to a 600-grit finish, and the desert-ironwood handle to a 1200-grit finish. Then he applied Ben Gay (to his muscles, not the blade).** *(SharpByCoop.com photo)*

▶ **ANDERS HOGSTROM: Such a swarthy sword is the artifact-walrus-tusk-handled piece showcasing a clay-tempered 1050 blade and bronze fittings.** *(BladeGallery.com photo)*

▲ **DAVID BRODZIAK: Explain how someone looks at a drive chain and says, "You know I could forge a far-out, 15-inch blade from that." Well, that's just what Garry Wood did, and David Brodziak went with the moment, adding bronze guards and a mammoth-ivory and York-gum-burl handle.**

▶ **DON NORRIS:** The fantasy sword escapes to dreamland donning a Jim Ferguson damascus blade and a fossil-walrus-ivory handle. *(Weyer photo)*

▶ **SCOTT SLOBODIAN:** He hafted the walking staff in Brazilian walnut, then he inlaid Merlin gold and forged a 25-inch blade for it (in case he needed to talk while he walked).

▲ **DAVID SCHLUETER:** The colossal katana cuts it up with a John Lundemo blade. *(SharpByCoop.com photo)*

▶ **ROB DOUGLAS:** You couldn't trace the movements of a bouncing ball any better than how the temper line of the forged 1050 blade showed up after etching. *(PointSeven photo)*

# Customary Pocketknives

Why do some folks still carry pocket watches when wrist watches, with lights, digital readouts, dates, alarms and compasses are just as comfortable to wear, easier to see and even more durable? Why would anyone cook on a charcoal grill when gas grills are cleaner and less work? Why plant, grow, weed, water, prune, pick and can vegetables when they're easier and nearly as inexpensive to buy already canned?

Why buy or make a slip-joint folding knife that opens via a nail nick when you could just as easily, and for probably less money, get your hands on an assisted-opening, one-hand, locking-liner folder with a safety, a partially serrated blade and a pocket clip? Why carve a wooden canoe when plastic and fiberglass models are available for the cost of your time and materials?

Have you seen a modern wrist watch and compared it to a gold pocket watch? When's the last time you became nostalgic over the smell of a gas grill? Have you really looked at the store-bought, canned vegetables lately? And how about the workmanship, fit, finish, sound, pull and snap of the modern versions of old pocketknives? Wooden canoes, by the way, are just cool.

It's a combination of workmanship, nostalgia, history and quite frankly the style and cutting capabilities of traditional pocketknife patterns that keeps makers interested and busy building them. These aren't the pocketknives your daddy carried. The springs, pivots, bushings and materials are better. The designs are well executed, the quality is as good, if not better, and the blade, bolster, handle and mechanical materials have advanced. Some good things have gotten better. They're not old-fashioned pocketknives. They're just fashioned to resemble the old ones.

It's customary to carry pocketknives. Apples can still be sliced with them, sticks whittled, little boys' airplanes carved with them, loose threads cut, and, best of all, memories made.

*Joe Kertzman*

◀ **SALVATORE PUDDU:** The "Crisscross" model, featuring tortoise-shell inlays framed in 14-carat gold, is a double-blade lockback that can be completely dismantled.

◀ **MARK LARAMIE:** With a giraffe-leg-bone handle, the trapper is off to a good start. The damascus makers include Devin Thomas (blade) and Bob Eggerling (bolsters). *(Hoffman photo)*

◀ **JEFF CLAIBORNE:** There he goes manicuring those toenails again, and this one polished up with 52100 blades, nickel silver bolsters and red stag to boot.

◀ **EUGENE SHADLEY:** For old time's sake, Shadley sat down on the front porch with a coke bottle and a whittler, both pocketknives, of course, and featuring German bone and stag handles, respectively. *(PointSeven photo)*

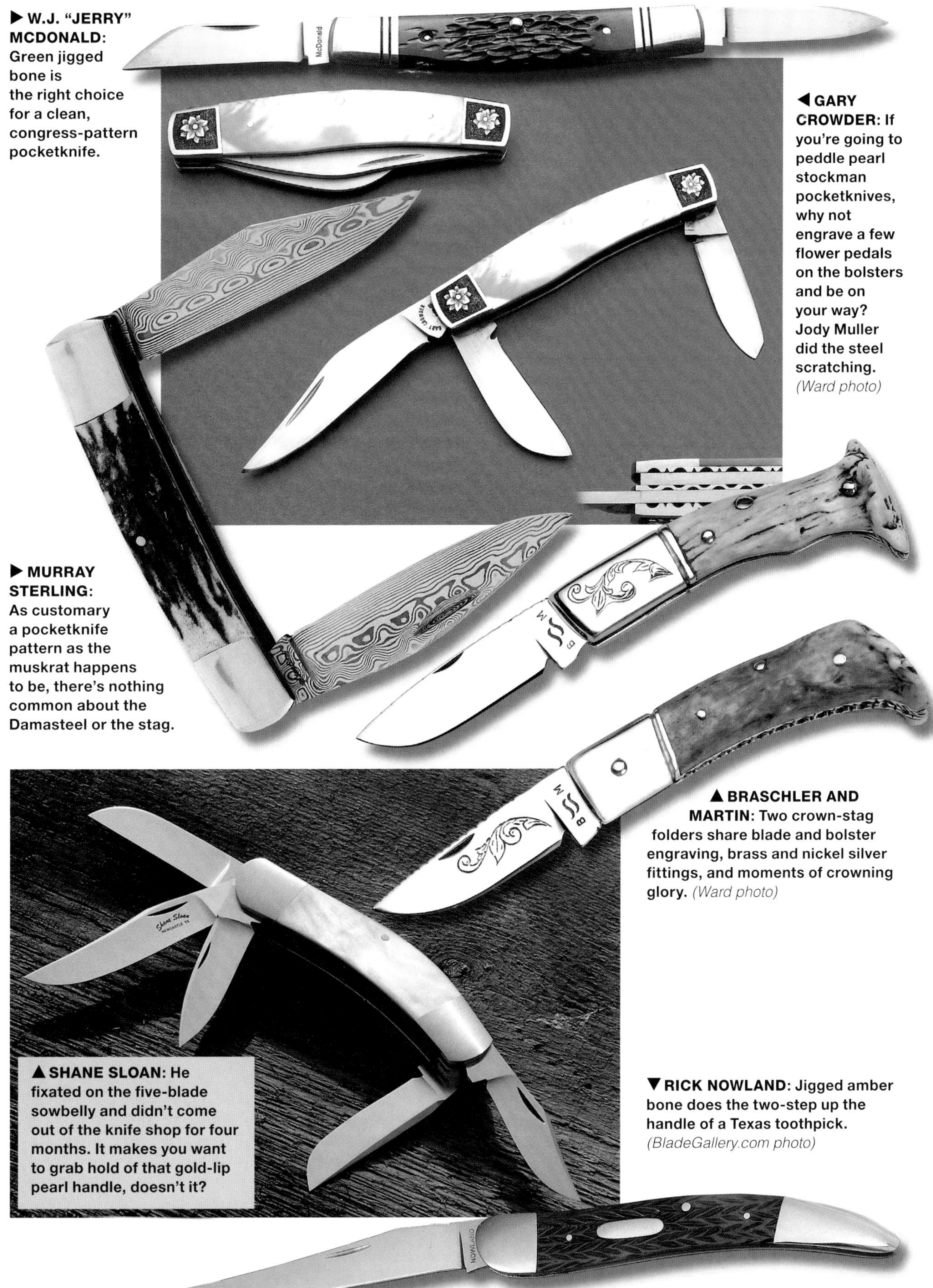

▶ **W.J. "JERRY" MCDONALD:** Green jigged bone is the right choice for a clean, congress-pattern pocketknife.

◀ **GARY CROWDER:** If you're going to peddle pearl stockman pocketknives, why not engrave a few flower pedals on the bolsters and be on your way? Jody Muller did the steel scratching. *(Ward photo)*

▶ **MURRAY STERLING:** As customary a pocketknife pattern as the muskrat happens to be, there's nothing common about the Damasteel or the stag.

▲ **BRASCHLER AND MARTIN:** Two crown-stag folders share blade and bolster engraving, brass and nickel silver fittings, and moments of crowning glory. *(Ward photo)*

▲ **SHANE SLOAN:** He fixated on the five-blade sowbelly and didn't come out of the knife shop for four months. It makes you want to grab hold of that gold-lip pearl handle, doesn't it?

▼ **RICK NOWLAND:** Jigged amber bone does the two-step up the handle of a Texas toothpick. *(BladeGallery.com photo)*

▼ **BOB SIMS:** A simple stag lockback is superiorly styled.

▲ **TOMONARI HAMADA:** If he can carve black-lip mother-of-pearl like that, imagine what he can do with a couple ATS-34 blades, a pick and scissors. *(PointSeven photo)*

▲ **JACK DAVENPORT:** There's a moose pattern in pearl and a swayback jack in stag. *(PointSeven photo)*

▲ **BOB SIMS:** Swedish damascus comes alive and thrives on three ivory-handle lockback folders in incremental sizes. *(PointSeven photo)*

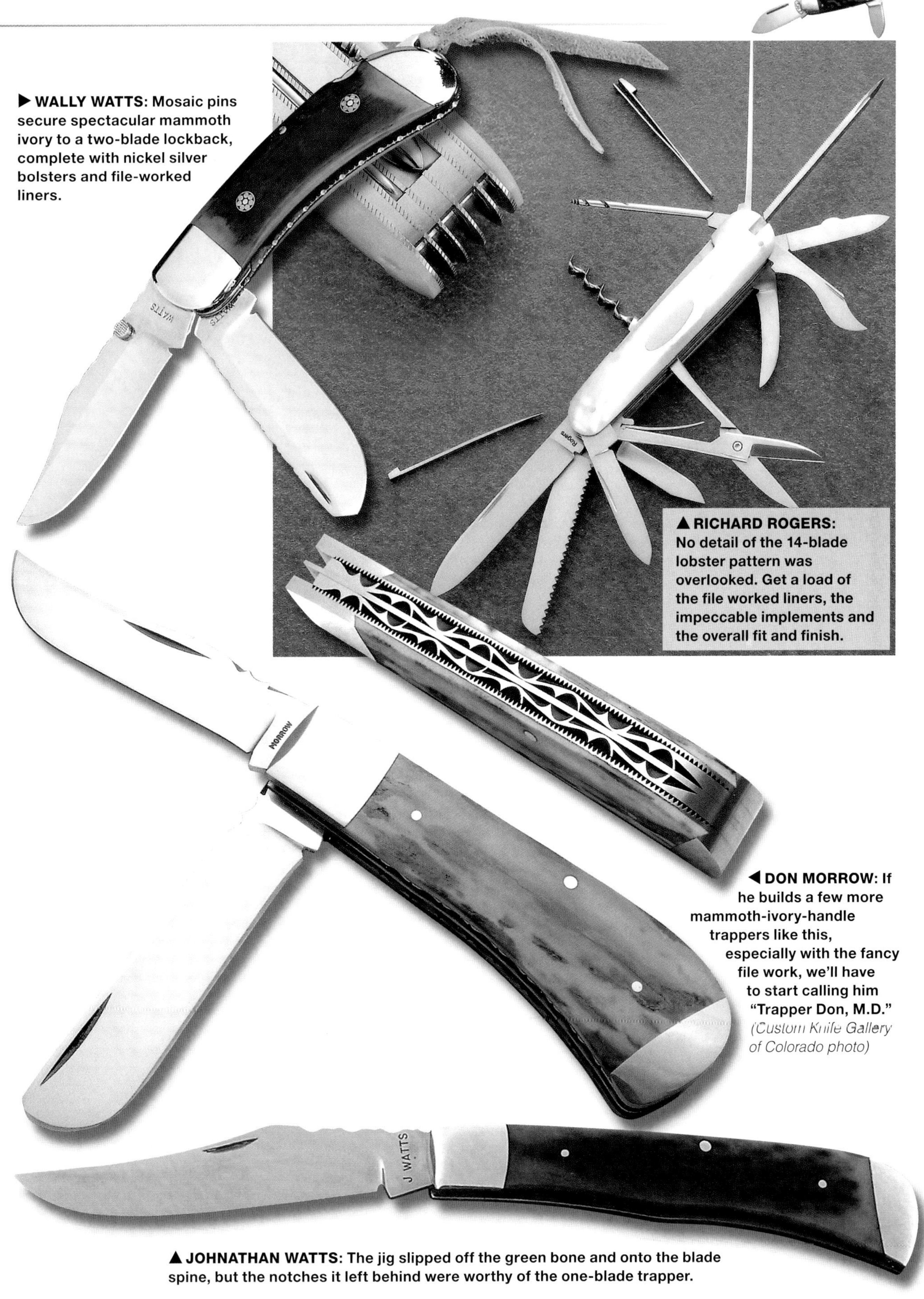

▶ **WALLY WATTS**: Mosaic pins secure spectacular mammoth ivory to a two-blade lockback, complete with nickel silver bolsters and file-worked liners.

▲ **RICHARD ROGERS**: No detail of the 14-blade lobster pattern was overlooked. Get a load of the file worked liners, the impeccable implements and the overall fit and finish.

◀ **DON MORROW**: If he builds a few more mammoth-ivory-handle trappers like this, especially with the fancy file work, we'll have to start calling him "Trapper Don, M.D." *(Custom Knife Gallery of Colorado photo)*

▲ **JOHNATHAN WATTS**: The jig slipped off the green bone and onto the blade spine, but the notches it left behind were worthy of the one-blade trapper.

# The Cutlery Corner

We've come a long way since Julia Childs, Betty Crocker and Sara Lee. Today we have the Food Channel, Food Network, and chefs like Emeril Lagasse, Wolfgang Puck and Rachael Ray. Many knife companies blame Ray, herself, for starting the Granton edge and Santoku kitchen knife craze. During her show on the Food Network, Ray uses a Granton-edge Santoku knife. Granton edges have dimples along the sides of the blades, down to the edges, and air is trapped between the food and the knife blades, thus eliminating the food sticking to the knives when slicing and dicing.

It's difficult to figure out which came first—the chicken casserole or the egg omelet—but the best we can figure out, it was a combination of things. First, people started building and buying newer houses, or restoring historic buildings, and entertaining more in the home. Kitchens began bustling.

As Joyce Laituri of Spyderco recently said, it doesn't matter how big a TV and entertainment center she and her husband have, when they invite guests over, their friends seem to naturally congregate in the kitchen. So, people are buying nicer things for their kitchens. Add to that the host of new cooking shows, channels, and even a network, and you can see why more people are buying, and, thus offering and making, kitchen knives.

Usually in the knife industry, factories keep an eye on what the custom knifemakers are doing and incorporate their ideas into factory knives. As far as kitchen knives go, it may be the other way around. Just to name a few of the companies that traditionally sell sporting knives and are now offering kitchen knife lines, they include Spyderco, Al Mar Knives, Benchmade, William Henry Knives, Cold Steel, Kershaw, Taylor Cutlery, A.G. Russell Knives, Kellam Knives and SOG Specialty Knives.

The list is not complete and continues to grow. Several of the companies named have unveiled expensive laminated blades and fancy wood display racks. Still others showcase damascus blades and knives designed by known custom knifemakers.

All roads lead toward more useful and innovative kitchen knives. Whether custom knifemakers or factories are leading the pack is inconsequential. What matters is that there is a kitchen knife craze out there and a bevy of beautiful blades you can buy for your next potluck.

*Joe Kertzman*

**◀ MIKE MOONEY:** **Here is one for the chef and one for her little helper.** *(Hoffman photo)*

**◀ NENOX USA: Let me at the salmon, russet potatoes, broccoli and wine bottle.** *(PointSeven photo)*

▶ **PER BILLGREN:** In hopes of being invited over for supper, Julius Kirschner forged the blade steel.

▶ **BURT FOSTER:** No, the acidic dishwasher soap didn't wash away the damascus. He wasn't cutting too many lemons. It's a composite blade made up of an O-1 and L-6 damascus core laminated between layers of 304 stainless steel.

◀ **ED SCHEMPP:** He dazzles the dinner party with damascus and steel laminates, allows them to feel the ironwood grips and sends them home with their tummies full. *(Mitch Lum photo)*

▲ **TOM BLACK:** A set of eight steak knives is outfitted in damascus blades and ironwood handles. *(Hoffman photo)*

▲ **JOE CORDOVA:** Some standout pieces of cutlery make up the set of six steak knives. *(PointSeven photo)*

# Pearl Power

▶ **JASON TIENSVOLD: The magic of mosaic damascus meets the inherent beauty of gold-lip pearl head on, and both emerge unscathed.** *(Custom Knife Gallery of Colorado photo)*

▲ **T.R. OVEREYNDER: An inter-frame handle and sculpted bolsters surround black-lip-pearl and mother-of-pearl inlays.** *(PointSeven photo)*

◀ **BILL HERNDON: The art dagger was pre-approved by the initial designer, Herman Schneider, and handcrafted to include a black-oxide-treated 5160 blade, a mother-of-pearl handle and gold inlay work by John Baraclough.** *(Hiro Sogo photo)*

▶ **STEVE HILL: The "Spaced" art folder broke through the atmosphere after the Robert Eggerling and Daryl Meier damascus blade and bolsters were applied, and went into orbit as soon as the pearl was pierced to reveal the gold leaf "sun" underlay. There's a comet sculpted into the rocker release button, and Saturn lies on the bolster, complete with 24k-gold rings.** *(PointSeven photo)*

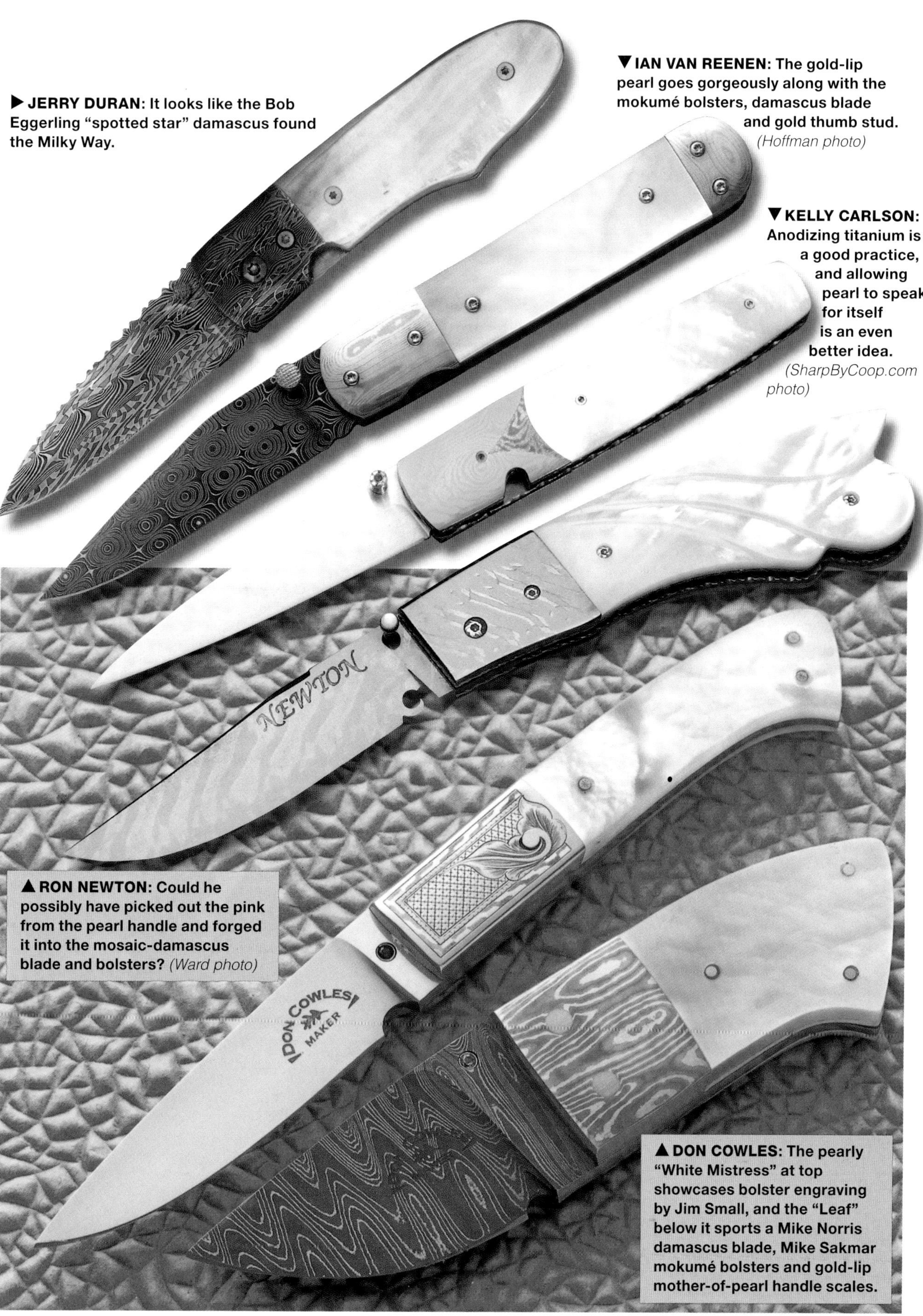


▶ **JERRY DURAN:** It looks like the Bob Eggerling "spotted star" damascus found the Milky Way.

▼ **IAN VAN REENEN:** The gold-lip pearl goes gorgeously along with the mokumé bolsters, damascus blade and gold thumb stud. *(Hoffman photo)*

▼ **KELLY CARLSON:** Anodizing titanium is a good practice, and allowing pearl to speak for itself is an even better idea. *(SharpByCoop.com photo)*

▲ **RON NEWTON:** Could he possibly have picked out the pink from the pearl handle and forged it into the mosaic-damascus blade and bolsters? *(Ward photo)*

▲ **DON COWLES:** The pearly "White Mistress" at top showcases bolster engraving by Jim Small, and the "Leaf" below it sports a Mike Norris damascus blade, Mike Sakmar mokumé bolsters and gold-lip mother-of-pearl handle scales.

# Beastly Blades

Decay, dry rot, cracking, chipping and discoloration are rarely good things, unless you are referring to the tusks and teeth that elephants, wooly mammoths and walruses left behind upon their demise. Then such elemental breakdowns are godsends. Walking around with blue and green teeth is a scary and unsanitary practice, but if a little discoloration sets in postmortem, then no man or beast suffers.

Such things as ancient-walrus or elephant teeth and tusks make for splendid knife handles. If they turned blue, green, yellow, orange, beige, black or gold with age, they just lend a little more color and character to the knives they grace. Like fine wine, ivory gets better with age. It's as if the color is inside the stuff, and when it dies, hues rise from the decaying remains like corpses giving up their ghosts. As spirits elevate toward the heavens, so too do chocolate-colored lines rise to the surface of rotting elephant tusks.

Purple, green, yellow, blue, gold and tan pigments push their way to the surface, and upon their arrival, they permeate their colorful characters all over the surfaces of the ivory-like extensions.

And when it comes to pushing up through surfaces, that's how most of the ancient ivory is harvested in the first place. As if the tusks and teeth know their calling, as if they are reincarnated to live many lifetimes, they push upward from the core of the frozen tundra in places like northern Alaska, breaking through the earth's crust and poking out of the ground like chick beaks through eggshells. Once visible, native Alaskans, and only native Alaskans, harvest it. Many of the fine northern Alaskan Indians are kind enough to sell the colorful teeth and tusks to entrepreneur knifemakers who build some of the most inviting ivory handled knives this side of the Ice Age. The beastly blades of teeth and tusks are cracked, discolored, dry rotted, chipped, decayed and cavity-ridden cutters of only the coolest kind.

*Joe Kertzman*

▲ **DON NORRIS: Etched by Francine Larstein, the blade tells the story of a land where elephants once roamed, while the handle is evidence of their existence.** *(ScreenSurge photo)*

▲ **ROBERT DODD: The mammoth that lost this tooth must have been one colorful character. Trav Winn engraved the knife bolster.** *(ScreenSurge photo)*

▲ **DUSTY MOULTON: He squeezed the mammoth ivory until he left finger grooves, engraved a bolster to butt up against it and asked Jim Ferguson to forge steel for the occasion.** *(SharpByCoop.com photo)*

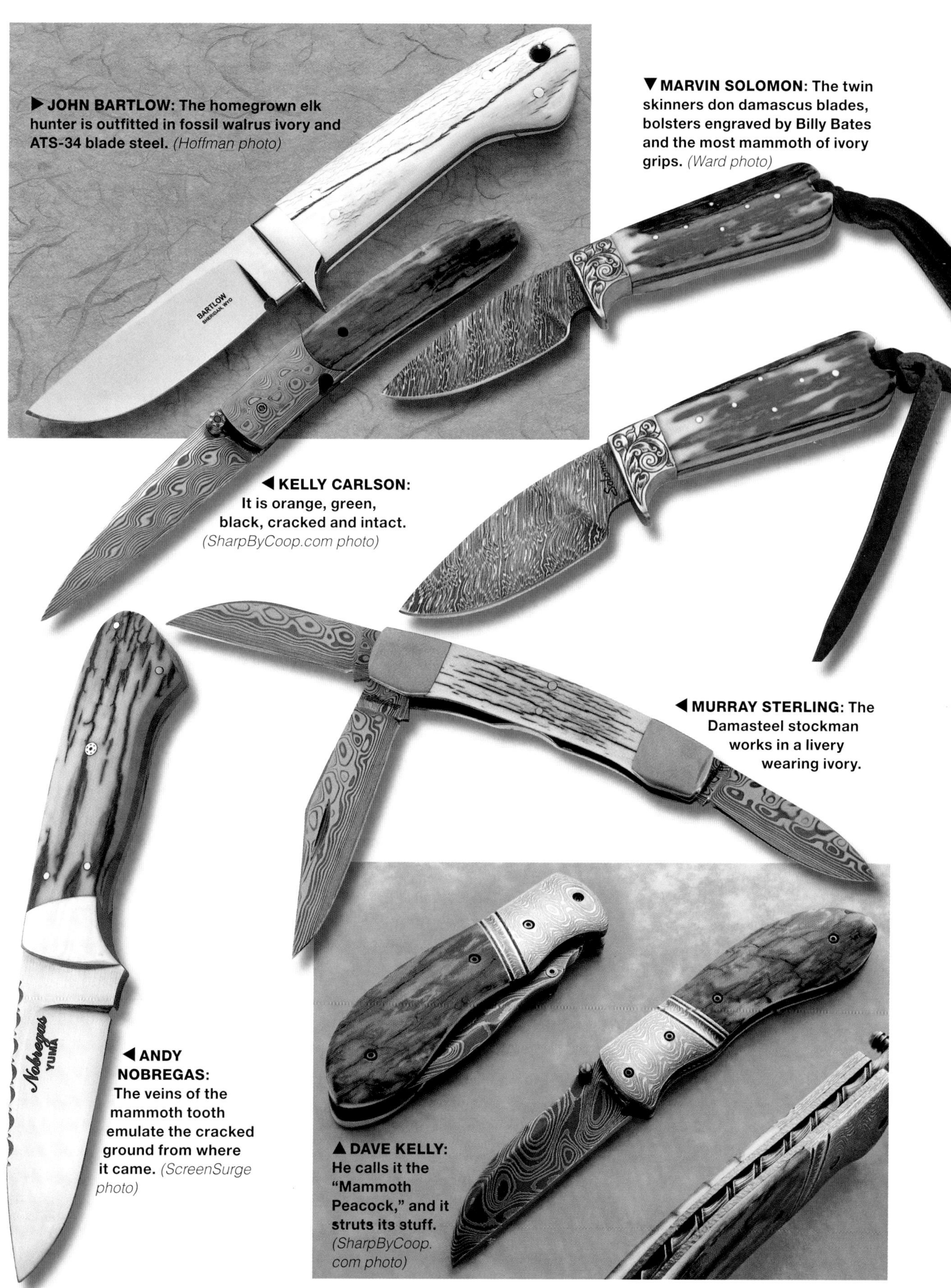


▶ **JOHN BARTLOW: The homegrown elk hunter is outfitted in fossil walrus ivory and ATS-34 blade steel.** *(Hoffman photo)*

▼ **MARVIN SOLOMON: The twin skinners don damascus blades, bolsters engraved by Billy Bates and the most mammoth of ivory grips.** *(Ward photo)*

◀ **KELLY CARLSON: It is orange, green, black, cracked and intact.** *(SharpByCoop.com photo)*

◀ **MURRAY STERLING: The Damasteel stockman works in a livery wearing ivory.**

◀ **ANDY NOBREGAS: The veins of the mammoth tooth emulate the cracked ground from where it came.** *(ScreenSurge photo)*

▲ **DAVE KELLY: He calls it the "Mammoth Peacock," and it struts its stuff.** *(SharpByCoop.com photo)*

▲ **LOYD THOMSEN: The rings of mammoth tooth complement the ovals of ladder-pattern damascus.**

◀ **BILL SOWELL: Heck, if there are pink elephants, why not blue wooly mammoths, or are their tusks just that way?** *(Hoffman photo)*

▲ **STEVE HILL: The "Delta Blues" folder, complete with carved music notes and resonator guitar in the handle spine, pays tribute to bluesmen and women past and present, so the blue/gold mammoth ivory was a good choice. While Steve Schwarzer blued the mosaic damascus bolsters, Robert Eggerling belted out the blade steel.** *(SharpByCoop.com photo)*

▶ **CLIFTON POLK: Do you trumpet loudly when you release the blade of your mammoth-ivory-handled scale-release auto?**

◀ **JIM DAVIS JR.: The blade tang is hidden deep within the pores of fossil walrus ivory.** *(photo courtesy of Dan Delavan/Plaza Cutlery)*

▶ **J.D. BARTH: Like an old school desk marred by pencil marks, ink spills, engraved initials and clumsy kids, the highly figured mammoth ivory stands in stark contrast to the newness of the Spirograph damascus blade.**

▶ **THOMAS HASLINGER:** The Ammolite thumb stud and anodized-titanium bolsters bring out the blues and greens of the mammoth ivory. That's a Damasteel blade and it is darned delightful. *(SharpByCoop.com photo)*

▲ **LEON TREIBER:** Imagine the wail when the wooly mammoth let go of that tooth! Mike Norris complemented the bicuspid with a stainless damascus blade.

◀ **JONATHAN WATTS:** As the rains fell, leaving permanent pools on the steel that lay there, a mammoth tusk rose from the sodden earth, peeking its tip out as an earthworm feels the air.

▲ **ROGER GAMBLE:** The bowie is bowed like a mammoth tusk, and there are traces of elephant all over the piece. *(PointSeven photo)*

◀ **LARRY DOWNING:** You've gotta love "The Dove," complete with olive-branch-like Michael Dubber scroll engraving, a Devin Thomas Spirograph-damascus beak and the most peaceful fossil mammoth ivory this side of Central Park.

▲ **KEVIN HOFFMAN:** Snap, crackle, pop!

◀ **MIKE ROCHFORD:** Cracks in the ivory are reminiscent of the spidery fingers that form on ice cubes when submerged in warm liquid. Bill Fiorini forged the blade steel, and Robert Eggerling did the bolster steel honors.

▶ **CORRIE SCHOEMAN:** The purple people-eater devours his prey with one mammoth tooth.

▶ **KAJ EMBRETSEN:** A circle of mammoth ivory on the thumb stud is just the kind of attention to detail that sets the file-worked folding dagger apart, much like a three-bar-damascus blade, milky mammoth handle and shiny gold bail would have done to the piece. *(PointSeven photo)*

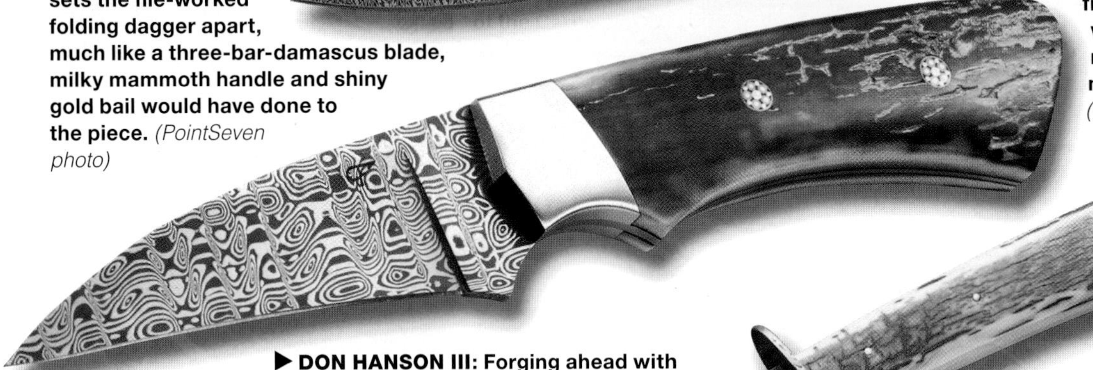

▼ **COLTEN TIPPETTS:** The "Griffyn Claw" is a scrappy fighter and flavored with Damasteel, nickel silver and mammoth ivory. *(PointSeven photo)*

▶ **DON HANSON III:** Forging ahead with damascus bowie in hand, he stopped to admire the mammoth grip. *(PointSeven photo)*

▲ **MICHAEL KANTER:** With teeth stained orange from battle, the wooly beast bent down in defeat to the edged steel and blew one last battle cry. *(SharpByCoop.com photo)*

# STATE OF THE ART

Imagine the early blacksmith—a man of brute strength, true grit; a tough character, someone accustomed to heat, dirt, dust, oil, hard work, heavy lifting, repetitive motion, smoke and suffocating enclosures. He sweated for a living: pounded, poured, fired, heated, quenched, shaped and muscled steel into useful shapes. He was a blade smith, toolmaker, horse farrier, handyman, die caster, mechanic, ironworker and mechanical engineer. He was into multi-tasking before it was a word.

A good number of modern knifemakers choose to forge their own knife blades, but few do ironwork on the side. Not many cast their own dies or make tools for the townspeople. Those knifemakers who fashion art knives do multi-task, however. They scrimshaw, engrave, carve, etch and color coordinate. They are artists, jewelers, sculptors and goldsmiths. They are men and women of brute strength, true grit, incredible character, and they're accustomed to heat, dirt, dust, oil, hard work, heavy lifting, repetitive motion, smoke and suffocating enclosures. They also create edged art, edged jewelry and one-of-a-kind collectibles.

The knives made today might have been scoffed at in the 1800s, but after the scoffing subsided, the socialites might have pocketed a couple of the edged gems when no one was looking. They would have taken them to church services, perhaps, and showed them to their neighbors and friends—much the way modern knife collectors handle and treat their edged collectibles. Things are not so terribly different today. People still carry and use knives. Modern knifemakers have figured out ways to make the edged tools incredibly beautiful and functional. The state of the art is alive and well in the knife industry.

*Joe Kertzman*

# Gravers Gone Wild

▼ **BILLY BATES:** The Devin Thomas Spirograph damascus had a few swirls that could be somewhat simulated in the bolster engraving of an A.T. Barr locking-liner folder. *(Hoffman photo)*

▲ **RICK DUNKERLEY:** He forges his own damascus, inlays his own gemstones and engraves his own handles in Western themes. Go cowboy! *(PointSeven photo)*

▼ **SIMON LYTTON:** Knifemaker Bob Terzuola knew of Lytton's talents and built an all-steel folder so the engraver would have more canvas on which to work his dragon-slaying magic. *(PointSeven photo)*

▼ **BAILEY BRADSHAW:** Could it be the grouse that laid the golden egg? *(PointSeven photo)*

▶ **RALPH DEWEY HARRIS:** He classically combined scroll, leaf and freeform engraving. *(PointSeven photo)*

◀ **JERE DAVIDSON:** The Ronald Best knife was so sweet that Davidson planted eye candy all around it. *(BladeGallery.com photo)*

▼ **JIM SMALL:** Knifemaker Don Cowles didn't have to pretty up the pearl any more than it already was. The damascus needed no complementary embellishment. But he knew the engraver could add a third dimension to the knife, one that tied all the elements together as a whole. *(PointSeven photo)*

▶ **JOE MASON:** Golden stems produce the sweetest leaves. Johnny Stout fashioned the "Baron" knife, and Jerry Rados forged the Turkish twist-damascus blade. *(Hoffman photo)*

▶ **ANTONIO FOGARIZZO:** Golden locks fall upon the bare shoulders of a sensuous lady adorning the handle of a lock-back folder. *(PointSeven photo)*

◀ **RON SKAGGS: The man who rubbed the bottle was granted a wish by the genie, and what a wish it was! Joe Kious is the other man behind the knifemaking.** *(PointSeven photo)*

▶ **SIMON LYTTON: This is how beasts fought before the advent of coliseums. Howard Hitchmough built the locking-liner folder before Lytton took a good-gosh-darn graver to it.** *(PointSeven photo)*

◀ **RAY COVER JR.: Someone was in a bad mood after being banished for life onto the bolster of a Don Hanson III folder, complete with a mosaic-damascus blade and a black-lip-pearl handle.** *(SharpByCoop.com photo)*

▲ **HARRY LIMING: Old Golden Eyebrow peeked his head out from the shrubbery only to stare down the edge of a Gene Baskett blade.** *(PointSeven photo)*

▶ **MANRICO TORCOLI: With fantasies like these, who needs reality? Charles Bennica brings us back to earth with the stunning knife fashioned from ATS-34 blade steel and a red-coral handle.** *(PointSeven photo)*

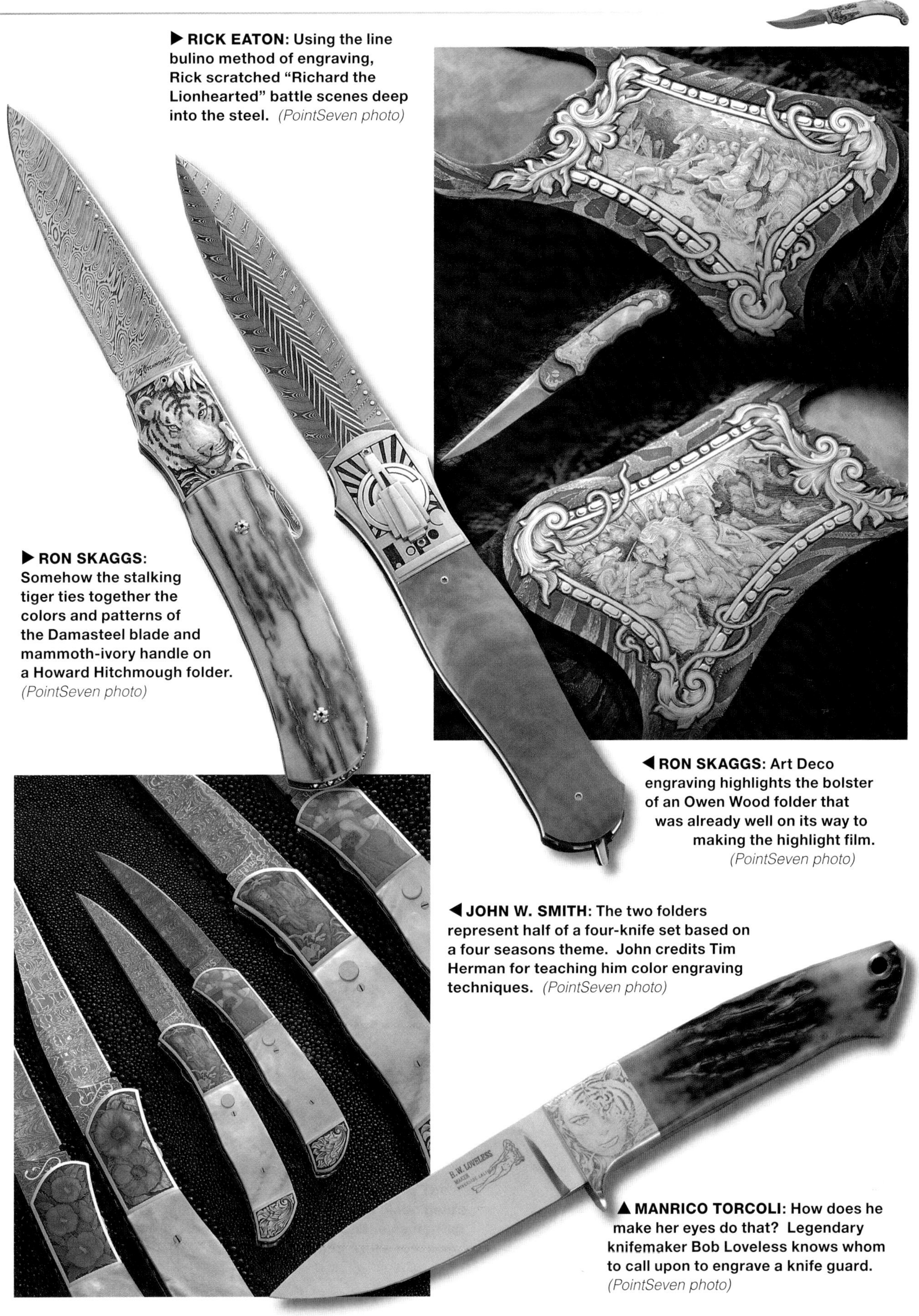


▶ **RICK EATON:** Using the line bulino method of engraving, Rick scratched "Richard the Lionhearted" battle scenes deep into the steel. *(PointSeven photo)*

▶ **RON SKAGGS:** Somehow the stalking tiger ties together the colors and patterns of the Damasteel blade and mammoth-ivory handle on a Howard Hitchmough folder. *(PointSeven photo)*

◀ **RON SKAGGS:** Art Deco engraving highlights the bolster of an Owen Wood folder that was already well on its way to making the highlight film. *(PointSeven photo)*

◀ **JOHN W. SMITH:** The two folders represent half of a four-knife set based on a four seasons theme. John credits Tim Herman for teaching him color engraving techniques. *(PointSeven photo)*

▲ **MANRICO TORCOLI:** How does he make her eyes do that? Legendary knifemaker Bob Loveless knows whom to call upon to engrave a knife guard. *(PointSeven photo)*

▼**JODY AND PAT MULLER:** Whether etching or engraving, some makers just know how to decorate a knife. *(Ward photo)*

▲**BERTIL AASLAND:** The engraving intertwines within itself, and the knife is a Warren Osborne inter-frame folder ala the way Ron Lake makes them. *(PointSeven photo)*

▼**RAY COVER JR.:** The seawater was as green as algae, the sky as gray as slate, and the Viking as bold as gold. Joe Kious mastered the folding dagger before loaning it to a master engraver. *(PointSeven photo)*

▲**TIM GEORGE:** A gentleman's pocketknife fashioned by Gray Taylor called for another gentleman's fine touch with an engraving tool or two. *(PointSeven photo)*

▼**C.J. CAI:** Engraved on the titanium handle of a curvaceous Ken Onion folder are Samurai swordsmen sending steel singing through the Eastern wind. *(Mitch Lum photo)*

◀**GIL RUDOLPH:** It's deep-relief engraving because the guy holding the graver gives a deep sigh of relief when he can finally set it down. W.E. Ankrom fashioned the foxy pearl-handle folder with a Robert Eggerling damascus blade. *(Custom Knife Gallery of Colorado photo)*

**▶ NESTOR LORENZO RHO:** The blade was born from a place where horses run free and gravers go wild.

**▲ FRANCESCO AMADORI:** Knifemaker Ron Lake knew a hepcat when he saw one. *(PointSeven photo)*

**◀ JANDY SHINOSKY:** Pearl parts the waving engraving.

**▶ GIL RUDOLPH:** The handle of the W.E. Ankrom knife is designed to emulate a Beretta S-O over/under shotgun action, including a niter-blued bolster, and the engraving is as traditional as a fine shotgun.

**▲ JOHN BUSFIELD:** Your deep-sea pad, or mine? *(PointSeven photo)*

▶ **JULIUS MOJZIS: Sharks, squid, seashells, sails and sailors are sunk into the steel of a fine knife for fighting.**

▼ **JERE DAVIDSON: The engraver copiously cut into the steel of an all-integral Edmund Davidson sub-hilt fighter fashioned after a Bob Loveless original design.** *(PointSeven photo)*

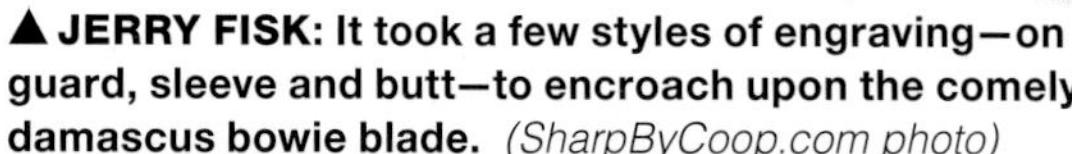

▲ **JERRY FISK: It took a few styles of engraving—on guard, sleeve and butt—to encroach upon the comely damascus bowie blade.** *(SharpByCoop.com photo)*

▲ **RON NOTT: Don't get sore, dinosaur, the fields are golden and the leaf-eaters plentiful. Reese Weiland is the author of the "Raptor" knife.** *(SharpByCoop.com photo)*

◀ **BERTIL AASLAND: There's plenty of prettiness in the fine, precise, uninterrupted integral knife design, yet the bolster engraving gives it a dimension it couldn't accomplish on its own.** *(PointSeven photo)*

# Golden Rods

When imagining what Nirvana might be like, people get faraway looks in their eyes and talk about streets paved in gold. In describing row upon row of wheat, stretching as far as the eye can see, folks often refer to "fields of gold." If you want to accomplish a goal, you "reach for the golden ring," a phrase dating back to when kids practically stretched their arms out of their sockets trying to snag a golden ring on early merry-go-rounds. A "gold digger" is someone who marries for money, and a "golden child" is one born into prosperity or destined for greatness.

Knifemakers, reaching for the golden ring, build knives as beautiful as streets paved in gold and fields of golden wheat. The edged objects are gold inlaid and encrusted, given golden overlays and undertones, inset and adorned with good old fashioned gold––gold that's as gold as honey, as gold as the sun, as golden as the waning years of a long-lasting marriage. These knives pay tribute to gold itself. They represent 1800s prospectors with big dreams and strong backbones. The golden rods of the knife industry stand for dreams, whether broken or fulfilled. They symbolize the good things in life—wealth, prosperity, luxury and high class.

They attract, not gold diggers, not golden children, but collectors with sophisticated tastes and deep pocketbooks. Knives parading golden exteriors put glimmers in all our eyes. They are as stunning as a rain-soaked valley during sunrise, birds chirping their morning tunes, leaves blowing in the wind, sunrays peeking through tree branches and creating sporadic golden spotlights on green grasses. They can be likened to hillsides of goldenrod on hot summer days.

*Joe Kertzman*

**▲ VAN BARNETT: As if the eye-popping Persian wasn't appealing enough with the ladder-pattern damascus blade and carved-ebony handle, Van went ahead and gave it gold inlays and a gold wire wrap.** *(SharpByCoop.com photo)*

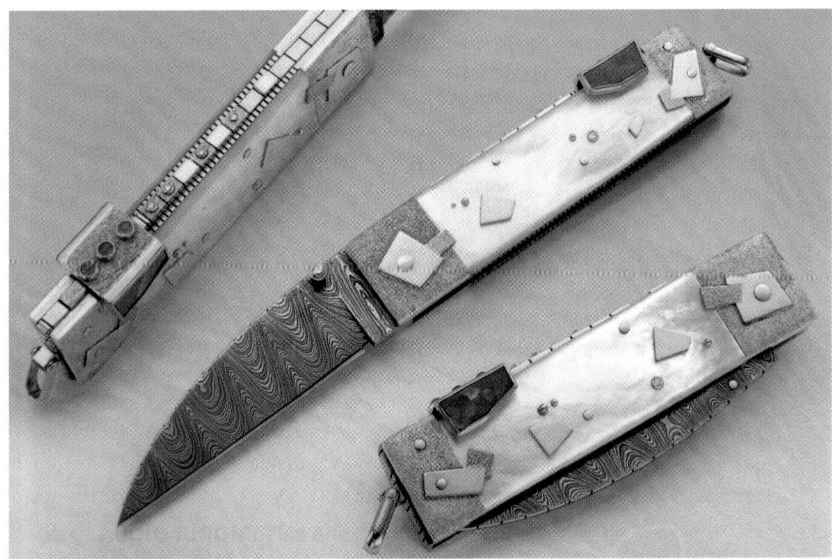

**▲ DELLANA: Islands of gold float dreamily along a river of pearl. There's also an emerald isle or two, a few stray diamonds and some black opals.** *(SharpByCoop.com photo)*

**▲ JEROME ANDERS: Get a 'lode' of the "Clamshell" bowie's gold-hued damascus blade.** *(Hoffman photo)*

▶ **BILL KELLER: Eureka! Gold plating covers the mosaic-damascus blade, carved-mild-steel bolsters and back spacer, all complemented by a solid-gold thumb stud.** *(Custom Knife Gallery of Colorado photo)*

▶ **MICHAEL WALKER: If there are such things as lighthearted gold inlays, these would be them, but the Damasteel folder is a seriously stunning cutting tool.** *(PointSeven photo)*

◀ **DONALD BELL: Cleverly carved and pierced 18-carat gold frames the pink-pearl handle of a fine folder. Gary House forged the damascus.** *(PointSeven photo)*

▲ **SCOTT SLOBODIAN: Follow the golden-brick road to the carved silver stud and Paul Strand explosion-damascus blade; the precious piece was engraved by B. Slobodian.**

◀ **STEVE DUNN: Rich veins of gold run along the bolster, spine and back spacer of a damascus folder, all outlining a goldenrod of a flower planted in the middle.** *(PointSeven photo)*

▲ **RICK EATON:** Ladies with real golden locks discreetly peek out from a mosaic-damascus masterpiece, which includes gold-lip-pearl, abalone and platinum inlays, among other amenities. *(PointSeven photo)*

▶ **DAVID BRODZIAK:** Richard Chapman complemented the gold-plated-damascus blade of the medieval dagger with guard and pommel engraving. More gold plating was added to the fittings, and a gold chain was inlaid along the fluted-mammoth-ivory grip. Carol O'Connor exquisitely painted the scabbard.

▲ **PETER MARTIN:** Prospectors Beware: A mosaic-damascus scorpion with golden handle, legs, claws and stinger guards the precious loot.

# Pin and Ink Drawings

◀ **RONI DIETRICH:** When mermaids that marvelous swim to shore, you carve sterling silver seashells, you allow the rains to drop damascus from the heavens above, and you scrimshaw using the most brilliant inks in your inventory. Howard Hitchmough built the beautiful knife. *(SharpByCoop.com photo)*

▲ **LINDA KARST STONE:** Here's a raven beauty—not only the scrimshaw, but also the all-integral knife by Edmund Davidson and the engraving by Jere Davidson. *(PointSeven photo)*

▲ **LORI RISTINEN:** Revel in reverse scrimshaw on a black buffalo horn handle, and take in the Turkish damascus blade before bowing to the Kirk Rexroat knife. *(PointSeven photo)*

▶ **DIANE HECHT:** The knife fashioned by A.T. Barr, the damascus made by Devin Thomas, the bolsters engraved by Billy Bates and the mastodon ivory scrimshawed by Diane Hecht are all trophy catches. *(Hoffman photo)*

▲ **RONI DIETRICH:** A ravishing beauty snuggles up to her tiger and tells it tall tales. Willy Rigney rigged the knife. *(SharpByCoop.com photo)*

▲ **WILLY B. ELLIS:** What better to scrimshaw on a walrus tooth than an Eskimo and a sailing ship?

▲ **MICHELLE CLAIR:** The character of a big cat comes alive on the pre-ban ivory handle of a Norman Sandow folder.

◀ **LINDA KARST STONE:** Somewhere a Native American is nodding approval of the Leon Treiber lockback folder. *(Ward photo)*

▲ **RICK HUTCHINGS:** One baring its teeth and one with motionless muzzle are married on the ivory grip of a Randall-made knife. *(PointSeven photo)*

▼ **TURNING BEAR MASON:** Mike Mann fashioned a 5160 steel, copper and fossil-mastodon-ivory Doc Togden bowie, and Turning Bear Mason made it more than it already was. *(BladeGallery.com photo)*

◀ **GUY DAHL:** A polar bear, grizzly, cougar and wolf stare out of ivory and into the souls of the prey they stalk. Bob Lay built the knives, and Bruce Shaw engraved the guards and pommels. *(Weyer photo)*

▲ **RONI DIETRICH:** Don't you wish you could capture the beauty of a butterfly, put it in a safe place and save it forever. Your wish came true. Bob Barber is the lucky maker of the knife.

◀ **SHARON BURGER:** The ferociousness, free spiritedness and wildness of Africa's "Big Five" are captured on the ivory handles of William Burger knives. *(Weyer photo)*

▼**SANDRA BRADY:** Once Sandra gets oriented on a knife handle, beautiful blades abound like butterflies on summer days. Tom Watson's knife was the recipient of such embellishment.

◀**LINDA KARST STONE:** As war drums beat, a native dancer treads where only eagles dare. Mike Norris forged the stainless steel damascus, and Leon Treiber honored us with the knife.

▲**DIANE HECHT:** The bee is headed toward the sweet honeycomb bolsters of a Jim Downs folder. Bob Eggerling did up the damascus. *(Hoffman photo)*

▶**JOHN STAHL:** The jungle king and queen get comfortable on the ivory grip of a Jim Elliot damascus fixed-blade. *(SharpByCoop.com photo)*

▲ **LINDA KARST STONE:** You wouldn't want to be skewered by the elephant, the rhino or the Devin Thomas damascus blade of the Carlton Evans folder.

▲ **SHARON BURGER:** When knifemaker Rob Brown commissioned Sharon to scrimshaw the elephant ivory, he got a guinea fowl and a yellow-bird duck, and that was more than enough to satisfy him, and us.

▲ **STEPHEN MACKRILL:** The scrimshaw is true to the tusk from which the handle was born. *(PointSeven photo)*

▶ **MIRELLA PACHI:** It is the dream of all hunters who visit Africa to come face-to-face with one of the "Big Five" beasts, and thanks to a skilled scrimshaw artist, all are adorned on the handle of the Francesco Pachi fixed blade.

▲ **STEPHEN MACKRILL:** Two dinosaur scenes scrimshawed on hippo-tooth ivory come together when the damascus blade is sheathed. *(PointSeven photo)*

◀ **SHARON BURGER:** I hope Sharon took a bow after poking holes in elephant ivory until a stunning crowned martial eagle appeared on a Rob Brown knife. The martial eagle, by the way, is the largest eagle in Africa, weighing nearly 14 pounds.

▶ **MATT STOTHART:** When Matt saw the mastodon ivory, he imagined Japanese Kabuki actors. Using needles and ink, he planted their pictures beneath the surface of the ivory grips, copying their likenesses from original Japanese Toyokuni III prints dating back to 1856. Kelly Carlson built the knife, and Delbert Ealy forged the mosaic damascus bolsters. *(PointSeven photo)*

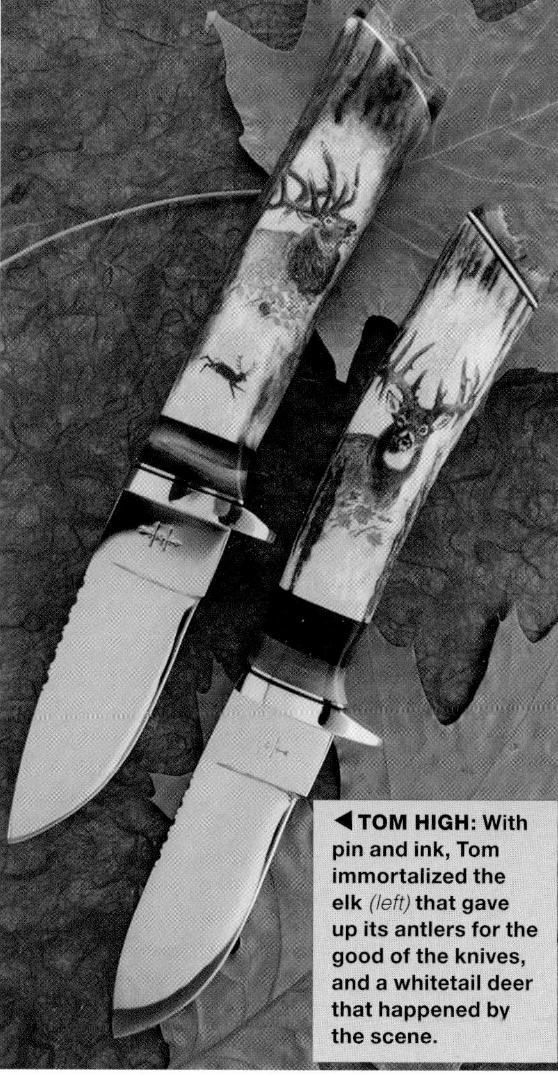

◀ **TOM HIGH:** With pin and ink, Tom immortalized the elk *(left)* that gave up its antlers for the good of the knives, and a whitetail deer that happened by the scene.

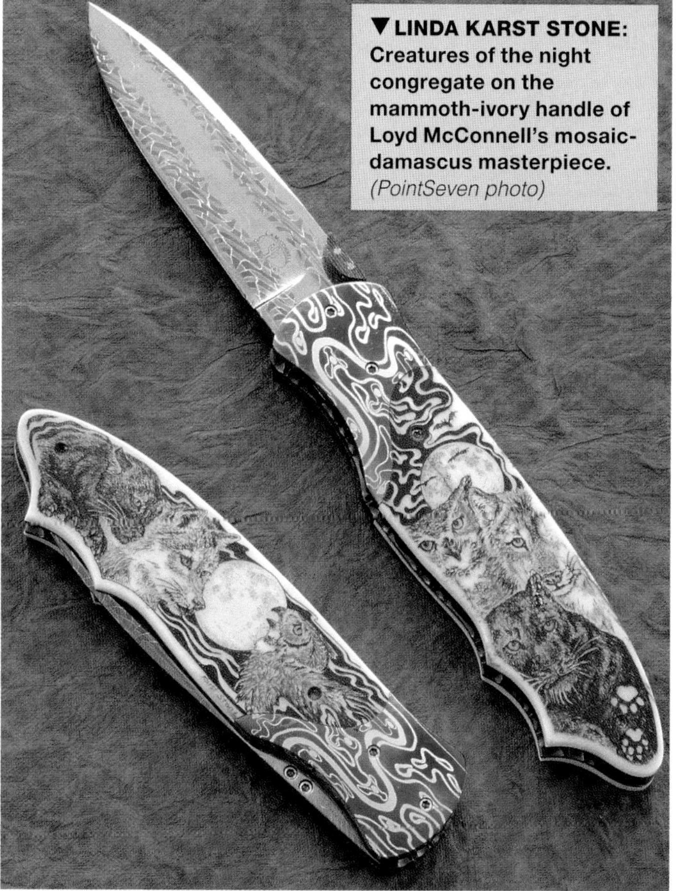

▼ **LINDA KARST STONE:** Creatures of the night congregate on the mammoth-ivory handle of Loyd McConnell's mosaic-damascus masterpiece. *(PointSeven photo)*

# Scenic Steel

People can say what they want about there not being anything new in knives. Folks with a hankering for history will expound on damascus blades that are thousands of years old, on sword blades that were coal-forged, clay-tempered and outlasted several samurai insurgencies. They'll find knives similar to the American bowie that were built in places like Argentina, Italy, France or England hundreds of years prior to the taming of the Wild West. Those wishing to preserve heritage—a good virtue—talk about obsidian knives, iron-ore blades, steel made from dirt and laminated-steel pieces uncovered and made long before it became fashionable.

Few, though, will find early, historic edged examples that have images of spider webs forged into mosaics of damascus. Excavators in Rome haven't unearthed pattern-welded blades featuring Sylvester and Tweety cartoon characters. Even though some ancient Japanese blades have seen or caused faces of death, none that are over a decade old were ever made from steel layers that, when etched, revealed faces of death within the steel.

Wavy temper lines have been around since the advent of differential heat-treating, hundreds, if not thousands of years. But, "shock-wave" damascus is a recent phenomenon.

Just the idea of cutting, etching, forge welding and generally manipulating steel until images are born from within it is astounding. It is new. Scenic steel is not historic. It is here now, for the first time in history, and imaginative blade smiths have started something that has no limits or bounds. Any image, no matter how detailed, can be recreated in the way steels that etch differently are forged together. Use your imagination. What would you like to see in your blade—a butterfly, a dragon, devil, the face of your enemy, or perhaps an image of your own likeness?

*Joe Kertzman*

**▲ GARY HOUSE: This blade billet will make your mustache wiggle.** *(PointSeven photo)*

**▲ TED MOORE: He pulled out his knife to cut through the web of deceit.** *(SharpByCoop.com photo)*

**▲ DON HANSON III: The faces of death were permanently etched into the blade.**

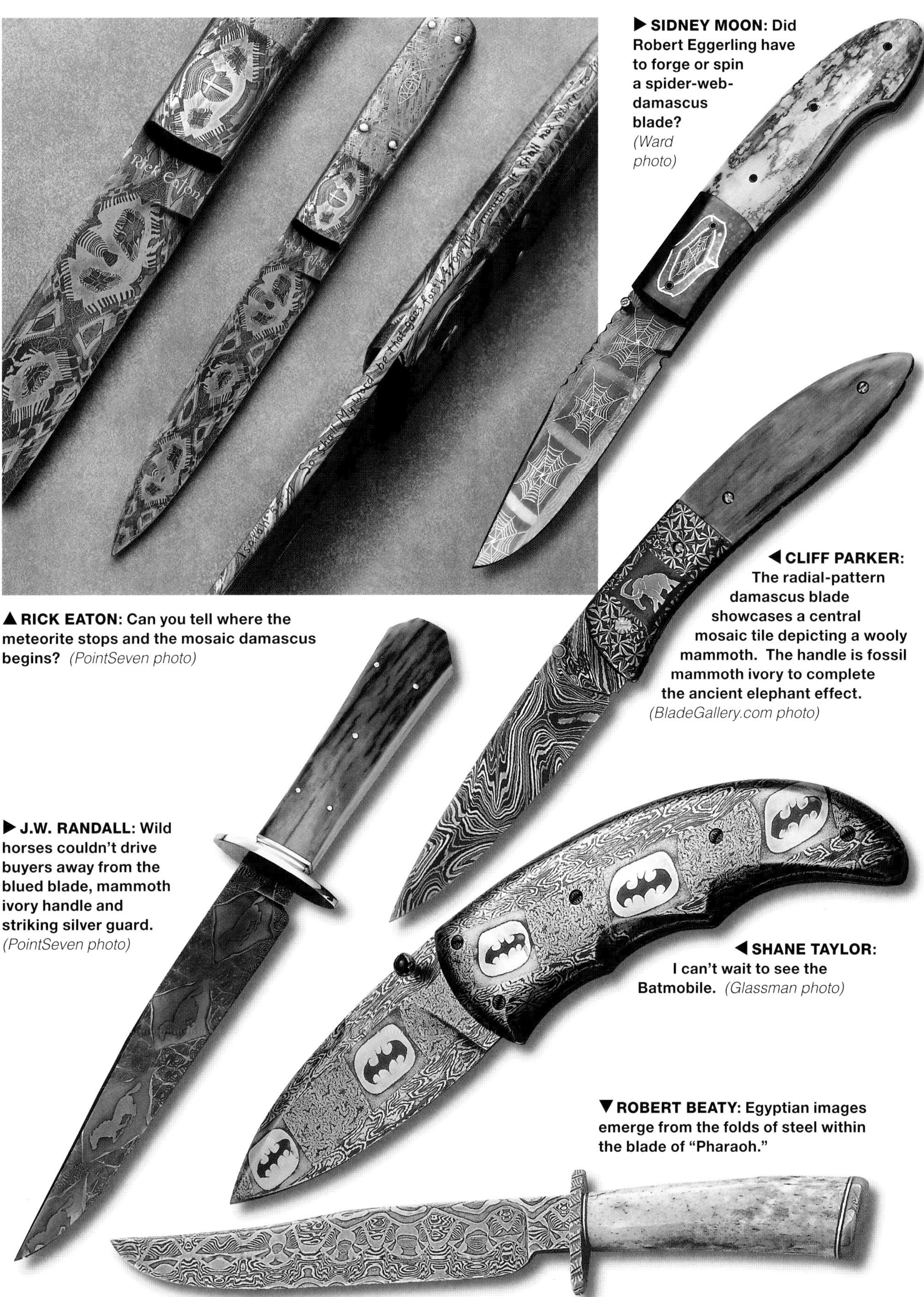


▶ **SIDNEY MOON: Did Robert Eggerling have to forge or spin a spider-web-damascus blade?** *(Ward photo)*

▲ **RICK EATON: Can you tell where the meteorite stops and the mosaic damascus begins?** *(PointSeven photo)*

◀ **CLIFF PARKER: The radial-pattern damascus blade showcases a central mosaic tile depicting a wooly mammoth. The handle is fossil mammoth ivory to complete the ancient elephant effect.** *(BladeGallery.com photo)*

▶ **J.W. RANDALL: Wild horses couldn't drive buyers away from the blued blade, mammoth ivory handle and striking silver guard.** *(PointSeven photo)*

◀ **SHANE TAYLOR: I can't wait to see the Batmobile.** *(Glassman photo)*

▼ **ROBERT BEATY: Egyptian images emerge from the folds of steel within the blade of "Pharaoh."**

▶ **TOM FERRY:** Who'd have thought that perfection would come in the form of a "ball-and-chain" damascus Persian integral fixed-blade? *(Mitch Lum photo)*

◀ **PETER MARTIN:** This one morphs from a stinger into a beautiful butterfly. *(SharpByCoop.com photo)*

▲ **MATT DISKIN:** The "virus" damascus blade is infectious. *(Mitch Lum photo)*

▶ **SHANE TAYLOR:** The "griz-track" damascus blade is fur-colored and complemented incredibly well by a mammoth-ivory grip of similar patina and pattern. *(PointSeven photo)*

▲ **LOYD MCCONNELL:** Made in the U.S.A., the bowie proudly parades the stars and stripes. *(PointSeven photo)*

◀ **TOM FERRY:** This is a whale of a Koi damascus knife, complete with a textured damascus grip. *(Mitch Lum photo)*

▶ **JOE OLSON:** Check out the "Grim Reaper" relief engraving on the bolsters and handle, the morbid images around the pool of pearl, and especially the "apocalypse" damascus blade. *(BladeGallery.com photo)*

▶ **BILL BUXTON:** As if forging stars, stripes and an eagle into a bowie blade weren't enough, the maker inlaid silver wire stars into curly maple for effect. *(BladeGallery.com photo)*

▶ **JERRY MCCLURE:** "Shockwave" mosaic damascus bolsters are the aftereffects of a Joel Davis "lightning strike" blade. *(Hoffman photo)*

◀ **JOEL DAVIS:** The "shockwave" mosaic damascus blade is electrifying. *(PointSeven photo)*

▲ **HANK KNICKMEYER:** The five-bar composite blade bears female figures in the center bar and is coupled with a fossll-walrus handle. *(PointSeven photo)*

# Hued Blue and Honed True

There's something about blue and steel that makes you want to lump them together. There was even a movie, starring Jamie Lee Curtis, named "Blue Steel." Of course, the title refers to the way a blued pistol barrel looks, and possibly feels. Using word association, some people automatically think of cold when they hear the word "blue." Imagine that—there's a knife company named Cold Steel, isn't there? The name, of course, refers to the way steel feels in the hand.

Bluing steel is a way of protecting it from oxidation. It is also a way of making it beautiful. Some blades were just born to be blue. Blue is a boy color, and knives are often referred to as "boy toys." Oceans and skies are blue, and some birds, gemstones, candies and berries are blue. It's an awesome color to emulate, and knives have much in common with the things that share the color blue.

Knifemakers inlay blades and handles with gemstones, they shape the blades like bird beaks, they give them shell handles and interplanetary designs. They get their inspiration from the waters below and the heavens above. Blades and grips are given blue hues so bright that sunny days feel cheated, the Caribbean Sea turns cold in protest and the feathers of bluebirds all over the world are ruffled.

Knives are born from steel, sweat and tears, and there's nothing bluer than that. Take a good look at some fine knives that were hued blue and honed true.

*Joe Kertzman*

▼**GEORGE MULLER: To get the blues to come out of the mammoth ivory, he heat colored the mosaic damascus and hot blued the twist damascus. Then reds started shining through that he didn't know were there in the first place.** *(Custom Knife Gallery of Colorado photo)*

▲**TED MOORE: Red rubies raised the bar as far as blade bluing went.** *(SharpByCoop.com photo)*

▶**JOHN DAVIS: He calls it "wine country" mosaic damascus, and it was obviously a good year for grapes. The handle is redwood burl to complete the Californian theme.** *(Mitch Lum photo)*

**▼TOM FERRY:** Ferry needed a ferry to get across that ocean of handle material. *(Mitch Lum photo)*

**▲TODD BEGG:** The handle is textured like the fibers of fiberglass, only thick, smooth and much more handsome. *(SharpByCoop.com photo)*

**▲KELLY CARLSON:** He huffed and puffed and blued the blade and bolsters. *(SharpByCoop.com photo)*

**▲KELLY CARLSON:** Purple ringlets form in the blue pools. *(SharpByCoop.com photo)*

**▼GAIL LUNN:** The Robert Eggerling damascus was etched deeply for high contrast, so deep it took on aspects of the ocean where rays of sun scarcely shine.

**▲JOSH SMITH:** For his fourth automatic knife, Josh blued out all the stops. *(PointSeven photo)*

▶ **RICK DUNKERLEY:** How does Rick know what the world looks like from space? The heat-blued Gibeon meteorite handle is inlaid with diamonds, sapphire, ruby, moonstone, hematite and 24-carat gold. *(BladeGallery.com photo)*

▲ **GAIL LUNN:** The "crisscross" mosaic damascus will appeal as much to the bluebloods as the mother-of-pearl handle, diamond thumb stud and 14k-gold filed spacers. *(PointSeven photo)*

▲ **KELLY CARLSON:** The three-bar damascus blade by Andre Andersson of Sweden was niter-blued to display the flame-patterned edges and gold Celtic patterns down the center. The bolsters are forged Turkish damascus by Delbert Ealy with 24k-gold inlays by Ron Nott. *(SharpByCoop.com photo)*

▲ **JASON MAGRUDER:** The blue blade was begotten from blue flames, ball-peen hammer and bare knuckles. *(SharpByCoop.com photo)*

▶ **A.T. BARR:** Like a blue marlin, the Persian folder borrows some of its colors from the sea—perhaps the Persian Gulf. The knife sports a Devin Thomas damascus blade and bolsters. *(SharpByCoop.com photo)*

▶ **MATT DISKIN:** The "Night Sky" folder features niter-blued damascus, presentation-grade abalone and gold dual thumb studs. *(Custom Knife Gallery of Colorado photo)*

▲ **MICHAEL KANTER:** George Werth made the damascus, Jerry Rados hot-blued it, and Kanter capped it off with mammoth tooth, amber stag and a mild steel nut.

▶ **RICHARD S. WRIGHT:** If I didn't know better, I'd say those are Celtic knots, blue bonnets and purple petticoats. *(SharpByCoop.com photo)*

▼ **ANDRE VAN HEERDEN:** There's something about blue wooly mammoth bark ivory that makes you want to niter-blue Robert Eggerling and Devin Thomas damascus before calling it a day. *(Custom Knife Gallery of Colorado photo)*

▲ **CLAUDIO RIBONI:** This one bleeds purple, blue, white and red, and we hope that is all that's bleeding.

◀ **RON NEWTON:** The feather pattern damascus resembles a blue goose I once knew. The filework, on the other hand, is like nothing I've ever seen. *(PointSeven photo)*

▼ **JOSH SMITH:** While carving the black-lip pearl, he wondered how blue, green and pink would get along. Then, when they joined forces, it was an automatic match. *(PointSeven photo)*

▲ **TODD BEGG:** The handle is Timascus by Tom Ferry, and fairly fiery Timascus at that. *(SharpByCoop.com photo)*

▶ **JOSH SMITH:** No, it's not a ladder pattern, but the blade is blue enough to ascend into heaven. *(PointSeven photo)*

▲ **FRED DURIO:** Robert Eggerling damascus is dazzling in black or blue, and the mammoth ivory handle is hot in orange. *(Ward photo)*

▶ **RICK DUNKERLEY:** Blue blazes, that's some special steel hunkered right up against some of the boldest black-lip pearl this town's ever seen. *(PointSeven photo)*

▶ **TOM FERRY:** The Timascus wharncliffe is almost too cool to cut with ... almost. *(Mitch Lum photo)*

▶ **PAUL FOX:** Is it a blue Fox? *(PointSeven photo)*

▶ **DANIEL STEPHAN:** Damascus that is this drop-dead gorgeous could only be sculpted, filed, inlaid and displayed. *(PointSeven photo)*

▲ **BRIAN TIGHE:** It's a carved-damascus and Timascus cutup, and no one is laughing. *(PointSeven photo)*

▲ **ED CAFFREY:** Ed's "Blue Saturday" folder is a mosaic-damascus masterpiece, including three rubies inset into each side of the textured handle. *(BladeGallery.com photo)*

# Bezels and Bevels

In the Mexican jungle villages where Mayans still live in much the same way their ancestors did in the 17th century—without electricity, running water, concrete or steel—there is a bit of folklore that is passed down from generation to generation. Mayan tradition holds that a man courting a lady would present her with a rather large jungle beetle, and, believe it or not, a tiny cloak of sorts was sewn for the beetle and adorned with precious stones. Mind you, the beetle was still alive at the time.

The lady would graciously accept the cloak-wearing beetle and place it on front of her dress at about shoulder height, near where a woman would wear a corsage. The beetle clung onto the dress and stayed there, probably scared half to death. The jeweled beetle indicated that the lady was spoken for, or that the man and lady were engaged, much the same way a diamond engagement ring symbolizes a marriage proposal in North American culture.

Jewels mean many things to many people. For some they indicate wealth or prosperity, for others hierarchy or royalty, and for still more people they are decoration or embellishment. Jeweled knives tend to be fancier, perhaps classier, and more expensive than those sans precious stones. Settings that hold the gemstones are often handmade, and of silver, gold or bronze. Precious metals and precious jewels go together like fine china and fine silver. Some engraving, carving, etching, scrimshaw or sculpting is a nice touch to complement a jeweled piece.

In the sleepy mountain towns where English noblemen still stroll cobblestone streets, cane swords tapping a beat as they walk, there is a bit of folklore that is passed down from generation to generation. Tradition holds that real works of art are handcrafted using methods that are hundreds, if not thousands, of years old, and only the rarest, most expensive and exquisite jewels are worthy of the finer things in life, like jewelry, statuettes ... and knives.

*Joe Kertzman*

▶ **MARK STEINBRECHER:** Since he went to the trouble of carving the Jerry Rados damascus blade, the Delbert Ealy bolsters and the walrus-ivory handle, he might as well have covered the screws with rubies. *(SharpByCoop.com photo)*

▶ **KENNETH KING:** Like many knifemakers, Kenneth crossed over into the business from the jewelry designing trade, and he deserves a purple heart for his efforts. *(PointSeven photo)*

▲ **MICHAEL WATTELET:** The sterling silver and 14k-gold handle is set with carnelian cabochons, making for one jewel of a knife.

▲ **TEX SKOW:** The rubes had best beware of the rubies, because this is no rustic cutter, as the Ron Nott engraving would indicate.

▶ **BILL KELLER:** Few knifemakers apply piquet work to knife handles, but those who do usually carve the ivory into little checks and painstakingly set a gold or silver pin into the center of each check. But, no, that wasn't good enough for Bill, who went with white topazes, rubies and sapphires just to show off. *(Custom Knife Gallery of Colorado photo)*

▶ **KENNETH KING:** Having gold, sapphires and diamonds is one thing, but knowing what to do with them when you get them is quite another. The damascus completes the dressy delivery. *(PointSeven photo)*

▼ **JOVAN DEBRAGA:** The red areas on the ends of the guard, which, by the way, was carved from a solid block of stainless steel, are cloisonné of ruby red composite. A red cabochon garnet was set on top of the blade sleeve and another on the faceplate of the guard. It rocks!

◀ **RAINY VALLOTTON:** A lone sapphire was set dead center in a sea of damascus. *(PointSeven photo)*

▲ **STEVE JERNIGAN:** Scaling the castle walls were golden vines with malachite ivy leaves. *(PointSeven photo)*

▲ **JOSE DEBRAGA:** "Old Blue Eye" won them over with his good looks and sharp dress.

# Knive Wires

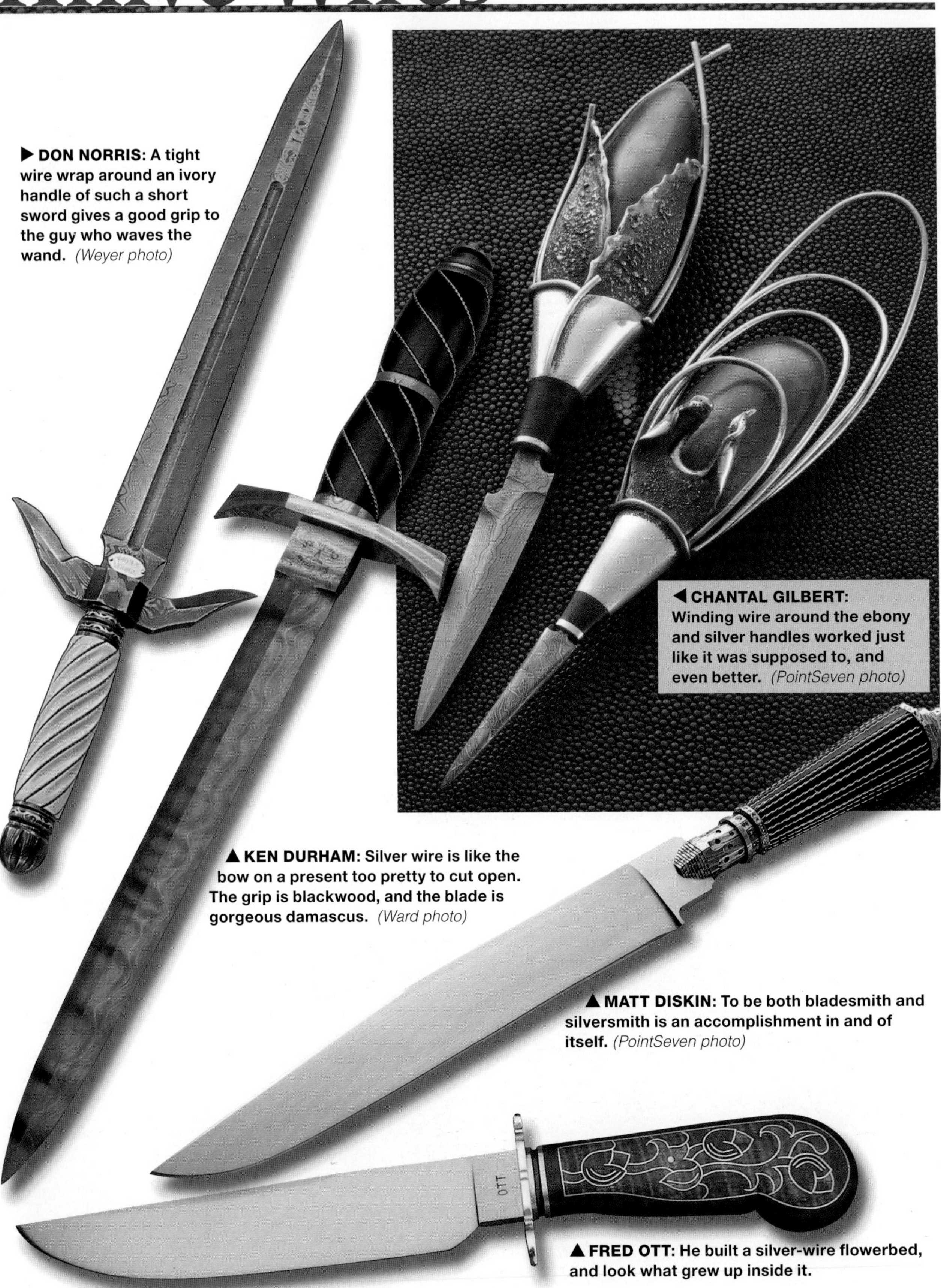


▶ **DON NORRIS:** A tight wire wrap around an ivory handle of such a short sword gives a good grip to the guy who waves the wand. *(Weyer photo)*

◀ **CHANTAL GILBERT:** Winding wire around the ebony and silver handles worked just like it was supposed to, and even better. *(PointSeven photo)*

▲ **KEN DURHAM:** Silver wire is like the bow on a present too pretty to cut open. The grip is blackwood, and the blade is gorgeous damascus. *(Ward photo)*

▲ **MATT DISKIN:** To be both bladesmith and silversmith is an accomplishment in and of itself. *(PointSeven photo)*

▲ **FRED OTT:** He built a silver-wire flowerbed, and look what grew up inside it.

◀ **JOE KEESLAR:** The "Paradox" fixed blade looked more like a peacock after the silver wire was inlaid within the grain of the curly maple handle. *(PointSeven photo)*

▶ **TODD KOPP:** He wrapped wire around the mammoth ivory grip of the full-size dagger, and wee wire around the itty-bitty ivory grip of the diminutive dagger. *(ScreenSurge photo)*

▲ **HOWARD HITCHMOUGH:** Gold wires cut across a pearl handle like a Damasteel knife blade into a cardboard box. *(PointSeven photo)*

◀ **CHARLIE AND HARRY MATTHEWS:** What do you know—white and gold go together just as well as black and silver. That's a carved sambar-stag handle, by the way.

# Of Cutlers Who Carve

◀ **VAN BARNETT:** The "Ivory Coast" dagger is destined for greatness, starting with the incredible carved-ivory handle, to the way the guard is engraved to continue the leafy pattern, and how the ladder-pattern damascus blade brings the knife to a final, emphatic point. *(SharpByCoop.com photo)*

▼ **JEROME ANDERS:** The bowie knife embodies all the right checks and balances. *(Mitch Lum photo)*

▶ **MARK STEINBRECHER:** Even though Jerry Rados and Delbert Ealy forged the blade and bolsters, respectively, Mark carved them into a copasetic cutting machine. *(SharpByCoop.com photo)*

▲ **JULIUS MOJZIS:** The sky shown pearly white as the bird of freedom soared overhead on that summer day in the desert of Mohave.

◀ **JOSEF RUSNAK:** A fantastic forest, seemingly silhouetted by the aurora borealis, grew where Josef Rusnak laid his carving tool upon the handle of a Bud West Damasteel knife. *(BladeGallery.com photo)*

▼ **JOHN W. SMITH:** If he can change gold-lip pearl into diamonds, imagine how deep he can make mosaic damascus cut. *(Custom Knife Gallery of Colorado photo)*

▲ **RICK PALM:** Rick's "Thunderbird" is carved from 100-year-old Alaskan yellow cedar, yet it glides with the greatest of ease. When carved, the wood smells like spice, so that's an added benefit.

▲ **KEN STEIGERWALT:** Scalloping damascus, or sculpting steel, is not for the faint at heart, nor is gazing at such a powerful piece of work. Mike Norris provided the ladder-pattern damascus of the blade, and Robert Eggerling forged the twist-damascus bolsters (before the scalloping began). *(Custom Knife Gallery of Colorado photo)*

▲ **ARPAD BOJTOS:** Prometheus was a Greek mythological titan who stole fire from Olympus and gave it to human beings. Now we know where Arpad gets the fire that feeds his forge.

▼ **VLADIMIR PULIS:** Vladimir's thematic approach to knifemaking has never been so stunning as on this mosaic damascus masterpiece, complete with carved bear roaring on the damascus blade; a bear-tooth handle carved to depict early man drawing on a cave wall; and a leather-and-bear-tooth sheath showcasing not only an embossed-leather cave drawing, but also a carved cavemen-versus-bear scene.

▶ **BOB CROWDER:** The mammoth-ivory handle of the "Rose Dagger" is carved so daintily, the bed of roses looks soft enough to sleep on. Devin Thomas forged the "fireball" damascus. *(BladeGallery.com photo)*

▼ **DONALD BELL:** The Robert Eggerling damascus blade and bolsters, and the gold-lip-pearl handle, are carved in deep relief to look like living leaves and petals splayed out and displayed for their inherent beauty. *(PointSeven photo)*

▲ **JERRY LAIRSON:** Let the "Dove" knife bring peace to your day. The smooth grip is giraffe bone, and the bold blade traces its origin back to cable damascus. *(Ward photo)*

▶ **JOSEF RUSNAK:** The carbon damascus is grooved, the antique bronze is sculpted and the mammoth tusk is carved, all making for one embellished knife. *(BladeGallery.com photo)*

▶ **STACY APELT:** The damascus blade is forged in a snake pattern, and the handle is snakewood, but the grip and sheath are carved into a fire-breathing dragon. *(Hoffman photo)*

▲ **VIRGIL ENGLAND:** The "Saddle Knife" puts on a solemn face and is clad "from head to tip" in damascus, silver, bronze, meteorite and fossil bone.

▶ **ROBERT WEINSTOCK:** The folding dagger is outfitted in damascus, gold and a suit of armor carefully formed to fit his fantastic frame. *(PointSeven photo)*

◀ **AL DIPPOLD:** The mammoth ivory grip sprouts from the knife bolster as a flower bud pushes forth and opens in the spring. *(PointSeven photo)*

▶ **JOSE DE BRAGA:** The dagger parades a carved pink-ivory handle. Do you see Witch Mountain, a castle tower, a fiery battle scene or something else entirely?

▲ **JOSE DE BRAGA:** "Perseus" (the son of Zeus and Danae who slew Medusa) is a D-guard short glaive stretching 23 inches overall and featuring a carved jet stone handle with 14k-gold and oxidized-fine-silver appliqués where garnets were set. The figure of Medusa is carved in 14-carat gold on the pommel face.

▶ **DAVID BROADWELL:** Enthusiasts talk about the "lines of a knife," but rarely does a knifemaker point them out so well for his customers. The entire integral damascus sub-hilt fighter is carved, including the blade, guard and handle. *(PointSeven photo)*

▲ **LADISLAV SANTA-LASKY:** The blade was forged from dragon's breath and a hellacious hammer.

▶ **ROBERT WEINSTOCK:** Files, folks, he did that with hand files! *(PointSeven photo)*

▲ **RICK EATON:** Carved Celtic knots emerge from the guard and pommel areas of a stunning damascus folding dagger. *(PointSeven photo)*

▶ **DONALD VOGT:** The blade and bolsters are fully carved using chisels and a chase hammer, and the handle sprouts carved gold flower overlays. *(PointSeven photo)*

▲ **LARRY FUEGEN:** The knife was inspired by the famous Spanish explorer, Hernando Cortes, but even the knifemaker's inspiration can't match his talent. Everything is carved and gold-plated, including the blade.

▶ **DONALD VOGT:** The knifemaker knew just what to carve away and what to leave where it lay. *(PointSeven photo)*

▲ **CHARLIE AND HARRY MATTHEWS:** Even the color was carved off the red stag, and you could say it's staggering.

# A Shout Out to Sheaths

There's nothing standard about the sheaths on this and the following two pages. The sheath makers were not required to meet a set standard, and once met, relish in a job well done. There were no quotas, no minimum requirements, no standardized rules and regulations. That's why the sheaths are so stunning. It's why such things as innovation, state of the art materials, creative snap closures, artwork, handiwork and overall quality workmanship exist.

No one was watching over the sheath makers' shoulders. The boss didn't blow a whistle for lunch or a break. No clock was punched. The inspector didn't stop by to see that everything was running smoothly.

The only motivations to excel at sheath making … the only reasons to fashion some of the prettiest, most utilitarian, well made, quality sheaths available were pride in workmanship, dedication to a craft, will to succeed, vested interest, pride and desire to provide useful tools. Rarely does a knife- and sheath-maker get a great deal of extra money for a knife because it comes with a fine sheath. The sheath might help sell the knife, but it is not the prime money-getter.

No, the sheaths are the extras. They're proof that the knifemakers, whether they made the sheaths themselves or hired out the jobs, took pride in their work, offered a little more, went the extra mile and gave good customer service. Few parts plants boast that kind of dedication to the customer. And that's why it is of utmost importance to give a loud, enthusiastic shout out to sheaths.

*Joe Kertzman*

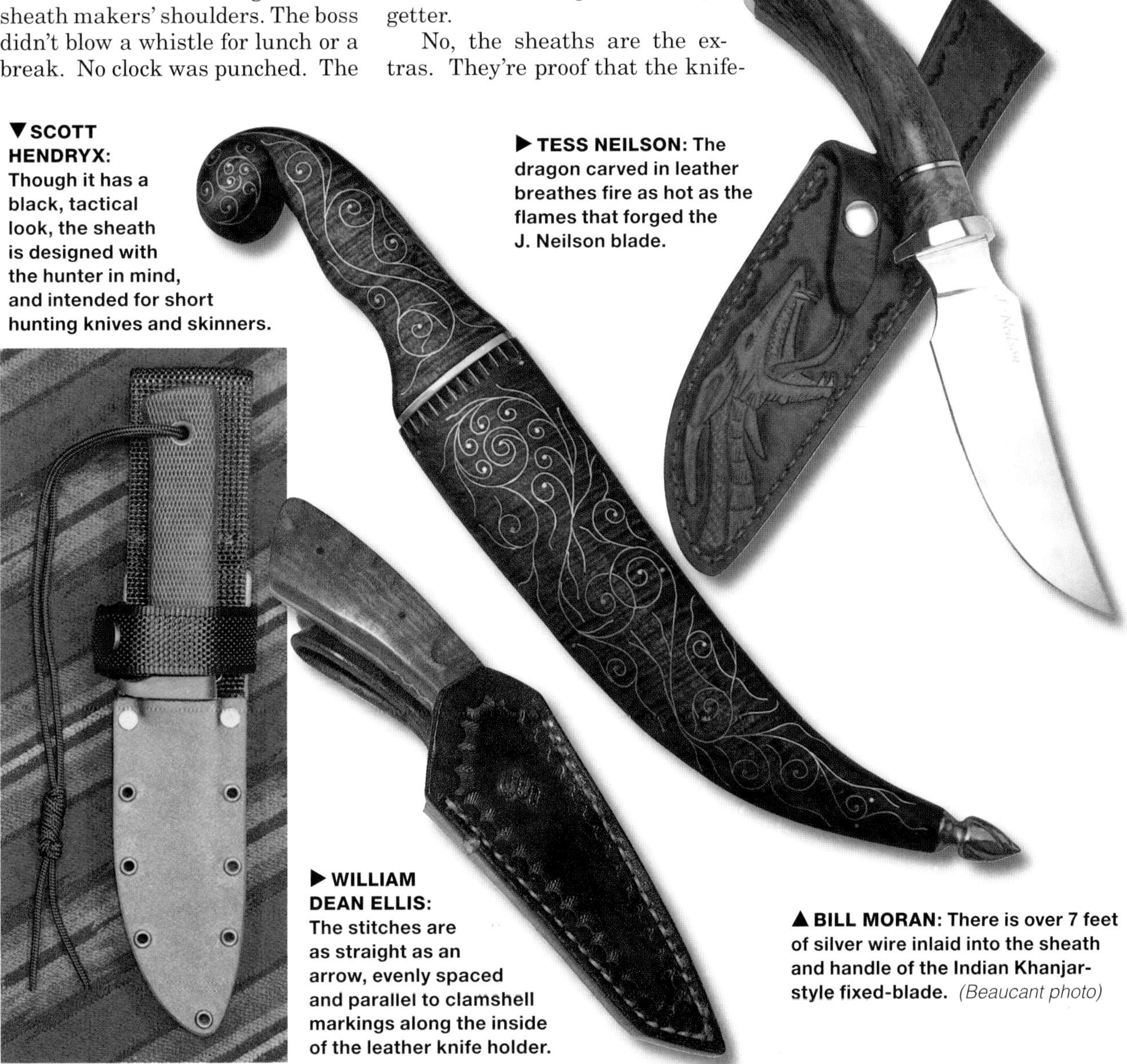

▼**SCOTT HENDRYX:** Though it has a black, tactical look, the sheath is designed with the hunter in mind, and intended for short hunting knives and skinners.

▶ **TESS NEILSON:** The dragon carved in leather breathes fire as hot as the flames that forged the J. Neilson blade.

▶ **WILLIAM DEAN ELLIS:** The stitches are as straight as an arrow, evenly spaced and parallel to clamshell markings along the inside of the leather knife holder.

▲ **BILL MORAN:** There is over 7 feet of silver wire inlaid into the sheath and handle of the Indian Khanjar-style fixed-blade. *(Beaucant photo)*

▶ **RIC CARTER:** Red, white and blue beaded is the beautiful sheath that accompanies a Mike Mann bowie. *(BladeGallery.com photo)*

▼ **FRED ROWE:** Smooth leather is a badge of honor for a fine fixed-blade.

▲ **LOYD THOMSEN:** No one thought the blade was leaf-shaped until they saw the stunning sheath.

▶ **KENNY ROWE:** Leather embellished in such a spectacular fashion could start a stampede. The knife, with African blackwood handle, is from the hands of Lin Rhea. *(Ward photo)*

▲ **MARK NEVLING:** With bolsters pointed upward, knives fit snugly into three folder sheaths: one inlaid with boa skin, another in beavertail skin and a final blade buddy in rattlesnake hide.

▶ **ROBERT SCHRAP:** Cowhide and boa skin, expertly formed, stitched and generally fashioned, protect body parts from the sharp edge when the blade is not in use.

◀ **CHRIS KRAVITT:** If you ever see a black Malaysian horned frog, don't touch it, just call Chris and he'll catch it for sheath material.

▶ **CAROL ANN O'CONNOR:** The Dorcas gazelle on the scabbard of a David Brodziak knife was hand-painted by Carol.

▶ **JIM GARDNER:** The gentleman's bowie benefits from an Indian-style Western sheath trailing leather fringe and beadwork, that bodes well for he who carries it.

▼ **JACQUELINE DAVIS:** A couple Jerry Duran bowie-style neck knives are the beneficiaries of some incredible beadwork and leatherwork.

# FACTORY TRENDS

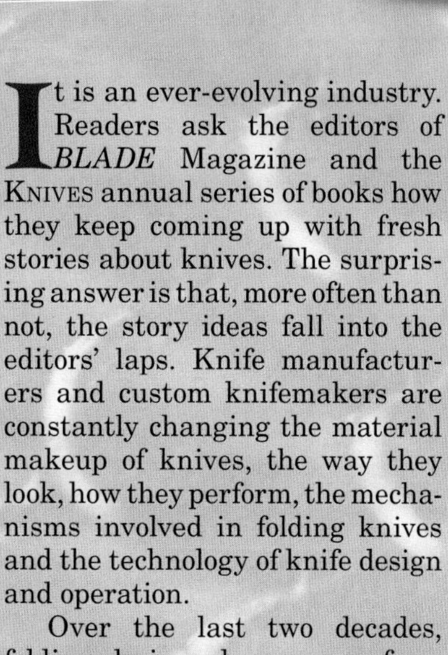

It is an ever-evolving industry. Readers ask the editors of *BLADE* Magazine and the Knives annual series of books how they keep coming up with fresh stories about knives. The surprising answer is that, more often than not, the story ideas fall into the editors' laps. Knife manufacturers and custom knifemakers are constantly changing the material makeup of knives, the way they look, how they perform, the mechanisms involved in folding knives and the technology of knife design and operation.

Over the last two decades, folding knives have gone from having no blade locks at all (slip joints) or unsophisticated locking mechanisms, to having high-tech, innovative locks, and now to having not only bank-vault-tight locks, but safeties to further avoid lock failure.

Hunting knives are no longer high-carbon-steel or stainless fixed blades and folders. They, too, have locks, whether locking blades or locking sheaths, replaceable blades, blades that rarely need sharpening and handles that look and feel good.

Even field saws have evolved. They fold now, and they often accompany complete sets of hunting and camp knives that can tackle any job from camp setup to the butchering, field dressing and skinning of deer and other game, to food preparation.

Tactical knives are no longer made for Rambo "wannabes," but for the police, military and emergency medical professionals. They are designed for specific cutting tasks and duties, and include such features as window punches, seat belt cutters, wire cutters and blunt blade tips for safety. All has changed in the knife industry. Factory trends are established by changes in technology and the evolving, duty-specific needs of professionals or other knife enthusiasts in the field.

*Joe Kertzman*

# Stand and Salute the CQC -7

***It's been more than 10 years since Ernest Emerson's CQC-7 arrived on the knife scene, and the story unfolds from there ...***

*By Dexter Ewing*

**Pictured are two Emerson CQC-7s—the 7B tanto and 7A utilitarian spear point. Both have green G-10 handles, which were in production only a couple years, then discontinued.**

It is arguably one of the best-selling production tactical folders of all time. It has seen action in all corners of the globe. The tactical folding knife has been found in the pockets of some of the most elite armed forces in the far reaches of the world. It is one of the most popular tactical folding knives among military and law enforcement personnel, and just as gaga over it are everyday knife enthusiasts.

Of course, "it" is Ernest Emerson's CQC-7 knife model—the tactical folder that rode a wave of popularity generated by Richard Marcinko's *Rogue Warrior* book series, in which the main character employed the predecessor to the CQC-7, the CQC-6.

The CQC-7 is truly a knife that has "been there, done that." And with 2004 having come and gone as the 10th anniversary of the tactical folder, KNIVES 2006 would like to salute the CQC-7 by taking a look back at where the knife has been, where it is now and where design enhancements will take it in the future.

When asked for his design philosophies behind the CQC-7, Emerson was quick to credit his inspiration for the CQC-7's chisel-ground tanto blade. "Phil Hartsfield was the father of the modern chisel grind," Emerson noted.

A chisel-ground tanto, like the 3.3-inch blade of the CQC-7, not only exhibits lateral strength and a reinforced tip, but also a general blade design that excels in performing piercing cuts.

"This chisel grind is very efficient and strong, and is also easy to maintain," explained Emerson. "The CQC-6 was the father of the CQC-7. It had a 'neutral' handle and I had customers who requested a knife with a handle shape that allowed for indexing of the cutting edge [by feel of the handle shape]."

The CQC-7's handle was born out of necessity. Emerson also pointed out that the handle shape

*ALL PHOTOS BY JOHN HOLLISTER, HOLLISTER IMAGING*

**The Benchmade 975 was the predecessor of what is now the Emerson Knives Super CQC-7. It stretches to an overall length of about 9 inches, giving the user extended reach and cutting capacity.**

**The Mini CQC-7B offers the same design and performance advantages of the regular CQC-7 except in a more pocket-friendly, scaled-down size.**

is one that people can use in any grip configuration, regardless of it being a reverse grip or hammer grip. "The handle design was a good marriage for the CQC-7 blade," he said.

Another marriage made in heaven was that between Emerson and Benchmade Knife Co., a twosome that paired on a production version of the CQC-7. In the mid 1990s, Benchmade introduced its Emerson-designed model 970 CQC-7, a knife that featured an ATS-34 blade, a textured G-10 handle, dual titanium liners and a thumb disk for easy one-hand opening.

## Compact and Quick to Deploy

The Benchmade model captured the essence of the CQC-7 design, being compact, quick to deploy, and easy to carry and use. Immediately, the 970 was a big hit with the knife buying public, so much so, in fact, that Benchmade produced variations of the model 970 in subsequent years.

Such model variations included the 975, with a 4-inch blade; the highly specialized 970ST, complete with a titanium blade and carbide-coated edge; and the 9700 automatic version of the 975, purpose-designed for military and law enforcement personnel.

"We had a huge ground swell of support from the Special Forces guys," enthused Emerson. "The CQC-7 attained legendary status in the law enforcement and military circles. The knife saw use in all circles, from guys in high command to regular operators."

The Emerson and Benchmade collaboration was a win-win situation for both sides. Benchmade helped elevate Emerson's status in the production knife industry, and Emerson made a great number of custom-knife buyers aware of Benchmade. In part, the CQC-7's success helped pave the way for the formation of Emerson Knives Inc. The company's formation, in 1997, was a sign of things to come.

Year 1999 marked yet another milestone for the CQC-7 tactical folder. With Emerson at the helm of his own production knife company, it seemed only fitting that Emerson Knives would take over the production of the CQC-7. Thus, the Benchmade CQC-7 was discontinued and Emerson Knives picked up the pace from there. The Emerson CQC-7 retained the Benchmade design and performance characteristics, while at the same time embodying minor improvements.

The edges of the G-10 handles were radiused instead of chamfered, thereby offering a more comfortable grip. All screws on the knives were changed, including Phillips heads for the handle screws and a flathead screw for the pivot, eliminating the need for specialty drivers to adjust the pivot or field-strip the knife for thorough cleaning when necessary.

Emerson reports that the CQC-7 remained a top seller for the company throughout the years. It was, after all, his signature design! Things could not have gotten any better. Or could they?

In 2002, Emerson enhanced the CQC-7, making the tactical folder available with a patented Wave remote-pocket opener. What's the Wave? The Wave is a hook extending from the base of the blade nearest the handle. With the folder closed and the knife clipped via a pocket clip inside the front pants pocket of the average knife user, the Wave extension rides just below the pocket hem. When the folder is extracted from the pocket, the Wave almost naturally hooks onto the hem, opening the blade as the knife is pulled from the pocket, all in one swift, smooth motion.

At top is a Benchmade 970SBT black-bladed CQC-7, and below it is the original prototype of the CQC-7, a handmade knife by Ernest Emerson. The handmade Emerson is the very knife that Benchmade used as a model for its highly successful production model.

## The Knife World Does the Wave

The Emerson Commander was the first production knife to feature the Wave, and since its inception in 1998, the knife world has been "doin' the Wave." According to Emerson, after the CQC-7 Wave was introduced, the company experienced another huge surge in knife sales.

For people who were more utilitarian in their knife use, Emerson also introduced the CQC-7A, a knife virtually identical to the CQC-7, but with a more friendly spear-point blade. The CQC-7A was aimed at the outdoors and utility crowd who were looking for a sturdy folder that would stand up to heavy use.

The Super CQC-7 is the beefiest of all the CQC-7 designs, including a blade that stretches to nearly 4 inches. The knife is a handful, yet carries well due to its flat profile.

Emerson and crew just weren't satisfied with producing the CQC-7 in its original dimensions. Based on feedback from loyal customers all over the globe, 2004 saw the introduction of the Mini CQC-7. With a 2.9-inch blade, the Mini CQC-7 solved the dilemma for those who liked the CQC-7 but lived in municipalities where a 3.3-inch blade exceeded the legal size limit.

While the Mini CQC-7 is more pocket friendly in terms of physical size, it retains the bite and attitude of its bigger brother! And speaking of big brothers, the Emerson Super CQC-7 is a behemoth of a folding beauty, complete with a 3.78-inch blade made longer yet by a Wave remote pocket opener.

Amongst all the CQC-7 variations are several "flavors" of the models from which to choose. Optional blade finishes include a bead blasted, Black T, Green T, hard chrome, chromium nitride, and ceramic coatings in black or silver. For a couple years, Emerson offered the CQC-7 in a green G-10 handle, in addition to the standard black grip. There have been non-sharpened, blunt-tipped training-knife versions of the CQC-7, and pre-production hand-ground models for collectors seeking limited editions.

Derek Russell, sales manager of Emerson Knives, says that some of the most ardent of Emerson fans aren't even aware that there were damascus-blade versions of

**Benchmade's 9700 automatic was in production for only a short time. An auto-opening version of the 975, the blade was fired via a coil spring and the handles were thick G-10 sans liners.**

of an already tough-looking knife, the HD-7 just oozes testosterone!

What does the future hold for the CQC-7? In addition to offering the regular CQC-7, Mini CQC-7, Super CQC-7 and HD-7, and based on customer demand, Derek Russell hints at the possibility of bringing back the utilitarian CQC-7A. So, if this sounds good to you, let your voice be heard!

No other production tactical folder on record has enjoyed such a long run of success as the Emerson-designed CQC-7, and it's easy to see why, with its no-nonsense design and execution, the knife will stand up to any cutting task. Those who have used the CQC-7 extensively over the years know it like an old friend, and like man's other best friend, it's there with

the CQC-7. Made in extremely limited numbers, they sported Devin Thomas stainless-damascus blades. Collectors gobbled them up as fast as they were produced, Russell claims, and never again did Emerson make damascus variations of the storied tactical folder

**The HD-7 (Heavy Duty-7) is the next evolution of the legendary CQC-7 design. It's a beefed-up folder featuring a titanium integral lock mated with a G-10 handle and offering reduced weight and strength. The HD-7's blade is a bit wider than the regular CQC-7, as well, making it a beefier knife all the way around.**

## A Shout Out to Heavy D

In 2004, Emerson Knives celebrated the 10th anniversary of the CQC-7 by further refining and changing the venerable CQC-7. Enter the Heavy Duty 7 (HD-7), a beefed-up version of the CQC-7 with an integral lock.

"We changed some of the nuances of the basic CQC-7 design," Emerson remarked, adding that many of his customers had been asking him to make an integral-lock folder. The titanium, integral lock of the HD-7 added brute strength to an already strong design. Other noteworthy changes include a flared front end of the handle, forming a simple yet effective hand guard, and a blade made a bit longer to fill out the beefed-up look and construction.

Now a standard model in the Emerson production lineup, the HD-7 comes in two versions—an all-titanium, limited-edition model with a satin-finished blade and a 10th-anniversary logo; and a hybrid G-10/titanium version for a more subdued look and a reduction in overall weight.

The hybrid G-10/titanium model is available with either a black- or silver-ceramic-coated blade. The all-titanium HD-7 retails for $429, while the G-10/titanium combo is a much-easier-to-digest $364.95. A bulky version

you when you need it most, no matter what happens.

With Emerson's variations, including minor overall improvements, a great knife is made even better, further increasing its demand. There is no other tactical folder like the often imitated, never duplicated Emerson CQC-7. There never has been and never will be.

# Steel Sophisticates

◀ **XIKAR:** XIKAR has taken its 730 Express open-frame mid-lock folder and upgraded it with a selection of attractive natural materials, including a snakewood handle and a 440A stainless steel blade.

▲ **WILLIAM HENRY FINE KNIVES:** Part of the Da Vinci collection, the B05-WMD folder showcases a ZDP-stainless-damascus-laminate blade, a mokumé bolster/frame, an ancient walrus ivory handle, a thumb stud inset with a diamond and an 18k-gold bail.

▶ **C.A.S. IBERIA:** Here's one pearl of a folder, complete with an ATS-34 blade, a mother-of-pearl handle, engraved bolsters and an unusual locking mechanism that releases by moving the top side plate.

▶ **KERSHAW KNIVES:** The Nakamura folder employs a clad VG-10 and 420J2 stainless blade, a quince-wood handle and steel-and-copper bolsters.

▼ **CHRIS REEVE KNIVES:** The 21st Anniversary Sebenza is a frame-lock folder featuring a Gary House zebra-pattern mosaic damascus blade, a braided-leather lanyard, and a titanium handle inlaid with an Idaho star garnet and a 1.5mm diamond in a 14k-gold bezel. *(PointSeven photo)*

▲ **BUCK KNIVES:** The 777 Lumina features a 5mm LED light programmed for high, medium, low and flash beams, a 420HC stainless blade and a translucent-nylon handle.

# Pivotal Saws

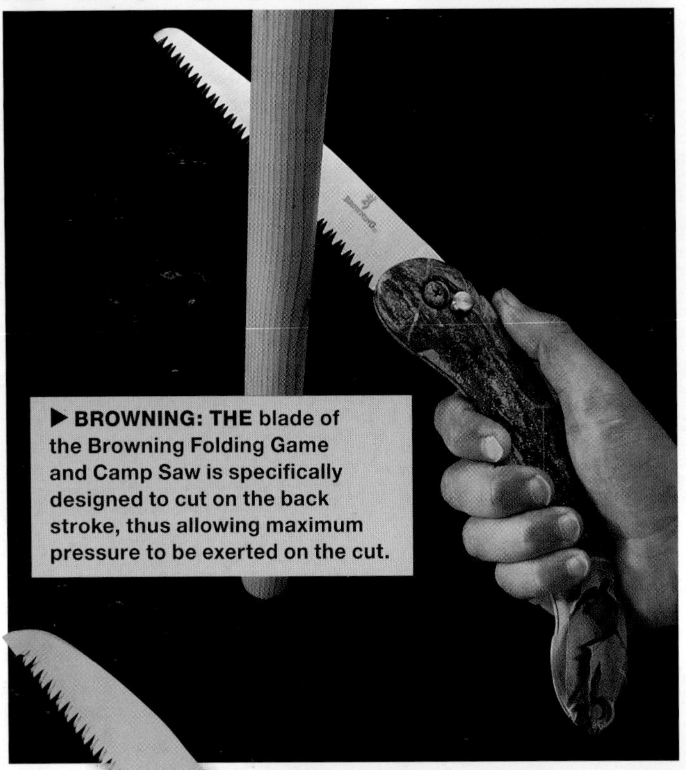

▶ **BROWNING: THE** blade of the Browning Folding Game and Camp Saw is specifically designed to cut on the back stroke, thus allowing maximum pressure to be exerted on the cut.

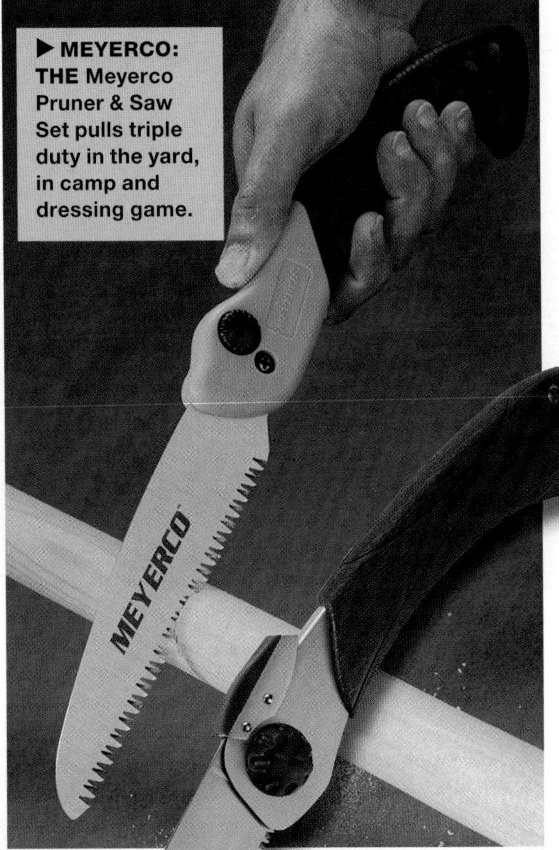


▶ **MEYERCO: THE** Meyerco Pruner & Saw Set pulls triple duty in the yard, in camp and dressing game.

▲ **GERBER LEGENDARY BLADES:** The Gerber Exchange-A-Blade comes with optional wood and bone-cutting blades. It's a dependable tool that locks up firmly and is comfortable to use.

▶ **SPYDERCO:** at an overall weight of 3 ounces, the SpyderSaw is designed for backpack hunters who need to shed every ounce.

◀ **SOG SPECIALTY KNIVES:** The SOG Revolver provides a robust hunting blade suitable for dressing deer and large game, along with an effective saw in the same package.

▶ **KERSHAW KNIVES:** The Swedish-steel teeth of the Kershaw folding saw are sharp and well suited for rapid cuts.

# The Tomahawk Team

▲ **COLD STEEL:** The primary bit of the Cold Steel Vietnam Tomahawk has a sharpened beard for hook cutting, and the rear of the head is a V-shaped spike. The piece also sports a hickory handle.

▼ **TOPS KNIVES:** Mike Fuller of TOPS Knives said the Outfitter's Axe can handle everything from heavy-duty chopping to detail work as fine as sharpening a pencil, the latter possible through the use of a "choke-up" hole in the axe head.

▲ **JEFF HALL:** Designed by Joel Pirela and made by Jeff Hall, the DETA2 is fashioned more like a sharpened pry bar than an axe.

▲ **EMERSON KNIVES INC.:** Made by American Tomahawk for Emerson Knives Inc., the CQC-T is an Ernest Emerson design including a 2 7/8-inch curved head of 4140 carbon steel. The "hawk" weighs 1 pound and stretches 13 3/4 inches.

▲ **STRIDER KNIVES:** Strider's new axe has a titanium body with an S-7 head and contact bits, and an electrically insulated handle.Its primary job is as a crash/ breacher's axe.

▲ **AMERICAN TOMAHAWK:** The LaGana Tactical Tomahawk has a drop-forged head of 1060 carbon steel and a modified-nylon handle. It weighs 1 pound.

# Lock, Stock and Safeties

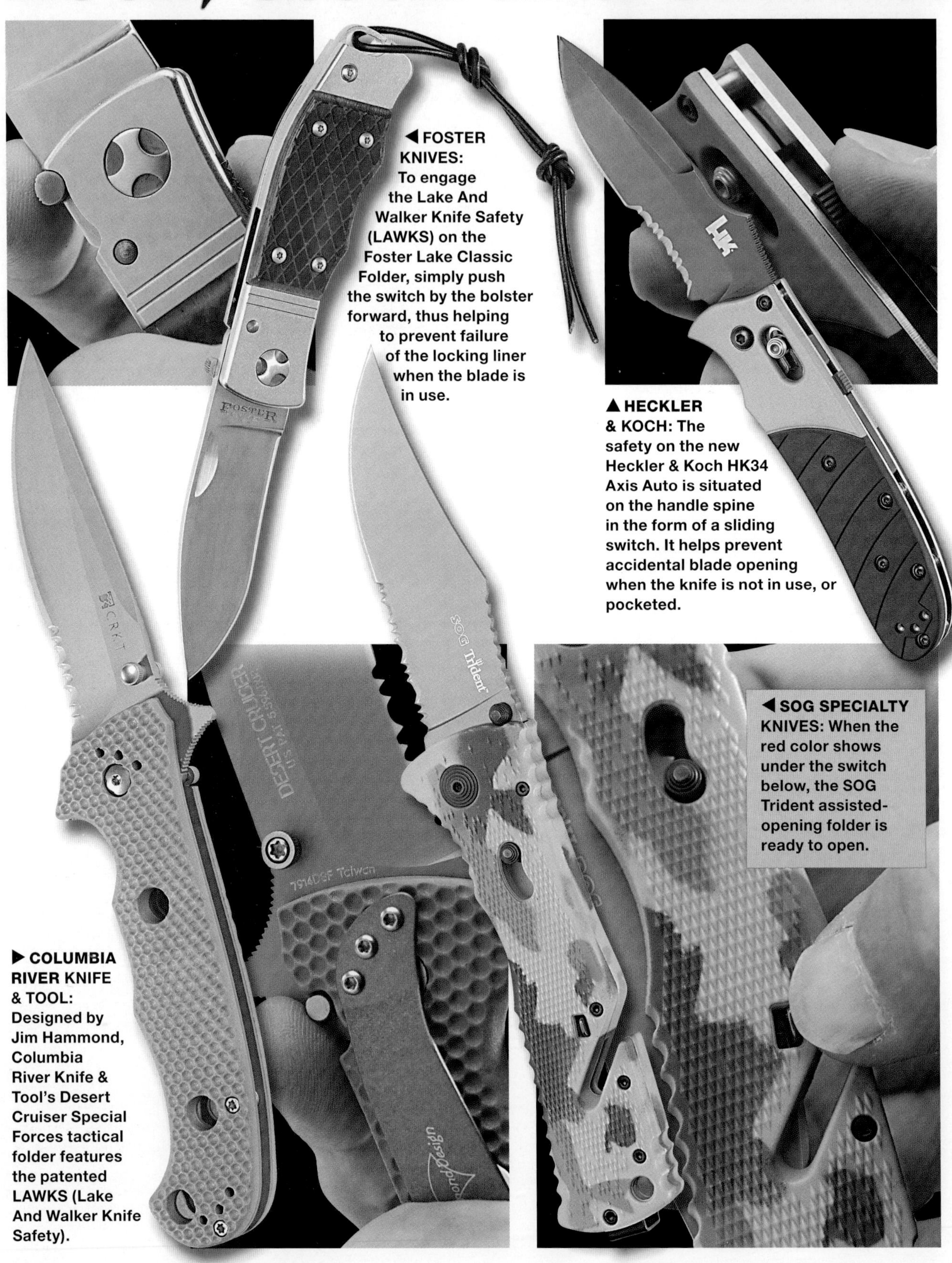


◀ **FOSTER KNIVES:** To engage the Lake And Walker Knife Safety (LAWKS) on the Foster Lake Classic Folder, simply push the switch by the bolster forward, thus helping to prevent failure of the locking liner when the blade is in use.

▲ **HECKLER & KOCH:** The safety on the new Heckler & Koch HK34 Axis Auto is situated on the handle spine in the form of a sliding switch. It helps prevent accidental blade opening when the knife is not in use, or pocketed.

◀ **SOG SPECIALTY KNIVES:** When the red color shows under the switch below, the SOG Trident assisted-opening folder is ready to open.

▶ **COLUMBIA RIVER KNIFE & TOOL:** Designed by Jim Hammond, Columbia River Knife & Tool's Desert Cruiser Special Forces tactical folder features the patented LAWKS (Lake And Walker Knife Safety).

▲ **BUCK KNIVES:** Situated on the handle spine just behind the centerline of the blade's pivot, the Cam Lock safety of the Buck Tempest works off its own pivot to trap the blade tang in the closed position. The safety keeps the blade from opening until the user pulls back on the Cam Lock to move it out of the way.

▲ **PRODUCTS: THE** ALSR (Air Land Sea Rescue) is the first rescue knife to feature the LAWKS safety so that the locking-liner of the two-blade folder, including a saw, does not fail. Some of the knife's features include a replaceable seat belt cutting blade, a window punch and a serrated N690 Co cobalt-stainless-steel, serrated, clip-point blade.

# Folders of Forward Thinking

▶ **KERSHAW KNIVES:** Made in the USA, the Offset features a state-of-the-art Metal Injection Molded and Hot Isostatic Pressed 440C blade. It also dons the latest SpeedSafe assisted-opening mechanism, the "Double Pumper," designed especially for the opening of large blades. *(PointSeven photo)*

▲ **COLUMBIA RIVER** KNIFE & TOOL: Ed Van Hoy designed the lock of the Snap Fire so that the locking blade is released when the pivot wheel is pressed down. *(PointSeven photo)*

▶ **BRADLEY CUTLERY** CO.: A folder that is just as cool as it looks, the Alias I sports a 3.6-inch CPM S30V blade, a 6AL-4V titanium handle, blue-anodized-aluminum barrel spacers, a blue thumb stud and a pocket clip.

▼ **SPYDERCO AND KERSHAW KNIVES:** A true knife-factory-to-knife-factory collaboration, the SpyKer combines Spyderco's ergonomics and patented one-hand-opening round hole in the blade with the looks of Kershaw/Ken Onion's "Bump" design. *(PointSeven photo)*

▶ **GERBER LEGENDARY** BLADES: The Fast Draw folder incorporates Forward Action Spring Technology (F.A.S.T.), a mechanism developed and patented by Butch Vallotton to release the locked blade via the slide of a button.

▼ **BUCK KNIVES:** With exceedingly smooth blade action and tight lock-up, the Buck/Mayo Cutback represents an excellent opportunity to obtain a Tom Mayo design for $45.

▶ **BOKER USA:** Designed by Dietmar Pohl, the Speedlock 3000 boasts a 3 3/8-inch 4034 stainless steel blade, a matte-finished aluminum handle and a walnut grip insert.

▲ **BENCHMADE KNIFE** CO.: A Mel Pardue design, the Mini Presidio showcases a 6061-T6 aluminum handle with bi-directional grooves, a 2.95-inch 154CM blade, double 420J stainless steel liners, dual thumb studs, a pocket clip and Benchmade's AXIS Lock mechanism.

# Heavy-Hitting Hunters

▶ **BROWNING:** The new Mirage knives employ replaceable blades of GIN5 stainless steel that can be switched out for fresh edges as quickly as the blades of the average razor.

▶ **FOX CUTLERY:** Knifemaker Allen Elishewitz designed the heavy-hitting hunter, complete with a bead-blasted N690C cobalt steel blade, a European stag handle inlay and stainless steel liners.

▶ **WILD BOAR BLADES:** Fresh from Kopromed and Wild Boar Blades is the Model 22 lock-back hunter, including a blade etch of running wild boars and an African hardwood handle.

▶ **WINCHESTER KNIVES:** The John Primble Muskrat gives the hunter handle choices that include mother-of-pearl, stag and two colors of jigged bone—burnt orange and antique green.

▶ **OUTDOOR EDGE:** Hunters should take a liking to the Caper-Lite featuring a 2 1/2-inch AUS-8 blade with a deep choil for choking up while working the edge, double stainless steel liners, dual thumb studs and a pocket clip.

◀ **BEAR AND SON CUTLERY:** Blackie Collins designed the CB87 Feathermate, a high-carbon stainless steel hunter with a cocobolo handle and oversized brass rivets.

# Top-of-the-Heap Tacticals

▶ **SPYDERCO:** Part of Spyderco's Byrd series of well-built but inexpensive knives, the Black Meadowlark features a stainless steel blade with a comet-shaped one-hand-opening hole and a fiberglass-reinforced-nylon handle.

▶ **SIGARMS: THE** Model SS02 locking-liner folder is patterned after the company's SIG Sauer P226 handgun.

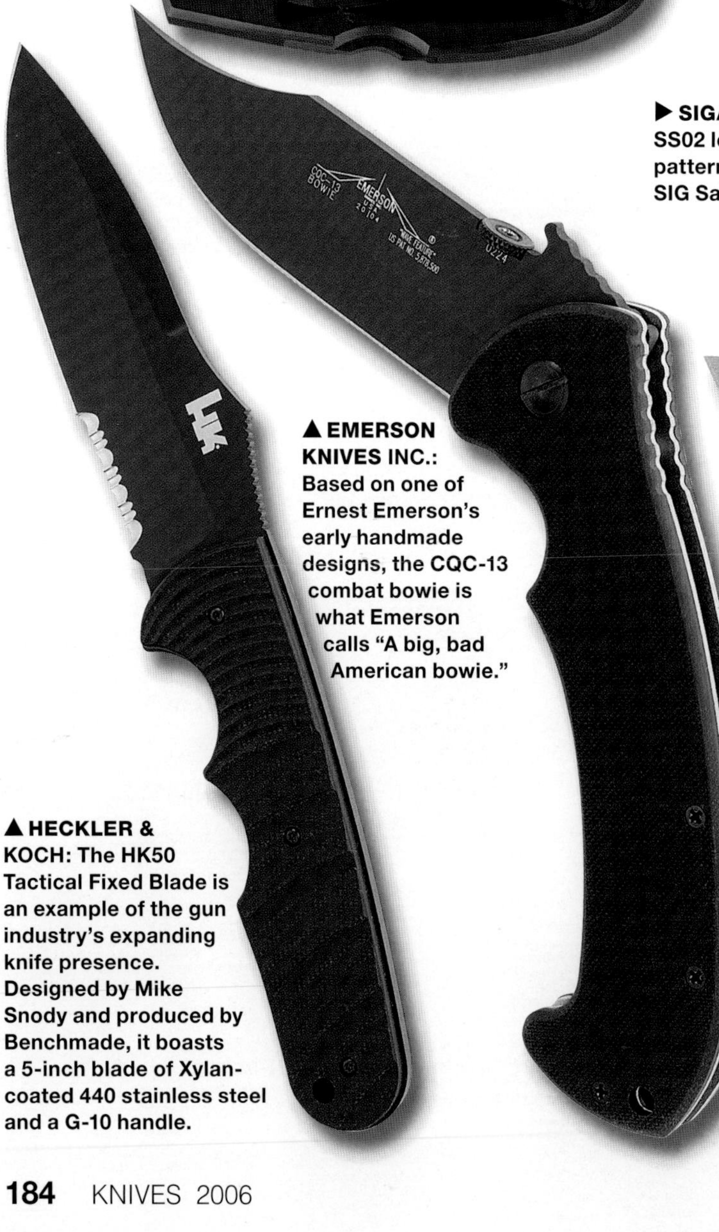

▲ **EMERSON KNIVES INC.:** Based on one of Ernest Emerson's early handmade designs, the CQC-13 combat bowie is what Emerson calls "A big, bad American bowie."

▶ **STRIDER KNIVES:** With a CPM S30V blade, a G-10 handle and a titanium sidelock, the PT Folder is anything but a retro model, it's a top-of-the-heap tactical.

▲ **HECKLER & KOCH:** The HK50 Tactical Fixed Blade is an example of the gun industry's expanding knife presence. Designed by Mike Snody and produced by Benchmade, it boasts a 5-inch blade of Xylan-coated 440 stainless steel and a G-10 handle.

▶ **CHRIS REEVE KNIVES:** New from Chris Reeve Knives is a variation on a classic design—the Classic Sebenza—but with sectional Micarta handle inlays, a bead-blasted-titanium handle frame and a stone-washed CPM S30V blade.

▲ **ONTARIO KNIFE CO.:** Catering to an ever-increasing police, military and rescue population, Ontario debuted the RAT-3 fixed blade that sports a 3.3-inch, full-tang, gray, textured, drop-point D-2 blade and a black-linen-Micarta® handle.

▶ **TAYLOR CUTLERY:** Smith & Wesson adds an assisted-opening folder to its line with the Black Ops tactical folder available from Taylor Cutlery.

◀ **UNITED CUTLERY:** Designed by Fred Carter for police, EMTs and firefighters, the Colt Rescue Knife from United features a blue-anodized 6061-T6 aluminum handle, a 420HC blade with a blunt tip for safety, an extra-large thumb disc for ease of use with gloved handles, a seat-belt cutter, a large lanyard hole, a carbide glass breaker and a stainless pocket clip.

◀ **THREE COMPANIES:** Several companies have unveiled knives designed to satisfy the needs of the military. Such pieces include, clockwise from the top, the Timberline N.S.W. (Navy Special Warfare), the Blackhawk Blades Kalista and the Simonich Knives Salish.

# KNIVES MARKETPLACE

## INTERESTING PRODUCT NEWS FOR BOTH THE CUTLER AND THE KNIFE ENTHUSIAST

The companies and individuals represented on the following pages will be happy to provide additional information — feel free to contact them.

# KNIVES MARKETPLACE

## SHARPEN YOUR KNIFE THE PROFESSIONAL WAY

You've seen them demonstrated at knife, gun and craft shows, State Fairs, sharpening booths in your local gun and pawn shops, major sporting retailers and by friends in their workshops. These knife sharpening wheels have been designed to help professional knifemakers to put a perfect edge on any knife, old or new. Perfected by Jantz Supply, these wheels are now the perfect size and grit to bring you the ultimate sharpening system available. In just seconds you can restore an old rusty knife to an unbelievably sharp useful tool. The two wheel set includes everything needed to start sharpening with your buffer or grinder. Each wheel is 8x3/4" and can be used on a 1/2" or 5/8" shaft. Complete sharpening outfits are available which include a Baldor buffer along with the wheels and compounds necessary to set up a professional sharpening center in your shop.

Visit their showroom located at 309 West Main, Davis, OK. Call 1-800-351-8900 to order yours today. Dealers inquire.

**JANTZ SUPPLY**
P.O. Box 584
Davis, OK 73030-0584
Phone: 800-351-8900 • Fax: 580-369-3082
Web: www.knifemaking.com

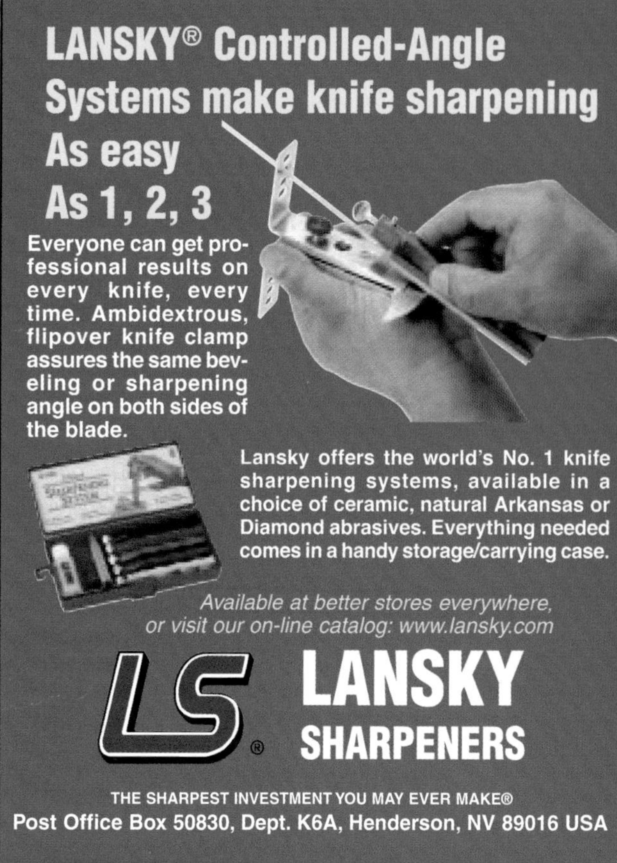

*"Handles With Care"*
*from*
**MASECRAFT SUPPLY COMPANY**

**Pearl, Horn, Bone, Exotic Woods, Micarta, G-10's, Carbon Fiber, Celluloids, Stag, ImiStag, Laminated Pearl Veneer Sheets, Color Ply Laminated Veneer Wood, Imitation Pearl, Alternative Ivory, Recon Stone and More**

***Call to order our catalog***
**P.O. Box 423 BL**
**254 Amity St.,**
**Meriden, CT 06450**
**Phone: (203) 238-3049**
E-mail: masecraft@masecraftsupply.necoxmail.com

# KNIVES MARKETPLACE

## GARY LEVINE FINE KNIVES
## A DEALER OF HANDMADE KNIVES

Gary's goal is to offer the collector the best custom knives available, in stock and ready for delivery. He has the best makers as well as the rising stars at fair prices. Gary enjoys working with collectors who want to enhance their collections, as well as someone who just wants a great knife to carry. Gary is also always on the lookout for collections, as well as single custom knives to purchase. Please stop by his Web site.

**GARY LEVINE FINE KNIVES**
P.O. Box 416, Ridgefield, CT 06877
Phone: 203-438-5294
Web: http://www.levineknives.com
E-mail: gary@levineknives.com

Timeless ~ Elegant ~ Functional

## MNANDI

Chris Reeve Knives' legacy of quality combined with performance is evident in this variation of the Mnandi.

Snakewood, inset with gold and diamonds, is inlaid on both sides into titanium handles. S30V blade, pocket clip of titanium and Integral Lock©.

The Mnandi is part of the CRK family that includes the One Piece Range, Sebenzas and Green Beret knives.

**www.chrisreeve.com**
**208-375-0367**

## KOVAL KNIVES

*The Finest in Knifemaking Equipment & Supplies For Over 25 Years!*

### The "Little Sharpie"

*Professional Knife Sharpening System*

**FEATURES:**
- 12" W x 18" L x 8" H & Weighs 28 lbs.
- 110V/1725 RPM, 1/4-HP Motor
- Uses Standard 1 x 30" Belts

**No. LSM1**..........................**$295**

### Evenheat Set-Pro Ovens

*Setpoint Control with Infinite Switch & Gauge*

**FEATURES:**
- New 3-Button Controller
- Simple Programming for Controlled Firings
- 240 Volts • 2300 degree F Max. Temp

**KF-13.55TP** ACI Set-Pro Control..........**$860**
**KF-18STP** ACI Set-Pro Control..........**$905**
**KF-22.55TP** ACI Set-Pro Control..........**$950**

Evenheat Set-Pro Oven

### Three Burner Whisper Low Boy Forge

*Uniform Heat-Self Regulating to 2350 Degrees*

**FEATURES:**
- Fuel of Choice-comes fitted for propane but may be configured for natural gas • Low profile/Open End Ports • 3" x 12" x 9" Firebox • Push Button Ignition • Hose, Gauge & Regulator Included • No blower Required-Venture Design • Weighs 55 lbs.

**KNC-3 1-HP, 120V**..................**$545**

Square Wheel Grinder

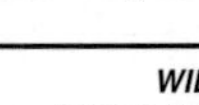

### WILTON
### Square Wheel Grinder

*Saves Costly Production Time & Money*

**FEATURES:**
- 2" x 72" Belt • Bench model, 1-HP 1 Phase, 115/230V TEFC motor • Belt speed of 4600 SFPM • Weighs 125 lbs.

**W-4103**..................................**$1,035**

**SLOW DOWN PULLY**
Converts high to low speed
30% reduction
**W-410375**..................................**$135**

CATALOG 2003/2004
KOVAL KNIVES

ORDER TODAY!
1-800-556-4837
For technical advice, please call 614-855-0777

KOVAL KNIVES

*For a complete Catalog of knifemaking supplies send $4.00 to:*
*Koval Knives • P.O. Box 492 • New Albany, OH 43054*

*Vist our Showroom at: 5819 Zarley St., New Albany, Ohio*
*Or Visit us online at: www.kovalknives.com • e mail: koval@kovalknives.com*

## PRO-TECH

**The Original Italian American**
**Proudly Made in the USA**

**Superior Spring Action**
**www.protechknives.com**

***FROM DUTY ON THE FRONT LINES...***

**Godfather™ Model 921 - USMC ($280)**

**Godson™ Model 752 ($290)**

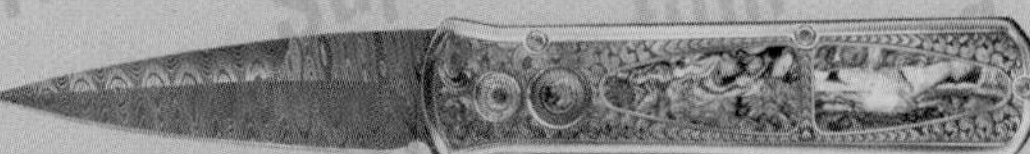

**Godson™ Ultimate Custom ($2,500)**

**Pro-Tech Knives, LLC**
**Santa Fe Springs, California**
**(562) 903-0678**

***...TO THE FRONT ROW OF YOUR COLLECTION***

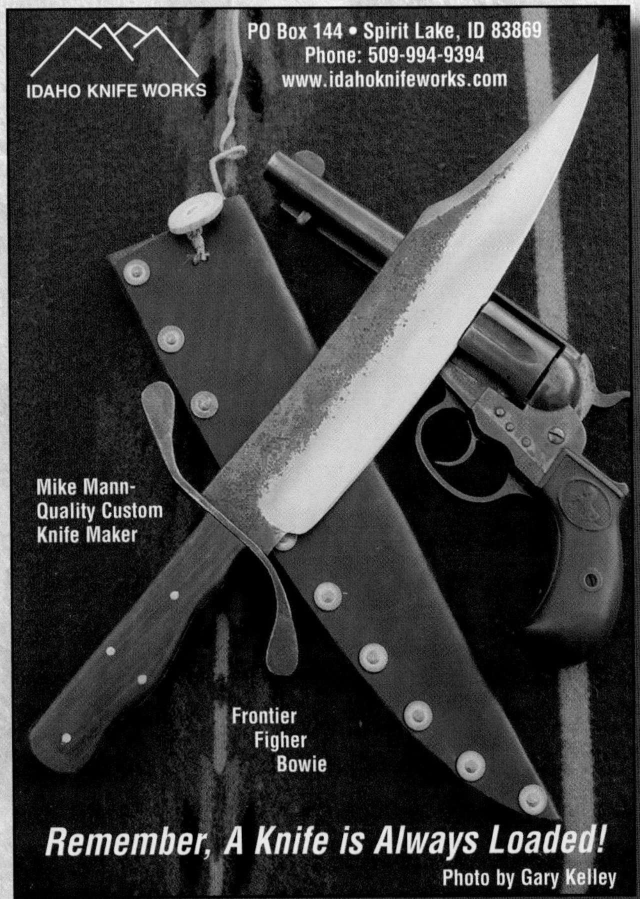
IDAHO KNIFE WORKS
PO Box 144 • Spirit Lake, ID 83869
Phone: 509-994-9394
www.idahoknifeworks.com
Mike Mann-
Quality Custom
Knife Maker
Frontier
Figher
Bowie
Remember, A Knife is Always Loaded!
Photo by Gary Kelley

# Knives Marketplace

# Knives Marketplace

WWW.BLADEGALLERY.COM
The Online Source for Fine Custom Knives
Mammouth Nouveau by Laurent Doussot
Mammoth Birdwing by Rick Dunkerley, M.S.
Model 17: Scagel Style Hunter by PJ Tomes, M.S.
BladeGallery.com, founded in 1998, is the premier source for fine custom knives on the internet. The best work from over 300 top makers from around the world is brought together and displayed with professional photographs. All these knives are competitively priced and may be purchased either online or at our retail gallery.
Continuing a tradition of excellence, The Epicurean Edge provides a gallery setting for the highest quality chef's knives and cutlery found anywhere. Among the many knives available are exquisitely handcrafted cutlery by Shigefusa, Thomas Haslinger, Kansui, Kobayashi, Ryusen, Hattori, Fiorini and many other renowned masters.
107 Central Way • Kirkland, WA 98033
877-562-5233 • 425-889-5980
Damascus San Mai Fruit Knife by Hattori
Shigefusa Deba Hocho, Damascus by Tokifusa Iizuka
eGallery.com
BG
ine Knives
Damasteel Santoku by WMF
Osage Orange Chef's Knife by Thomas Haslinger
The Epicurean Edge
The Knife that Makes the Meal ~ Cutlery for the Discerning Chef
WWW.EPICUREANEDGE.COM

# DIRECTORY



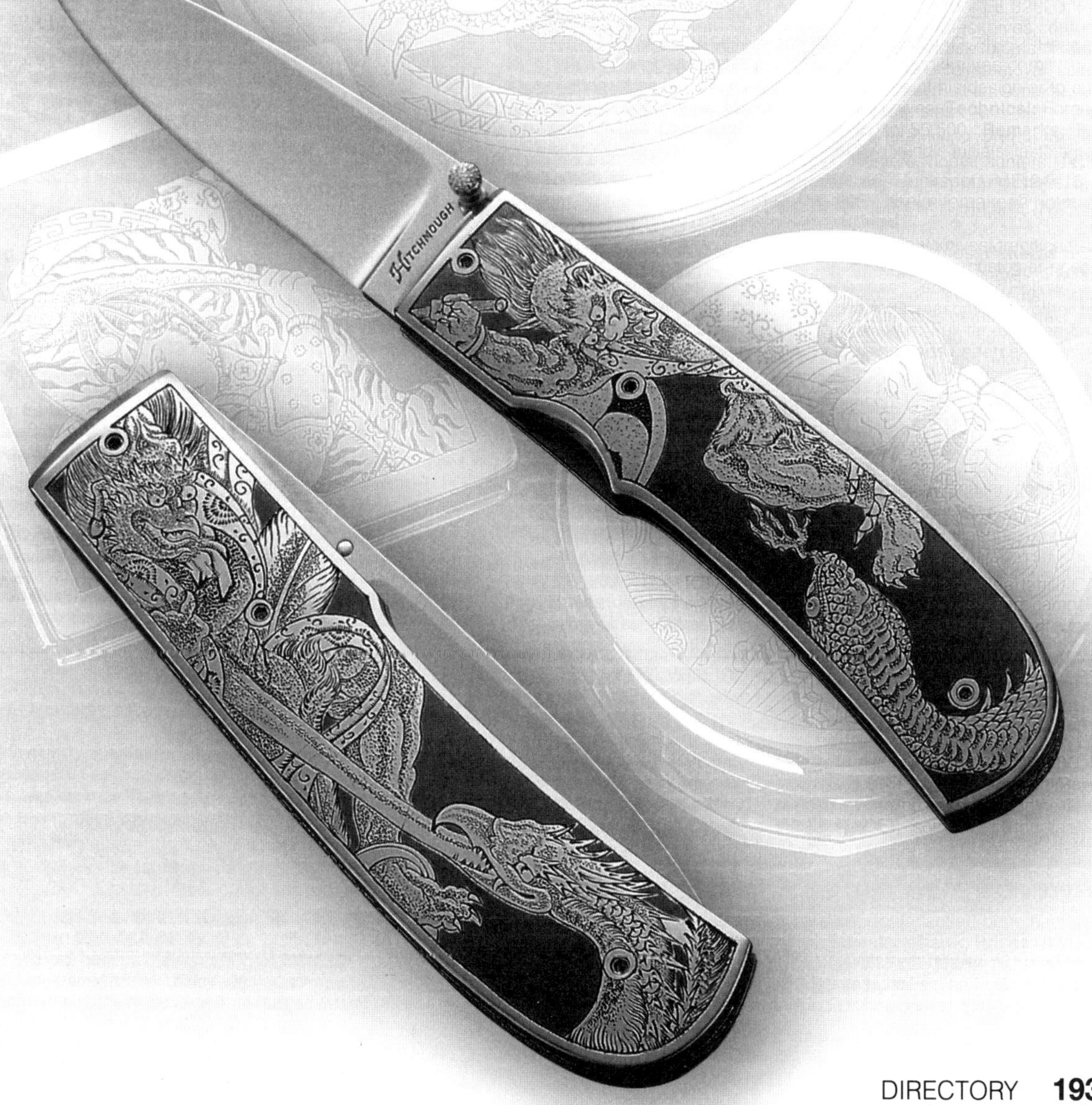

# A

**ABBOTT, WILLIAM M.,** Box 102A, RR #2, Chandlerville, IL 62627, Phone: 217-458-2325
**Specialties:** High-grade edged weapons. **Patterns:** Locking folders, Bowies, working straight knives, kitchen cutlery, minis. **Technical:** Grinds D2, ATS-34, 440C and commercial Damascus. Heat-treats; Rockwell tests. Prefers natural handle materials. **Prices:** $100 to $1,000. **Remarks:** Part-time maker; first knife sold in 1984. **Mark:** Name.

**ABEGG, ARNIE,** 5992 Kenwick Cr., Huntington Beach, CA 92648, Phone: 714-848-5697

**ABERNATHY, PAUL J.,** 3033 Park St., Eureka, CA 95501, Phone: 707-442-3593
**Specialties:** Period pieces and traditional straight knives of his design and in standard patterns. **Patterns:** Miniature daggers, fighters and swords. **Technical:** Forges and files SS, brass and sterling silver. **Prices:** $100 to $250; some to $500. **Remarks:** Part-time maker. Doing business as Abernathy's Miniatures. **Mark:** Stylized initials.

**ACKERSON, ROBIN E.,** 119 W Smith St., Buchanan, MI 49107, Phone: 616-695-2911

**ADAMS, LES,** 6413 NW 200 St., Hialeah, FL 33015, Phone: 305-625-1699
**Specialties:** Working straight knives of his design. **Patterns:** Fighters, tactical folders, waw enforcing autos. **Technical:** Grinds ATS-34, 440C and D2. **Prices:** $100 to $500. **Remarks:** Part-time maker; first knife sold in 1989. **Mark:** First initial, last name, Custom Knives.

**ADAMS, WILLIAM D.,** PO Box 439, Burton, TX 77835, Phone: 713-855-5643, Fax: 713-855-5638
**Specialties:** Hunter scalpels and utility knives of his design. **Patterns:** Hunters and utility/camp knives. **Technical:** Grinds 1095, 440C and 440V. Uses stabilized wood and other stabilized materials. **Prices:** $100 to $200. **Remarks:** Part-time maker; first knife sold in 1994. **Mark:** Last name in script.

**ADDISON, KYLE A.,** 809 N. 20th St, Murray, KY 42071, Phone: 270-759-1564, kylest2@yahoo.com
**Specialties:** Hand forged blades including Bowies, fighters and hunters. **Patterns:** Custom leather sheaths. **Technical:** Forges 5160, 1084, and his own Damascus. **Prices:** $175 to $1,500. **Remarks:** Part-time maker, first knife sold in 1996. **Mark:** First and middle initial, last name under "Trident" with knife and hammer. **Other:** ABS member.

**ADKINS, RICHARD L.,** 138 California Ct., Mission Viejo, CA 92692-4079

**AIDA, YOSHIHITO,** 26-7 Narimasu 2-chome, Itabashi-ku, Tokyo 175-0094, JAPAN, Phone: 81-3-3939-0052, Fax: 81-3-3939-0058
**Specialties:** High-tech working straight knives and folders of his design. **Patterns:** Bowies, lockbacks, hunters, fighters, fishing knives, boots. **Technical:** Grinds CV-134, ATS-34; buys Damascus; works in traditional Japanese fashion for some handles and sheaths. **Prices:** $400 to $900; some higher. **Remarks:** Full-time maker; first knife sold in 1978. **Mark:** Initial logo and Riverside West.

**ALBERICCI, EMILIO,** 19 Via Masone, 24100, Bergamo, ITALY, Phone: 01139-35-215120
**Specialties:** Folders and Bowies. **Patterns:** Collector knives. **Technical:** Uses stock removal with extreme lavoration accuracy; offers exotic and high-tech materials. **Prices:** Not currently selling. **Remarks:** Part-time maker. **Mark:** None.

**ALDERMAN, ROBERT,** 2655 Jewel Lake Rd., Sagle, ID 83860, Phone: 208-263-5996
**Specialties:** Classic and traditional working straight knives in standard patterns or to customer specs and his design; period pieces. **Patterns:** Bowies, fighters, hunters and utility/camp knives. **Technical:** Casts, forges and grinds 1084; forges and grinds L6 and O1. Prefers an old appearance. **Prices:** $100 to $350; some to $700. **Remarks:** Full-time maker; first knife sold in 1975. Doing business as Trackers Forge. **Mark:** Deer track. **Other:** Knife-making school. Two-week course for beginners; will cover forging, stock removal, hardening, tempering, case making. All materials supplies - $1,250.

**ALDRETE, BOB,** PO Box 1471, Lomita, CA 90717, Phone: 310-326-3041

**ALEXANDER, DARREL,** Box 381, Ten Sleep, WY 82442, Phone: 307-366-2699, daleywyo@tctwest.net
**Specialties:** Traditional working straight knives. **Patterns:** Hunters, boots and fishing knives. **Technical:** Grinds D2, 440C, ATS-34 and 154CM. **Prices:** $75 to $120; some to $250. **Remarks:** Full-time maker; first knife sold in 198[illegible] **Mark:** Name, city, state.

**ALEXANDER, JERED,** 213 Hogg Hill Rd., Dierks, AR 71833, Phone: 870-286-2981

**ALEXANDER, EUGENE,** Box 540, Ganado, TX 77962-0540, Phone: 512-771-3727

**ALLEN, MIKE "WHISKERS",** 12745 Fontenot Acres Rd., Malakoff, TX 75148, Phone: 903-489-1026, whiskersknives@aol.com Web: www.whiskersknives.com
**Specialties:** Working and collector-quality lockbacks, liner locks and aut[illegible] matic folders to customer specs. **Patterns:** Hunters, tantos, Bowies, swor[illegible] and miniatures. **Technical:** Grinds Damascus, 440C and ATS-34, engrave[illegible] **Prices:** $200 and up. **Remarks:** Full-time maker; first knife sold in 198[illegible] **Mark:** Whiskers and date.

**ALLRED, BRUCE F.,** 1764 N. Alder, Layton, UT 84041, Phone: 801-825-4612, allredbf@msn.com
**Specialties:** Custom hunting and utility knives. **Patterns:** Custom desig[illegible] that include a unique grind line, thumb and mosaic pins. **Technical:** ATS-3[illegible] 154CM and 440C. **Remarks:** The handle material include but not limited Micarta (in various colors), natural woods and reconstituted stone.

**ALVERSON, TIM (R.V.),** 4874 Bobbits Bench Rd., Peck, ID 83545, Phone: 208-476-3999, trvasma@orofino-id.com
**Specialties:** Fancy working knives to customer specs; other types on reque[illegible] **Patterns:** Bowies, daggers, folders and miniatures. **Technical:** Grinds 440[illegible] ATS-34; buys some Damascus. **Prices:** Start at $175. **Remarks:** Full-tir[illegible] maker; first knife sold in 1981. **Mark:** R.V.A. around rosebud.

**AMERI, MAURO,** Via Riaello No. 20, Trensasco St. Olcese, 16010 Ge[illegible] ova, ITALY, Phone: 010-8357077
**Specialties:** Working and using knives of his design. **Patterns:** Hunters, Bo[illegible] ies and utility/camp knives. **Technical:** Grinds 440C, ATS-34 and 154C[illegible] Handles in wood or Micarta; offers sheaths. **Prices:** $200 to $1,2[illegible] **Remarks:** Spare-time maker; first knife sold in 1982. **Mark:** Last name, city[illegible]

**AMMONS, DAVID C.,** 6225 N. Tucson Mtn. Dr., Tucson, AZ 85743, Phone: 520-307-3585
**Specialties:** Will build to suit. **Patterns:** Yours or mine. **Prices:** $250 [illegible] $2,000. **Mark:** AMMONS.

**AMOR JR., MIGUEL,** 10730 NW 7th St. Apt B, Miami, FL 33172, Phon[illegible] 305-812-3477
**Specialties:** Working and fancy straight knives in standard patterns; some[illegible] customer specs. **Patterns:** Bowies, hunters, fighters and tantos. **Technic[illegible]** Grinds 440C, ATS-34, carbon steel and commercial Damascus; forges so[illegible] in high-carbon steels. **Prices:** $125 to $500; some to $1,500 and high[illegible] **Remarks:** Part-time maker; first knife sold in 1983. **Mark:** Last name. On c[illegible] lectors' pieces: last name, city, state.

**AMOS, CHRIS,** , 550 S Longfellow, Tucson, AZ 85711, Phone: 520-2[illegible] 9752
**Specialties:** Traditional and custom, user-friendly working knives. **Patter[illegible]** Hunters, utility, camp, and primitive. Your design or mine. **Technical:** For[illegible] high-carbon steel, multiple quench differential hardening. **Prices:** $150 [illegible] up. **Remarks:** Part-time maker, member ABS, first knife sold in 1999. **Ma[illegible]** CAK (Chris Amos Knives).

**AMOUREUX, A.W.,** PO Box 776, Northport, WA 99157, Phone: 509-732-6292
**Specialties:** Heavy-duty working straight knives. **Patterns:** Bowies, fight[illegible] camp knives and hunters for world-wide use. **Technical:** Grinds 440C, A[illegible] 34 and 154CM. **Prices:** $80 to $2,000. **Remarks:** Full-time maker; first k[illegible] sold in 1974. **Mark:** ALSTAR.

**ANDERS, DAVID,** 157 Barnes Dr., Center Ridge, AR 72027, Phone: 501-893-2294
**Specialties:** Working straight knives of his design. **Patterns:** Bowies, figh[illegible] and hunters. **Technical:** Forges 5160, 1080 and Damascus. **Prices:** $22[illegible] $3200. **Remarks:** Part-time maker; first knife sold in 1988. Doing busines[illegible] Anders Knives. **Mark:** Last name/MS.

**ANDERS, JEROME,** 155 Barnes Dr., Center Ridge, AR 72027, Phon[illegible] 501-893-9981, Web: www.andersknives.com
**Specialties:** Case handles and pin work. **Patterns:** Layered and mo[illegible] steel. **Prices:** $275 and up. **Remarks:** All his knives are truly one-of-a-k[illegible] **Mark:** J. Anders in half moon.

**ANDERSEN, HENRIK LEFOLII,** Jagtvej 8, Groenholt, 3480, Fredens[illegible] borg, DENMARK, Phone: 0011-45-48483026
**Specialties:** Hunters and matched pairs for the serious hunter. **Techni[illegible]** Grinds A2; uses materials native to Scandinavia. **Prices:** Start at $[illegible] **Remarks:** Part-time maker; first knife sold in 1985. **Mark:** Initials with arro[illegible]

**ANDERSON, TOM,** 955 Canal Rd. Extd., Manchester, PA 17345, Phone: 717-266-6475, andersontech@suscom.net, Web: www.andersoncustomknives.com
**Specialties:** High-tech one-hand folders. **Patterns:** Fighters, utility, and dress knives. **Technical:** Grinds BG-42, S30V and Damascus. Uses titanium, carbon fiber and select natural handle materials. **Prices:** Start at $400. **Remarks:** First knife sold in 1996. **Mark:** Stylized A over T logo with maker's name.

**ANDERSON, MEL,** 17158 Lee Lane, Cedaredge, CO 81413-8247, Phone: 970-856-6465, Fax: 970-856-6463, artnedge1@wmconnect.com
**Specialties:** Full-size, miniature and one-of-a-kind straight knives and folders of his design. **Patterns:** Bowies, daggers, fighters, hunters and pressure folders. **Technical:** Grinds 440C, 5160, D2, 1095 and Damascus; offers antler, ivory and wood carved handles. **Prices:** Start at $145. **Remarks:** Knife maker and sculptor, full-time maker; first knife sold in 1987. **Mark:** Scratchy Hand.

**ANDERSON, MARK ALAN,** 1176 Poplar St, Denver, CO 80220, Phone: 720-941-9276, mcantdrive65@comcast.net Web: wwwmalancustomknives.com
**Specialties:** Stilettos. **Prices:** $750 to $1,800. **Remarks:** Most of my kives are automatic. **Mark:** Dragon head.

**ANDERSON, GARY D.,** 2816 Reservoir Rd., Spring Grove, PA 17362-9802, Phone: 717-229-2665
**Specialties:** From working knives to collectors quality blades, some folders. **Patterns:** Traditional and classic designs; customer patterns welcome. **Technical:** Forges Damascus carbon and stainless steels. Offers silver inlay, mokume, filework, checkering. **Prices:** $250 and up. **Remarks:** Part-time maker; first knife sold in 1985. **Mark:** GAND, MS. **Other:** Some engraving, scrimshaw and stone work.

**ANDRESS, RONNIE,** 415 Audubon Dr. N, Satsuma, AL 36572, Phone: 251-675-7604
**Specialties:** Working straight knives in standard patterns. **Patterns:** Boots, Bowies, hunters, friction folders and camp knives. **Technical:** Forges 1095, 5160, O1 and his own Damascus. Offers filework and inlays. **Prices:** $125 to $500. **Remarks:** Part-time maker; first knife sold in 1983. Doing business as Andress Knives. **Mark:** Last name, J.S. **Other:** Jeweler, goldsmith, gold work, stone setter. Not currently making knives.

**ANDREWS, ERIC,** 132 Halbert Street, Grand Ledge, MI 48837, Phone: 517-627-7304
**Specialties:** Traditional working and using straight knives of his design. **Patterns:** Full-tang hunters, skinners and utility knives. **Technical:** Forges carbon steel; heat-treats. All knives come with sheath; most handles are of wood. **Prices:** $80 to $160. **Remarks:** Part-time maker; first knife sold in 1990. Doing business as The Tinkers Bench.

**ANGELL, JON,** 22516 East C .R .1474, Hawthorne, FL 32640, Phone: 352-475-5380, syrjon@aol.com

**ANKROM, W.E.,** 14 Marquette Dr., Cody, WY 82414, Phone: 307-587-3017, Fax: 307-587-3017
**Specialties:** Best quality folding knives of his design. **Patterns:** Lock backs, liner locks, single high art. **Technical:** ATS-34 commercial Damascus. **Prices:** $500 and up. **Remarks:** Full-time maker; first knife sold in 1975. **Mark:** Name or name, city, state.

**ANSO, JENS,** GL. Skanderborgvej, 116, 8472 Sporup, DENMARK, Phone: 45 86968826, info@ansoknives.com Web: www.ansoknives.com
**Specialties:** Working knives of his own design. **Patterns:** Folders, baliaongs and fixedblades: Droppoints, sheepsfoots, hawkbill, tanto, recurve.**Technical:** Grinds RWL-34 Damasteel 530V. Hand rubbed or beadblasted finish. **Price:** $175 to $795, some up to $2,500. **Remarks:** Full-time maker since January 2002. First knife sold 1997. Doing business as ANSOKNIVES. **Mark:** ANSO and/or ANSO with logo.

**ANTONIO JR., WILLIAM J.,** 6 Michigan State Dr., Newark, DE 19713-1161, Phone: 302-368-8211, antonioknives@aol.com
**Specialties:** Fancy working straight knives of his design. **Patterns:** Hunting, survival and fishing knives. **Technical:** Grinds D2, 440C and 154CM; offers stainless Damascus. **Prices:** $125 to $395; some to $900. **Remarks:** Part-time maker; first knife sold in 1978. **Mark:** Last name.

**AOUN, CHARLES,** 69 Nahant St., Wakefield, MA 01880, Phone: 781-224-3353
**Specialties:** Classic and fancy straight knives of his design. **Patterns:** Fighters, hunters and personal knives. **Technical:** Grinds W2, 1095, ATS-34 and Damascus. Uses natural handle materials; embellishes with silver and semi-precious stones. **Prices:** Start at $290. **Remarks:** Part-time maker; first knife sold in 1995. Doing business as Galeb Knives. **Mark:** G stamped on ricasso or choil.

**APELT, STACY E.,** 8076 Moose Ave., Norfolk, VA 23518, Phone: 757-583-5872, sapelt@cox.net
**Specialties:** Exotic wood and burls, ivories, bowies, custom made knives to order. **Patterns:** Bowies, hunters, fillet, professional cutlery. **Technical:** Hand forging, stock removal, scrimshaw, carbon, stainless and Damascus steels. **Prices:** $65 to $3,500. **Remarks:** Professional Goldsmith. **Mark:** Stacy E. Apelt - Norfolk VA

**APPLEBY, ROBERT,** 43 N. Canal St., Shickshinny, PA 18655, Phone: 570-542-4335, r.appleby@juno.com Web: www.angelfire.com/pe2/applebyknives
**Specialties:** Working using straight knives and folders of his own and popular and historical designs. **Patterns:** Variety of straight knives and folders. **Technical:** Hand forged or grinds O-1, 1084, 5160, 440C, ATS-34, commercial Damascus, makes own sheaths. **Prices:** Starting at $75. **Remarks:** Part-time maker, first knife sold in 1995. **Mark:** APPLEBY over SHICKSHINNY, PA.

**APPLETON, RAY,** 244 S. Fetzer St., Byers, CO 80103-9748, rapltn@fone.net; Web: http://www.texinet.net/ray
**Specialties:** One-of-a-kind folding knives. **Patterns:** Unique folding multi-locks and high-tech patterns. **Technical:** All parts machined; D2, S7, 440C, and 6a14v. **Prices:** Start at $8,500. **Remarks:** Spare-time maker; first knife sold in 1986. **Mark:** Initials within arrowhead, signed and dated.

**ARBUCKLE, JAMES M.,** 114 Jonathan Jct., Yorktown, VA 23693, Phone: 757-867-9578, a_r_bukckle@hotmail.com
**Specialties:** One-of-a-kind of his design; working knives. **Patterns:** Mostly chefs knives and hunters. **Technical:** Forged and stock removal blades using exotic hardwoods, natural materials, Micarta and stabilized woods. Forge 5160, 1084 and 01; stock remove D2, ATS-34, 440C. Make own pattern welded steel. Prices; $150 to $700. **Remarks:** Forge, grind, heat-treat, finish and embellish all knives myself. Do own leatherwork and wood work. Part-time maker. **Mark:** J. Arbuckle or Arbuckle with maker below it. **Other:** ABS member; ASM member.

**ARCHER, RAY AND TERRI,** PO Box 129, Medicine Bow, WY 82329, Phone: 307-379-2567, archert@trib.com Web: http://www.archersknives.com
**Specialties:** High finish working straight knives and small one-of-a-kind. **Patterns:** Hunters/skinners, camping. **Technical:** ATS-34, 440C, S30V. Buys Damascus. **Price:** $75 to $650. **Remarks:** Make own sheaths; first knife sold 1994. **Mark:** Last name over city and state. **Other:** Member of PKA & OK CA (Oregon Knife Collector Assoc.)

**ARDWIN, COREY,** 4700 North Cedar, North Little Rock, AR 72116, Phone: 501-791-0301, Fax: 501-791-2974, Boog@hotmail.com

**ARM-KO KNIVES, ,** PO Box 76280, Marble Ray 4035 KZN, South Africa, Phone: 27 31 5771451, arm-koknives.co.za Web: www.arm-koknives.co.za
**Specialties:** They will make what your fastidious taste desires. Be it cool collector or tenacious tactical with handles of mother of pearl, fossil & local ivories. Exotic dye/stabilized burls, giraffe bone, horns, carbon fiber, g 10, and titanium etc. **Technical:** Via stock removal, grinding Damasteel, carbon & mosaic. Damascus, ATS-34, N690, 440A, 440B, 12 C 27 RWL34 and high carbon EN 8, 5160 all heat treated in house. **Prices:** From $200 and up. **Remarks:** Father a part-time maker for well over 10 years and member of knifemakers guild in SA. Son full-time maker over 3 years. **Mark:** Logo of initials A R M and H A R M "Edged Tools".

**ARNOLD, JOE,** 47 Patience Cres., London, Ont., CANADA N6E 2K7, Phone: 519-686-2623
**Specialties:** Traditional working and using straight knives of his design and to customer specs. **Patterns:** Fighters, hunters and Bowies. **Technical:** Grinds 440C, ATS-34 and 5160. **Prices:** $75 to $500; some to $2,500. **Remarks:** Part-time maker; first knife sold in 1988. **Mark:** Last name, country.

**ARROWOOD, DALE,** 556 Lassetter Rd., Sharpsburg, GA 30277, Phone: 404-253-9672
**Specialties:** Fancy and traditional straight knives of his design and to customer specs. **Patterns:** Bowies, fighters and hunters. **Technical:** Grinds ATS-34 and 440C; forges high-carbon steel. Engraves and scrimshaws. **Prices:** $125 to $200; some to $245. **Remarks:** Part-time maker; first knife sold in 1989. **Mark:** Anvil with an arrow through it; Old English "Arrowood Knives".

**ASHBY, DOUGLAS,** 10123 Deermont, Dallas, TX 75243, Phone: 214-238-7531
**Specialties:** Traditional and fancy straight knives of his design or to customer specs. **Patterns:** Hunters, fighters and utility/camp knives. **Technical:** Grinds 440C, ATS-34 and commercial Damascus. **Prices:** $75 to $200; some to $500. **Remarks:** Part-time maker; first knife sold in 1990. **Mark:** Name, city.

**ASHWORTH, BOYD,** 1510 Bullard Place, Powder Springs, GA 30127, Phone: 770-422-9826, boydashworth@comcast.net Web: www.boydashworthknives.com
**Specialties:** Turtle folders. Fancy Damascus locking folders. **Patterns:** Fighters, hunters and gents. **Technical:** Forges own Damascus; offers filework; uses exotic handle materials. **Prices:** $500 to $2,500. **Remarks:** Part-time maker; first knife sold in 1993. **Mark:** Last name.

**ATHEY, STEVE,** 3153 Danube, Riverside, CA 92503, Phone: 951-850-8618
**Specialties:** One of a kind designs. **Patterns:** Bowies, hunters.**Technical:** Stock removal. **Prices:** $125 to $500. **Remarks:** Part-time maker. **Mark:** Last name on blade.

**ATKINSON, DICK,** General Delivery, Wausau, FL 32463, Phone: 850-638-8524
**Specialties:** Working straight knives and folders of his design; some fancy. **Patterns:** Hunters, fighters, boots; locking folders in interframes. **Technical:** Grinds A2, 440C and 154CM. Likes filework. **Prices:** $85 to $300; some exceptional knives. **Remarks:** Full-time maker; first knife sold in 1977. **Mark:** Name, city, state.

**AYARRAGARAY, CRISTIAN L.,** Buenos Aires 250, (3100) Parana-Entre Rios, ARGENTINA, Phone: 043-231753
**Specialties:** Traditional working straight knives of his design. **Patterns:** Fishing and hunting knives. **Technical:** Grinds and forges carbon steel. Uses native Argentine woods and deer antler. **Prices:** $150 to $250; some to $400. **Remarks:** Full-time maker; first knife sold in 1980. **Mark:** Last name, signature.

**BAARTMAN, GEORGE,** PO Box 1116, Bela-Bela 0480, Limpopo, SOUTH AFRICA, Phone: 27 14 736 4036, Fax: 27 14 736 4036, baartmanknives@hotmail.com
**Specialties:** Fancy and working liner lock folders of own design and to customers specs. Specialize in pattern filework on liners. Specialize in pattern filework on liners. **Patterns:** Liner lock folders. **Technical:** Grinds 12C27, ATS-34, and Damascus, prefer working with stainless damasteel. Hollow grinds to hand-rubbed and polished satin finish. Enjoys working with mammoth, warthog tusk and pearls. **Prices:** Folders from $260 to $800. **Remarks:** Part-time maker. Member of the Knifemakers Guild of South Africa since 1993. **Mark:** BAARTMAN.

**BABCOCK, RAYMOND G.,** 179 Lane Rd., Vincent, OH 45784, Phone: 614-678-2688
**Specialties:** Plain and fancy working straight knives.Will make knives to his design and to custom specifications. **Patterns:** Hunting knives and Bowies. **Technical:** Hollow grinds L6. **Prices:** $100 to $500. **Remarks:** Part-time maker; first knife sold in 1973. **Mark:** First initial and last name; R. Babcock.

**BACHE-WIIG, TOM,** N-5966, Eivindvik, NORWAY, Phone: 4757784290, Fax: 4757784122
**Specialties:** High-art and working knives of his design. **Patterns:** Hunters, utility knives, hatchets, axes and art knives. **Technical:** Grinds Uddeholm Elmax, powder metallurgy tool stainless steel. Handles made of rear burls of Nordic woods stabilized with vacuum/high-pressure technique. **Prices:** $430 to $900; some to $2,300. **Remarks:** Part-time maker; first knife sold 1988. **Mark:** Etched name and eagle head.

**BACON, DAVID R.,** 906 136th St. E., Bradenton, FL 34202-9694, Phone: 813-996-4289

**BAGLEY, R. KEITH,** Old Pine Forge, 4415 Hope Acres Dr., White Plains, MD 20695, Phone: 301-932-0990, oldpineforge@hotmail.com
**Specialties:** High-carbon Damascus with semi-precious stones set in exotic wood handle; tactical and skinner knives. **Technical:** Use ATS-34, 5160, 01, 1085, 1095. **Patterns:** Various patterns; prefer all Tool-Steel and Nickel Damascus. **Price:** Damascus from $250 to $500; stainless from $100 to $225. **Remarks:** Farrier for 25 years, blacksmith for 25 years, knife maker for 10 years.

**BAILEY, RYAN,** 4185 S. St. Rt. 605, Galena, OH 43021, Phone: 740-965-9970, dr@darrelralph.com Web: www.darrelralph.com
**Specialties:** Fancy, high-art, high-tech, collectible straight knives and folders of his design and to customer specs; unique mechanisms, some disassemble. **Patterns:** Daggers, fighters and swords. **Technical:** Does own Damascus and forging from high-carbon. Embellishes with file work and gold work. **Prices:** $200 to $2,500. **Remarks:** Full-time maker; first knife sold in 1999. Doing business as Briar Knives. **Mark:** RLB.

**BAILEY, JOSEPH D.,** 3213 Jonesboro Dr., Nashville, TN 37214, Phone: 615-889-3172, jbknfemkr@aol.com
**Specialties:** Working and using straight knives; collector pieces. **Patterns** Bowies, hunters, tactical, folders. **Technical:** 440C, ATS-34, Damascus an wire Damascus. Offers scrimshaw. **Prices:** $85 to $1,200. **Remarks:** Part time maker; first knife sold in 1988. **Mark:** Joseph D Bailey Nashville Tennessee.

**BAILEY, KIRBY C.,** 2055 F.M. 2790 W., Lytle, TX 78052, Phone: 830-772-3376
**Specialties:** All kinds of knives folders, fixed blade, fighters. **Patterns:** Hun ers, folders, fighters, Bowies, miniatures. **Technical:** Does all his own wor heat treating, file work etc. **Prices:** $200 to $1,000. **Remarks:** Builds any kin of hand cutlery. Have made knives for 45 years; sold knives for 28 years **Mark:** K.C.B. and serial #. **Other:** Have sold knives in Asia and all states i US.

**BAKER, HERB,** 14104 NC 87 N., Eden, NC 27288, Phone: 336-627-0338

**BAKER, RAY,** PO Box 303, Sapulpa, OK 74067, Phone: 918-224-8013
**Specialties:** High-tech working straight knives. **Patterns:** Hunters, fighter Bowies, skinners and boots of his design and to customer specs. **Technica** Grinds 440C, 1095 spring steel or customer request; heat-treats. Custon made scabbards for any knife. **Prices:** $125 to $500; some to $1,00 **Remarks:** Full-time maker; first knife sold in 1981. **Mark:** First initial, la name.

**BAKER, VANCE,** 574 Co. Rd. 675, Riceville, TN 37370, Phone: 423-745-9157
**Specialties:** Traditional working straight knives of his design and to custom specs. Prefers drop-point hunters and small Bowies. **Patterns:** Hunters, util and kitchen knives. **Technical:** Forges Damascus, cable, L6 and 516 **Prices:** $100 to $250; some to $500. **Remarks:** Part-time maker; first kni sold in 1985. **Mark:** Initials connected.

**BAKER, WILD BILL,** Box 361, Boiceville, NY 12412, Phone: 914-657-8646
**Specialties:** Primitive knives, buckskinners. **Patterns:** Skinners, camp kniv and Bowies. **Technical:** Works with L6, files and rasps. **Prices:** $100 to $35 **Remarks:** Part-time maker; first knife sold in 1989. **Mark:** Wild Bill Baker, O Leaf Forge, or both.

**BALBACH, MARKUS,** Heinrich - Worner - Str. 3, 35789 Weilmunster-Laubuseschbach/Ts., GERMANY 06475-8911, Fax: 912986, Web: www.schmiede-balbach.de
**Specialties:** High-art knives and working/using straight knives and folders his design and to customer specs. **Patterns:** Hunters and daggers. **Tech cal:** Stainless steel, one of Germany's greatest Smithies. Supplier for t forges of Solingen. **Remarks:** Full-time maker; first knife sold in 1984. Doi business as Schmiedewerkstatte M. Balbach. **Mark:** Initials stamped ins the handle.

**BALDWIN, PHILLIP,** PO Box 563, Snohomish, WA 98290, Phone: 42 334-5569, phb@drizzle.com
**Specialties:** One-of-a-kind elegant table cutlery; exotics. **Patterns:** Elegant exotic knives. Likes the challenge of axes, spears and specialty tools. **Tech cal:** Forges W2, W1 and his own pattern welded steel and mokume-ga **Prices:** Start at $1,000. **Remarks:** Full-time maker; first knife sold in 19 **Mark:** Last initial marked with chisel.

**BALL, KEN,** 127 Sundown Manor, Mooresville, IN 46158, Phone: 317 834-4803
**Specialties:** Classic working/using straight knives of his design and to c tomer specs. **Patterns:** Hunters and utility/camp knives. **Technical:** F grinds ATS-34. Offers filework. **Prices:** $150 to $400. **Remarks:** Part-ti maker; first knife sold in 1994. Doing business as Ball Custom Knives. **Ma** Last name.

**BALLESTRA, SANTINO,** via D. Tempesta 11/17, 18039 Ventimiglia (IM), ITALY 0184-215228, ladasin@libero.it
**Specialties:** Using and collecting straight knives. **Patterns:** Hunting, fighti skinners, Bowies, medieval daggers and knives. **Technical:** Forges ATS-D2, O2, 1060 and his own Damascus. Uses ivory and silver. **Prices:** $50 $2,000; some higher. **Remarks:** Full-time maker; first knife sold in 19 **Mark:** First initial, last name.

**BALLEW, DALE,** PO Box 1277, Bowling Green, VA 22427, Phone: 8 633-5701
**Specialties:** Miniatures only to customer specs. **Patterns:** Bowies, dagg and fighters. **Technical:** Files 440C stainless; uses ivory, abalone, ex woods and some precious stones. **Prices:** $100 to $800. **Remarks:** Part-t maker; first knife sold in 1988. **Mark:** Initials and last name.

**BANKS, DAVID L.,** 99 Blackfoot Ave., Riverton, WY 82501, Phone: 307-856-3154/Cell:307-851-5599
**Specialties:** Heavy-duty working straight knives. **Patterns:** Hunters, Bowies and camp knives. **Technical:** Forges Damascus 1084-15N20, L-6-W1 pure nickel, 5160, 52100 and his own Damascus; differential heat treat and tempers. Handles made of horn, antlers and exotic wood. Hand-stitched harness leather sheaths. **Prices:** $300 to $2,000. **Remarks:** Part-time maker. **Mark:** Banks Blackfoot forged Dave Banks and initials connected.

**BARDSLEY, NORMAN P.,** 197 Cottage St., Pawtucket, RI 02860, Phone: 401-725-9132, www.bardsleydistinctiveweaponry.com or www.bardsleycustomknives.com
**Specialties:** Working and fantasy knives. **Patterns:** Fighters, boots, fantasy, renaissance and native American in upscale and presentation fashion. **Technical:** Grinds all steels and Damascus. Uses exotic hides for sheaths. **Prices:** $100 to $15,000. **Remarks:** Full-time maker. **Mark:** Last name in script with logo.

**BAREFOOT, JOE W.,** 117 Oakbrook Dr., Liberty, SC 29657
**Specialties:** Working straight knives of his design. **Patterns:** Hunters, fighters and boots; tantos and survival knives. **Technical:** Grinds D2, 440C and ATS-34. Mirror finishes. Uses ivory and stag on customer request only. **Prices:** $50 to $160; some to $500. **Remarks:** Part-time maker; first knife sold in 1980. **Mark:** Bare footprint.

**BARKER, REGGIE,** 603 S. Park Dr., Springhill, LA 71075, Phone: 318-539-2958, wrbarker@cmaaccess.com Web: www.reggiebarkerknives.com
**Specialties:** Camp knives and hatchets. **Patterns:** Bowie, skinning, hunting, camping, fighters, kitchen or customer design. **Technical:** Forges carbon steel and own pattern welded steels. **Prices:** $225 to $2,000. **Remarks:** Full-time maker. Winner of 1999 and 2000 Spring Hammering Cutting contest. Winner of Best Value of Show 2001; Arkansas Knife Show and Journeyman-Smith. **Mark:** Barker JS. **Other:** Border Guard Forge.

**BARKER, ROBERT G.,** 2311 Branch Rd., Bishop, GA 30621, Phone: 706-769-7827
**Specialties:** Traditional working/using straight knives of his design. **Patterns:** Bowies, hunters and utility knives, ABS Journeyman Smith. **Technical:** Hand forged carbon and Damascus. Forges to shape high-carbon 5160, cable and chain. Differentially heat-treats. **Prices:** $200 to $500; some to $1,000. **Remarks:** Spare-time maker; first knife sold in 1987. **Mark:** BARKER/J.S.

**BARLOW, JANA POIRIER,** 3820 Borland Cir., Anchorage, AK 99517, Phone: 907-243-4581

**BARNES, AUBREY G.,** 11341 Rock Hill Rd., Hagerstown, MD 21740, Phone: 301-223-4587, a.barnes@myactv.net
**Specialties:** Classic Moran style reproductions and using knives of his own design. **Patterns:** Bowies, hunters, fighters, daggers and utility/camping knives. **Technical:** Forges 5160, 1085, L6 and Damascus, Silver wire inlays. **Prices:** $300 to $2,500. **Remarks:** Full-time maker; first knife sold in 1992. Doing business as Falling Waters Forge. **Mark:** First and middle initials, last name, M.S.

**BARNES, GARY L.,** Box 138, New Windsor, MD 21776-0138, Phone: 410-635-6243, Fax: 410-635-6243
**Specialties:** Ornate button lock Damascus folders. **Patterns:** Barnes original. **Technical:** Forges own Damascus. **Prices:** Average $2,500. **Remarks:** ABS Master Smith since 1983. **Mark:** Hand engraved logo of letter B pierced by dagger.

**BARNES, JACK,** PO Box 1315, Whitefish, MT 59937-1315, Phone: 406-862-6078

**BARNES, WENDELL,** PO Box 272, Clinton, MT 59825, Phone: 406-825-0908
**Specialties:** Working straight knives. **Patterns:** Hunters, folders, neck knives. **Technical:** Grinds 440C, ATS-34, D2 and Damascus. **Prices:** Start at $75. **Remarks:** Spare-time maker; first knife sold in 1996. **Mark:** First initial and last name around broken heart.

**BARNES, GREGORY,** 266 W. Calaveras St., Altadena, CA 91001, Phone: 626-398-0053, snake@annex.com

**BARNES, WILLIAM,** 591 Barnes Rd., Wallingford, CT 06492-1805, Phone: 860-349-0443

**BARNES, MARLEN R.,** 904 Crestview Dr.S., Atlanta, TX 75551-1854, Phone: 903-796-3668, MRBlives@worldnet.att.net
**Specialties:** Hammer forges random and mosaic Damascus. **Patterns:** Hatchets, straight and folding knives. **Technical:** Hammer forges carbon steel using 5160, 1084 and 52100 with 15N20 and 203E nickel. **Prices:** $150 and up. **Remarks:** Part-time maker; first knife sold 1999. **Mark:** Script M.R.B., other side J.S.

**BARNES, ERIC,** H C 74 Box 41, Mountain View, AR 72560, Phone: 501-269-3358

**BARNES JR., CECIL C.,** 141 Barnes Dr., Center Ridge, AR 72027, Phone: 501-893-2267

**BARNETT, VAN,** Barnett Int'l Inc., 1135 Terminal Way Ste. #209, Reno, NV 89502, Phone: 866 ARTKNIFE or 304-727-5512, Fax: 775-201-0038, Artknife@vanBarnett.com Web: www.VanBarnett.com
**Specialties:** Collector grade one-of-a-kind / embellished high art daggers and art folders. **Patterns:** Art daggers and folders. **Technical:** Forges and grinds own Damascus. **Prices:** Upscale. **Remarks:** Designs and makes one-of-a-kind highly embellished art knives using high karat gold, diamonds and other gemstones, pearls, stone and fossil ivories, carved steel guards and blades, all knives are carved and or engraved, does own engraving, carving and other embellishments, sole authorship; full-time maker since 1981. **Mark:** V. H. Barnett or Van Barnett in script. **Other:** Does one high art collaboration a year with Dellana. Voting Member of Knifemakers Guild. Member of ABS.

**BARNGROVER, JERRY,** RR. #4, Box 1230, Afton, OK 74331, Phone: 918-257-5076

**BARR, A.T.,** 153 Madonna Dr., Nicholasville, KY 40356, Phone: 859-887-5400, Web: www.customknives.com
**Specialties:** Fine Gent's user and collector grade liner lock folders and sheat knives. **Patterns:** Liner lock folders and sheath knives. **Technical:** Flat grinds S30V, ATS-34, D-2 commercial Damascus; all knives have a hand rubbed satin finish. Does all leather work. **Prices:** Start at $250 for folders and $200 for sheath knives. **Remarks:** Full-time maker, first knife sold in 1979. **Mark:** Full name. **Other:** Knifemakers' Guild Voting member. "Don't you buy no ugly knife."

**BARR, JUDSON C.,** 1905 Pickwick Circle, Irving, TX 75060, Phone: 972-790-7195
**Specialties:** Bowies. **Patterns:** Sheffield and Early American. **Technical:** Forged carbon steel and Damascus. Also stock removal. **Remarks:** Journeyman member of ABS **Mark:** Barr.

**BARRETT, CECIL TERRY,** 2514 Linda Lane, Colorado Springs, CO 80909, Phone: 719-473-8325
**Specialties:** Working and using straight knives and folders of his design, to customer specs and in standard patterns. **Patterns:** Bowies, hunters, kitchen knives, locking folders and slip-joint folders. **Technical:** Grinds 440C, D2 and ATS-34. Wood and leather sheaths. **Prices:** $65 to $500; some to $750. **Remarks:** Full-time maker. **Mark:** Stamped middle name.

**BARRETT, RICK L. (TOSHI HISA),** 18943 CR .18, Goshen, IN 46528, Phone: 574-533-4297, barrettrick@hotmail.com
**Specialties:** Japanese-style blades from sushi knives to katana and fantasy pieces. **Patterns:** Swords, axes, spears/lances, hunter and utility knives. **Technical:** Forges and grinds Damascus and carbon steels, occasionally uses stainless. **Prices:** $250 to $4,000+. **Remarks:** Full-time bladesmith, jeweler. **Mark:** Japanese mei on Japanese pieces and stylized initials.

**BARRON, BRIAN,** 123 12th Ave., San Mateo, CA 94402, Phone: 650-341-2683
**Specialties:** Traditional straight knives. **Patterns:** Daggers, hunters and swords. **Technical:** Grinds 440C, ATS-34 and 1095. Sculpts bolsters using an S-curve. **Prices:** $130 to $270; some to $1,500. **Remarks:** Part-time maker; first knife sold in 1993. **Mark:** Diamond Drag "Barron".

**BARRY III, JAMES J.,** 115 Flagler Promenade No., West Palm Beach, FL 33405, Phone: 561-832-4197
**Specialties:** High-art working straight knives of his design also high art tomahawks. **Patterns:** Hunters, daggers and fishing knives. **Technical:** Grinds 440C only. Prefers exotic materials for handles. Most knives embellished with filework, carving and scrimshaw. Many pieces designed to stand unassisted. **Prices:** $500 to $10,000. **Remarks:** Part-time maker; first knife sold in 1975. Guild member (knifemakers) since 1991. **Mark:** Branded initials as a J and B together.

**BARTH, J.D.,** 101 4th St., PO Box 186, Alberton, MT 59820, Phone: 406-722-4557, mtdeerhunter@blackfoot.net Web: www.jdbarthcustomknives.com
**Specialties:** Working and fancy straight knives of his design. Liner lock folders, stainless and Damascus, fully file worked, nitre blueing. **Technical:** Grinds ATS-34, 440-C, stainless and carbon Damascus. Uses variety of natural handle materials and Micarta. Likes dovetailed bolsters. Filework on most knives, full and tapered tangs. Makes custom fit sheaths for each knife. **Mark:** Name over maker, city and state.

**BARTLOW, JOHN,** 5078 Coffeen Ave., Sheridan, WY 82801, Phone: 307 673-4941, jbartlow@vcn
**Specialties:** New liner locks, working hunters, skinners, bird and trouts. **Patterns:** Working hunters, skinners, capers, bird and trout knives. **Technical:** Working on 6 new liner lock designs. **Prices:** $200 to $2,000. **Remarks:** Full-

time maker; first knife sold in 1979. Field-tests knives. **Mark:** Bartlow Sheridan, Wyo.

**BARTRUG, HUGH E.,** 2701 34th St. N., #142, St. Petersburg, FL 33713, Phone: 813-323-1136

**Specialties:** Inlaid straight knives and exotic folders; high-art knives and period pieces. **Patterns:** Hunters, Bowies and daggers; traditional patterns. **Technical:** Diffuses mokume. Forges 100 percent nickel, wrought iron, mosaic Damascus, shokeedo and O1 tool steel; grinds. **Prices:** $210 to $2,500; some to $5,000. **Remarks:** Retired maker; first knife sold in 1980. **Mark:** Ashley Forge or name.

**BASKETT, LEE GENE,** 427 Sutzer Ck. Rd., Eastview, KY 42732, Phone: 270-862-5019, baskettknives@hotmail.com Web: www.geocities.com/baskettknives

**Specialties:** Fancy working knives and fantasy pieces, often set up in desk stands. **Patterns:** Fighters, Bowies and survival knives; locking folders and traditional styles. **Technical:** Liner locks. Grinds O1, 440C, S-30-V; buys Damascus. Filework provided on most knives. **Prices:** Start at $250 and up. **Remarks:** Part-time maker; first knife sold in 1980. **Mark:** Last name.

**BATLEY, MARK S.,** PO Box 217, Wake, VA 23176, Phone: 804 776-7794

**BATSON, RICHARD G.,** 6591 Waterford Rd., Rixeyville, VA 22737, Phone: 540-937-2318

**Specialties:** Military, utility and fighting knives in working and presentation grade. **Patterns:** Daggers, combat and utility knives. **Technical:** Grinds O1, 1095 and 440C. Etches and scrimshaws; offers polished, Parkerized finishes. **Prices:** Active military, please inquire. **Remarks:** Semi-retired, limit production. First knife sold in 1958. **Mark:** Bat in circle, hand-signed and serial numbered.

**BATSON, JAMES,** 176 Brentwood Lane, Madison, AL 35758, Phone: 540-937-2318

**Specialties:** Forged Damascus blades and fittings in collectible period pieces. **Patterns:** Integral art knives, Bowies, folders, American-styled blades and miniatures. **Technical:** Forges carbon steel and his Damascus. **Prices:** $150 to $1,800; some to $4,500. **Remarks:** Semi retired full-time maker; first knife sold in 1978. **Mark:** Name, bladesmith with horse's head.

**BATTS, KEITH,** 450 Manning Rd., Hooks, TX 75561, Phone: 903-832-1140, kbatts@quixnet.net

**Specialties:** Working straight knives of his design or to customer specs. **Patterns:** Bowies, hunters, skinners, camp knives and others. **Technical:** Forges 5160 and his Damascus; offers filework. **Prices:** $245 to $895. **Remarks:** Part-time maker; first knife sold in 1988. **Mark:** Last name.

**BAUCHOP, PETER,** c/o Beck's Cutlery Specialties, 107 Edinburgh S #109, Cary, NC 27511, Phone: 919-460-0203, Fax: 919-460-7772, beckscutlery@mindspring.com

**Specialties:** Working straight knives and period pieces. **Patterns:** Fighters, swords and survival knives. **Technical:** Grinds O1, D2, G3, 440C and AST-34. Scrimshaws. **Prices:** $100 to $350; some to $1,500. **Remarks:** Full-time maker; first knife sold in 1980. **Mark:** Bow and axe (BOW-CHOP).

**BAUCHOP, ROBERT,** PO Box 330, Munster, Kwazulu-Natal 4278, SOUTH AFRICA, Phone: +27 39 3192449

**Specialties:** Fantasy knives; working and using knives of his design and to customer specs. **Patterns:** Hunters, swords, utility/camp knives, diver's knives and large swords. **Technical:** Grinds Sandvick 12C27, D2, 440C. Uses South African hardwoods red ivory, wild olive, African blackwood, etc. on handles. **Prices:** $200 to $800; some to $2,000. **Remarks:** Full-time maker; first knife sold in 1986. Doing business as Bauchop Custom Knives and swords. **Mark:** Viking helmet with Bauchop (bow and chopper) crest.

**BAUM, RICK,** 435 North Center St., Lehi, UT 84043, Phone: 801-431-7290, rick_baum@modusmedia.com

**BAUMGARDNER, ED,** 128 E. Main St., Glendale, KY 42740, Phone: 502-435-2675

**Specialties:** Working fixed blades, some folders. **Patterns:** Drop point and clip point hunters, fighters, small Bowies, traditional slip joint folders and lockbacks. **Technical:** Grinds O-1, 154CM, ATS-34, and Damascus likes using natural handle materials. **Prices:** $100 to $700. **Remarks:** Part-time maker, first knife sold in 2001. **Mark:** Last name.

**BAXTER, DALE,** 291 County Rd. 547, Trinity, AL 35673, Phone: 256-355-3626, dale@baxterknives.com

**Specialties:** Bowies, fighters, and hunters. **Patterns:** No patterns: all unique true customs. **Technical:** Hand forge and hand finish. Steels: 1095 and L-6 for carbon blades, 1095/L-6 for Damascus. **Remarks:** Full-time bladesmith and sold first knife in 1998. **Mark:** Dale Baxter (script) and J.S. on reverse.

**BEAM, JOHN R.,** 1310 Foothills Rd., Kalispell, MT 59901, Phone: 406-755-2593

**Specialties:** Classic, high-art and working straight knives of his design. **Patterns:** Bowies and hunters. **Technical:** Grinds 440C, Damascus and scrap. **Prices:** $175 to $600; some to $3,000. **Remarks:** Part-time maker; first knife sold in 1950. Doing business as Beam's Knives. **Mark:** Beam's Knives.

**BEASLEY, GENEO,** PO Box 339, Wadsworth, NV 89442, Phone: 775-575-2584

**BEATTY, GORDON H.,** 121 Petty Rd., Seneca, SC 29672, Phone: 864-882-6278

**Specialties:** Working straight knives, some fancy. **Patterns:** Traditional patterns, mini-skinners and letter openers. **Technical:** Grinds 440C, D2 and ATS-34; makes knives one-at-a-time. **Prices:** $75 to $450. **Remarks:** Part time maker; first knife sold in 1982. **Mark:** Name.

**BEATY, ROBERT B.,** CUTLER, 1995 Big Flat Rd., Missoula, MT 59804, Phone: 406-549-1818

**Specialties:** Plain and fancy working knives and collector pieces; will accep custom orders. **Patterns:** Hunters, Bowies, utility, kitchen and camp knives locking folders. **Technical:** Grinds D-2, ATS-34, Dendritie D-2, makes all too steel Damascus, forges 1095, 5160, 52100. **Prices:** $100 to $450; some t $1,100. **Remarks:** Full-time maker; first knife sold 1995. **Mark:** Stainless: Firs name, middle initial, last name, city and state. Carbon: Last name stamped o Ricasso.

**BEAUCHAMP, GAETAN,** 125, de la Rivire, Stoneham, PQ, CANADA G0A 4P0, Phone: 418-848-1914, Fax: 418-848-6859, gaetanbeauchamp@videotron.ca Web: www.beauchamp.cjb.net

**Specialties:** Working knives and folders of his design and to customer specs **Patterns:** Hunters, fighters, fantasy knives. **Technical:** Grinds ATS-34, 440C Damascus. Scrimshaws on ivory; specializes in buffalo horn and black back grounds. Offers a variety of handle materials. **Prices:** Start at $125. **Remarks** Full-time maker; first knife sold in 1992. **Mark:** Signature etched on blade.

**BECKER, STEVE,** 201 1st Ave. N.W., Conrad, MT 59425, Phone: 406-278-7753, scbecker@marsweb.com

**BECKER, FRANZ,** AM Kreuzberg 2, 84533, Marktl/Inn, GERMANY 08678-8020

**Specialties:** Stainless steel knives in working sizes. **Patterns:** Semi- and fu integral knives; interframe folders. **Technical:** Grinds stainless steels; like natural handle materials. **Prices:** $200 to $2,000. **Mark:** Name, country.

**BECKETT, NORMAN L.,** 102 Tobago Ave., Satsuma, FL 32189, Phone 386-325-3539, nbknives@yahoo.com

**Specialties:** Fancy, traditional and working folders and straight knives of h design. **Patterns:** Bowies, fighters, folders and hunters. **Technical:** Grinc CPM-S30V and Damascus. Fileworks blades; hollow and flat grinds. Prefe mirror finish; satin finish on working knives. Uses exotic handle material, stab lized woods and Micarta. Hand-tooled or inlaid sheaths. **Prices:** $125 to $90 some to $2,500 and up. **Remarks:** Full-time maker; first knife sold in 199 Doing business as Norm Beckett Knives. **Mark:** First and last name, make city and state.

**BEERS, RAY,** 8 Manorbrook Rd., Monkton, MD 21111, Phone: Summe 410-472-2229, Fax: 410-472-9136

**BEERS, RAY,** 2501 Lakefront Dr., Lake Wales, FL 33898, Phone: Winte 863-696-3036, Fax: 863-696-9421, rbknives@copper.net

**BEETS, MARTY,** 390 N. 5th Ave., Williams Lake, BC, CANADA V2G 2G4, Phone: 250-392-7199

**Specialties:** Working and collectable straight knives of his own design. **Pa terns:** Hunter, skinners, Bowies and utility knives. **Technical:** Grinds 440 does all his own work including heat treating Uses a variety of handle mater specializing in exotic hardwoods, antler and horn. **Price:** $125 to $40 **Remarks:** Wife, Sandy does handmade/hand stitched sheaths. First kn sold in 1988.Business name Beets Handmade Knives.

**BEGG, TODD M.,** 420 169 St. S, Spanaway, WA 98387, Phone: 253-531-2113, Web: www.beggknives.com

**Specialties:** Hand rubbed satin finished 440c stainless steel. Mirror polish 426 stainless steel. Stabilized mardrone wood.

**BEHNKE, WILLIAM,** 8478 Dell Rd., Kingsley, MI 49649, Phone: 231-263-7447, wbehnke@michweb.net

**Specialties:** Hunters, belt knives and folders. **Patterns:** Traditional styling moderate-sized straight and folding knives. **Technical:** Forges his own Da ascus, W-2 and 1095; likes natural material. **Prices:** $150 to $2,0 **Remarks:** Part-time maker. **Mark:** Bill Behnke Knives.

**BELL, DONALD,** 2 Division St., Bedford, Nova Scotia, CANADA B4A 1Y8, Phone: 902-835-2623, donbell@accesswave.ca Web: www.bellknives.com
**Specialties:** Fancy knives: carved and pierced folders of his own design. **Patterns:** Locking folders, pendant knives, jewelry knives. **Technical:** Grinds Damascus, pierces and carves blades. **Prices:** $500 to $2,000; some to $3,000. **Remarks:** Spare-time maker; first knife sold in 1993. **Mark:** Bell symbol with first initial inside.

**BELL, MICHAEL,** 88321 N. Bank Lane, Coquille, OR 97423, Phone: 541-396-3605, michael@dragonflyforge.com Web: www. Dragonfly-forge.com
**Specialties:** Full line of combat quality Japanese swords. **Patterns:** Traditional tanto to katana. **Technical:** Handmade steel and welded cable. **Prices:** Swords from bare blades to complete high art $4,500 to $28,000.**Remarks:** Studied with Japanese master Nakajima Mineyoshi. **Mark:** Dragonfly in shield or tombo kunimitsu.

**BENDIK, JOHN,** 7076 Fitch Rd., Olmsted Falls, OH 44138

**BENJAMIN JR., GEORGE,** 3001 Foxy Ln., Kissimmee, FL 34746, Phone: 407-846-7259
**Specialties:** Fighters in various styles to include Persian, Moro and military. **Patterns:** Daggers, skinners and one-of-a-kind grinds. **Technical:** Forges O1, D2, A2, 5160 and Damascus. Favors Pakkawood, Micarta, and mirror or Parkerized finishes. Makes unique para-military leather sheaths. **Prices:** $150 to $600; some to $1,200. **Remarks:** Doing business as The Leather Box. **Mark:** Southern Pride Knives.

**BENNETT, BRETT C.,** 1922 Morrie Ave., Cheyenne, WY 82001, Phone: 307-220-3919, brett@bennettknives.com Web: www.bennettknives.com
**Specialties:** Hand-rubbed finish on all blades. **Patterns:** Most fixed blade patterns. **Technical:** ATS-34, D-2, 1080/15N20 Damascus, 1080 forged. **Prices:** $100 and up. **Mark:** "B.C. Bennett" in script or "Bennett" stamped in script.

**BENNETT, PETER,** PO Box 143, Engadine N.S.W. 2233, AUSTRALIA, Phone: 02-520-4975 (home), Fax: O2-528-8219 (work)
**Specialties:** Fancy and embellished working and using straight knives to customer specs and in standard patterns. **Patterns:** Fighters, hunters, bird/trout and fillet knives. **Technical:** Grinds 440C, ATS-34 and Damascus. Uses rare Australian desert timbers for handles. **Prices:** $90 to $500; some to $1,500. **Remarks:** Full-time maker; first knife sold in 1985. **Mark:** First and middle initials, last name; country.

**BENNETT, GLEN C.,** 5821 S. Stewart Blvd., Tucson, AZ 85706

**BENNICA, CHARLES,** Chemin du Salet, 34190 Moules et Baucels, FRANCE, Phone: +33 4 67 73 42 40, b-ni-k@club-internet.fr
**Specialties:** Fixed blades and folding knives; the latter with slick closing mechanisms with push buttons to unlock blades. Unique handle shapes, signature to the maker. **Technical:** 416 stainless steel frames for folders and ATS-34 blades. Also specializes in Damascus.

**BENSON, DON,** 2505 Jackson St., #112, Escalon, CA 95320, Phone: 209-838-7921
**Specialties:** Working straight knives of his design. **Patterns:** Axes, Bowies, tantos and hunters. **Technical:** Grinds 440C. **Prices:** $100 to $150; some to $400. **Remarks:** Spare-time maker; first knife sold in 1980. **Mark:** Name.

**BENTLEY, C.L.,** 2405 Hilltop Dr., Albany, GA 31707, Phone: 912-432-6656

**BER, DAVE,** 656 Miller Rd., San Juan Island, WA 98250, Phone: 206-378-7230
**Specialties:** Working straight and folding knives for the sportsman; welcomes customer designs. **Patterns:** Hunters, skinners, Bowies, kitchen and fishing knives. **Technical:** Forges and grinds saw blade steel, wire Damascus, O1, L6, 5160 and 440C. **Prices:** $100 to $300; some to $500. **Remarks:** Full-time maker; first knife sold in 1985. **Mark:** Last name.

**BERG, LOTHAR,** 37 Hillcrest Ln., Kitchener ON, CANADA NZK 1S9, Phone: 519-745-3260
519-745-3260

**BERGER, MAX A.,** 5716 John Richard Ct., Carmichael, CA 95608, Phone: 916-972-9229, bergerknives@aol.com
**Specialties:** Fantasy and working/using straight knives of his design. **Patterns:** Fighters, hunters and utility/camp knives. **Technical:** Grinds ATS-34 and 440C. Offers fileworks and combinations of mirror polish and satin finish blades. **Prices:** $200 to $600; some to $2,500. **Remarks:** Part-time maker; first knife sold in 1992. **Mark:** Last name.

**BERGH, ROGER,** Dalkarlsa 291, 91598 Bygdea, SWEDEN, Phone: 46693430061, knivroger@hotmail.com Web: www.roger-bergh.nu
**Specialties:** Collectible all-purpose straight-blade knives. Damascus steel blades, carving and artistic design knives are heavily influenced by nature and have an organic hand crafted feel.

**BERGLIN, BRUCE D.,** 17441 Lake Terrace Place, Mount Vernon, WA 98274, Phone: 360-422-8603, bdb@fishersons.com
**Specialties:** Working and using straight knives of his own design. **Patterns:** Hunters, boots, Bowies, utility/camp knives and period pieces, some made to look old. **Technical:** Forges carbon steel, grinds carbon and stainless steel. Prefers natural handle material and micarta. **Prices:** Start at $300. **Remarks:** Part-time maker since 1998. **Mark:** First initial, middle initial and last name, sometimes surrounded with an oval.

**BERTHOLUS, BERNARD,** Atelier Du Brute, De Forge 21, Rue Fersen 06600, Antibes, FRANCE, Phone: 04 93 34 95 90
**Specialties:** Traditional working and using straight knives of his design. **Patterns:** Bowies, daggers and hunters. **Technical:** Forges ATS-34, 440, D2 and carbon steels. **Prices:** $750 to $7,500. **Remarks:** Full-time maker; first knife sold in 1990. **Mark:** City and last name.

**BERTOLAMI, JUAN CARLOS,** Av San Juan 575, Neuquen, ARGENTINA 8300, fliabertolami@infovia.com.ar
**Specialties:** Hunting and country labor knives. All of them unique high quality pieces and supplies collectors too. **Technical:** Austrian stainless steel and elephant, hippopotamus and orca ivory, as well as ebony and other fine woods for the handles.

**BERTUZZI, ETTORE,** Via Partigiani 3, 24068 Seriate (Bergamo), ITALY, Phone: 035-294262, Fax: 035-294262
**Specialties:** Classic straight knives and folders of his design, to customer specs and in standard patterns. **Patterns:** Bowies, hunters and locking folders. **Technical:** Grinds ATS-34, D3, D2 and various Damascus. **Prices:** $300 to $500. **Remarks:** Part-time maker; first knife sold in 1993. **Mark:** Name etched on ricasso.

**BESEDICK, FRANK E.,** 195 Stillwagon Rd, Ruffsdale, PA 15679, Phone: 724-696-3312, bxtr.bez3@verizon.net
**Specialties:** Traditional working and using straight knives of his design. **Patterns:** Hunters, utility/camp knives and miniatures; buckskinner blades and tomahawks. **Technical:** Forges and grinds 5160, O1 and Damascus. Offers filework and scrimshaw. **Prices:** $75 to $300; some to $750. **Remarks:** Part-time maker; first knife sold in 1990. **Mark:** Name or initials.

**BESHARA, BRENT,** 207 Cedar St., PO Box 1046, Stayner, ON, CANADA L0M 1S0, Phone: 705-428-3152, Fax: 705-428-5961, beshknives@sympatico.ca Web: www.beshknives.com
**Specialties:** Tactical fighting fixed knives. **Patterns:** Tantos, fighters, neck and custom designs. **Technical:** Grinds 0-1, L-6 and stainless upon request. Offers Kydex sheaths, does own Paragon heat treating. **Prices:** Start at $150. **Remarks:** Part-time maker. Active serving military bomb tech driver. **Mark:** "BESH" stamped.

**BETHKE, LORA SUE,** 13420 Lincoln St., Grand Haven, MI 49417, Phone: 616-842-8268, Fax: 616-844-2696, lspb@compuserve.com
**Specialties:** Classic and traditional straight knives of her design. **Patterns:** Boots, Bowies and hunters. **Technical:** Forges 1084 and Damascus. **Prices:** Start at $400. **Remarks:** Part-time maker; first knife sold in 1997. **Mark:** Full name - JS on reverse side. **Other:** Journeyman bladesmith, American Bladesmith Society.

**BEUKES, TINUS,** 83 Henry St., Risiville, Vereeniging 1939, SOUTH AFRICA, Phone: 27 16 423 2053
**Specialties:** Working straight knives. **Patterns:** Hunters, skinners and kitchen knives. **Technical:** Grinds D2, 440C and chain, cable and stainless Damascus. **Prices:** $80 to $180. **Remarks:** Part-time maker; first knife sold in 1993. **Mark:** Full name, city, logo.

**BEVERLY II, LARRY H.,** PO Box 741, Spotsylvania, VA 22553, Phone: 540-898-3951
**Specialties:** Working straight knives, slip-joints and liner locks. Welcomes customer designs. **Patterns:** Bowies, hunters, guard less fighters and miniatures. **Technical:** Grinds 440C, A2 and O1. **Prices:** $125 to $1,000. **Remarks:** Part-time maker; first knife sold in 1986. **Mark:** Initials or last name in script.

**BEZUIDENHOUT, BUZZ,** 30 Surlingham Ave., Malvern, Queensburgh, Natal 4093, SOUTH AFRICA, Phone: 031-4632827, Fax: 031-3631259
**Specialties:** Traditional working and using straight knives of his design and to customer specs. **Patterns:** Boots, hunters, kitchen knives and utility/camp knives. **Technical:** Grinds 12C27, 440C and ATS-34. Uses local hardwoods, horn - kudu, impala, buffalo - giraffe bone and ivory for handles. **Prices:** $150 to $200; some to $1,500. **Remarks:** Spare-time maker; first knife sold in 1988. **Mark:** First name with a bee emblem.

**BIGGERS, GARY,** Ventura Knives, 1278 Colina Vista, Ventura, CA 93003, Phone: 805-658-6610, Fax: 805-658-6610
**Specialties:** Fixed blade knives of his design. **Patterns:** Hunters, boots/fighters, Bowies and utility knives. **Technical:** Grinds ATS-34, 01 and commercial Damascus. **Prices:** $150 to $550. **Remarks:** Part-time maker; first knife sold

in 1996. Doing business as Ventura Knives. **Mark:** First and last name, city and state.

**BILLGREN, PER,** STALLGATAN 9, S815 76 Soderfors, SWEDEN, Phone: +46 293 30600, Fax: +46 293 30124, mail@damasteel.se

**Specialties:** Damasteel, stainless Damascus steels. **Patterns:** Bluetounge, Heimskringla, Muhammed's ladder, Rose twist, Odin's eye, Vinland, Hakkapelliitta. **Technical:** Modern Damascus steel made by patented powder metallurgy method. **Prices:** $80 to $180. **Remarks:** Damasteel is available through distributors around the globe.

**BIRDWELL, IRA LEE,** PO Box 1135, Bagdad, AZ 86321, Phone: 520-633-2516

**Specialties:** Special orders. **Mark:** Engraved signature.

**BIRNBAUM, EDWIN,** 9715 Hamocks Blvd. I 206, Miami, FL 33196

**BISH, HAL,** 9347 Sweetbriar Trace, Jonesboro, GA 30236, Phone: 770-477-2422, hal-bish@hp.com

**BIZZELL, ROBERT,** 145 Missoula Ave., Butte, MT 59701, Phone: 406-782-4403, patternweld2@cs.com

**Specialties:** Damascus. **Patterns:** Composite, mosaic and traditional. **Technical:** Only fixed blades at this time. **Prices:** Start at $150. **Mark:** Hand signed.

**BLACK, SCOTT,** 27100 Leetown Rd., Picayune, MS 39466, Phone: 601-799-5939, copperheadforge@telepak.net

**Specialties:** Friction folders; fighters. **Patterns:** Bowies, fighters, hunters, smoke hawks, friction folders, daggers. **Technical:** All forged, all work done by me, own hand-stitched leather work; own heat-treating. **Prices:** $100 to $2200. **Remarks:** ABS Journeyman Smith. **Mark:** Hot Mark - Copperhead Snake. **Other:** Cabel / Damascus/ High Carbone.

**BLACK, EARL,** 3466 South, 700 East, Salt Lake City, UT 84106, Phone: 801-466-8395

**Specialties:** High-art straight knives and folders; period pieces. **Patterns:** Boots, Bowies and daggers; lockers and gents. **Technical:** Grinds 440C and 154CM. Buys some Damascus. Scrimshaws and engraves. **Prices:** $200 to $1,800; some to $2,500 and higher. **Remarks:** Full-time maker; first knife sold in 1980. **Mark:** Name, city, state.

**BLACK, SCOTT,** 570 Malcom Rd., Covington, GA 30209

**Specialties:** Working/using folders of his design. **Patterns:** Daggers, hunters, utility/camp knives and friction folders. **Technical:** Forges pattern welded, cable, 1095, O1 and 5160. **Prices:** $100 to $500. **Remarks:** Part-time maker; first knife sold in 1992. Doing business as Copperhead Forge. **Mark:** Hot mark on blade, copperhead snake.

**BLACK, TOM,** 921 Grecian N.W., Albuquerque, NM 87107, Phone: 505-344-2549, tblackknives@aol.com

**Specialties:** Working knives to fancy straight knives of his design. **Patterns:** Drop-point skinners, folders, using knives, Bowies and daggers. **Technical:** Grinds 440C, 154CM, ATS-34, A2, D2 and Damascus. Offers engraving and scrimshaw. **Prices:** $250 and up; some over $8,500. **Remarks:** Full-time maker; first knife sold in 1970. **Mark:** Name, city.

**BLACKTON, ANDREW E.,** 12521 Fifth Isle, Bayonet Point, FL 34667, Phone: 727-869-1406

**Specialties:** Straight and folding knives, some fancy. **Patterns:** Hunters, Bowies and daggers. **Technical:** Grinds D2, 440C and 154CM. Offers some embellishment. **Prices:** $125 to $450; some to $2,000. **Remarks:** Full-time maker. **Mark:** Last name in script.

**BLACKWOOD, NEIL,** 7032 Willow Run, Lakeland, FL 33813, Phone: 863-701-0126, neil@blackwoodknives.com Web: www.blackwood-knives.com

**Specialties:** Fixed blades and folders. **Technical:** Blade steels d-2 Talonite, Stellite, CPM S30V and RWL 34. Handle Materials G-10 carbon fiber and Micarta in the synthetics: giraffe bone and exotic woods on the natural side. **Remarks:** Makes everything from the frames to the stop pins, pivot pins-everything but the stainless screws; one factory/custom collaboration (the Hybrid Hunter) with Outdoor Edge is in place and negotiations were under way at press time for one with Benchmade.

**BLANCHARD, G.R. (GARY),** PO Box 709, Pigeon Forge, TN 37868, Phone: 865-908-7466, Fax: 865-908-7466, blanchardscutlery@yahoo.com Web: www.blanchardscutlery.com

**Specialties:** Fancy folders with patented button blade release and high-art straight knives of his design. **Patterns:** Boots, daggers and locking folders. **Technical:** Grinds 440C and ATS-34 and Damascus. Engraves his knives. **Prices:** $1,500 to $18,000 or more. **Remarks:** Full-time maker; first knife sold in 1989. **Mark:** First and middle initials, last name or last name only.

**BLASINGAME, ROBERT,** 281 Swanson, Kilgore, TX 75662, Phone: 903-984-8144

**Specialties:** Classic working and using straight knives and folders of his design and to customer specs. **Patterns:** Bowies, daggers, fighters and hunters; one-of-a-kind historic reproductions. **Technical:** Hand-forges P.W. Damascus, cable Damascus and chain Damascus. **Prices:** $150 to $1,000; some to $2,000. **Remarks:** Full-time maker; first knife sold in 1968. **Mark:** 'B' inside anvil.

**BLAUM, ROY,** 319 N. Columbia St., Covington, LA 70433, Phone: 985-893-1060

**Specialties:** Working straight knives and folders of his design; lightweight easy-open folders. **Patterns:** Hunters, boots, fishing and woodcarving/whittling knives. **Technical:** Grinds A2, D2, O1, 154CM and ATS-34. Offers leatherwork. **Prices:** $40 to $800; some higher. **Remarks:** Full-time maker; first knife sold in 1976. **Mark:** Engraved signature or etched logo.

**BLOOMER, ALAN T.,** 116 E. 6th St., Maquon, IL 61458, Phone: 309-875-3583

**Specialties:** All Damascus folders, making own Damascus. **Patterns:** Bowies, Folders, chef etc. **Technical:** Does own heat treating. **Prices:** $400 to $1,000. **Remarks:** Part-time maker; Guild member. **Mark:** Stamp Bloomer. **Other:** No orders.

**BLOOMQUIST, R. GORDON,** 6206 Tiger Trail Dr., Olympia, WA 98512, Phone: 360-352-7162, bloomquistr@energy.wsu.edu

**BLUM, CHUCK,** 743 S. Brea Blvd., #10, Brea, CA 92621, Phone: 714-529-0484

**Specialties:** Art and investment daggers and Bowies. **Technical:** Flat-grinds; hollow-grinds 440C, ATS-34 on working knives. **Prices:** $125 to $8,500. **Remarks:** Part-time maker; first knife sold in 1985. **Mark:** First and middle initials and last name with sailboat logo.

**BLUM, KENNETH,** 1729 Burleson, Brenham, TX 77833, Phone: 979-836-9577

**Specialties:** Traditional working straight knives of his design. **Patterns:** Camp knives, Hunters and Bowies. **Technical:** Forges 5160; grinds 440C and D2. Uses exotic woods and Micarta for handles. **Prices:** $150 to $300. **Remarks:** Part-time maker; first knife sold in 1978. **Mark:** Last name on ricasso.

**BOARDMAN, GUY,** 39 Mountain Ridge R., New Germany 3619, SOUTH AFRICA, Phone: 031-726-921

**Specialties:** American and South African-styles. **Patterns:** Bowies, American and South African hunters, plus more. **Technical:** Grinds Bohler steels, some ATS-34. **Prices:** $100 to $600. **Remarks:** Part-time maker; first knife sold 1986. **Mark:** Name, city, country.

**BOATRIGHT, BASEL,** 11 Timber Point, New Braunfels, TX 78132, Phone: 210-609-0807

**Specialties:** Working and using knives of his design. **Patterns:** Hunters, skinners and utility/camp knives. **Technical:** Grinds and hand-tempers 5160. **Prices:** $75 to $300. **Remarks:** Part-time maker. **Mark:** Stamped BBB.

**BOCHMAN, BRUCE,** 183 Howard Place, Grants Pass, OR 97526, Phone: 503-471-1985

**Specialties:** Working straight knives in standard patterns. **Patterns:** Bowies, hunters, fishing and bird knives. **Technical:** 440C; mirror or satin finish. **Prices:** $140 to $250; some to $750. **Remarks:** Part-time maker; first knife sold in 1977. **Mark:** Custom blades by B. Bochman.

**BODEN, HARRY,** Via Gellia Mill, Bonsall Matlock, Derbyshire DE4 2A, ENGLAND, Phone: 0629-825176

**Specialties:** Traditional working straight knives and folders of his design. **Patterns:** Hunters, locking folders and utility/camp knives. **Technical:** Grinds Sandvik 12C27, D2 and O1. **Prices:** £70 to £150; some to £300. **Remarks:** Full-time maker; first knife sold in 1986. **Mark:** Full name.

**BODNER, GERALD "JERRY",** 4102 Spyglass Ct., Louisville, KY 4022 Phone: 502-968-5946

**Specialties:** Fantasy straight knives in standard patterns. **Patterns:** Bowies, fighters, hunters and micro-miniature knives. **Technical:** Grinds Damascus, 440C and D2. Offers filework. **Prices:** $35 to $180. **Remarks:** Part-time maker; first knife sold in 1993. **Mark:** Last name in script and JAB in o above knives.

**BODOLAY, ANTAL,** Rua Wilson Soares Fernandes #31, Planalto, Be Horizonte MG-31730-700, BRAZIL, Phone: 031-494-1885

**Specialties:** Working folders and fixed blades of his design or to custom specs; some art daggers and period pieces. **Patterns:** Daggers, hunters, locking folders, utility knives and Khukris. **Technical:** Grinds D6, high-carbon steels and 420 stainless. Forges files on request. **Prices:** $30 to $3 **Remarks:** Full-time maker; first knife sold in 1965. **Mark:** Last name in scri

**BOEHLKE, GUENTER,** Parkstrasse 2, 56412 Grossholbach, GERMANY 2602-5440, Boehlke-Messer@t-online.de Web: www.boehlke-messer.de

**Specialties:** Classic working/using straight knives of his design. **Patterns:** Hunters, utility/camp knives and ancient remakes. **Technical:** Grinds Damascus, CPM-T-440V and 440C. Inlays gemstones and ivory. **Prices:** $220 to $700; some to $2,000. **Remarks:** Spare-time maker; first knife sold in 1985. **Mark:** Name, address and bow and arrow.

**BOGUSZEWSKI, PHIL,** PO Box 99329, Lakewood, WA 98499, Phone: 253-581-7096, knives01@aol.com

**Specialties:** Working folders—some fancy—mostly of his design. **Patterns:** Folders, slip-joints and lockers; also makes anodized titanium frame folders. **Technical:** Grinds BG42 and Damascus; offers filework. **Prices:** $550 to $3,000. **Remarks:** Full-time maker; first knife sold in 1979. **Mark:** Name, city and state.

**BOJTOS, ARPA D.,** Dobsinskeho 10, 98403 Lucenec, Slovakia, Phone: 00421-47 4333512, botjos@stonline.sk

**Specialties:** Art Knives. **Patterns:** Daggers, fighters and hunters. **Technical:** Grinds ATS-34. Carves on steel, handle materials and sheaths. **Prices:** $2,000 to $5,000; some to $8,000. **Remarks:** Full-time maker; first knife sold in 1990. **Mark:** AB

**BOLD, STU,** 63 D'Andrea Tr., Sarnia, Ont., CANADA N7S 6H3, Phone: 519-383-7610, sbold@sar.hookup.net

**Specialties:** Traditional working/using straight knives in standard patterns and to customer specs. **Patterns:** Boots, Bowies and hunters. **Technical:** Grinds ATS-34, 440C and Damascus; mosaic pins. Offers scrimshaw and hand-tooled leather sheaths. **Prices:** $140 to $500; some to $2,000. **Remarks:** Part-time maker; first knife sold in 1983. **Mark:** Name, city, province.

**BOLEWARE, DAVID,** PO Box 96, Carson, MS 39427, Phone: 601-943-5372

**Specialties:** Traditional and working/using straight knives of his design, to customer specs and in standard patterns. **Patterns:** Bowies, hunters and utility/camp knives. **Technical:** Grinds ATS-34, 440C and Damascus. **Prices:** $85 to $350; some to $600. **Remarks:** Part-time maker; first knife sold in 1989. **Mark:** First and last name, city, state.

**BOLTON, CHARLES B.,** PO Box 6, Jonesburg, MO 63351, Phone: 636-488-5785

**Specialties:** Working straight knives in standard patterns. **Patterns:** Hunters, skinners, boots and fighters. **Technical:** Grinds 440C and ATS-34. **Prices:** $100 to $300; some to $600. **Remarks:** Full-time maker; first knife sold in 1973. **Mark:** Last name.

**BONASSI, FRANCO,** Via Nicoletta 4, Pordenone 33170, ITALY, Phone: 434-550821, bonassi.f@schmidt.it

**Specialties:** Fancy and working one-of-a-kind straight knives of his design. **Patterns:** Hunters,utility and folders liner locks. **Technical:** Grinds CPM, ATS-34, 154CM and commercial Damascus. Uses only titanium foreguards and pommels. **Prices:** Start at $250. **Remarks:** Spare-time maker; first knife sold in 1988. Has made cutlery for several celebrities; Gen. Schwarzkopf, Fuzzy Zoeller, etc. **Mark:** FRANK.

**BOOCO, GORDON,** 175 Ash St., PO Box 174, Hayden, CO 81639, Phone: 970-276-3195

**Specialties:** Fancy working straight knives of his design and to customer specs. **Patterns:** Hunters and Bowies. **Technical:** Grinds 440C, D2 and A2. Heat-treats. **Prices:** $150 to $350; some $600 and higher. **Remarks:** Part-time maker; first knife sold in 1984. **Mark:** Last name with push dagger artwork.

**BOOS, RALPH,** 5107 40 Ave., Edmonton, Alberta, CANADA T6L 1B3, Phone: 780-463-7094

**Specialties:** Classic, fancy and fantasy miniature knives and swords of his design or to customer specs. **Patterns:** Bowies, daggers and swords. **Technical:** Hand files O1, stainless and Damascus. Engraves and carves. Does heat bluing and acid etching. **Prices:** $125 to $350; some to $1,000. **Remarks:** Part-time maker; first knife sold in 1982. **Mark:** First initials back to back.

**BOOTH, PHILIP W.,** 301 S. Jeffery Ave., Ithaca, MI 48847, Phone: 989-875-2844

**Specialties:** Folding knives, various mechanisms, maker of the "minnow" series small folding knife. **Patterns:** Auto lock backs, liner locks, classic pattern multi-blades. **Technical:** Grinds ATS-34, 440C, 1095 and commercial Damascus. Prefers natural materlals, offers flle work and scrlmshaw. **Prlces:** $200 and up. **Remarks:** Full-time maker; first knife sold in 1991. **Mark:** Last name or name with city and map logo.

**BORGER, WOLF,** Benzstrasse 8, 76676 Graben-Neudorf, GERMANY, Phone: 07255-72303, Fax: 07255-72304, wolfgmesserschmied.de Web: www.messerschmied.de

**Specialties:** High-tech working and using straight knives and folders, many with corkscrews or other tools, of his design. **Patterns:** Hunters, Bowies and folders with various locking systems. **Technical:** Grinds 440C, ATS-34 and CPM. Uses stainless Damascus. **Prices:** $250 to $900; some to $1,500. **Remarks:** Full-time maker; first knife sold in 1975. **Mark:** Howling wolf and name; first name on Damascus blades.

**BOSE, REESE,** PO Box 61, Shelburn, IN 47879, Phone: 812-397-5114

**Specialties:** Traditional working and using knives in standard patterns and multi-blade folders. **Patterns:** Multi-blade slip-joints. **Technical:** ATS-34, D2 and CPM 440V. **Prices:** $275 to $1,500. **Remarks:** Full-time maker; first knife sold in 1992. Photos by Jack Busfield. **Mark:** R. Bose.

**BOSE, TONY,** 7252 N. County Rd., 300 E., Shelburn, IN 47879-9778, Phone: 812-397-5114

**Specialties:** Traditional working and using knives in standard patterns; multi-blade folders. **Patterns:** Multi-blade slip-joints. **Technical:** Grinds commercial Damascus, ATS-34 and D2. **Prices:** $400 to $1,200. **Remarks:** Full-time maker; first knife sold in 1972. **Mark:** First initial, last name, city, state.

**BOSSAERTS, CARL,** Rua Albert Einstein 906, 14051-110, Ribeirao Preto, S.P. BRAZIL, Phone: 016 633 7063

**Specialties:** Working and using straight knives of his design, to customer specs and in standard patterns. **Patterns:** Hunters, fighters and utility/camp knives. **Technical:** Grinds ATS-34, 440V and 440C; does filework. **Prices:** 60 to $400. **Remarks:** Part-time maker; first knife sold in 1992. **Mark:** Initials joined together.

**BOST, ROGER E.,** 30511 Cartier Dr, Palos Verdes, CA 90275-5629, Phone: 310- 541-6833, rogerbost@cox.net

**Specialties:** Hunters, fighters, boot, utility. **Patterns:** Loveless-style. **Technical:** ATS-34, 60-61RC, stock removal and forge. **Prices:** $300 and up. **Remarks:** First knife sold in 1990. **Mark:** Diamond with initials inside and Palos Verdes California around outside. **Other:** Cal. Knifemakers Assn, ABS.

**BOSTWICK, CHRIS T.,** 341 Robins Run, Burlington, WI 53105, c.bostwick@wi.rr.com or ceebozz @hotmail.com

**Specialties:** Slipjoints ATS-34. **Patterns:** English jack, gunstock jack, doctors, stockman. **Prices:** $300 and up. **Remarks:** Enjoy traditional patterns/history multiblade slipjoints. **Mark:** CTB.

**BOSWORTH, DEAN,** 329 Mahogany Dr., Key Largo, FL 33037, Phone: 305-451-1564

**Specialties:** Free hand hollow ground working knives with hand rubbed satin finish, filework and inlays. **Patterns:** Bird and Trout, hunters, skinners, filet, Bowies, miniatures. **Technical:** Using 440C, ATS-34, D2, Meier Damascus, custom wet formed sheaths. **Prices:** $250 and up. **Remarks:** Part-time maker; first knife made in 1985. **Mark:** BOZ stamped in block letters. **Other:** Member: Florida Knifemakers Assoc.

**BOURBEAU, JEAN YVES,** 15 Rue Remillard, Notre Dame, Ile Perrot, Quebec, CANADA J7V 8M9, Phone: 514-453-1069

**Specialties:** Fancy/embellished and fantasy folders of his design. **Patterns:** Bowies, fighters and locking folders. **Technical:** Grinds 440C, ATS-34 and Damascus. Carves precious wood for handles. **Prices:** $150 to $1,000. **Remarks:** Part-time maker; first knife sold in 1994. **Mark:** Interlaced initials.

**BOUSE, D. MICHAEL,** 1010 Victoria Pl., Waldorf, MD 20602, Phone: 301-843-0449

**Specialties:** Traditional and working/using straight knives of his design. **Patterns:** Daggers, fighters and hunters. **Technical:** Forges 5160 and Damascus; grinds D2; differential hardened blades; decorative handle pins. **Prices:** $125 to $350. **Remarks:** Spare-time maker; first knife sold in 1992. Doing business as Michael's Handmade Knives. **Mark:** Etched last name.

**BOWEN, TILTON,** 189 Mt Olive Rd., Baker, WV 26801, Phone: 304-897-6159

**Specialties:** Straight, stout working knives. **Patterns:** Hunters, fighters and boots; also offers buckskinner and throwing knives. All his D2-blades since 1st of year, 1997 are Deep Cryogenic processed. **Technical:** Grinds D2 and 4140. **Prices:** $60 to $275. **Remarks:** Full-time maker; first knife sold in 1982-1983. Sells wholesale to dealers. **Mark:** Initials and BOWEN BLADES, WV.

**BOWLES, CHRIS,** PO Box 985, Reform, AL 35481, Phone: 205-375-6162

**Specialties:** Working/using straight knives, and period pieces. **Patterns:** Utillty, tactlcal, huntlng, neck knlves, machetes, and swords. **Grlnds:** 0-1, 154 cm, BG-42, 440V. **Prices:** $50 to $400 some higher. **Remarks:** Full-time maker. **Mark:** Bowles stamped or Bowles etched in script.

**BOXER, BO,** LEGEND FORGE, 6477 Hwy. 93 S #134, Whitefish, MT 59937, Phone: 505-799-0173, legendforge@aol.com Web: www.legendforgesknives.com

**Specialties:** Handmade hunting knives, Damascus hunters. Most are antler handled. Also, hand forged Damascus steel. **Patterns:** Hunters and Bowies. **Prices:** $125 to $2,500 on some very exceptional Damascus knives. **Mark:** The name "Legend Forge" hand engraved on every blade. Additional: Makes his own custom leather sheath stamped with maker stamp. His knives are used by the outdoorsman of the Smoky Mountains, North Carolina, and the Rockies of Montana and New Mexico. **Other:** Spends one-half of the year in Montana and the other part of the year in Taos New Mexico.

**BOYD, FRANCIS,** 1811 Prince St., Berkeley, CA 94703, Phone: 510-841-7210

**Specialties:** Folders and kitchen knives; Japanese swords. **Patterns:** Push-button sturdy locking folders; San Francisco-style chef's knives. **Technical:** Forges and grinds; mostly uses high-carbon steels. **Prices:** Moderate to heavy. **Remarks:** Designer. **Mark:** Name.

**BOYE, DAVID,** PO Box 1238, Dolan Springs, AZ 86441, Phone: 800-853-1617, Fax: 928-767-3030, boye@ctaz.com Web: ww.boyeknives.com

**Specialties:** Folders, hunting and kitchen knives. Forerunner in the use of dendritic steel and dendritic cobalt for blades. **Patterns:** Lockback folders, kitchen knives and hunting knives. **Technical:** Casts blades in stainless 440Cand cobalt. **Prices:** From $129 to $500. **Remarks:** Full-time maker; author of *Step-by-Step Knifemaking*; **Mark:** Name.

**BOYER, MARK,** 10515 Woodinville Dr., #17, Bothell, WA 98011, Phone: 206-487-9370, boyerbl@mail.eskimo.com

**Specialties:** High-tech and working/using straight knives of his design. **Patterns:** Fighters and utility/camp knives. **Technical:** Grinds 1095 and D2. Offers Kydex sheaths; heat-treats. **Prices:** $45 to $120. **Remarks:** Part-time maker; first knife sold in 1994. Doing business as Boyer Blades. **Mark:** Eagle holding two swords with name.

**BOYSEN, RAYMOND A.,** 125 E. St. Patrick, Rapid Ciy, SD 57701, Phone: 605-341-7752

**Specialties:** Hunters and Bowies. **Technical:** High performance blades forged from 52100 and 5160. **Prices:** $200 and up. **Remarks:** American Bladesmith Society JourneymanSmith. **Mark:** BOYSEN. **Other:** Part-time bladesmith.

**BRACK, DOUGLAS D.,** 119 Camino Ruiz, #71, Camirillo, CA 93012, Phone: 805-987-0490

**Specialties:** Working straight knives of his design. **Patterns:** Heavy-duty skinners, fighters and boots. **Technical:** Grinds 440C, ATS-34 and 5160; forges cable. **Prices:** $90 to $180; some to $300. **Remarks:** Part-time maker; first knife sold in 1984. **Mark:** tat.

**BRADBURN, GARY,** BRADBURN CUSTOM CUTLERY, 1714 Park Place, Wichita, KS 67203, Phone: 316-269-4273, steeldust5@aol.com Web: www.angelfire.com/bc2bradburnknives/

**Specialties:** Specialize in clay-tempered Japanese-style knives and swords. **Patterns:** Also Bowies and fighers. **Technical:** Forge and/or grind carbon steel only. **Prices:** $150 to $1,200. **Mark:** Initials GB stylized to look like Japanese character.

**BRADFORD, GARRICK,** 582 Guelph St., Kitchener ON, CANADA N2H-5Y4, Phone: 519-576-9863

**BRADLEY, DENNIS,** 2410 Bradley Acres Rd., Blairsville, GA 30512, Phone: 706-745-4364

**Specialties:** Working straight knives and folders, some high-art. **Patterns:** Hunters, boots and daggers; slip-joints and two-blades. **Technical:** Grinds ATS-34, D2, 440C and commercial Damascus. **Prices:** $100 to $500; some to $2,000. **Remarks:** Part-time maker; first knife sold in 1973. **Mark:** BRADLEY KNIVES in double heart logo.

**BRADLEY, JOHN,** PO Box 37, Pomona Park, FL 32181, Phone: 904-649-4739

**Specialties:** Fixed-blade using knives. **Patterns:** Skinners, Bowies, camp knives and Sgian Dubhs. **Technical:** Hand forged from 52100, 1095 and own Damascus. **Prices:** $125 to $500; some higher. **Remarks:** Part-time maker; first knife sold in 1988. **Mark:** Last name.

**BRADSHAW, BAILEY,** PO Box 564, Diana, TX 75640, Phone: 903-968-2029, bailey@bradshawcutlery.com

**Specialties:** Traditional folders and contemporary front lock folders. **Patterns:** Single or multi-blade folders, Bowies. **Technical:** Grind CPM 3V, CPM 440V, CPM 420V, Forge Damascus, 52100. **Prices:** $250 to $3,000. **Remarks:** Engraves, carves and does sterling silver sheaths. **Mark:** Tori arch over initials back to back.

**BRANDON, MATTHEW,** 4435 Meade St., Denver, CO 80211, Phone: 303-458-0786, MTBRANDON@HOTMAIL.COM

**Specialties:** Hunters, skinners, full-tang Bowies. **Prices:** $100 to $250 **Remarks:** Satisfaction or full refund. **Mark:** MTB.

**BRANDSEY, EDWARD P.,** 335 Forest Lake Dr., Milton, WI 53563, Phone: 608-868-9010, edchar2@ticon.net

**Specialties:** Large Bowies. Does own scrimshaw. See Egnath's second book **Patterns:** Hunters, fighters, Bowies and daggers, some buckskinner-styles Native American influence on some. An occasional tanto. **Technical:** ATS-34 440-C, 0-1, and some Damascus. Paul Bos treating past 20 years. **Prices** $250 to $600; some to $3,000. **Remarks:** Full-time maker. First knife sold i 1973. **Mark:** Initials connected - registered Wisc. Trademark since Marc 1983.

**BRANDT, MARTIN W.,** 833 Kelly Blvd., Springfield, OR 97477, Phone: 541-747-5422, oubob747@aol.com

**BRANTON, ROBERT,** 4976 Seewee Rd., Awendaw, SC 29429, Phone 843-928-3624

**Specialties:** Working straight knives of his design or to customer spec throwing knives. **Patterns:** Hunters, fighters and some miniatures. **Technica** Grinds ATS-34, A2 and 1050; forges 5160, O1. Offers hollow- or conve grinds. **Prices:** $25 to $400. **Remarks:** Part-time maker; first knife sold 1985. Doing business as Pro-Flyte, Inc. **Mark:** Last name; or first and la name, city, state.

**BRATCHER, BRETT,** 11816 County Rd. 302, Plantersville, TX 77363, Phone: 936-894-3788, Fax: (936) 894-3790, brett_bratcher@msn.com

**Specialties:** Hunting and skinning knives. **Patterns:** Clip and Drop Poi Hand forged. **Technical:** Material 5160, D2, 1095 and Damascus. **Pric** $200 to $500. **Mark:** Bratcher.

**BRAY JR., W. LOWELL,** 6931 Manor Beach Rd., New Port Richey, FL 34652, Phone: 727-846-0830, brayknives@aol.com

**Specialties:** Traditional working and using straight knives and folders of h design. **Patterns:** Hunters, fighters and utility knives. **Technical:** Grinds 44C and ATS-34; forges 52100 and Damascus. **Prices:** $100 to $500. **Remark** Spare-time maker; first knife sold in 1992. **Mark:** Lowell Bray Knives in shiel

**BREED, KIM,** 733 Jace Dr., Clarksville, TN 37040, Phone: 931-645-9171, sfbreed@yahoo.com Web: www.bwbladeworks.com

**Specialties:** High end through working folders and straight knives. **Pattern** Hunters, fighters, daggers, Bowies. His design or customers. Likes one-of-kind designs. **Technical:** Makes own Mosiac and regular Damascus, but w use stainless steels. Offers filework and sculpted material. **Prices:** $150 $2,000. **Remarks:** Full-time maker. First knife sold in 1990. **Mark:** Last nam

**BREND, WALTER,** 353 Co. Rd. 1373, Vinemont, AL 35179, Phone: 25 739-1987

**Specialties:** Tactical-style knives, fighters, automatics. **Technical:** Grinds Z and 440C blade steels, 154CM steel. **Prices:** Micarta handles, titanium ha dles.

**BRENNAN, JUDSON,** PO Box 1165, Delta Junction, AK 99737, Phon 907-895-5153, Fax: 907-895-5404

**Specialties:** Period pieces. **Patterns:** All kinds of Bowies, rifle knives, da gers. **Technical:** Forges miscellaneous steels. **Prices:** Upscale, good valu **Remarks:** Muzzle-loading gunsmith; first knife sold in 1978. **Mark:** Name.

**BRESHEARS, CLINT,** 1261 Keats, Manhattan Beach, CA 90266, Phone: 310-372-0739, Fax: 310-372-0739, breshears@mindspring.co Web: www.clintknives.com

**Specialties:** Working straight knives and folders. **Patterns:** Hunters, Bow and survival knives. Folders are mostly hunters. **Technical:** Grinds 44C 154CM and ATS-34; prefers mirror finishes. **Prices:** $125 to $750; some $1,800. **Remarks:** Part-time maker; first knife sold in 1978. **Mark:** First nan

**BREUER, LONNIE,** PO Box 877384, Wasilla, AK 99687-7384

**Specialties:** Fancy working straight knives. **Patterns:** Hunters, camp kni and axes, folders and Bowies. **Technical:** Grinds 440C, AEB-L and D2; li wire inlay, scrimshaw, decorative filing. **Prices:** $60 to $150; some to $3 **Remarks:** Part-time maker; first knife sold in 1977. **Mark:** Signature.

**BRIGHTWELL, MARK,** 21104 Creekside Dr., Leander, TX 78641, Phone: 512-267-4110

**Specialties:** Fancy and plain folders of his design. **Patterns:** Fighters, hu ers and gents, some traditional. **Technical:** Hollow- or flat-grinds ATS-34, custom Damascus; elaborate filework; heat-treats. Extensive choice of natu handle materials; no synthetics. **Prices:** $300 to $1,500. **Remarks:** Full-ti maker. **Mark:** Last name.

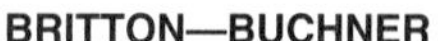

**BRITTON, TIM,** 5645 Murray Rd., Winston-Salem, NC 27106, Phone: 336-922-9582
336-922-9582, Fax: 336-923-2062, tim@trimbritton.com Web: www.trim-britton.com
**Specialties:** Small and simple working knives, sgian dubhs and special tactical designs. **Technical:** Forges and grinds stainless steel. **Prices:** $110 to $600. **Remarks:** Veteran knife maker. **Mark:** Etched signature.

**BROADWELL, DAVID,** PO Box 4314, Wichita Falls, TX 76308, Phone: 940-692-1727, Fax: 940-692-4003, david@broadwell.com Web: www.david.broadwell.com
**Specialties:** Sculpted high-art straight and folding knives. **Patterns:** Daggers, sub-hilted fighters, folders, sculpted art knives and some Bowies. **Technical:** Grinds mostly Damascus; carves; prefers natural handle materials, including stone. Some embellishment. **Prices:** $350 to $3,000; some higher. **Remarks:** Full-time maker; first knife sold in 1982. **Mark:** Stylized emblem bisecting "B"/ with last name below.

**BROCK, KENNETH L.,** PO Box 375, 207 N Skinner Rd., Allenspark, CO 80510, Phone: 303-747-2547, brockknives@nedernet.net
**Specialties:** Custom designs, Full-tang working knives and button lock folders of his design. **Patterns:** Hunters, miniatures and minis. **Technical:** Flat-grinds D2 and 440C; makes own sheaths; heat-treats. **Prices:** $50 to $500. **Remarks:** Full-time maker; first knife sold in 1978. **Mark:** Last name, city, state and serial number.

**BRODZIAK, DAVID,** 27 Stewart St, Albany, WESTERN AUSTRALIA 6330, Phone: 61 8 9841 3314, Fax: 61898115065, brodziakomninet.net.au. Web: www.brodziakcustomknives.com

**BROMLEY, PETER,** Bromley Knives, 1408 S Bettman, Spokane, WA 99212, Phone: 509-534-4235, Fax: 509-536-2666
**Specialties:** Period Bowies, folder, hunting knives - all sizes and shapes. **Patterns:** Bowies, boot knives, hunters, utility, folder, working knives. Technical; High-carbon steel (1084, 1095 and 5160). Stock removal and forge. **Prices:** $85 to $750. **Remarks:** Almost full-time, first knife sold in 1987. A.B.S. JourneymanSmith. **Mark:** Bromley, Spokane, WA.

**BROOKER, DENNIS,** Rt. 1, Box 12A, Derby, IA 50068, Phone: 515-533-2103
**Specialties:** Fancy straight knives and folders of his design. **Patterns:** Hunters, folders and boots. **Technical:** Forges and grinds. Full-time engraver and designer; instruction available. **Prices:** Moderate to upscale. **Remarks:** Part-time maker. Takes no orders; sells only completed work. **Mark:** Name.

**BROOKS, MICHAEL,** 2811 64th St, Lubbock, TX 79413, Phone: 806-799-3088, chiang@nts-online.net
**Specialties:** Working straight knives of his design or to customer specs. **Patterns:** Martial art, Bowies, hunters, and fighters. **Technical:** Grinds 440C, D2 and ATS-34; offers wide variety of handle materials. **Prices:** $75 & up. **Remarks:** Part-time maker; first knife sold in 1985. **Mark:** Initials.

**BROOKS, STEVE R.,** 1610 Dunn Ave., Walkerville, MT 59701, Phone: 406-782-5114
**Specialties:** Working straight knives and folders; period pieces. **Patterns:** Hunters, Bowies and camp knives; folding lockers; axes, tomahawks and buckskinner knives; swords and stilettos. **Technical:** Forges O1, Damascus and mosaic Damascus. Some knives come embellished. **Prices:** $150 to $2,000. **Remarks:** Full-time maker; first knife sold in 1982. **Mark:** Lazy initials.

**BROOKS, BUZZ,** 2345 Yosemite Dr., Los Angles, CA 90041, Phone: 323-256-2892

**BROOME, THOMAS A.,** 1212 E. Aliak Ave., Kenai, AK 99611-8205, Phone: 907-283-9128, tomlei@ptialaska.ent Web: www.alaskanknives.com
**Specialties:** Working hunters and folders **Patterns:** Traditional and custom orders. **Technical:** Grinds ATS-34, BG-42, CPM-S30V. **Prices:** $175 to $350. **Remarks:** Full-time maker; first knife sold in 1979. Doing business as Thom's Custom Knives. **Mark:** Full name, city, state. **Other:** Doing business as: Alaskan Man O; Steel Knives.

**BROTHERS, ROBERT L.,** 989 Philpott Rd., Colville, WA 99114, Phone: 509-684-8922
**Specialties:** Traditional working and using straight knives and folders of his design and to customer specs. **Patterns:** Bowies, fighters and hunters. **Technical:** Grinds D2; forges Damascus. Makes own Damascus from saw steel wire rope and chain; part-time goldsmith and stone-setter. **Prices:** $100 to $400; some higher. **Remarks:** Part-time maker; first knife sold in 1986. **Mark:** Initials and year made.

**BROWER, MAX,** 2016 Story St., Boone, IA 50036, Phone: 515-432-2938
**Specialties:** Working/using straight knives. **Patterns:** Bowies, hunters and boots. **Technical:** Grinds 440C and ATS-34. **Prices:** Start at $150. **Remarks:** Spare-time maker; first knife sold in 1981. **Mark:** Last name.

**BROWN, DENNIS G.,** 1633 N. 197TH Pl., Shoreline, WA 98133, Phone: 206-542-3997, denjilbro@msn.com

**BROWN, ROB E.,** PO Box 15107, Emerald Hill 6011, Port Elizabeth, SOUTH AFRICA, Phone: 27-41-3661086, Fax: 27-41-4511731, rbknives@global.co.za
**Specialties:** Contemporary-designed straight knives and period pieces. **Patterns:** Utility knives, hunters, boots, fighters and daggers. **Technical:** Grinds 440C, D2, ATS-34 and commercial Damascus. Knives mostly mirror finished; African handle materials. **Prices:** $100 to $1,500. **Remarks:** Full-time maker; first knife sold in 1985. **Mark:** Name and country.

**BROWN, TROY L.,** 22945 W. 867 Rd., Park Hill, OK 74451, Phone: 918-457-4128
**Specialties:** Working and using knives and folders. **Patterns:** Bowies, hunters, folders and scagel-style. **Technical:** Forges 5160, 52100, 1084; makes his own Damascus. Prefers stag, wood and Micarta for handles. Offers engraved bolsters and guards. **Prices:** $150 to $750. **Remarks:** Full-time maker; first knife sold in 1994. Knives. **Mark:** Troy Brown. **Other:** Doing business as Elk Creek Forge.

**BROWN, JIM,** 1097 Fernleigh Cove, Little Rock, AR 72210

**BROWN, HAROLD E.,** 3654 N.W. Hwy. 72, Arcadia, FL 34266, Phone: 863-494-7514, brknives@strato.net
**Specialties:** Fancy and exotic working knives. **Patterns:** Folders, slip-lock, locking several kinds. **Technical:** Grinds D2, 440C and ATS-34. Embellishment available. **Prices:** $175 to $1,000. **Remarks:** Part-time maker; first knife sold in 1976. **Mark:** Name and city with logo.

**BROWNE, RICK,** 980 West 13th St., Upland, CA 91786, Phone: 909-985-1728
**Specialties:** Sheffield pattern pocket knives. **Patterns:** Hunters, fighters and daggers. No heavy-duty knives. **Technical:** Grinds ATS-34. **Prices:** Start at $450. **Remarks:** Part-time maker; first knife sold in 1975. **Mark:** R.E. Browne, Upland, CA.

**BROWNING, STEVEN W.,** 3400 Harrison Rd., Benton, AR 72015, Phone: 501-316-2450

**BRUNCKHORST, LYLE,** Country Village, 23706 7th Ave. SE, Ste. B, Bothell, WA 98021, Phone: 425-402-3484, bronks@net-tech.com Web: bronks.com or bronksknifeworks.com
**Specialties:** Traditional working and using straight knives and folders of his design. **Patterns:** Bowies, hunters and locking folders. **Technical:** Grinds ATS-34; forges 5160 and his own Damascus. Iridescent RR spike knives. Offers scrimshaw, inlays and animal carvings in horn handles. **Prices:** $225 to $750; some to $3,750. **Remarks:** Full-time maker; first knife sold in 1976. Doing business as Bronk's Knife works. **Mark:** Bucking horse.

**BRUNER JR., FRED, BRUNER BLADES,** E10910W Hilldale Dr., Fall Creek, WI 54742, Phone: 715-877-2496, brunerblades@msn.com
**Specialties:** Pipe tomahawks, swords, may my own. **Patterns:** Drop point hunters. **Prices:** $65.00 to $1,500.00. **Remarks:** Voting member of the knifemakers guild. **Mark:** Fred Bruner.

**BRUNETTA, DAVID,** PO Box 4972, Laguna Beach, CA 92652, Phone: 714-497-9611
**Specialties:** Straights, folders and art knives. **Patterns:** Bowies, camp/hunting, folders, fighters. **Technical:** Grinds ATS-34, D2, BG42. forges O1, 52100, 5160, 1095, makes own Damascus. **Prices:** $300 to $9,000. **Mark:** Circle DB logo with last name straight or curved.

**BRYAN, TOM,** 14822 S Gilbert Rd., Gilbert, AZ 85296, Phone: 480-812-8529
**Specialties:** Straight and folding knives. **Patterns:** Drop-point hunter fighters. **Technical:** ATS-34, 154CM, 440C and A2. **Prices:** $150 to $800. **Remarks:** Part-time maker; sold first knife in 1994. **Mark:** T. Bryan. **Other:** DBA as T. Bryan Knives.

**BUCHMAN, BILL,** 63312 South Rd., Bend, OR 97701, Phone: 503-382-8851
**Specialties:** Working straight knives. **Patterns:** Hunters, Bowies, fighters and boots. Makes full line of leather craft and saddle maker knives. **Technical:** Forges 440C and Sandvik 15N20. Prefers 440C for saltwater. **Prices:** $95 to $400. **Remarks:** Full-time maker; first knife sold in 1982. **Mark:** Initials or last name.

**BUCHNER, BILL,** PO Box 73, Idleyld Park, OR 97447, Phone: 541-498-2247, blazinhammer@earthlink.net Web: www.home.earthlin.net/~blazinghammer
**Specialties:** Working straight knives, kitchen knives and high-art knives of his design. **Technical:** Uses W1, L6 and his own Damascus. Invented "spectrum metal" for letter openers, folder handles and jewelry. Likes sculpturing and carving in Damascus. **Prices:** $40 to $3,000; some higher. **Remarks:** Full-time maker; first knife sold in 1978. **Mark:** Signature.

**BUCHOLZ, MARK A.,** PO Box 82, Holualoa, HI 96725, Phone: 808-322-4045
**Specialties:** Liner lock folders. **Patterns:** Hunters and fighters. **Technical:** Grinds ATS-34. **Prices:** Upscale. **Remarks:** Full-time maker; first knife sold in 1976. **Mark:** Name, city and state in buffalo skull logo or signature.

**BUCKBEE, DONALD M.,** 243 South Jackson Trail, Grayling, MI 49738, Phone: 517-348-1386
**Specialties:** Working straight knives, some fancy, in standard patterns; concentrating on kitchen knives. **Patterns:** Kitchen knives, hunters, Bowies. **Technical:** Grinds D2, 440C, ATS-34. Makes ultra-lights in hunter patterns. **Prices:** $100 to $250; some to $350. **Remarks:** Part-time maker; first knife sold in 1984. **Mark:** Antlered bee—a buck bee.

**BUCKNER, JIMMIE H.,** PO Box 162, Putney, GA 31782, Phone: 229-436-4182
**Specialties:** Camp knives, Bowies (one-of-a-kind), liner-lock folders, tomahawks, camp axes, neck knives for law enforcement and hide-out knives for body guards and professional people. **Patterns:** Hunters, camp knives, Bowies. **Technical:** Forges 1084, 5160 and Damascus (own), own heat treats. **Prices:** $195 to $795 and up. **Remarks:** Full-time maker; first knife sold in 1980, ABS Master Smith. **Mark:** Name over spade.

**BUEBENDORF, ROBERT E.,** 108 Lazybrooke Rd., Monroe, CT 06468, Phone: 203-452-1769
**Specialties:** Traditional and fancy straight knives of his design. **Patterns:** Hand-makes and embellishes belt buckle knives. **Technical:** Forges and grinds 440C, O1, W2, 1095, his own Damascus and 154CM. **Prices:** $200 to $500. **Remarks:** Full-time maker; first knife sold in 1978. **Mark:** First and middle initials, last name and MAKER.

**BULLARD, RANDALL,** 7 Mesa Dr., Canyon, TX 79015, Phone: 806-655-0590
**Specialties:** Working/using straight knives and folders of his design or to customer specs. **Patterns:** Hunters, locking folders and slip-joint folders. **Technical:** Grinds O1, ATS-34 and 440C. Does file work. **Prices:** $125 to $300; some to $500. **Remarks:** Part-time maker; first knife sold in 1993. Doing business as Bullard Custom Knives. **Mark:** First and middle initials, last name, maker, city and state.

**BULLARD, TOM,** 117 MC 8068, Flippin, AR 72634, Phone: 870-453-3421, tbullard@bullshoals.net Web: www.natconet.com/~tbullard
**Specialties:** Armadillo handle material on hunter and folders. **Patterns:** Bowies, hunters, single and 2-blade trappers, lockback folders. **Technical:** Grinds 440-C, ATS-34, 0-1, commercial Damascus. **Prices:** $150 and up. **Remarks:** Offers filework and engraving by Norvell Foster and Terry Thies. Does not make screw-together knives. **Mark:** T Bullard.

**BULLARD, BILL,** Rt. 5, Box 35, Andalusia, AL 36420, Phone: 334-222-9003
**Specialties:** Traditional working and using straight knives and folders of his design. **Patterns:** Hunters, slip-joint folders and utility/camp knives and folders to customer specs. **Technical:** Forges Damascus, cable. Offers filework. **Prices:** $100 to $500; some to $1,500. **Remarks:** Part-time maker; first knife sold in 1974. Doing business as Five Runs Forge. **Mark:** Last name stamped on ricasso.

**BUMP, BRUCE D.,** 1103 Rex Ln., Walla Walla, WA 99362, Phone: 509 522-2219, bruceandkaye@charter.net Web: www.brucebumpknives.com
**Specialties:** Traditional and Mosaic Damascus. **Patterns:** Black powder pistol/knife combinations also gun/hawk. **Technical:** Enjoy the 15th-18th century "dual threat" weapons. **Prices:** $350 to $10,000. **Remarks:** American Bladesmith Society Master Smith 2003. **Mark:** Bruce D. Bump Bruce D Bump Custom Walla Walla WA.

**BURAK, CHET,** KNIFE SERVICES PHOTOGRAPHER, PO Box 14383, E Providence, RI 02914, Phone: 401-431-0625, Fax: 401-434-9821

**BURDEN, JAMES,** 405 Kelly St., Burkburnett, TX 76354

**BURGER, FRED,** Box 436, Munster 4278, Kwa-Zulu Natal, SOUTH AFRICA, Phone: 27 393216, Web: www.swordcane.com
**Specialties:** Sword canes and tactical walking sticks. **Patterns:** 440C and carbon steel blades. **Technical:** Double hollow ground and Poniard-style blades. **Prices:** $190 to $600. **Remarks:** Full-time maker with son, Barry, since 1987. **Mark:** Last name in oval pierced by a dagger. **Other:** Member South African Guild.

**BURGER, PON,** 12 Glenwood Ave., Woodlands, Bulawayo, Zimbabwe 75514
**Specialties:** Collector's items. **Patterns:** Fighters, locking folders of traditional styles, buckles. **Technical:** Scrimshaws 440C blade. Uses polished buffalo horn with brass fittings. Cased in buffalo hide book. **Prices:** $450 to $1,100. **Remarks:** Full-time maker; first knife sold in 1973. Doing business as Burg[e] Products. **Mark:** Spirit of Africa.

**BURKE, BILL,** 12 chapman ln., Boise, ID 83716, Phone: 208-756-3797 burke531@salmoninternet.com
**Specialties:** Hand-forged working knives. **Patterns:** Fowler pronghorn, cl[ip] point and drop point hunters. **Technical:** Forges 52100 and 5160. Makes ow[n] Damascus from 15N20 and 1084. **Prices:** $450 and up. **Remarks:** Dedicate[d] to fixed-blade high-performance knives. ABS journey man. **Mark:** Initials co[n]nected. **Other:** Also make "Ed Fowler" miniatures.

**BURKE, DAN,** 22001 Ole Barn Rd., Edmond, OK 73034, Phone: 405-341-3406, Fax: 405-340-3333
**Specialties:** Slip joint folders. **Patterns:** Traditional folders. **Technica[l]:** Grinds D2 and BG-42. Prefers natural handle materials; heat-treats. **Price[s]:** $440 to $1,900. **Remarks:** Full-time maker; first knife sold in 1976. **Mark:** Fi[rst] initial and last name.

**BURNETT, MAX,** 537 Old Dug Mtn. Rd., Paris, AR 72855, Phone: 501 963-2767, mburnett@cswnet.com
**Specialties:** Forging with coal/charcoal; some stock removal. **Patterns:** Hu[nt]ers, Bowies, camp, tactical, neck knives and kydex sheaths. **Technic[al]:** Steels used: 1084, 1095, 52100, 5160, L6, 01 and others available. **Price[s]:** $50 and up for neck knives/Bowies $250 and up. **Remarks:** Full-time sin[ce] March 2000. **Mark:** M.OGG and omega symbol.

**BURRIS, PATRICK R.,** 11078 Crystal Lynn C.t, Jacksonville, FL 3222[6] Phone: 904-757-3938, keenedge@comcast.net
**Specialties:** Traditional straight knives. **Patterns:** Hunters, bowies, locki[ng] liner folders. **Technical:** Flat grinds CPM stainless and Damascus. **Remar[ks]:** Charter member Florida Knifemakers Association. Member Knifemak[ers] Guild. **Mark:** Last name in script.

**BURROWS, CHUCK,** Wild Rose Trading Co, PO Box 5174, Durango, CO 81301, Phone: 970-259-8396, chuck@wrtcleather.com Web: www.wrtcleather.com
**Specialties:** Presentation knives, hawks, and sheaths based on the styles [of] the American frontier incorporating carving, beadwork, rawhide, braintan, a[nd] other period correct materials. We also make other period style knives such [as] Scottish Dirks and Moorish jambiyahs. **Patterns:** Bowies, Dags, tomahaw[ks,] war clubs, and all other 18th and 19th century frontier style edged weapo[ns] and tools. **Prices:** $500.00 plus. **Remarks:** Full-time maker, first knife sol[d] [in] 1973. 40+ years experience working leather. **Technical:** Carbon steel o[r] 5160, 1080/1084, 1095, O1, Damascus-Our Frontier Shear Steel, plus ot[her] styles - available on request. Forged knives, hawks, etc. are made in colla[bo]rations with bladesmiths. Gib Guignard (under the name of Cactus Rose) a[nd] Mark Williams (under the name UB Forged). Blades are usually forge finis[h] and all items are given an aged period look. **Mark:** A lazy eight or lazy ei[ght] with a capital T at the center. On leather either the lazy eight with T o[r] WRTC makers stamp.

**BURROWS, STEPHEN R.,** 3532 Michigan, Kansas City, MO 64109, Phone: 816-921-1573
**Specialties:** Fantasy straight knives of his design, to customer specs an[d] standard patterns; period pieces. **Patterns:** Fantasy, bird and trout kni[ves,] daggers, fighters and hunters. **Technical:** Forges 5160 and 1095 high-car[bon] steel, O1 and his Damascus. Offers lost wax casting in bronze or silve[r] cross guards and pommels. **Prices:** $65 to $600; some to $2,000. **Remar[ks]:** Full-time maker; first knife sold in 1983. Doing business as Gypsy Silk. **Ma[rk]:** Etched name.

**BUSFIELD, JOHN,** 153 Devonshire Circle, Roanoke Rapids, NC 278[..] Phone: 252-537-3949, Fax: 252-537-8704, busfield@charter.net Web[:] www.busfieldknives.com
**Specialties:** Investor-grade folders; high-grade working straight knives. **P[at]terns:** Original price-style and trailing-point interframe and sculpted-fra[me] folders, drop-point hunters and semi-skinners. **Technical:** Grinds 154CM [and] ATS-34. Offers interframes, gold frames and inlays; uses jade, agate [and] lapis. **Prices:** $275 to $2,000. **Remarks:** Full-time maker; first knife sol[d in] 1979. **Mark:** Last name and address.

**BUSSE, JERRY,** 11651 Co. Rd. 12, Wauseon, OH 43567, Phone: 41[9] 923-6471
**Specialties:** Working straight knives. **Patterns:** Heavy combat knives [and] camp knives. **Technical:** Grinds D2, A2, INFI. **Prices:** $1,100 to $3,[..] **Remarks:** Full-time maker; first knife sold in 1983. **Mark:** Last name in lo[go].

**BUTLER, JOHN,** 777 Tyre Rd., Havana, FL 32333, Phone: 850-539-5742
**Specialties:** Hunters, Bowies, period. **Technical:** Damascus, 52100, 5[160,] L6 steels. **Prices:** $80 and up. **Remarks:** Making knives since 1986. **M[ark]:** JB. **Other:** Journeyman (ABS).

**BUTLER, BART,** 822 Seventh St., Ramona, CA 92065, Phone: 760-789-6431

**BUTLER, JOHN R.,** 20162 6th Ave. N.E., Shoreline, WA 98155, Phone: 206-362-3847, rjjjrb@sprynet.com

**BUXTON, BILL,** 155 Oak Bend Rd, Kaiser, MO 65047, Phone: 573-348-3577, camper@yhti.net Web: www.geocites.com/buxtonknives
**Specialties:** Forged fancy and working straight knives and folders. Mostly one-of-a-kind pieces. **Patterns:** Fighters, daggers, bowies, hunters, linerlock folders, axes and tomahawks. **Technical:** Forges 52100, 0-1, 1080. Makes own Damascus (mosaic and random patterns) from 1080, 1095, 15n20, and powdered metals 1084 and 4800a. Offers sterling silver inlay, n/s pin pattern-ing and pewter pouring on axe and hawk handles. **Prices:** $300 to $1,500. **Remarks:** Full-time maker, sold first knife in 1998. **Mark:** First ad last name.

**BYBEE, BARRY J.,** 795 Lock Rd. E., Cadiz, KY 42211-8615
**Specialties:** Working straight knives of his design. **Patterns:** Hunters, fight-ers, boot knives, tantos and Bowies. **Technical:** Grinds ATS-34, 440C. Likes stag and Micarta for handle materials. **Prices:** $125 to $200; some to $1,000. **Remarks:** Part-time maker; first knife sold in 1968. **Mark:** Arrowhead logo with name, city and state.

**BYRD, WESLEY L.,** 189 Countryside Dr., Evensville, TN 37332, Phone: 423-775-3826, w.l.byrd@worldnet.att.net
**Specialties:** Hunters, fighters, Bowies, dirks, sign dubh, utility, and camp knives. **Patterns:** Wire rope, random patterns.Twists, W's, Ladder, Kite Tail. **Technical:** Uses 52100, 1084, 5160, L6, and 15n20. **Prices:** Starting at $180. **Remarks:** Prefer to work with customer for their design preferences. **Mark:** BYRD, WB<X. **Other:** ABS JourneymanSmith.

# C

**CABE, JERRY (BUDDY),** 62 McClaren Ln., Hattieville, AR 72063, Phone: 501-354-3581

**CABRERA, SERGIO B.,** 25711 Frampton Ave. Apt. 113, Harbor City, CA 90710

**CAFFREY, EDWARD J.,** 2608 Central Ave. West, Great Falls, MT 59404, Phone: 406-727-9102, ed@caffreyknives.net Web: www.caf-freyknives.net
**Specialties:** One-of-a-kind, collector quality pieces, working/using knives; will accept some customer designs. **Patterns:** Folders, Bowies, hunters, fighters, camp/utility, some hawks and hatchets. **Technical:** Forges his own mosaic Damascus, 52100, 6150, 1080/1084, W-1, W-2, some cable and/or chain Damascus. Offers S30V for those who demand stainless. **Prices:** Starting at $140; typical hunters start at $350; prices for exotic mosaic Damascus pieces can range to $5,000. **Remarks:** Retired military; ABS Master Smith. Full-time maker; first knife sold in 1989. **Mark:** Stamped last name with MS on straight knives. Etched last name with MS on folders.

**CAIRNES JR., CARROLL B.,** RT. 1 Box 324, Palacios, TX 77465, Phone: 369-588-6815

**CALDWELL, BILL,** 255 Rebecca, West Monroe, LA 71292, Phone: 318-323-3025
**Specialties:** Straight knives and folders with machined bolsters and liners. **Patterns:** Fighters, Bowies, survival knives, tomahawks, razors and push knives. **Technical:** Owns and operates a very large, well-equipped blacksmith and bladesmith shop extant with six large forges and eight power hammers. **Prices:** $400 to $3,500; some to $10,000. **Remarks:** Full-time maker and self-styled blacksmith; first knife sold in 1962. **Mark:** Wild Bill and Sons.

**CALLAHAN, F. TERRY,** PO Box 880, Boerne, TX 78006, Phone: 830-981-8274, Fax: 830-981-8279, ftclaw@gvtc.com
**Specialties:** Custom hand-forged edged knives, collectible and functional. **Patterns:** Bowies, folders, daggers, hunters & camp knives. **Technical:** Forges 5160, 1095 and his own Damascus. Offers filework and handmade sheaths. **Prices:** $125 to $2,000. **Remarks:** First knife sold in 1990. **Mark:** Initials inside a keystone symbol. **Other:** ABS/Journeyman Bladesmith.

**CALLAHAN, ERRETT,** 2 Fredonia, Lynchburg, VA 24503, Phone: 434-528-3444
**Specialties:** Obsidian knives. **Patterns:** Modern-styles and Stone Age replicas. **Technical:** Flakes and knaps to order. **Prices:** $100 to $3400. **Remarks:** Part-time maker; first flint blades sold in 1974. **Mark:** Blade—engraved name, year and arrow; handle—signed edition, year and unit number.

**CALVERT JR., ROBERT W. (BOB),** 911 Julia, PO Box 858, Rayville, LA 71269, Phone: 318-728-4113, Fax: (318) 728-0000, rcalvert@bayou.com
**Specialties:** Using and hunting knives; your design or mine. Since 1990. **Patterns:** Forges own Damascus; all patterns. **Technical:** 5160, D2, 52100, 1084. Prefers natural handle material. **Prices:** $150 and up. **Remarks:** TOMB Member ABS, Journeyman Smith. **Mark:** Calvert (Block) J S.

**CAMERER, CRAIG,** 3766 Rockbridge Rd, Chesterfield, IL 62630, Phone: 618-753-2147, craig@camererknives.com Web: www.cam-ererknives.com
**Specialties:** Everyday carry knives, hunters and Bowies. **Patterns:** D-guard, historical recreations and fighters. **Technical:** Most of his knives are forged to shape. **Prices:** $100 and up. **Remarks:** Member of the ABS and PKA. Jouneymen smith ABS

**CAMERON, RON G.,** PO Box 183, Logandale, NV 89021, Phone: 702-398-3356, rntcameron@mvdsl.com
**Specialties:** Fancy and embellished working/using straight knives and folders of his design. **Patterns:** Bowies, hunters and utility/camp knives. **Technical:** Grinds ATS-34, AEB-L and Devin Thomas Damascus or my own Damascus from 1084 and 15N20. Does filework, fancy pins, mokume fittings. Uses exotic hardwoods, stag and Micarta for handles. Pearl & mammoth ivory. **Prices:** $175 to $850; some to $1,000. **Remarks:** Part-time maker; first knife sold in 1994. Doing business as Cameron Handmade Knives. **Mark:** Last name, town, state or last name.

**CAMERON HOUSE,** 2001 Delaney Rd. Se., Salem, OR 97306, Phone: 503-585-3286
**Specialties:** Working straight knives. **Patterns:** Hunters, Bowies, Fighters. **Technical:** Grinds ATS-34, 530V, 154CM. **Remarks:** Part-time maker, first knife. sold in 1993. **Prices:** $150 and up. **Mark:** HOUSE.

**CAMPBELL, DICK,** 196 Garden Homes Dr, Colville, WA 99114, Phone: 509-684-6080, dicksknives@aol.com
**Specialties:** Working straight knives, period pieces. **Patterns:** Hunters, fight-ers, boots: 19th century Bowies. **Technical:** Grinds 440C, 154CM. **Prices:** $200 to $2,500. **Remarks:** Full-time maker. First knife sold in 1975. **Mark:** Name.

**CAMPBELL, COURTNAY M.,** PO Box 23009, Columbia, SC 29224, Phone: 803-787-0151

**CAMPOS, IVAN,** R.XI de Agosto, 107, Tatui, SP, BRAZIL 18270-000, Phone: 00-55-15-2518092, Fax: 00-55-15-2594368, ivan@ivancam-pos.com Web: www.ivancompos.com
**Specialties:** Brazilian handmade and antique knives.

**CANDRELLA, JOE,** 1219 Barness Dr., Warminster, PA 18974, Phone: 215-675-0143
**Specialties:** Working straight knives, some fancy. **Patterns:** Daggers, boots, Bowies. **Technical:** Grinds 440C and 154CM. **Prices:** $100 to $200; some to $1,000. **Remarks:** Part-time maker; first knife sold in 1985. Does business as Franjo. **Mark:** FRANJO with knife as J.

**CANNADY, DANIEL L.,** Box 301, Allendale, SC 29810, Phone: 803-584-2813, Fax: 803-584-2813
**Specialties:** Working straight knives and folders in standard patterns. **Patterns:** Drop-point hunters, Bowies, skinners, fishing knives with concave grind, steak knives and kitchen cutlery. **Technical:** Grinds D2, 440C and ATS-34. **Prices:** $65 to $325; some to $1,000. **Remarks:** Full-time maker; first knife sold in 1980. **Mark:** Last name above Allendale, S.C.

**CANNON, RAYMOND W.,** PO Box 1412, Homer, AK 99603, Phone: 907-235-7779
**Specialties:** Fancy working knives, folders and swords of his design or to customer specs; many one-of-a-kind pieces. **Patterns:** Bowies, daggers and skinners. **Technical:** Forges and grinds O1, A6, 52100, 5160, his combinations for his own Damascus. **Remarks:** First knife sold in 1984. **Mark:** Cannon Alaska or "Hand forged by Wes Cannon".

**CANNON, DAN,** 9500 Leon, Dallas, TX 75217, Phone: 972-557-0268
**Specialties:** Damascus, hand forged. **Patterns:** Bowies, hunters, folders. **Prices:** $300. **Remarks:** Full-time maker. **Mark:** CANNON D.

**CANOY, ANDREW B.,** 3420 Fruchey Ranch Rd., Hubbard Lake, MI 49747, Phone: 810-266-6039, canoy1@shianet.org

**CANTER, RONALD E.,** 96 Bon Air Circle, Jackson, TN 38305, Phone: 731-668-1780, canterr@charter.net
**Specialties:** Traditional working knives to customer specs. **Patterns:** Beaver-tail skinners, Bowies, hand axes and folding lockers. **Technical:** Grinds A1, 440C and 154CM. **Prices:** $65 to $250; some $500 and higher. **Remarks:** Spare-time maker; first knife sold in 1973. **Mark:** Three last initials intertwined.

**CANTRELL, KITTY D.,** 19720 Hwy. 78, Ramona, CA 92076, Phone: 760-788-8304

**CAPDEPON, ROBERT,** 829 Vatican Rd., Carencro, LA 70520, Phone: 337-896-8753, Fax: 318-896-8753
**Specialties:** Traditional straight knives and folders of his design. **Patterns:** Boots, hunters and locking folders. **Technical:** Grinds ATS-34, 440C and D2. Hand-rubbed finish on blades. Likes natural horn materials for handles, including ivory. Offers engraving. **Prices:** $250 to $750. **Remarks:** Full-time maker; first knife made in 1992. **Mark:** Last name.

**CAPDEPON, RANDY,** 553 Joli Rd., Carencro, LA 70520, Phone: 318-896-4113, Fax: 318-896-8753
**Specialties:** Straight knives and folders of his design. **Patterns:** Hunters and locking folders. **Technical:** Grinds ATS-34, 440C and D2. **Prices:** $200 to $600. **Remarks:** Part-time maker; first knife made in 1992. Doing business as Capdepon Knives. **Mark:** Last name.

**CAREY JR., CHARLES W.,** 1003 Minter Rd., Griffin, GA 30223, Phone: 770-228-8994
**Specialties:** Working and using knives of his design and to customer specs; period pieces. **Patterns:** Fighters, hunters, utility/camp knives and forged-to-shape miniatures. **Technical:** Forges 5160, old files and cable. Offers filework; ages some of his knives. **Prices:** $35 to $400. **Remarks:** Part-time maker; first knife sold in 1991. **Mark:** Knife logo.

**CARILLO, DWAINE,** C/O AIRKAT KNIVES, 1021 SW 15th St, Moore, OK 73160, Phone: 405-503-5879, Web: www.airkatknives.com

**CARLISLE, FRANK,** 5930 Hereford, Detroit, MI 48224, Phone: 313-882-8349
**Specialties:** Fancy/embellished and fantasy folders of his design. **Patterns:** Hunters, locking folders and swords. **Technical:** Grinds Damascus and stainless. **Prices:** $80 to $300. **Remarks:** Full-time maker; first knife sold in 1993. Doing business as Carlisle Cutlery. **Mark:** Last name.

**CARLISLE, JEFF,** PO Box 282 12753 Hwy. 200, Simms, MT 59477, Phone: 406-264-5693

**CARLSON, KELLY,** 54 S. Holt Hill, Antrim, NH 03440, Phone: 603-588-2765, kellycarlson@tds.net Web: www.carlsonknives.com
**Specialties:** Unique folders of maker's own design. **Patterns:** One-of-a-kind, artistic folders, mostly of liner-lock design, along with interpretations of traditional designs. **Technical:** Grinds and heat treats S30V, D2, ATS-34, stainless and carbon Damascus steels. Prefers hand sanded finishes and natural ivories and pearls, in conjunction with decorative accents obtained from mosaic Damascus, Damascus and various exotic materials. **Prices:** $600 to $3,500. **Remarks:** Full-time maker as of 2002, first knife sold in 1975.

**CARNAHAN, CHARLES A.,** 27 George Arnold Lane, Green Spring, WV 26722, Phone: 304-492-5891
**Specialties:** Hand forged fixed blade knives. **Patterns:** Bowies and hunters. **Technical:** Steels used; 5160, 1095, 1085, L6 and A023-E. **Prices:** $300 to $2,000. **Remarks:** Part-time maker. First knife sold in 1991. Knives all made by hand forging, no stock removal. **Mark:** Last name.

**CAROLINA CUSTOM KNIVES, SEE TOMMY MCNABB**

**CARPENTER, RONALD W.,** RT. 4 Box 323, Jasper, TX 75951, Phone: 409-384-4087

**CARR, TIM,** 3660 Pillon Rd., Muskegon, MI 49445, Phone: 231-766-3582
**Specialties:** Hunters, camp knives. **Patterns:** Mine or yours. **Technical:** Hand forged 52100 and Damascus. **Prices:** $125 to $700. **Remarks:** Part-time maker. **Mark:** The letter combined from maker's initials TRC.

**CARROLL, CHAD,** 12182 McClelland, Grant, MI 49327, Phone: 231-834-9183, CHAD724@msn.com
**Specialties:** Hunters, Bowies, folders, swords, tomahawks. **Patterns:** Fixed blades, folders. **Prices:** $100 to $2,000. **Remarks:** ABS Journeyman-May 2002. **Mark:** (a backward C next to a forward C, maker's initials).

**CARSON, HAROLD J. "KIT",** 1076 Brizendine Lane, Vine Grove, KY 40175, Phone: 270 877-6300, Fax: 270 877 6338, KCKnives@bbtel.com Web: http://ww.kvnet.org/knives Web: album- www.kitcarsonknives.com/album
**Specialties:** Military fixed blades and folders; art pieces. **Patterns:** Fighters, D handles, daggers, combat folders and Crosslock-styles, tactical folders, tactical fixed blades. **Technical:** Grinds Stellite 6K, Talonite, CPM steels, Damascus. **Prices:** $400 to $750; some to $5,000. **Remarks:** Full-time maker; first knife sold in 1973. **Mark:** Name stamped or engraved.

**CARTER, MURRAY M.,** PO Box 307, Vernonia, OR 97064, Phone: 503-429-0447, m_carter-cutlery@pop06.odn.ne.jp
**Specialties:** Traditional Japanese cutlery, utilizing San soh ko (3 layer) or Kata-ha (two layer) blade construction. Laminated neck knives, traditional Japanese etc. **Patterns:** Works from over 200 standard Japanese and North American designs. **Technical:** Hot Forges and cold forges Hitachi white steel #1, Hitachi blue super steel exclusively. **Prices:** $30 to $3,000. **Remarks:** Full-time maker. First knife sold in 1989. Owner and designer of "Muteki" brand knives. **Mark:** Name with Japanese character on forged pieces. "Muteki" with Japanese characters on stock-removal blades.

**CARTER, FRED,** 5219 Deer Creek Rd., Wichita Falls, TX 76302, Phone: 904-723-4020
**Specialties:** High-art investor-class straight knives; some working hunters and fighters. **Patterns:** Classic daggers, Bowies; interframe, stainless and blued steel folders with gold inlay. **Technical:** Grinds a variety of steels. Us no glue or solder. Engraves and inlays. **Prices:** Generally upscale. **Remark** Full-time maker. **Mark:** Signature in oval logo.

**CASHEN, KEVIN R.,** 5615 Tyler St., Hubbardston, MI 48845, Phone: 989-981-6780, krcashen@mvcc.com Web: www.cashenblades.com
**Specialties:** Working straight knives, high art pattern welded swords, tra tional renaissance and ethnic pieces. **Patterns:** Hunters, Bowies, uti knives, swords, daggers. **Technical:** Forges 1095, 1084 and his own O1/ Damascus. **Prices:** $100 to $4,000+. **Remarks:** Full-time maker; first kn sold in 1985. Doing business as Matherton Forge. **Mark:** Black letter C English initials and Master Smith stamp.

**CASTEEL, DOUGLAS,** PO Box 63, Monteagle, TN 37356, Phone: 931-723-0851, Fax: 931-723-1856, ddcasteel@charter.net Web: www.caste customknives.com
**Specialties:** One-of-a-kind collector-class period pieces. **Patterns:** Dagge Bowies, swords and folders. **Technical:** Grinds 440C. Offers gold and sil castings. **Prices:** Upscale. **Remarks:** Full-time maker; first knife sold in 19 **Mark:** Last name.

**CASTEEL, DIANNA,** P.O .Box 63, Monteagle, TN 37356, Phone: 931-723-0851, ddcasteel@charter.net Web: wwwcasteelcustomknives.com
**Specialties:** Small, delicate daggers and miniatures; most knives one-of kind. **Patterns:** Daggers, boot knives, fighters and miniatures. **Technic** Grinds 440C. **Prices:** Start at $350; miniatures start at $250. **Remarks:** F time maker. **Mark:** Di in script.

**CASTON, DARRIEL,** 3725 Duran Circle, Sacramento, CA 95821, Phone: 916-359-0613, dcaston@surewest.net
**Specialties:** Investment grade jade handle folders of his design and gen man folders. **Patterns:** Folders - slipjoints and lockback. Will be making erlocks in the near future. **Technical:** Small gentleman folders for office desk warriors. Grinds ATS-34, 154CM, S30V and Damascus. **Prices:** $25 $900. **Remarks:** Part-time maker; won best new maker at first show in S 2004. **Mark:** Etched rocket ship with "Darriel Caston" or just "Caston" inside spring on Damascus and engraved knives.

**CATOE, DAVID R.,** 4024 Heutte Dr., Norfolk, VA 23518, Phone: 757-480-3191
**Technical:** Does own forging, Damascus and heat treatments. **Price:** $20 $500; some higher. **Remarks:** Part-time maker; trained by Dan Maragni 19 1988; first knife sold 1989. **Mark:** Leaf of a camillia.

**CAWTHORNE, CHRISTOPHER A.,** PO Box 604, Wrangell, AK 9992
**Specialties:** High-carbon steel, cable wire rope, silver wire inlay. **Patter** Forge welded Damascus and wire rope, random pattern. **Technical:** H forged, 50 lb little giant power hammer, W-2, 0-1, L6, 1095. **Prices:** $65 $2,500. **Remarks:** School ABS 1985 w/bill moran, hand forged, heat tr **Mark:** Cawthorne, forged in stamp.

**CENTOFANTE, FRANK,** PO Box 928, Madisonville, TN 37354-0928, Phone: 423-442-5767, frankcentofante@bellsouth.net
**Specialties:** Fancy working folders. **Patterns:** Lockers and liner locks. **Te nical:** Grinds ATS-34; hand-rubbed satin finish on blades. **Prices:** $60 $1,200. **Remarks:** Full-time maker; first knife sold in 1968. **Mark:** Name, state.

**CHAFFEE, JEFF L.,** 14314 N. Washington St., PO Box 1, Morris, IN 47033, Phone: 812-934-6350
**Specialties:** Fancy working and utility folders and straight knives. **Patte** Fighters, dagger, hunter and locking folders. **Technical:** Grinds comme Damascus, 440C, ATS-34, D2 and O1. Prefers natural handle mate **Prices:** $350 to $2,000. **Remarks:** Part-time maker; first knife sold in 1 **Mark:** Last name.

**CHAMBERLAIN, JON A.,** 15 S. Lombard, E. Wenatchee, WA 98802 Phone: 509-884-6591
**Specialties:** Working and kitchen knives to customer specs; exotics on cial order. **Patterns:** Over 100 patterns in stock. **Technical:** Prefers ATS D2, L6 and Damascus. **Prices:** Start at $50. **Remarks:** First knife so 1986. Doing business as Johnny Custom Knifemakers. **Mark:** Name in with city and state enclosing.

**CHAMBERLAIN, JOHN B.,** 1621 Angela St., Wenatchee, WA 9880 Phone: 509-663-6720
**Specialties:** Fancy working and using straight knives mainly to cust specs, though starting to make some standard patterns. **Patterns:** Hur Bowies and daggers. **Technical:** Grinds D2, ATS-34, M2, M4 and L6. **Pr** $60 to $190; some to $2,500. **Remarks:** Full-time maker; first knife sc 1943. **Mark:** Name, city, state.

**CHAMBERLAIN, CHARLES R.,** PO Box 156, Barren Springs, VA 24313-0156, Phone: 703-381-5137

**CHAMBERLIN, JOHN A.,** 11535 Our Rd., Anchorage, AK 99516, Phone: 907-346-1524, Fax: 907-562-4583
**Specialties:** Art and working knives. **Patterns:** Daggers and hunters; some folders. **Technical:** Grinds ATS-34, 440C, A2, D2 and Damascus. Uses Alaskan handle materials such as oosic, jade, whale jawbone, fossil ivory. **Prices:** Start at $150. **Remarks:** Does own heat treating and cryogenic deep freeze. Full-time maker; first knife sold in 1984. **Mark:** Name over English shield and dagger.

**CHAMBLIN, JOEL,** 960 New Hebron Church Rd., Concord, GA 30206, Phone: 770-884-9055, Web: chamblinknives.com
**Specialties:** Fancy and working folders. **Patterns:** Fancy locking folders, traditional, multi-blades and utility. **Technical:** Grinds ATS-34, 440V, BG-42 and commercial Damascus. Offers filework. **Prices:** Start at $300. **Remarks:** Full-time maker; first knife sold in 1989. **Mark:** Last name.

**CHAMPAGNE, PAUL,** 48 Brightman Rd., Mechanicville, NY 12118, Phone: 518-664-4179
**Specialties:** Rugged, ornate straight knives in the Japanese tradition. **Patterns:** Katanas, wakizashis, tantos and some European daggers. **Technical:** Forges and hand-finishes carbon steels and his own Damascus. Makes Tamahagane for use in traditional blades; uses traditional heat-treating techniques. **Prices:** Start at $750. **Remarks:** Has passed all traditional Japanese cutting tests. Doing business as Twilight Forge. **Mark:** Three diamonds over a stylized crown.

**CHAMPION, ROBERT,** 1806 Plateau Ln, Amarillo, TX 79106, Phone: 806-359-0446, championknives@arn.net
**Specialties:** Traditional working straight knives. **Patterns:** Hunters, skinners, camp knives, Bowies, daggers. **Technical:** Grinds 440C and D2. **Prices:** $100 to $600. **Remarks:** Part-time maker; first knife sold in 1979. **Mark:** Last name with dagger logo, city and state. **Other:** Stream-line hunters.

**CHAPO, WILLIAM G.,** 45 Wildridge Rd., Wilton, CT 06897, Phone: 203-544-9424
**Specialties:** Classic straight knives and folders of his design and to customer specs; period pieces. **Patterns:** Boots, Bowies and locking folders. **Technical:** Forges stainless Damascus. Offers filework. **Prices:** $750 and up. **Remarks:** Full-time maker; first knife sold in 1989. **Mark:** First and middle initials, last name, city, state.

**CHARD, GORDON R.,** 104 S. Holiday Lane, Iola, KS 66749, Phone: 620-365-2311, Fax: 620-365-2311, gchard@cox.net
**Specialties:** High tech folding knives in one-of-a-kind styles. **Patterns:** Liner locking folders of own design Some fixed blades. **Technical:** Clean work with attention to fit and finish. **Prices:** $150 to $2,000. **Remarks:** First knife sold in 1983. **Other:** Blade steel mostly ATS-34 and 154CM, some CPM440V Vaso Wear and Damascus.

**CHASE, ALEX,** 208 E. Pennsylvania Ave., DeLand, FL 32724, Phone: 386-734-9918
**Specialties:** Historical steels, classic and traditional straight knives of his design and to customer specs. **Patterns:** Art, fighters and hunters. **Technical:** Forges O1-L6 Damascus, meteoric Damascus, 52100, 5160; uses fossil walrus and mastodon ivory etc. **Prices:** $150 to $1,000; some to $3,500. **Remarks:** Part-time maker; first knife sold in 1990. Doing business as Confederate Forge. **Mark:** Stylized initials-A.C.

**CHASE, JOHN E.,** 217 Walnut, Aledo, TX 76008, Phone: 817-441-8331, jchaseknives@earthlink.net
**Specialties:** Straight high-tech working knives in standard patterns or to customer specs. **Patterns:** Hunters, fighters, daggers and Bowies. **Technical:** Grinds D2, 01, 440C; offers mostly satin finishes. **Prices:** Start at $235. **Remarks:** Part-time maker; first knife sold in 1974. **Mark:** Last name in logo.

**CHASTAIN, WADE,** Rt. 2, Box 137-A, Horse Shoe, NC 28742, Phone: 704-891-4803
**Specialties:** Fancy fantasy and high-art straight knives of his design; period pieces. Known for unique mounts. **Patterns:** Bowies, daggers and fighters. **Technical:** Grinds 440C, ATS-34 and O1. Engraves; offers jewelling. **Prices:** $400 to $1,200; some to $2,000. **Remarks:** Full-time maker; first knife sold in 1984. Doing business as The Iron Master. **Mark:** Engraved last name.

**CHAUVIN, JOHN,** 200 Anna St., Scott, LA 70583, Phone: 337-237-6138, Fax: 337-230-7980
**Specialties:** Traditional working and using straight knives of his design, to customer specs and in standard patterns. **Patterns:** Bowies, fighters, and hunters. **Technical:** Grinds ATS-34, 440C and O1 high-carbon. Paul Bos heat treating. Uses ivory, stag, oosic and stabilized Louisiana swamp maple for handle materials. Makes sheaths using alligator and ostrich. **Prices:** $200 and up. Bowies start at $500. **Remarks:** Part-time maker; first knife sold in 1995. **Mark:** Full name, city, state.

**CHAUZY, ALAIN,** 1 Rue de Paris, 21140 Seur-en-Auxios, FRANCE, Phone: 03-80-97-03-30, Fax: 03-80-97-34-14
**Specialties:** Fixed blades, folders, hunters, Bowies-scagel-style. **Technical:** Forged blades only. Steels used XC65, 07C, and own Damascus. **Prices:** Contact maker for quote. **Remarks:** Part-time maker. **Mark:** Number 2 crossed by an arrow and name.

**CHAVAR, EDWARD V.,** 1830 Richmond Ave., Bethlehem, PA 18018, Phone: 610-865-1806
**Specialties:** Working straight knives to his or customer design specifications, folders, high art pieces and some forged pieces. **Patterns:** Fighters, hunters, tactical, straight and folding knives and high art straight and folding knives for collectors. **Technical:** Grinds ATS-34, 440C, L6, Damascus from various makers and uses Damascus Steel and Mokume of his own creation. **Prices:** Standard models range from $95 to $1,500, custom and specialty up to $3,000. **Remarks:** Full-time maker; first knife sold in 1990. **Mark:** Name, city, state or signature.

**CHEATHAM, BILL,** PO Box 636, Laveen, AZ 85339, Phone: 602-237-2786, blademan76@aol.com
**Specialties:** Working straight knives and folders. **Patterns:** Hunters, fighters, boots and axes; locking folders. **Technical:** Grinds 440C. **Prices:** $150 to $350; exceptional knives to $600. **Remarks:** Full-time maker; first knife sold in 1976. **Mark:** Name, city, state.

**CHELQUIST, CLIFF,** PO Box 91, Arroyo Grande, CA 93421, Phone: 805-489-8095
**Specialties:** Stylish pratical knives for the outdoorsman. **Patterns:** Trout and bird to camp knives. **Technical:** Grinds ATS-34. **Prices:** $90 to $250 and up. **Remarks:** Part-time maker, first knife sold in 1983. **Mark:** First initial and last name.

**CHERRY, FRANK J.,** 3412 Tiley N.E., Albuquerque, NM 87110, Phone: 505-883-8643

**CHEW, LARRY,** 515 Cleveland Rd Unit A-9, Granbury, TX 76049, Phone: 817-326-0165, larry@larrychew.com Web: www.larrychew.com
**Specialties:** High-tech folding knives. **Patterns:** Double action automatic and manual folding patterns of my design. **Technical:** CAD designed folders utilizing my roller bearing pivot design known as my "VooDoo". Double action automatic folders with a variety of obvious and disguised release mechanisms, some with lock-outs. **Prices:** Manual folders start at $475, double action autos start at $675. **Remarks:** Made and sold first knife in 1988, first folder in 1989. Full-time maker since 1997. **Mark** Name and location etched in blade, Damascus autos marked on spring inside frame. Earliest knives stamped LC.

**CHOATE, MILTON,** 1665 W. County 17-1/2, Somerton, AZ 85350, Phone: 928-627-7251, mccustom@juno.com
**Specialties:** Classic working and using straight knives of his design, to customer specs and in standard patterns. **Patterns:** Bowies, hunters and utility/camp knives. **Technical:** Grinds 440C; grinds and forges 1095 and 5160. Does filework on top and guards on request. **Prices:** $200 to $800. **Remarks:** Full-time maker, first knife made in 1990. All knives come with handmade sheaths by Judy Choate. **Mark:** Knives marked "Choate".

**CHRISTENSEN, JON P.,** 7814 Spear Dr., Shepherd, MT 59079, Phone: 406-373-0253, jbchris@aol.com Web: www.jonchristensenknives.com
**Specialties:** Patch knives, hunter/utility knives, Bowies, tomahawks. **Technical:** All blades forged, does all own work including sheaths. Forges 0-1, 1084, 52100, 5160. Damascus from 1084/15N20. **Prices:** $170 on up. **Remarks:** ABS JourneymanSmith, First knife sold in 1999. **Mark:** First and middle initial surrounded by last initial.

**CHURCHMAN, T.W. (TIM),** 475 Saddle Horn Drive, Bandera, TX 78003, Phone: 210-690-8641
**Specialties:** Fancy and traditional straight knives and single blade liner locking folders. Bird/trout knives of his design and to customer specs. **Patterns:** Bird/trout knives, fillet, Bowies, daggers, fighters, boot knives, some miniatures. **Technical:** Grinds 440C and D2. Offers stainless fittings, fancy filework, exotic and stabilized woods and hand sewed lined sheaths. Also flower pins as a style. **Prices:** $80 to $650; some to $1,500. **Remarks:** Part-time maker; first knife made n 1981 after reading "*KNIVES '81*". Doing business as "Custom Knives Churchman Made". **Mark:** Last name, dagger.

**CLAIBORNE, RON,** 2918 Ellistown Rd., Knox, TN 37924, Phone: 615-524-2054, Bowie@icy.net
**Specialties:** Multi-blade slip joints, swords, straight knives. **Patterns:** Hunters, daggers, folders. **Technical:** Forges Damascus: mosaic, powder mosaic. Prefers bone and natural handle materials; some exotic woods. **Prices:** $125 to $2,500. **Remarks:** Part-time maker; first knife sold in 1979. Doing business as Thunder Mountain Forge Claiborne Knives. **Mark:** Claiborne.

**CLAIBORNE, JEFF,** 1470 Roberts Rd., Franklin, IN 46131, Phone: 317-736-7443

**Specialties:** Multi blade slip joint folders. All one-of-a-kind by hand—no jigs or fixtures—swords, straight knives, period pieces, camp knives, hunters, fighters, ethnic swords all periods. Handle—uses stag, pearl, oosic, bone ivory, mastadon-mammoth, elephant or exotic woods. **Technical:** Forges high-carbon steel, makes Damascus, forges cable grinds, 01, 1095, 5160, 52100, L-6. **Prices:** $100 and up. **Remarks:** Part-time maker; first knife sold in 1989. **Mark:** Stylized initials in an oval.

**CLARK, NATE,** 604 Baird Dr, Yoncalla, OR 97499, Phone: 541-680-5677, nateclarkknives@hotmail.com Web: www.nateclarkknives.com

**Specialties:** Automatics (Push button and hidden release) ATS-34 mirror polish or satin finish, Damascus, Pearl, Ivory, Abalone, Woods, Bone, Micarta, G-10, filework and carving and sheath knives. **Prices:** $100. to $2,500. **Remarks:** Fulltime knife maker since 1996. **Mark:** Nate Clark (located inside on spring).

**CLARK, R.W.,** R.W. CLARK CUSTOM KNIVES, 1069 Golden Meadow, Corona, CA 92882, Phone: 909-279-3494, Fax: 909-279-4394, info@rwclarkknives.com Web: www.rwclarkknives.com

**Specialties:** Military field knives and Asian hybrids. Hand carved leather sheaths. **Patterns:** Fixed blade hunters, field utility and military. Also presentation and collector grade knives. **Technical:** First maker to use liquid metals LM1 material in knives. Other materials include S30V, O1, stainless and carbon Damascus. **Prices:** $75 to $2,000. Average price $300. **Remarks:** Started knife making in 1990 full-time in 2000. **Mark:** R.W. Clark., Custom., Corona, CA in standard football shape. Also uses three Japanese characters, spelling Clark, on Asian Hybrids.

**CLARK, D.E. (LUCKY),** 126 Woodland St., Mineral Point, PA 15942, Phone: 814-322-4725

**Specialties:** Working straight knives and folders to customer specs. **Patterns:** Customer designs. **Technical:** Grinds D2, 440C, 154CM. **Prices:** $100 to $200; some higher. **Remarks:** Part-time maker; first knife sold in 1975. **Mark:** Name on one side; "Lucky" on other.

**CLARK, HOWARD F.,** 115 35th Pl., Runnells, IA 50237, Phone: 515-966-2126, howard@mvforge.com Web: mvforge.com

**Specialties:** Currently Japanese-style swords. **Patterns:** Katana. **Technical:** Forges 1086, L6, 52100 and his own all tool steel Damascus; bar stock; forged blanks. **Prices:** $500 to $3,000. **Remarks:** Full-time maker; first knife sold in 1979. Doing business as Morgan Valley Forge. **Prior Mark:** Block letters and serial number on folders; anvil/initials logo on straight knives. **Current Mark:** Two character kanji "Big Ear".

**CLAY, J.D.,** 65 Ellijay Rd, Greenup, KY 41144, Phone: 606-473-6769

**Specialties:** Long known for cleanly finished, collector quality knives of functional design. **Patterns:** Practical hunters and locking folders. **Technical:** Grinds 440C - high mirror finishes. **Prices:** Start at $95. **Remarks:** Full-time maker; first knife sold in 1972. **Mark:** Name stamp in script on blade.

**CLAY, WAYNE,** Box 125B, Pelham, TN 37366, Phone: 931-467-3472, Fax: 931-467-3076

**Specialties:** Working straight knives and folders in standard patterns. **Patterns:** Hunters and kitchen knives; gents and hunter patterns. **Technical:** Grinds ATS-34. **Prices:** $125 to $500; some to $1,000. **Remarks:** Full-time maker; first knife sold in 1978. **Mark:** Name.

**COCKERHAM, LLOYD,** 1717 Carolyn Ave., Denham Springs, IA 70726, Phone: 225-665-1565

**COFER, RON,** 188 Ozora Rd., Loganville, GA 30052

**Specialties:** Fancy working and using straight knives of his design. **Patterns:** Hunters, Bowies and fighters. **Technical:** Grinds 440C and ATS-34. Heat-treats. Some knives have carved stag handles or scrimshaw. Makes leather sheath for each knife and walnut and deer antler display stands for art knives. **Prices:** $125 to $250; some to $600. **Remarks:** Spare-time maker; first knife sold in 1991. **Mark:** Name, serial number.

**COFFEY, BILL,** 68 Joshua Ave, Clovis, CA 93611

**Specialties:** Working and fancy straight knives and folders of his design. **Patterns:** Hunters, fighters, utility, linerlock folders and fantasy knives. **Technical:** Grinds 440C, ATS-34, A-Z and commercial Damascus. **Prices:** $250 to $1,000 some to $2,500. **Remarks:** Full-time maker first knife sold in 1993. **Mark:** First & Last name, city, state.

**COFFMAN, DANNY,** 541 Angel Dr. S., Jacksonville, AL 36265-5787, Phone: 256-435-1619

**Specialties:** Straight knives and folders of his design. Now making liner locks for $650 to $1,200 with natural handles and contrasting Damascus blades and bolsters. **Patterns:** Hunters, locking and slip-joint folders. **Technical:** Grinc Damascus, 440C and D2. Offers filework and engraving. **Prices:** $100 $400; some to $800. **Remarks:** Spare-time maker; first knife sold in 199 Doing business as Customs by Coffman. **Mark:** Last name stamped engraved.

**COHEN, N.J. (NORM),** 2408 Sugarcone Rd., Baltimore, MD 21209, Phone: 410-484-3841, njck528@bcpl.net Web: www.njcknives.com

**Specialties:** Working class knives. **Patterns:** Hunters, skinners, bird knive push daggers, boots, kitchen and practical customer designs. **Technic** Stock removal 440C, ATS-34. Uses Micarta, Corian. Some woods in handle **Prices:** $50 to $250. **Remarks:** Part-time maker; first knife sold in 198 **Mark:** Etched initials or NJC MAKER.

**COHEN, TERRY A.,** PO Box 406, Laytonville, CA 95454

**Specialties:** Working straight knives and folders. **Patterns:** Bowies to bc knives and locking folders; mini-boot knives. **Technical:** Grinds stainles hand rubs; tries for good balance. **Prices:** $85 to $150; some to $32 **Remarks:** Part-time maker; first knife sold in 1983. **Mark:** TERRY KNIVE city and state.

**COIL, JIMMIE J.,** 2936 Asbury Pl., Owensboro, KY 42303, Phone: 27C 684-7827

**Specialties:** Traditional working and straight knives of his design. **Patterr** Hunters, Bowies and fighters. **Technical:** Grinds 440C, ATS-34 and D Blades are flat-ground with brush finish; most have tapered tang. Offers fi work. **Prices:** $65 to $250; some to $750. **Remarks:** Spare-time maker; f knife sold in 1974. **Mark:** Name.

**COLE, JAMES M.,** 505 Stonewood Blvd., Bartonville, TX 76226, Phon 817-430-0302, dogcole@swbell.net

**COLE, DAVE,** 620 Poinsetta Dr., Satellite Beach, FL 32937, Phone: 32 773-1687

**Specialties:** Fixed blades and friction folders of his design or customers. **P terns:** Utility, hunters, and Bowies. **Technical:** Grinds 01, 1095. 440C sta less Damascus; prefers natural handle materials, handmade sheaths. **Pric** $100 and up. **Remarks:** Part-time maker, member of FKA; first knife solc 1991. **Mark:** D Cole.

**COLE, WELBORN I.,** 3284 Inman Dr. N.E., Atlanta, GA 30319, Phone 404-261-3977

**Specialties:** Traditional straight knives of his design. **Patterns:** Hunt **Technical:** Grinds 440C, ATS-34 and D2. Good wood scales. **Prices:** **Remarks:** Full-time maker; first knife sold in 1983. **Mark:** Script initials.

**COLEMAN, KEITH E.,** 5001 Starfire Pl. N.W., Albuquerque, NM 8712 2010, Phone: 505-899-3783, keith@kecenterprises.com Web: kecent prises.com

**Specialties:** Affordable collector-grade straight knives and folders; so fancy. **Patterns:** Fighters, tantos, combat folders, gents folders and bo **Technical:** Grinds ATS-34 and Damascus. Prefers specialty woods; of filework. **Prices:** $150 to $700; some to $1,500. **Remarks:** Full-time ma first knife sold in 1980. **Mark:** Name, city and state.

**COLEMAN, JOHN A,** 7233 Camel Rock Way, Citrus Heightss, CA 95610, Phone: 916-335-1568

**Specialties:**Traditional working straight knives of my design or yours. **terns:** Plain to fancy file back working knives hunters, bird, trout, camp kni skinners. Trout knives miniatures of bowies and cappers. **Technical:** Gr 440-C, ATS34, 145-CM and D2. Exotic woods bone, antler and some iv **Prices:** $80 to $200 some to $450. **Remarks:** Part-time maker. First knife in 1989. Doing business as Slim's Custom Knives. **Mark:** Cowboy settinc log whittling Slim's Custom Knives above cowboy and name and state u cowboy. **Other:** Enjoy making knives to your specs all knives come with ha made sheath by Slim's Leather.

**COLLINS, HAROLD,** 503 First St., West Union, OH 45693, Phone: 5 544-2982

**Specialties:** Traditional using straight knives and folders of his design c customer specs. **Patterns:** Hunters, Bowies and locking folders. **Techni** Forges and grinds 440C, ATS-34, D2, O1 and 5160. Flat-grinds standard; work available. **Prices:** $75 to $300. **Remarks:** Full-time maker; first sold in 1989. **Mark:** First initial, last name.

**COLLINS, LYNN M.,** 138 Berkley Dr., Elyria, OH 44035, Phone: 440 366-7101

**Specialties:** Working straight knives. **Patterns:** Field knives, boots and f ers. **Technical:** Grinds D2, 154CM and 440C. **Prices:** Start at $ **Remarks:** Spare-time maker; first knife sold in 1980. **Mark:** Initials, asteri

**COLTER, WADE,** PO Box 2340, Colstrip, MT 59323, Phone: 406-748-4573
**Specialties:** Fancy and embellished straight knives, folders and swords of his design; historical and period pieces. **Patterns:** Bowies, swords and folders. **Technical:** Hand forges 52100 ball bearing steel and L6, 1090, cable and chain Damascus from 5N20 and 1084. Carves and makes sheaths. **Prices:** $250 to $3,500. **Remarks:** Part-time maker; first knife sold in 1990. Doing business as "Colter's Hell" Forge. **Mark:** Initials on left side ricasso.

**COLTRAIN, LARRY D.,** PO Box 1331, Buxton, NC 27920

**COMPTON, WILLIAM E.,** 106 N. Sequoia Ct., Sterling, VA 20164, Phone: 703-430-2129
**Specialties:** Working straight knives of his design or to customer specs; some fancy knives. **Patterns:** Hunters, camp knives, Bowies and some kitchen knives. **Technical:** Also forges 5160, 1095 and make his own Damascus. **Prices:** $150 to $750; some to $1,500. **Remarks:** Part-time maker, ABS JourneymanSmith. first knife sold in 1994. Doing business as Comptons Custom Knives. **Mark:** Stock removal—first and middle initials, last name, city and state. Forged first and middle initials, last name, city and state, anvil in middle.

**COMUS, STEVE,** PO Box 68040, Anaheim, CA 92817-9800

**CONKEY, TOM,** 9122 Keyser Rd., Nokesville, VA 22123, Phone: 703-791-3867
**Specialties:** Classic straight knives and folders of his design and to customer specs. **Patterns:** Boots, hunters and locking folders. **Technical:** Grinds ATS-34, O1 and commercial Damascus. Lockbacks have jeweled scales and locking bars with dovetailed bolsters. Folders utilize unique 2-piece bushing of his design and manufacture. Sheaths are handmade. Presentation boxes made upon request. **Prices:** $100 to $500. **Remarks:** Part-time maker; first knife sold in 1991. Collaborates with Dan Thomas. **Mark:** Last name with "handcrafted" underneath.

**CONKLIN, GEORGE L.,** Box 902, Ft. Benton, MT 59442, Phone: 406-622-3268, Fax: 406-622-3410, 7bbgrus@3rivers.net
**Specialties:** Designer and manufacturer of the "Brisket Breaker." **Patterns:** Hunters, utility/camp knives and hatchets. **Technical:** Grinds 440C, ATS-34, D2, 1095, 154CM and 5160. Offers some forging and heat-treats for others. Offers some jewelling. **Prices:** $65 to $200; some to $1,000. **Remarks:** Full-time maker. Doing business as Rocky Mountain Knives. **Mark:** Last name in script.

**CONLEY, BOB,** 1013 Creasy Rd., Jonesboro, TN 37659, Phone: 423-753-3302
**Specialties:** Working straight knives and folders. **Patterns:** Lockers, two-blades, gents, hunters, traditional-styles, straight hunters. **Technical:** Grinds 440C, 154CM and ATS-34. Engraves. **Prices:** $250 to $450; some to $600. **Remarks:** Full-time maker; first knife sold in 1979. **Mark:** Full name, city, state.

**CONN JR., C.T.,** 206 Highland Ave., Attalla, AL 35954, Phone: 205-538-7688
**Specialties:** Working folders, some fancy. **Patterns:** Full range of folding knives. **Technical:** Grinds O2, 440C and 154CM. **Prices:** $125 to $300; some to $600. **Remarks:** Part-time maker; first knife sold in 1982. **Mark:** Name.

**CONNER, ALLEN L.,** 6399 County Rd. 305, Fulton, MO 65251, Phone: 573-642-9200, emmorris@sockets.net

**CONNOLLY, JAMES,** 2486 Oro-Quincy Hwy., Oroville, CA 95966, Phone: 916-534-5363, jim@histumyani.com Web: http://www.quiknet.com/~connolly
**Specialties:** Classic working and using knives of his design. **Patterns:** Boots, Bowies and daggers. **Technical:** Grinds ATS-34; forges 5160; forges and grinds O1. **Prices:** $100 to $500; some to $1,500. **Remarks:** Part-time maker; first knife sold in 1980. Doing business as Gold Rush Designs. **Mark:** First initial, last name, Handmade.

**CONNOR, MICHAEL,** Box 502, Winters, TX 79567, Phone: 915-754-5602
**Specialties:** Straight knives, period pieces, some folders. **Patterns:** Hunters to camp knives to traditional locking folders to Bowies. **Technical:** Forges 5160, O1, 1084 steels and his own Damascus. **Prices:** Moderate to upscale. **Remarks:** Spare-time maker; first knife sold in 1974. **Mark:** Last name, M.S. **Other:** ABS Master Smith 1983.

**CONNOR, JOHN W.,** PO Box 12981, Odessa, TX 79768-2981, Phone: 915-362-6901

**CONTI, JEFFREY D.,** 21104 75th St E, Bonney Lake, WA 98390, Phone: 253-447-4660, Fax: 253-512-8629
**Specialties:** Working straight knives. **Patterns:** Fighters and survival knives; hunters, camp knives and fishing knives. **Technical:** Grinds D2, 154CM and O1. Engraves. **Prices:** Start at $80. **Remarks:** Part-time maker; first knife sold in 1980. Do my own heat treating. **Mark:** Initials, year, steel type, name and number of knife.

**COOGAN, ROBERT,** 1560 Craft Center Dr., Smithville, TN 37166, Phone: 615-597-6801, http://iweb.tntech.edu/rcoogan/
**Specialties:** One-of-a-kind knives. **Patterns:** Unique items like ooloo-style Appalachian herb knives. **Technical:** Forges; his Damascus is made from nickel steel and W1. **Prices:** Start at $100. **Remarks:** Part-time maker; first knife sold in 1979. **Mark:** Initials or last name in script.

**COOK, MIKE A.,** 10927 Shilton Rd., Portland, MI 48875, Phone: 517-647-2518
**Specialties:** Fancy/embellished and period pieces of his design. **Patterns:** Daggers, fighters and hunters. **Technical:** Stone bladed knives in agate, obsidian and jasper. Scrimshaws; opal inlays. **Prices:** $60 to $300; some to $800. **Remarks:** Part-time maker; first knife sold in 1988. Doing business as Art of Ishi. **Mark:** Initials and year.

**COOK, MIKE,** 475 Robinson Ln., Ozark, IL 62972, Phone: 618-777-2932
**Specialties:** Traditional working and using straight knives of his design and to customer specs. **Patterns:** Bowies, hunters and utility/camp knives. **Technical:** Forges 5160. Filework; pin work. **Prices:** Start at $50/inch. **Remarks:** Spare-time maker; first knife sold in 1991. **Mark:** First initial, last name and Journeyman stamp on one side; panther head on the other.

**COOK, LOUISE,** 475 Robinson Ln., Ozark, IL 62972, Phone: 618-777-2932
**Specialties:** Working and using straight knives of her design and to customer specs; period pieces. **Patterns:** Bowies, hunters and utility/camp knives. **Technical:** Forges 5160. Filework; pin work; silver wire inlay. **Prices:** Start at $50/inch. **Remarks:** Part-time maker; first knife sold in 1990. Doing business as Panther Creek Forge. **Mark:** First name and Journeyman stamp on one side; panther head on the other.

**COOK, JAMES R.,** 3611 Hwy. 26 W., Nashville, AR 71852, Phone: 870 845 5173, jrcook@cswnet.com Web: www.jrcrookknives.com
**Specialties:** Working straight knives and folders of his design or to customer specs. **Patterns:** Bowies, hunters and camp knives. **Technical:** Forges 1084 and high-carbon Damascus. **Prices:** $195 to $5,500. **Remarks:** Full-time maker; first knife sold in 1986. **Mark:** First and middle initials, last name.

**COOMBS JR., LAMONT,** 546 State Rt. 46, Bucksport, ME 04416, Phone: 207-469-3057, Fax: 207-469-3057, theknifemaker@hotmail.com Web: www.knivesby.com/coomb-knives.html
**Specialties:** Classic fancy and embellished straight knives; traditional working and using straight knives. Knives of his design and to customer specs. **Patterns:** Hunters, folders and utility/camp knives. **Technical:** Hollow- and flat-grinds ATS-34, 440C, A2, D2 and O1; grinds Damascus from other makers. **Prices:** $100 to $500; some to $3,500. **Remarks:** Full-time maker; first knife sold in 1988. **Mark:** Last name on banner, handmade underneath.

**COON, RAYMOND C.,** 21135 S.E. Tillstrom Rd., Gresham, OR 97080, Phone: 503-658-2252, Raymond@damascusknife.com Web: Damascusknife.com
**Specialties:** Working straight knives in standard patterns. **Patterns:** Hunters, Bowies, daggers, boots and axes. **Technical:** Forges high-carbon steel and Damascus. **Prices:** Start at $135. **Remarks:** Full-time maker; does own leatherwork, makes own Damascus, daggers; first knife sold in 1995. **Mark:** First initial, last name.

**COPELAND, THOM,** 171 Country Line Rd. S., Nashville, AR 71852, tcope@cswnet.com
**Specialties:** Hand forged fixed blades; hunters, Bowies and camp knives. **Mark:** Copeland. **Other:** Member of ABS and AKA (Arkansas Knifemakers Association).

**COPELAND, GEORGE STEVE,** 220 Pat Carr Lane, Alpine, TN 38543, Phone: 931-823-5214, nifmakr@twlakes.net
**Specialties:** Traditional and fancy working straight knives and folders. **Patterns:** Friction folders, Congress two- and four-blade folders, button locks and one- and two-blade automatics. **Technical:** Stock removal of 440C, S300, ATS-34 and A2; heat-treats. **Prices:** $180 to $950; some higher. **Remarks:** Full-time maker; first knife sold in 1979. Doing business as Alpine Mountain Knives. **Mark:** G.S. Copeland (HANDMADE); some with four-leaf clover stamp.

**COPPINS, DANIEL,** 7303 Sherrard Rd., Cambridge, OH 43725, Phone: 740-439-4199
**Specialties:** Grinds 440 C and etching toll steels, antler, bone handles. **Patterns:** Hunters patch, neck knives, primitive, tomahawk. **Prices:** $20 and up; some to $600. **Remarks:** Sold first knife in 2002. **Mark:** DC. **Other:** Made tomahawk + knives + walking stick for country music band Confederate Railroad.

**CORBY, HAROLD,** 218 Brandonwood Dr., Johnson City, TN 37604, Phone: 615-926-9781
**Specialties:** Large fighters and Bowies; self-protection knives; art knives. Along with art knives and combat knives, Corby now has a all new automatic MO.PB1, also side lock MO LL-1 with titanium liners G-10 handles. **Patterns:** Sub-hilt fighters and hunters. **Technical:** Grinds 154CM, ATS-34 and 440C. **Prices:** $200 to $6,000. **Remarks:** Full-time maker; first knife sold in 1969. Doing business as Knives by Corby. **Mark:** Last name.

**CORDOVA, JOSEPH G.,** PO Box 977, Peralta, NM 87042, Phone: 505-869-3912, kcordova@rt66.com
**Specialties:** One-of-a-kind designs, some to customer specs. **Patterns:** Fighter called the 'Gladiator', hunters, boots and cutlery. **Technical:** Forges 1095, 5160; grinds ATS-34, 440C and 154CM. **Prices:** Moderate to upscale. **Remarks:** Full-time maker; first knife sold in 1953. Past chairman of American Bladesmith Assoc. **Mark:** Cordova made.

**CORKUM, STEVE,** 34 Basehoar School Rd., Littlestown, PA 17340, Phone: 717-359-9563, sco7129849@aol.com Web: www.hawknives.com

**CORRIGAN, DAVID P.,** HCR 65 Box 67, Bingham, ME 04920, Phone: 207-672-4879, outfarm@tdstelme.net

**COSGROVE, CHARLES G.,** 2314 W. Arbook Blvd., Arlington, TX 76015, Phone: 817-472-6505
**Specialties:** Traditional fixed or locking blade working knives. **Patterns:** Hunters, Bowies and locking folders. **Technical:** Stock removal using 440C, ATS-34 and D2; heat-treats. Makes heavy, hand-stitched sheaths. **Prices:** $250 to $2,500. **Remarks:** Full-time maker; first knife sold in 1968. No longer accepting customer designs. **Mark:** First initial, last name, or full name over city and state.

**COSTA, SCOTT,** 409 Coventry Rd., Spicewood, TX 78669, Phone: 830-693-3431
**Specialties:** Working straight knives. **Patterns:** Hunters, skinners, axes, trophy sets, custom boxed steak sets, carving sets and bar sets. **Technical:** Grinds D2, ATS-34, 440 and Damascus. Heat-treats. **Prices:** $225 to $2,000. **Remarks:** Full-time maker; first knife sold in 1985. **Mark:** Initials connected.

**COTTRILL, JAMES I.,** 1776 Ransburg Ave., Columbus, OH 43223, Phone: 614-274-0020
**Specialties:** Working straight knives of his design. **Patterns:** Caters to the boating and hunting crowd; cutlery. **Technical:** Grinds O1, D2 and 440C. Likes filework. **Prices:** $95 to $250; some to $500. **Remarks:** Full-time maker; first knife sold in 1977. **Mark:** Name, city, state, in oval logo.

**COUGHLIN, MICHAEL M.,** 414 Northridge Lane, Winder, GA 30680, Phone: 770-307-9509, sandman223@msn.com
**Specialties:** One-of-a-kind large folders and daily carry knives. **Remarks:** Likes customer input and involvement.

**COURTNEY, ELDON,** 2718 Bullinger, Wichita, KS 67204, Phone: 316-838-4053
**Specialties:** Working straight knives of his design. **Patterns:** Hunters, fighters and one-of-a-kinds. **Technical:** Grinds and tempers L6, 440C and spring steel. **Prices:** $100 to $500; some to $1,500. **Remarks:** Full-time maker; first knife sold in 1977. **Mark:** Full name, city and state.

**COURTOIS, BRYAN,** 3 Lawn Avenue, Saco, ME 04072, Phone: 207-282-3977, Web: WWW.GWI.NET/~COURTOIS/
**Specialties:** Working straight knives; prefers customer designs, no standard patterns. **Patterns:** Functional hunters; everyday knives. **Technical:** Grinds 440C or customer request. Hollow-grinds with a variety of finishes. Specializes in granite handles and custom skeleton knives. **Prices:** Start at $75. **Remarks:** Part-time maker; first knife sold in 1988. Doing business as Castle Knives. **Mark:** A rook chess piece machined into blade using electrical discharge process.

**COUSINO, GEORGE,** 7818 Norfolk, Onsted, MI 49265, Phone: 517-467-4911, Fax: 517-467-4911, gcousino1@aol.com Web: www.cousinoknives.com
**Specialties:** Hunters, Bowies using knives. **Patterns:** Hunters, Bowies, buckskinners, folders and daggers. **Technical:** Grinds 440C. **Prices:** $95 to $300. **Remarks:** Part-time maker; first knife sold in 1981. **Mark:** Last name.

**COVER, RAYMOND A.,** Rt. 1, Box 194, Mineral Point, MO 63660, Phone: 573-749-3783
**Specialties:** High-tech working straight knives and folders in standard patterns. **Patterns:** Slip joint folders, two-bladed folders. **Technical:** Grinds D2, and ATS-34. **Prices:** $165 to $250; some to $400. **Remarks:** Part-time maker; first knife sold in 1974. **Mark:** Name.

**COWLES, DON,** 1026 Lawndale Dr., Royal Oak, MI 48067, Phone: 248-541-4619, don@cowlesknives.com Web: www.cowlesknives.com
**Specialties:** Straight, non-folding pocket knives of his design. **Patterns:** Gentlemen's pocket knives. **Technical:** Grinds ATS-34, RWL34, S30V, stainless Damascus, Talonite. Scrimshaws; pearl inlays in some handles. **Prices:** $300 to $1,200. **Remarks:** Full-time maker; first knife sold in 1994. **Mark:** Full name with oak leaf.

**COX, COLIN J.,** 107 N. Oxford Dr., Raymore, MO 64083, Phone: 816-322-1977
**Specialties:** Working straight knives and folders of his design; period pieces. **Patterns:** Hunters, fighters and survival knives. Folders, two-blades, gents and hunters. **Technical:** Grinds D2, 440C, 154CM and ATS-34. **Prices:** $125 to $750; some to $4,000. **Remarks:** Full-time maker; first knife sold in 1981. **Mark:** Full name, city and state.

**COX, SAM,** 1756 Love Springs Rd., Gaffney, SC 29341, Phone: 864-489-1892, Fax: 864-489-0403, artcutlery@yahoo.com Web: www.sam-cox.us
**Specialties:** Classic high-art working straight knives of his design. Duc knives copyrighted. **Patterns:** Diverse. **Technical:** Grinds 154CM. **Prices:** $300 to $1,400. **Remarks:** Full-time maker; first knife sold in 1983. **Mark:** Co Call, Sam, Sam Cox, unique 2000 logo.

**CRAIG, ROGER L.,** 2617 SW Seabrook Ave, Topeka, KS 66614, Phone: 785-249-4109
**Specialties:** Working and camp knives, some fantasy; all his design. **Patterns:** Fighters, hunter. **Technical:** Grinds 1095 and 5160. Most knives have file work. **Prices:** $50 to $250. **Remarks:** Part-time maker; first knife sold 1991. Doing business as Craig Knives. **Mark:** Last name-Craig.

**CRAIN, JACK W.,** PO Box 212, Granbury, TX 76048, Phone: 817-599-6414, Web: www.crainknives.com - Site 9291 jackwcrain@crainknives.com
**Specialties:** Fantasy and period knives; combat and survival knives. **Patterns:** One-of-a-kind art or fantasy daggers, swords and Bowies; survival knives. **Technical:** Forges Damascus; grinds stainless steel. Carves. **Prices:** $350 to $2,500; some to $20,000. **Remarks:** Full-time maker; first knife sold 1969. Designer and maker of the knives seen in the films *Dracula 2000*, *Executive Decision*, *Demolition Man*, *Predator I and II*, *Commando*, *Die Hard I* and *II*, *Road House*, *Ford Fairlane* and *Action Jackson*, and television shows *W of the Worlds*, *Air Wolf*, *Kung Fu: The Legend Cont.* and *Tales of the Cryp* **Mark:** Stylized crane.

**CRAIN, FRANK,** 1127 W. Dalke, Spokane, WA 99205, Phone: 509-32 1596

**CRAWFORD, PAT AND WES,** 205 N. Center, West Memphis, AR 72301, Phone: 870-732-2452, patcrawford1@earthlink.com
**Specialties:** Stainless steel Damascus. High-tech working self-defense a combat types and folders. **Patterns:** Tactical-more fancy knives now. **Technical:** Grinds ATS-34, D2 and 154CM. **Prices:** $400 to $2,000. **Remarks:** Fu time maker; first knife sold in 1973. **Mark:** Last name.

**CRAWLEY, BRUCE R.,** 16 Binbrook Dr., Croydon 3136 Victoria, AUSTRALIA
**Specialties:** Folders. **Patterns:** Hunters, lockback folders and Bowies. **Technical:** Grinds 440C, ATS-34 and commercial Damascus. Offers filework a mirror polish. **Prices:** $160 to $3,500. **Remarks:** Part-time maker; first kn sold in 1990. **Mark:** Initials.

**CRENSHAW, AL,** Rt. 1, Box 717, Eufaula, OK 74432, Phone: 918-452 2128
**Specialties:** Folders of his design and in standard patterns. **Patterns:** Hu ers, locking folders, slip-joint folders, multi blade folders. **Technical:** Grin 440C, D2 and ATS-34. Does filework on back springs and blades; off scrimshaw on some handles. **Prices:** $150 to $300; some higher. **Remarks:** Full-time maker; first knife sold in 1981. Doing business as A. Crensh Knives. **Mark:** First initial, last name, Lake Eufaula, state stamped; first ini last name in rainbow; Lake Eufaula across bottom with Okla. in middle.

**CROCKFORD, JACK,** 1859 Harts Mill Rd., Chamblee, GA 30341, Phone: 770-457-4680
**Specialties:** Lockback folders. **Patterns:** Hunters, fishing and camp kniv traditional folders. **Technical:** Grinds A2, D2, ATS-34 and 440C. Engra and scrimshaws. **Prices:** Start at $175. **Remarks:** Part-time maker; first kn sold in 1975. **Mark:** Name.

**CROSS, ROBERT,** RMB 200B, Manilla Rd., Tamworth 2340, NSW AU TRALIA, Phone: 067-618385

**CROSSMAN, DANIEL C.,** Box 5236, Blakely Island, WA 98222, Phon 360-375-6542

**CROWDER, ROBERT,** Box 1374, Thompson Falls, MT 59873, Phone 406-827-4754
**Specialties:** Traditional working knives to customer specs. **Patterns:** Hu ers, Bowies, fighters and fillets. **Technical:** Grinds ATS-34, 154CM, 44 Vascowear and commercial Damascus. **Prices:** $160 to $250; some $2,500. **Remarks:** Part-time maker; first knife sold in 1985. **Mark:** First ini last name.

**CROWELL, JAMES L.,** PO Box 822, Mtn. View, AR 72560, Phone: 870-746-4215, crowellknives@yahoo.com
**Specialties:** Bowie knives; fighters and working knives. **Patterns:** Hunters, fighters, Bowies, daggers and folders. Period pieces: War hammers, Japanese and European. **Technical:** Forges 10 series carbon steels as well as 0-1, L-6 and his own Damascus. **Prices:** $425 to $4,500; some to $7,500. **Remarks:** Full-time maker; first knife sold in 1980. Earned ABS Master Bladesmith in 1986. **Mark:** A shooting star.

**CROWTHERS, MARK F.,** PO Box 4641, Rolling Bay, WA 98061-0641, Phone: 206-842-7501

**CULPEPPER, JOHN,** 2102 Spencer Ave., Monroe, LA 71201, Phone: 318-323-3636
**Specialties:** Working straight knives. **Patterns:** Hunters, Bowies and camp knives in heavy-duty patterns. **Technical:** Grinds O1, D2 and 440C; hollow-grinds. **Prices:** $75 to $200; some to $300. **Remarks:** Part-time maker; first knife sold in 1970. Doing business as Pepper Knives. **Mark:** Pepper.

**CULVER, STEVE,** 5682 94th St., Meriden, KS 66512, Phone: 866-505-0146, Web: www.culverart.com
**Specialties:** Edged tools and weapons, collectible and functional. **Patterns:** Bowies, daggers, swords, hunters, folders and edged tools. **Technical:** Forges carbon steels and his own pattern welded steels. **Prices:** $200 to $1,500; some to $4,000. **Remarks:** Full-time maker; first knife sold in 1989. **Mark:** Last name, J.S.

**CUMMING, BOB,** CUMMING KNIVES, 35 Manana Dr., Cedar Crest, NM 87008, Phone: 505-286-0509, cumming@comcast.net Web: www.cummingknives.com
**Specialties:** One of a kind exhibition grade custom bowie knives, exhibition grade and working hunters, bird & trout knives, salt and fresh water filet knives. Low country oyster knives, custom tanto's plains Indian style sheaths & custom leather, all types of exotic handle materials, scrimshaw and engraving. Coming in 206 Folders. **Prices:** $90 to $2,500 and up. **Remarks:** Mentored by the late Jim Nolen, sold first knife in 1978 in Denmark. Retired U.S. Foreign Service Office. Member NCCKG **Mark:** Stylized CUMMING.

**CUTCHIN, ROY D.,** 960 Hwy. 169 S., Seale, AL 36875, Phone: 334-855-3080
**Specialties:** Fancy and working folders of his design. **Patterns:** Locking folders. **Technical:** Grinds ATS-34 and commercial Damascus; uses anodized titanium. **Prices:** Start at $250. **Remarks:** Part-time maker. **Mark:** First initial, last name, city and state, number.

**CUTE, THOMAS,** State Rt. 90-7071, Cortland, NY 13045, Phone: 607-749-4055
**Specialties:** Working straight knives. **Patterns:** Hunters, Bowies and fighters. **Technical:** Grinds O1, 440C and ATS-34. **Prices:** $100 to $1,000. **Remarks:** Full-time maker; first knife sold in 1974. **Mark:** Full name.

# D

**DAILEY, G.E.,** 577 Lincoln St., Seekonk, MA 02771, Phone: 508-336-5088, gedailey@msn.com Web: www.gedailey.com
**Specialties:** One-of-a-kind exotic designed edged weapons. **Patterns:** Folders, daggers and swords. **Technical:** Reforges and grinds Damascus; prefers hollow-grinding. Engraves, carves, offers filework and sets stones and uses exotic gems and gold. **Prices:** Start at $1,100. **Remarks:** Full-time maker. First knife sold in 1982. **Mark:** Last name or stylized initialed logo.

**DAKE, MARY H.,** RT. 5 Box 287A, New Orleans, LA 70129, Phone: 504-254-0357

**DAKE, C.M.,** 19759 Chef Menteur Hwy., New Orleans, LA 70129-9602, Phone: 504-254-0357, Fax: 504-254-9501
**Specialties:** Fancy working folders. **Patterns:** Front-lock lockbacks, button-lock folders. **Technical:** Grinds ATS-34 and Damascus. **Prices:** $500 to $2,500; some higher. **Remarks:** Full-time maker; first knife sold in 1988. Doing business as Bayou Custom Cutlery. **Mark:** Last name.

**DALAND, B. MACGREGOR,** RT. 5 Box 196, Harbeson, DE 19951, Phone: 302-945-2609

**DALLYN, KELLY,** 14695 Deerridge Dr. S.E., Calgary AB, CANADA T2J 4A8, Phone: 403-278-3056

**DAMLOVAC, SAVA,** 10292 Bradbury Dr., Indianapolis, IN 46231, Phone: 317-839-4952
**Specialties:** Period pieces, Fantasy, Viking, Moran type all Damascus daggers. **Patterns:** Bowies, fighters, daggers, Persian-style knives. **Technical:** Uses own Damascus, some stainless, mostly hand forges. **Prices:** $150 to $2,500; some higher. **Remarks:** Full-time maker; first knife sold in 1993. **Mark:** "Sava" stamped in Damascus or etched in stainless. **Other:** Specialty, Bill Moran all Damascus dagger sets, in Moran-style wood case.

**D'ANDREA, JOHN,** 9321 M Santos, Citrus Springs, FL 34434, Phone: 570-420-6050
**Specialties:** Fancy working straight knives and folders with filework and distinctive leatherwork. **Patterns:** Hunters, fighters, daggers, folders and an occasional sword. **Technical:** Grinds ATS-34, 154CM, 440C and D2. **Prices:** $180 to $600; some to $1,000. **Remarks:** Part-time maker; first knife sold in 1986. **Mark:** First name, last initial imposed on samurai sword.

**D'ANGELO, LAURENCE,** 14703 N.E. 17th Ave., Vancouver, WA 98686, Phone: 360-573-0546
**Specialties:** Straight knives of his design. **Patterns:** Bowies, hunters and locking folders. **Technical:** Grinds D2, ATS-34 and 440C. Hand makes all sheaths. **Prices:** $100 to $200. **Remarks:** Full-time maker; first knife sold in 1987. **Mark:** Football logo—first and middle initials, last name, city, state, Maker.

**DANIEL, TRAVIS E.,** 1655 Carrow Rd., Chocowinity, NC 27817, Phone: 252-940-0807, dorispaul@email.com
**Specialties:** Traditional working straight knives of his design or to customer specs. **Patterns:** Hunters, fighters and utility/camp knives. **Technical:** Grinds ATS-34, D-2, 440-C, 154CM, forges his own Damascus. **Prices:** $90 to $1,250; some to $2,000. **Remarks:** Full-time maker; first knife sold in 1976. **Mark:** Carolina Custom Knives or "TED".

**DANIELS, ALEX,** 1416 County Rd. 415, Town Creek, AL 35672, Phone: 256-685-0943, akdknives@aol.com
**Specialties:** Working and using straight knives and folders; period pieces, reproduction Bowies. **Patterns:** Mostly reproduction Bowies but offer full line of knives. **Technical:** Now also using BG-42 along with 440C and ATS-34. **Prices:** $200 to $2,500. **Remarks:** Full-time maker; first knife sold in 1963. **Mark:** First and middle initials, last name, city and state.

**DARBY, JED,** 7878 E. Co. Rd. 50 N., Greensburg, IN 47240, Phone: 812-663-2696
**Specialties:** Traditional working/using straight knives of his design and to customer specs. **Patterns:** Bowies, hunters and utility/camp knives. **Technical:** Grinds 440C, ATS-34 and Damascus. **Prices:** $70 to $550; some to $1,000. **Remarks:** Full-time maker; first knife sold in 1992. Doing business as Darby Knives. **Mark:** Last name and year.

**DARBY, RICK,** 71 Nestingrock Ln., Levittown, PA 19054
**Specialties:** Working straight knives. **Patterns:** Boots, fighters and hunters with mirror finish. **Technical:** Grinds 440C and CPM440V. **Prices:** $125 to $300. **Remarks:** Part-time maker; first knife sold in 1974. **Mark:** First and middle initials, last name.

**DARBY, DAVID T.,** 30652 S 533 Rd., Cookson, OK 74427, Phone: 918-457-4868, knfmkr@fullnet.net
**Specialties:** Forged blades only-All styles. **Prices:** $350.00 and up. **Mark:** Stylized quillion dagger incorporates last name (Darby). **Other:** ABS journeyman smith.

**DARCEY, CHESTER L.,** 1608 Dominik Dr., College Station, TX 77840, Phone: 979-696-1656, DarceyKnives@yahoo.com
**Specialties:** Lockback, liner lock and scale release folders. **Patterns:** Bowies, hunters and utilities. **Technical:** Stock removal on carbon and stainless steels, forge own Damascus. **Prices:** $200 to $1,000. **Remarks:** Part-time maker, first knife sold in 1999. **Mark:** Last name in script.

**DARK, ROBERT,** 2218 Huntington Court, Oxford, AL 36203, Phone: 256-831-4645, Web: www.darknives.com
**Specialties:** Fixed blade working knives of maker's designs. Works with customer designed specifications. **Patterns:** Hunters, Bowies, Camp Knives, Kitchen/utility, bird and trout. Standard patterns and customer designed. **Technical:** Forged and stock removal. Works with high carbon, stainless and Damascus steels. Hollow and flat grinds. **Prices:** $175 to $750. **Remarks:** Sole authorship knives and custom leather sheaths. Part-time maker. **Mark:** "R Dark" on left side of blade.

**DARPINIAN, DAVE,** 15219 W. 125th, Olathe, KS 66062, Phone: 913-397-8914, darpo1956@yahoo.com Web: www.darpinianknives.com
**Specialties:** Working knives and fancy pieces to customer specs. **Patterns:** Full range of straight knives including art daggers and short swords. **Technical:** Art grinds ATS-34, 440C, 154 CM, 5160, 1095. **Prices:** $200 to $1,000. **Remarks:** First knife sold in 1996, part-time maker. **Mark:** Last name.

**DAVENPORT, JACK,** 36842 W. Center Ave., Dade City, FL 33525, Phone: 352-521-4088
**Specialties:** Titanium liner lock, button-lock and release. **Patterns:** Boots and double-ground fighters. **Technical:** Grinds ATS-34, 12C27 SS and Damascus; liquid nitrogen quench; heat-treats. **Prices:** $250 to $5,000. **Remarks:** Full-time maker; first knife sold in 1986. **Mark:** Last name.

**DAVIDSON, EDMUND,** 3345 Virginia Ave., Goshen, VA 24439, Phone: 540-997-5651, Web: www.edmunddavidson.com
**Specialties:** Working straight knives; many integral patterns and upgraded models. **Patterns:** Heavy-duty skinners and camp knives. **Technical:** Grinds A2, ATS-34, BG-42, S7, 440C. **Prices:** $100 to infinity. **Remarks:** Full-time maker; first knife sold in 1986. **Mark:** Name in deer head or custom logos.

**DAVIDSON, LARRY,** 921 Bennett St., Cedar Hill, TX 75104, Phone: 972-291-3904, dson@swbell.net Web: www.davidsonknives.com

**DAVIS, DON,** 8415 Coyote Run, Loveland, CO 80537-9665, Phone: 970-669-9016, Fax: 970-669-8072
**Specialties:** Working straight knives in standard patterns or to customer specs. **Patterns:** Hunters, utility knives, skinners and survival knives. **Technical:** Grinds 440C, ATS-34. **Prices:** $75 to $250. **Remarks:** Full-time maker; first knife sold in 1985. **Mark:** Signature, city and state.

**DAVIS, JESSE W.,** 7398A Hwy. 3, Sarah, MS 38665, Phone: 662-382-7332, jandddvais1@earthlink.net
**Specialties:** Working straight knives and boots in standard patterns and to customer specs. **Patterns:** Boot knives, daggers, fighters, subhilts & bowies. **Technical:** Grinds A2, D2, 440C and commercial Damascus. **Prices:** $125 to $1,000. **Remarks:** Full-time maker; first knife sold in 1977. Former member Knife Makers Guild (in good standing). **Mark:** Name or initials.

**DAVIS, JOHN,** 235 Lampe Rd., Selah, WA 98942, Phone: 509-697-3845, Fax: 509-697-8087
**Specialties:** Working and using straight knives of his own design, to customer specs and in standard patterns. **Patterns:** Boots, hunters, kitchen and utility/camp knives. **Technical:** Grinds ATS-34, 440C and commercial Damascus; makes own Damascus and mosaic Damascus. Embellishes with stabilized wood, mokume and nickel-silver. **Prices:** Start at $150. **Remarks:** Part-time maker; first knife sold in 1996. **Mark:** Name city and state on Damascus stamp initials.

**DAVIS, STEVE,** 3370 Chatsworth Way, Powder Springs, GA 30127, Phone: 770-427-5740
**Specialties:** Traditional Gents and Ladies folders of his design and to customer specs. **Patterns:** Slip-joint folders, locking-liner folders, lock back folders. **Technical:** Grinds ATS-34, 440C and Damascus. Offers filework; prefers hand-rubbed finishes and natural handle materials. Uses pearl, ivory, stag and exotic woods. **Prices:** $250 to $600; some to $1,500. **Remarks:** Part-time maker; first knife sold in 1988. Doing business as Custom Knives by Steve Davis. **Mark:** Name engraved on blade.

**DAVIS, TERRY,** Box 111, Sumpter, OR 97877, Phone: 541-894-2307
**Specialties:** Traditional and contemporary folders. **Patterns:** Multi-blade folders, whittlers and interframe multiblades; sunfish patterns. **Technical:** Flat-grinds ATS-34. **Prices:** $400 to $1,000; some higher. **Remarks:** Full-time maker; first knife sold in 1985. **Mark:** Name in logo.

**DAVIS, VERNON M.,** 2020 Behrens Circle, Waco, TX 76705, Phone: 254-799-7671
**Specialties:** Presentation-grade straight knives. **Patterns:** Bowies, daggers, boots, fighters, hunters and utility knives. **Technical:** Hollow-grinds 440C, ATS-34 and D2. Grinds an aesthetic grind line near choil. **Prices:** $125 to $550; some to $5,000. **Remarks:** Part-time maker; first knife sold in 1980. **Mark:** Last name and city inside outline of state.

**DAVIS, W.C.,** 19300 S. School Rd., Raymore, MO 64083, Phone: 816-331-4491
**Specialties:** Fancy working straight knives and folders. **Patterns:** Folding lockers and slip-joints; straight hunters, fighters and Bowies. **Technical:** Grinds A2, ATS-34, 154, CPM T490V and CPM 530V. **Prices:** $100 to $300; some to $1,000. **Remarks:** Full-time maker; first knife sold in 1972. **Mark:** Name.

**DAVIS, CHARLIE,** ANZA Knives, PO Box 710806, Santee, CA 92072, Phone: 619-561-9445, Fax: 619-390-6283, sales@anzaknives.com Web: www.anzaknives.com
**Specialties:** Fancy and embellished working straight knives of his design. **Patterns:** Hunters, camp and utility knives. **Technical:** Grinds high-carbon files. **Prices:** $20 to $185 - custom depends. **Remarks:** Full-time maker; first knife sold in 1980. **Mark:** ANZA U.S.A. **Other:** we now offer custom.

**DAVIS, BARRY L.,** 4262 U.S. 20, Castleton, NY 12033, Phone: 518-477-5036
**Specialties:** Complete sole authorship presentation grade highly complex pattern welded mosaic Damascus blade and bolster stock. **Patterns:** To date Joel has executed over 900 different mosaic Damascus patterns in the past four years anything conceived by makers imagination. Duplication of makers patterns is very rarely done, but can be if necessary. **Technical:** Uses various heat colorable "high vibranc steels, nickel 200 and some powdered metal for bolster stock only and uses 1095, 1075 and 15N20 high carbon steels for cutting edge blade stock only. **Prices:** 15 to $50 per square inch and up, depending on complexity of patterns. **Remarks:** Full-time mosaic Damascus meta smith. Focusing strictly on never before seen mosaic patterns. Most of maker work is used for art knives ranging between $1,500 to $4,500.

**DAVIS, JOEL,** 74538 165th, Albert Lea, MN 56007, Phone: 507-377-0808, joelknives@yahoo.com
**Specialties:** Complete sole authorship presentation grade highly comple pattern-welded mosaic Damascus blade and bolster stock. **Patterns:** To dat Joel has executed over 900 different mosaic Damascus patterns in the pas four years. Anything conceived by makers imagination. Duplication of make patterns is very rarely done, but can be if necessary. **Technical:** Uses variou heat colorable "high vibrancy" steels, nickel 200 and some powdered metal fc bolster stock only. And uses 1095, 1075 and 15N20. High carbon steels f cutting edge blade stock only. **Prices:** 15 to $50 per square inch and u depending on complexity of pattern. **Remarks:** Full-time mosaic Damascu metal smith focusing strictly on never before seen mosaic patterns. Most makers work is used for art knives ranging between $1,500 to $4,500.

**DAVIS JR., JIM,** 5129 Ridge St., Zephyrhills, FL 33541, Phone: 813-779-9213 813-469-4241 Cell, jimdavisknives@aol.com
**Specialties:** Presentation-grade fixed blade knives w/composite hidden ta handles. Employs a variety of ancient and contemporary ivories. **Pattern** One-of-a-kind gents, personal, and executive knives and hunters w/uniq cam-lock pouch sheaths and display stands. **Technical:** Flat grinds ATS- and stainless Damascus w/most work by hand w/assorted files. **Prices:** $3C and up. **Remarks:** Full-time maker, first knives sold in 2000. **Mark:** Signatu w/printed name over "HANDCRAFTED".

**DAVISSON, COLE,** 25939 Casa Loma Ct., Hemet, CA 92544, Phone: 909-652-8588, cmd@koan.com

**DAWKINS, DUDLEY L.,** 221 NW Broadmoor Ave., Topeka, KS 66606-1254, Phone: 785-235-0468, Fax: 785-235-3871, dawkind@sbcglobal.net
**Specialties:** Stylized old or "Dawkins Forged" with anvil in center. New Ta Stamps. **Patterns:** Straight knives. **Technical:** Mostly carbon steel; sor Damascus-all knives forged. **Prices:** $175 and up. **Remarks:** All knives su plied with wood-lined sheaths. Also make custom wood-lined sheaths $55 a up. **Mark:** Stylized "DLD or Dawkins Forged with anvil in center. **Other:** AE Member - sole authorship.

**DAWSON, LYNN,** 10A Town Plaza, Suite 303, Durango, CO 81301, Fax: 928-772-1729, LINDAD@NORTHLINK.COM Web: www.knives.com
**Specialties:** Swords, hunters, utility, and art pieces. **Patterns:** Over 25 p terns to choose from. **Technical:** Grinds 440C, ATS-34, own heat treati **Prices:** $80 to $1,000. **Remarks:** Custom work and her own designs. **Ma** The name "Lynn" in print or script.

**DAWSON, BARRY,** 10A Town Plaza, Suite 303, Durango, CO 81301, LINDAD@NORTHLINK.COM Web: www.knives.com
**Specialties:** Samurai swords, combat knives, collector daggers, tactical, fc ing and hunting knives. **Patterns:** Offers over 60 different models. **Technic** Grinds 440C, ATS-34, own heat-treatment. **Prices:** $75 to $1,500; some $5,000. **Remarks:** Full-time maker; first knife sold in 1975. **Mark:** Last nan USA in print or last name in script.

**DE MARIA JR., ANGELO,** 12 Boronda Rd., Carmel Valley, CA 93924 Phone: 831-659-3381, Fax: 831-659-1315, ang@mbay.net
**Specialties:** Damascus, fixed and folders, sheaths. **Patterns:** Mosiac a random. **Technical:** Forging 5160, 1084 and 15N20. **Prices:** $20 **Remarks:** Part-time maker. **Mark:** Angelo de Maria Carmel Valley, CA etc AdM stamp.

**DE VILLIERS, ANDRE AND KIRSTEN,** Postnet Suite 263, Private Ba X6, Cascades 3202, SOUTH AFRICA, Phone: 27 33 4133312, andre@knifemaker.co.za Web: www.knifemaker.co.za
**Specialties:** Tactical and up-market folders. **Technical:** Linerlock, butt locks and fixed blades. **Prices:** $300 to $1,200. **Remarks:** Collectors kni are artful with filework and individual specifications. **Mark:** ADV.

**DEAN, HARVEY J.,** 3266 CR 232, Rockdale, TX 76567, Phone: 512-446-3111, Fax: 512-446-5060, dean@tex1.net Web: www.harvey-dean.com
**Specialties:** Collectible, functional knives. **Patterns:** Bowies, hunters, fold daggers, swords, battle axes, camp and combat knives. **Technical:** For 1095, O1 and his Damascus. **Prices:** $350 to $10,000. **Remarks:** Full-t maker; first knife sold in 1981. **Mark:** Last name and MS.

**DEBRAGA, JOSE C.,** 76 Rue de La Pointe, Aux Lievres Quebec, CA ADA G1K 5Y3, Phone: 418-948-0105, Fax: 418-948-0105, josecde-bragaglovetrotter.net Web: www.gcaq.ga
**Specialties:** Art knives, fantasy pieces and working knives of his design c customer specs. **Patterns:** Knives with sculptured or carved handles, f miniatures to full-size working knives. **Technical:** Grinds and hand-files 4

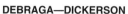

and ATS-34. A variety of steels and handle materials available. Offers lost wax casting. **Prices:** Start at $300. **Remarks:** Full-time maker; wax modeler, sculptor and knife maker; first knife sold in 1984. **Mark:** Initials in stylized script and serial number.

**DEBRAGA, JOVAN,** 141 Notre Dame des Victoir, Quebec, CANADA G2G 1J3, Phone: 418-948-0105, jovancdebraga@msn.com

**Specialties:**Art knives, fantasy pieces and working knives of his design or to customer specs. **Patterns:** Knives with sculptured or carved handles, from miniatures to full-sized working knives. **Technical:** Grinds and hand-files 440C, and Ats-34. A variety of steels and handle materials available. **Prices:** Start at $300. **Remarks:** Part-time maker. Sculptor and knife maker. First knife sold in 2003. **Mark:** Initials in stylized script and serial number.

**DEFEO, ROBERT A.,** 403 Lost Trail Dr., Henderson, NV 89014, Phone: 702-434-3717

**Specialties:** Working straight knives and period pieces. **Patterns:** Hunters, fighters, daggers and Bowies. **Technical:** Grinds ATS-34 and Damascus. **Prices:** $250 to $500; some higher. **Remarks:** Part-time maker; first knife sold in 1982. **Mark:** Last name.

**DEFREEST, WILLIAM G.,** PO Box 573, Barnwell, SC 29812, Phone: 803-259-7883

**Specialties:** Working straight knives and folders. **Patterns:** Fighters, hunters and boots; locking folders and slip-joints. **Technical:** Grinds 440C, 154CM and ATS-34; clean lines and mirror finishes. **Prices:** $100 to $700. **Remarks:** Full-time maker; first knife sold in 1974. **Mark:** GORDON.

**DEL RASO, PETER,** 28 Mayfield Dr., Mt. Waverly, Victoria, 3149, AUSTRALIA, Phone: 613 98060644, delrasofamily@optusnet.com.au

**Specialties:** Fixed Blades, some folders, art knives. **Patterns:** Daggers, Bowies, tactical, boot, personal and working knives. **Technical:** Grinds ATS-34, commercial Damascus and any other type of steel on request. **Prices:** $100 to $1,500. **Remarks:** Part-time maker, first show in 1993. **Mark:** Makers surname stamped.

**DELAROSA, JIM,** 343 S Eden Ct, Whitewater, WI 53190, Phone: 262-473-5652

**Specialties:** Working straight knives and folders of his design or customer specs. **Patterns:** Hunters, skinners, fillets, utility and locking folders. **Technical:** Grinds ATS-34, 440-C, D2, 01 and commercial Damascus. **Prices:** $75 to $450; some higher. **Remarks:** Part-time maker. **Mark:** First and last name, city and state.

**DELL, WOLFGANG,** Am Alten Berg 9, D-73277 Owen-Teck, GERMANY, Phone: 49-7021-81802, dellknives@compuserve.de Web: www.dell-knives.de

**Specialties:** Fancy high-art straight of his design and to customer specs. **Patterns:** Fighters, hunters, Bowies and utility/camp knives. **Technical:** Grinds ATS-34, RWL-34, Elmax, Damascus (Fritz Schneider). Offers high gloss finish and engraving. **Prices:** $500 to $1,000; some to $1,600. **Remarks:** Full-time maker; first knife sold in 1992. **Mark:** Hopi hand of peace. **Other:** Member of German Knife maker Guild since 1993. Member of the Italian Knife maker Guild since 2000.

**DELLANA, ,** Starlani Int'l. Inc., 1135 Terminal Way Ste. #209, Reno, NV 89502, Phone: 877-88dellana or 304-727-5512, Fax: 303-362-7901, Dellana@KnivesByDellana.com Web: www.knivesbydellana.com

**Specialties:** Collector grade fancy/embellished high art folders and art daggers. **Patterns:** Locking folders and art daggers. **Technical:** Forges her own Damascus and W-2. Engraves, does stone setting, filework, carving and gold/platinum fabrication. Prefers exotic, high karat gold, platinum, silver, gemstone and mother-of-pearl handle materials. **Price:** Upscale. **Remarks:** Sole authorship, full-time maker, first knife sold in 1994. **Mark:** First name. **Other:** Also does one high art collaboration a year with Van Barnett. Member: Art Knife Invitational and ABS; voting member: Knifemakers Guild.

**DELONG, DICK,** 17561 E. Ohio Circle, Aurora, CO 80017, Phone: 303-745-2652

**Specialties:** Fancy working knives and fantasy pieces. **Patterns:** Hunters and small skinners. **Technical:** Grinds and files O1, D2, 440C and Damascus. Offers cocobolo and Osage orange for handles. **Prices:** Start at $50. **Remarks:** Part-time maker. **Mark:** Last name; some unmarked. **Other:** Member of Art Knife Invitational. Voting member of Knifemakers Guild. Member of ABS.

**DEMENT, LARRY,** PO Box 1807, Prince Fredrick, MD 20678, Phone: 410-586-9011

**Specialties:** Fixed blades. **Technical:** Forged and stock removal. **Prices:** $75 to $200. **Remarks:** Affordable, good feelin, quality knives. **Other:** Part-time maker.

**DEMPSEY, GORDON S.,** PO Box 7497, N. Kenai, AK 99635, Phone: 907-776-8425

**Specialties:** Working straight knives. **Patterns:** Pattern welded Damascus and carbon steel blades. **Technical:** Pattern welded Damascus and carbon steel. **Prices:** $80 to $250. **Remarks:** Part-time maker; first knife sold in 1974. **Mark:** Name.

**DEMPSEY, DAVID,** 103 Chadwick Dr., Macon, GA 31210, Phone: 478-474-4948, dempsey@dempseyknives.com Web: www.dempseyknives.com

**Specialties:** Tactical, Utility, Working, Classic straight knives. **Patterns:** Fighters, Tantos, Hunters, Neck, Utility or Customer design. **Technical:** Grinds carbon steel and stainless including S30V. (differential heat treatment), Stainless Steels. **Prices:** Start at $150 for Neck Knives. **Remarks:** Full-time maker. First knife sold 1998. **Mark:** First and last name over knives.

**DENNEHY, JOHN D,** 8463 Woodlands Way, Wellington, CO 80549, Phone: 970-568-3697, jd@thewildirishrose.com

**Specialties:** Working straight knives, throwers, and leatherworkers knives. **Technical:** 440C, & 01, heat treats own blades, part-time maker, 1st knife sold in 1989. **Patterns:** Small hunting to presentation bowies, leatherworks round and head knives. **Prices:** $200 and up. **Remarks:** Custom sheath maker, sheath making seminars at the Blade Show.

**DENNEHY, DAN,** PO Box 2F, Del Norte, CO 81132, Phone: 719-657-2545

**Specialties:** Working knives, fighting and military knives, throwing knives. **Patterns:** Full range of straight knives, tomahawks, buckle knives. **Technical:** Forges and grinds A2, O1 and D2. **Prices:** $200 to $500. **Remarks:** Full-time maker; first knife sold in 1942. **Mark:** First name and last initial, city, state and shamrock.

**DENNING, GENO,** Caveman Engineering, 135 Allenvalley Rd., Gaston, SC 29053, Phone: 803-794-6067, cden101656@aol.com Web: www.cavemanengineering.com

**Specialties:** Mirror finish. **Patterns:** Hunters, fighters, folders. **Technical:** ATS-34, 440V, S-30-V D-2. **Prices:** $100 and up. **Remarks:** Full-time maker since 1996. Sole income since 1999. Instructor at montgomery Community College (Grinding Blades). **Mark:** Troy NC. **Other:** A director of SCAK. South Carolina Association of Knifemakers.

**DENT, DOUGLAS M.,** 1208 Chestnut St., S. Charleston, WV 25309, Phone: 304-768-3308

**Specialties:** Straight and folding sportsman's knives. **Patterns:** Hunters, boots and Bowies, interframe folders. **Technical:** Forges and grinds D2, 440C, 154CM and plain tool steels. **Prices:** $70 to $300; exceptional knives to $800. **Remarks:** Part-time maker; first knife sold in 1969. **Mark:** Last name.

**DERINGER, CHRISTOPH,** 625 Chemin Lower, Cookshire Quebec, CANADA J0B 1M0, Phone: 819-345-4260, cdsab@sympatico.ca

**Specialties:** Traditional working/using straight knives and folders of his design and to customer specs. **Patterns:** Boots, hunters, folders, art knives, kitchen knives and utility/camp knives. **Technical:** Forges 5160, O1 and Damascus. Offers a variety of filework. **Prices:** Start at $250. **Remarks:** Full-time maker; first knife sold in 1989. **Mark:** Last name stamped/engraved.

**DERR, HERBERT,** 413 Woodland Dr., St. Albans, WV 25177, Phone: 304-727-3866

**Specialties:** Damascus one-of-a-kind knives, carbon steels also. **Patterns:** Birdseye, Ladder back, Mosaics. **Technical:** All styles functional as well as artistically pleasing. **Prices:** $90 to $175 carbon, Damascus $250 to $800. **Remarks:** All Damascus made by maker. **Mark:** H.K. Derr.

**DETMER, PHILLIP,** 14140 Bluff Rd., Breese, IL 62230, Phone: 618-526-4834

**Specialties:** Working knives. **Patterns:** Bowies, daggers and hunters. **Technical:** Grinds ATS-34 and D2. **Prices:** $60 to $400. **Remarks:** Part-time maker; first knife sold in 1977. **Mark:** Last name with dagger.

**DI MARZO, RICHARD,** 1417 10th St So, Birmingham, AL 35205, Phone: 205-252-3331

**Specialties:** Handle artist. Scrimshaw carvings.

**DICKERSON, GORDON S.,** 152 Laurel Ln., Hohenwald, TN 38462, Phone: 931-796-1187

**Specialties:** Traditional working straight knives; Civil War era period pieces. **Patterns:** Bowies, hunters, tactical, camp/utility knives; some folders. **Technical:** Forges carbon steel; pattern welded and cable Damascus. **Prices:** $150 to $500; some to $3,000. **Mark:** Last name. **Other:** ABS member.

**DICKERSON, GAVIN,** PO Box 7672, Petit 1512, SOUTH AFRICA, Phone: +27 011-965-0988, Fax: +27 011-965-0988

**Specialties:** Straight knives of his design or to customer specs. **Patterns:** Hunters, skinners, fighters and Bowies. **Technical:** Hollow-grinds D2, 440C, ATS-34, 12C27 and Damascus upon request. Prefers natural handle materials; offers synthetic handle materials. **Prices:** $190 to $2,500. **Remarks:** Part-time maker; first knife sold in 1982. **Mark:** Name in full.

**DICKISON, SCOTT S.,** 179 Taylor Rd., Fisher Circle, Portsmouth, RI 02871, Phone: 401-847-7398, squared22@cox .net; Web: http://members.cox.net/squared22
**Specialties:** Working and using straight knives and locking folders of his design and automatics. **Patterns:** Trout knives, fishing and hunting knives. **Technical:** Forges and grinds commercial Damascus and D2, O1. Uses natural handle materials. **Prices:** $400 to $750; some higher. **Remarks:** Part-time maker; first knife sold in 1989. **Mark:** Stylized initials.

**DICRISTOFANO, ANTHONY P.,** PO Box 2369, Northlake, IL 60164, Phone: 847-845-9598
**Specialties:** Japanese-style swords. **Patterns:** Katana, Wakizashi, Otanto, Kozuka. **Technical:** Tradition and some modern steels. All clay tempered and traditionally hand polished using Japanese wet stones. **Remarks:** Part-time maker. **Prices:** Varied, available on request. **Mark:** Blade tang signed in "Masatoni" Japanese.

**DIEBEL, CHUCK,** PO Box 13, Broussard, LA 70516-0013

**DIETZ, HOWARD,** 421 Range Rd., New Braunfels, TX 78132, Phone: 830-885-4662
**Specialties:** Lock-back folders, working straight knives. **Patterns:** Folding hunters, high-grade pocket knives. ATS-34, 440C, CPM 440V, D2 and stainless Damascus. **Prices:** $300 to $1,000. **Remarks:** Full-time gun and knife maker; first knife sold in 1995. **Mark:** Name, city, and state.

**DIETZEL, BILL,** PO Box 1613, Middleburg, FL 32068, Phone: 904-282-1091
**Specialties:** Forged straight knives and folders. **Patterns:** His interpretations. **Technical:** Forges his Damascus and other steels. **Prices:** Middle ranges. **Remarks:** Likes natural materials; uses titanium in folder liners. **Mark:** Name. **Other:** Master Smith (1997).

**DIGANGI, JOSEPH M.,** Box 950, Santa Cruz, NM 87567, Phone: 505-753-6414, Fax: 505-753-8144
**Specialties:** Kitchen and table cutlery. **Patterns:** French chef's knives, carving sets, steak knife sets, some camp knives and hunters. Holds patents and trademarks for "System II" kitchen cutlery set. **Technical:** Grinds ATS-34. **Prices:** $150 to $595; some to $1,200. **Remarks:** Full-time maker; first knife sold in 1983. **Mark:** DiGangi Designs.

**DILL, DAVE,** 7404 NW 30th St., Bethany, OK 73008, Phone: 405-789-0750
**Specialties:** Folders of his design. **Patterns:** Various patterns. **Technical:** Hand-grinds 440C, ATS-34. Offers engraving and filework on all folders. **Prices:** Starting at $450. **Remarks:** Full-time maker; first knife sold in 1987. **Mark:** First initial, last name.

**DILL, ROBERT,** 1812 Van Buren, Loveland, CO 80538, Phone: 970-667-5144, Fax: 970-667-5144
**Specialties:** Fancy and working knives of his design. **Patterns:** Hunters, Bowies and fighters. **Technical:** Grinds 440C and D2. **Prices:** $100 to $800. **Remarks:** Full-time maker; first knife sold in 1984. **Mark:** Logo stamped into blade.

**DILLUVIO, FRANK J.,** 7544 Ravenswood, Warren, MI 48093, Phone: 810-531-7003, fjdknives@hotmail.com Web: www.fdilluviocustomknives.com
**Specialties:** Traditional working straight knives, some high-tech. **Patterns:** Hunters, Bowies, fishing knives, sub-hilts, liner lock folders and miniatures. **Technical:** Grinds D2, 440C, CPM; works for precision fits—no solder. **Prices:** $95 to $450; some to $800. **Remarks:** Full-time maker; first knife sold in 1984. **Mark:** Name and state.

**DION, GREG,** 3032 S. Jackson St., Oxnard, CA 93033, Phone: 805-483-1781
**Specialties:** Working straight knives, some fancy. Welcomes special orders. **Patterns:** Hunters, fighters, camp knives, Bowies and tantos. **Technical:** Grinds ATS-34, 154CM and 440C. **Prices:** $85 to $300; some to $600. **Remarks:** Part-time maker; first knife sold in 1985. **Mark:** Name.

**DIOTTE, JEFF,** Diotte Knives, 159 Laurier Dr., LaSalle Ontario, CANADA N9J 1L4, Phone: 519-978-2764

**DIPPOLD, AL,** 90 Damascus Ln., Perryville, MO 63775, Phone: 573-547-1119, adippold@midwest.net
**Specialties:** Fancy one-of-a-kind locking folders. **Patterns:** Locking folders. **Technical:** Forges and grinds mosaic and pattern welded Damascus. Offers filework on all folders. **Prices:** $500 to $3,500; some higher. **Remarks:** Full-time maker; first knife sold in 1980. **Mark:** Last name in logo inside of liner.

**DISKIN, MATT,** PO Box 653, Freeland, WA 98249, Phone: 360-730-0451
**Specialties:** Damascus autos. **Patterns:** Dirks and daggers. **Technica** Forges mosaic Damascus using 15N20, 1084, 02, 06, L6; pure nickel. **Prices** Start at $500. Remarks; Full-time maker. **Mark:** Last name.

**DIXON JR., IRA E.,** PO Box 2581, Ventura, CA 93002-2581, Phone: 805-659-5867
**Specialties:** Utilitarian straight knives of his design. **Patterns:** Camp, hunters boot, fighters. **Technical:** Grinds ATS-34, 440C, D2, 5160. **Prices:** $150 $400. **Remarks:** Part-time maker; first knife sold in 1993. **Mark:** First name Handmade.

**DODD, ROBERT F.,** 4340 E Canyon Dr., Camp Verde, AZ 86322, Phone: 928-567-3333, bob@rfdknives.com Web: www.rfdknives.com
**Specialties:** Useable fixed blade hunter/skinners, some Bowies and collectables. **Patterns:** Drop point. **Technical:** ATS-34 stainless and Damascu **Prices:** $250 and up. **Remarks:** Hand tooled leather sheaths, users and cc lectables. **Mark:** R. F. Dodd, Camp Verde AZ.

**DOGGETT, BOB,** 1310 Vinetree Rd., Brandon, FL 33510, Phone: 813-786-9057, dogman@tampabay.rr.com Web: www.doggettcustomknives.com
**Specialties:** Clean, functional working knives. **Patterns:** Classic-style hunter, fighter and utility fixed blades; liner locking folders. **Technical:** Us stainless steel and commercial Damascus, 416 stainless for bolsters a hardware, hand-rubbed satin finish, top quality handle materials and titaniu liners on folders. **Prices:** Start at $175. **Remarks:** Part-time maker. **Ma** Last name.

**DOIRON, DONALD,** 6 CHEMIN PETIT LAC DES CED, Messines PQ, CANADA JOX-2JO, Phone: 819-465-2489

**DOLAN, ROBERT L.,** 220—B Naalae Rd., Kula, HI 96790, Phone: 808-878-6406
**Specialties:** Working straight knives in standard patterns, his designs or customer specs. **Patterns:** Fixed blades and potter's tools, ceramic saw **Technical:** Grinds O1, D2, 440C and ATS-34. Heat-treats and engrave **Prices:** Start at $75. **Remarks:** Full-time tool and knife maker; first knife sc in 1985. **Mark:** Last name, USA.

**DOLE, ROGER,** DOLE CUSTOM KNIFE WORKS, PO Box 323, Buckley, WA 98321, Phone: 253-862-6770
**Specialties:** Folding knives. They include slip joint, lock back and locking li type knives. Most have integral bolster and liners. The locking liner kniv have a removable titanium side lock that is machined into the integral lin they are also available with a split liner lock. **Technical:** Makes ATS-34, 44 C and BG-42 stainless steel. Has in stock or available all types of natural a synthetic handle materials. Uses 416, 303, and 304 stainless steel, 7075-aluminum and titanium for the guards on the fixed blade knives and integ liners on the folding knives. The locking liner lock mechanisms are made fr 6AL4V titanium. Uses the stock removal method to fabricate all of the blac produced. The blades are ground on a 2 X 72 inch belt grinder. Not a bla smith. **Patterns:** 51 working designs for fixed blade knives. They include sm bird and trout knives to skinning axes. Most are working designs. All co with hand crafted leather sheath Kydex sheaths; can be special order **Remarks:** First knife sold in 1975.

**DOMINY, CHUCK,** PO Box 593, Colleyville, TX 76034, Phone: 817-49 4527
**Specialties:** Titanium liner lock folders. **Patterns:** Hunters, utility/camp kni and liner lock folders. **Technical:** Grinds 440C and ATS-34. **Prices:** $25C $3,000. **Remarks:** Full-time maker; first knife sold in 1976. **Mark:** Last nam

**DOOLITTLE, MIKE,** 13 Denise Ct., Novato, CA 94947, Phone: 415-8 3246
**Specialties:** Working straight knives in standard patterns. **Patterns:** Hunt and fishing knives. **Technical:** Grinds 440C, 154CM and ATS-34. **Pric** $125 to $200; some to $750. **Remarks:** Part-time maker; first knife sol 1981. **Mark:** Name, city and state.

**DORNELES, LUCIANO OLIVERIRA,** Rua 15 De Novembro 2222, No Petropolis, RS, BRAZIL 95150-000, Phone: 011-55-54-303-303-90, tc bufalo@hotmail.com
**Specialties:** Traditional "true" Brazilian-style working knives and to custo specs. **Patterns:** Brazilian hunters, utility and camp knives, Bowies, Dirk master at the making of the true "Faca Campeira Gaucha," the true ca knife of the famous Brazilian Gauchos. A Dorneles knife is 100% hand-for with sledge hammers only. Can makes spectacular Damascus hunters/c gers. **Technical:** Forges only 52100 and his own Damascus, can put si wire inlay on customer design handles on special orders; uses only nat handle materials. **Prices:** $250 to $1,000. **Mark:** Symbol with L. Dorneles.

**DOTSON, TRACY,** 1280 Hwy. C-4A, Baker, FL 32531, Phone: 850-537-2407
**Specialties:** Folding fighters and small folders. **Patterns:** Liner lock and lockback folders. **Technical:** Hollow-grinds ATS-34 and commercial Damascus. **Prices:** Start at $250. **Remarks:** Part-time maker; first knife sold in 1995. **Mark:** Last name.

**DOUCETTE, R,** CUSTOM KNIVES, 112 Memorial Dr, Brantford Ontario, CANADA N3R 5S3, Phone: 519-756-9040, randy@randydoucetteknives.com Web: www.randydoucetteknives.com
**Specialties:** Filework, tactical designs, multiple grinds. **Patterns:** Bowies, daggers, tantos, karambits, short swords. **Technical:** All my knives are handmade. The only out sourcing is heat treatment. **Prices:** $200 to $2,500. **Remarks:** Custom orders welcome. **Mark:** R. Doucette

**DOUGLAS, JOHN J.,** 506 Powell Rd., Lynch Station, VA 24571, Phone: 804-369-7196
**Specialties:** Fancy and traditional straight knives and folders of his design and to customer specs. **Patterns:** Locking folders, swords and sgian dubhs. **Technical:** Grinds 440C stainless, ATS-34 stainless and customer's choice. Offers newly designed non-pivot uni-lock folders. Prefers highly polished finish. **Prices:** $160 to $1,400. **Remarks:** Full-time maker; first knife sold in 1975. Doing business as Douglas Keltic. **Mark:** Stylized initial. Folders are numbered; customs are dated.

**DOURSIN, GERARD,** Chemin des Croutoules, F 84210, Pernes les Fontaines, FRANCE
**Specialties:** Period pieces. **Patterns:** Liner locks and daggers. **Technical:** Forges mosaic Damascus. **Prices:** $600 to $4,000. **Remarks:** First knife sold in 1983. **Mark:** First initial, last name and I stop the lion.

**DOUSSOT, LAURENT,** 6262 De La Roche, Montreal, Quebec, CANADA H2H 1W9, Phone: 516-270-6992, Fax: 516-722-1641
**Specialties:** Fancy and embellished folders and fantasy knives. **Patterns:** Fighters and locking folders. **Technical:** Grinds ATS-34 and commercial Damascus. Scale carvings on all knives; most bolsters are carved titanium. **Prices:** $350 to $3,000. **Remarks:** Part-time maker; first knife was sold in 1992. **Mark:** Stylized initials inside circle.

**DOWELL, T.M.,** 139 NW St. Helen's Pl., Bend, OR 97701, Phone: 541-382-8924
**Specialties:** Integral construction in hunting knives. **Patterns:** Limited to featherweights, lightweights, integral hilt and caps. **Technical:** Grinds D-2, BG-42 and Vasco wear. **Prices:** $185 and up. **Remarks:** Full-time maker; first knife sold in 1967. **Mark:** Initials logo.

**DOWNIE, JAMES T.,** 10076 Estate Dr., Port Franks, Ont., CANADA NOM 2LO, Phone: 519-243-1488, Fax: 519-243-1487, Web: www.kdg.org click on members page
**Specialties:** Serviceable straight knives and folders; period pieces. **Patterns:** Hunters, Bowies, camp knives and miniatures. **Technical:** Grinds D2, 440C and ATS-34, Damasteel, stainless steel Damascus. **Prices:** $100 to $500; some higher. **Remarks:** Full-time maker, first knife sold in 1978. **Mark:** Signature of first and middle initials, last name.

**DOWNING, TOM,** 2675 12th St., Cuyahoga Falls, OH 44223, Phone: 330-923-7464
**Specialties:** Working straight knives; period pieces. **Patterns:** Hunters, fighters and tantos. **Technical:** Grinds 440C, ATs-34 and CPM-T-440V. Prefers natural handle materials. **Prices:** $150 to $900; some to $1,500. **Remarks:** Part-time maker; first knife sold in 1979. **Mark:** First and middle initials, last name.

**DOWNING, LARRY,** 12268 Hwy. 181N, Bremen, KY 42325, Phone: 270-525-3523, Fax: 270-525-3372, larrdowning@bellsout.net Web: www.downingcustomknives.com
**Specialties:** Working straight knives and folders. **Patterns:** From mini-knives to daggers, folding lockers to interframes. **Technical:** Forges and grinds 154CM, ATS-34 and his own Damascus. **Prices:** $195 to $950; some higher. **Remarks:** Part-time maker; first knife sold in 1979. **Mark:** Name in arrowhead.

**DOWNS, JAMES F.,** 35 Sunset Rd., Londonderry, OH 45647, Phone: 740-887-2099, jfdowns1@yahoo.com
**Specialties:** Working straight knives of his design or to customer specs. **Patterns:** Folders, Bowies, boot, hunters, utility. **Technical:** Grinds 440C and other steels. Prefers mastodon ivory, all pearls, stabilized wood and elephant ivory. **Prices:** $75 to $1,200. **Remarks:** Full-time maker; first knife sold in 1980. Brochures $2. **Mark:** Last name.

**DOX, JAN,** Zwanebloemlaan 27, B 2900 Schoten, BELGIUM, Phone: 32 3 658 77 43, jan.dox@pi.be
**Specialties:** Working/using knives, from kitchen to battlefield. **Patterns:** Own designs, some based on traditional ethnic patterns (Scots, Celtic, Scandinavian and Japanese) or to customer specs. **Technical:** Grinds D2/A2 and stainless, forges carbon steels, convex edges. Handles: Wrapped in modern or traditional patterns, resin impregnated if desired. Natural or synthetic materials, some carved. **Prices:** Start at 25 to 50 Euro (USD) and up. **Remarks:** Spare-time maker, first knife sold 2001. **Mark:** Name or stylized initials.

**DOZIER, BOB,** PO Box 1941, Springdale, AR 72765, Phone: 888-823-0023/479-756-0023, Fax: 479-756-9139, info@dozierknives.com Web www.dozierknives.com
**Specialties:** Using knives (fixed blades and folders). **Patterns:** Some fine collector-grade knives. **Technical:** Uses D2. Prefers Micarta handle material. **Prices:** Using knives: $145 to $595. **Remarks:** Full-time maker; first knife sold in 1965. **Mark:** State, made, last name in a circle (for fixed blades); Last name with arrow through 'D' and year over name (for folders). **Other:** Also sells a semi-handmade line of fixed blade with mark; state, knives, last name in circle.

**DRAPER, AUDRA,** #10 Creek Dr., Riverton, WY 82501, Phone: 307-856-6807 or 307-851-0426 cell, adraper@wyoming.com Web: www.draperknives.com
**Specialties:** One-of-a-kind straight and folding knives. Also pendants, earring and bracelets of Damascus. **Patterns:** Design custom knives, using, Bowies, and mini's. **Technical:** Forge Damascus; heat-treats all knives. **Prices:** Vary depending on item. **Remarks:** Full-time maker; master bladesmith in the ABS. Member of the PKA; first knife sold in 1995. **Mark:** Audra.

**DRAPER, MIKE,** #10 Creek Dr., Riverton, WY 82501, Phone: 307-856-6807, adraper@wyoming.com
**Specialties:** Mainly folding knives in tactical fashion, occasonal fixed blade. **Patterns:** Hunters, Bowies and camp knives, tactical survival. **Technical:** Grinds S30V stainless steel . **Prices:** Starting at $250+. **Remarks:** Full-time maker; first knife sold in 1996. **Mark:** Initials M.J.D. or name, city and state.

**DREW, GERALD,** 2 Glenn Cable, Asheville, NC 28805, Phone: 828-299-7821
**Specialties:** Blade ATS-34 5 1/2". Handle spalted Maple. 10" OAL. Straight knives. **Patterns:** Hunters, camp knives, some Bowies and tactical. **Technical:** ATS-34 preferred. **Price:** $110 to $200. **Mark:** GL DREW.

**DRISCOLL, MARK,** 4115 Avoyer Pl., La Mesa, CA 91941, Phone: 619-670-0695
**Specialties:** High-art, period pieces and working/using knives of his design or to customer specs; some fancy. **Patterns:** Swords, Bowies, Fighters, daggers, hunters and primitive (mountain man-styles). **Technical:** Forges 52100, 5160, O1, L6, 1095, and maker his own Damascus and mokume; also does multiple quench heat treating. Uses exotic hardwoods, ivory and horn, offers fancy file work, carving, scrimshaws. **Prices:** $150 to $550; some to $1,500. **Remarks:** Part-time maker; first knife sold in 1986. Doing business as Mountain Man Knives. **Mark:** Double "M".

**DRISKILL, BERYL,** PO Box 187, Braggadocio, MO 63826, Phone: 573-757-6262
**Specialties:** Fancy working knives. **Patterns:** Hunting knives, fighters, Bowies, boots, daggers and lockback folders. **Technical:** Grinds ATS-34. **Prices:** Start at $200. **Remarks:** Part-time maker; first knife sold in 1984. **Mark:** Name.

**DROST, MICHAEL B.,** Rt. 2, Box 49, French Creek, WV 26218, Phone: 304-472-7901
**Specialties:** Working/using straight knives and folders of all designs. **Patterns:** Hunters, locking folders and utility/camp knives. **Technical:** Grinds ATS-34, D2 and CPM-T-440V. Offers dove-tailed bolsters and spacers, filework and scrimshaw. **Prices:** $125 to $400; some to $740. **Remarks:** Full-time maker; first knife sold in 1990. Doing business as Drost Custom Knives. **Mark:** Name, city and state.

**DROST, JASON D.,** Rt. 2, Box 49, French Creek, WV 26218, Phone: 304-472-7901
**Specialties:** Working/using straight knives of his design. **Patterns:** Hunters and utility/camp knives. **Technical:** Grinds 154CM and D2. **Prices:** $125 to $5,000. **Remarks:** Spare-time maker; first knife sold in 1995. **Mark:** First and middle initials, last name, maker, city and state.

**DUBLIN, DENNIS,** 728 Stanley St., Box 986, Enderby, BC, CANADA V0E 1V0, Phone: 604-838-6753
**Specialties:** Working straight knives and folders, plain or fancy. **Patterns:** Hunters and Bowies, locking hunters, combination knives/axes. **Technical:** Forges and grinds high-carbon steels. **Prices:** $100 to $400; some higher. **Remarks:** Full-time maker; first knife sold in 1970. **Mark:** Name.

**DUFF, BILL,** 14380 Ghost Rider Dr., Reno, NV 89511, Phone: 775-851-9331
**Specialties:** Straight knives and folders, some fancy. **Patterns:** Hunters, folders and miniatures. **Technical:** Grinds 440-C and commercial Damascus. **Prices:** $200 to $1,000; some higher. **Remarks:** First knife some in 1976. **Mark:** Bill Duff.

**DUFOUR, ARTHUR J.,** 8120 De Armoun Rd., Anchorage, AK 99516, Phone: 907-345-1701
**Specialties:** Working straight knives from standard patterns. **Patterns:** Hunters, Bowies, camp and fishing knives—grinded thin and pointed. **Technical:** Grinds 440C, ATS-34, AEB-L. Tempers 57-58R; hollow-grinds. **Prices:** $135; some to $250. **Remarks:** Part-time maker; first knife sold in 1970. **Mark:** Prospector logo.

**DUGAN, BRAD M.,** 422 A Cribbage Ln., San Marcos, CA 92069, Phone: 760-752-4417

**DUGGER, DAVE,** 2504 West 51, Westwood, KS 66205, Phone: 913-831-2382
**Specialties:** Working straight knives; fantasy pieces. **Patterns:** Hunters, boots and daggers in one-of-a-kind styles. **Technical:** Grinds D2, 440C and 154CM. **Prices:** $75 to $350; some to $1,200. **Remarks:** Part-time maker; first knife sold in 1979. Not currently accepting orders. Doing business as Dog Knives. **Mark:** DOG.

**DUNKERLEY, RICK,** PO Box 582, Seeley Lake, MT 59868, Phone: 406-677-5496, rick@dunkerleyhandmadedknives.com
**Specialties:** Mosaic Damascus folders and carbon steel utility knives. **Patterns:** One-of-a-kind folders, standard hunters and utility designs. **Technical:** Forges 52100, Damascus and mosaic Damascus. Prefers natural handle materials. **Prices:** $200 and up. **Remarks:** Full-time maker; first knife sold in 1984, ABS Master Smith. Doing business as Dunkerley Custom Knives. Dunkerley handmade knives, sole authorship. **Mark:** Dunkerley, MS.

**DUNN, STEVE,** 376 Biggerstaff Rd., Smiths Grove, KY 42171, Phone: 270-563-9830
**Specialties:** Working and using straight knives of his design; period pieces. **Patterns:** Hunters, skinners, Bowies, fighters, camp knives, folders, swords and battle axes. **Technical:** Forges his Damascus, O1, 5160, L6 and 1095. **Prices:** Moderate to upscale. **Remarks:** Full-time maker; first knife sold in 1990. **Mark:** Last name and MS.

**DUNN, CHARLES K.,** 17740 GA Hwy. 116, Shiloh, GA 31826, Phone: 706-846-2666
**Specialties:** Fancy and working straight knives and folders of his design and to customer specs. **Patterns:** Bowies, hunters and locking folders. **Technical:** Grinds 440C and ATS-34. Engraves; filework offered. **Prices:** $75 to $300. **Remarks:** Part-time maker; first knife sold in 1988. **Mark:** First initial, last name, city, state.

**DURAN, JERRY T.,** PO Box 80692, Albuquerque, NM 87198-0692, Phone: 505-873-4676, jtdknives@hotmail.com Website: www.kmg.org/jtdknives
**Specialties:** Tactical folders, Bowies, fighters, liner locks and hunters. **Patterns:** Folders, Bowies, hunters and tactical knives. **Technical:** Forges own Damascus and forges carbon steel. **Prices:** Moderate to upscale. **Remarks:** Full-time maker; first knife sold in 1978. **Mark:** Initials in elk rack logo.

**DURHAM, KENNETH,** BUZZARD ROOST FORGE, 10495 White Pike, Cherokee, AL 35616, Phone: 256-359-4287, www.home.hiwaay.net/~jamesd/
**Specialties:** Bowies, dirks, hunters. **Patterns:** Traditional patterns. **Technical:** Forges 1095, 5160, 52100 and makes own Damascus. **Prices:** $85 to $1,600. **Remarks:** Began making knives about 1995. Received Journeyman stamp 1999. **Mark:** Bull's head with Ken Durham above and Cherokee AL below.

**DURIO, FRED,** 144 Gulino St., Opelousas, LA 70570, Phone: 337-948-4831
**Specialties:** Folders. **Patterns:** Liner locks; plain and fancy. **Technical:** Makes own Damascus. **Prices:** Moderate to upscale. **Remarks:** Full-time maker. **Mark:** Last name-Durio.

**DUVALL, FRED,** 10715 Hwy. 190, Benton, AR 72015, Phone: 501-778-9360
**Specialties:** Working straight knives and folders. **Patterns:** Locking folders, slip joints, hunters, fighters and Bowies. **Technical:** Grinds D2 and CPM440V; forges 5160. **Prices:** $100 to $400; some to $800. **Remarks:** Part-time maker; first knife sold in 1973. **Mark:** Last name.

**DYER, DAVID,** 4531 Hunters Glen, Granbury, TX 76048, Phone: 817-573-1198
**Specialties:** Working skinners and early period knives. **Patterns:** Customer designs, his own patterns. **Technical:** Coal forged blades; 5160 and 52100 steels. **Prices:** $150 for neck-knives and small (3" to 3-1/2"). To $600 for large blades and specialty blades. **Mark:** Last name DYER electro etched. **Other:** Grinds D-2, 1095, L-6.

**DYESS, EDDIE,** 1005 Hamilton, Roswell, NM 88201, Phone: 505-623-5599
**Specialties:** Working and using straight knives in standard patterns. **Patterns:** Hunters and fighters. **Technical:** Grinds 440C, 154CM and D2 on request. **Prices:** $85 to $135; some to $250. **Remarks:** Spare-time maker; first knife sold in 1980. **Mark:** Last name.

**DYRNOE, PER,** Sydskraenten 10, Tulstrup, DK 3400 Hilleroed, DENMARK, Phone: +45 42287041
**Specialties:** Hand-crafted knives with zirconia ceramic blades. **Patterns:** Hunters, skinners, Norwegian-style tolle knives, most in animal-like ergonomic shapes. **Technical:** Handles of exotic hardwood, horn, fossil ivory, etc. Norwegian-style sheaths. **Prices:** Start at $500. **Remarks:** Part-time maker in cooperation with Hans J. Henriksen; first knife sold in 1993. **Mark:** Initial logo.

# E

**EAKER, ALLEN L.,** 416 Clinton Ave., Dept KI, Paris, IL 61944, Phone: 217-466-5160
**Specialties:** Traditional straight knives and folders of his design. **Patterns:** Hunters, locking folders and slip-joint folders. **Technical:** Grinds 440C; inlays. **Prices:** $125 to $325; some to $500. **Remarks:** Spare-time maker; first knife sold in 1994. **Mark:** Initials in tankard logo stamped on tang, serial number on back side.

**EALY, DELBERT,** PO Box 121, Indian River, MI 49749, Phone: 231-238-4705

**EASLER JR., RUSSELL O.,** PO Box 301, Woodruff, SC 29388, Phone: 864-476-7830
**Specialties:** Working straight knives and folders. **Patterns:** Hunters, tanto and boots; locking folders and interframes. **Technical:** Grinds 440C, 154C and ATS-34. **Prices:** $100 to $350; some to $800. **Remarks:** Part-time maker; first knife sold in 1973. **Mark:** Name or name with bear logo.

**EATON, RICK,** 9944 McCranie St., Shepherd, MT 59079 3126
**Specialties:** Interframe folders and one-hand-opening side locks. **Patterns:** Bowies, daggers, fighters and folders. **Technical:** Grinds 154CM, ATS-34, 440C and other maker's Damascus. Offers high-quality hand engraving, Bulino and gold inlay. **Prices:** Upscale. **Remarks:** Full-time maker; first knife sold in 1982. **Mark:** Full name or full name and address.

**EBISU, HIDESAKU,** 3-39-7 KOI OSAKO NISHI KU, Hiroshima City, JAPAN 733 0816

**ECHOLS, ROGER,** 46 Channing Rd., Nashville, AR 71852-8588, Phone: 870-451-9089, blademanechols@aol.com
**Specialties:** Liner locks, auto-scale release, lock backs. **Patterns:** My own or yours. **Technical:** Autos. **Prices:** $500 to $1,700. **Remarks:** Likes to use pearl, ivory and Damascus the most. **Mark:** Name. **Other:** Made first knife in 1984. **Remarks:** Part-time maker; tool and die maker by trade.

**EDDY, HUGH E.,** 211 E Oak St., Caldwell, ID 83605, Phone: 208-459-0536

**EDEN, THOMAS,** PO Box 57, Cranbury, NJ 08512, Phone: 609-371-0774
**Patterns:** Fixed blade, working patterns, hand forged. **Technical:** Damascus. **Mark:** Eden (script). **Remarks:** ABS Smith.

**EDGE, TOMMY,** 1244 County Road 157, Cash, AR 72421, Phone: 501-477-5210, tedge@tex.net
**Specialties:** Fancy/embellished working knives of his design. **Patterns:** Bowies, hunters and utility/camping knives. **Technical:** Grinds 440C, ATS-34 and D2. Makes own cable Damascus; offers filework. **Prices:** $70 to $250; some to $1,500. **Remarks:** Part-time maker; first knife sold in 1973. **Mark:** Stamped first initial, last name and stenciled name, city and state in oval shape.

**EDWARDS, MITCH,** 303 New Salem Rd., Glasgow, KY 42141, Phone: 270-651-9257, medwards@glasgow-ky.com Web: www.traditionalknives.com
**Specialties:** Period pieces. **Patterns:** Neck knives, camp, rifleman and Bowie knives. **Technical:** All hand forged, forges own Damascus 01, 1084, 1095, L-6, 15N20. **Prices:** $200 to $1,000. **Remarks:** JourneymanSmith. **Mark:** Broken heart.

**EDWARDS, FAIN E.,** PO Box 280, Topton, NC 28781, Phone: 828-321-3127

**EHRENBERGER, DANIEL ROBERT,** 6192 Hwy 168, Shelbyville, MO 63469, Phone: 573-633-2010
**Specialties:** Affordable working/using straight knives of his design and to custom specs. Patterns: 10" western Bowie, fighters, hunting and skinning knives. **Technical:** Forges 1085, 1095, his own Damascus and cable Damascus. **Prices:** $80 to $500. **Remarks:** Full-time maker, first knife sold 1994. **Mark:** Ehrenberger JS.

**KLUND, MAIHKEL,** Föne 1111, S-820 41 Farila, SWEDEN, info@art-nives.com Web: www.art-knives.com
**pecialties:** Collector-grade working straight knives. **Patterns:** Hunters, Bow-s and fighters. **Technical:** Grinds ATS-34, Uddeholm and Dama steel. ngraves and scrimshaws. **Prices:** $150 to $700. **Remarks:** Full-time maker; ·st knife sold in 1983. **Mark:** Initials or name.

**LDER JR., PERRY B.,** 1321 Garretsburg Rd., Clarksville, TN 37042-516, Phone: 931-647-9416, pbebje@aol.com
**pecialties:** Hunters, combat Bowies bird and trout. **Technical:** High-carbon eel and Damascus blades. **Prices:** $250 and up depending on blade esired. **Mark:** ELDER.

**LDRIDGE, ALLAN,** 7731 Four Winds Dr., Ft Worth, TX 76133, Phone: 17-370-7778
**pecialties:** Fancy classic straight knives in standard patterns. **Patterns:** unters, Bowies, fighters, folders and miniatures. **Technical:** Grinds O1 and amascus. Engraves silver-wire inlays, pearl inlays, scrimshaws and offers ework. **Prices:** $50 to $500; some to $1,200. **Remarks:** Spare-time maker; ·st knife sold in 1965. **Mark:** Initials.

**LISHEWITZ, ALLEN,** PO Box 3059, Canyon Lake, TX 78133, Phone: 30-899-5356, allen@elishewitzknives.com Web: elishewitzknives.com
**pecialties:** Collectible high-tech working straight knives and folders of his esign. **Patterns:** Working, utility and tactical knives. **Technical:** Grinds 54CM and stainless steel Damascus. All designs drafted and field-tested. **rices:** $400 to $600. **Remarks:** Full-time maker; first knife sold in 1989. **ark:** Last name with a Japanese crane.

**LKINS, R. VAN,** PO Box 156, Bonita, LA 71223, Phone: 318-823-2124, ax: 318-283-6802
**pecialties:** High-art Bowies, fighters, folders and period daggers; all one-of-kind pieces. **Patterns:** Welcomes customer designs. **Technical:** Forges his wn Damascus in several patterns, O1 and 5160. **Prices:** $250 to $2800. **emarks:** First knife sold in 1984. **Mark:** Last name.

**LLEFSON, JOEL,** PO Box 1016, 310 S. 1st St., Manhattan, MT 59741, hone: 406-284-3111
**pecialties:** Working straight knives, fancy daggers and one-of-a-kinds. **Pat-rns:** Hunters, daggers and some folders. **Technical:** Grinds A2, 440C and TS-34. Makes own mokume in bronze, brass, silver and shibuishi; makes ·ass/steel blades. **Prices:** $75 to $500; some to $2,000. **Remarks:** Part-time aker; first knife sold in 1978. **Mark:** Stylized last initial.

**LLERBE, W.B.,** 3871 Osceola Rd., Geneva, FL 32732, Phone: 407-49-5818
**pecialties:** Period and primitive knives and sheaths. **Patterns:** Bowies to atch knives, some tomahawks. **Technical:** Grinds Sheffield O1 and files. **rices:** Start at $35. **Remarks:** Full-time maker; first knife sold in 1971. Doing usiness as Cypress Bend Custom Knives. **Mark:** Last name or initials.

**LLIOTT, JERRY,** 4507 Kanawha Ave., Charleston, WV 25304, Phone: )4-925-5045
**pecialties:** Classic and traditional straight knives and folders of his design nd to customer specs. **Patterns:** Hunters, locking folders and Bowies. **Tech-ical:** Grinds ATS-34, 154CM, O1, D2 and T-440-V. All guards silver-sol-ered; bolsters are pinned on straight knives, spot-welded on folders. **Prices:** 30 to $265; some to $1,000. **Remarks:** Full-time maker; first knife sold in 972. **Mark:** First and middle initials, last name, knife maker, city, state.

**LLIOTT, MARCUS,** Pen Dinas, Wyddfydd Rd., Great Orme, Llandudno wynedd, GREAT BRITAIN LL30 2QL, Phone: 01492-872747
**pecialties:** Fancy working knives. **Patterns:** Boots and small hunters. **Tech-ical:** Grinds O1, 440C and ATS-34. **Prices:** $160 to $250. **Remarks:** Spare-me maker; first knife sold in 1981. Makes only a few knives each year. **Mark:** rst name, middle initial, last name, knife maker, city, state.

**LLIS, WILLY B.,** WILLY B CUSTOM STICKS and PICKS, 4941 Cardi-al Trail, Palm Harbor, FL 34683, Phone: 727-942-6420, Web: www.wil-b.com
**pecialties:** One-of-a-kind high art and fantasy knives of his design. Occa-onal customs full size and miniatures. **Patterns:** Bowies, fighters, hunters nd others. **Technical:** Grinds 440C, ATS-34, 1095, carbon Damascus, ivory one, stone and metal carving. **Prices:** $175 to $15,000. **Remarks:** Full-time aker, first knife made in 1973.Probationary member Knifemakers Guild. **ark:** Willy B. or WB"S C etched or carved. **Other:** Jewel setting inlays.

**LLIS, WILLIAM DEAN,** 8875 N. Barton, Fresno, CA 93720, Phone: )9-299-0303, urleebird@comcast.net Web: www.billysblades.com
**pecialties:** Classic and fancy knives of his design. **Patterns:** Boots, fighters nd utility knives. **Technical:** Grinds ATS-34, D2 and Damascus. Offers pered tangs and six patterns of filework; tooled multi-colored sheaths. **rices:** $250 to $500; some to $1,500. **Remarks:** Part-time maker; first knife old in 1991. Doing business as Billy's Blades. **Mark:** "B" in a five-point star ext to "Billy," city and state within a rounded-corner rectangle.

**ELLIS, DAVE/ABS MASTERSMITH,** 380 South Melrose Dr. #407, Vista, CA 92083, Phone: 760-643-4032 Eves: 760-945-7177, www.exquisiteknives.com
**Specialties:** Bowies, utility and combat knives. **Patterns:** Using knives to art quality pieces. **Technical:** Forges 5160, L-6, 52100, cable and his own Damascus steels. **Prices:** $300 to $4,000. **Remarks:** Part-time maker. California's first ABS Master Smith. **Mark:** Dagger-Rose with name and M.S. mark.

**ELROD, ROGER R.,** 58 Dale Ave., Enterprise, AL 36330, Phone: 334-347-1863

**EMBRETSEN, KAJ,** FALUVAGEN 67, S-82821 Edsbyn, SWEDEN, Phone: 46-271-21057, Fax: 46-271-22961
**Specialties:** High quality folders. **Patterns:** Scandinavian-style knives. **Technical:** Forges Damascus. Uses only his blades; natural materials. **Prices:** Upscale. **Remarks:** Full-time maker. **Mark:** Name.

**EMERSON, ERNEST R.,** PO Box 4180, Torrance, CA 90510-4180, Phone: 310-212-7455, info@emersonknives.com Web: www.emersonknives.com
**Specialties:** High-tech folders and combat fighters. **Patterns:** Fighters, liner lock combat folders and SPECWAR combat knives. **Technical:** Grinds 154CM and Damascus. Makes folders with titanium fittings, liners and locks. Chisel grind specialist. **Prices:** $550 to $850; some to $10,000. **Remarks:** Full-time maker; first knife sold in 1983. **Mark:** Last name and Specwar knives.

**ENCE, JIM,** 145 S 200 East, Richfield, UT 84701, Phone: 435-896-6206
**Specialties:** High-art period pieces (spec in California knives) art knives. **Patterns:** Art, boot knives, fighters, Bowies and occasional folders. **Technical:** Grinds 440C for polish and beauty boys'; makes own Damascus. **Prices:** Upscale. **Remarks:** Full-time maker; first knife sold in 1977. Does own engraving, gold work and stone work. **Mark:** Ence, usually engraved. **Other:** Guild member since 1977. Founding member of the AKI.

**ENGLAND, VIRGIL,** 1340 Birchwood St., Anchorage, AK 99508, Phone: 907-274-9494, Web: www.virgilengland.com
**Specialties:** Edged weapons and equipage, one-of-a-kind only. **Patterns:** Axes, swords, lances and body armor. **Technical:** Forges and grinds as pieces dictate. Offers stainless and Damascus. **Prices:** Upscale. **Remarks:** A veteran knife maker. No commissions. **Mark:** Stylized initials.

**ENGLE, WILLIAM,** 16608 Oak Ridge Rd., Boonville, MO 65233, Phone: 816-882-6277
**Specialties:** Traditional working and using straight knives of his design. **Patterns:** Hunters, Bowies and fighters. **Technical:** Grinds 440C, ATS-34 and 154 CM. **Prices:** $250 to $500; some higher. **Remarks:** Part-time maker; first knife sold in 1982. All knives come with certificate of authenticity. **Mark:** Last name in block lettering.

**ENGLEBRETSON, GEORGE,** 1209 NW 49th St., Oklahoma City, OK 73118, Phone: 405-840-4784
**Specialties:** Working straight knives. **Patterns:** Hunters and Bowies. **Technical:** Grinds A2, D2, 440C and ATS-34. **Prices:** Start at $150. **Remarks:** Full-time maker; first knife sold in 1967. **Mark:** "By George," name and city.

**ENGLISH, JIM,** 14586 Olive Vista Dr., Jamul, CA 91935, Phone: 619-669-0833
**Specialties:** Traditional working straight knives to customer specs. **Patterns:** Hunters, Bowies, fighters, tantos, daggers, boot and utility/camp knives. **Technical:** Grinds 440C, ATS-34, commercial Damascus and customer choice. **Prices:** $130 to $350. **Remarks:** Part-time maker; first knife sold in 1985. In addition to custom line, also does business as Mountain Home Knives. **Mark:** Double "A," Double "J" logo.

**ENNIS, RAY,** 1220S 775E, Ogden, UT 84404, Phone: 800-410-7603, Fax: 501-621-2683, nifmakr@hotmail.com Web: www.ennis-entrekusa.com

**ENOS III, THOMAS M.,** 12302 State Rd. 535, Orlando, FL 32836, Phone: 407-239-6205, tmenos3@att.net
**Specialties:** Heavy-duty working straight knives; unusual designs. **Patterns:** Swords, machetes, daggers, skinners, filleting, period pieces. **Technical:** Grinds 440C, D2, 154CM. **Prices:** $75 to $1,500. **Remarks:** Full-time maker; first knife sold in 1972. **Mark:** Name in knife logo and year, type of steel and serial number. **Other:** No longer accepting custom requests. Will be making his own designs. Send SASE for listing of items for sale.

**ENTIN, ROBERT,** 127 Pembroke St. 1, Boston, MA 02118

**EPTING, RICHARD,** 4021 Cody Dr., College Station, TX 77845, Phone: 979-690-6496, rgeknives@hotmail.com
**Specialties:** Folders and working straight knives. **Patterns:** Hunters, Bowies, and locking folders. **Technical:** Forges high-carbon steel and his own Damascus. **Prices:** $200 to $800; some to $1,800. **Remarks:** Part-time maker, first knife sold 1996. **Mark:** Name in arch logo.

**ERICKSON, L.M.,** PO Box 132, Liberty, UT 84310, Phone: 801-745-2026

**Specialties:** Straight knives; period pieces. **Patterns:** Bowies, fighters, boots and hunters. **Technical:** Grinds 440C, 154CM and commercial Damascus. **Prices:** $200 to $900; some to $5,000. **Remarks:** Part-time maker; first knife sold in 1981. **Mark:** Name, city, state.

**ERICKSON, WALTER E.,** 22280 Shelton Tr., Atlanta, MI 49709, Phone: 989-785-5262

**Specialties:** Unusual survival knives and high-tech working knives. **Patterns:** Butterflies, hunters, tantos. **Technical:** Grinds ATS-34 or customer choice. **Prices:** $150 to $500; some to $1,500. **Remarks:** Full-time maker; first knife sold in 1981. **Mark:** Last name in depressed area on blade.

**ERIKSEN, JAMES THORLIEF,** dba VIKING KNIVES, 3830 Dividend Dr., Garland, TX 75042, Phone: 972-494-3667, Fax: 972-235-4932, VikingKnives@aol.com

**Specialties:** Heavy-duty working and using straight knives and folders utilizing traditional, Viking original and customer specification patterns. Some high-tech and fancy/embellished knives available. **Patterns:** Bowies, hunters, skinners, boot and belt knives, utility/camp knives, fighters, daggers, locking folders, slip-joint folders and kitchen knives. **Technical:** Hollow-grinds 440C, D2, ASP-23, ATS-34, 154CM, Vascowear. **Prices:** $150 to $300; some to $600. **Remarks:** Full-time maker; first knife sold in 1985. Doing business as Viking Knives. For a color catalog showing 50 different models, mail $5 to above address. **Mark:** VIKING or VIKING USA for export.

**ESSEGIAN, RICHARD,** 7387 E. Tulare St., Fresno, CA 93727, Phone: 309-255-5950

**Specialties:** Fancy working knives of his design; art knives. **Patterns:** Bowies and some small hunters. **Technical:** Grinds A2, D2, 440C and 154CM. Engraves and inlays. **Prices:** Start at $600. **Remarks:** Part-time maker; first knife sold in 1986. **Mark:** Last name, city and state.

**ETZLER, JOHN,** 11200 N. Island, Grafton, OH 44044, Phone: 440-748-2460, jetzler@bright.net Web: members.tripod.com/~etzlerknives/

**Specialties:** High-art and fantasy straight knives and folders of his design and to customer specs. **Patterns:** Folders, daggers, fighters, utility knives. **Technical:** Forges and grinds nickel Damascus and tool steel; grinds stainless steels. Prefers exotic, natural materials. **Prices:** $250 to $1,200; some to $6,500. **Remarks:** Full-time maker; first knife sold in 1992. **Mark:** Name or initials.

**EVANS, CARLTON,** PO Box 815, Aledo, TX 76008, Phone: 817-441-1363, carlton@crevanscustomkives.com Web: crevancustomknives.com

**Specialties:** In high end folders and fixe bald that are collectible but durable enough to carry everyday. **Patterns:** Working and hunting. **Technical:** Uses the stock removal methods. The materials used are of the highest quality. **Prices:** Start from $650. **Remarks:** Part-time knifemaker. A 2003 Probationary member, eligible for voting membership August 2005 to the Knifemakers Guild.

**EVANS, RONALD B.,** 209 Hoffer St., Middleton, PA 17057-2723, Phone: 717-944-5464

**EVANS, VINCENT K. AND GRACE,** 35 Beaver Creek Rd, Cathlamet, WA 98612, Phone: 360-795-0096, vevans@localnet.com

**Specialties:** Period pieces; swords. **Patterns:** Scottish, Viking, central Asian. **Technical:** Forges 5160 and his own Damascus. **Prices:** $300 to $2,000; some to $8,000. **Remarks:** Full-time maker; first knife sold in 1983. **Mark:** Last initial with fish logo.

**EVANS, BRUCE A.,** 409 CR 1371, Booneville, MS 38829, Phone: 662-720-0193, beknives@avsia.com Web: www.bruceevans.homestead.com/open.html

**Specialties:** Forges blades. **Patterns:** Hunters, Bowies, or will work with customer. **Technical:** 5160, cable Damascus, pattern welded Damascus. **Prices:** $200 and up. **Mark:** Bruce A. Evans Same with JS on reverse of blade.

**EWING, JOHN H.,** 3276 Dutch Valley Rd., Clinton, TN 37716, Phone: 615-457-5757

**Specialties:** Working straight knives, hunters, camp knives. **Patterns:** Hunters. **Technical:** Grinds 440, Forges 5160 52100; prefers forging. **Prices:** $150 to $2,000. **Remarks:** Part-time maker; first knife sold in 1985. **Mark:** First initial, last name, some embellishing done on knives.

# F

**FAGAN, JAMES A.,** 109 S 17 Ave., Lake Worth, FL 33460, Phone: 5 585-9349

**FANT JR., GEORGE,** 1983 CR 3214, Atlanta, TX 75551-6515, Phon (903) 846-2938

**FARR, DAN,** 285 Glen Ellyn Way, Rochester, NY 14618, Phone: 585 721-1388

**Specialties:** Hunting, camping, fighting and utility. **Patterns:** Fixed bla **Technical:** Forged or stock removal. **Prices:** $150 to $750.

**FASSIO, MELVIN G.,** 420 Tyler Way, Lolo, MT 59847, Phone: 406-2 9143

**Specialties:** Working folders to customer specs. **Patterns:** Locking fold hunters and traditional-style knives. **Technical:** Grinds 440C. **Prices:** $12 $350. **Remarks:** Part-time maker; first knife sold in 1975. **Mark:** Name city, dove logo.

**FAUCHEAUX, HOWARD J.,** PO Box 206, Loreauville, LA 70552, Phone: 318-229-6467

**Specialties:** Working straight knives and folders; period pieces. Als hatchet with capping knife in the handle. **Patterns:** Traditional locking folc hunters, fighters and Bowies. **Technical:** Forges W2, 1095 and his own D ascus; stock removal D2. **Prices:** Start at $200. **Remarks:** Full-time ma first knife sold in 1969. **Mark:** Last name.

**FAUST, JOACHIM,** Kirchgasse 10, 95497 Goldkronach, GERMANY

**FAUST, DICK,** 624 Kings Hwy. N, Rochester, NY 14617, Phone: 585 544-1948

**Specialties:** High-performance working straight knives. **Patterns:** Hur and utility/camp knives. **Technical:** Hollow grinds ATS-34 and 154CM tang. Exotic woods, stag and Micarta handles. Provides a custom lea sheath with each knife. **Prices:** From $200 to $600, some higher. **Rema** Full-time maker. **Mark:** Signature.

**FECAS, STEPHEN J.,** 1312 Shadow Lane, Anderson, SC 29625, Phone: 864-287-4834, Fax: 864-287-4834

**Specialties:** Front release lock backs, liner locks. Folders only. **Patte** Gents folders. **Technical:** Grinds ATS-34, Damascus-Ivories and pearl h dles. **Prices:** $650 to $1,200. **Remarks:** Full-time maker since 1980. knife sold in 1977. **Mark:** Last name signature. **Other:** All knives hand finis to 1500 grit.

**FEIGIN, B.,** Liir Corp, 3037 Holly Mill Run, Marietta, GA 30062, Phon 770-579-1631, Fax: 770-579-1199, fabei@abraxis.com

**FELIX, ALEXANDER,** PO Box 4036, Torrance, CA 90510, Phone: 31 320-1836

**Specialties:** Straight working knives, fancy ethnic designs. **Patterns:** H ers, Bowies, daggers, period pieces. **Technical:** Forges carbon steel Damascus; forged stainless and titanium jewelry, gold and silver cas **Prices:** $110 and up. **Remarks:** Jeweler, ABS JourneymanSmith. **Mark:** name.

**FELLOWS, MIKE,** PO Box 166, Velddrie 7365, SOUTH AFRICA, Pho 27 82 960 3868

**Specialties:** Miniatures, art knives, subhilt fighters and folders. **Patte** Original designs and client's specs. **Technical:** Uses own Damascus (L6 nickel). **Other:** All knives carry strong, reliable thru-tang handles screwed bonded together. Uses only indigenous materials for handles, i.e., var hard woods, selected horns, ivory, warthog tusk, hippo tooth, etc. Lov carve animal heads; favorite-Roses. **Mark:** "Shin" letter from Hebrew alph in front of Hebrew word "Karat". **Prices:** R800 - R5500 (approximately $1C $700).

**FERDINAND, DON,** PO Box 1564, Shady Cove, OR 97539-1564, Phone: 503-560-3355

**Specialties:** One-of-a-kind working knives and period pieces; all tool s Damascus. **Patterns:** Bowies, push knives and fishing knives. **Techni** Forges high-carbon alloy steels L6, D2; makes his own Damascus. E handle materials offered. **Prices:** $100 to $500. **Remarks:** Full-time m since 1980. Does business as Wyvern. **Mark:** Initials connected.

**FERGUSON, JIM,** 32131 Via Bande, Temecula, CA 92592, Phone: 9 719-1552, jim@twistednickel.com Web: www.twisterdnickel.com

**Specialties:** Nickel Damascus - Bowies - Daggers - Push Blades. **Patte** All styles. **Technical:** Forges Damascus and sells in U.S. and Can **Prices:** $120 to $5,000. **Remarks:** 1,200 sq. ft. commercial shop - 75 press. Have mad over 10,000 lbs. of Damascus. **Mark:** Jim Ferguson push blade. Also make swords, battle axes and utilities.

**FERGUSON, JIM,** PO Box 764, San Angelo, TX 76902, Phone: 915-651-6656
**Specialties:** Straight working knives and folders. **Patterns:** Working belt knives, hunters, Bowies and some folders. **Technical:** Grinds ATS-34, D2 and Vascowear. Flat-grinds hunting knives. **Prices:** $200 to $600; some to $1,000. **Remarks:** Full-time maker; first knife sold in 1987. **Mark:** First and middle initials, last name.

**FERGUSON, LEE,** 1993 Madison 7580, Hindsville, AR 72738, Phone: 479-443-0084, info@fergusonknives.com Web: www.fergusonknives.com
**Specialties:** Straight working knives and folders, some fancy. **Patterns:** Hunters, daggers, swords, locking folders and slip-joints. **Technical:** Grinds D2, 440C and ATS-34; heat-treats. **Prices:** $50 to $600; some to $4,000. **Remarks:** Full-time maker; first knife sold in 1977. **Mark:** Full name.

**FERRARA, THOMAS,** 122 Madison Dr., Naples, FL 33942, Phone: 813-597-3363, Fax: 813-597-3363
**Specialties:** High-art, traditional and working straight knives and folders of all designs. **Patterns:** Boots, Bowies, daggers, fighters and hunters. **Technical:** Grinds 440C, D2 and ATS-34; heat-treats. **Prices:** $100 to $700; some to $1,300. **Remarks:** Part-time maker; first knife sold in 1983. **Mark:** Last name.

**FERRIER, GREGORY K.,** 3119 Simpson Dr., Rapid City, SD 57702, Phone: 605-342-9280

**FERRIS, BILL,** 186 Thornton Dr., Palm Beach Garden, FL 33418

**FERRY, TOM,** 16005 SE 322nd St., Auburn, WA 98092, Phone: 253-939-4468, KNFESMTH71@AOL.COM
**Specialties:** Damascus, fixed blades and folders. **Patterns:** Folders Damascus, and fixed blades. **Technical:** Specialize in Damascus and timascus TM (Titanium Damascus). **Prices:** $400 to $2,000. **Remarks:** Name Tom Ferry DBA: Soos Creek Ironworks. **Mark:** Combined T and F in a circle and/or last name on folders. **Other:** Co-developer of Timascus TM (Titanium Damascus).

**FIKES, JIMMY L.,** PO Box 3457, Jasper, AL 35502, Phone: 205-387-9302, Fax: 205-221-1980, oleyfermo@aol.com
**Specialties:** High-art working knives; artifact knives; using knives with cord-wrapped handles; swords and combat weapons. **Patterns:** Axes to buckskinners, camp knives to miniatures, tantos to tomahawks; spring less folders. **Technical:** Forges W2, O1 and his own Damascus. **Prices:** $135 to $3,000; exceptional knives to $7,000. **Remarks:** Full-time maker. **Mark:** Stylized initials.

**FILIPPOU, IOANNIS-MINAS,** 7 KRINIS STR NEA SMYRNI, ATHENS 17122, GREECE, Phone: ( 1) 935-2093

**FINCH, RICKY D.,** 2446 HWY 191, West Liberty, KY 41472, Phone: 606-743-7151, finchknives@mrtc.com Web: www.finchknives.com
**Specialties:** Traditional working/using straight knives of his design or to customer spec. **Patterns:** Hunters, skinners and utility/camp knives. **Technical:** Grinds 440C and ATS-34, hand rubbed stain finish, use Micarta, stabilized wood - natural and exotic. **Prices:** $55 to $175; some $250. **Remarks:** Part-time maker, first knife made 1994. Doing business as Finch Knives. **Mark:** Last name inside outline of state of Kentucky.

**FIORINI, BILL,** E2173 Axlen Rd., DeSoto, WI 54624, Phone: 608-780-5898, fiorini.will@uwlax.edu Web: www.billfiorini.com
**Specialties:** Fancy working knives. **Patterns:** Hunters, boots, Japanese-style knives and kitchen/utility knives and folders. **Technical:** Forges own Damascus, mosaic and mokune-gane. **Prices:** Full range. **Remarks:** Full-time metal smith researching pattern materials. **Mark:** Orchid crest with name KOKA in Japanese.

**FISHER, JAY,** 1405 Edwards, Clovis, NM 88101, Phone: 505-763-2268, Fax: 505-463-2346, Web: www.JayFisher.com
**Specialties:** High-art, ancient and exact working and using straight knives of his design and client's designs. Military working and commemoratives. **Patterns:** Hunters, daggers, folding knives, museum pieces and high-art sculptures. **Technical:** Grinds 440C, ATS-34, 01and D2. Prolific maker of stone-handled knives and swords. **Prices:** $250 to $50,000; some higher. **Remarks:** Full-time maker; first knife sold in 1980. **Mark:** Very fine—JaFisher—Quality Custom Knives. **Other:** High resolution etching, computer and manual engraving.

**FISHER, THEO (TED),** 8115 Modoc Lane, Montague, CA 96064, Phone: 916-459-3804
**Specialties:** Moderately priced working knives in carbon steel. **Patterns:** Hunters, fighters, kitchen and buckskinner knives, Damascus miniatures. **Technical:** Grinds ATS-34, L6 and 440C. **Prices:** $65 to $165; exceptional knives to $300. **Remarks:** First knife sold in 1981. **Mark:** Name in banner logo.

**FISK, JERRY,** 10095 Hwy. 278 W, Nashville, AR 71852, Phone: 870-845-4456, jfisk@alltel.net Web: fisk-knives.com
**Specialties:** Edged weapons, collectible and functional. **Patterns:** Bowies, daggers, swords, hunters, camp knives and others. **Technical:** Forges carbon steels and his own pattern welded steels. **Prices:** $250 to $15,000. **Remarks:** National living treasure. **Mark:** Name, MS.

**FISTER, JIM,** PO Box 307, Simpsonville, KY 40067
**Specialties:** One-of-a-kind collectibles and period pieces. **Patterns:** Bowies, camp knives, hunters, buckskinners, and daggers. **Technical:** Forges, 1085, 5160, 52100, his own Damascus, pattern and turkish. **Prices:** $150 to $2,500. **Remarks:** Part-time maker; first knife sold in 1982. **Mark:** Name and MS.

**FITCH, JOHN S.,** 45 Halbrook Rd., Clinton, AR 72031-8910, Phone: 501-893-2020

**FITZGERALD, DENNIS M.,** 4219 Alverado Dr., Fort Wayne, IN 46816-2847, Phone: 219-447-1081
**Specialties:** One-of-a-kind collectibles and period pieces. **Patterns:** Skinners, fighters, camp and utility knives; period pieces. **Technical:** Forges 1085, 1095, L6, 5160, 52100, his own pattern and Turkish Damascus. **Prices:** $100 to $500. **Remarks:** Part-time maker; first knife sold in 1985. Doing business as The Ringing Circle. **Mark:** Name and circle logo.

**FLINT, ROBERT,** 2902 Aspen, Anchorage, AK 99517, Phone: 907-243-6706
**Specialties:** Working straight knives and folders. **Patterns:** Utility, hunters, fighters and gents. **Technical:** Grinds ATS-34, BG-42, D2 and Damascus. **Prices:** $150 and up. **Remarks:** Part-time maker, first knife sold in 1998. **Mark:** Last name; stylized initials.

**FLOURNOY, JOE,** 5750 Lisbon Rd., El Dorado, AR 71730, Phone: 870-863-7208, flournoy@ipa.net
**Specialties:** Working straight knives and folders. **Patterns:** Hunters, Bowies, camp knives, folders and daggers. **Technical:** Forges only high-carbon steel, steel cable and his own Damascus. **Prices:** $350 Plus. **Remarks:** First knife sold in 1977. **Mark:** Last name and MS in script.

**FOGARIZZU, BOITEDDU,** via Crispi, 6, 07016 Pattada, ITALY
**Specialties:** Traditional Italian straight knives and folders. **Patterns:** Collectible folders. **Technical:** forges and grinds 12C27, ATS-34 and his Damascus. **Prices:** $200 to $3,000. **Remarks:** Full-time maker; first knife sold in 1958. **Mark:** Full name and registered logo.

**FOGG, DON,** 40 Alma Rd., Jasper, AL 35501-8813, Phone: 205-483-0822, dfogg@dfoggknives.com; Web: www.dfoggknives.com
**Specialties:** Swords, daggers, Bowies and hunting knives. **Patterns:** Collectible folders. **Technical:** Hand-forged high-carbon and Damascus steel. **Prices:** $200 to $5,000. **Remarks:** Full-time maker; first knife sold in 1976. **Mark:** 24K gold cherry blossom.

**FONTENOT, GERALD J.,** 901 Maple Ave., Mamou, LA 70554, Phone: 318-468-3180

**FORREST, BRIAN,** FORREST KNIVES, PO Box 203, Descanso, CA 91916, Phone: 619-445-6343, Web: www.forrestknives.com
**Specialties:** Working straight knives, some fancy made to customer order. **Patterns:** Traditional patterns, Bowies, hunters, skinners and daggers. **Technical:** Grinds 440C, files and rasps. **Prices:** $125 and up. **Remarks:** Member of California Knifemakers Association. Full-time maker. First knife sold in 1971. **Mark:** Forrest USA.

**FORSTALL, AL,** 38379 Aunt Massey Rd., Pearl River, LA 70452, Phone: 504-863-2930
**Specialties:** Traditional working and using straight knives of his design or to customer specs. **Patterns:** Fighters, hunters and utility/camp knives. **Technical:** Grinds ATS-34, 440C, commercial Damascus and others upon request. **Prices:** $75 to $250. **Remarks:** Spare-time maker; first knife sold in 1991. **Mark:** Fleur-di-lis with name.

**FORTHOFER, PETE,** 5535 Hwy. 93S, Whitefish, MT 59937, Phone: 406-862-2674
**Specialties:** Interframes with checkered wood inlays; working straight knives. **Patterns:** Interframe folders and traditional-style knives; hunters, fighters and Bowies. **Technical:** Grinds D2, 440C, 154CM and ATS-34. **Prices:** $350 to $2,500. **Remarks:** Part-time maker; full-time gunsmith. First knife sold in 1979. **Mark:** Name and logo.

**FORTUNE PRODUCTS, INC.,** 205 Hickory Creek Rd., Marble Falls, TX 78654, Phone: 830-693-6111, Fax: 830-693-6394, Web: www.accusharp.com
**Specialties:** Knife sharpeners.

**FOSTER, NORVELL C.,** 619 Holmgreen Rd., San Antonio, TX 78220, Phone: 210-333-1675
**Specialties:** Engraving; ivory handle carving. **Patterns:** American-large and small scroll-oak leaf and acorns. **Prices:** $25 to $400. **Mark:** N.C. Foster - S.A., TX and current year.

**FOSTER, RONNIE E.,** 95 Riverview Rd., Morrilton, AR 72110, Phone: 501-354-5389
**Specialties:** Working, using knives, some period pieces, work with customer specs. **Patterns:** Hunters, fighters, Bowies, liner-lock folders, camp knives. **Technical:** Forge-5160, 1084, 01, 15N20-makes own Damascus. **Prices:** $200 (start). **Remarks:** Part-time maker. First knife sold 1994. **Mark:** Ronnie Foster MS.

**FOSTER, TIMOTHY L.,** 723 Sweet Gum Acres Rd., El Dorado, AR 71730, Phone: 870-863-6188

**FOSTER, BURT,** 23697 Archery Range Rd., Bristol, VA 24202, Phone: 276-669-0121, Web: www.burtfoster.com
**Specialties:** Working straight knives, Laminated blades, and some art knives of his design. **Patterns:** Bowies, hunters, daggers. **Technical:** Forges 52100, W-2 and makes own Damascus. Does own heat treating. **Remarks:** ABS MasterSmith. Full-time maker, believes in sole authorship. **Mark:** Signed "BF" initials.

**FOSTER, AL,** 118 Woodway Dr., Magnolia, TX 77355, Phone: 936-372-9297
**Specialties:** Straight knives and folders. **Patterns:** Hunting, fishing, folders and Bowies. **Technical:** Grinds 440-C, ATS-34 and D2. **Prices:** $100 to $1,000. **Remarks:** Full-time maker; first knife sold in 1981. **Mark:** Scorpion logo and name.

**FOSTER, R.L. (BOB),** 745 Glendale Blvd., Mansfield, OH 44907, Phone: 419-756-6294

**FOWLER, CHARLES R.,** 226 National Forest Rd. 48, Ft McCoy, FL 32134-9624, Phone: 904-467-3215

**FOWLER, ED A.,** Willow Bow Ranch, PO Box 1519, Riverton, WY 82501, Phone: 307-856-9815
**Specialties:** High-performance working and using straight knives. **Patterns:** Hunter, camp, bird, and trout knives and Bowies. New model, the gentleman's Pronghorn. **Technical:** Low temperature forged 52100 from virgin 5 1/2 round bars, multiple quench heat treating, engraves all knives, all handles domestic sheep horn processed and aged at least 5 years. Makes heavy duty hand-stitched waxed harness leather pouch type sheathes. **Prices:** $800 to $7,000. **Remarks:** Full-time maker. First knife sold in 1962. **Mark:** Initials connected.

**FOWLER, JERRY,** 610 FM 1660 N., Hutto, TX 78634, Phone: 512-846-2860, fowler@inetport.com
**Specialties:** Using straight knives of his design. **Patterns:** A variety of hunting and camp knives, combat knives. Custom designs considered. **Technical:** Forges 5160, his own Damascus and cable Damascus. Makes sheaths. Prefers natural handle materials. **Prices:** Start at $150. **Remarks:** Part-time maker; first knife sold in 1986. Doing business as Fowler Forge Knife works. **Mark:** First initial, last name, date and J.S.

**FOWLER, RICKY AND SUSAN,** FOWLER CUSTOM KNIVES, 18535-B Co. Rd. 48, Robertsdale, AL 36567, Phone: 251-947-5648, theknife-shop@gulftel.com Web: www.fowlerknives.net
**Specialties:** Traditional working/using straight knives of his design or to customer specifications. **Patterns:** Skinners, fighters, tantos, Bowies and utility/camp knives. **Technical:** Grinds O1, exclusively. **Prices:** Start at $150. **Remarks:** Full-time maker; first knife sold in 1994. Doing business as Fowler Custom Knives. **Mark:** Last name tang stamped and serial numbered.

**FOX, PAUL,** 4721 Rock Barn Rd., Claremont, NC 28610, Phone: 828-459-2000, Fax: 828-459-9200
**Specialties:** Hi-Tech. **Patterns:** Naibsek, Otnat, and Zorro (tactical) knives. **Technical:** Grinds ATS-34, 440C and D2. **Prices:** $500. **Remarks:** Spare-time maker; first knife sold in 1985. Doing business as Fox Knives. **Mark:** Laser engraved.

**FOX, WENDELL,** 1480 S 39th St., Springfield, OR 97478, Phone: 541-747-2126, WfoxForge@aol.com
**Specialties:** Large camping knives and friction folders of his design and to customer specs. One-of-a-kind prices. **Patterns:** Hunters, locking folders, slip-joint folders and utility/camp knives. **Technical:** Forges and grinds high-carbon steel only. **Prices:** $200 and up. **Remarks:** Full-time maker; first knife sold in 1952. **Mark:** Stamped name or logo. **Other:** All one-of-a-kind pieces. Specializing in early American.

**FOX, JACK L.,** 7085 Canelo Hills Dr., Citrus Heights, CA 95610, Phone: 916-723-8647
**Specialties:** Traditional working/using straight knives of all designs. **Patterns:** Hunters, utility/camp knives and bird/fish knives. **Technical:** Grinds ATS-34, 440C and D2. **Prices:** $125 to $225; some to $350. **Remarks:** Spare-tim maker; first knife sold in 1985. Doing business as Fox Knives. **Mark:** Stylize fox head.

**FRALEY, D.B.,** 1355 Fairbanks Ct., Dixon, CA 95620, Phone: 707-678-0393, dbfknives@aol
**Specialties:** Traditional working/using straight knives and folders of h design and in standard patterns. **Patterns:** Fighters, hunters, utility/cam knives. **Technical:** Grinds ATS-34. Offers hand-stitched sheaths. **Price** Start at $100. **Remarks:** Part-time maker; first knife sold in 1990. **Mark:** Fir and middle initials, last name over buffalo.

**FRAMSKI, WALTER P.,** 24 Rek Ln., Prospect, CT 06712, Phone: 203-758-5634

**FRANCE, DAN,** Box 218, Cawood, KY 40815, Phone: 606-573-6104
**Specialties:** Traditional working and using straight knives of his design. **Pa terns:** Hunters, Bowies and utility/camp knives. **Technical:** Forges and grin O1, 5160 and L6. **Prices:** $35 to $125; some to $350. **Remarks:** Spare-tin maker; first knife sold in 1985. **Mark:** First name.

**FRANCIS, JOHN D.,** FRANCIS KNIVES, 18 Miami St., Ft. Loramie, OH 45845, Phone: 937-295-3941, fscjohn@wcoil.com
**Specialties:** Utility and hunting-style fixed bladed knives of ATS-34 ste micarta, exotic woods, and other types of handle materials. **Prices:** $100 $150 range. **Remarks:** Exceptional quality and a value at factory price **Mark:** Francis-Ft. Loramie, OH stamped on tang.

**FRANCIS, VANCE,** 2612 Alpine Blvd., Alpine, CA 91901, Phone: 619-445-0979
**Specialties:** Working straight knives. **Patterns:** Bowies and utility knive **Technical:** Uses ATS-34, A2, D2 and Damascus; differentially tempers lar blades. **Prices:** $175 to $600. **Remarks:** Part-time maker. **Mark:** First nam last name, city and state under feather in oval.

**FRANK, HEINRICH H.,** 13868 NW Keleka Pl., Seal Rock, OR 97376, Phone: 541-563-3041, Fax: 541-563-3041
**Specialties:** High-art investor-class folders, handmade and engraved. **Pa terns:** Folding daggers, hunter-size folders and gents. **Technical:** Grinds and O1. **Prices:** $4,800 to $16,000. **Remarks:** Full-time maker; first knife so in 1965. Doing business as H.H. Frank Knives. **Mark:** Name, address a date.

**FRANKL, JOHN M.,** 12 Holden St., Cambridge, MA 02138, Phone: 61 547-0359
**Specialties:** Hand forged tool steel and Damascus. **Patterns:** Camp knive Bowies, hunters and fighters. **Technical:** Forge own Damascus, 5160 and 1084. **Prices:** $150 to $1,000. **Mark:** Last name "Frankl" on ricasso.

**FRANKLIN, MIKE,** 9878 Big Run Rd., Aberdeen, OH 45101, Phone: 937-549-2598
**Specialties:** High-tech tactical folders. **Patterns:** Tactical folders. **Technic** Grinds CPM-T-440V, 440-C, ATS-34; titanium liners and bolsters; carbon fi scales. Uses radical grinds and severe serrations. **Prices:** $275 to $6 **Remarks:** Full-time maker; first knife sold in 1969. **Mark:** Stylized boar w HAWG.

**FRAPS, JOHN R.,** 3810 Wyandotte Tr., Indianpolis, IN 46240-3422, Phone: 317-849-9419, Fax: 317-842-2224, jfraps@att.net Web: www.frapsknives.com
**Specialties:** Working and Collector Grade liner lock and slip joint folders. **P terns:** One-of-a kind linerlocks and traditional slip joints. **Technical:** Flat a hollow grinds ATS-34, Damascus, Talonite, CPM S30V, 154Cm, Stellite hand rubbed or mirror finish. **Prices:** $200 to $1,500; some higher. **Remar** Full-time maker; first knife sold in 1997. **Mark:** Cougar Creek Knives and name.

**FRAZIER, RON,** 2107 Urbine Rd., Powhatan, VA 23139, Phone: 804-794-8561
**Specialties:** Classy working knives of his design; some high-art strai knives. **Patterns:** Wide assortment of straight knives, including miniatures a push knives. **Technical:** Grinds 440C; offers satin, mirror or sand finish **Prices:** $85 to $700; some to $3,000. **Remarks:** Full-time maker; first k sold in 1976. **Mark:** Name in arch logo.

**FRED, REED WYLE,** 3149 X S., Sacramento, CA 95817, Phone: 916 739-0237
**Specialties:** Working using straight knives of his design. **Patterns:** Hun and camp knives. **Technical:** Forges any 10 series, old files and car steels. Offers initialing upon request; prefers natural handle materials. **Pric** $30 to $300. **Remarks:** Part-time maker; first knife sold in 1994. Doing b ness as R.W. Fred Knife maker. **Mark:** Engraved first and last initials.

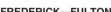

**FREDERICK, AARON,** 459 Brooks Ln, West Liberty, KY 41472-8961, Phone: 606-7432015, aaronf@mrtc.com Web: www.frederickknives.com

**Specialties:** I make most types of knives, but as for now I specialize in the Damascus folder. I do all my Damascus and forging of the steel. I also prefer natural handle material such as ivory and pearl. I prefer 14K gold screws in most of the knives I do. I also offer several types of file work on blades, spacers, and liners. I have just recently started doing carving and can do a limited amount of engraving.

**FREEMAN, JOHN,** 160 Concession St., Cambridge, Ont., CANADA N1R 2H7, Phone: 519-740-2767, Fax: 519-740-2785, freeman@golden.net; Web: www.freemanknives.com

**Specialties:** Kitchen knives, outdoor knives, sharpeners and folders. **Patterns:** Hunters, skinners, utilities, backpackers. **Technical:** Flat ground 440C. **Prices:** Start at $135 and up. **Remarks:** Full-time maker; first knife sold in 1985. **Mark:** Last name, country.

**FREER, RALPH,** 114 12th St., Seal Beach, CA 90740, Phone: 562-493-4925, Fax: same, ralphfreer@adelphia.net

**Specialties:** Exotic folders, liner locks, folding daggers, fixed blades. **Patters:** All original. **Technical:** Lots of Damascus, ivory, pearl, jeweled, thumb studs, carving ATS-34, 420V, 530V. **Prices:** $400 to $2,500; and up. **Mark:** Freer in German-style text, also Freer shield.

**FREILING, ALBERT J.,** 3700 Niner Rd., Finksburg, MD 21048, Phone: 301-795-2880

**Specialties:** Working straight knives and folders; some period pieces. **Patterns:** Boots, Bowies, survival knives and tomahawks in 4130 and 440C; some locking folders and interframes; ball-bearing folders. **Technical:** Grinds O1, 440C and 154CM. **Prices:** $100 to $300; some to $500. **Remarks:** Part-time maker; first knife sold in 1966. **Mark:** Initials connected.

**FREY, STEVE,** 19103 131st Drive SE, Snohomish, WA 98296, Phone: 360-668-7351, sfrey2@aol.com

**Remarks:** Custom crafted knives-all styles.

**FREY JR., W. FREDERICK,** 305 Walnut St., Milton, PA 17847, Phone: 570-742-9576, wffrey@guidescape.net

**Specialties:** Working straight knives and folders, some fancy. **Patterns:** Wide rangeminiatures, boot knives and lock back folders. **Technical:** Grinds A2, O1 and D2; vaseo wear, cru-wear and CPM 440V. **Prices:** $100 to $250; $1,200. **Remarks:** Spare-time maker; first knife sold in 1983. All knives include quality and stitched sheaths. **Mark:** Last name in script.

**FRIEDLY, DENNIS E.,** 12 Cottontail Ln. - E, Cody, WY 82414, Phone: 307-527-6811, friedly_knives@hotmail.com

**Specialties:** Fancy working straight knives and daggers, lock back folders and liner locks. **Patterns:** Hunters, fighters, short swords, minis and miniatures; new line of full-tang hunters/boots. **Technical:** Grinds 440C, commercial Damascus, mosaic Damascus and ATS-34 blades; prefers hidden tangs. **Prices:** $135 to $900; some to $2,500. **Remarks:** Full-time maker; first knife sold in 1972. **Mark:** D.E. Friedly

**FRIGAULT, RICK,** 3584 Rapidsview Dr., Niagara Falls ON, CANADA L2G 6C4, Phone: 905-295-6695, rfigault@cogeco.ca Web: www.rfrigaultknives.com

**Specialties:** Fixed blades. **Patterns:** Hunting, tactical and large Bowies. **Technical:** Grinds ATS-34, 440-C, D-2, CPMS30V, CPMS60V, CPMS90V, BG42 and Damascus. Use G-10, Micarta, ivory, antler, ironwood and other stabilized woods for carbon fiber handle material. Makes leather sheaths by hand. Tactical blades include a Concealex sheath made by "On Scene Tactical". **Remarks:** Sold first knife in 1997. Member of Canadian Knifemakers Guild. **Mark:** RFRIGAULT.

**FRITZ, JESSE,** 900 S. 13th St., Slaton, TX 79364, Phone: 806-828-5083

**Specialties:** Working and using straight knives in standard patterns. **Patterns:** Hunters, utility/camp knives and skinners with gut hook, bowie knives, kitchen carving sets by request. **Technical:** Grinds 440C, O1 and 1095. Uses 1095 steel. Fline-napped steel design, blued blades, filework and machine jewelling. Inlays handles with turquoise, coral and mother-of-pearl. Makes sheaths. **Prices:** $85 to $275; some to $500. **Mark:** Last name only (FRITZ).

**FRIZZELL, TED,** 14056 Low Gap Rd., West Fork, AR 72774, Phone: 501-839-2516

**Specialties:** Swords, axes and self-defense weapons. **Patterns:** Small skelen knives to large swords. **Technical:** Grinds 5160 almost exclusively—1/4" 1/2"— bars some O1 and A2 on request. All knives come with Kydex sheaths. **Prices:** $45 to $1,200. **Remarks:** Full-time maker; first knife sold in 1984. Doing business as Mineral Mountain Hatchet Works. Wholesale orders welcome. **Mark:** A circle with line in the middle; MM and HW within the circle.

**FRONEFIELD, DANIEL,** 137 Catherine Dr., Hampton Cove, AL 35763-9732, Phone: 256-536-7827, dfronfld@hiwaay.com

**Specialties:** Fixed and folding knives featuring meteorites and other exotic materials. **Patterns:** San-mai Damascus, custom Damascus. **Prices:** $500 to $3,000.

**FROST, DEWAYNE,** 1016 Van Buren Rd., Barnesville, GA 30204, Phone: 770-358-1426, lbrtyhill@aol.com

**Specialties:** Working straight knives and period knives. **Patterns:** Hunters, Bowies and utility knives. **Technical:** Forges own Damascus, cable, etc. as well as stock removal. **Prices:** $150 to $500. **Remarks:** Part-time maker ABS JourneymanSmith. **Mark:** Liberty Hill Forge Dewayne Frost w/liberty bell.

**FRUHMANN, LUDWIG,** Stegerwaldstr 8, 84489 Burghausen, GERMANY

**Specialties:** High-tech and working straight knives of his design. **Patterns:** Hunters, fighters and boots. **Technical:** Grinds ATS-34, CPM-T-440V and Schneider Damascus. Prefers natural handle materials. **Prices:** $200 to $1,500. **Remarks:** Spare-time maker; first knife sold in 1990. **Mark:** First initial and last name.

**FUEGEN, LARRY,** 617 N. Coulter Circle, Prescott, AZ 86303, Phone: 928-776-8777, fuegen@cableone.net Web: www.larryfuegen.com

**Specialties:** High-art folders and classic and working straight knives. **Patterns:** Forged scroll folders, lockback folders and classic straight knives. **Technical:** Forges 5160, 1095 and his own Damascus. Works in exotic leather; offers elaborate filework and carving; likes natural handle materials, now offers own engraving. **Prices:** $575 to $9,000. **Remarks:** Full-time maker; first knife sold in 1975. **Mark:** Initials connected. Other: Sole authorship on all knives. ABS mastersmith.

**FUJIKAWA, SHUN,** Sawa 1157 Kaizuka, Osaka 597 0062, JAPAN, Phone: 81-724-23-4032, Fax: 81-726-23-9229

**Specialties:** Folders of his design and to customer specs. **Patterns:** Locking folders. **Technical:** Grinds his own steel. **Prices:** $450 to $2,500; some to $3,000. **Remarks:** Part-time maker.

**FUJISAKA, STANLEY,** 45-004 Holowai St., Kaneohe, HI 96744, Phone: 808-247-0017

**Specialties:** Fancy working straight knives and folders. **Patterns:** Hunters, boots, personal knives, daggers, collectible art knives. **Technical:** Grinds 440C, 154CM and ATS-34; clean lines, inlays. **Prices:** $150 to $1,200; some to $3,000. **Remarks:** Full-time maker; first knife sold in 1984. **Mark:** Name, city, state.

**FUKUTA, TAK,** 38-Umeagae-cho, Seki-City, Gifu-Pref, JAPAN, Phone: 0575-22-0264

**Specialties:** Bench-made fancy straight knives and folders. **Patterns:** Sheffield-type folders, Bowies and fighters. **Technical:** Grinds commercial Damascus. **Prices:** Start at $300. **Remarks:** Full-time maker. **Mark:** Name in knife logo.

**FULLER, BRUCE A.,** 1305 Airhart Dr., Baytown, TX 77520, Phone: 281-427-1848, fullcoforg@aol.com

**Specialties:** One-of-a-kind working/using straight knives and folders of his designs. **Patterns:** Bowies, hunters, folders, and utility/camp knives. **Technical:** Forges high-carbon steel and his own Damascus. Prefers El Solo Mesquite and natural materials. Offers filework. **Prices:** $200 to $500; some to $1,800. **Remarks:** Spare-time maker; first knife sold in 1991. Doing business as Fullco Forge. **Mark:** Fullco, M.S.

**FULLER, JACK A.,** 7103 Stretch Ct., New Market, MD 21774, Phone: 301-798-0119

**Specialties:** Straight working knives of his design and to customer specs. **Patterns:** Fighters, camp knives, hunters, tomahawks and art knives. **Technical:** Forges 5160, O1, W2 and his own Damascus. Does silver wire inlay and own leather work, wood lined sheaths for big camp knives. **Prices:** $300 to $850. **Remarks:** Part-time maker. Master Smith in ABS; first knife sold in 1979. **Mark:** Fuller's Forge, MS.

**FULTON, MICKEY,** 406 S Shasta St., Willows, CA 95988, Phone: 530-934-5780

**Specialties:** Working straight knives and folders of his design. **Patterns:** Hunters, Bowies, lockback folders and steak knife sets. **Technical:** Hand-filed, sanded, buffed ATS-34, 440C and A2. **Prices:** $65 to $600; some to $1,200. **Remarks:** Full-time maker; first knife sold in 1979. **Mark:** Signature.

# G

**GADBERRY, EMMET,** 82 Purple Plum Dr., Hattieville, AR 72063, Phone: 501-354-4842

**GADDY, GARY LEE,** 205 Ridgewood Lane, Washington, NC 27889, Phone: 252-946-4359
**Specialties:** Working/using straight knives of his design; period pieces. **Patterns:** Bowies, hunters, utility/camp knives. **Technical:** Grinds ATS-34, 01; forges 1095**Prices:** $100 to $225; some to $400. **Remarks:** Spare-time maker; first knife sold in 1991. **Mark:** Quarter moon logo.

**GAETA, ROBERTO,** Rua Mandi Ssununha 41, Sao Paulo, BRAZIL 05619-010, Phone: 11-37684626
**Specialties:** Wide range of using knives. **Patterns:** Brazilian and North American hunting and fighting knives. **Technical:** Grinds stainless steel; likes natural handle materials. **Prices:** $100 to $250; some to $600. **Remarks:** Full-time maker; first knife sold in 1979. **Mark:** BOB'G.

**GAETA, ANGELO,** R. Saldanha Marinho, 1295 Centro Jau, SP-17201-310, BRAZIL, Phone: 0146-224543, Fax: 0146-224543
**Specialties:** Straight using knives to customer specs. **Patterns:** Hunters, fighting, daggers, belt push dagger. **Technical:** Grinds D6, ATS-34 and 440C stainless. titanium nitride golden finish upon request. **Prices:** $60 to $300. **Remarks:** Full-time maker; first knife sold in 1992. **Mark:** First initial, last name.

**GAGSTAETTER, PETER,** Nibelungenschmiede, Bergstrasse 2, 9306 Freidorf Tg, SWITZERLAND

**GAINES, BUDDY,** GAINES KNIVES, 155 Red Hill Rd., Commerce, GA 30530, Web: www.gainesknives.com
**Specialties:** Collectible and working folders and straight knives. **Patterns:** Folders, hunters, Bowies, tactical knives. **Technical:** Forges own Damascus, grinds ATS-34, D2, commercial Damascus. Prefers mother-of-pearl and stag. **Prices:** Start at $200. **Remarks:** Part-time maker, sold first knife in 1985. **Mark:** Last name.

**GAINEY, HAL,** 904 Bucklevel Rd., Greenwood, SC 29649, Phone: 864-223-0225, Web: www.scak.org
**Specialties:** Traditional working and using straight knives and folders. **Patterns:** Hunters, slip-joint folders and utility/camp knives. **Technical:** Hollow-grinds ATS-34 and D2; makes sheaths. **Prices:** $95 to $145; some to $500. **Remarks:** Full-time maker; first knife sold in 1975. **Mark:** Eagle head and last name.

**GALLAGHER, BARRY,** 135 Park St., Lewistown, MT 59457, Phone: 406-538-7056, Web: www.gallagherknives.com
**Specialties:** One-of-a-kind Damascus folders. **Patterns:** Folders - utility to high art, some straight knives - hunter, Bowies, and art pieces. **Technical:** Forges own mosaic Damascus and carbon steel, some stainless. **Prices:** $400 to $5,000+. **Remarks:** Full-time maker; first knife sold in 1993. Doing business as Gallagher Custom Knives. **Mark:** Last name.

**GALLAGHER, SEAN,** 24828 114th PL SE, Monroe, WA 98272-7685

**GAMBLE, FRANK,** 3872 Dunbar Pl., Fremont, CA 94536, Phone: 510-797-7970
**Specialties:** Fantasy and high-art straight knives and folders of his design. **Patterns:** Daggers, fighters, hunters and special locking folders. **Technical:** Grinds 440C and ATS-34; forges Damascus. Inlays; offers jewelling. Prices $150 to $10,000. **Remarks:** Full-time maker; first knife sold in 1976. **Mark:** First initial, last name.

**GAMBLE, ROGER,** 2801 65 Way N., St. Petersburg, FL 33710, Phone: 727-384-1470, rlgamble2@netzero.net
**Specialties:** Traditional working/using straight knives and folders of his design. **Patterns:** Liner locks and hunters. **Technical:** Grinds ATS-34 and Damascus. **Prices:** $150 to $2,000. **Remarks:** Part-time maker; first knife sold in 1982. Doing business as Gamble Knives. **Mark:** First name in a fan of cards over last name.

**GANSTER, JEAN-PIERRE,** 18, Rue du Vieil Hopital, F-67000 Strasbourg, FRANCE, Phone: (0033) 388 32 65 61, Fax: (0033) 388 32 52 79
**Specialties:** Fancy and high-art miniatures of his design and to customer specs. **Patterns:** Bowies, daggers, fighters, hunters, locking folders and miniatures. **Technical:** Forges and grinds stainless Damascus, ATS-34, gold and silver. **Prices:** $100 to $380; some to $2,500. **Remarks:** Part-time maker; first knife sold in 1972. **Mark:** Stylized first initials.

**GARCIA, MARIO EIRAS,** R. Edmundo Scanapieco, 300 Caxingui, Sao Paulo SP-05516-070, BRAZIL, Fax: 011-37214528
**Specialties:** Fantasy knives of his design; one-of-a-kind only. **Patterns:** Fighters, daggers, boots and two-bladed knives. **Technical:** Forges car leaf springs. Uses only natural handle material. **Prices:** $100 to $200. **Remarks:** Part-time maker; first knife sold in 1976. **Mark:** Two "B"s, one opposite th other.

**GARDNER, ROB,** 3381 E Rd., Loxahatchee, FL 33470, Phone: 561-784-4994
**Specialties:** High-art working and using knives of his design and to custom specs. **Patterns:** Daggers, hunters and ethnic-patterned knives. **Technica** Forges Damascus, L6 and 10-series steels. Engraves and inlays. Handle and fittings may be carved. **Prices:** $175 to $500; some to $2,500. **Remark** Full-time maker; artist blacksmith, first knife sold in 1987. Knives made by cu tom order only. **Mark:** Engraved or stamped initials.

**GARNER, LARRY W.,** 13069 FM 14, Tyler, TX 75706, Phone: 903-597 6045, lwgarner@classicnet.net
**Specialties:** Fixed blade hunters and Bowies. **Patterns:** My designs or you **Technical:** Hand forges 5160. **Prices:** $200 to $500. **Remarks:** Apprenti bladesmith. **Mark:** Last name.

**GARNER JR., WILLIAM O.,** 2803 East DeSoto St., Pensacola, FL 32503, Phone: 850-438-2009
**Specialties:** Working straight and art knives. **Patterns:** Hunters and folde **Technical:** Grinds 440C and ATS-34 steels. **Prices:** $235 to $600. **Remark** Full-time maker; first knife sold in 1985. **Mark:** First and last name in oval lo or last name.

**GARVOCK, MARK W.,** RR 1, Balderson, Ontario, CANADA K1G 1A0, Phone: 613-833-2545, Fax: 613-833-2208, garvock@travel-net.com
**Specialties:** Hunters, Bowies, Japanese, daggers and swords. **Patterr** Cable Damascus, random pattern welded or to suit. **Technical:** Forg blades; hi-carbon. **Prices:** $250 to $900. **Remarks:** Also CKG member a ABS member. **Mark:** Big G with M in middle. **Other:** Shipping and taxes ext

**GAUDETTE, LINDEN L.,** 5 Hitchcock Rd., Wilbraham, MA 01095, Phone: 413-596-4896
**Specialties:** Traditional working knives in standard patterns. **Patterns:** Broa bladed hunters, Bowies and camp knives; wood carver knives; locking folde **Technical:** Grinds ATS-34, 440C and 154CM. **Prices:** $150 to $400; so higher. **Remarks:** Full-time maker; first knife sold in 1975. **Mark:** Last name Gothic logo; used to be initials in circle.

**GAULT, CLAY,** #1225 PR 7022, Lexington, TX 78947, Phone: 979-77 3305
**Specialties:** Classic straight and folding hunting knives and multi-blade fo ers of his design. **Patterns:** Folders and hunting knives. **Technical:** Grir BX-NSM 174 steel, custom rolled from billets to his specifications. Uses exe leathers for sheaths, and fine natural materials for all knives. **Prices:** $325 $600; some higher. **Remarks:** Full-time maker; first knife sold in 1970. **Ma** Name or name with cattle brand.

**GEDRAITIS, CHARLES J.,** GEDRAITIS HAND CRAFTED KNIVES, 4 Shrewsbuyn St, Holden, MA 01520, Phone: 508-886-0221, knifemaker_1999@yahoo.com Web: http://cgknives.blademakers.com
**Specialties:** One of a kind folders & automatics of my own design. **Patter** One of a kind.**Technical:** Forges to shape mostly stock removal. **Prices:** $ to $2,500. **Remarks:** Full-time maker. **Mark:** 3 scallop shells with an in inside each one. CJG

**GEISLER, GARY R.,** PO Box 294, Clarksville, OH 45113, Phone: 937 383-4055, ggeisler@in-touch.net
**Specialties:** Period Bowies and such; flat ground. **Patterns:** Working kni usually modeled close after an existing antique. **Technical:** Flat grinds 44 A2 and ATS-34. **Prices:** $300 and up. **Remarks:** Part-time maker; first k sold in 1982. **Mark:** G.R. Geisler Maker; usually in script on reverse s because I'm left-handed.

**GENSKE, JAY,** 283 Doty St., Fond du Lac, WI 54935, Phone: 920-92 8019/Cell Phone 920-579-0144, jaygenske@hotmail.com
**Specialties:** Working/using knives and period pieces of his design and to c tomer specs. **Patterns:** Bowies, fighters, hunters. **Technical:** Grinds ATS and 440C, 01 and 1095 forges and grinds Damascus and 1095. Offers tom-tooled sheaths, scabbards and hand carved handles. **Prices:** $95 $500; some to $1,000. **Remarks:** Full-time maker; first knife sold in 19 Doing business as Genske Knives. **Mark:** Stamped or engraved last name

**GEORGE, HARRY,** 3137 Old Camp Long Rd., Aiken, SC 29805, Pho 803-649-1963, hdkk-george@scescape.net
**Specialties:** Working straight knives of his design or to customer specs. terns: Hunters, skinners and utility knives. **Technical:** Grinds ATS-34. Pre natural handle materials, hollow-grinds and mirror finishes. **Prices:** Sta $70. **Remarks:** Part-time maker; first knife sold in 1985. Trained ur George Herron. Member SCAK. Member Knifemakers Guild. **Mark:** Na city, state.

**GEORGE, LES,** 1703 Payne, Wichita, KS 67203, Phone: 316-267-07
**Specialties:** Classic, traditional and working/using straight knives of design and to customer specs. **Patterns:** Fighters, hunters, swords and mi

tures. **Technical:** Grinds D2; forges 5160 and Damascus. Uses mosaic handle pins and his own mokume-gane. **Prices:** $35 to $200; some to $800. **Remarks:** No orders taken at this time due to enlistment in the U.S. Marine Corps.; first knife sold in 1992. Doing business as George Custom Knives. **Mark:** Last name or initials stacked.

**GEORGE, TOM,** 550 Aldbury Dr., Henderson, NV 89014, tagmaker@aol.com
**Specialties:** Working straight knives, display knives and folders of his design. **Patterns:** Hunters, Bowies, daggers, buckskinners, swords and folders. **Technical:** Uses D2, 440C, ATS-34 and 154CM. **Prices:** $250 to $10,000. **Remarks:** Custom orders 'not' accepted. Full-time maker. **Mark:** Tom George maker.

**GEPNER, DON,** 2615 E. Tecumseh, Norman, OK 73071, Phone: 405-364-2750
**Specialties:** Traditional working and using straight knives of his design. **Patterns:** Bowies and daggers. **Technical:** Forges his Damascus, 1095 and 5160. **Prices:** $100 to $400; some to $1,000. **Remarks:** Spare-time maker; first knife sold in 1991. Has been forging since 1954; first edged weapon made at 9 years old. **Mark:** Last initial.

**GERNER, THOMAS,** 939 German Rd., Glentui RD, Oxford, NEW ZEALAND 8253
**Specialties:** Forged working knives; plain steel and pattern welded. **Patterns:** Tries most patterns heard or read about. **Technical:** 5160, L6, 01, 52100 steels; Australian hardwood handles. **Prices:** $160 and up. **Remarks:** Achieved ABS Master Smith rating in 2001. **Mark:** Like a standing arrow and a leaning cross, T.G. in the Runic (Viking) alphabet.

**GERUS, GERRY,** PO Box 2295, G.P.O. Cairns, Qld. 4870, AUSTRALIA 070-341451, Phone: 019 617935
**Specialties:** Fancy working and using straight knives of his design. **Patterns:** Hunters, Bowies and fighters. **Technical:** Uses 440C, ATS-34 and commercial Damascus. **Prices:** $275 to $600; some to $1,200. **Remarks:** Part-time maker; first knife sold in 1988. **Mark:** Last name; or last name, Hand Made, city, country.

**GEVEDON, HANNERS (HANK),** 1410 John Cash Rd., Crab Orchard, KY 40419-9770
**Specialties:** Traditional working and using straight knives. **Patterns:** Hunters, swords, utility and camp knives. **Technical:** Forges and grinds his own Damascus, 5160 and L6. Cast aluminum handles. **Prices:** $50 to $250; some to $400. **Remarks:** Part-time maker; first knife sold in 1983. **Mark:** Initials and BF tang stamp.

**GIAGU, SALVATORE AND DEROMA MARIA ROSARIA,** Via V. Emanuele 64, 07016 Pattada (SS), ITALY, Phone: 079-755918, Fax: 079-755918, coltelligiagu@jumpy.it
**Specialties:** Using and collecting traditional and new folders from Sardegna. **Patterns:** Folding, hunting, utility, skinners and kitchen knives. **Technical:** Forges ATS-34, 440, D2 and Damascus. **Prices:** $200 to $2,000; some higher. **Mark:** First initial, last name and name of town and muflon's head.

**GIBERT, PEDRO,** Gutierrez 5189, 5603 Rama Caida, San Rafael Mendoza, ARGENTINA, Phone: 054-2627-441138, rosademayo@infovia.com.ar
**Specialties:** Hand forges: Stock removal and integral. High quality artistic knives of his design and to customer specifications. **Patterns:** Country (Argentine gaucho-style), knives, folders, Bowies, daggers, hunters. Others upon request. **Technical:** Blade: Bohler k110 Austrian steel (high resistance to waste). Handles: (Natural materials) ivory elephant, killer whale, hippo, walrus tooth, deer antler, goat, ram, buffalo horn, bone, rhea, goat, sheep, cow, exotic woods ( South America native woods) hand carved and engraved guards and blades. Stainless steel guards, finely polished: semi-matte or shiny finish. Sheaths: Raw or tanned leather, hand-stitched; rawhide or cotton yarn embroidered. Box: One wood piece, hand carved. Wooden hinges and locks. **Prices:** $400 and up. **Remarks:** Full-time maker. Supply contractors. **Mark:** Only a rose logo.Buyers initials upon request.

**GIBO, GEORGE,** PO Box 4304, Hilo, HI 96720, Phone: 808-987-7002, geogibo@interpac.net
**Specialties:** Straight knives and folders. **Patterns:** Hunters, bird and trout, utility, gentlemen and tactical folders. **Technical:** Grinds ATS-34, BG-42, Talonite, Stainless Steel Damascus. **Prices:** $250 to $1,000. **Remarks:** Spare-time maker; first knife sold in 1995. **Mark:** Name, city and state around Hawaiian "Shaka" sign.

**GIBSON SR., JAMES HOOT,** 90 Park Place Ave., Bunnell, FL 32110, Phone: 904-437-4383
**Specialties:** Bowies, folders, daggers, and hunters. **Patterns:** Most all. **Technical:** ATS-440C hand cut and grind. **Prices:** $1,250 to $3,000. **Remarks:** 100% handmade. **Mark:** Hoot.

**GILBERT, CHANTAL,** 291 Rue Christophe-Colomb est. #105, Quebec City Quebec, CANADA G1K 3T1, Phone: 418-525-6961, Fax: 418-525-4666, gilbertc@medion.qc.ca Web: www.chantalgilbert.com
**Specialties:** Straight art knives that may resemble creatures, often with wings, shells and antennae, always with a beak of some sort, fixed blades in a feminine style. **Technical:** ATS-34 and Damascus. Handle materials usually silver that she forms to shape via special molds and a press; ebony and fossil ivory. **Prices:** Range from $500 to $4,000. **Other:** Often embellishes her art knives with rubies, meteorite, 18k gold and similar elements.

**GILBREATH, RANDALL,** 55 Crauswell Rd., Dora, AL 35062, Phone: 205-648-3902
**Specialties:** Damascus folders and fighters. **Patterns:** Folders and fixed blades. **Technical:** Forges Damascus and high-carbon; stock removal stainless steel. **Prices:** $300 to $1,500. **Remarks:** Full-time maker; first knife sold in 1979. **Mark:** Name in ribbon.

**GILJEVIC, BRANKO,** 35 Hayley Crescent, Queanbeyan 2620, N.S.W., AUSTRALIA 0262977613
**Specialties:** Classic working straight knives and folders of his design. **Patterns:** Hunters, Bowies, skinners and locking folders. **Technical:** Grinds 440C. Offers acid etching, scrimshaw and leather carving. **Prices:** $150 to $1,500. **Remarks:** Part-time maker; first knife sold in 1987. Doing business as Sambar Custom Knives. **Mark:** Company name in logo.

**GIRTNER, JOE,** 409 Catalpa Ave, Brea, CA 92821, Phone: 714-529-2388

**GITTINGER, RAYMOND,** 6940 S Rt. 100, Tiffin, OH 44883, Phone: 419-397-2517

**GLOVER, WARREN D.,** dba BUBBA KNIVES, PO Box 475, Cleveland, GA 30528, Phone: 706-865-3998, Fax: 706-348-7176
**Specialties:** Traditional and custom working and using straight knives of his design and to customer request. **Patterns:** Hunters, skinners, bird and fish, utility and kitchen knives. **Technical:** Grinds 440, ATS-34 and stainless steel Damascus. **Prices:** $75 to $400 and up. **Remarks:** Part-time maker; sold first knife in 1995. **Mark:** Bubba, year, name, state.

**GLOVER, RON,** 7702 Misty Springs Ct., Mason, OH 45040, Phone: 513-398-7857
**Specialties:** High-tech working straight knives and folders. **Patterns:** Hunters to Bowies; some interchangeable blade models; unique locking mechanisms. **Technical:** Grinds 440C, 154CM; buys Damascus. **Prices:** $70 to $500; some to $800. **Remarks:** Part-time maker; first knife sold in 1981. **Mark:** Name in script.

**GODDARD, WAYNE,** 473 Durham Ave., Eugene, OR 97404, Phone: 541-689-8098, wgoddard44@comcast.net
**Specialties:** Working/using straight knives and folders. **Patterns:** Hunters and folders. **Technical:** Works exclusively with wire Damascus and his own-pattern welded material. **Prices:** $250 to $4,000. **Remarks:** Full-time maker; first knife sold in 1963. Three-year backlog on orders. **Mark:** Blocked initials on forged blades; regular capital initials on stock removal.

**GOERS, BRUCE,** 3423 Royal Ct. S., Lakeland, FL 33813, Phone: 941-646-0984
**Specialties:** Fancy working and using straight knives of his design and to customer specs. **Patterns:** Hunters, fighters, Bowies and fantasy knives. **Technical:** Grinds ATS-34, some Damascus. **Prices:** $195 to $600; some to $1,300. **Remarks:** Part-time maker; first knife sold in 1990. Doing business as Vulture Cutlery. **Mark:** Buzzard with initials.

**GOERTZ, PAUL S.,** 201 Union Ave. SE, #207, Renton, WA 98059, Phone: 425-228-9501
**Specialties:** Working straight knives of his design and to customer specs. **Patterns:** Hunters, skinners, camp, bird and fish knives, camp axes, some Bowies, fighters and boots. **Technical:** Grinds ATS-34, BG42, and CPM420V. **Prices:** $75 to $500. **Remarks:** Full-time maker; first knife sold in 1985. **Mark:** Signature.

**GOFOURTH, JIM,** 3776 Aliso Cyn Rd., Santa Paula, CA 93060, Phone: 805-659-3814
**Specialties:** Period pieces and working knives. **Patterns:** Bowies, locking folders, patent lockers and others. **Technical:** Grinds A2 and 154CM. **Prices:** Moderate. **Remarks:** Spare-time maker. **Mark:** Initials interconnected.

**GOGUEN, SCOTT,** 166 Goguen Rd., Newport, NC 28570, Phone: 252-393-6013, goguenknives.com
**Specialties:** Classic and traditional working knives. **Patterns:** Kitchen, camp, hunters, Bowies. **Technical:** Forges high-carbon steel and own Damascus. Offers clay tempering and cord wrapped handles. **Prices:** $85 to $1,500. **Remarks:** Spare-time maker; first knife sold in1988. **Mark:** Last name or name in Japanese characters.

**GOLDBERG, DAVID,** 1120 Blyth Ct., Blue Bell, PA 19422, Phone: 215-654-7117

**Specialties:** Japanese-style designs, will work with special themes in Japanese Genre. **Patterns:** Kozuka, Tanto, Wakazashi, Katana, Tachi, Sword canes, Yari and Naginata. **Technical:** Forges his own Damascus and makes his own handmade steel from straw ash, iron, carbon and clay. Uses traditional materials, carves fittings handles and cases. Hardens all blades in traditional Japanese clay differential technique. **Remarks:** Full-time maker; first knife sold in 1987. **Mark:** Name (kinzan) in Japanese Kanji on Tang under handle. **Other:** Japanese swordsmanship teacher (jaido) and Japanese self-defense teach (aikido).

**GOLDING, ROBIN,** PO Box 267, Lathrop, CA 95330, Phone: 209-982-0839

**Specialties:** Working straight knives of his design. **Patterns:** Survival knives, Bowie extractions, camp knives, dive knives and skinners. **Technical:** Grinds 440C, 154CM and ATS-34. **Prices:** $95 to $250; some to $500. **Remarks:** Full-time maker; first knife sold in 1985. Up to 1-1/2 year waiting period on orders. **Mark:** Signature of last name.

**GOLTZ, WARREN L.,** 802 4th Ave. E., Ada, MN 56510, Phone: 218-784-7721, sspexp@loretel.net

**Specialties:** Fancy working knives in standard patterns. **Patterns:** Hunters, Bowies and camp knives. **Technical:** Grinds 440C and ATS-34. **Prices:** $120 to $595; some to $950. **Remarks:** Part-time maker; first knife sold in 1984. **Mark:** Last name.

**GONZALEZ, LEONARDO WILLIAMS,** Ituzaingo 473, Maldonado, CP 20000, URUGUAY, Phone: 598 4222 1617, Fax: 598 4222 1617, willyknives@hotmail.com

**Specialties:** Classic high-art and fantasy straight knives; traditional working and using knives of his design, in standard patterns or to customer specs. **Patterns:** Hunters, Bowies, daggers, fighters, boots, swords and utility/camp knives. **Technical:** Forges and grinds high-carbon and stainless Bohler steels. **Prices:** $100 to $2,500. **Remarks:** Full-time maker; first knife sold in 1985. **Mark:** Willy, whale, R.O.U.

**GOO, TAI,** 5920 W Windy Lou Ln., Tucson, AZ 85742, Phone: 520-744-9777, taigoo@msn.com Web: www.taigoo.com

**Specialties:** High art, neo-tribal, bush and fantasy. **Technical:** hand forges, does own heat treating, makes own Damascus. **Prices:** $150 to $500; some to $10,000. **Remarks:** Full-time maker; first knife sold in 1978. **Mark:** Chiseled signature.

**GOODE, BEAR,** PO Box 6474, Navajo Dam, NM 87419, Phone: 505-632-8184

**Specialties:** Working/using straight knives of his design and in standard patterns. **Patterns:** Bowies, hunters and utility/camp knives. **Technical:** Grinds 440C, ATS-34, 154-CM; forges and grinds 1095, 5160 and other steels on request; uses Damascus. **Prices:** $60 to $225; some to $500 and up. **Remarks:** Part-time maker; first knife sold in 1993. Doing business as Bear Knives. **Mark:** First and last name with a three-toed paw print.

**GOODE, BRIAN,** 104 Cider Dr., Shelby, NC 28152, Phone: 704-484-9020, Web: www.bgoodeknives.com

**Specialties:** Flat ground working knives with etched/antique finish or hand rubbed. **Patterns:** Field, camp, hunters, skinners, survival, maker's design or yours. Currently full tang only with supplied leather sheath. Kydex can be outsourced if desired. **Technical:** 0-1, 1095, or similar high-carbon ground flatstock. Stock removal and differential heat treat preferred. Will offer handforged with the same differential heat treat method in future. Etched antique/etched satin working finish preferred. Micarta and hardwoods for strength. **Prices:** $115 to $680. **Remarks:** Part-time maker and full-time knife lover. First knife sold in 2004. **Mark:** B. Goode with NC separated by a feather.

**GOODLING, RODNEY W.,** 6640 Old Harrisburg Rd., York Springs, PA 17372

**GORDON, LARRY B.,** 23555 Newell Cir. W, Farmington Hills, MI 48336, Phone: 248-477-5483, lbgordon1@aol.com

**Specialties:** Folders, small fixed blades. **Patterns:** Rotating handle locker. **Prices:** $450 minimmum. **Mark:** Gordon. **Other:** High line materials preferred.

**GORENFLO, JAMES T. (JT),** 9145 Sullivan Rd., Baton Rouge, LA 70818, Phone: 225-261-5868

**Specialties:** Traditional working and using straight knives of his design. **Patterns:** Bowies, hunters and utility/camp knives. **Technical:** Forges 5160, 1095, 52100 and his own Damascus. **Prices:** Start at $200. **Remarks:** Part-time maker; first knife sold in 1992. **Mark:** Last name or initials, J.S. on reverse.

**GORENFLO, GABE,** 9145 Sullivan Rd, Baton Rouge, LA 70818, Phone 504-261-5868

**GOSSMAN, SCOTT,** RAZORBACK KNIVES, PO Box 815, Forest Hill, MD 21050, Phone: 410-452-8456, scott@razorback-knives.com Web: www.razorback-knives.com

**Specialties:** Heavy duty knives for big game hunting and survival. **Pattern** Drop point hunters, semi-skinners and spear point hunters. **Technical:** Grin D-2, A2 and 5160 convex and flatgrind filework standard around full tang ha dles. **Price:** $100 to $350 some higher. **Remarks:** Part-time maker does bu ness as Razorback Knives. **Mark:** First and last initials and year.

**GOTTAGE, JUDY,** 43227 Brooks Dr., Clinton Twp., MI 48038-5323, Phone: 810-286-7275

**Specialties:** Custom folders of her design or to customer specs. **Pattern** Interframes or integral. **Technical:** Stock removal. **Prices:** $300 to $3,0C **Remarks:** Full-time maker; first knife sold in 1980. **Mark:** Full name, maker script.

**GOTTAGE, DANTE,** 43227 Brooks Dr., Clinton Twp., MI 48038-5323, Phone: 810-286-7275

**Specialties:** Working knives of his design or to customer specs. **Patterr** Large and small skinners, fighters, Bowies and fillet knives. **Technical:** Grin O1, 440C and 154CM and ATS-34. **Prices:** $150 to $600. **Remarks:** Pa time maker; first knife sold in 1975. **Mark:** Full name in script letters.

**GOTTSCHALK, GREGORY J.,** 12 First St. (Ft. Pitt), Carnegie, PA 15106, Phone: 412-279-6692

**Specialties:** Fancy working straight knives and folders to customer spe **Patterns:** Hunters to tantos, locking folders to minis. **Technical:** Grinds 44C 154CM, ATS-34. Now making own Damascus. Most knives have mirror ishes. **Prices:** Start at $150. **Remarks:** Part-time maker; first knife sold 1977. **Mark:** Full name in crescent.

**GOUKER, GARY B.,** PO Box 955, Sitka, AK 99835, Phone: 907-747-3476

**Specialties:** Hunting knives for hard use. **Patterns:** Skinners, semi-skinne and such. **Technical:** Likes natural materials, inlays, stainless steel. **Pric** Moderate. **Remarks:** New Alaskan maker. **Mark:** Name.

**GOYTIA, ENRIQUE,** 2120 E Paisano Ste. 276, El Paso, TX 79905

**GRAFFEO, ANTHONY I.,** 100 Riess Place, Chalmette, LA 70043, Phone: 504-277-1428

**Specialties:** Traditional working and using straight knives of his design customer specs and in standard patterns. **Patterns:** Hunters, utility/ca knives and fishing knives. **Technical:** Hollow- and flat-grinds ATS-34, 44 and 154CM. Handle materials include Pakkawood, Micarta and sambar st **Prices:** $65 to $100; some to $250. **Remarks:** Part-time maker; first knife s in 1991. Doing business as Knives by: Graf. **Mark:** First and middle initi last name city, state, Maker.

**GRAHAM, GORDON,** Rt. 3 Box 207, New Boston, TX 75570, Phone: 903-628-6337

**GRANGER, PAUL J.,** 2820 St. Charles Ln., Kennesaw, GA 30144, Phone: 770-426-6298, grangerknives@hotmail.com Web: www.geocities.com/grangerknives Web: www.grangerknives.com

**Specialties:** Working straight knives of his own design and a few folders. **terns:** 2.75" - 4.0" work knives, skinners, tactical knives and Bowies from 9". **Technical:** Forges 52100 and 5160 and his own carbon steel Damas Offers filework. **Prices:** $95 to $400. **Remarks:** Part-time maker since 1 Sold first knife in 1997. Doing business as Granger Knives and Pale H Fighters. **Mark:** "Granger" or "Palehorse Fighters". **Other:** Member of and OBG.

**GRAVELINE, PASCAL AND ISABELLE,** 38, Rue de Kerbrezillic, 29 Moelan-sur-Mer, FRANCE, Phone: 33 2 98 39 73 33, Fax: 33 2 98 39 33, atelier.graveline@wanadso.fr

**Specialties:** French replicas from the 17th, 18th and 19th centuries. **terns:** Traditional folders and multi-blade pocket knives; traveling knives, knives and fork sets; puzzle knives and friend's knives; rivet less kni **Technical:** Grind 12C27, ATS-34, Damascus and carbon steel. **Prices:** $ to $5,000. **Remarks:** Full-time makers; first knife sold in 1992. **Mark:** name over head of ram.

**GRAY, DANIEL,** GRAY KNIVES, 686 Main Rd., Brownville, ME 0441 Phone: 207-965-2191, mail@grayknives.com Web: www.grayknives. **Specialties:** Straight knives, Fantasy, folders, automatics and tradition his own design. **Patterns:** Automatics, fighters, hunters. **Technical:** Grinc 154CM and D2. **Prices:** From $155 to $750. **Remarks:** Full-time maker; knife sold in 1974. **Mark:** Gray Knives.

**GRAY, BOB,** 8206 N. Lucia Court, Spokane, WA 99208, Phone: 509 468-3924

**Specialties:** Straight working knives of his own design or to customer sp **Patterns:** Hunter, fillet and carving knives. **Technical:** Forges 5160, L6

some 52100; grinds 440C. **Prices:** $100 to $600. **Remarks:** Part-time knife maker; first knife sold in 1991. Doing business as Hi-Land Knives. **Mark:** HI-L.

**GREBE, GORDON S.,** PO Box 296, Anchor Point, AK 99556-0296, Phone: 907-235-8242
**Specialties:** Working straight knives and folders, some fancy. **Patterns:** Tantos, Bowies, boot fighter sets, locking folders. **Technical:** Grinds stainless steels; likes 1/4" inch stock and glass-bead finishes. **Prices:** $75 to $250; some to $2,000. **Remarks:** Full-time maker; first knife sold in 1968. **Mark:** Initials in lightning logo.

**GRECO, JOHN,** 100 Mattie Jones Rd., Greensburg, KY 42743, Phone: 270-932-3335, Fax: 270-932-2225, greco@kfbol.com Web: www.grecoknives.com
**Specialties:** Limited edition knives and swords. **Patterns:** Tactical, fighters, camp knives, short swords. **Technical:** Stock removal carbon steel. **Prices:** Affordable. **Remarks:** Full-time maker since 1986. First knife sold in 1979. **Mark:** Greco and steroc w/mo mark.

**GREEN, RUSS,** 6013 Briercrest Ave., Lakewood, CA 90713, Phone: 562-867-2305
**Specialties:** Sheaths and using knives. **Technical:** Knives 440C, ATS-34, 5160, 01, cable Damascus. **Prices:** Knives: $135 to $850; sheaths: $30 to $200. **Mark:** Russ Green and year.

**GREEN, MARK,** 1523 S Main St. PO Box 20, Graysville, AL 35073, Phone: 205-647-9353

**GREEN, BILL,** 706 Bradfield, Garland, TX 75042, Phone: 972-272-4748
**Specialties:** High-art and working straight knives and folders of his design and to customer specs. **Patterns:** Bowies, hunters, kitchen knives and locking folders. **Technical:** Grinds ATS-34, D2 and 440V. Hand-tooled custom sheaths. **Prices:** $70 to $350; some to $750. **Remarks:** Part-time maker; first knife sold in 1990. **Mark:** Last name.

**GREEN, WILLIAM (BILL),** 46 Warren Rd., View Bank Vic., AUSTRALIA 3084, Fax: 03-9459-1529
**Specialties:** Traditional high-tech straight knives and folders. **Patterns:** Japanese-influenced designs, hunters, Bowies, folders and miniatures. **Technical:** Forges O1, D2 and his own Damascus. Offers lost wax castings for bolsters and pommels. Likes natural handle materials, gems, silver and gold. **Prices:** $400 to $750; some to $1,200. **Remarks:** Full-time maker. **Mark:** Initials.

**GREENAWAY, DON,** 3325 Dinsmore Tr., Fayetteville, AR 72704, Phone: 501-521-0323

**GREENE, DAVID,** 570 Malcom Rd., Covington, GA 30209, Phone: 770-784-0657
**Specialties:** Straight working using knives. **Patterns:** Hunters. **Technical:** Forges mosaic and twist Damascus. Prefers stag and desert ironwood for handle material.

**GREENE, STEVE,** DUNN KNIVES INC., PO Box 204, Rossville, KS 66533, Phone: 785-584-6856, Fax: 785-584-6856

**GREENE, CHRIS,** 707 Cherry Lane, Shelby, NC 28150, Phone: 704-434-5620

**GREENFIELD, G.O.,** 2605 15th St. #522, Everett, WA 98201, Phone: 425-258-1551, garyg1946@yahoo.com
**Specialties:** High-tech and working straight knives and folders of his design. **Patterns:** Boots, daggers, hunters and one-of-a-kinds. **Technical:** Grinds ATS-34, D2, 440C and T-440V. Makes sheaths for each knife. **Prices:** $100 to $800; some to $10,000. **Remarks:** Part-time maker; first knife sold in 1978. **Mark:** Springfield®, serial number.

**GREGORY, MICHAEL,** 211 Calhoun Rd., Belton, SC 29627, Phone: 864-338-8898
**Specialties:** Working straight knives and folders. **Patterns:** Hunters, tantos, locking folders and slip-joints, boots and fighters. **Technical:** Grinds 440C, 154CM and ATS-34; mirror finishes. **Prices:** $95 to $200; some to $1,000. **Remarks:** Part-time maker; first knife sold in 1980. **Mark:** Name, city in logo.

**GREINER, RICHARD,** 1073 E. County Rd. 32, Green Springs, OH 44836

**GREISS, JOCKL,** Herrenwald 15, D 77773 Schenkenzell, GERMANY, Phone: +49 7836 95 71 69 or +49 7836 95 55 76, www.jockl-greissmesser.de
**Specialties:** Classic and working using straight knives of his design. **Patterns:** Bowies, daggers and hunters. **Technical:** Uses only Jerry Rados Damascus. All knives are one-of-a-kind made by hand; no machines are used. **Prices:** $700 to $2,000; some to $3,000. **Remarks:** Full-time maker; first knife sold in 1984. **Mark:** An "X" with a long vertical line through it.

**GREY, PIET,** PO Box 363, Naboomspruit 0560, SOUTH AFRICA, Phone: 014-743-3613
**Specialties:** Fancy working and using straight knives of his design. **Patterns:** Fighters, hunters and utility/camp knives. **Technical:** Grinds ATS-34 and AEB-L; forges and grinds Damascus. Solder less fitting of guards. Engraves and scrimshaws. **Prices:** $125 to $750; some to $1,500. **Remarks:** Part-time maker; first knife sold in 1970. **Mark:** Last name.

**GRIFFIN, RENDON AND MARK,** 9706 Cedardale, Houston, TX 77055, Phone: 713-468-0436
**Specialties:** Working folders and automatics of their designs. **Patterns:** Standard lockers and slip-joints. **Technical:** Most blade steels; stock removal. **Prices:** Start at $350. **Remarks:** Rendon's first knife sold in 1966; Mark's in 1974. **Mark:** Last name logo.

**GRIFFIN, THOMAS J.,** 591 Quevli Ave., Windom, MN 56101, Phone: 507-831-1089
**Specialties:** Period pieces and fantasy straight knives of his design. **Patterns:** Daggers and swords. **Technical:** Forges 1095, 52100 and L6. Most blades are his own Damascus; turned fittings and wire-wrapped grips. **Prices:** $250 to $800; some to $2,000. **Remarks:** Full-time maker; first knife sold in 1991. Doing business as Griffin Knives. **Mark:** Last name etched.

**GRIFFIN JR., HOWARD A.,** 14299 SW 31st Ct., Davie, FL 33330, Phone: 954-474-5406, mgriffin18@aol.com
**Specialties:** Working straight knives and folders. **Patterns:** Hunters, Bowies, locking folders with his own push-button lock design. **Technical:** Grinds 440C. **Prices:** $100 to $200; some to $500. **Remarks:** Part-time maker; first knife sold in 1983. **Mark:** Initials.

**GRIFFITH, LYNN,** 5103 S Sheridan Rd. #402, Tulsa, OK 74145-7627, Phone: 918-366-8303, GriffithKN@aol.com Web: www.griffithknives.com
**Specialties:** Flat ground, full tang tactical knives. **Patterns:** Neck and multi-carry knives, drop and clip points, tantos and Wharncliffes. **Technical:** Grinds ATS-34 and Talonite. **Prices:** $125 to $400; some to $700. **Remarks:** Full-time knife maker; first knife sold in 1987. **Mark:** Last name over year made.

**GROSPITCH, ERNIE,** 18440 Amityville Dr., Orlando, FL 32820, Phone: 407-568-5438, shrpknife@aol.com Web: www.ernieskives.com
**Specialties:** Bowies, hunting, fishing, kitchen, lockback folders, leather craft. **Patterns:** His design or customer. **Technical:** Stock removal using most available steels. **Prices:** $140 and up. **Remarks:** Full-time maker, sold first knife in 1990. Mark: Etched name/maker city and state.

**GROSS, W.W.,** 109 Dylan Scott Dr., Archdale, NC 27263-3858
**Specialties:** Working knives. **Patterns:** Hunters, boots, fighters. **Technical:** Grinds. **Prices:** Moderate. **Remarks:** Full-time maker. **Mark:** Name.

**GROSSMAN, STEWART,** 24 Water St., #419, Clinton, MA 01510, Phone: 508-365-2291; 800-mysword
**Specialties:** Miniatures and full-size knives and swords. **Patterns:** One-of-a-kind miniatures—jewelry, replicas—and wire-wrapped figures. Full-size art, fantasy and combat knives, daggers and modular systems. **Technical:** Forges and grinds most metals and Damascus. Uses gems, crystals, electronics and motorized mechanisms. **Prices:** $20 to $300; some to $4,500 and higher. **Remarks:** Full-time maker; first knife sold in 1985. **Mark:** G1.

**GRUSSENMEYER, PAUL G.,** 310 Kresson Rd., Cherry Hill, NJ 08034, Phone: 856-428-1088, pgrussentne@comcast.net Web: www.pgcarvings.com
**Specialties:** Assembling fancy and fantasy straight knives with his own carved handles. **Patterns:** Bowies, daggers, folders, swords, hunters and miniatures. **Technical:** Uses forged steel and Damascus, stock removal and knapped obsidian blades. **Prices:** $250 to $4,000. **Remarks:** Spare-time maker; first knife sold in 1991. **Mark:** First and last initial hooked together on handle.

**GUARNERA, ANTHONY R.,** 42034 Quail Creek Dr., Quartzhill, CA 93536, Phone: 661-722-4032
**Patterns:** Hunters, camp, Bowies, kitchen, fighter knives. **Technical:** Forged and stock removal. **Prices:** $100 and up.

**GUESS, RAYMOND L.,** 7214 Salineville Rd. NE, Mechanicstown, OH 44651, Phone: 330-738-2793
**Specialties:** Working straight knives and folders of his design or to customer specs. **Patterns:** Hunters, Bowies, fillet knives, steak and paring knife sets. **Technical:** Grinds 440C. Offers silver inlay work and mirror finishes. Custom-made leather sheath for each knife. **Prices:** $65 to $850; some to $700. **Remarks:** Spare-time maker; first knife sold in 1985. **Mark:** First initial, last name.

**GUIDRY, BRUCE,** 24550 Adams Ave., Murrieta, CA 92562, Phone: 909-677-2384

**GUIGNARD, GIB,** Box 3413, Quartzsite, AZ 85359, Phone: 928-927-4831, http://www.cactusforge.com
**Specialties:** Rustic finish on primitive Bowies with stag or ironwood handles and turquoise inlay. **Patterns:** Very large in 5160 and ATS-34 - Small and med. size hunting knives in ATS-34. **Technical:** Forges 5160 and grind ATS-34. **Prices:** $100 to $1,000. **Remarks:** Full-time maker first knife sold in 1989.

Doing business as Cactus Forge. Also do collaborations with Chuck Burrows of Wild Rose Trading Co. these collaborations are done under the name of Cactus Rose. **Mark:** Last name or G+ on period pieces and primitive.

**GUNN, NELSON L.,** 77 Blake Rd., Epping, NH 03042, Phone: 603-679-5119
**Specialties:** Classic and working/using straight knives of his design. **Patterns:** Bowies, fighters and hunters. **Technical:** Grinds O1 and 440C. Carved stag handles with turquoise inlays. **Prices:** $125 to $300; some to $700. **Remarks:** Part-time maker; first knife sold in 1996. Doing business as Nelson's Custom Knives. **Mark:** First and last initial.

**GUNTER, BRAD,** 13 Imnaha Rd., Tijeras, NM 87059, Phone: 505-281-8080

**GURGANUS, CAROL,** 2553 N.C. 45 South, Colerain, NC 27924, Phone: 252-356-4831, Fax: 252-356-4650
**Specialties:** Working and using straight knives. **Patterns:** Fighters, hunters and kitchen knives. **Technical:** Grinds D2, ATS-34 and Damascus steel. Uses stag, and exotic wood handles. **Prices:** $100 to $300. **Remarks:** Part-time maker; first knife sold in 1992. **Mark:** Female symbol, last name, city, state.

**GURGANUS, MELVIN H.,** 2553 N.C. 45 South, Colerain, NC 27924, Phone: 252-356-4831, Fax: 252-356-4650
**Specialties:** High-tech working folders. **Patterns:** Leaf-lock and back-lock designs, bolstered and interframe. **Technical:** D2 and 440C; Heat-treats, carves and offers lost wax casting. **Prices:** $300 to $3,000. **Remarks:** Part-time maker; first knife sold in 1983. **Mark:** First initial, last name and maker.

**GUTHRIE, GEORGE B.,** 1912 Puett Chapel Rd., Bassemer City, NC 28016, Phone: 704-629-3031
**Specialties:** Working knives of his design or to customer specs. **Patterns:** Hunters, boots, fighters, locking folders and slip-joints in traditional styles. **Technical:** Grinds D2, 440C and 154CM. **Prices:** $105 to $300; some to $450. **Remarks:** Part-time maker; first knife sold in 1978. **Mark:** Name in state.

# H

**HAGEN, PHILIP L.,** PO Box 58, 41780 Kansas Point Ln, Pelican Rapids, MN 56572, Phone: 218-863-8503, dhagen@prtel.com Web: www.dochagencustomknives.com
**Specialties:** Folders. **Patterns:** Defense-related straight knives; wide variety of folders. **Technical:** Dual action scale release, holster release autos.**Prices:** $300 to $800; some to $3,000. **Remarks:** Part-time maker; first knife sold in 1975. Make my own Damascus. **Mark:** DOC HAGEN in shield, knife, banner logo; or DOC.

**HAGGERTY, GEORGE S.,** PO Box 88, Jacksonville, VT 05342, Phone: 802-368-7437, swewater@sover.net
**Specialties:** Working straight knives and folders. **Patterns:** Hunters, claws, camp and fishing knives, locking folders and backpackers. **Technical:** Forges and grinds W2, 440C and 154CM. **Prices:** $85 to $300. **Remarks:** Part-time maker; first knife sold in 1981. **Mark:** Initials or last name.

**HAGUE, GEOFF,** The Malt House, Hollow Ln., Wilton Marlborough, Wiltshire, ENGLAND SN8 3SR, Phone: (+44) 01672-870212, Fax: (+44) 01672 870212, geoff@hagueknives.com Web: www.hagueknives.com
**Specialties:** Fixed blade and folding knives. **Patterns:** Locking and friction folders, hunters and small knives. **Technical:** Grinds ATS-34, RWL34 and Damascus; others by agreement. **Prices:** Start at $200. **Remarks:** Full-time maker. **Mark:** Last name. **Other:** British voting member of the Knife Makers Guild.

**HAINES, JEFF, HAINES CUSTOM KNIVES,** 302 N. Mill St., Wauzeka, WI 53826, Phone: 608-875-5002
**Patterns:** Hunters, skinners, camp knives, customer designs welcome. **Technical:** Forges 1095, 5160, and Damascus, grinds A2. **Prices:** $40 and up. **Remarks:** Part-time maker since 1995. **Mark:** Last name.

**HALFRICH, JERRY,** 340 Briarwood, San Marcos, TX 78666, Phone: 512-353-2582, jerryhalfrich@earthlink.com
**Specialties:** Working knives and specialty utility knives for the professional and serious hunter. Uses proven designs in both straight and folding knives. Plays close attention to fit and finish. Art knives on special request. **Patterns:** Hunters, skinners, lock back liner lock. **Technical:** Grinds both flat and hollow D2, damasteel, BG42 makes high precision folders. **Prices:**$300 to $600, sometimes $1,000. **Remarks:** Full-time maker since 2000. DBA Halfrich Custom Knives. **Mark:** Halfrich, San Marcos, TX in a football shape

**HALL, JEFF,** PO Box 435, Los Alamitos, CA 90720, Phone: 562-594-4740, jhall10176@aol.com
**Specialties:** Collectible and working folders of his design. **Technical:** Grinds S30V, ATS-34, and various makers' Damascus. **Patterns:** Fighters, gentleman's, hunters and utility knives. **Prices:** $300 to $500; some to $1,00 **Remarks:** Full-time maker. First knife sold 1998. **Mark:** Last name.

**HALLIGAN, ED,** 14 Meadow Way, Sharpsburg, GA 30277, Phone: 77C 251-7720, Fax: 770-251-7720
**Specialties:** Working straight knives and folders, some fancy. **Patterns:** Lin locks, hunters, skinners, boots, fighters and swords. **Technical:** Grinds AT 34; forges 5160; makes cable and pattern Damascus. **Prices:** $160 to $2,5C **Remarks:** Full-time maker; first knife sold in 1985. Doing business as Hallig Knives. **Mark:** Last name, city, state and USA.

**HAMLET JR., JOHNNY,** 300 Billington, Clute, TX 77531, Phone: 979-265-6929, nifeman@swbell.net Web: www.hamlets-handmade-knives.com
**Specialties:** Working straight knives and folders. **Patterns:** Hunters, fighte fillet and kitchen knives, locking folders. Likes upswept knives and trailir points. **Technical:** Grinds 440C, D2, ATS-34. Makes sheaths. **Prices:** $1 and up. **Remarks:** Part-time maker; first knife sold in 1988. **Mark:** Hamle Handmade in script.

**HAMMOND, JIM,** PO Box 486, Arab, AL 35016, Phone: 256-586-4151 Fax: 256-586-0170, hammondj@otelco.net Web: www.jimhammondknives.com
**Specialties:** High-tech fighters and folders. **Patterns:** Proven-design fighte **Technical:** Grinds 440C, 440V, ATS-34 and other specialty steels. **Pric** $385 to $1,200; some to $8,500. **Remarks:** Full-time maker; first knife solc 1977. Designer for Columbia River Knife and Tool. **Mark:** Full name, city, st in shield logo.

**HANCOCK, TIM,** 10805 N. 83rd St., Scottsdale, AZ 85260, Phone: 48 998-8849
**Specialties:** High-art and working straight knives and folders of his des and to customer preferences. **Patterns:** Bowies, fighters, daggers, tant swords, folders. **Technical:** Forges Damascus and 52100; grinds ATS- Makes Damascus. Silver-wire inlays; offers carved fittings and file w **Prices:** $500 to $10,000. **Remarks:** Full-time maker; first knife sold in 19 **Mark:** Last name or heart. **Other:** Master Smith ABS.

**HAND, BILL,** PO Box 773, 1103 W. 7th St., Spearman, TX 79081, Phone: 806-659-2967, Fax: 806-659-5117, klinker@arn.net
**Specialties:** Traditional working and using straight knives and folders of design or to customer specs. **Patterns:** Hunters, Bowies, folders and fighte **Technical:** Forges 5160, 52100 and Damascus. **Prices:** Start at $1 **Remarks:** Part-time maker; Journeyman Smith. Current delivery time 12 to months. **Mark:** Stylized initials.

**HANKINS, R.,** 9920 S Rural Rd. #10859, Tempe, AZ 85284, Phone: 480-940-0559, PAMHANKINS@USWEST.NET Web: http://albums.ph topoint.com/j/
**Specialties:** Completely hand-made tactical, practical and custom Bo knives. **Technical:** Use Damascus, ATS-34 and 440C stainless steel blades. Stock removal method of grinding. Handle material varies from iv stag to Micarta, depending on application and appearance. **Remarks:** P time maker applying for Knifemakers Guild Int'l membership in June 2001.

**HANSEN, LONNIE,** PO Box 4956, Spanaway, WA 98387, Phone: 25 847-4632, LONNIEHANSEN@MSN.COM Web: lchansen.com
**Specialties:** Working straight knives of his design. **Patterns:** Tomahav tantos, hunters, filet. **Technical:** Forges 1086, 52100, grinds 440V, BG **Prices:** Starting at $300. **Remarks:** Part-time maker since 1989. **Mark:** F initial and last name. Also first and last initial.

**HANSEN, ROBERT W.,** 35701 University Ave. N.E., Cambridge, MN 55008, Phone: 612-689-3242
**Specialties:** Working straight knives, folders and integrals. **Patterns:** F hunters to minis, camp knives to miniatures; folding lockers and slip-join original styles. **Technical:** Grinds O1, 440C and 154CM; likes filew **Prices:** $75 to $175; some to $550. **Remarks:** Part-time maker; first knife in 1983. **Mark:** Fish with last initial inside.

**HANSON III, DON L.,** PO Box 13, Success, MO 65570-0013, Phone: 573-674-3045, Web: www.sunfishforge.com, www.donhansonknives.c
**Specialties:** One-of-a-kind Damascus folders and forged fixed blades. terns: Small, fancy pocket knives, large folding fighters and bowies. **Tec cal:** Forges own pattern welded Damascus, file work and carving also ca steel bades with hamons. **Prices:** $800 and up. **Remarks:** Full-time ma first knife sold in 1984. **Mark:** Sunfish.

**HARA, KOUJI,** 292-2 Ohsugi, Seki-City, Gifu-Pref. 501-32, JAPAN, Phone: 0575-24-7569, Fax: 0575-24-7569
**Specialties:** High-tech and working straight knives of his design; some ers. **Patterns:** Hunters, locking folders and utility/camp knives. **Techn** Grinds Cowry X, Cowry Y and ATS-34. Prefers high mirror polish; pearl ha inlay. **Prices:** $80 to $500; some to $1,000. **Remarks:** Full-time maker;

knife sold in 1980. Doing business as Knife House "Hara". **Mark:** First initial, last name in fish.

**HARDY, SCOTT,** 639 Myrtle Ave., Placerville, CA 95667, Phone: 530-622-5780, Web: www.innercite.com/~shardy
**Specialties:** Traditional working and using straight knives of his design. **Patterns:** Most anything with an edge. **Technical:** Forges carbon steels. Japanese stone polish. Offers mirror finish; differentially tempers. **Prices:** $100 to $1,000. **Remarks:** Part-time maker; first knife sold in 1982. **Mark:** First initial, last name and Handmade with bird logo.

**HARDY, DOUGLAS E.,** 114 Cypress Rd., Franklin, GA 30217, Phone: 706-675-6305

**HARKINS, J.A.,** PO Box 218, Conner, MT 59827, Phone: 406-821-1060, kutter@customknives.net Web: customknives.net
**Specialties:** Investment grade folders. **Patterns:** flush buttons, lockers. **Technical:** Grinds ATS-34. Engraves; offers gem work. **Prices:** Start at $550. **Remarks:** Full-time maker and engraver; first knife sold in 1988. **Mark:** First and middle initials, last name.

**HARLEY, RICHARD,** 348 Deerfield Dr., Bristol, TN 37620, Phone: 423-878-5368/423-571-0638
**Specialties:** Hunting knives, Bowies, friction folders, one-of-a-kind. **Technical:** Forges 1084, S160, 52100, Lg. **Prices:** $150 to $1,000. **Mark:** Pine Tree with name.

**HARLEY, LARRY W.,** 348 Deerfield Dr., Bristol, TN 37620, Phone: 423-878-5368 (shop)/Cell 423-571-0638, Fax: 276-466-6771, Web: www.lonesomepineknives.com
**Specialties:** One-of-a-kind Persian in one-of-a-kind Damascus. Working knives, period pieces. **Technical:** Forges and grinds ATS-34, 440c, L6, 15, 20, 1084, and 52100. **Patterns:** Full range of straight knives, tomahawks, razors, buck skinners and hog spears. **Prices:** $200 and up. **Mark:** Pine tree.

**HARM, PAUL W.,** 818 Young Rd., Attica, MI 48412, Phone: 810-724-5582, harm@blclinks.net
**Specialties:** Early American working knives. **Patterns:** Hunters, skinners, patch knives, fighters, folders. **Technical:** Forges and grinds 1084, 01, 52100 and own Damascus. **Prices:** $75 to $1,000. **Remarks:** First knife sold in 1990. **Mark:** Connected initials.

**HARMON, JAY,** 462 Victoria Rd., Woodstock, GA 30189, Phone: 770-928-2734
**Specialties:** Working straight knives and folders of his design or to customer specs; collector-grade pieces. **Patterns:** Bowies, daggers, fighters, boots, hunters and folders. **Technical:** Grinds 440C, 440V, ATS-34, D2 1095 and Damascus; heat-treats; makes own mokume. **Prices:** Start at $185. **Remarks:** Part-time maker; first knife sold in 1984. **Mark:** Last name.

**HARRINGTON, ROGER,** 3 Beech Farm Cottages, Bugsell Ln., East Sussex, ENGLAND TN 32 5 EN, Phone: 44 0 1580 882194, info@bisonbushcraft.co.uk Web: www.bisonbushcraft.co.uk
**Specialties:** Working straight knives to his or customer's designs, flat saber Scandinavia-style grinds on full tang knives, also hollow and convex grinds. **Technical:** Grinds 01, D2, Damascus. **Prices:** $200 to $800. **Remarks:** First knife made by hand in 1997 whilst traveling around the world. **Mark:** Bison with bison written under.

**HARRIS, JEFFERY A.,** 705 Olive St. Ste. 325, St. Louis, MO 63101, Phone: 314-241-2442, jeffro135@aol.com
**Remarks:** Purveyor and collector of handmade knives.

**HARRIS, CASS,** 19855 Fraiser Hill Ln., Bluemont, VA 20135, Phone: 540-554-8774, Web: www.tdogforge.com
**Prices:** $160 to $500.

**HARRIS, JOHN,** 14131 Calle Vista, Riverside, CA 92508, Phone: 951-653-2755, johnharris@yahoo.com
**Specialties:** Hunters, Daggers, Bowies, Bird and Trout, period pieces, Damascus and carbon steel knives, forged and stock removal. **Prices:** $200 to $1,000.

**HARRIS, RALPH DEWEY,** 2607 Bell Shoals Rd., Brandon, FL 33511, Phone: 813-681-5293, Fax: 813-654-8175
**Specialties:** Collector quality interframe folders. **Patterns:** High tech locking folders of his own design with various mechanisms. **Technical:** Grinds 440C, ATS-34 and commercial Damascus. Offers various frame materials including 416ss, and titanium; file worked frames and his own engraving. **Prices:** $400 to $3,000. **Remarks:** Full-time maker; first knife sold in 1978. **Mark:** Last name, or name and city.

**HARRIS, JAY,** 991 Johnson St., Redwood City, CA 94061, Phone: 415-366-6077
**Specialties:** Traditional high-tech straight knives and folders of his design. **Patterns:** Daggers, fighters and locking folders. **Technical:** Uses 440C, ATS-34 and CPM. **Prices:** $250 to $850. **Remarks:** Spare-time maker; first knife sold in 1980.

**HARRISON, JIM (SEAMUS),** 721 Fairington View Dr., St. Louis, MO 63129, Phone: 314-894-2525, seamusknives@msn.com Web: www.seamusknives.com
**Specialties:** Gents and fancy tactical locking-liner folders. Compact straight blades for hunting, backpacking and canoeing. **Patterns:** Liner lock folders. Compact 3 fingered fixed blades often with modified wharncliffes. Survival knife with mortised handles. **Technical"** Grinds 440C, talonite, S-30V, Mike Norris and Devin Thomas S.S. Damascus. Heat treats. **Prices:** Folders $325 to $700. Fixed flades $300 to $400. **Remarks:** Soon to be full time. **Mark:** Seamus

**HARSEY, WILLIAM H.,** 82710 N. Howe Ln., Creswell, OR 97426, Phone: 519-895-4941, harseyjr@cs.com
**Specialties:** High-tech kitchen and outdoor knives. **Patterns:** Folding hunters, trout and bird folders; straight hunters, camp knives and axes. **Technical:** Grinds; etches. **Prices:** $125 to $300; some to $1,500. Folders start at $350. **Remarks:** Full-time maker; first knife sold in 1979. **Mark:** Full name, state, U.S.A.

**HART, BILL,** 647 Cedar Dr., Pasadena, MD 21122, Phone: 410-255-4981
**Specialties:** Fur-trade era working straight knives and folders. **Patterns:** Springbuck folders, skinners, Bowies and patch knives. **Technical:** Forges and stock removes 1095 and 5160 wire Damascus. **Prices:** $100 to $600. **Remarks:** Part-time maker; first knife sold in 1986. **Mark:** Name.

**HARTMAN, ARLAN (LANNY),** 340 Ruddiman, N. Muskegon, MI 49445, Phone: 231-744-3635
**Specialties:** Working straight knives and folders. **Patterns:** Drop-point hunters, coil spring lockers, slip-joints. **Technical:** Flat-grinds D2, 440C and ATS-34. **Prices:** $300 to $2,000. **Remarks:** Part-time maker; first knife sold in 1982. **Mark:** Last name.

**HARTSFIELD, PHILL,** PO Box 1637, Newport Beach, CA 92659-0637, Phone: 949-722-9792 and 714-636-7633, phillhartsfield@mind-spring.com Web: www.phillhartsfield.com
**Specialties:** Heavy-duty working and using straight knives. **Patterns:** Fighters, swords and survival knives, most in Japanese profile. **Technical:** Grinds A2. **Prices:** $350 to $20,000. **Remarks:** Full-time maker; first knife sold about 1976. Doing business as A Cut Above. **Mark:** Initials, chiseled character plus register mark. **Other:** Color catalog $10.

**HARVEY, HEATHER,** HEAVIN FORGE, PO Box 768, Belfast 1100, SOUTH AFRICA, Phone: 27-13-253-0914, heavin.knives@mweb.co.za Web: www.africut.co.za
**Specialties:** Integral hand forged knives, traditional African weapons, primitive folders and by-gone forged-styles. **Patterns:** All forged knives, war axes, spears, arrows, forks, spoons, and swords. **Technical:** Own carbon Damascus and mokume. Also forges stainless, brass, copper and titanium. Traditional forging and heat-treatment methods used. **Prices:** $300 to $5,000, average $1,000. **Remarks:** Full-time maker and knifemaking instructor. Master bladesmith with ABS. First Damascus sold in 1995, first knife sold in 1998. Often collaborate with husband, Kevin (ABS MS) using the logo "Heavin". **Mark:** First name and sur name - oval shape with "M S" in middle.

**HARVEY, KEVIN,** HEAVIN FORGE, PO Box 768, Belfast 1100, SOUTH AFRICA, Phone: 27-13-253-0914, heavin.knives@mweb.co.za Web: www.africut.co.za
**Specialties:** Large knives of presentation quality and creative art knives. **Patterns:** Fixed blades of Bowie, dagger and fighter-styles, occasionally folders. **Technical:** Stock removal of stainless and forging of carbon steel and own Damascus. Indigenous African handle materials preferred. Stacked file worked handles. Ostrich, bull frog, fish, crocodile and snake leathers used on unique sheaths. Surface texturing and heat coloring of materials. Often collaborate with wife, Heather (ABS MS) under the logo "Heavin". **Prices:** $500 to $5,000 average $1,500. **Remarks:** Full-time maker and knifemaking instructor. Master bladesmith with ABS. First knife sold in 1984. **Mark:** First name and surname - oval with "M S" in the middle.

**HARVEY, MAX,** 14 Bass Rd., Bull Creek, Perth 6155, WESTERN AUSTRALIA, Phone: 09-332-7585
**Specialties:** Daggers, Bowies, fighters and fantasy knives. **Patterns:** Hunters, Bowies, tantos and skinners. **Technical:** Hollow-and flat-grinds 440C, ATS-34, 154CM and Damascus. Offers gem work. **Prices:** $250 to $4,000. **Remarks:** Part-time maker; first knife sold in 1981. **Mark:** First and middle initials, last name.

**HASLINGER, THOMAS,** 164 Fairview Dr. SE, Calgary AB, CANADA T2H 1B3, Phone: 403-253-9628, Web: www.haslinger-knives.com
**Specialties:** One-of-a-kind using, working and art knives HCK signature sweeping grind liners. Differential heat treated stainless steel. **Patterns:** No

fixed patterns, likes to work with customers on design. **Technical:** Grinds Various specialty alloys, including Damascus, High end satin finish. Prefers natural handle materials e.g. ancient ivory stag, pearl, abalone, stone and exotic woods. Does inlay work with stone, some sterling silver, niobium and gold wire work. Custom sheaths using matching woods or hand stitched with unique leather like sturgeon, Nile perch or carp. Offers engraving. **Prices:** Starting at $150. **Remarks:** Full-time maker; first knife sold in 1994. Doing business as Haslinger Custom Knives. **Mark:** Two marks used, high end work uses stylized initials, other uses elk antler with Thomas Haslinger, Canada, Handcrafted above.

**HATCH, KEN,** PO Box 203, Dinosaur, CO 81610
**Specialties:** Indian and early trade knives. **Patterns:** Buckskinners and period Bowies. **Technical:** Forges and grinds 1095, O1, W2, ATS-34. Prefers natural handle materials. **Prices:** $85 to $400. **Remarks:** Part-time maker, custom leather and bead work; first knife sold in 1977. **Mark:** Last name or dragonfly stamp.

**HAWES, CHUCK,** HAWES FORGE, PO Box 176, Weldon, IL 61882, Phone: 217-736-2479
**Specialties:** 95% of all work in own Damascus. **Patterns:** Slip-joints liner locks, hunters, Bowie's, swords, anything in between. **Technical:** Forges everything, uses all high-carbon steels, no stainless. **Prices:** $150 to $4,000. **Remarks:** Like to do custom orders, his style or yours. Sells Damascus. **Mark:** Small football shape. Chuck Hawes maker Weldon,IL. **Other:** Full-time maker sine 1995.

**HAWK, GRANT AND GAVIN,** Box 401, Idaho City, ID 83631, Phone: 208-392-4911, Web: www.9-hawkknives.com
**Specialties:** Large folders with unique locking systems D.O.G. lock, toad lock. **Technical:** Grinds ATS-34, titanium folder parts. **Prices:** $450 and up. **Remarks:** Full-time maker. **Mark:** First initials and last names.

**HAWK, JACK L.,** Rt. 1, Box 771, Ceres, VA 24318, Phone: 703-624-3878
**Specialties:** Fancy and embellished working and using straight knives of his design or to customer specs. **Patterns:** Hunters, Bowies and daggers. **Technical:** Hollow-grinds 440C, ATS-34 and D2; likes bone and ivory handles. **Prices:** $75 to $1,200. **Remarks:** Full-time maker; first knife sold in 1982. **Mark:** Full name and initials.

**HAWK, JOEY K.,** Rt. 1, Box 196, Ceres, VA 24318, Phone: 703-624-3282
**Specialties:** Working straight knives, some fancy. Welcomes customer designs. **Patterns:** Hunters, fighters, daggers, Bowies and miniatures. **Technical:** Grinds 440C or customer preference. Offers some knives with jewelling. **Prices:** $100 to $250; some to $500. **Remarks:** Part-time maker; first knife sold in 1983. **Mark:** First and middle initials, last name stamped.

**HAWKINS, RADE,** 110 Buckeye Rd., Fayetteville, GA 30214, Phone: 770-964-1023, Fax: 770-306-2877, sales@hawkinsknifemakingsupplies.com Web: www.hawkinsknifemakingsupplies.com
**Specialties:** Full line of knife making supplies and equipment. Catalog available $2.00. **Patterns:** All styles. **Technical:** Grinds and forges. Makes own Damascus**Prices:** Start at $190. **Remarks:** Full-time maker; first knife sold in 1972. Member knifemakers guild, ABS journeyman smith. **Mark:** Rade Hawkins Custom Knives.

**HAWKINS, BUDDY,** PO Box 5969, Texarkana, TX 75505-5969, Phone: 903-838-7917, buddyhawkins@cableone.net

**HAYES, DOLORES,** PO Box 41405, Los Angeles, CA 90041, Phone: 213-258-9923
**Specialties:** High-art working and using straight knives of her design. **Patterns:** Art knives and miniatures. **Technical:** Grinds 440C, stainless AEB, commercial Damascus and ATS-34. **Prices:** $50 to $500; some to $2,000. **Remarks:** Spare-time maker; first knife sold in 1978. **Mark:** Last name.

**HAYES, WALLY,** 1026 Old Montreal Rd., Orleans, Ont., CANADA K4A-3N2, Phone: 613-824-9520, Web: www.hayesknives.com
**Specialties:** Classic and fancy straight knives and folders. **Patterns:** Daggers, Bowies, fighters, tantos. **Technical:** Forges own Damascus and O1; engraves. **Prices:** $150 to $14,000. **Mark:** Last name, M.S. and serial number.

**HAYES, SCOTTY,** Texarkana College, 2500 N Robinson Rd., Tesarkana, TX 75501, Phone: 903-838-4541, ext. 3236, Fax: 903-832-5030, shayes@texakanacollege.edu Web: www.americanbladesmith.com/2005ABSo/o20schedule.htm
**Specialties:** ABS School of Bladesmithing.

**HAYNES, JERRY,** 6902 Teton Ridge, San Antonio, TX 78233, Phone: 210-599-2928
**Specialties:** Working straight knives and folders of his design, also historical blades. **Patterns:** Hunters, skinners, carving knives, fighters, renaissance daggers, locking folders and kitchen knives. **Technical:** Grinds ATS-34, CPM, Stellite 6K, D2 and acquired Damascus. Prefers exotic handle materials. Ha B.A. in design. Studied with R. Buckminster Fuller. **Prices:** $200 to $1,20C **Remarks:** Part-time maker - will go full-time after retirement in 2007. Firs knife sold in 1953. **Mark:** Arrowhead and last name.

**HAYNIE, CHARLES,** 125 Cherry Lane, Toccoa, GA 30577, Phone: 706 886-8665

**HAYS, MARK,** Hays Handmade Knives, 1008 Kavanagh Dr., Austin, TX 78748, Phone: 512-292-4410, markhays@austin.rr.com Web: www,
**Specialties:** Working straight knives and folders. Patterns inspired by Randa and Stone. **Patterns:** Bowies, hunters and slip-joint folders. **Technical:** 440 stock removal. Repairs and restores Stone knives. **Prices:** Start at $20C **Remarks:** Part-time maker, brochure available, with Stone knives 1974-198 1990-1991. **Mark:** First initial, last name, state and serial number.

**HAZEN, MARK,** 9600 Surrey Rd., Charlotte, NC 28227, Phone: 704-573-0904, Fax: 704-573-0052, mhazen@carolina.rr.com
**Specialties:** Working/using straight knives of his design and to custome specs. **Patterns:** Hunters/skinners, fillet, utility/camp, fighters, short sword **Technical:** Grinds 154 CM, ATS-34, 440C. **Prices:** $75 to $450; some t $1,500. **Remarks:** Part-time maker. First knife sold 1982. **Mark:** Name wi cross in it, stamped in blade.

**HEADRICK, GARY,** 122 Wilson Blvd., Juane Les Pins, FRANCE 06160 Phone: 033 0610282885
**Specialties:** Hi-tech folders with natural furnishings. Back lock & back sprin **Patterns:** Damascus and Mokumes. **Technical:** Self made Damascus a steel (no nickel). **Prices:** $500 to $2,000. **Remarks:** Full-time maker for last years. **Mark:** G/P in a circle. **Other:** 10 years active.

**HEARN, TERRY L.,** Rt. 14 Box 7676, Lufkin, TX 75904, Phone: 936-632-5045, hearn1@lufkntx.com

**HEASMAN, H.G.,** 28 St. Mary's Rd., Llandudno, N. Wales U.K. LL302UB, Phone: (UK)0492-876351
**Specialties:** Miniatures only. **Patterns:** Bowies, daggers and swords. **Techn cal:** Files from stock high-carbon and stainless steel. **Prices:** $400 to $60 **Remarks:** Part-time maker; first knife sold in 1975. Doing business Reduced Reality. **Mark:** NA.

**HEATH, WILLIAM,** PO Box 131, Bondville, IL 61815, Phone: 217-863-2576
**Specialties:** Classic and working straight knives, folders. **Patterns:** Hunte and Bowies liner lock folders. **Technical:** Grinds ATS-34, 440C, 154C Damascus, handle materials micarta, woods to exotic materials snake ski cobra, rattle snake, African flower snake. Does own heat treating. **Prices:** $ to $300; some $1,000. **Remarks:** Full-time maker. First knife sold in 19 **Mark:** W. D. HEATH.

**HEDRICK, DON,** 131 Beechwood Hills, Newport News, VA 23608, Phone: 757-877-8100, dhknife@cox.net or donaldhedrick@cox.net
**Specialties:** Working straight knives; period pieces and fantasy knives. **P terns:** Hunters, boots, Bowies and miniatures. **Technical:** Grinds 440C a commercial Damascus. Also makes micro-mini Randall replicas. **Prices:** $1 to $550; some to $1,200. **Remarks:** Part-time maker; first knife sold in 19 **Mark:** First initial, last name in oval logo.

**HEFLIN, CHRISTOPHER M.,** 6013 Jocely Hollow Rd., Nashville, TN 37205, Phone: 615-352-3909, blix@bellsouth.net

**HEGWALD, J.L.,** 1106 Charles, Humboldt, KS 66748, Phone: 316-47 3523
**Specialties:** Working straight knives, some fancy. **Patterns:** Makes Bowi miniatures. **Technical:** Forges or grinds O1, L6, 440C; mixes materials handles. **Prices:** $35 to $200; some higher. **Remarks:** Part-time maker; f knife sold in 1983. **Mark:** First and middle initials.

**HEHN, RICHARD KARL,** Lehnmuehler Str. 1, 55444 Dorrebach, GERMANY, Phone: 06724 3152
**Specialties:** High-tech, full integral working knives. **Patterns:** Hunters, fig ers and daggers. **Technical:** Grinds CPM T-440V, CPM T-420V, forges own stainless Damascus. **Prices:** $1,000 to $10,000. **Remarks:** Full-ti maker; first knife sold in 1963. **Mark:** Runic last initial in logo.

**HEINZ, JOHN,** 611 Cafferty Rd., Upper Black Eddy, PA 18972, Phone 610-847-8535, Web: www.herugrim.com
**Specialties:** Historical pieces / copies. **Technical:** Makes his own st **Prices:** $150 to $800. **Mark:** "H"

**HEITLER, HENRY,** 8106 N Albany, Tampa, FL 33604, Phone: 813-93 1645
**Specialties:** Traditional working and using straight knives of his design an customer specs. **Patterns:** Fighters, hunters, utility/camp knives and f knives. **Technical:** Flat-grinds ATS-34; offers tapered tangs. **Prices:** $13 $450; some to $600. **Remarks:** Part-time maker; first knife sold in 19 **Mark:** First initial, last name, city, state circling double H's.

**HELSCHER, JOHN W.,** 2645 Highway 1, Washington, IA 52353, Phone: 319-653-7310

**HELTON, ROY,** Helton Knives, 2941 Comstock St., San Diego, CA 92111, Phone: 858-277-5024

**HEMBROOK, RON,** HEMBROOK KNIVES, PO Box 201, Neosho, WI 53059, Phone: 920-625-3607, knifemkr@nconnect.net Web: www.hembrookcustomknives.com
**Specialties:** Hunters, working knives. **Technical:** Grinds ATS-34, 440C, 01 and Damascus. **Prices:** $125 to $750; some to $1,000. **Remarks:** First knife sold in 1980. **Mark:** Hembrook plus a serial number. Part-time maker, makes hunters, daggers, Bowies, folders and miniatures.

**HEMPERLEY, GLEN,** 13322 Country Run Rd., Willis, TX 77318, Phone: 936-228-5048, hemperley.com
**Specialties:** Specializes in hunting knives, does fixed and folding knives.

**HENDRICKS, SAMUEL J.,** 2162 Van Buren Rd., Maurertown, VA 22644, Phone: 703-436-3305
**Specialties:** Integral hunters and skinners of thin design. **Patterns:** Boots, hunters and locking folders. **Technical:** Grinds ATS-34, 440C and D2. Integral liners and bolsters of N-S and 7075 T6 aircraft aluminum. Does leatherwork. **Prices:** $50 to $250; some to $500. **Remarks:** Full-time maker; first knife sold in 1992. **Mark:** First and middle initials, last name, city and state in football-style logo.

**HENDRICKSON, E. JAY,** 4204 Ballenger Creek Pike, Frederick, MD 21703, Phone: 301-663-6923, jhendrickson@xecu.net
**Specialties:** Classic collectors and working straight knives of his design. **Patterns:** Bowies, Kukri's, camp, hunters, and fighters. **Technical:** Forges 06, 1084, 5160, 52100, D2, L6 and W2; makes Damascus; offers silver wire inlay. Moran-styles on order. **Prices:** $400 to $5,000. **Remarks:** Full-time maker; first knife sold in 1975. **Mark:** Last name, M.S.

**HENDRICKSON, SHAWN,** 2327 Kaetzel Rd., Knoxville, MD 21758, Phone: 301-432-4306
**Specialties:** Hunting knives. **Patterns:** Clip points, drop points and trailing point hunters. **Technical:** Forges 5160, 1084 and L6. **Prices:** $175 to $400.

**HENDRIX, JERRY,** HENDRIX CUSTOM KNIVES, 175 Skyland Dr. Ext., Clinton, SC 29325, Phone: 864-833-2659, jhendrix@backroads.net
**Specialties:** Traditional working straight knives of all designs. **Patterns:** Hunters, utility, boot, bird and fishing. **Technical:** grinds ATS-34 and 440C. **Prices:** $85 to $275. **Remarks:** Full-time maker. **Mark:** Full name in shape of knife. **Other:** Hand stitched, waxed leather sheaths.

**HENDRIX, WAYNE,** 9636 Burton's Ferry Hwy., Allendale, SC 29810, Phone: 803-584-3825, Fax: 803-584-3825, knives@barnwellsc.com Web: www.hendrixknives.com
**Specialties:** Working/using knives of his design. **Patterns:** Hunters and fillet knives. **Technical:** Grinds ATS-34, D2 and 440C. **Prices:** $70 to $600. **Remarks:** Full-time maker; first knife sold in 1985. **Mark:** Last name.

**HENNICKE, METALLGESTALTUNG,** Wassegasse 4, 55578 Wallerheim, GERMANY, Phone: 0049 6732 930414, Fax: 0049 6732 930415, hennicke.metall@gmx.de Web: www.hennickemesser.de
**Specialties:** All kinds of knives folder with titanium leiner and inlaid springs. **Patterns:** Huntingknives, Bowies, kukris, swords, daggers, camp knives. **Technical:** Forge damststeels mostly wild pattern and sanmai pattern to get strong blades. **Prices:** 400 Euro till 3000 Euro swords about 3000 to 6000 Euro. **Mark:** Is an Mamuth walking out of the ricasso to the blade ore an UH in a circle.

**HENRIKSEN, HANS J.,** Birkegaardsvej 24, DK 3200 Helsinge, DENMARK, Fax: 45 4879 4899
**Specialties:** Zirconia ceramic blades. **Patterns:** Customer designs. **Technical:** Slip-cast zirconia-water mix in plaster mould; offers hidden or full tang. **Prices:** White blades start at $10cm; colored +50 percent. **Remarks:** Part-time maker; first ceramic blade sold in 1989. **Mark:** Initial logo.

**HENSLEY, WAYNE,** PO Box 904, Conyers, GA 30012, Phone: 770-483-8938
**Specialties:** Period pieces and fancy working knives. **Patterns:** Boots to Bowies, locking folders to miniatures. Large variety of straight knives. **Technical:** Grinds ATS-34, 440C, D2 and commercial Damascus. **Prices:** $85 and up. **Remarks:** Full-time maker; first knife sold in 1974. **Mark:** Last name.

**HERBST, PETER,** Komotauer Strasse 26, 91207 Lauf a.d. Pegn., GERMANY, Phone: 09123-13315, Fax: 09123-13379
**Specialties:** Working/using knives and folders of his design. **Patterns:** Hunters, fighters and daggers; interframe and integral. **Technical:** Grinds CPM-T-440V, UHB-Elmax, ATS-34 and stainless Damascus. **Prices:** $300 to $3,000; some to $8,000. **Remarks:** Full-time maker; first knife sold in 1981. **Mark:** First initial, last name.

**HERMAN, TIM,** 7721 Foster, Overland Park, KS 66204, Phone: 913-649-3860, Fax: 913-649-0603
**Specialties:** Investment-grade folders of his design; interframes and bolster frames. **Patterns:** Interframes and new designs in carved stainless. **Technical:** Grinds ATS-34 and damasteel Damascus. Engraves and gold inlays with pearl, jade, lapis and Australian opal. **Prices:** $1,000 to $15,000. **Remarks:** Full-time maker; first knife sold in 1978. **Mark:** Etched signature.

**HERNDON, WM. R. "BILL",** 32520 Michigan St., Acton, CA 93510, Phone: 661-269-5860, bherndons1@earthlink.net
**Specialties:** Straight knives, plain and fancy. **Technical:** Carbon steel (white and blued), Damascus, stainless steels. **Prices:** Start at $120. **Remarks:** Full-time maker; first knife sold in 1976. American Bladesmith Society journeyman smith. **Mark:** Signature and/or helm logo.

**HERRING, MORRIS,** Box 85, 721 W Line St., Dyer, AR 72935, Phone: 501-997-8861, morrish@ipa.com

**HERRON, GEORGE,** 474 Antonio Way, Springfield, SC 29146, Phone: 803-258-3914
**Specialties:** High-tech working and using straight knives; some folders. **Patterns:** Hunters, fighters, boots in personal styles. **Technical:** Grinds 154CM, ATS-34. **Prices:** $400 to $2,500. **Remarks:** Full-time maker; first knife sold in 1963. About 12 year back log. Not excepting orders. No catalog. **Mark:** Last name in script.

**HESSER, DAVID,** PO Box 1079, Dripping Springs, TX 78620, Phone: 512-894-0100
**Specialties:** High-art daggers and fantasy knives of his design; court weapons of the Renaissance. **Patterns:** Daggers, swords, axes, miniatures and sheath knives. **Technical:** Forges 1065, 1095, O1, D2 and recycled tool steel. Offers custom lapidary work and stone-setting, stone handles and custom hardwood scabbards. **Prices:** $95 to $500; some to $6,000. **Remarks:** Full-time maker; first knife sold in 1989. Doing business as Exotic Blades. **Mark:** Last name, year.

**HETHCOAT, DON,** Box 1764, Clovis, NM 88101, Phone: 505-762-5721, dhethcoat@plateautel.net
**Specialties:** Liner lock-locking and multi-blade folders **Patterns:** Hunters, Bowies. **Technical:** Grinds stainless; forges Damascus. **Prices:** Moderate to upscale. **Remarks:** Full-time maker; first knife sold in 1969. **Mark:** Last name on all.

**HIBBEN, WESTLEY G.,** 14101 Sunview Dr., Anchorage, AK 99515
**Specialties:** Working straight knives of his design or to customer specs. **Patterns:** Hunters, fighters, daggers, combat knives and some fantasy pieces. **Technical:** Grinds 440C mostly. Filework available. **Prices:** $200 to $400; some to $3,000. **Remarks:** Part-time maker; first knife sold in 1988. **Mark:** Signature.

**HIBBEN, JOLEEN,** PO Box 172, LaGrange, KY 40031, Phone: 502-222-0983, dhibben1@bellsouth.net
**Specialties:** Miniature straight knives of her design; period pieces. **Patterns:** Hunters, axes and fantasy knives. **Technical:** Grinds Damascus, 1095 tool steel and stainless 440C or ATS-34. Uses wood, ivory, bone, feathers and claws on/for handles. **Prices:** $60 to $200. **Remarks:** Spare-time maker; first knife sold in 1991. **Mark:** Initials or first name.

**HIBBEN, DARYL,** PO Box 172, LaGrange, KY 40031-0172, Phone: 502-222-0983, dhibben1@bellsouth.net
**Specialties:** Working straight knives, some fancy to customer specs. **Patterns:** Hunters, fighters, Bowies, short sword, art and fantasy. **Technical:** Grinds 440C, ATS-34, 154CM, Damascus; prefers hollow-grinds. **Prices:** $175 to $3,000. **Remarks:** Full-time maker; first knife sold in 1979. **Mark:** Etched full name in script.

**HIBBEN, GIL,** PO Box 13, LaGrange, KY 40031, Phone: 502-222-1397, Fax: 502-222-2676
**Specialties:** Working knives and fantasy pieces to customer specs. **Patterns:** Full range of straight knives, including swords, axes and miniatures; some locking folders. **Technical:** Grinds ATS-34, 440C and 154CM. **Prices:** $300 to $2,000; some to $10,000. **Remarks:** Full-time maker; first knife sold in 1957. Maker and designer of *Rambo III* knife; made swords for movie *Marked for Death* and throwing knife for movie *Under Seige*; made belt buckle knife and knives for movie *Perfect Weapon*; made knives featured in movie *Star Trek the Next Generation* Star Trek Nemesis 1990 inductee cutlery hall of fame; designer for United Cutlery. Official klingon armourer for Star Trek, over 34 movies and TV productions. **Mark:** Hibben Knives. City and state, or signature.

**HIGGINS, J.P. DR.,** ART KNIVES BY, 120 N Pheasant Run, Coupeville, WA 98239, Phone: 360-678-9269, Fax: 360-678-9269, netsuke @whidbey.net Web: www.bladegallery.com or www.2.whidbey.net/netsuke
**Specialties:** Since 2003 Dr. J.P. Higgins and Tom Sterling have created a unique collaboration of one-of-a-kind, ultra-quality art knives with percussion

or pressured flaked stone blades and creatively sculpted handles. Their knives are often highly influenced by the traditions of Japanese netsuke and unique fusions of cultures, reflecting stylistically integrated choices of exotic hardwoods, fossil ivories and semi-precious materials, contrasting inlays and polychromed and pyrographed details. **Prices:** $300 to $900. **Remarks:** Limited output ensures highest quality artwork and exceptional levels of craftsmanship. **Mark:** Signatures Sterling and Higgins.

**HIGH, TOM,** 5474 S. 112.8 Rd., Alamosa, CO 81101, Phone: 719-589-2108, www.rockymountainscrimshaw.com
**Specialties:** Hunters, some fancy. **Patterns:** Drop-points in several shapes; some semi-skinners. Knives designed by and for top outfitters and guides. **Technical:** Grinds ATS-34; likes hollow-grinds, mirror finishes; prefers scrim able handles. **Prices:** $175 to $8,000. **Remarks:** Full-time maker; first knife sold in 1965. Limited edition wildlife series knives. **Mark:** Initials connected; arrow through last name.

**HILKER, THOMAS N.,** PO Box 409, Williams, OR 97544, Phone: 541-846-6461
**Specialties:** Traditional working straight knives and folders. **Patterns:** Folding skinner in two sizes, Bowies, fork and knife sets, camp knives and interchangeable. **Technical:** Grinds D2, 440C and ATS-34. Heat-treats. **Prices:** $50 to $350; some to $400. Doing business as Thunderbolt Artisans. Only limited production models available; not currently taking orders. **Remarks:** Full-time maker; first knife sold in 1983. **Mark:** Last name.

**HILL, STEVE E.,** 40 Rand Pond Rd., Goshen, NH 03752, Phone: 603-863-4762, Fax: 603-863-4762, kingpirateboy2@juno.com
**Specialties:** Fancy manual and automatic liner lock folders, some working grade. **Patterns:** Classic to cool folding and fixed blade designs. **Technical:** Grinds Damascus and occasional 440C, D2. Prefers natural handle materials; offers elaborate filework, carving, and inlays. **Prices:** $375 to $5,000; some higher. **Remarks:** Full-time maker; first knife sold in 1978. **Mark:** First initial, last name and handmade. (4400, D2). Damascus folders: mark inside handle. **Other:** Google search: Steve Hill custom knives.

**HILL, RICK,** 20 Nassau, Maryville, IL 62062-5618, Phone: 618-288-4370
**Specialties:** Working knives and period pieces to customer specs. **Patterns:** Hunters, locking folders, fighters and daggers. **Technical:** Grinds D2, 440C and 154CM; forges his own Damascus. **Prices:** $75 to $500; some to $3,000. **Remarks:** Part-time maker; first knife sold in 1983. **Mark:** Full name in hill shape logo.

**HILL, HOWARD E.,** 111 Mission Lane, Polson, MT 59860, Phone: 406-883-3405, Fax: 406-883-3486, knifeman@bigsky.net
**Specialties:** Autos, complete new design, legal in Montana (with permit). **Patterns:** Bowies, daggers, skinners and lockback folders. **Technical:** Grinds 440C; uses micro and satin finish. **Prices:** $150 to $1,000. **Remarks:** Full-time maker; first knife sold in 1981. **Mark:** Persuader.

**HILLMAN, CHARLES,** 225 Waldoboro Rd., Friendship, ME 04547, Phone: 207-832-4634
**Specialties:** Working knives of his own or custom design. Heavy Scagel influence. **Patterns:** Hunters, fishing, camp and general utility. Occasional folders. **Technical:** Grinds D2 and 440C. File work, blade and handle carving, engraving. Natural handle materials-antler, bone, leather, wood, horn. Sheaths made to order. **Prices:** $60 to $500. **Remarks:** Part-time maker; first knife sold 1986. **Mark:** Last name in oak leaf.

**HINDERER, RICK,** 5423 Kister Rd., Wooster, OH 44691, Phone: 216-263-0962, rhind64@earthlink.net Web: www.rhknives.com
**Specialties:** Working tactical knives, and some one-of-a kind. **Patterns:** Make my own. **Technical:** Grinds CPM S30V. **Prices:** $150 to $4,000. **Remarks:** Full-time maker doing business as Rick Hinderer Knives, first knife sold in 1988. **Mark:** R. Hinderer.

**HINK III, LES,** 1599 Aptos Lane, Stockton, CA 95206, Phone: 209-547-1292
**Specialties:** Working straight knives and traditional folders in standard patterns or to customer specs. **Patterns:** Hunting and utility/camp knives; others on request. **Technical:** Grinds carbon and stainless steels. **Prices:** $80 to $200; some higher. **Remarks:** Part-time maker; first knife sold in 1980. **Mark:** Last name, or last name 3.

**HINMAN, TED,** 183 Highland Ave., Watertown, MA 02472

**HINSON AND SON, R.,** 2419 Edgewood Rd., Columbus, GA 31906, Phone: 706-327-6801
**Specialties:** Working straight knives and folders. **Patterns:** Locking folders, liner locks, combat knives and swords. **Technical:** Grinds 440C and commercial Damascus. **Prices:** $100 to $350; some to $1,500. **Remarks:** Part-time maker; first knife sold in 1983. Son Bob is co-worker. **Mark:** HINSON, city and state.

**HINTZ, GERALD M.,** 5402 Sahara Ct., Helena, MT 59602, Phone: 406 458-5412
**Specialties:** Fancy, high-art, working/using knives of his design. **Pattern** Bowies, hunters, daggers, fish fillet and utility/camp knives. **Technic** Forges ATS-34, 440C and D2. Animal art in horn handles or in the blac **Prices:** $75 to $400; some to $1,000. **Remarks:** Part-time maker; first kn sold in 1980. Doing business as Big Joe's Custom Knives. Will take custo orders. **Mark:** F.S. or W.S. with first and middle initials and last name.

**HIRAYAMA, HARUMI,** 4-5-13 Kitamachi, Warabi City, Saitama Pref. 335-0001, JAPAN, Phone: 048-443-2248, Fax: 048-443-2248, Web: www.ne.jp/asahi/harumi/knives
**Specialties:** High-tech working knives of her design. **Patterns:** Locking fo ers, interframes, straight gents and slip-joints. **Technical:** Grinds 440C equivalent; uses natural handle materials and gold. **Prices:** Start at $1,5( **Remarks:** Part-time maker; first knife sold in 1985. **Mark:** First initial, la name.

**HIROTO, FUJIHARA,** , 2-34-7 Koioosako Nishi-ku Hiroshima-city, Hiroshima, JAPAN, Phone: 082-271-8389, fjhr8363@crest.ocn.ne.jp

**HITCHMOUGH, HOWARD,** 95 Old Street Rd., Peterborough, NH 0345 1637, Phone: 603-924-9646, Fax: 603-924-9595, howard@hitchmougl knives.com Web: www.hitchmoughknives.com
**Specialties:** High class folding knives. **Patterns:** Lockback folders, lir locks, pocket knives. **Technical:** Uses ATS-34, stainless Damascus, titaniu gold and gemstones. Prefers hand-rubbed finishes and natural handle mate als. **Prices:** $850 to $3,500; some to $4,500. **Remarks:** Full-time maker; fi knife sold in 1967. **Mark:** Last name.

**HOBART, GENE,** 100 Shedd Rd., Windsor, NY 13865, Phone: 607-65 1345

**HOCKENBARY, WARREN E.,** 1806 Vallecito Dr., San Pedro, CA 907

**HOCKENSMITH, DAN,** 33514 CR 77, Crook, CO 80726, Phone: 970-886-3404, Web: hockensmithknives.com
**Specialties:** Traditional working and using straight knives of his design. **P terns:** Hunters, Bowies, folders and utility/camp knives. **Technical:** Uses Damascus, 5160, carbon steel, 52100 steel and 1084 steel. Hand forg **Prices:** $250 to $1,500. **Remarks:** Part-time maker; first knife sold in 19 **Mark:** Last name or stylized "D" with H inside.

**HODGE, J.B.,** 1100 Woodmont Ave. SE, Huntsville, AL 35801, Phone 205-536-8388
**Specialties:** Fancy working folders. **Patterns:** Slip-joints. **Technical:** Grir 154CM and ATS-34. **Prices:** Start at $175. **Remarks:** Part-time maker; fi knife sold in 1978. Not currently taking orders. **Mark:** Name, city and state.

**HODGE III, JOHN,** 422 S. 15th St., Palatka, FL 32177, Phone: 904-32 3897
**Specialties:** Fancy straight knives and folders. **Patterns:** Various. **Technic** Pattern-welded Damascus—"Southern-style." **Prices:** To $1,000. **Remar** Part-time maker; first knife sold in 1981. **Mark:** JH3 logo.

**HODGSON, RICHARD J.,** 9081 Tahoe Lane, Boulder, CO 80301, Phone: 303-666-9460
**Specialties:** Straight knives and folders in standard patterns. **Patterns:** Hi tech knives in various patterns. **Technical:** Grinds 440C, AEB-L and CF **Prices:** $850 to $2200. **Remarks:** Part-time maker. **Mark:** None.

**HOEL, STEVE,** PO Box 283, Pine, AZ 85544, Phone: 602-476-4278
**Specialties:** Investor-class folders, straight knives and period pieces of design. **Patterns:** Folding interframes lockers and slip-joints; straight Bowi boots and daggers. **Technical:** Grinds 154CM, ATS-34 and commercial Da ascus. **Prices:** $600 to $1,200; some to $7,500. **Remarks:** Full-time mak **Mark:** Initial logo with name and address.

**HOFER, LOUIS,** GEN DEL, Rose Prairie BC, CANADA V0C 2H0, Phone: 250-630-2513

**HOFFMAN, KEVIN L.,** 28 Hopeland Dr., Savannah, GA 31419, Phone 912-920-3579, Fax: 912-920-3579, kevh052475@aol.com Web: www.KLHoffman.com
**Specialties:** Distinctive folders and fixed blades. **Patterns:** Titanium fra lock folders. **Technical:** Sculpted guards and fittings cast in sterling silver a 14k gold. Grinds ATS-34, Damascus. Makes kydex sheaths for his fixed bla working knives. **Prices:** $400 and up. **Remarks:** Full-time maker since 19 **Mark:** KLH.

**HOFFMANN, UWE H.,** PO Box 60114, Vancouver, BC, CANADA V5V 4B5, Phone: 604-572-7320 (after 5 p.m.)
**Specialties:** High-tech working knives, folders and fantasy knives of design or to customer specs. **Patterns:** Hunters, fishing knives, combat a survival knives, folders and diver's knives. **Technical:** Grinds 440C, ATS-D2 and commercial Damascus. **Prices:** $95 to $900; some to $2,000 a

higher. **Remarks:** Full-time maker; first knife sold in 1985. **Mark:** Hoffmann Handmade Knives.

**HOGAN, THOMAS R.,** 2802 S. Heritage Ave., Boise, ID 83709, Phone: 208-362-7848

**HOGSTROM, ANDERS T.,** Granvagen 2, 135 52 Tyreso, SWEDEN, Phone: 46 8 798 5802, andershogstrom@hotmail.com or andershogstrom@rixmail.se Web: www.andershogstrom.com
**Specialties:** Short and long daggers, fighters and swords For select pieces makes wooden display boxes. **Patterns:** Daggers, fighters, short knives and swords and an occasional sword. **Technical:** Grinds 1050 High Carbon, Damascus and stanless, forges own Damasus on occasion. Does clay tempering and uses exotic hardwoods. **Prices:** Start at $500. **Marks:** Last name in various typefaces.

**HOKE, THOMAS M.,** 3103 Smith Ln., LaGrange, KY 40031, Phone: 502-222-0350
**Specialties:** Working/using knives, straight knives. Own designs and customer specs. **Patterns:** Daggers, Bowies, hunters, fighters, short swords. **Technical:** Grind 440C, Damascus and ATS-34. Filework on all knives. Tooling on sheaths (custom fit on all knives). Any handle material - mostly exotic. **Prices:** $100 to $700; some to $1,500. **Remarks:** Full-time maker, first knife sold in 1986. **Mark:** Dragon on banner which says T.M. Hoke.

**HOLBROOK, H.L.,** PO Box 483, Sandy Hook, KY 41171, Phone: 606-738-9922 home/606-738-6842 Shop, hhknives@mrtc.com
**Specialties:** Traditional working using straight knives and folders of his design, to customer specs and in standard patterns. Stablized wood. **Patterns:** Hunters, folders. **Technical:** Grinds 440C, ATS-34 and D2. Blades have hand-rubbed satin finish. Uses exotic woods, stag and Micarta. Handsewn sheath with each straight knife. **Prices:** $90 to $270; some to $400. **Remarks:** Part-time maker; first knife sold in 1983. Doing business as Holbrook knives. **Mark:** Name, city, state.

**HOLDER, D'ALTON,** 7148 W. Country Gables Dr., Peoria, AZ 85381, Phone: 623-878-3064, Fax: 623-878-3964, dholderknives@cox.net Web: d'holder.com
**Specialties:** Deluxe working knives and high-art hunters. **Patterns:** Droppoint hunters, fighters, Bowies. **Technical:** Grinds ATS-34; uses amber and other materials in combination on stick tangs. **Prices:** $400 to $1,000; some to $2,000. **Remarks:** Full-time maker; first knife sold in 1966. **Mark:** D'HOLDER, city and state.

**HOLLAND, JOHN H.,** 1580 Nassau St., Titusville, FL 32780, Phone: 321-267-4378
**Specialties:** Traditional and fancy working/using straight knives and folders of his design, to customer specs and in standard patterns. **Patterns:** Hunters, and slip-joint folders. **Technical:** Grinds 440V and 440C. Offers engraving. **Prices:** $200 to $500; some to $1,000. **Remarks:** Part-time maker; first knife sold in 1988. doing business as Holland Knives. **Mark:** First and last name, city, state.

**HOLLAR, BOB,** 701 2nd Ave. SW, Great Falls, MT 59404, Phone: 406-268-8252, goshawk@imt.net
**Specialties:** Working/using straight knives and folders of his design and to customer specs; period pieces. **Patterns:** Fighters, hunters, liners and back lock folders. **Technical:** Forges 52100, 5160, 15N20 and 1084 (Damascus)*. **Prices:** $225 to $650; some to $1,500. **Remarks:** Full-time maker. Doing business as Goshawk Knives. **Mark:** Goshawk stamped. **Other:** *Burled woods, stag, ivory; all stabilized material for handles.

**HOLLOWAY, PAUL,** 714 Burksdale Rd., Norfolk, VA 23518, Phone: 804-588-7071
**Specialties:** Working straight knives and folders to customer specs. **Patterns:** Lockers and slip-joints; fighters and boots; fishing and push knives, from swords to miniatures. **Technical:** Grinds A2, D2, 154CM, 440C and ATS-34. **Prices:** $125 to $400; some to $1,200. **Remarks:** Part-time maker; first knife sold in 1981. **Mark:** Last name, or last name and city in logo.

**HOLMES, ROBERT,** 1431 S Eugene St., Baton Rouge, LA 70808-1043, Phone: 504-291-4864
**Specialties:** Using straight knives and folders of his design or to customer specs. **Patterns:** Bowies, utility hunters, camp knives, skinners, slip-joint and lock-back folders. **Technical:** Forges 1065, 1095 and L6. Makes his own Damascus and cable Damascus. Offers clay tempering. **Prices:** $150 to $1,500. **Remarks:** Part-time maker; first knife sold in 1988. **Mark:** DOC HOLMES, or anvil logo with last initial inside.

**HORN, DES,** PO Box 322, NEWLANDS, 7700 Cape Town, SOUTH AFRICA, Phone: 27283161795, Fax: 27283161795, deshorn@usa.net
**Specialties:** Folding knives. **Patterns:** Ball release side lock mechanism and interframe automatics. **Technical:** Prefers working in totally stainless materials. **Prices:** $600 to $3,000. **Remarks:** Full-time maker. Enjoys working in gold, titanium, meteorite, pearl and mammoth. **Mark:** Des Horn.

**HORN, JESS,** 2526 Lansdown Rd., Eugene, OR 97404, Phone: 541-463-1510, jandahorn@earthlink.net
**Specialties:** Investor-class working folders; period pieces; collectibles. **Patterns:** High-tech design and finish in folders; liner locks, traditional slip-joints and featherweight models. **Technical:** Grinds ATS-34, 154CM. **Prices:** Start at $1,000. **Remarks:** Full-time maker; first knife sold in 1968. **Mark:** Full name or last name.

**HORNE, GRACE,** 182 Crimicar Ln., Sheffield Britian, UNITED KINGDOM S10 4EJ, grace.horne@student.shu.ac.uk Web: www.gracehorne.co.uk
**Specialties:** Knives of own design including kitchen and utility knives for people with reduced hand use. **Technical:** Working at Sheffield Hallam University researching innovative, contemporary Damascus steels using non-traditional methods of manufacture. **Remarks:** Spare-time maker/full-time researcher. **Mark:** 'gH' and 'Sheffield'.

**HORTON, SCOT,** PO Box 451, Buhl, ID 83316, Phone: 208-543-4222
**Specialties:** Traditional working stiff knives and folders. **Patterns:** Hunters, skinners, utility and show knives. **Technical:** Grinds ATS-34. Uses stag, abalone and exotic woods. **Prices:** $200 to $2,500. **Remarks:** First knife sold in 1990. **Mark:** Full name in arch underlined with arrow, city, state.

**HOSSOM, JERRY,** 3585 Schilling Ridge, Duluth, GA 30096, Phone: 770-449-7809, knives@attbi.com Web: www.hossom.com
**Specialties:** Working straight knives of his own design. **Patterns:** Fighters, combat knives, modern Bowies and daggers, modern swords, concealment knives for military and LE uses. **Technical:** Grinds 154CM, S30V, CPM-3V and stainless Damascus. Uses natural and synthetic handle materials. **Prices:** $250-1500, some higher. **Remarks:** Full-time maker since 1997. First knife sold in 1983. **Mark:** First initial and last name, includes city and state since 2002.

**HOUSE, LAWRENCE,** 932 Eastview Dr., Canyon Lake, TX 78133, Phone: 830-899-6932

**HOUSE, GARY,** 2851 Pierce Rd., Ephrata, WA 98823, Phone: 509-754-3272, spindry101@aol.com
**Specialties:** Mosaic Damascus bar stock. Forged blades. **Patterns:** Unlimited, SW Indian designs, geometric patterns, using 1084, 15N20 and some nickel. Bowies, hunters and daggers.**Technical:** Forge mosaic Damascus.**Prices:** $500 & up. **Remarks:** Some of the finest and most unique patterns available. ABS journeyman smith. **Marks:** Initials GTH, G hanging T, H

**HOWARD, DURVYN M.,** 4220 McLain St. S., Hokes Bluff, AL 35903, Phone: 256-492-5720
**Specialties:** Collectible upscale folders; one of kinds, gentlemen's folders. Multiple patents. **Patterns:** Conceptual designs; each unique and different. **Technical:** Uses natural and exotic materials and precious metals. **Prices:** $5,000 to $25,000. **Remarks:** Full-time maker; by commission or available work. **Mark:** Howard: new for 2000; Howard in Garamond Narrow "etched". **Other:** Work displayed at select shows, K.G. Show etc.

**HOWE, TORI,** 13000 E Stampede Rd., Athol, ID 83801

**HOWELL, LEN,** 550 Lee Rd. 169, Opelika, AL 36804, Phone: 334-749-1942
**Specialties:** Traditional and working knives of his design and to customer specs. **Patterns:** Buckskinner, hunters and utility/camp knives. **Technical:** Forges cable Damascus, 1085 and 5160; makes own Damascus. **Mark:** Engraved last name.

**HOWELL, ROBERT L.,** Box 1617, Kilgore, TX 75663, Phone: 903-986-4364
**Specialties:** Straight knives and folders of his design. **Patterns:** Hunters and locking folders. **Technical:** Grinds D2 and ATS-34; forges and grinds Damascus. **Prices:** $75 to $200; some to $2,500. **Remarks:** Part-time maker; first knife sold in 1978. Doing business as Howell Knives. **Mark:** Last name.

**HOWELL, TED,** 1294 Wilson Rd., Wetumpka, AL 36092, Phone: 205-569-2281, Fax: 205-569-1764
**Specialties:** Working/using straight knives and folders of his design; period pieces. **Patterns:** Bowies, fighters, hunters. **Technical:** Forges 5160, 1085 and cable. Offers light engraving and scrimshaw; filework. **Prices:** $75 to $250; some to $450. **Remarks:** Part-time maker; first knife sold in 1991. Doing business as Howell Co. **Mark:** Last name, Slapout AL.

**HOWELL, JASON G.,** 213 Buffalo Trl., Lake Jackson, TX 77566, Phone: 979-297-9454
**Specialties:** Fixed blades and liner lock folders. Makes own Damascus. **Patterns:** Clip and drop point. **Prices:** $150 to $750. **Remarks:** Likes making Mosaic Damascus out of the ordinary stuff. Member of TX Knifemakers and Collectors Association; apprentice in ABS; working towards Journeyman Stamp. **Mark:** Name, city, state.

**HOWSER, JOHN C.,** 54 Bell Ln., Frankfort, KY 40601, Phone: 502-875-3678
**Specialties:** Slip joint folders (old patterns-multi blades). **Patterns:** traditional slip joint folders, lockbacks, hunters and fillet knives. **Technical:** ATS-34, S-30V, drop 440-V standard steel, will use D-2, 440V-hand rubbed satin finish natural materials. **Prices:** $100 to $400; some to $500. **Remarks:** Full-time maker; first knife sold in 1974. **Mark:** Signature or stamp.

**HOY, KEN,** 54744 Pinchot Dr., North Fork, CA 93643, Phone: 209-877-7805

**HRISOULAS, JIM,** 330 S. Decatur Ave., Suite 109, Las Vegas, NV 89107, Phone: 702-566-8551
**Specialties:** Working straight knives; period pieces. **Patterns:** Swords, daggers and sgian dubhs. **Technical:** Double-edged differential heat treating. **Prices:** $85 to $175; some to $600 and higher. **Remarks:** Full-time maker; first knife sold in 1973. Author of *The Complete Bladesmith*, *The Pattern Welded Blade* and *The Master Bladesmith*. Doing business as Salamander Armory. **Mark:** 8R logo and sword and salamander.

**HUCKABEE, DALE,** 254 Hwy 260, Maylene, AL 35114, Phone: 205-664-2544, dalehuckabee@hotmail.com
**Specialties:** Fixed blade hunter and Bowies of his design. **Technical:** Steel used: 5160, 1095, 1084 and some Damascus. **Prices:** Starting at $150 and up, depending on materials used. **Remarks:** Hand forged. JourneymanSmith. **Mark:** Stamped Huckabee J.S. **Other:** Part-time maker.

**HUCKS, JERRY,** KNIVES BY HUCKS, 1807 Perch Road, Moncks Corner, SC 29461, Phone: 843-761-6481, kinvesbyhucks@dycon.com
**Specialties:** Oyster knives, hunters, bowies, fillets, Bowies being makers favorite with stag & ivory. **Patterns:** Yours and mine. **Technical:** ATS-34, BG-42, makers cable Damascus also 1084 & 15N20. **Prices:** $95.00 and up. **Remarks:** Full-time maker, retired as a machinist in 1990. **Mark:** Robin Hood hat with monck corner in oval. **Other:** Making folders 4" closed, titanium liners anodized) 2-56 torx screws.

**HUDSON, ROB,** 340 Roush Rd., Northumberland, PA 17857, Phone: 570-473-9588, robscustknives@aol.com
**Specialties:** Custom hunters and bowies **Technical:** Grinds ATS-34, stainless, Damascus hollow grinds or flat. Filework finger groves. Engraving and scrimshaw available. (Stainless). **Prices:** $300 to $1,200. **Remarks:** Full-time maker. Does business as Rob's Custom Knives. **Mark:** Capital R, Capital H in script.

**HUDSON, ANTHONY B.,** PO Box 368, Amanda, OH 43102, Phone: 740-969-4200, jjahudson@wmconnect.com
**Specialties:** Hunting knives, fighters, survival. **Remarks:** ABS Journeyman Smith. **Mark:** A.B. HUDSON.

**HUDSON, ROBERT,** 3802 Black Cricket Ct., Humble, TX 77396, Phone: 713-454-7207
**Specialties:** Working straight knives of his design. **Patterns:** Bowies, hunters, skinners, fighters and utility knives. **Technical:** Grinds D2, 440C, 154CM and commercial Damascus. **Prices:** $85 to $350; some to $1,500. **Remarks:** Part-time maker; first knife sold in 1980. **Mark:** Full name, handmade, city and state.

**HUDSON, C. ROBBIN,** 22280 Frazier Rd., Rock Hall, MD 21661, Phone: 410-639-7273
**Specialties:** High-art working knives. **Patterns:** Hunters, Bowies, fighters and kitchen knives. **Technical:** Forges W2, nickel steel, pure nickel steel, composite and mosaic Damascus; makes knives one-at-a-time. **Prices:** 500 to $1,200; some to $5,000. **Remarks:** Full-time maker; first knife sold in 1970. **Mark:** Last name and MS.

**HUGHES, ED,** 280 1/2 Holly Lane, Grand Junction, CO 81503, Phone: 970-243-8547, edhughes26@msn.com
**Specialties:** Working and art folders. **Patterns:** Buys Damascus. **Technical:** Grinds stainless steels. Engraves. **Prices:** $300 and up. **Remarks:** Full-time maker; first knife sold in 1978. **Mark:** Name or initials.

**HUGHES, LAWRENCE,** 207 W. Crestway, Plainview, TX 79072, Phone: 806-293-5406
**Specialties:** Working and display knives. **Patterns:** Bowies, daggers, hunters, buckskinners. **Technical:** Grinds D2, 440C and 154CM. **Prices:** $125 to $300; some to $2,000. **Remarks:** Full-time maker; first knife sold in 1979. **Mark:** Name with buffalo skull in center.

**HUGHES, DARYLE,** 10979 Leonard, Nunica, MI 49448, Phone: 616-837-6623
**Specialties:** Working knives. **Patterns:** Buckskinners, hunters, camp knives, kitchen and fishing knives. **Technical:** Forges and grinds W2, O1 and D2. **Prices:** $40 to $100; some to $400. **Remarks:** Part-time maker; first knife sold in 1979. **Mark:** Name and city in logo.

**HUGHES, DAN,** 13743 Persimmon Blvd., West Palm Beach, FL 33411
**Specialties:** Working straight knives to customer specs. **Patterns:** Hunters fighters, fillet knives. **Technical:** Grinds 440C and ATS-34. **Prices:** $55 t $175; some to $300. **Remarks:** Part-time maker; first knife sold in 198 **Mark:** Initials.

**HUGHES, BILL,** 110 Royale Dr., Texarkana, TX 75503, Phone: 903-838-0134, chughes@tc.cc.tx.us

**HULETT, STEVE,** 115 Yellowstone Ave., West Yellowstone, MT 59758, Phone: 406-646-4116, Web: www.seldomseenknives.com
**Specialties:** Classic, working/using knives, straight knives, folders. Yo design, custom specs. **Patterns:** Utility/camp knives, hunters, and liner lo folders. **Technical:** Grinds 440C stainless steel, O1 Carbon, 1095. Shop retail and knife shop—people watch their knives being made. We do ever thing in house—"all but smelt the ore, or tan the hide." **Prices:** $125 to $7,00 **Remarks:** Full-time maker; first knife sold in 1994. **Mark:** Seldom seen knive West Yellowstone Montana.

**HULL, MICHAEL J.,** 1330 Hermits Circle, Cottonwood, AZ 86326, Phone: 928-634-2871, mjwhull@earthlink.net
**Specialties:** Period pieces and working knives. **Patterns:** Hunters, fighter Bowies, camp and Mediterranean knives, etc. **Technical:** Grinds 440C, AT 34 and BG42 and S30V. **Prices:** $125 to $750; some to $1,000. **Remark** Full-time maker; first knife sold in 1983. **Mark:** Name, city, state.

**HULSEY, HOYT,** 379 Shiloh, Attalla, AL 35954, Phone: 256-538-6765
**Specialties:** Traditional working straight knives and folders of his design. **Pa terns:** Hunters and utility/camp knives. **Technical:** Grinds 440C, ATS-34, C and A2. **Prices:** $75 to $250. **Remarks:** Part-time maker; first knife sold 1989. **Mark:** Hoyt Hulsey Attalla AL.

**HUME, DON,** , 2731 Tramway Cir. NE, Albuquerque, NM 87122, Phon 505-796-9451

**HUMENICK, ROY,** PO Box 55, Rescue, CA 95672
**Specialties:** Multiblade folders. **Patterns:** Original folder and fixed bla designs, also traditional patterns. **Technical:** Grinds premium steels a Damascus. **Prices:** $350 and up; some to $1,500. **Remarks:** First knife sc in 1984. **Mark:** Last name in ARC.

**HUMPHREYS, JOEL,** 3260 Palmer Rd., Bowling Green, FL 33834-980 Phone: 863-773-0439
**Specialties:** Traditional working/using straight knives and folders of h design and in standard patterns. **Patterns:** Hunters, folders and utility/car knives. **Technical:** Grinds ATS-34, D2, 440C. All knives have tapered tan mitered bolster/handle joints, handles of horn or bone fitted sheaths. **Price** $135 to $225; some to $350. **Remarks:** Part-time maker; first knife sold 1990. Doing business as Sovereign Knives. **Mark:** First name or "H" pierc by arrow.

**HUNT, MAURICE,** 10510 N CR 650 E, Winter: 2925 Argyle Rd. Venic FL 34293, Brownsburg, IN 46112, Phone: 317-892-2982/Winter: 941-493-4027, mdhuntknives@juno.com
**Patterns:** Bowies, hunters, fighters. **Prices:** $200 to $800. **Remarks:** Pa time maker. **Other:** JourneymanSmith.

**HUNTER, HYRUM,** 285 N. 300 W, PO Box 179, Aurora, UT 84620, Phone: 435-529-7244
**Specialties:** Working straight knives of his design or to customer specs. **P terns:** Drop and clip, fighters dagger, some folders. **Technical:** Forged fr two piece Damascus. **Prices:** Prices are adjusted according to size, compl ity and material used. **Remarks:** Will consider any design you have. Part-ti maker; first knife sold in 1990. **Mark:** Initials encircled with first initial and l name and city, then state. Some patterns are numbered.

**HUNTER, RICHARD D.,** 7230 NW 200th Ter., Alachua, FL 32615, Phone: 386-462-3150
**Specialties:** Traditional working/using knives of his design or customer s gestions; filework. **Patterns:** Folders of various types, Bowies, hunters, d gers. **Technical:** Traditional blacksmith; hand forges high-carbon steel (51 1084, 52100) and makes own Damascus; grinds 440C and ATS-34. **Pric** $200 and up. **Remarks:** Part-time maker; first knife sold in 1992. **Mark:** L name in capital letters.

**HURST, JEFF,** PO Box 247, Rutledge, TN 37861, Phone: 865-828-572 jhurst@esper.com
**Specialties:** Working straight knives and folders of his design. **Patter** Tomahawks, hunters, boots, folders and fighters. **Technical:** Forges W2, and his own Damascus. Makes mokume. **Prices:** $175 to $350; some $500. **Remarks:** Full-time maker; first knife sold in 1984. Doing business Buzzard's Knob Forge. **Mark:** Last name; partnered knives are marked Newman L. Smith, handle artisan, and SH in script.

**HURST, COLE,** 1583 Tedford, E. Wenatchee, WA 98802, Phone: 509-884-9206
**Specialties:** Fantasy, high-art and traditional straight knives. **Patterns:** Bowies, daggers and hunters. **Technical:** Blades are made of stone; handles are made of stone, wood or ivory and embellished with fancy woods, ivory or antlers. **Prices:** $100 to $300; some to $2,000. **Remarks:** Spare-time maker; first knife sold in 1985. **Mark:** Name and year.

**HURT, WILLIAM R.,** 9222 Oak Tree Cir., Frederick, MD 21701, Phone: 301-898-7143
**Specialties:** Traditional and working/using straight knives. **Patterns:** Bowies, hunters, fighters and utility knives. **Technical:** Forges 5160, O1 and O6; makes own Damascus. Offers silver wire inlay. **Prices:** $200 to $600; some higher. **Remarks:** Full-time maker; first knife sold in 1989. **Mark:** First and middle initials, last name.

**HUSIAK, MYRON,** PO Box 238, Altona 3018, Victoria, AUSTRALIA, Phone: 03-315-6752
**Specialties:** Straight knives and folders of his design or to customer specs. **Patterns:** Hunters, fighters, lock-back folders, skinners and boots. **Technical:** forges and grinds his own Damascus, 440C and ATS-34. **Prices:** $200 to $900. **Remarks:** Part-time maker; first knife sold in 1974. **Mark:** First initial, last name in logo and serial number.

**HUTCHESON, JOHN,** SURSUM KNIFE WORKS, 1237 Brown's Ferry Rd., Chattanooga, TN 37419, Phone: 423-667-6193, sursum5071@aol.com Web: www.sursumknife.com
**Specialties:** Straight working knives, hunters. **Patterns:** Customer designs, hunting, speciality working knives. **Technical:** Grinds D2, S7, 01 and 5160, ATS-34 on request. **Prices:** $100 to $300; some to $600. **Remarks:** First knife sold 1985, also produces a mid-tech line. **Mark:** Family crest boar's head over 3 arrows. **Other:** Doing business as Sursum Knife Works.

**HYDE, JIMMY,** 5094 Stagecoach Rd., Ellenwood, GA 30049, Phone: 404-968-1951, Fax: 404-209-1741
**Specialties:** Working straight knives of any design; period pieces. **Patterns:** Bowies, hunters and utility knives. **Technical:** Grinds 440C; forges 5160, 1095 and O1. Makes his own Damascus and cable Damascus. **Prices:** $150 to $600. **Remarks:** Part-time maker; first knife sold in 1978. **Mark:** First initial, last name.

**HYTOVICK, JOE"HY",** 14872 SW 111th St., Dunnellon, FL 34432, Phone: 800-749-5339, Fax: 352-489-3732, hyclassknives@aol.com
**Specialties:** Straight, Folder and Miniature. **Technical:** Blades from Wootz, Damascus and Alloy steel. **Prices:** To $5,000. **Mark:** HY.

# I

**IKOMA, FLAVIO YUJI, R. MANOEL R. TEIXEIRA, 108,** 108, Centro Presidente Prudente, SP-19031-220, BRAZIL, Phone: 0182-22-0115, ikomaknives@hotmail.com
**Specialties:** Straight knives and folders of all designs. **Patterns:** Fighters, hunters, Bowies, swords, folders, skinners, utility and defense knives. **Technical:** Grinds and forges D6, 440C, high-carbon steels and Damascus. **Prices:** $60 to $350; some to $3,300. **Remarks:** Full-time maker; first knife sold in 1991. All stainless steel blades are ultra sub-zero quenched. **Mark:** Ikoma Knives beside eagle.

**IMBODEN II, HOWARD L.,** 620 Deauville Dr., Dayton, OH 45429, Phone: 513-439-1536
**Specialties:** One-of-a-kind hunting, flint, steel and art knives. **Technical:** Forges and grinds stainless, high-carbon and Damascus. Uses obsidian, cast sterling silver, 14K and 18K gold guards. Carves ivory animals and more. **Prices:** $65 to $25,000. **Remarks:** Full-time maker; first knife sold in 1986. Doing business as Hill Originals. **Mark:** First and last initials, II.

**IMEL, BILLY MACE,** 1616 Bundy Ave., New Castle, IN 47362, Phone: 765-529-1651
**Specialties:** High-art working knives, period pieces and personal cutlery. **Patterns:** Daggers, fighters, hunters; locking folders and slip-joints with interframes. **Technical:** Grinds D2, 440C and 154CM. **Prices:** $300 to $2,000; some to $6,000. **Remarks:** Part-time maker; first knife sold in 1973. **Mark:** Name in monogram.

**IRIE, MICHAEL L.,** MIKE IRIE HANDCRAFT, 1606 Auburn Dr., Colorado Springs, CO 80909, Phone: 719-572-5330, mikeirie@aol.com
**Specialties:** Working fixed blade knives and handcrafted blades for the do-it-yourselfer. **Patterns:** Twenty standard designs along with custom. **Technical:** Blades are ATS-34, BG-43, 440C with some outside Damascus. **Prices:** Fixed blades $95 and up, blade work $45 and up. **Remarks:** Formerly dba Wood, Irie and Co. with Barry Wood. Full-time maker since 1991. **Mark:** Name.

**IRON WOLF FORGE, SEE NELSON, KEN**

**ISAO, OHBUCHI,** , 702-1 Nouso Yame-City, Fukuoka, JAPAN, Phone: 0943-23-4439, www.5d.biglobe.ne.jp/~ohisao/

**ISGRO, JEFFERY,** 1516 First St., West Babylon, NY 11704, Phone: 631-587-7516
**Specialties:** File work, glass beading, kydex, leather. **Patterns:** Tactical use knives, skinners, capers, Bowies, camp, hunters. **Technical:** ATS-34, 440C and D2. **Price:** $120 to $600. **Remarks:** Part-time maker. **Mark:** First name, last name, Long Island, NY.

**ISHIHARA, HANK,** 86-18 Motomachi, Sakura City, Chiba Pref., JAPAN, Phone: 043-485-3208, Fax: 043-485-3208
**Specialties:** Fantasy working straight knives and folders of his design. **Patterns:** Boots, Bowies, daggers, fighters, hunters, fishing, locking folders and utility camp knives. **Technical:** Grinds ATS-34, 440C, D2, 440V, CV-134, COS25 and Damascus. Engraves. **Prices:** $250 to $1,000; some to $10,000. **Remarks:** Full-time maker; first knife sold in 1987. **Mark:** HANK.

# J

**JACKS, JIM,** 344 S. Hollenbeck Ave., Covina, CA 91723-2513, Phone: 626-331-5665
**Specialties:** Working straight knives in standard patterns. **Patterns:** Bowies, hunters, fighters, fishing and camp knives, miniatures. **Technical:** Grinds Stellite 6K, 440C and ATS-34. **Prices:** Start at $100. **Remarks:** Spare-time maker; first knife sold in 1980. **Mark:** Initials in diamond logo.

**JACKSON, DAVID,** 214 Oleander Ave., Lemoore, CA 93245, Phone: 559-925-8547, jnbcrea@lemoorenet.com
**Specialties:** Forged steel. **Patterns:** Hunters, camp knives, Bowies. **Prices:** $150 and up. **Mark:** G.D. Jackson - Maker - Lemoore CA.

**JACKSON, JIM,** 7 Donnington Close, Chapel Row Bucklebury RG7 6PU, ENGLAND, Phone: 011-89-712743, Fax: 011-89-710495, jlandsejackson@aol.com
**Specialties:** Large Bowies, concentrating on form and balance; collector quality Damascus daggers. **Patterns:** With fancy filework and engraving available. **Technical:** Forges O1, 5160 and CS70 and 15N20 Damascus. **Prices:** From $1,000. **Remarks:** Part-time maker. **Mark:** Jackson England with in a circle M.S. **Other:** All knives come with a custom tooled leather swivel sheath or exotic materials.

**JACKSON, CHARLTON R.,** 6811 Leyland Dr., San Antonio, TX 78239, Phone: 210-601-5112

**JAKSIK JR., MICHAEL,** 427 Marschall Creek Rd., Fredericksburg, TX 78624, Phone: 830-997-1119
**Mark:** MJ or M. Jaksik.

**JANIGA, MATTHEW A.,** 2090 Church Rd., Hummelstown, PA 17036-9796, Phone: 717-533-5916
**Specialties:** Period pieces, swords, daggers. **Patterns:** Daggers, fighters and swords. **Technical:** Forges and Damascus. Does own heat treating. Forges own pattern-welded steel. **Prices:** $100 to $1,000; some to $5,000. **Remarks:** Spare-time maker; first knife sold in 1991. **Mark:** Interwoven initials.

**JARVIS, PAUL M.,** 30 Chalk St., Cambridge, MA 02139, Phone: 617-547-4355 or 617-666-9090
**Specialties:** High-art knives and period pieces of his design. **Patterns:** Japanese and Mid-Eastern knives. **Technical:** Grinds Myer Damascus, ATS-34, D2 and O1. Specializes in height-relief Japanese-style carving. Works with silver, gold and gems. **Prices:** $200 to $17,000. **Remarks:** Part-time maker; first knife sold in 1978.

**JEAN, GERRY,** 25B Cliffside Dr., Manchester, CT 06040, Phone: 860-649-6449
**Specialties:** Historic replicas. **Patterns:** Survival and camp knives. **Technical:** Grinds A2, 440C and 154CM. Handle slabs applied in unique tongue-and-groove method. **Prices:** $125 to $250; some to $1,000. **Remarks:** Spare-time maker; first knife sold in 1973. **Mark:** Initials and serial number.

**JEFFRIES, ROBERT W.,** Route 2, Box 227, Red House, WV 25168, Phone: 304-586-9780
**Specialties:** Straight knives and folders. **Patterns:** Hunters, skinners and folders. **Technical:** Uses 440C, ATS-34; makes his own Damascus. **Prices:** Moderate. **Remarks:** Part-time maker; first knife sold in 1988. **Mark:** NA.

**JENSEN, JOHN LEWIS,** dba MAGNUS DESIGN STUDIO, PO Box 60547, Pasadena, CA 91116, Phone: 626-449-1148, Fax: 626-449-1148, john@jensenknives.com Web: www.jensenknives.com
**Specialties:** Designer and fabricator of modern, unique, elegant, innovative, original, one-of-a-kind, hand crafted, custom ornamental edged weaponry. Combines skill, precision, distinction and the finest materials, geared toward the discriminating art collector. **Patterns:** Folding knives and fixed blades,

daggers, fighters and swords. **Technical:** High embellishment, BFA 96 Rhode Island School of Design: Jewelry and metalsmithing. Grinds 440C, ATS-34, Damascus. Works with custom made Damascus to his specs. Uses gold, silver, gemstones, pearl, titanium, fossil mastodon and walrus ivories. Carving, file work, soldering, deep etches Damascus, engraving, layers, bevels, blood grooves Also forges his own Damascus. **Prices:** Start at $3,500. **Remarks:** Available on a first come basis and via commission based on his designs Knifemakers guild voting member and ABS apprenticesmith and member of the Society of North American Goldsmiths. **Mark:** Maltese cross/butterfly shield.

**JENSEN JR., CARL A.,** 1130 Colfax St., Blair, NE 68008, Phone: 402-426-3353
**Specialties:** Working knives of his design; some customer designs. **Patterns:** Hunters, fighters, boots and Bowies. **Technical:** Grinds A2, D2, O1, 440C, 5160 and ATS-34; recycles old files, leaf springs; heat-treats. **Prices:** $35 to $350. **Remarks:** Part-time maker; first knife sold in 1980. **Mark:** Stamp "BEAR'S CUTLERY" or etch of letters "BEAR" forming silhouette of a Bear.

**JERNIGAN, STEVE,** 3082 Tunnel Rd., Milton, FL 32571, Phone: 850-994-0802, Fax: 850-994-0802, jernigankives@mchsi.com
**Specialties:** Investor-class folders and various theme pieces. **Patterns:** Array of models and sizes in side plate locking interframes and conventional liner construction. **Technical:** Grinds ATS-34, CPM-T-440V and Damascus. Inlays mokume (and minerals) in blades and sculpts marble cases. **Prices:** $650 to $1,800; some to $6,000. **Remarks:** Full-time maker; first knife sold in 1982. Takes orders for folders only. **Mark:** Last name.

**JOBIN, JACQUES,** 46 St. Dominique, Levis Quebec, CANADA G6V 2M7, Phone: 418-833-0283, Fax: 418-833-8378
**Specialties:** Fancy and working straight knives and folders; miniatures. **Patterns:** Minis, fantasy knives, fighters and some hunters. **Technical:** ATS-34, some Damascus and titanium. Likes native snake wood. Heat-treats. **Prices:** Start at $250. **Remarks:** Full-time maker; first knife sold in 1986. **Mark:** Signature on blade.

**JOEHNK, BERND,** Posadowskystrasse 22, 24148 Kiel, GERMANY, Phone: 0431-7297705, Fax: 0431-7297705
**Specialties:** One-of-a-kind fancy/embellished and traditional straight knives of his design and from customer drawing. **Patterns:** Daggers, fighters, hunters and letter openers. **Technical:** Grinds and file 440C, ATS-34, powder metal orgical, commercial Damascus and various stainless and corrosion-resistant steels. **Prices:** Upscale. **Remarks:** Likes filework. Leather sheaths. Offers engraving. Part-time maker; first knife sold in1990. **Other:** Doing business as metal design kiel. All knives made by hand. **Mark:** From 2005 full name and city, with certificate.

**JOHANNING CUSTOM KNIVES, TOM,** 1735 Apex Rd., Sarasota, FL 34240 9386, Phone: 941-371-2104, Fax: 941-378-9427, Web: www.survivalknives.com
**Specialties:** Survival knives. **Prices:** $375 to $775.

**JOHANSSON, ANDERS,** Konstvartarevagen 9, S-772 40 Grangesberg, SWEDEN, Phone: 46 240 23204, Fax: +46 21 358778, www.scrimart.u.se
**Specialties:** Scandinavian traditional and modern straight knives. **Patterns:** Hunters, fighters and fantasy knives. **Technical:** Grinds stainless steel and makes own Damascus. Prefers water buffalo and mammoth for handle material. **Prices:** Start at $100. **Remarks:** Spare-time maker; first knife sold in 1994. Works together with scrimshander Viveca Sahlin. **Mark:** Stylized initials.

**JOHNS, ROB,** 1423 S. Second, Enid, OK 73701, Phone: 405-242-2707
**Specialties:** Classic and fantasy straight knives of his design or to customer specs; fighters for use at Medieval fairs. **Patterns:** Bowies, daggers and swords. **Technical:** Forges and grinds 440C, D2 and 5160. Handles of nylon, walnut or wire-wrap. **Prices:** $150 to $350; some to $2,500. **Remarks:** Full-time maker; first knife sold in 1980. **Mark:** Medieval Customs, initials.

**JOHNSON, RUFFIN,** 215 LaFonda Dr., Houston, TX 77060, Phone: 281-448-4407
**Specialties:** Working straight knives and folders. **Patterns:** Hunters, fighters and locking folders. **Technical:** Grinds 440C and 154CM; hidden tangs and fancy handles. **Prices:** $200 to $400; some to $1,095. **Remarks:** Full-time maker; first knife sold in 1972. **Mark:** Wolf head logo and signature.

**JOHNSON, MIKE,** 38200 Main Rd, Orient, NY 11957, Phone: 631-323-3509, mjohnsoncustomknives@hotmail.com
**Specialties:** Large bowie knives and cutters, fighters and working knives to customer specs. **Technical:** Forges 5160, O1. **Prices:** $325 to $1,200. **Remarks:** Full-time bladesmith. **Mark:** Johnson.

**JOHNSON, R.B.,** Box 11, Clearwater, MN 55320, Phone: 320-558-6128
**Specialties:** Liner Locks with Titanium - Mosaic Damascus. **Patterns:** Liner lock folders, skeleton hunters, frontier Bowies. **Technical:** Damascus, Mosaic Damascus, A-2, O-1, 1095. **Prices:** $200 and up. **Remarks:** Full-time maker since 1973. Not accepting orders. **Mark:** R B Johnson (signature).

**JOHNSON, DURRELL CARMON,** PO Box 594, Sparr, FL 32192, Phone: 352-622-5498
**Specialties:** Old-fashioned working straight knives and folders of his design or to customer specs. **Patterns:** Bowies, hunters, fighters, daggers, camp knives and Damascus miniatures. **Technical:** Forges 5160, his own Damascus, W2, wrought iron, nickel and horseshoe rasps. Offers filework. **Prices:** $100 to $2,000. **Remarks:** Full-time maker and blacksmith; first knife sold in 1957. **Mark:** Middle name.

**JOHNSON, GORDEN W.,** 5426 Sweetbriar, Houston, TX 77017, Phone: 713-645-8990
**Specialties:** Working knives and period pieces. **Patterns:** Hunters, boots and Bowies. **Technical:** Flat-grinds 440C; most knives have narrow tang. **Prices:** $90 to $450. **Remarks:** Full-time maker; first knife sold in 1974. **Mark:** Name, city, state.

**JOHNSON, STEVEN R.,** 202 E. 200 N., PO Box 5, Manti, UT 84642, Phone: 435-835-7941, srj@mail.manti.com Web: www.srjknives.com
**Specialties:** Investor-class working knives. **Patterns:** Hunters, fighters, boots and folders of locking liner variety. **Technical:** Grinds ATS-34, 440-C, RWL-34. **Prices:** $500 to $5,000. **Remarks:** Full-time maker; first knife sold in 197[illegible] **Mark:** Name, city, state and optional signature mark.

**JOHNSON, RANDY,** 2575 E. Canal Dr., Turlock, CA 95380, Phone: 209-632-5401
**Specialties:** Folders. **Patterns:** Locking folders. **Technical:** Grinds Damascus. **Prices:** $200 to $400. **Remarks:** Spare-time maker; first knife sold in 1989. Doing business as Puedo Knifeworks. **Mark:** PUEDO.

**JOHNSON, RYAN M.,** 7320 Foster Hixson Cemetery Rd., Hixson, TN 37343, Phone: 615-842-9323
**Specialties:** Working and using straight knives of his design and to customer specs. **Patterns:** Bowies, hunters and utility/camp knives. **Technical:** Forges 5160, Damascus and files. Prices; $70 to $400; some to $800. **Remarks:** Full-time maker; first knife sold in 1986. **Mark:** Sledge-hammer with halo.

**JOHNSON, C.E. GENE,** 5648 Redwood Ave., Portage, IN 46368, Phone: 219-762-5461
**Specialties:** Lock-back folders and springers of his design or to customer specs. **Patterns:** Hunters, Bowies, survival lock-back folders. **Technical:** Grinds D2, 440C, A18, O1, Damascus; likes filework. **Prices:** $100 to $2,000. **Remarks:** Full-time maker; first knife sold in 1975. **Mark:** "Gene" city, state and serial number.

**JOHNSON, RICHARD,** W165 N10196 Wagon Trail, Germantown, WI 53022, Phone: 262-251-5772, rlj@execpc.com Web: http://www.execpc.com/~rlj/index.html
**Specialties:** Custom knives and knife repair.

**JOHNSON, JOHN R.,** 5535 Bob Smith Ave., Plant City, FL 33565, Phone: 813-986-4478, rottyjohn@msn.com
**Specialties:** Hand forged and stock removal. **Technical:** High tec. Folders. **Mark:** J.R. Johnson Plant City, FL.

**JOHNSON, DAVID A.,** 1791 Defeated Creek Rd., Pleasant Shade, TN 37145, Phone: 615-774-3596, artsmith@mwsi.net

**JOHNSTON, DR. ROBT.,** PO Box 9887, 1 Lomb Mem Dr., Rochester, NY 14623

**JOKERST, CHARLES,** 9312 Spaulding, Omaha, NE 68134, Phone: 402-571-2536
**Specialties:** Working knives in standard patterns. **Patterns:** Hunters, fighters and pocketknives. **Technical:** Grinds 440C, ATS-34. **Prices:** $90 to $1[illegible] **Remarks:** Spare-time maker; first knife sold in 1984. **Mark:** Early work marked RCJ; current work marked with last name and city.

**JONES, BOB,** 6219 Aztec NE, Albuquerque, NM 87110, Phone: 505-881-4472
**Specialties:** Fancy working knives of his design. **Patterns:** Mountain man/buckskinner-type knives; multi-blade folders, locking folders, and slip-joints. **Technical:** Grinds A2, O1, 1095 and commercial Damascus; uses no stainless steel. Engraves. **Prices:** $100 to $500; some to $1,500. **Remarks:** Full-time maker; first knife sold in 1960. **Mark:** Initials on fixed blades; initials encircled on folders.

**JONES, JOHN,** 12 Schooner Circuit, Manly West, QLD 4179, AUSTRALIA, Phone: 07-339-33390
**Specialties:** Straight knives and folders. **Patterns:** Working hunters, folders, lockbacks, fancy daggers and miniatures. **Technical:** Grinds 440C, O1 and L6. **Prices:** $180 to $1,200; some to $2,000. **Remarks:** Part-time maker; first knife sold in 1986. **Mark:** Jones.

**JONES, ENOCH,** 7278 Moss Ln., Warrenton, VA 20187, Phone: 540-341-0292

**Specialties:** Fancy working straight knives. **Patterns:** Hunters, fighters, boots and Bowies. **Technical:** Forges and grinds O1, W2, 440C and Damascus. **Prices:** $100 to $350; some to $1,000. **Remarks:** Part-time maker; first knife sold in 1982. **Mark:** First name.

**JONES, CURTIS J.,** 39909 176th St. E., Palmdale, CA 93591, Phone: 805-264-2753

**Specialties:** Big Bowies, daggers, his own style of hunters. **Patterns:** Bowies, daggers, hunters, swords, boots and miniatures. **Technical:** Grinds 440C, ATS-34 and D2. Fitted guards only; does not solder. Heat-treats. Custom sheaths-hand-tooled and stitched. **Prices:** $125 to $1,500; some to $3,000. **Remarks:** Full-time maker; first knife sold in 1975. Mail orders accepted. **Mark:** Stylized initials on either side of three triangles interconnected.

**JONES, FRANKLIN (FRANK) W.,** 6030 Old Dominion Rd., Columbus, GA 31909, Phone: 706-563-6051, frankscuba@peoplepc.com

**Specialties:** Traditional/working/tactical/period straight knives of his or your design. **Patterns:** Hunters, skinners, utility/camp, Bowies, fighters, kitchen, neck knives. **Technical:** Forges using 5160, 01, 52100, 1084 1095 and Damascus. Also stock removal of stainless steel. **Prices:** $150 to $1,000. **Remarks:** Full-time, American Bladesmith Society Journeyman Smith. **Mark:** F.W. Jones, Columbus, GA.

**JONES, CHARLES ANTHONY,** 36 Broadgate Close, Bellaire Barnstable, No. Devon E31 4AL, ENGLAND, Phone: 0271-75328

**Specialties:** Working straight knives. **Patterns:** Simple hunters, fighters and utility knives. **Technical:** Grinds 440C, O1 and D2; filework offered. Engraves. **Prices:** $100 to $500; engraving higher. **Remarks:** Spare-time maker; first knife sold in 1987. **Mark:** Tony engraved.

**JONES, BARRY M. AND PHILLIP G.,** 221 North Ave., Danville, VA 24540, Phone: 804-793-5282

**Specialties:** Working and using straight knives and folders of their design and to customer specs; combat and self-defense knives. **Patterns:** Bowies, fighters, daggers, swords, hunters and liner lock folders. **Technical:** Grinds 440C, ATS-34 and D2; flat-grinds only. All blades hand polished. **Prices:** $100 to $1,000; some higher. **Remarks:** Part-time makers; first knife sold in 1989. **Mark:** Jones Knives, city, state.

**JONES, ROGER MUDBONE,** GREENMAN WORKSHOP, PO Box 367, Waverly, OH 45690, Phone: 740-947-5684, greenmanworkshop@yahoo.com

**Specialties:** Working in cutlery to suit working woodsman and fine collector. **Patterns:** Bowies, hunters, folders, hatchets in both period and modern style, scale miniatures a specialty. **Technical:** All cutlery hand forged to shape with traditional methods; multiple quench and draws, limited Damascus production and carves wildlife and historic themes in stag/antler/ivory, full line of functional and high art leather. All work sole authorship. **Prices:** $50 to $5,000 **Remarks:** Full-time maker/first knife sold in 1979. **Mark:** Stamped R. Jones and made or hand engraved sig. W/Bowie knife mark.

**JONES, JOHN A.,** 779 SW 131 HWY, Holden, MO 64040, Phone: 816-850-4318

**Specialties:** Working, using knives. Hunters, skinners and fighters. **Technical:** Grinds D2, 01, 440C, 1095. Prefers forging; creates own Damascus. File working on most blades. **Prices:** $50 to $500. **Remarks:** Part-time maker; first knife sold in 1996. Doing business as Old John Knives. **Mark:** OLD JOHN and serial number.

**JUSTICE, SHANE,** 425 South Brooks St., Sheridan, WY 82801, Phone: 307-673-4432

**Specialties:** Fixed blade working knives. **Patterns:** Hunters, skinners and camp knives. Other designs produced on a limited basis. **Technical:** Hand forged 5160 and 52100. **Remarks:** Part-time maker. Sole author. **Mark:** Cross over a Crescent.

# K

**K B S, KNIVES,** RSD 181, North Castlemaine, Vic 3450, AUSTRALIA, Phone: 0011 61 3 54 705864, Fax: 0011 61 3 54 706233

**Specialties:** Bowies, daggers and miniatures. **Patterns:** Art daggers, traditional Bowies, fancy folders and miniatures. **Technical:** Hollow or flat grind, most steels. **Prices:** $200 to $600+. **Remarks:** Full-time maker; first knife sold 1983. **Mark:** Initials and address in Southern Cross motif.

**KACZOR, TOM,** 375 Wharncliffe Rd. N., Upper London, Ont., CANADA N6G 1E4, Phone: 519-645-7640

**KADASAH, AHMED BIN,** PO Box 1969, Jeddah 21441, SAUDI ARABIA, Phone: ( 26) 913-0082

**KAGAWA, KOICHI,** 1556 Horiyamashita, Hatano-Shi, Kanagawa, JAPAN

**Specialties:** Fancy high-tech straight knives and folders to customer specs. **Patterns:** Hunters, locking folders and slip-joints. **Technical:** Uses 440C and ATS-34. **Prices:** $500 to $2,000; some to $20,000. **Remarks:** Part-time maker; first knife sold in 1986. **Mark:** First initial, last name-YOKOHAMA.

**KAIN, CHARLES,** KAIN DESIGNS, 38 South Main St, Indianapolis, IN 4627, Phone: 317-781-8556, Web: www.kaincustomknives.com

**Specialties:** Unique damascus Art Folders. **Patterns:** Any. **Technical:** Specialized & Patented Mechanisms. **Remarks:** Unique knife & knife mechanism desgin. **Mark:** Kain and Signet stamp for unique pieces.

**KAJIN, AL,** PO Box 1047, Forsyth, MT 59327, Phone: 406-346-2442, kajinknives@calemt.net

**Specialties:** Utility/working knives, kitchen cutlery; makes own Damascus steel. **Patterns:** All types except fantasy styles. **Technical:** Maker since 1989, ABS member since 1995. Does won differential heat treating on carbon steel and Damascus with double tempering. Cryogenic soaking on stainless with double tempering. **Prices:** Stock removal starting at $250. Forged blades/Damascus start at #300. Kitchen cutlery starts at $100. **Remarks:** Likes to work with customer on designs. **Mark:** Interlocked AK on forged blades. Stylized Kajin in outline of Montana on stock removal knives.

**KANDA, MICHIO,** 7-32-5 Shinzutumi-cho, Shunan-shi, Yamaguchi 7460033, JAPAN, Phone: 0834-62-1910, Fax: 011-81-83462-1910

**Specialties:** Fantasy knives of his design. **Patterns:** Animal knives. **Technical:** Grinds ATS-34. **Prices:** $300 to $3,000. **Remarks:** Full-time maker; first knife sold in 1985. Doing business as Shusui Kanda. **Mark:** Last name inside "M".

**KANKI, IWAO,** 14-25 3-CHOME FUKUI MIKI, Hydugo, JAPAN 673-0433, Phone: 07948-3-2555

**Specialties:** Plane, knife. **Prices:** Not determined yet. **Mark:** Chiyozuru Sadahide. **Other:** Masters of traditional crafts designated by the Minister of International Trade and Industry (Japan).

**KANSEI, MATSUNO,** 109-8 Uenomachi Nishikaiden, Gitu-city, JAPAN 501-1168, Phone: 81-58-234-8643

**Specialties:** Folders of original design. **Patterns:** Liner lock folder. **Technical:** Grinds VG-10, Damascus. **Prices:** $350 to $2,000. **Remarks:** Full-time maker. First knife sold in 1993. **Mark:** Name.

**KANTER, MICHAEL,** ADAM MICHAEL KNIVES, 14550 West Honey Ln., New Berlin, WI 53151, Phone: 262-860-1136, mike@adam-michaelknives.com Web: www.adammichaelknives.com

**Specialties:** Fixed blades and liner lock folders. **Patterns:** Drop Point hunters, and Bowies. **Technical:** My own Damascus, BG42, ATS-34 and CPMS60V. **Prices:** $200 to $1,000. **Mark:** Adam Michael over wavy line or engraved Adam Michael. **Other:** Ivory, Mamoth Ivory, stabilized woods, and pearl handles.

**KARP, BOB,** PO Box 47304, Phoenix, AZ 85068, Phone: 602 870-1234 602 870-1234, Fax: 602-331-0283

**KATO, SHINICHI,** 3233-27-5-410 Kikko Taikogane, Moriyama-ku Nagoya, JAPAN 463-0004, Phone: 81-52-736-6032

**Specialties:** Flat grind and hand finish. **Patterns:** Bowie, fighter. Hunting knife. **Technical:** Flat grind ATS-34. **Prices:** $100 to $1,500. **Remarks:** Part-time maker. First knife sold in 1995. **Mark:** Name.

**KATO, KIYOSHI,** 4-6-4 Himonya Meguro-ku, Tokyo 152, JAPAN

**Specialties:** Swords, Damascus knives, working knives and paper knives. **Patterns:** Traditional swords, hunters, Bowies and daggers. **Technical:** Forges his own Damascus and carbon steel. Grinds ATS-34. **Prices:** $260 to $700; some to $4,000. **Remarks:** Full-time maker. **Mark:** First initial, last name.

**KATSUMARO, SHISHIDO,** , 2-6-11 Kamiseno Aki-ku, Hiroshima, JAPAN, Phone: 090-3634-9054, Fax: 082-227-4438, shishido@d8.dion.ne.jp

**KAUFFMAN, DAVE,** 120 Clark Creek Loop, Montana City, MT 59634, Phone: 406-442-9328

**Specialties:** Field grade and exhibition grade hunting knives and ultra light folders. **Patterns:** Fighters, Bowies and drop-point hunters. **Technical:** ATS-34 and Damascus. **Prices:** $60 to $1,200. **Remarks:** Full-time maker; first knife sold in 1989. On the cover of Knives '94. **Mark:** First and last name, city and state.

**KAUFMAN, SCOTT,** 302 Green Meadows Cr., Anderson, SC 29624, Phone: 864-231-9201, scott.kaufman@ces.clemson.edu
**Specialties:** Classic and working/using straight knives in standard patterns. **Patterns:** Fighters, hunters and utility/camp knives. Technical Grinds ATS-34, 440C, O1. **Prices:** $100 to $500. **Remarks:** Part-time maker; first knife sold in 1987. **Mark:** Kaufman Knives with Bible in middle.

**KAWASAKI, AKIHISA,** 11-8-9 Chome Minamiamachi, Suzurandai Kita-Ku, Kobe, JAPAN, Phone: 078-593-0418, Fax: 078-593-0418
**Specialties:** Working/using knives of his design. **Patterns:** Hunters, kit camp knives. **Technical:** Forges and grinds Molybdenum Panadium. Grinds ATS-34 and stainless steel. Uses Chinese Quince wood, desert ironwood and cow leather. **Prices:** $300 to $800; some to $1,000. **Remarks:** Full-time maker. **Mark:** A.K.

**KAY, J. WALLACE,** 332 Slab Bridge Rd., Liberty, SC 29657

**KAZSUK, DAVID,** PO Box 39, Perris, CA 92572-0039, Phone: 909-780-2288, ddkaz@hotmail.com
**Specialties:** Hand forged. **Prices:** $150+. **Mark:** Last name.

**KEARNEY, JAROD,** 7200 Townsend Forest Ct., Brown Summit, NC 27214, Phone: 336-656-4617, jarodk@mindspring.com Web: www.jarodsworkshop.com

**KEESLAR, JOSEPH F.,** 391 Radio Rd., Almo, KY 42020, Phone: 270-753-7919, Fax: 270-753-7919, sjkees@apex.net
**Specialties:** Classic and contemporary Bowies, combat, hunters, daggers and folders. **Patterns:** Decorative filework, engraving and custom leather sheaths available. **Technical:** Forges 5160, 52100 and his own Damascus steel. **Prices:** $300 to $3,000. **Remarks:** Full-time maker; first knife sold in 1976. **Mark:** First and middle initials, last name in hammer, knife and anvil logo, M.S. **Other:** ABS Master Smith.

**KEESLAR, STEVEN C.,** 115 Lane 216, Hamilton, IN 46742, Phone: 260-488-3161, skeeslar@juno.com
**Specialties:** Traditional working/using straight knives of his design and to customer specs. **Patterns:** Bowies, hunters, utility/camp knives. **Technical:** Forges 5160, files 52100 Damascus. **Prices:** $100 to $600; some to $1,500. **Remarks:** Part-time maker; first knife sold in 1976. A.B.S. members. **Mark:** Fox lead in flames over Steven C Keeslar.

**KEETON, WILLIAM L.,** 6095 Rehobeth Rd. SE, Laconia, IN 47135-9550, Phone: 812-969-2836
**Specialties:** Plain and fancy working knives. **Patterns:** Hunters and fighters; locking folders and slip-joints. Names patterns after Kentucky Derby winners. **Technical:** Grinds D2, ATS-34, 440C, 440V and 154CM; mirror and satin finishes. **Prices:** $95 to $2,000. **Remarks:** Full-time maker; first knife sold in 1971. **Mark:** Logo of key.

**KEHIAYAN, ALFREDO,** Cuzco 1455, Ing. Maschwitz, CP B1623GXU Buenos Aires, ARGENTINA, Phone: 03488-4-42212, alfredo@kehiayan.com.ar Web: www.kehiayan.com.ar
**Specialties:** Functional straight knives. **Patterns:** Utility knives, skinners, hunters and boots. **Technical:** Forges and grinds SAE 52.100, SAE 6180, SAE 9260, SAE 5160, 440C and ATS-34, titanium with nitride. All blades mirror-polished; makes leather sheath and wood cases. **Prices:** $70 to $800; some to $6,000. **Remarks:** Full-time maker; first knife sold in 1983. **Mark:** Name. **Other:** Some knives are satin finish (utility knives).

**KEIDEL, GENE W. AND SCOTT J.,** 4661 105th Ave. SW, Dickinson, ND 58601
**Specialties:** Fancy/embellished and working/using straight knives of his design. **Patterns:** Bowies, hunters and miniatures. **Technical:** Grind 440C and O1 tool steel. Offer scrimshaw and filework. **Prices:** $95 to $500. **Remarks:** Full-time makers; first knife sold in1990. Doing business as Keidel Knives. **Mark:** Last name.

**KEISUKE, GOTOH,** 105 Cosumo-City, Otozu 202 Ohita-city, Ohita, JAPAN, Phone: 097-523-0750, k-u-an@ki.rim.or.jp

**KELLEY, GARY,** 17485 SW Pheasant Lane, Aloha, OR 97006, Phone: 503-649-7867, Web: www.reproductionblades.com
**Specialties:** Primitive knives and blades. **Patterns:** Fur trade era rifleman's knives, fur trade, cowboy action, hunting knives. **Technical:** Hand-forges and precision investment casts. **Prices:** $35 to $125. **Remarks:** Family business, reproduction blades. Doing business as Reproduction Blades. **Mark:** Fir tree logo.

**KELLEY, THOMAS P.,** 4711 E Ashler Hill Dr., Cave Creek, AZ 85331, Phone: 480-488-3101

**KELLOGG, BRIAN R.,** 19048 Smith Creek Rd., New Market, VA 22844, Phone: 540-740-4292
**Specialties:** Fancy and working straight knives of his design and to customer specs. **Patterns:** Fighters, hunters and utility/camp knives. **Technical:** Grinds 440C, D2 and A2. Offers filework and fancy pin and cable pin work. Prefers natural handle materials. **Prices:** $75 to $225; some to $350. **Remarks:** Pa time maker; first knife sold in 1983. **Mark:** Last name.

**KELLY, LANCE,** 1723 Willow Oak Dr., Edgewater, FL 32132, Phone: 904-423-4933
**Specialties:** Investor-class straight knives and folders. **Patterns:** Kelly-sty in contemporary outlines. **Technical:** Grinds O1, D2 and 440C; engrave inlays gold and silver. **Prices:** $600 to $3,500. **Remarks:** Full-time engrav and knife maker; first knife sold in 1975. **Mark:** Last name.

**KELSEY, NATE,** 3400 E Zion Rd, Springdale, AR 72764, nkelsey@cox.net
**Specialties:** Hand forges or stock removal traditional working knives of o or customer design. Forges own Damascus, makes custom leather sheath does fine engraving and scrimshaw. **Technical:** Forges 52100, 1084/15N2 5160. Grinds ATS-34, 154CM. Prefers natural handle materials. Prices $1 to $750. **Remarks:** Part-time maker since 1990. **Mark:** Name and city. Doi business as Ozark Mountain Forge. **Other:** Member ABS, Arkansas knifema ers assoc.

**KELSO, JIM,** 577 Collar Hill Rd., Worcester, VT 05682, Phone: 802-22 4254, Fax: 802-229-0595
**Specialties:** Fancy high-art straight knives and folders that mix Eastern a Western influences. Only uses own designs, but accepts suggestions themes. **Patterns:** Daggers, swords and locking folders. **Technical:** Grin only custom Damascus. Works with top Damascus blade smiths. **Price** $3,000 to $8,000; some to $15,000. **Remarks:** Full-time maker; first knife s in 1980. **Mark:** Stylized initials.

**KENNEDY JR., BILL,** PO Box 850431, Yukon, OK 73085, Phone: 405 354-9150
**Specialties:** Working straight knives. **Patterns:** Hunters, fighters, minis a fishing knives. **Technical:** Grinds D2, 440C and Damascus. **Prices:** $80 a higher. **Remarks:** Part-time maker; first knife sold in 1980. **Mark:** Last na and year made.

**KERN, R. W.,** 20824 Texas Trail W, San Antonio, TX 78257-1602, Phone: 210-698-2549, rkern@ev1.net
**Specialties:** Damascus, straight and folders. **Patterns:** Hunters, Bowies a folders. **Technical:** Grinds ATS-34, 440C and BG42. Forge own Damasc **Prices:** $200 and up. **Remarks:** First knives 1980; retired; work as time p mits. **Mark:** Outline of Alamo with kern over outline. **Other:** Member AE Texas Knifemaker and Collectors Association.

**KESSLER, RALPH A.,** PO Box 61, Fountain Inn, SC 29644-0061
**Specialties:** Traditional-style knives. **Patterns:** Folders, hunters, fighte Bowies and kitchen knives. **Technical:** Grinds D2, O1, A2 and ATS- Forges 1090 and 1095. **Prices:** $100 to $500. **Remarks:** Part-time mak first knife sold in 1982. **Mark:** Last name or initials with last name.

**KEYES, DAN,** 6688 King St., Chino, CA 91710, Phone: 909-628-8329

**KHALSA, JOT SINGH,** 368 Village St., Millis, MA 02054, Phone: 508-376-8162, Fax: 508-376-8081, jotkhalsa@aol.com Web: www.lifeknives.com Coming soon; www.khalsakirpans.com
**Specialties:** Liner locks, one-of-a-kind daggers, swords, and kirpans (S daggers) all original designs. **Technical:** Forges own Damascus, uses oth high quality Damascus including stainless, and grinds stainless steels. U natural handle materials frequently unusual minerals. Pieces are freque engraved and more recently carved. **Prices:** Start at $700.

**KHARLAMOV, YURI,** Oboronnay 46, 2, Tula, 300007, RUSSIA
**Specialties:** Classic, fancy and traditional knives of his design. **Patter** Daggers and hunters. **Technical:** Forges only Damascus with nickel. U natural handle materials; engraves on metal, carves on nut-tree; silver pearl inlays. **Prices:** $600 to $2,380; some to $4,000. **Remarks:** Full-t maker; first knife sold in 1988. **Mark:** Initials.

**KI, SHIVA,** 5222 Ritterman Ave., Baton Rouge, LA 70805, Phone: 22 356-7274, shivakicustomeknives@netzero.net Web: www.shivakicustomknives.com
**Specialties:** Fancy working straight knives and folders to customer sp **Patterns:** Emphasis on personal defense knives, martial arts weapons. **Te nical:** Forges and grinds; makes own Damascus; prefers natural handle m rials. **Prices:** $135 to $850; some to $1,800. **Remarks:** Full-time maker; knife sold in 1981. **Mark:** Name with logo.

**KIEFER, TONY,** 112 Chateaugay Dr., Pataskala, OH 43062, Phone: 740-927-6910
**Specialties:** Traditional working and using straight knives in standard terns. **Patterns:** Bowies, fighters and hunters. **Technical:** Grinds 440C D2; forges D2. Flat-grinds Bowies; hollow-grinds drop-point and trailing-p hunters. **Prices:** $95 to $140; some to $200. **Remarks:** Spare-time ma first knife sold in 1988. **Mark:** Last name.

**KILBY, KEITH,** 1902 29th St., Cody, WY 82414, Phone: 307-587-2732
**Specialties:** Works with all designs. **Patterns:** Mostly Bowies, camp knives and hunters of his design. **Technical:** Forges 52100, 5160, 1095, Damascus and mosaic Damascus. **Prices:** $250 to $3,500. **Remarks:** Part-time maker; first knife sold in 1974. Doing business as Foxwood Forge. **Mark:** Name.

**KIMBERLEY, RICHARD L.,** 86-B Arroyo Hondo Rd., Santa Fe, NM 87508, Phone: 505-820-2727
**Specialties:** Fixed-blade and period knives. **Technical:** O1, 52100, 9260 steels. **Remarks:** Member ABS. **Mark:** "By D. KIMBERLEY SANTA FE NM". **Other:** Marketed under "Kimberleys of Santa Fe".

**KIMSEY, KEVIN,** 198 Cass White Rd. NW, Cartersville, GA 30121, Phone: 770-387-0779 and 770-655-8879
**Specialties:** Tactical fixed blades and folders. **Patterns:** Fighters, folders, hunters and utility knives. **Technical:** Grinds 440C, ATS-34 and D2 carbon. **Prices:** $100 to $400; some to $600. **Remarks:** Three-time "Blade" award winner, Knife maker since 1983. **Mark:** Rafter and stylized KK.

**KING, HERMAN,** PO Box 122, Millington, TN 38083, Phone: 901-876-3062

**KING, BILL,** 14830 Shaw Rd., Tampa, FL 33625, Phone: 813-961-3455
**Specialties:** Folders, lockbacks, liner locks and stud openers. **Patterns:** Wide varieties; folders. **Technical:** ATS-34 and some Damascus; single and double grinds. Offers filework and jewel embellishment; nickel-silver Damascus and mokume bolsters. **Prices:** $150 to $475; some to $850. **Remarks:** Full-time maker; first knife sold in 1976. All titanium fitting on liner-locks; screw or rivet construction on lock-backs. **Mark:** Last name in crown.

**KING, JASON M.,** 5170 Rockenham Rd, St George, KS 66423, Phone: 785-494-8377, Web: www.jasonmkingknives.com
**Specialties:** Working and using straight knives of his design and sometimes to customer specs. Some slip joint and lockback folders. **Patterns:** Hunters, Bowies, tacticals, fighters; some miniatures. **Technical:** Grinds D2, 440C and other Damascus. **Prices:** $75 to $200; some up to $500. **Remarks:** First knife sold in 1998. **Mark:** JMK. **Other:** Likes to use height quality stabilized wood.

**KING, FRED,** 430 Grassdale Rd., Cartersville, GA 30120, Phone: 770-382-8478, Web: http://www.fking83264@aol.com
**Specialties:** Fancy and embellished working straight knives and folders. **Patterns:** Hunters, Bowies and fighters. **Technical:** Grinds ATS-34 and D2: forges 5160 and Damascus. Offers filework. **Prices:** $100 to $3,500. **Remarks:** Spare-time maker; first knife sold in 1984. **Mark:** Kings Edge.

**KING JR., HARVEY G.,** 32266 Hwy K4, Alta Vista, KS 66423-0184, Phone: 785-499-5207, Web: www.harveykingknives.com
**Specialties:** Traditional working and using straight knives of his design and to customer specs. **Patterns:** Hunters, Bowies and fillet knives. **Technical:** Grinds O1, A2 and D2. Prefers natural handle materials; offers leatherwork. **Prices:** Start at $70. **Remarks:** Part-time maker; first knife sold in 1988. **Mark:** Name and serial number based on steel used, year made and number of knives made that year.

**KINKADE, JACOB,** 197 Rd. 154, Carpenter, WY 82054, Phone: 307-649-2446
**Specialties:** Working/using knives of his design or to customer specs; some miniature swords, daggers and battle axes. **Patterns:** Hunters, daggers, boots; some miniatures. **Technical:** Grinds carbon and stainless and commercial Damascus. Prefers natural handle material. **Prices:** Start at $30. **Remarks:** Part-time maker; first knife sold in 1990. **Mark:** Connected initials or none.

**KINKER, MIKE,** 8755 E County Rd. 50 N, Greensburg, IN 47240, Phone: 812-663-5277, Fax: 812-662-8131, mokinker@hsonline.net
**Specialties:** Working/using knives, Straight knives. Starting to make folders. Your design. **Patterns:** Boots, daggers, hunters, skinners, hatchets. **Technical:** Grind 440C and ATS 34, others if required. Damascus, dovetail bolsters, jeweled blade. **Prices:** $125 to 375; some to $1,000. **Remarks:** Part-time maker; first knife sold in 1991. Doing business as Kinker Knives. **Mark:** Kinker and Kinker plus year.

**KINNIKIN, TODD,** Eureka Forge, 8356 John McKeever Rd., House Springs, MO 63051, Phone: 314-938-6248
**Specialties:** Mosaic Damascus. **Patterns:** Hunters, fighters, folders and automatics. **Technical:** Forges own mosaic Damascus with tool steel Damascus edge. Prefers natural, fossil and artifact handle materials. **Prices:** $400 to $1,400. **Remarks:** Full-time maker; first knife sold in 1994. **Mark:** Initials connected.

**KIOUS, JOE,** 1015 Ridge Pointe Rd., Kerrville, TX 78028, Phone: 830-367-2277, Fax: 830-367-2286, kious@ktc.com
**Specialties:** Investment-quality interframe and bolstered folders. **Patterns:** Folder specialist - all types. **Technical:** Both stainless and non stainless Damascus. **Prices:** $650 to $3,000; some to $10,000. **Remarks:** Full-time maker; first knife sold in 1969. **Mark:** Last name, city and state or last name only.

**KIRK, RAY,** PO Box 1445, Tahlequah, OK 74465, Phone: 918-456-1519, ray@rakerknives.com Web: www.rakerknives.com
**Specialties:** Folders, skinners fighters, and bowies. **Patterns:** Neck knives and small hunters and skinners. **Technical:** Forges all knives from 52100 and own Damascus. **Prices:** $65 to $3,000. **Remarks:** Started forging in 1989; makes own Damascus. Does custom steel rolling. Has some 52100 and Damascus in custom flat bar 512E3 for sale **Mark:** Stamped "Raker" on blade.

**KITSMILLER, JERRY,** 67277 Las Vegas Dr., Montrose, CO 81401, Phone: 970-249-4290
**Specialties:** Working straight knives in standard patterns. **Patterns:** Hunters, boots. **Technical:** Grinds ATS-34 and 440C only. **Prices:** $75 to $200; some to $300. **Remarks:** Spare-time maker; first knife sold in 1984. **Mark:** JandS Knives.

**KNICKMEYER, HANK,** 6300 Crosscreek, Cedar Hill, MO 63016, Phone: 314-285-3210
**Specialties:** Complex mosaic Damascus constructions. **Patterns:** Fixed blades, swords, folders and automatics. **Technical:** Mosaic Damascus with all tool steel Damascus edges. **Prices:** $500 to $2,000; some $3,000 and higher. **Remarks:** Part-time maker; first knife sold in 1989. Doing business as Dutch Creek Forge and Foundry. **Mark:** Initials connected.

**KNICKMEYER, KURT,** 6344 Crosscreek, Cedar Hill, MO 63016, Phone: 314-274-0481

**KNIGHT, JASON,** 110 Paradie Pond Ln., Harleyville, SC 29448, Phone: 843-452-1163
**Specialties:** Bowies. **Patterns:** Bowies and anything from history or his own design. **Technical:** 1084, 5160, 01, 52102, Damascus/forged blades. **Prices:** $200 and up. **Remarks:** Bladesmith. **Mark:** KNIGHT.

**KNIPSCHIELD, TERRY,** 808 12th Ave. NE, Rochester, MN 55906, Phone: 507-288-7829, knipper01@charter.net Web: http://webpages.charter.net/knipper01
**Specialties:** Folders and fixed blades. Woodcarving knives. **Patterns:** Variations of traditional patterns and my own new designs. **Technical:** Stock removal. Uses ATS-34 and stainless Damascus. **Prices:** $350 to $800 on folders. $150 to $400 for fixed blades. **Mark:** Knife with shield.

**KNIPSTEIN, R.C. (JOE),** 731 N. Fielder, Arlington, TX 76012, Phone: 817-265-0573;817-265-2021, Fax: 817-265-3410
**Specialties:** Traditional pattern folders along with custom designs. **Patterns:** Hunters, Bowies, folders, fighters, utility knives. **Technical:** Grinds 440C, D2, 154CM and ATS-34. Natural handle materials and full tangs are standard. **Prices:** Start at $300. **Remarks:** Part-time maker; first knife sold in 1989. **Mark:** Last name.

**KNOTT, STEVE,** KNOTT KNIVES, 203 Wild Rose, Guyton, GA 31312, Phone: 912-772-7655
**Technical:** Uses ATS-34/440C and some commercial Damascus, single and double grinds with mirror or satin finishes. **Patters:** Hunters, boot knives, Bowies, and tantos, slip joint and lock-back folders. Uses a wide variety of handle materials to include ironwood, coca-bola and colored stabilized wood, also horn, bone and ivory upon customer request. **Remarks:** First knife sold in 1991. Part-time maker.

**KNUTH, JOSEPH E.,** 3307 Lookout Dr., Rockford, IL 61109, Phone: 815-874-9597
**Specialties:** High-art working straight knives of his design or to customer specs. **Patterns:** Daggers, fighters and swords. **Technical:** Grinds 440C, ATS-34 and D2. **Prices:** $150 to $1,500; some to $15,000. **Remarks:** Full-time maker; first knife sold in 1989. **Mark:** Initials on bolster face.

**KOHLS, JERRY,** N4725 Oak Rd., Princeton, WI 54968, Phone: 920-295-3648
**Specialties:** Working knives and period pieces. **Patterns:** Hunters-boots and Bowies - your designs or his. **Technical:** Grinds, ATS-34 440c 154CM and 1095 and commercial Damascus. **Remarks:** Part-time maker. **Mark:** Last name.

**KOJETIN, W.,** 20 Bapaume Rd., Delville, Germiston 1401, SOUTH AFRICA, Phone: 27118733305/mobile 27836256208
**Specialties:** High-art and working straight knives of all designs. **Patterns:** Daggers, hunters and his own Man hunter Bowie. **Technical:** Grinds D2 and ATS-34; forges and grinds 440B/C. Offers "wrap-around" pava and abalone handles, scrolled wood or ivory, stacked filework and setting of faceted semi-precious stones. **Prices:** $185 to $600; some to $11,000. **Remarks:** Spare-time maker; first knife sold in 1962. **Mark:** Billy K.

**KOLITZ, ROBERT,** W9342 Canary Rd., Beaver Dam, WI 53916, Phone: 920-887-1287
**Specialties:** Working straight knives to customer specs. **Patterns:** Bowies, hunters, bird and trout knives, boots. **Technical:** Grinds O1, 440C; commercial Damascus. **Prices:** $50 to $100; some to $500. **Remarks:** Spare-time maker; first knife sold in 1979. **Mark:** Last initial.

**KOMMER, RUSS,** 9211 Abbott Loop Rd., Anchorage, AK 99507, Phone: 907-346-3339

**Specialties:** Working straight knives with the outdoorsman in mind. **Patterns:** Hunters, semi-skinners, fighters, folders and utility knives, art knives. **Technical:** Hollow-grinds ATS-34, 440C and 440V. **Prices:** $125 to $850; some to $3,000. **Remarks:** Full-time maker; first knife sold in 1995. **Mark:** Bear paw—full name, city and state or full name and state.

**KOPP, TODD M.,** PO Box 3474, Apache Jct., AZ 85217, Phone: 480-983-6143, tmkopp@msn.com

**Specialties:** Classic and traditional straight knives. Fluted handled daggers. **Patterns:** Bowies, boots, daggers, fighters, hunters, swords and folders. **Technical:** Grinds 5160, 440C, ATS-34. All Damascus steels, or customers choice. Some engraving and filework. **Prices:** $200 to $1,200; some to $4,000. **Remarks:** Part-time maker; first knife sold in 1989. **Mark:** Last name in old english, some others name, city and state.

**KOSTER, STEVEN C.,** 16261 Gentry Ln., Huntington Beach, CA 92647, Phone: 714-840-8621

**Specialties:** Bowies, daggers, skinners, camp knives. **Technical:** Use 5160, 52100, 1084, 1095 steels. **Prices:** $200 to $1,000. **Remarks:** Wood and leather sheaths with silver furniture. **Mark:** Koster squeezed between lines. **Other:** ABS Journeyman 2003.

**KOVACIK, ROBERT,** Druzstevna 301, 98556, Tomasovce, Slovakia, Web: www.e-2brane.sk/kovacik

**Specialties:**Engraved hunting knives. **Prices:**USD 350, USD 1500.**Mark:** R.

**KOVAR, EUGENE,** 2626 W. 98th St., Evergreen Park, IL 60642, Phone: 708-636-3724

**Specialties:** One-of-a-kind miniature knives only. **Patterns:** Fancy to fantasy miniature knives; knife pendants and tie tacks. **Technical:** Files and grinds nails, nickel-silver and sterling silver. **Prices:** $5 to $35; some to $100. **Mark:** GK.

**KOYAMA, CAPTAIN BUNSHICHI,** 3-23 Shirako-cho, Nakamura-ku, Nagoya City 453-0817, JAPAN, Phone: 052-461-7070, Fax: 052-461-7070

**Specialties:** Innovative folding knife. **Patterns:** General purpose one hand. **Technical:** Grinds ATS-34 and Damascus. **Prices:** $400 to $900; some to $1,500. **Remarks:** Part-time maker; first knife sold in 1994. **Mark:** Captain B. Koyama and the shoulder straps of CAPTAIN.

**KRAFT, STEVE,** 315 S.E. 6th, Abilene, KS 67410, Phone: 785-263-1411

**Specialties:** Folders, lockbacks, scale release auto, push button auto. **Patterns:** Hunters, boot knives and fighters. **Technical:** Grinds ATS-34, Damascus; uses titanium, pearl, ivory etc. **Prices:** $500 to $2,500. **Remarks:** Part-time maker; first knife sold in 1984. **Mark:** Kraft.

**KRAFT, ELMER,** 1358 Meadowlark Lane, Big Arm, MT 59910, Phone: 406-849-5086, Fax: 406-883-3056

**Specialties:** Traditional working/using straight knives of all designs. **Patterns:** Fighters, hunters, utility/camp knives. **Technical:** Grinds 440C, D2. Custom makes sheaths. **Prices:** $125 to $350; some to $500. **Remarks:** Part-time maker; first knife sold in 1984. **Mark:** Last name.

**KRAPP, DENNY,** 1826 Windsor Oak Dr., Apopka, FL 32703, Phone: 407-880-7115

**Specialties:** Fantasy and working straight knives of his design. **Patterns:** Hunters, fighters and utility/camp knives. **Technical:** Grinds ATS-34 and 440C. **Prices:** $85 to $300; some to $800. **Remarks:** Spare-time maker; first knife sold in 1988. **Mark:** Last name.

**KRAUSE, ROY W.,** 22412 Corteville, St. Clair Shores, MI 48081, Phone: 810-296-3995, Fax: 810-296-2663

**Specialties:** Military and law enforcement/Japanese-style knives and swords. **Patterns:** Combat and back-up, Bowies, fighters, boot knives, daggers, tantos, wakazashis and katanas. **Technical:** Grinds ATS-34, A2, D2, 1045, O1 and commercial Damascus; differentially hardened Japanese-style blades. **Prices:** Moderate to upscale. **Remarks:** Full-time maker. **Mark:** Last name on traditional knives; initials in Japanese characters on Japanese-style knives.

**KREH, LEFTY,** 210 Wichersham Way, "Cockeysville", MD 21030

**KREIBICH, DONALD L.,** 1638 Commonwealth Circle, Reno, NV 89503, Phone: 775-746-0533, dmkreno@sbcglobal.net

**Specialties:** Working straight knives in standard patterns. **Patterns:** Bowies, boots and daggers; camp and fishing knives. **Technical:** Grinds 440C, 154CM and ATS-34; likes integrals. **Prices:** $100 to $200; some to $500. **Remarks:** Part-time maker; first knife sold in 1980. **Mark:** First and middle initials, last name.

**KRESSLER, D.F.,** Schloss Odetzhausen, Schlossberg 1-85235, Odetzhausen, GERMANY, Phone: 08134-998 7290, Fax: 08134-998 7290

**Specialties:** High-tech Integral and Interframe knives. **Patterns:** Hunters, fighters, daggers. **Technical:** Grinds new state-of-the-art steels; prefers natural handle materials. **Prices:** Upscale. **Mark:** Name in logo.

**KRETSINGER JR., PHILIP W.,** 17536 Bakersville Rd., Boonsboro, MD 21713, Phone: 301-432-6771

**Specialties:** Fancy and traditional period pieces. **Patterns:** Hunters, Bowies, camp knives, daggers, carvers, fighters. **Technical:** Forges W2, 5160 and his own Damascus. **Prices:** Start at $200. **Remarks:** Full-time knife maker. **Mark:** Name.

**KUBAIKO, HANK,** 10765 Northvale, Beach City, OH 44608, Phone: 330-359-2418

**Specialties:** Reproduce antique Bowies. Distal tapering and clay zone tempering. **Patterns:** Bowies, fighters, fishing knives, kitchen cutlery, lockers, slip joints, camp knives, axes and miniatures. Also makes American, European and traditional samurai swords and daggers. **Technical:** Grinds 440C, ATS-34 and D2; will use CPM-T-440V at extra cost. **Prices:** Moderate. **Remarks:** Full-time maker. Allow three months for sword order fulfillment. **Mark:** Alaskan Maid and name. **Other:** 25th year as a knife maker. Will be making 25 serial numbered knives-folder (liner-locks).

**KUBASEK, JOHN A.,** 74 Northhampton St., Easthampton, MA 01027, Phone: 413-532-3288

**Specialties:** Left- and right-handed liner lock folders of his design or to customer specs Also new knives made with Ripcord patent. **Patterns:** Fighters, tantos, drop points, survival knives, neck knives and belt buckle knives. **Technical:** Grinds ATS-34 and Damascus. **Prices:** $395 to $1,500. **Remarks:** Part-time maker; first knife sold in 1985. **Mark:** Name and address etched.

## L

**LADD, JIM S.,** 1120 Helen, Deer Park, TX 77536, Phone: 713-479-72[...]

**Specialties:** Working knives and period pieces. **Patterns:** Hunters, boots a[nd] Bowies plus other straight knives. **Technical:** Grinds D2, 440C and 154C[M]. **Prices:** $125 to $225; some to $550. **Remarks:** Part-time maker; first kn[ife] sold in 1965. Doing business as The Tinker. **Mark:** First and middle initi[als,] last name.

**LADD, JIMMIE LEE,** 1120 Helen, Deer Park, TX 77536, Phone: 713-479-7186

**Specialties:** Working straight knives. **Patterns:** Hunters, skinners and ut[ility] knives. **Technical:** Grinds 440C and D2. **Prices:** $75 to $225. **Remarks:** F[irst] knife sold in 1979. **Mark:** First and middle initials, last name.

**LAGRANGE, FANIE,** 12 Canary Crescent, Table View 7441, South Africa, Phone: 27 21 55 76 805

**Specialties:** African-influenced styles in folders and fixed blades. **Patte[rns:]** All original patterns with many one-of-a-kinds. **Technical:** Mostly st[ock] removal in 12c27, ATS-34, stainless Damascus. **Prices:** $350 to $3,0[00.] **Remarks:** Professional maker. S A Guild Member 13 years. **Mark:** Name o[n] spear.

**LAINSON, TONY,** 114 Park Ave., Council Bluffs, IA 51503, Phone: 7[12-]322-5222

**Specialties:** Working straight knives, liner locking folders. **Technical:** Gri[nds] 154CM, ATS-34, 440C buys Damascus. Handle materials include Mica[rta,] carbon fiber G-10 ivory pearl and bone. **Prices:** $95 to $600. **Remarks:** P[art-]time maker; first knife sold in 1987. **Mark:** Name and state.

**LAIRSON SR., JERRY,** H C 68 Box 970, Ringold, OK 74754, Phone: 580-876-3426, bladesmt@brightok.net Web: www.lairson-custom-knives.net

**Specialties:** Fighters and hunters. **Patterns:** Damascus, random, raind[rop,] ladder, twist and others. **Technical:** All knives hammer forged. **Prices:** [Car]bon steel $400 and up; Damascus $600 and up. **Remarks:** Makes any s[tyle] knife but prefer fighters and hunters.

**LAKE, RON,** 3360 Bendix Ave., Eugene, OR 97401, Phone: 541-484-2683

**Specialties:** High-tech working knives; inventor of the modern interfr[ame] folder. **Patterns:** Hunters, boots, etc.; locking folders. **Technical:** Gr[inds] 154CM and ATS-34. Patented interframe with special lock release. **Prices:** $2,200 to $3,000; some higher. **Remarks:** Full-time maker; first [knife] sold in 1966. **Mark:** Last name.

**LALA, PAULO RICARDO P. AND LALA, ROBERTO P.,** R. Daniel Martins, 636, Centro, Presidente Prudente, SP-19031-260, BRAZIL, Phone: 0182-210125, Web: http://www.orbita.starmedia/~korth
**Specialties:** Straight knives and folders of all designs to customer specs. **Patterns:** Bowies, daggers fighters, hunters and utility knives. **Technical:** Grinds and forges D6, 440C, high-carbon steels and Damascus. **Prices:** $60 to $400; some higher. **Remarks:** Full-time makers; first knife sold in 1991. All stainless steel blades are ultra sub-zero quenched. **Mark:** Sword carved on top of anvil under KORTH.

**LAMB, CURTIS J.,** 3336 Louisiana Ter., Ottawa, KS 66067-8996, Phone: 785-242-6657

**LAMBERT, JARRELL D.,** 2321 FM 2982, Granado, TX 77962, Phone: 512-771-3744
**Specialties:** Traditional working and using straight knives of his design and to customer specs. **Patterns:** Bowies, hunters, tantos and utility/camp knives. **Technical:** Grinds ATS-34; forges W2 and his own Damascus. Makes own sheaths. **Prices:** $80 to $600; some to $1,000. **Remarks:** Part-time maker; first knife sold in 1982. **Mark:** Etched first and middle initials, last name; or stamped last name.

**LAMEY, ROBERT M.,** 15800 Lamey Dr., Biloxi, MS 39532, Phone: 228-396-9066, Fax: 228-396-9022, rmlamey@ametro.net Web: www.lameyknives.com
**Specialties:** Bowies, fighters, hard use knives. **Patterns:** Bowies, fighters, hunters and camp knives. **Technical:** Forged and stock removal. **Prices:** $125 to $350. **Remarks:** Lifetime reconditioning; will build to customer designs, specializing in hard use, affordable knives. **Mark:** LAMEY.

**.AMPSON, FRANK G.,** 3215 Saddle Bag Circle, Rimrock, AZ 86335, Phone: 928-567-7395, fglampson@yahoo.com
**Specialties:** Working folders; one-of-a-kinds. **Patterns:** Folders, hunters, utility knives, fillet knives and Bowies. **Technical:** Grinds ATS-34, 440C and 154CM. **Prices:** $100 to $750; some to $3,500. **Remarks:** Full-time maker; irst knife sold in 1971. **Mark:** Name in fish logo.

**.ANCASTER, C.G.,** No 2 Schoonwinkel St., Parys, Free State, SOUTH AFRICA, Phone: 0568112090
**Specialties:** High-tech working and using knives of his design and to customer specs. **Patterns:** Hunters, locking folders and utility/camp knives. **Technical:** Grinds Sandvik 12C27, 440C and D2. Offers anodized titanium bolsters. **Prices:** $450 to $750; some to $1,500. **Remarks:** Part-time maker; rst knife sold in 1990. **Mark:** Etched logo.

**.ANCE, BILL,** PO Box 4427, Eagle River, AK 99577, Phone: 907-694-487
**Specialties:** Ooloos and working straight knives; limited issue sets. **Patterns:** Several ooloo patterns, drop-point skinners. **Technical:** Uses ATS-34, Vascomax 350; ivory, horn and high-class wood handles. **Prices:** $85 to $300; art sets to $3,000. **Remarks:** First knife sold in 1981. **Mark:** Last name over a ance.

**ANDERS, JOHN,** 758 Welcome Rd., Newnan, GA 30263, Phone: 404-53-5719
**Specialties:** High-art working straight knives and folders of his design. **Patterns:** hunters, fighters and slip-joint folders. **Technical:** Grinds 440C, ATS-4, 154CM and commercial Damascus. **Prices:** $85 to $250; some to $500. **Remarks:** Part-time maker; first knife sold in 1989. **Mark:** Last name.

**ANE, BEN,** 4802 Massie St., North Little Rock, AR 72218, Phone: 501-53-8238
**Specialties:** Fancy straight knives of his design and to customer specs; period pieces. **Patterns:** Bowies, hunters, utility/camp knives. **Technical:** Grinds D2 and 154CM; forges and grinds 1095. Offers intricate handle work including inlays and spacers. **Prices:** $120 to $450; some to $5,000. **Remarks:** Part-time maker; first knife sold in 1989. **Mark:** Full name, city, ate.

**ANER, DEAN,** 1480 Fourth St., Susanville, CA 96130, Phone: 530-310-917, laner54knives@yahoo.com
**Specialties:** Fancy working fixed blades, of his design, will do custom orders. **Patterns:** Hunters, fighters, combat, fishing, Bowies, utility, and kitchen knives. **Technical:** Grinds 154-CM, ATS-34, D-2, buys Damascus. Does mostly hallow grinding, some flat grinds. Uses Micata, mastodon ivory, hippo ory, exotic woods. Loves ding spacer work on stick tang knives. A leather or des sheath comes with every knife. Life-time warrantee and free sharpening so. **Remarks:** Pat-time maker, first knife sold in 1993. **Prices:** $150 to ,000. **Mark:** LANER CUSTOM KNIVES over D nest to a tree.

**ANG, KURT,** 4908 S. Wildwood Dr., McHenry, IL 60050, Phone: 708-6-4649
**Specialties:** High-art working knives. **Patterns:** Bowies, utilitarian-type knives th rough finishes. **Technical:** Forges welded steel in European and Japanese-styles. **Prices:** Moderate to upscale. **Remarks:** Part-time maker. **Mark:** "Crazy Eye" logo.

**LANGLEY, MICK,** 1015 Centre Rd, Crescent Qualicumm Beach BC, CANADA V9K 2G6, Phone: 250-752-4261
**Specialties:** Period Pieces and working knives. **Patterns:** Bowies, Push daggers, fighters, boots. Some folding lockers. **Technical:** Forges 5160, 1084, W2 and his own Damascus. **Prices:** $250 to $2,500. Some to $4,500. **Remarks:** Full-time maker, first knife sold in 1977. **Mark:** Langley with M.S. (For ABS. Master Smith)

**LANGLEY, GENE H.,** 1022 N. Price Rd., Florence, SC 29506, Phone: 843-669-3150
**Specialties:** Working knives in standard patterns. **Patterns:** Hunters, boots, fighters, locking folders and slip-joints. **Technical:** Grinds 440C, 154CM and ATS-34. **Prices:** $125 to $450; some to $1,000. **Remarks:** Part-time maker; first knife sold in 1979. **Mark:** Name.

**LANKTON, SCOTT,** 8065 Jackson Rd. R-11, Ann Arbor, MI 48103, Phone: 313-426-3735
**Specialties:** Pattern welded swords, krisses and Viking period pieces. **Patterns:** One-of-a-kind. **Technical:** Forges W2, L6 nickel and other steels. **Prices:** $600 to $12,000. **Remarks:** Part-time bladesmith, full-time smith; first knife sold in 1976. **Mark:** Last name logo.

**LAOISLAV, SANTA-LASKY,** Tatranska 32, 97401 Banska, Bystrica, Slovakia, santa.ladislav@pobox.sk Web: www.lasky.sk
**Specialties:**Damascus hunters, daggers and swords. **Patterns:**Carious Damascus patterns. **Prices:**300 USD - 6000 USD. **Mark:**L or Lasky

**LAPEN, CHARLES,** Box 529, W. Brookfield, MA 01585
**Specialties:** Chefs knives for the culinary artist. **Patterns:** camp knives, Japanese-style swords and wood working tools, hunters. **Technical:** Forges 1075, car spring and his own Damascus. Favors narrow and Japanese tangs. **Prices:** $200 to $400; some to $2,000. **Remarks:** Part-time maker; first knife sold in 1972. **Mark:** Last name.

**LAPLANTE, BRETT,** 4545 CR412, McKinney, TX 75071, Phone: 972-838-9191
**Specialties:** Working straight knives and folders to customer specs. **Patterns:** Survival knives, Bowies, skinners, hunters. **Technical:** Grinds D2 and 440C. Heat-treats. **Prices:** $175 to $600. **Remarks:** Part-time maker; first knife sold in 1987. **Mark:** Last name in Canadian maple leaf logo.

**LARAMIE, MARK,** 181 Woodland St., Fitchburg, MA 01420, Phone: 978-502-2726, laramieknives@verison.net Web: www.malknives.com
**Specialties:** Traditional folders & fancy everyday carry folders. **Patterns:**Slip-Joint, back lock L/L single and multi blades. **Technical:**Free hand ground blades of D2, 440, 8, and Damascus. **Mark:**Mall knives W/Fish Logo

**LARGIN, ,** KELGIN KNIVES, PO Box 151, Metamora, IN 47030, Phone: 765-969-5012, kelgin@hotmail.com Web: www.kelgin.com
**Specialties:** Meteorite knife blades. **Prices:** $100 to $8,000. **Mark:** KELGIN or K.C. LARGIN.

**LARSON, RICHARD,** 549 E. Hawkeye Ave., Turlock, CA 95380, Phone: 209-668-1615
**Specialties:** Traditional working/using straight knives in standard patterns. **Patterns:** Bowies, hunters and utility/camp knives. **Technical:** Grinds ATS-34, 440C, and 154CM. Engraves and scrimshaws holsters and handles. Hand-sews sheaths with tooling. **Prices:** $150 to $300; some to $1,000. **Remarks:** Part-time maker; first knife sold in 1986. Doing business as Larson Knives. **Mark:** Knife logo spelling last name.

**LARY, ED,** 651 Rangeline Rd., Mosinee, WI 54455, Phone: 715-693-3940, laryblades@hotmail.com
**Specialties:** Upscale hunters and art knives with display presentations. **Patterns:** Hunters, period pieces. **Technical:** Grinds all steels, heat treats, fancy file work and engraving. **Prices:** Upscale. **Remarks:** Since 1974. **Mark:** hand engraved "Ed Lary" in script.

**LAURENT, KERMIT,** 1812 Acadia Dr., LaPlace, LA 70068, Phone: 504-652-5629
**Specialties:** Traditional and working straight knives and folders of his design. **Patterns:** Bowies, hunters, utilities and folders. **Technical:** Forges own Damascus, plus uses most tool steels and stainless. Specializes in altering cable patterns. Uses stabilized handle materials, especially select exotic woods. **Prices:** $100 to $2,500; some to $50,000. **Remarks:** Full-time maker; first knife sold in 1982. Doing business as Kermit's Knife Works. Favorite material is meteorite Damascus **Mark:** First name.

**LAWRENCE, ALTON,** 201 W Stillwell, De Queen, AR 71832, Phone: 870-642-7643, Fax: 870-642-4023, uncleal@1pa.net Web: riversidemachine.net
**Specialties:** Classic straight knives and folders to customer specs. **Patterns:** Bowies, hunters, folders and utility/camp knives. **Technical:** Forges 5160,

1095, 1084, Damascus and railroad spikes. **Prices:** Start at $100. **Remarks:** Part-time maker; first knife sold in 1988. **Mark:** Last name inside fish symbol.

**LAY, L.J.,** 602 Mimosa Dr., Burkburnett, TX 76354, Phone: 817-569-1329
**Specialties:** Working straight knives in standard patterns; some period pieces. **Patterns:** Drop-point hunters, Bowies and fighters. **Technical:** Grinds ATS-34 to mirror finish; likes Micarta handles. **Prices:** Moderate. **Remarks:** Full-time maker; first knife sold in 1985. **Mark:** Name or name with ram head and city or stamp L J Lay.

**LAY, R.J. (BOB),** Box 122, Falkland BC, CANADA V0E 1W0, Phone: 250-379-2265, Fax: SAME
**Specialties:** Traditional-styled, fancy straight knifes of his design. Specializing in hunters. **Patterns:** Bowies, fighters and hunters. **Technical:** Grinds 440C, ATS-34, 530V, forges and grinds tool steels. Uses exotic handle and spacer material. File cut, prefers narrow tang. Sheaths available. **Price:** $200 to $500; some to $5,000. **Remarks:** Full-time maker, first knife sold in 1976. Doing business as Lay's Custom Knives. **Mark:** Signature acid etched.

**LEACH, MIKE J.,** 5377 W. Grand Blanc Rd., Swartz Creek, MI 48473, Phone: 810-655-4850
**Specialties:** Fancy working knives. **Patterns:** Hunters, fighters, Bowies and heavy-duty knives; slip-joint folders and integral straight patterns. **Technical:** Grinds D2, 440C and 154CM; buys Damascus. **Prices:** Start at $300 starting price. **Remarks:** Full-time maker; first knife sold in 1952. **Mark:** First initial, last name.

**LEAVITT JR., EARL F.,** Pleasant Cove Rd., Box 306, E. Boothbay, ME 04544, Phone: 207-633-3210
**Specialties:** 1500-1870 working straight knives and fighters; pole arms. **Patterns:** Historically significant knives, classic/modern custom designs. **Technical:** Flat-grinds O1; heat-treats. Filework available. **Prices:** $90 to $350; some to $1,000. **Remarks:** Full-time maker; first knife sold in 1981. Doing business as Old Colony Manufactory. **Mark:** Initials in oval.

**LEBATARD, PAUL M.,** 14700 Old River Rd., Vancleave, MS 39565, Phone: 228-826-4137, Fax: 228-826-2933
**Specialties:** Sound working knives; lightweight folder; practical tactical knives. **Patterns:** Hunters, trout and bird knives, fish fillet knives, kitchen knives, Bowies, one and two blade folders, plus a new line of tactical sheath knives. **Technical:** Grinds ATS-34, D-2, CPM 3-V, and commercial Damascus; forges and grinds 52100. Machines folder frames from aircraft aluminum. **Prices:** $50 to $650. **Remarks:** Part-time maker; celebrating 31 years of knifemaking; first knife made in 1974. Offers knife repair, restoration and sharpening. **Mark:** Stamped last name or etched logo of last name, city, and state. **Other:** All knives are serial numbered and registered in the name of the original purchaser.

**LEBER, HEINZ,** Box 446, Hudson's Hope, BC, CANADA V0C 1V0, Phone: 250-783-5304
**Specialties:** Working straight knives of his design. **Patterns:** 20 models, form capers to Bowies. **Technical:** Hollow-grinds D2 and M2 steel; mirror-finishes and full tang only. Likes moose, elk, stone sheep for handles. **Prices:** $175 to $1,000. **Remarks:** Full-time maker; first knife sold in 1975. **Mark:** Initials connected.

**LECK, DAL,** Box 1054, Hayden, CO 81639, Phone: 970-276-3663
**Specialties:** Classic, traditional and working knives of his design and in standard patterns; period pieces. **Patterns:** Boots, daggers, fighters, hunters and push daggers. **Technical:** Forges O1 and 5160; makes his own Damascus. **Prices:** $175 to $700; some to $1,500. **Remarks:** Part-time maker; first knife sold in 1990. Doing business as The Moonlight Smithy. **Mark:** Stamped: hammer and anvil with initials.

**LEE, RANDY,** PO Box 1873, St. Johns, AZ 85936, Phone: 928-337-2594, Fax: 928-337-5002, info@randyleenknives.com Web.wwwrandyleeknives.com
**Specialties:** Traditional working and using straight knives of his design. **Patterns:** Bowies, fighters, hunters, daggers and professional throwing knives. **Technical:** Grinds ATS-34, 440C and D2. Offers sheaths. **Prices:** $235 to $1,500. **Remarks:** Part-time maker; first knife sold in 1979. **Mark:** Full name, city, state.

**LELAND, STEVE,** 2300 Sir Francis Drake Blvd., Fairfax, CA 94930-1118, Phone: 415-457-0318, Fax: 415-457-0995, Web: wwwstephenleland@comcast.net
**Specialties:** Traditional and working straight knives and folders of his design. **Patterns:** Hunters, fighters, Bowies, chefs. **Technical:** Grinds O1, ATS-34 and 440C. Does own heat treat. Makes nickel silver sheaths. **Prices:** $150 to $750; some to $1,500. **Remarks:** Part-time maker; first knife sold in 1987. Doing business as Leland Handmade Knives. **Mark:** Last name.

**LEMCKE, JIM L.,** 10649 Haddington Ste 180, Houston, TX 77043, Phone: 888-461-8632, Fax: 713-461-8221, jimll@hal-pc.org Web: www.texasknife.com
**Specialties:** Large supply of custom ground and factory finished blades; kni kits; leather sheaths; in-house heat treating and cryogenic tempering; exo handle material (wood, ivory, oosik, horn, stabilized woods); machines ar supplies for knife making; polishing and finishing supplies; heat treat over etching equipment; bar, sheet and rod material (brass, stainless steel, nick silver); titanium sheet material. Catalog. $4.

**LEONARD, RANDY JOE,** 188 Newton Rd., Sarepta, LA 71071, Phone 318-994-2712

**LEONE, NICK,** 9 Georgetown, Pontoon Beach, IL 62040, Phone: 618-797-1179, nickleone@sbcglobal.net
**Specialties:** 18th century period straight knives. **Patterns:** skinners, hunte neck, leg and friction folders. **Technical:** Forges 5160, W2, O1, 1098, 521 and his own Damascus. **Prices:** $100 to $1,000; some to $3,500. **Remark** Full-time maker; first knife sold in 1987. Doing business as Anvil Head Forg **Mark:** Last name, NL, AHF.

**LEPORE, MICHAEL J.,** 66 Woodcutters Dr., Bethany, CT 06524, Phone: 203-393-3823
**Specialties:** One-of-a-kind designs to customer specs; mostly handma **Patterns:** Fancy working straight knives and folders. **Technical:** Forges a grinds W2, W1 and O1; prefers natural handle materials. **Prices:** Start $350. **Remarks:** Spare-time maker; first knife sold in 1984. **Mark:** Last nam

**LERCH, MATTHEW,** N88 W23462 North Lisbon Rd., Sussex, WI 5308 Phone: 262-246-6362, Web: www.lerchcustomknives.com
**Specialties:** Gentlemen's folders. **Patterns:** Interframe and integral folde lock backs, slip-joints, side locks, button locks and liner locks. **Technic** Grinds ATS-34, 1095, 440 and Damascus. Offers filework and embellish bolsters. **Prices:** $400 to $6,000. **Remarks:** Part-time maker; first knife sold 1995. **Mark:** Last name.

**LEVENGOOD, BILL,** 15011 Otto Rd., Tampa, FL 33624, Phone: 813-961-5688
**Specialties:** Working straight knives and folders. **Patterns:** Hunters, Bowi folders and collector pieces. **Technical:** Grinds ATS-34, BG-42 and Da ascus. **Prices:** $175 to $1,500. **Remarks:** Part-time maker; first knife sold 1983. **Mark:** Last name, city, state.

**LEVERETT, KEN,** PO Box 696, Lithia, FL 33547, Phone: 813-689-85
**Specialties:** High-tech and working straight knives and folders of his des and to customer specs. **Patterns:** Bowies, hunters and locking folders. **Te nical:** Grinds ATS-34, Damascus. **Prices:** $100 to $350; some to $1,5 **Remarks:** Part-time maker; first knife sold in 1991. **Mark:** Name, city, state

**LEVIN, JACK,** 7216 Bay Pkwy., Brooklyn, NY 11204, Phone: 718-232-8574
**Specialties:** Highly embellished collector knives.

**LEVINE, BOB,** 101 Westwood Dr., Tullahoma, TN 37388, Phone: 931-454-9943, levineknives@msn.com
**Specialties:** Working left- and right-handed Liner Lock® folders. **Patte** Hunters and folders. **Technical:** Grinds ATS-34, 440C, D2, O1 and sc Damascus; hollow and some flat grinds. Uses sheep horn, fossil ivory, Mic and exotic woods. Provides custom leather sheath with each fixed kr **Prices:** $125 to $500; some higher. **Remarks:** Full-time maker; first knife s in 1984. Voting member Knife Makers Guild. **Mark:** Name and logo.

**LEWIS, K.J.,** 374 Cook Rd., Lugoff, SC 29078, Phone: 803-438-4343

**LEWIS, MIKE,** 21 Pleasant Hill Dr., DeBary, FL 32713, Phone: 386-7 0936, dragonsteel@prodigy.net
**Specialties:** Traditional straight knives. **Patterns:** Swords and dagg **Technical:** Grinds 440C, ATS-34 and 5160. Frequently uses cast bronze cast nickel guards and pommels. **Prices:** $100 to $750. **Remarks:** Part-t maker; first knife sold in 1988. **Mark:** Dragon Steel and serial number.

**LEWIS, TOM R.,** 1613 Standpipe Rd., Carlsbad, NM 88220, Phone: 5 885-3616, Web: www.cavemen.net/lewisknives/
**Specialties:** Traditional working straight knives and pocketknives. **Patte** Outdoor knives, hunting knives and Bowies. **Technical:** Grinds ATS-34 fo 5168 and 01. Makes wire, pattern welded and chainsaw Damascus. **Pric** $100 to $900. **Remarks:** Part-time maker; first knife sold in 1980. Doing b ness as TR Lewis Handmade Knives. **Mark:** Lewis family crest.

**LEWIS, BILL,** PO Box 63, Riverside, IA 52327, Phone: 319-629-557
**Specialties:** Folders of all kins including those made from one-piece of w tail antler with or without the crown. **Patterns:** Hunters, folding hunters, f Bowies, push daggers, etc. **Prices:** $20 to $200. **Remarks:** Full-time ma first knife sold in 1978. **Mark:** W.E.L.

**LEWIS, STEVE,** Knife Dealer, PO Box 9056, Woodland Park, CO 80866, Phone: 719-686-1120 or 888-685-2322
**Specialties:** Buy, sell, trade and consign W. F. Moran and other fine custom-made knives. Mail order and major shows.

**LICATA, STEVEN,** LICATA CUSTOM KNIVES, 142 Orchard St., Garfield, NJ 07026, Phone: 973-341-4288, Web: steven.licata.home.att.net
**Prices:** $200 to $25,000.

**LIEBENBERG, ANDRE,** 8 Hilma Rd., Bordeauxrandburg 2196, SOUTH AFRICA, Phone: 011-787-2303
**Specialties:** High-art straight knives of his design. **Patterns:** Daggers, fighters and swords. **Technical:** Grinds 440C and 12C27. **Prices:** $250 to $500; some $4,000 and higher. Giraffe bone handles with semi-precious stones. **Remarks:** Spare-time maker; first knife sold in 1990. **Mark:** Initials.

**LIEGEY, KENNETH R.,** 132 Carney Dr., Millwood, WV 25262, Phone: 304-273-9545
**Specialties:** Traditional working/using straight knives of his design and to customer specs. **Patterns:** Hunters, utility/camp knives, miniatures. **Technical:** Grinds 440C. **Prices:** $75 to $150; some to $300. **Remarks:** Spare-time maker; first knife sold in 1977. **Mark:** First and middle initials, last name.

**LIGHTFOOT, GREG,** RR #2, Kitscoty AB, CANADA T0B 2P0, Phone: 780-846-2812, Pitbull@lightfootknives.com Web: www.lightfootknives.com
**Specialties:** Stainless steel and Damascus. **Patterns:** Boots, fighters and locking folders. **Technical:** Grinds BG-42, 440C, D2, CPM steels, Stellite 6K. Offers engraving. **Prices:** $250 to $500; some to $850. **Remarks:** Full-time maker; first knife sold in 1988. Doing business as Lightfoot Knives. **Mark:** Shark with Lightfoot Knives below.

**LIKARICH, STEVE,** PO Box 961, Colfax, CA 95713, Phone: 530-346-8480
**Specialties:** Fancy working knives; art knives of his design. **Patterns:** Hunters, fighters and art knives of his design. **Technical:** Grinds ATS-34, 154CM and 440C; likes high polishes and filework. **Prices:** $200 to $2,000; some higher. **Remarks:** Full-time maker; first knife sold in 1987. **Mark:** Name.

**LINKLATER, STEVE,** 8 Cossar Dr., Aurora, Ont., CANADA L4G 3N8, Phone: 905-727-8929, knifman@sympatico.ca
**Specialties:** Traditional working/using straight knives and folders of his design. **Patterns:** Fighters, hunters and locking folders. **Technical:** Grinds ATS-34, 440V and D2. **Prices:** $125 to $350; some to $600. **Remarks:** Part-time maker; first knife sold in 1987. Doing business as Links Knives. **Mark:** LINKS.

**LISTER JR., WELDON E.,** 9140 Sailfish Dr., Boerne, TX 78006, Phone: 210-981-2210
**Specialties:** One-of-a-kind fancy and embellished folders. **Patterns:** Locking and slip-joint folders. **Technical:** Commercial Damascus and O1. All knives embellished. Engraves, inlays, carves and scrimshaws. **Prices:** Upscale. **Remarks:** Spare-time maker; first knife sold in 1991. **Mark:** Last name.

**LITTLE, GUY A.,** 486 W Lincoln Ave., Oakhurst, NJ 07755

**LITTLE, LARRY,** 1A Cranberry Ln., Spencer, MA 01562, Phone: 508-885-2301
**Specialties:** Working straight knives of his design or to customer specs. Likes Scagel-style. **Patterns:** Hunters, fighters...can grind other patterns. **Technical:** Grinds L6 and O1, most have file work. Prefers natural handle material especially antler. Uses nickel silver. Makes own heavy duty leather sheath. **Prices:** start at $100. **Remarks:** Part-time maker. First knife sold in 1985. Offers knife repairs. **Mark:** Last name.

**LITTLE, GARY M.,** HC84 Box 10301, PO Box 156, Broadbent, OR 97414, Phone: 503-572-2656
**Specialties:** Fancy working knives. **Patterns:** Hunters, tantos, Bowies, axes and buckskinners; locking folders and interframes. **Technical:** Forges and grinds O1, L6, 1095; makes his own Damascus; bronze fittings. **Prices:** $85 to $300; some to $2,500. **Remarks:** Full-time maker; first knife sold in 1979. Doing business as Conklin Meadows Forge. **Mark:** Name, city and state.

**LITTLE, JIMMY L.,** PO Box 871652, Wasilla, AK 99687, Phone: 907-373-7831
**Specialties:** Working straight knives; fancy period pieces. **Patterns:** Bowies, bush swords and camp knives. **Technical:** Grinds 440C, 154CM and ATS-34. **Prices:** $100 to $1,000. **Remarks:** Full-time maker; first knife sold in 1984. **Mark:** First and middle initials, last name.

**LIVELY, TIM AND MARIAN,** PO Box 1172, Marble Falls, TX 78654, Web: www.livelyknives.com
**Specialties:** Multi-cultural primitive knives of their design on speculation. **Patterns:** Old world designs. **Technical:** Hand forges using ancient techniques; hammer finish. **Prices:** High. **Remarks:** Full-time makers; first knife sold in 1974. Offers knifemaking DVD online. **Mark:** Last name.

**LIVESAY, NEWT,** 3306 S. Dogwood St., Siloam Springs, AR 72761, Phone: 479-549-3356, Fax: 479-549-3357, newt@newtlivesay.com Web: www.newtlivesay.com
**Specialties:** Combat utility knives, hunting knives, titanium knives, swords, axes, KYDWX sheaths for knives and pistols, custom orders.

**LIVINGSTON, ROBERT C.,** PO Box 6, Murphy, NC 28906, Phone: 704-837-4155
**Specialties:** Art letter openers to working straight knives. **Patterns:** Minis to machetes. **Technical:** Forges and grinds most steels. **Prices:** Start at $20. **Remarks:** Full-time maker; first knife sold in 1988. Doing business as Mystik Knife works. **Mark:** MYSTIK.

**LOCKE, KEITH,** PMB 141, 7120 Rufe Snow Dr. Ste. 106, Watauga, TX 76148-1867, Phone: 817-514-7272
**Technical:** Forges carbon steel and handcrafts sheaths for his knives. **Remarks:** Sold first knife in 1996.

**LOCKETT, LOWELL C.,** 66653 Gunderson Rd., North Bend, OR 97459-9210, Phone: 541-756-1614, spur@outdrs.net
**Specialties:** Traditional and working/using knives. **Patterns:** Bowies, hunters, utility/camp knives. **Technical:** Forges 5160, 1095, 1084, 02, L6. Makes own guards and sheaths. **Prices:** Start at $90. **Remarks:** Full-time maker. **Mark:** L C lockett (on side of blade) ABS Journeyman Smith, member OKCA.

**LOCKETT, STERLING,** 527 E. Amherst Dr., Burbank, CA 91504, Phone: 818-846-5799
**Specialties:** Working straight knives and folders to customer specs. **Patterns:** Hunters and fighters. **Technical:** Grinds. **Prices:** Moderate. **Remarks:** Spare-time maker. **Mark:** Name, city with hearts.

**LOERCHNER, WOLFGANG,** WOLFE FINE KNIVES, PO Box 255, Bayfield, Ont., CANADA N0M 1G0, Phone: 519-565-2196
**Specialties:** Traditional straight knives, mostly ornate. **Patterns:** Small swords, daggers and stilettos; locking folders and miniatures. **Technical:** Grinds D2, 440C and 154CM; all knives hand-filed and flat-ground. **Prices:** $300 to $5,000; some to $10,000. **Remarks:** Part-time maker; first knife sold in 1983. Doing business as Wolfe Fine Knives. **Mark:** WOLFE.

**LONEWOLF, J. AGUIRRE,** 481 Hwy 105, Demorest, GA 30535, Phone: 706-754-4660, Fax: 706-754-8470, Web: http://hemc.net/~lonewolf
**Specialties:** High-art working and using straight knives of his design. **Patterns:** Bowies, hunters, utility/camp knives and fine steel blades. **Technical:** Forges Damascus and high-carbon steel. Most knives have hand-carved moose antler handles. **Prices:** $55 to $500; some to $2,000. **Remarks:** Full-time maker; first knife sold in 1980. Doing business as Lonewolf Trading Post. **Mark:** Stamp.

**LONG, GLENN A.,** 10090 SW 186th Ave., Dunnellon, FL 34432, Phone: 352-489-4272
**Specialties:** Classic working and using straight knives of his design and to customer specs. **Patterns:** Hunters, Bowies, utility. **Technical:** Grinds 440C D2 and 440V. **Prices:** $85 to $300; some to $800. **Remarks:** Part-time maker; first knife sold in 1990. **Mark:** Last name inside diamond.

**LONGWORTH, DAVE,** 1811 SR 774, Hamersville, OH 45130, Phone: 513-876-3637
**Specialties:** High-tech working knives. **Patterns:** Locking folders, hunters, fighters and elaborate daggers. **Technical:** Grinds O1, ATS-34, 440C; buys Damascus. **Prices:** $125 to $600; some higher. **Remarks:** Part-time maker; first knife sold in 1980. **Mark:** Last name.

**LOOS, HENRY C.,** 210 Ingraham, New Hyde Park, NY 11040, Phone: 516-354-1943, hcloos@optonline.net
**Specialties:** Miniature fancy knives and period pieces of his design. **Patterns:** Bowies, daggers and swords. **Technical:** Grinds O1 and 440C. Uses sterling, 18K, rubies and emeralds. All knives come with handmade hardwood cases. **Prices:** $90 to $195, some to $250. **Remarks:** Spare-time maker; first knife sold in 1990. **Mark:** Script last initial.

**LORO, GENE,** 2457 State Route 93 NE, Crooksville, OH 43731, Phone: 740-982-4521, Fax: 740-982-1249, geney@aol.com
**Specialties:** Hand forged knives. **Patterns:** Damascus, Random, Ladder, Twist, etc. **Technical:** ABS Journeyman Smith. **Prices:** $200 and up. **Remarks:** Loro and hand forged by Gene Loro. **Mark:** Loro. Retired engineer.

**LOTT-SINCLAIR, SHERRY,** 1100 Legion Park Road, Greensburg, KY 42743, Phone: 270-932-2212, 4sherrylott@msn.com
**Specialties:** One-of-a-kind, usually carved handles. **Patterns:** Art. **Technical:** Carbon steel, stock removal. Prices: Moderate. **Mark:** Sherry Lott. **Other:** First knife sold in 1994.

**LOVE, ED,** 19443 Mill Oak, San Antonio, TX 78258, Phone: 210-497-1021, edlove@co.bexar.tx.us
**Specialties:** Hunting, working knives and some art pieces. **Technical:** Grinds ATS-34, and 440C. **Prices:** $150 and up. **Remarks:** Part-time maker. First knife sold in 1980. **Mark:** Name in a weeping heart.

**LOVELESS, R.W.,** PO Box 7836, Riverside, CA 92503, Phone: 951-689-7800
**Specialties:** Working knives, fighters and hunters of his design. **Patterns:** Contemporary hunters, fighters and boots. **Technical:** Grinds 154CM and ATS-34. **Prices:** $850 to $4950. **Remarks:** Full-time maker since 1969. **Mark:** Name in logo.

**LOVESTRAND, SCHUYLER,** 1136 19th St. SW, Vero Beach, FL 32962, Phone: 561-778-0282, Fax: 561-466-1126
**Specialties:** Fancy working straight knives of his design and to customer specs; unusual fossil ivories. **Patterns:** Hunters, fighters, Bowies and fishing knives. **Technical:** Grinds stainless steel. **Prices:** $275 and up. **Remarks:** Part-time maker; first knife sold in 1982. **Mark:** Name in logo.

**LOZIER, DON,** 5394 SE 168th Ave., Ocklawaha, FL 32179, Phone: 352-625-3576
**Specialties:** Fancy and working straight knives of his design and in standard patterns. **Patterns:** Daggers, fighters, boot knives, and hunters. **Technical:** Grinds ATS-34, 440C and Damascus. Most pieces are highly embellished by notable artisans. Taking limited number of orders per annum. **Prices:** Start at $250; most are $1,250 to $3,000; some to $12,000. **Remarks:** Full-time maker. **Mark:** Name.

**LUCHAK, BOB,** 15705 Woodforest Blvd., Channelview, TX 77530, Phone: 281-452-1779
**Specialties:** Presentation knives; start of The Survivor series. **Patterns:** Skinners, Bowies, camp axes, steak knife sets and fillet knives. **Technical:** Grinds 440C. Offers electronic etching; filework. **Prices:** $50 to $1,500. **Remarks:** Full-time maker; first knife sold in 1983. Doing business as Teddybear Knives. **Mark:** Full name, city and state with Teddybear logo.

**LUCHINI, BOB,** 1220 Dana Ave., Palo Alto, CA 94301, Phone: 650-321-8095, rwluchin@bechtel.com

**LUCIE, JAMES R.,** 4191 E. Fruitport Rd., Fruitport, MI 49415, Phone: 231-865-6390, Fax: 231-865-3170, scagel@netonecom.net
**Specialties:** Hand-forges William Scagel-style knives. **Patterns:** Authentic scagel-style knives and miniatures. **Technical:** Forges 5160, 52100 and 1084 and forges his own pattern welded Damascus steel. **Prices:** Start at $750. **Remarks:** Full-time maker; first knife sold in 1975. Believes in sole authorship of his work. ABS Journeyman Smith. **Mark:** Scagel Kris with maker's name and address.

**LUCKETT, BILL,** 108 Amantes Ln., Weatherford, TX 76088, Phone: 817-613-9412
**Specialties:** Uniquely patterned robust straight knives. **Patterns:** Fighters, Bowies, hunters. **Technical:** Grinds 440C and commercial Damascus; makes heavy knives with deep grinding. **Prices:** $275 to $1,000; some to $2,000. **Remarks:** Part-time maker; first knife sold in 1975. **Mark:** Last name over Bowie logo.

**LUDWIG, RICHARD O.,** 57-63 65 St., Maspeth, NY 11378, Phone: 718-497-5969
**Specialties:** Traditional working/using knives. **Patterns:** Boots, hunters and utility/camp knives folders. Technical Grinds 440C, ATS-34 and BG42. File work on guards and handles; silver spacers. Offers scrimshaw. **Prices:** $325 to $400; some to $2,000. **Remarks:** Full-time maker. **Mark:** Stamped first initial, last name, state.

**LUI, RONALD M.,** 4042 Harding Ave., Honolulu, HI 96816, Phone: 808-734-7746
**Specialties:** Working straight knives and folders in standard patterns. **Patterns:** Hunters, boots and liner locks. **Technical:** Grinds 440C and ATS-34. **Prices:** $100 to $700. **Remarks:** Spare-time maker; first knife sold in 1988. **Mark:** Initials connected.

**LUM, ROBERT W.,** 901 Travis Ave., Eugene, OR 97404, Phone: 541-688-2737
**Specialties:** High-art working knives of his design. **Patterns:** Hunters, fighters, tantos and folders. **Technical:** Grinds 440C, 154CM and ATS-34; plans to forge soon. **Prices:** $175 to $500; some to $800. **Remarks:** Full-time maker; first knife sold in 1976. **Mark:** Chop with last name underneath.

**LUMAN, JAMES R.,** Clear Creek Trail, Anaconda, MT 59711, Phone: 406-560-1461
**Specialties:** San Mai and composite end patterns. **Patterns:** Pool and eye Spirograph southwest composite patterns. **Technical:** All patterns with blued steel; all made by him. **Prices:** $200 to $800. **Mark:** Stock blade removal. Pattern welded steel. Bottom ricasso JRL.

**LUNDSTROM, JAN-AKE,** Mastmostigen 8, 66010 Dals-Langed, SWEDEN, Phone: 0531-40270
**Specialties:** Viking swords, axes and knives in cooperation with handle makers. **Patterns:** All traditional-styles, especially swords and inlaid blades. **Technical:** Forges his own Damascus and laminated steel. **Prices:** $200 to $1,000. **Remarks:** Full-time maker; first knife sold in 1985; collaborates with museums. **Mark:** Runic.

**LUNN, LARRY A.,** PO Box 48931, St. Petersburg, FL 33743, Phone: 727-345-7455, larry@lunnknives.com Web: www.lunnknives.com
**Specialties:** Fancy folders and double action autos; some straight blades. **Patterns:** All types; his own designs. **Technical:** Stock removal; commercia Damascus. **Prices:** $125 and up. **Remarks:** File work inlays and exotic materials. **Mark:** Name in script.

**LUNN, GAIL,** PO Box 48931, St. Petersburg, FL 33743, Phone: 727-345-7455, gail@lunnknives.com Web: www.lunnknives.com
**Specialties:** Fancy folders and double action autos, some straight blades **Patterns:** One-of-a-kind - All types. **Technical:** Stock removal - Hand made **Prices:** $300 and up. **Remarks:** Fancy file work, exotic materials, inlays stone etc. **Mark:** Name in script.

**LUPOLE, JAMIE G.,** KUMA KNIVES, 285 Main St., Kirkwood, NY 13795, Phone: 607-775-9368, jlupole@stny.rr.com
**Specialties:** Working and collector grade fixed blades, ethnic-styled blades **Patterns:** Fighters, Bowies, tacticals, hunters, camp, utility, personal carr knives, some swords. **Technical:** Forges and grinds 10XX series and othe high-carbon steels, grinds ATS-34 and 440C, will use just about every handl material available. **Prices:** $80 to $500; and up. **Remarks:** Part-time make since 1999. **Marks:** "KUMA" hot stamped, name, city and state-etched, o "Daiguma saku" in kanji.

**LUTZ, GREG,** 127 Crescent Rd., Greenwood, SC 29646, Phone: 864-229-7340
**Specialties:** Working and using knives and period pieces of his design and t customer specs. **Patterns:** Fighters, hunters and swords. **Technical:** Forge 1095 and O1; grinds ATS-34. Differentially heat-treats forged blades; use cryogenic treatment on ATS-34. **Prices:** $50 to $350; some to $1,20 **Remarks:** Part-time maker; first knife sold in 1986. Doing business as Sco pion Forge. **Mark:** First initial, last name.

**LYLE III, ERNEST L.,** LYLE KNIVES, PO Box 1755, Chiefland, FL 32644, Phone: 352-490-6693, www.ernestlyleknives.com
**Specialties:** Fancy period pieces; one-of-a-kind and limited editions. **Pat terns:** Arabian/Persian influenced fighters, military knives, Bowies and Roma short swords; several styles of hunters. **Technical:** Grinds 440C, D2 and 15 CM. Engraves. **Prices:** Upscale. **Remarks:** Full-time maker; first knife sold i 1972. **Mark:** Last name in capital letters - LYLE over a much smaller Chie land.

**LYTTLE, BRIAN,** Box 5697, High River, AB, CANADA T1V 1M7, Phone 403-558-3638, brianlyttle@cadvision.com
**Specialties:** Fancy working straight knives and folders; art knives. **Patterns** Bowies, daggers, dirks, Sgian Dubhs, folders, dress knives. **Technica** Forges Damascus steel; engraving; scrimshaw; heat-treating; classe **Prices:** $200 to $1,000; some to $5,000. **Remarks:** Full-time maker; first kni sold in 1983. **Mark:** Last name, country.

## M

**MACDONALD, JOHN,** 9 David Dr., Raymond, NH 03077, Phone: 603-895-0918
**Specialties:** Working/using straight knives of his design and to custom specs. **Patterns:** Japanese cutlery, Bowies, hunters and working knive **Technical:** Grinds O1, L6 and ATS-34. Swords have matching handles a scabbards with Japanese flair. **Prices:** $70 to $250; some to $500. **Remark** Part-time maker; first knife sold in 1988. Wood/glass-topped custom case Doing business as Mac the Knife. **Mark:** Initials.

**MACDONALD, DAVID,** 2824 Hwy 47, Los Lunas, NM 87031, Phone: 505-866-5866

**MACKIE, JOHN,** 13653 Lanning, Whittier, CA 90605, Phone: 562-945-6104
**Specialties:** Forged. **Patterns:** Bowie and camp knives. **Technical:** Attend ABS Bladesmith School. **Prices:** $75 to $500. **Mark:** JSM in a triangle.

**MACKRILL, STEPHEN,** PO Box 1580, Pinegowrie 2123, Johannesbur SOUTH AFRICA, Phone: 27-11-886-2893, Fax: 27-11-334-6230, info@mackrill.co.za Web: www.mackrill.net
**Specialties:** Art fancy, historical, collectors and corporate gifts cutlery. **Pa terns:** Fighters, hunters, camp, custom lock back and liner lock folders. **Tec nical:** N690, 12C27, ATS-34, silver and gold inlay on handles; wooden a silver sheaths. **Prices:** $330 and upwards. **Remarks:** First knife sold in 19 **Mark:** Oval with first initial, last name, "Maker" country of origin.

**MADISON II, BILLY D.,** 2295 Tyler Rd., Remlap, AL 35133, Phone: 205-680-6722, littleh@bellsouth.net
**Specialties:** Traditional working and using straight knives and folders of his design or yours. **Patterns:** Hunters, locking folders, utility/camp knives, and fighters. **Technical:** Grinds 440C, ATS-34, D2 and BG-42; forges some high-carbons. Prefers natural handle material. Ivory, bone, exotic woods and horns. **Prices:** $250 to $500 depending on knife. My mirror finish has to be seen to aff. **Remarks:** Limited part-time maker (disabled machinist); first knife sold in 1978. Had first knife returned a folder needed buff! Horn re-epoxied. **Mark:** Last name and year. Offers sheaths. **Other:** Wife makes sheaths. All knives have unconditional lifetime warranty. Never had a knife returned in 27 years.

**MADRULLI, MME JOELLE,** RESIDENCE STE CATHERINE B1, Salon De Provence, FRANCE 13330

**MAE, TAKAO,** 1-119, 1-4 Uenohigashi, Toyonaka, Osaka, JAPAN 560-0013, Phone: 81-6-6852-2758, Fax: 81-6-6481-1649, taka-mae@nifty.com
**Remarks:** Distinction stylish in art-forged blades, with lacquered ergonomic handles.

**MAESTRI, PETER A.,** S11251 Fairview Rd., Spring Green, WI 53588, Phone: 608-546-4481
**Specialties:** Working straight knives in standard patterns. **Patterns:** Camp and fishing knives, utility green-river-styled. **Technical:** Grinds 440C, 154CM and 440A. **Prices:** $15 to $45; some to $150. **Remarks:** Full-time maker; first knife sold in 1981. Provides professional cutler service to professional cutters. **Mark:** CARISOLO, MAESTRI BROS., or signature.

**MAGEE, JIM,** 748 S Front #3, Salina, KS 67401, Phone: 785-820-6928
**Specialties:** Working and fancy folding knives. **Patterns:** Liner locking folders, favorite is his Persian. **Technical:** Grinds ATS-34, Devin Thomas & Eggerling Damascus, titanium. Liners Prefer mother-of-pearl handles. **Prices:** Start at $225 to $1,200. **Remarks:** Part-time maker, first knife sold in 2001. Purveyor since 1982. Currently President of the Professional Knifemakers Assn. **Mark:** Last name.

**MAGRUDER, JASON,** 10w Saint Elmo Ave, Colorado Springs, CO 80906, Phone: 719-210-1579, belstain@hotmail.com
**Specialties:**Fancy/embellished and working/using knives of his own design or to customer specs. Fancy filework and carving. **Patterns:** Tactical straight knives, hunters, bowies and lockback folders. **Technical:** Flats grinds S30V, CPM3V, and 1080. Forges own Damascus. **Prices:** $150 and up. **Remarks:** Part-time maker; first knife sold in 2000. **Mark:** Magruder, or initials J M.

**MAHOMEDY, A. R.,** PO Box 76280, Marble Ray KZN, 4035, SOUTH AFRICA, Phone: +27 31 577 1451, arm-koknives@mweb.co.za Web: www.arm-koknives.co.za
**Specialties:** Daggers, elegant folders, hunters & utilities. Prefers to work to commissions, collectons & presentations. With handles of mother of pearl, fossil & local ivories. Exotic dyed/stablized burls, giraffe bone and horns.**Technical:** Via stock removal grinds Damasteel, carbon and mosaic Damascus, ATS-34, N690, 440A, 440B, 12 C 27 and RWL 34. **Prices:** $500 and up. **Remarks:** Part-time maker. First knife sold in 1995. Member knifemakers Guild of SA. **Mark:** Logo of initials A R M crowned with a "Minaret".

**MAIENKNECHT, STANLEY,** 38648 S.R. 800, Sardis, OH 43946

**MAINES, JAY,** SUNRISE RIVER CUSTOM KNIVES, 5584 266th St., Wyoming, MN 55092, Phone: 651-462-5301, jaymaines@fronternet.net Web: http://www.sunrisecustomknives.com
**Specialties:** Heavy duty working, classic and traditional fixed blades. Some high-tech and fancy embellished knives available. **Patterns:** Hunters, skinners, Bowies, Tantos, fillet, fighters, daggers, boot and cutlery sets. **Technical:** Hollow ground, stock removal blades of 440C, ATS-34 and CPM S-90V. Prefers natural handle materials, exotic hard woods, and stag, rams and buffalo horns. Offers dovetailed bolsters in brass, stainless steel and nickel silver. Custom sheaths from matching wood or hand-stitched from heavy duty water buffalo hide. **Prices:** Moderate to up-scale. **Remarks:** Part-time maker; first knife sold in 1992. Color brochure available upon request. Doing business as Sunrise River Custom Knives. **Mark:** Full name under a Rising Sun logo. **Other:** Offers fixed blade knives repair and handle conversions.

**MAISEY, ALAN,** PO Box 197, Vincentia 2540, NSW AUSTRALIA, Phone: 2-4443 7829, tosanaji@excite.com
**Specialties:** Daggers, especially krisses; period pieces. **Technical:** Offers knives and finished blades in Damascus and nickel Damascus. **Prices:** $75 to $2,000; some higher. **Remarks:** Part-time maker; provides complete restoration service for krisses. Trained by a Javanese Kris smith. **Mark:** None, triangle in a box, or three peaks.

**MAJER, MIKE,** 50 Palmetto Bay Rd., Hilton Head, SC 29928, Phone: 843-681-3483

**MAKOTO, KUNITOMO,** 3-3-18 Imazu-cho, Fukuyama-city, Hiroshima, JAPAN, Phone: 084-933-5874, kunitomo@po.iijnet.or.jp

**MALABY, RAYMOND J.,** 835 Calhoun Ave., Juneau, AK 99801, Phone: 907-586-6981, Fax: 907-523-8031, malaby@gci.net
**Specialties:** Straight working knives. **Patterns:** Hunters, skiners, bowies, and camp knives. **Technical:** Hand forged 1084, 5160, O1 and grinds ATS-34 stainless.**Prices:** $195 to $400. **Remarks:** First knife sold in 1984. **Mark:** First initial, last name, city, and state.

**MALLETT, JOHN,** 760 E Francis St. #N, Ontario, CA 91761, Phone: 800-532-3336/ 909-923-4116, Fax: 909-923-9932, trugrit1@aol.com Web: www.trugrit.com
**Specialties:** Complete line of 3/M, Norton and Hermes belts for grinding and polishing 24-2000 grit; also hard core, Bader and Burr King grinders. Baldor motors and buffers. ATS-34, 440C, BG42 and 416 stainless steel.

**MALLOY, JOE,** 1039 Schwabe St., Freeland, PA 18224, Phone: 570-636-2781
**Specialties:** Working straight knives and lock back folders—plain and fancy—of his design. **Patterns:** Hunters, utility, Bowie, survival knives, folders. **Technical:** Grinds ATS-34, 440C, D2 and A2 and Damascus. Makes own leather and kyder sheaths. **Prices:** $100 to $1,800. **Remarks:** Part-time maker; first knife sold in 1982. **Mark:** First and middle initials, last name, city and state.

**MANABE, MICHAEL K.,** 3659 Tomahawk Lane, San Diego, CA 92117, Phone: 619-483-2416
**Specialties:** Classic and high-art straight knives of his design or to customer specs. **Patterns:** Bowies, fighters, hunters, utility/camp knives; all knives one-of-a-kind. **Technical:** Forges and grinds 52100, 5160 and 1095. Does multiple quenching for distinctive temper lines. Each blade triple-tempered. **Prices:** Start at $200. **Remarks:** Part-time maker; first knife sold in 1994. **Mark:** First and middle initials, last name and J.S. on other side.

**MANEKER, KENNETH,** RR 2, Galiano Island, B.C., CANADA V0N 1P0, Phone: 604-539-2084
**Specialties:** Working straight knives; period pieces. **Patterns:** Camp knives and hunters; French chef knives. **Technical:** Grinds 440C, 154CM and Vascowear. **Prices:** $50 to $200; some to $300. **Remarks:** Part-time maker; first knife sold in 1981. Doing business as Water Mountain Knives. **Mark:** Japanese Kanji of initials, plus glyph.

**MANKEL, KENNETH,** 7836 Cannonsburg Rd., Cannonsburg, MI 49317, Phone: 616-874-6955

**MANLEY, DAVID W.,** 3270 Six Mile Hwy., Central, SC 29630, Phone: 864-654-1125, nmanley@innova.net
**Specialties:** Working straight knives of his design or to custom specs. **Patterns:** Hunters, boot and fighters. **Technical:** Grinds 440C and ATS-34. **Prices:** $60 to $250. **Remarks:** Part-time maker; first knife sold in 1994. **Mark:** First initial, last name, year and serial number.

**MANN, MICHAEL L.,** IDAHO KNIFE WORKS, PO Box 144, Spirit Lake, ID 83869, Phone: 509 994-9394, Web: www.idahoknifeworks.com
**Specialties:** Good working blades-historical reproduction, modern or custom design. **Patterns:** Cowboy Bowies, Mountain Man period blades, old-style folders, designer and maker of "The Cliff Knife", hunter knives, hand ax and fish fillet.**Technical:** High-carbon steel blades-hand forged 5160. Stock removed 15N20 steel. Also Damascus **Prices:** $125 to $600+. **Remarks:** Made first knife in 1965. Full-time making knives as Idaho Knife Works since 1986. Functional as well as collectible. Each knife truly unique! **Mark:** Four mountain peaks are his initials MM.

**MANN, TIM,** BLADEWORKS, PO Box 1196, Honokaa, HI 96727, Phone: 808-775-0949, Fax: 808-775-0949, birdman@shaka.com
**Specialties:** Hand-forged knives and swords. **Patterns:** Bowies, Tantos, pesh kabz, daggers. **Technical:** Use 5160, 1050, 1075, 1095 and ATS-34 steels, cable Damascus. **Prices:** $200 to $800. **Remarks:** Just learning to forge Damascus. **Mark:** None yet.

**MARAGNI, DAN,** RD 1, Box 106, Georgetown, NY 13072, Phone: 315-662-7490
**Specialties:** Heavy-duty working knives, some investor class. **Patterns:** Hunters, fighters and camp knives, some Scottish types. **Technical:** Forges W2 and his own Damascus; toughness and edge-holding a high priority. **Prices:** $125 to $500; some to $1,000. **Remarks:** Full-time maker; first knife sold in 1975. **Mark:** Celtic initials in circle.

**MARKLEY, KEN,** 7651 Cabin Creek Lane, Sparta, IL 62286, Phone: 618-443-5284
**Specialties:** Traditional working and using knives of his design and to customer specs. **Patterns:** Fighters, hunters and utility/camp knives. **Technical:** Forges 5160, 1095 and L6; makes his own Damascus; does file work. **Prices:**

$150 to $800; some to $2,000. **Remarks:** Part-time maker; first knife sold in 1991. Doing business as Cabin Creek Forge. **Mark:** Last name, JS.

**MARLOWE, DONALD,** 2554 Oakland Rd., Dover, PA 17315, Phone: 717-764-6055
**Specialties:** Working straight knives in standard patterns. **Patterns:** Bowies, fighters, boots and utility knives. **Technical:** Grinds D2 and 440C. Integral design hunter models. **Prices:** $120 to $525. **Remarks:** Spare-time maker; first knife sold in 1977. **Mark:** Last name.

**MARLOWE, CHARLES,** 10822 Poppleton Ave., Omaha, NE 68144, Phone: 402-933-5065, cmarlowe1@cox.net Web: www.marloweknives.com
**Specialties:** Folding knives and balisong. **Patterns:** Tactical pattern folders. **Technical:** Grind ATS-34, S30V, others on request. Forges/grinds 1095 on occasion. **Prices:** Start at $350. **Remarks:** First knife sold in 1993. Full-time since 1999. **Mark:** MARLOWE.

**MARSHALL, STEPHEN R.,** 975 Harkreader Rd., Mt. Juliet, TN 37122

**MARSHALL, GLENN,** PO Box 1099, 1117 Hofmann St., Mason, TX 76856, Phone: 915-347-6207
**Specialties:** Working knives and period pieces. **Patterns:** Straight and folding hunters, fighters and camp knives. **Technical:** Steel used 440C, D2, CPM and 440V. **Prices:** $90 and up according to options. **Remarks:** Full-time maker; first knife sold in 1932. **Mark:** First initial, last name, city and state with anvil logo.

**MARTIN, GENE,** PO Box 396, Williams, OR 97544, Phone: 541-846-6755, bladesmith@customknife.com
**Specialties:** Straight knives and folders. **Patterns:** Fighters, hunters, skinners, boot knives, spring back and lock back folders. **Technical:** Grinds ATS-34, 440C, Damascus and 154CM. Forges; makes own Damascus; scrimshaws. **Prices:** $150 to $2,500. **Remarks:** Full-time maker; first knife sold in 1993. Doing business as Provision Forge. **Mark:** Name and/or crossed staff and sword.

**MARTIN, ROBB,** 7 Victoria St., Elmira, Ontario, CANADA N3B 1R9

**MARTIN, PETER,** 28220 N. Lake Dr., Waterford, WI 53185, Phone: 262-895-2815, Web: www.petermartinknives.com
**Specialties:** Fancy, fantasy and working straight knives and folders of his design and in standard patterns. **Patterns:** Bowies, fighters, hunters, locking folders and liner locks. **Technical:** Forges own Mosaic Damascus, powdered steel and his own Damascus. Prefers natural handle material; offers file work and carved handles. **Prices:** Moderate. **Remarks:** Part-time maker; first knife sold in 1988. Doing business as Martin Custom Products. Uses only natural handle materials. **Mark:** Martin Knives.

**MARTIN, BRUCE E.,** Rt. 6, Box 164-B, Prescott, AR 71857, Phone: 501-887-2023
**Specialties:** Fancy working straight knives of his design. **Patterns:** Bowies, camp knives, skinners and fighters. **Technical:** Forges 5160, 1095 and his own Damascus. Uses natural handle materials; filework available. **Prices:** $75 to $350; some to $500. **Remarks:** Full-time maker; first knife sold in 1979. **Mark:** Name in arch.

**MARTIN, JIM,** 1120 S. Cadiz Ct., Oxnard, CA 93035, Phone: 805-985-9849
**Specialties:** Fancy and working/using folders of his design. **Patterns:** Automatics, locking folders and miniatures. **Technical:** Grinds 440C, AEB-L, 304SS and Damascus. **Prices:** $350 to $700; some to $1,500. **Remarks:** Full-time maker; first knife sold in 1992. Doing business as Jim Martin Custom Knives.

**MARTIN, RANDALL J.,** 51 Bramblewood St, Bridgewater, MA 02324, Phone: 508-279-0682
**Specialties:** High tech folding and fixed blade tactical knives employing the latest blade steels and exotic materials. Employs a unique combination of 3d-CNC machining and hand work on both blades and handles. All knives are designed for hard use. Clean, radical grinds and ergonomic handles are hallmarks of RJ's work, as is his reputation for producing :Scary Sharp" knives. **Technical:** Grinds CPM30V, CPM 3V, CPM154CM, A2 and stainless Damascus. Other CPM alloys used on request. Performs all heat treating and cryogenic processing in-house. **Remarks:** Full-time maker since 2001 and materials engineer. Former helicopter designer. First knife sold in 1976.

**MARTIN, TONY,** 108 S. Main St., PO Box 324, Arcadia, MO 63621, Phone: 573-546-2254, arcadian@charter.net Web: www.arcadianforge.com
**Specialties:** Specializes in historical designs, esp. puukko, skean dhu. **Remarks:** Premium quality blades, exotic wood handles, unmatched fit and finish. **Mark:** RJ MARTIN incapital, outline letters.

**MARTIN, WALTER E.,** 570 Cedar Flat Rd., Williams, OR 97544, Phone: 541-846-6755

**MARTIN, HAL W.,** 781 Hwy. 95, Morrilton, AR 72110, Phone: 501-354-1682, hmartin@ipa.net

**MARTIN, JOHN ALEXANDER,** 821 N Grand Ave., Okmulgee, OK 74447, Phone: 918-758-1099, jam773054@yahoo.com Web: www.jamblades.com
**Specialties:** Inlaid and engraved handles. **Patterns:** Bowies, fighters, hunte[rs] and traditional patterns. **Technical:** Forges 5160, 1084, and his own Dam[ascus]. **Prices:** Start at $185. **Remarks:** Part-time maker. **Mark:** Initials or tw[o] initials and last name with JS.

**MARTIN, MICHAEL W.,** Box 572, Jefferson St., Beckville, TX 75631, Phone: 903-678-2161
**Specialties:** Classic working/using straight knives of his design and in sta[n]dard patterns. **Patterns:** Hunters. **Technical:** Grinds ATS-34, 440C, O1 a[nd] A2. Bead blasted, Parkerized, high polish and satin finishes. Sheaths a[re] handmade. Also hand forges cable Damascus. **Prices:** $185 to $280 so[me] higher. **Remarks:** Part-time maker; first knife sold in 1995. Doing business [as] Michael W. Martin Knives. **Mark:** Name and city, state in arch.

**MARZITELLI, PETER,** 19929 35A Ave., Langley, BC, CANADA V3A 2R1, Phone: 604-532-8899, marzitelli@shaw.ca
**Specialties:** Specializes in unique functional knife shapes and designs usi[ng] natural and synthetic handle materials. **Patterns:** Mostly folders, some da[g]gers and art knives. **Technical:** Grinds ATS-34, S/S Damascus and othe[rs]. **Prices:** $220 to $1,000 (average $375). **Remarks:** Full-time maker; first kn[ife] sold in 1984. **Mark:** Stylized logo reads "Marz."

**MASON, BILL,** 1114 St. Louis, #33, Excelsior Springs, MO 64024, Phone: 816-637-7335
**Specialties:** Combat knives; some folders. **Patterns:** Fighters to match kn[ife] types in book *Cold Steel.* **Technical:** Grinds O1, 440C and ATS-34. **Price[s]:** $115 to $250; some to $350. **Remarks:** Spare-time maker; first knife sold [in] 1979. **Mark:** Initials connected.

**MASSEY, RON,** 61638 El Reposo St., Joshua Tree, CA 92252, Phone: 760-366-9239 after 5 p.m., Fax: 763-366-4620
**Specialties:** Classic, traditional, fancy/embellished, high art, period piec[es], working/using knives, straight knives, folders, and automatics. Your desi[gn], customer specs, about 175 standard patterns. **Patterns:** Automatics, hunt[ers] and fighters. All folders are side-locking folders. Unless requested as l[ock] books slip joint he specializes or custom designs. **Technical:** ATS-34, 44[0C], D-2 upon request. Engraving, filework, scrimshaw, most of the exotic han[dle] materials. All aspects are performed by him: inlay work in pearls or sto[ne], hand made Pem' work. **Prices:** $110 to $2,500; some to $6,000. **Remar[ks]:** Part-time maker; first knife sold in 1976.

**MASSEY, AL,** Box 14, Site 15, RR#2, Mount Uniacke, Nova Scotia, CANADA B0N 1Z0, Phone: 902-866-4754, armjan@attcanada.ca
**Specialties:** Working knives and period pieces. **Patterns:** Swords and d[ag]gers of Celtic to medieval design, Bowies. **Technical:** Forges 5160, 1084 a[nd] 1095. Makes own Damascus. **Prices:** $100 to $400; some to $900. **Remar[ks]:** Part-time maker, first blade sold in 1988. **Mark:** Initials and JS on Ricasso.

**MASSEY, ROGER,** 4928 Union Rd., Texarkana, AR 71854, Phone: 8[70]-779-1018
**Specialties:** Traditional and working straight knives and folders of his des[ign] and to customer specs. **Patterns:** Bowies, hunters, daggers and utility kniv[es]. **Technical:** Forges 1084 and 52100, makes his own Damascus. Offers [file]work and silver wire inlay in handles. **Prices:** $200 to $1,500; some to $2,5[00]. **Remarks:** Part-time maker; first knife sold in 1991. **Mark:** Last name, M.S.

**MATA, LEONARD,** 3583 Arruza St., San Diego, CA 92154, Phone: 6[19]-690-6935

**MATHEWS, CHARLIE AND HARRY,** TWIN BLADES, 121 Mt Pisgah Church Rd., Statesboro, GA 30458, Phone: 912-865-9098, twinblades@bulloch.net Web: www.twinxblades.com
**Specialties:** Working straight knives. **Patterns:** Hunters, fighters, Bowies [and] period pieces. **Technical:** Grinds D2, BG42, CPMS30V, CPM3V, ATS-34 [and] commercial Damascus; handmade sheaths some with exotic leather, [file] work. **Prices:** Starting at $125. **Remarks:** Twin brothers making knives [full] time under the label of Twin Blades. Charter members Georgia Custom Kn[ife] maker's Guild. **Mark:** Twin Blades over crossed knives, reverse side s[teel] type.

**MATSUOKA, SCOT,** 94-415 Ukalialii Place, Mililani, HI 96789, Phone: 808-625-6658, scottym@hawaii.rr.com
**Specialties:**Folders, fixed blades with custom hand-stitched sheaths. **[Pat]terns:**Gentleman's knives, hunters, tactical folders. **Technical:**440C, 154[CM], BG42, bolsters, file work, and engraving. **Prices:**Starting price $125[.] **Remarks:**Part-time maker, first knife sold in 2002. **Mark:**Logo, name [and] state.

**MATSUSAKI, TAKESHI,** MATSUSAKI KNIVES, 151 Ono-Cho Sasebo-shi, Nagasaki, JAPAN, Phone: 0956-47-2938, Fax: 0956-47-2938
**Specialties:** Working and collector grade front look and slip joint. **Patterns:** Sheffierd type folders. **Technical:** Grinds ATS-34 k-120. **Price:** $250 to $1,000; some to $8,000. **Remarks:** Part-time maker, first knife sold in 1990. **Mark:** Name and initials.

**MAXEN, MICK,** 2 Huggins Welham Green, "Hatfield, Herts", UNITED KINGDOM AL97LR, Phone: 01707 261213, mmaxen@aol.com
**Specialties:** Damascus and Mosaic. **Patterns:** Medieval-style daggers and Bowies. **Technical:** Forges CS75 and 15N20 / nickel Damascus. **Mark:** Last name with axe above.

**MAXFIELD, LYNN,** 382 Colonial Ave., Layton, UT 84041, Phone: 801-544-4176, lcmaxfield@networld.com
**Specialties:** Sporting knives, some fancy. **Patterns:** Hunters, fishing, fillet, special purpose: some locking folders. **Technical:** Grinds 440-C, ATS-34, 154-CM, D2, CPM-S60V, S90V, 530V, CPM-3, Talonite, and Damascus. **Prices:** $125 to $400; some to $900. **Remarks:** Part-time maker; first knife sold in 1979. **Mark:** Name, city and state.

**MAXWELL, DON,** 1484 Celeste Ave, Clovis, CA 93611, Phone: 559-299-2197, maxwellknives@aol.com
**Specialties:** Fancy folding knives and fixed blades of my design. **Patterns:** Hunters, fighters, utility/camp knives, liner lock folders and fantasy knives. **Technical:** Grinds 440C, ATS-34, D2 and commercial Damascus. **Prices:** $250 to $1,000; some to $2,500. **Remarks:** Full-time maker; first knife sold in 1987. **Mark:** Last name only.

**MAYNARD, WILLIAM N.,** 2677 John Smith Rd., Fayetteville, NC 28306, Phone: 910-425-1615
**Specialties:** Traditional and working straight knives of all designs. **Patterns:** Combat, Bowies, fighters, hunters and utility knives. **Technical:** Grinds 440C, ATS-34 and commercial Damascus. Offers fancy filework; handmade sheaths. **Prices:** $100 to $300; some to $750. **Remarks:** Full-time maker; first knife sold in 1988. **Mark:** Last name.

**MAYNARD, LARRY JOE,** PO Box 493, Crab Orchard, WV 25827
**Specialties:** Fancy and fantasy straight knives. **Patterns:** Big knives; a Bowie with a full false edge; fighting knives. **Technical:** Grinds standard steels. **Prices:** $350 to $500; some to $1,000. **Remarks:** Full-time maker; first knife sold in 1986. **Mark:** Middle and last initials.

**MAYO JR., TOM,** 67-420 Alahaka St., Waialua, HI 96791, Phone: 808-637-6560, mayotool@hawaii.rr.com
**Specialties:** Framelocks/tactical knives. **Patterns:** Combat knives, hunters, Bowies and folders. **Technical:** Titanium/stellite/S30V. **Prices:** $500 to $1,000. **Remarks:** Part-time maker; first knife sold in 1983. **Mark:** Volcano logo with name and state.

**MAYVILLE, OSCAR L.,** 2130 E. County Rd. 910S., Marengo, IN 47140, Phone: 812-338-3103
**Specialties:** Working straight knives; period pieces. **Patterns:** Kitchen cutlery, Bowies, camp knives and hunters. **Technical:** Grinds A2, O1 and 440C. **Prices:** $50 to $350; some to $500. **Remarks:** Full-time maker; first knife sold in 1984. **Mark:** Initials over knife logo.

**MCABEE, WILLIAM,** 27275 Norton Grade, Colfax, CA 95713, Phone: 530-389-8163
**Specialties:** Working/using knives. **Patterns:** Fighters, Bowies, Hunters. **Technical:** Grinds ATS-34. **Prices:** $75 to $200; some to $350. **Remarks:** Part-time maker; first knife sold in 1990. **Mark:** Stylized WM stamped.

**MCCALLEN JR., HOWARD H.,** 110 Anchor Dr., So Seaside Park, NJ 08752

**MCCARLEY, JOHN,** 4165 Harney Rd., Taneytown, MD 21787
**Specialties:** Working straight knives; period pieces. **Patterns:** Hunters, Bowies, camp knives, miniatures, throwing knives. **Technical:** Forges W2, O1 and his own Damascus. **Prices:** $150 to $300; some to $1,000. **Remarks:** Part-time maker; first knife sold in 1977. **Mark:** Initials in script.

**MCCARTY, HARRY,** 1479 Indian Ridge Rd., Blaine, TN 37709
**Specialties:** Period pieces. **Patterns:** Trade knives, Bowies, 18th and 19th century folders and hunting swords. **Technical:** Forges and grinds high-carbon steel. **Prices:** $75 to $1,300. **Remarks:** Full-time maker; first knife sold in 1977. **Mark:** Stylized initials inside a shamrock. **Other:** Doing business as Indian Ridge Forge.

**MCCLURE, MICHAEL,** 803 17th Ave., Menlo Park, CA 94025, Phone: 650-323-2596, mikesknives@comcast.net
**Specialties:** Working/using straight knives of his design and to customer specs. **Patterns:** Bowies, hunters, skinners, utility/camp, tantos, fillets and boot knives. **Technical:** Forges high-carbon and Damascus; also grinds stainless, all grades. **Prices:** Start at $200. **Remarks:** Part-time maker; first knife sold in 1991. **Mark:** Mike McClure. **Other:** ABS JourneymanSmith.

**MCCONNELL, CHARLES R.,** 158 Genteel Ridge, Wellsburg, WV 26070, Phone: 304-737-2015
**Specialties:** Working straight knives. **Patterns:** Hunters, Bowies, daggers, minis and push knives. **Technical:** Grinds 440C and 154CM; likes full tangs. **Prices:** $65 to $325; some to $800. **Remarks:** Part-time maker; first knife sold in 1977. **Mark:** Name.

**MCCONNELL JR., LOYD A.,** 1710 Rosewood, Odessa, TX 79761, Phone: 915-363-8344, ccknives@ccknives.com Web: www.cck-nives.com
**Specialties:** Working straight knives and folders, some fancy. **Patterns:** Hunters, boots, Bowies, locking folders and slip-joints. **Technical:** Grinds CPM Steels, ATS-34 and BG-42 and commercial Damascus. **Prices:** $175 to $900; some to $10,000. **Remarks:** Full-time maker; first knife sold in 1975. Doing business as Cactus Custom Knives. Markets product knives under name: Lone Star Knives. **Mark:** Name, city and state in cactus logo.

**MCCORNOCK, CRAIG,** MCC MTN OUTFITTERS, 4775 Rte. 212, Willow, NY 12495, Phone: 914-679-9758, Mccmtn@aol.com Web: www.mccmtn.com

**MCCOUN, MARK,** 14212 Pine Dr., DeWitt, VA 23840, Phone: 804-469-7631, markmccoun@aol.com
**Specialties:** Working/using straight knives of his design and in standard patterns; custom miniatures. **Patterns:** Locking liners, integrals. **Technical:** Grinds Damascus, ATS-34 and 440C. **Prices:** $150 to $500. **Remarks:** Part-time maker; first knife sold in 1989. **Mark:** Name, city and state.

**MCCRACKIN, KEVIN,** 3720 Hess Rd., House Spings, MO 63051, Phone: 636-677-6066

**MCCRACKIN AND SON, V.J.,** 3720 Hess Rd., House Springs, MO 63051, Phone: 636-677-6066
**Specialties:** Working straight knives in standard patterns. **Patterns:** Hunters, Bowies and camp knives. **Technical:** Forges L6, 5160, his own Damascus, cable Damascus. **Prices:** $125 to $700; some to $1,500. **Remarks:** Part-time maker; first knife sold in 1983. Son Kevin helps make the knives. **Mark:** Last name, M.S.

**MCCULLOUGH, JERRY,** 274 West Pettibone Rd., Georgiana, AL 36033, Phone: 334-382-7644, ke4er@alaweb.com
**Specialties:** Standard patterns or custom designs. **Technical:** Forge and grind scrap-tool and Damascus steels. Use natural handle materials and turquoise trim on some. Filework on others. **Prices:** $65 to $250 and up. **Remarks:** Part-time maker. **Mark:** Initials (JM) combined.

**MCDERMOTT, MICHAEL,** 151 Hwy F, Defiance, MO 63341, Phone: 314-798-2077

**MCDONALD, ROBERT J.,** 14730 61 Court N., Loxahatchee, FL 33470, Phone: 561-790-1470
**Specialties:** Traditional working straight knives to customer specs. **Patterns:** Fighters, swords and folders. **Technical:** Grinds 440C, ATS-34 and forges own Damascus. **Prices:** $150 to $1,000. **Remarks:** Part-time maker; first knife sold in 1988. **Mark:** Electro-etched name.

**MCDONALD, W.J. "JERRY",** 7173 Wickshire Cove E., Germantown, TN 38138, Phone: 901-756-9924, wjmcdonaldknives@email.msn.com Web: www.mcdonaldknives.com
**Specialties:** Classic and working/using straight knives of his design and in standard patterns. **Patterns:** Bowies, hunters kitchen and traditional spring back pocket knives. **Technical:** Grinds ATS-34, 154CM, D2, 440V, BG42 and 440C. **Prices:** $125 to $1,000. **Remarks:** Full-time maker; first knife sold in 1989. **Mark:** First and middle initials, last name, maker, city and state. Some of his knives are stamped McDonald in script.

**MCDONALD, ROBIN J.,** 6509 E Jeffrey Dr., Fayetteville, NC 28314
**Specialties:** Working knives of maker's design. **Patterns:** Bowies, hunters, camp knives and fighters. **Technical:** Forges primarily 5160. **Prices:** $100 to $500. **Remarks:** Part-time maker; first knife sold in 1999. **Mark:** Initials RJM.

**MCDONALD, RICH,** 4590 Kirk Rd., Columbiana, OH 44408, Phone: 330-482-0007, Fax: 330-482-0007
**Specialties:** Traditional working/using and art knives of his design. **Patterns:** Bowies, hunters, folders, primitives and tomahawks. **Technical:** Forges 5160, 1084, 1095, 52100 and his own Damascus. Fancy filework. **Prices:** $200 to $1,500. **Remarks:** Full-time maker; first knife sold in 1994. **Mark:** First and last initials connected.

**MCFALL, KEN,** PO Box 458, Lakeside, AZ 85929, Phone: 928-537-2026, Fax: 928-537-8066, knives@citlink.net
**Specialties:** Fancy working straight knives and some folders. **Patterns:** Daggers, boots, tantos, Bowies; some miniatures. **Technical:** Grinds D2, ATS-34 and 440C. Forges his own Damascus. **Prices:** $200 to $1,200. **Remarks:** Part-time maker; first knife sold in 1984. **Mark:** Name, city and state.

**MCFARLIN, ERIC E.,** PO Box 2188, Kodiak, AK 99615, Phone: 907-486-4799
**Specialties:** Working knives of his design. **Patterns:** Bowies, skinners, camp knives and hunters. **Technical:** Flat and convex grinds 440C, A2 and AEB-L. **Prices:** Start at $200. **Remarks:** Part-time maker; first knife sold in 1989. **Mark:** Name and city in rectangular logo.

**MCFARLIN, J.W.,** 3331 Pocohantas Dr., Lake Havasu City, AZ 86404, Phone: 928-855-8095, Fax: 928-855-8095, aztheedge@redrivernet.com
**Technical:** Flat grinds, D2, ATS-34, 440C, Thomas and Peterson Damascus. **Remarks:** From working knives to investment. Customer designs always welcome. 100% hand made. **Prices:** $150 to $3,000. **Mark:** Hand written in the blade.

**MCGILL, JOHN,** PO Box 302, Blairsville, GA 30512, Phone: 404-745-4686
**Specialties:** Working knives. **Patterns:** Traditional patterns; camp knives. **Technical:** Forges L6 and 9260; makes Damascus. **Prices:** $50 to $250; some to $500. **Remarks:** Full-time maker; first knife sold in 1982. **Mark:** XYLO.

**MCGOWAN, FRANK E.,** 12629 Howard Lodge Dr., Sykesville, MD 21784, Phone: 410-489-4323, fmcgowan1@comcast.net
**Specialties:** Fancy working knives and folders to customer specs. **Patterns:** Survivor knives, fighters, fishing knives, folders and hunters. **Technical:** Grinds and forges O1, 440C, 5160, ATS-34, 52100, or customer choice. **Prices:** $100 to $1,000; some more. **Remarks:** Full-time maker; first knife sold in 1986. **Mark:** Last name.

**MCGRATH, PATRICK T.,** 8343 Kenyon Ave., Westchester, CA 90045, Phone: 310-338-8764, hidinginLA@excite.com

**MCGRODER, PATRICK J.,** 5725 Chapin Rd., Madison, OH 44057, Phone: 216-298-3405, Fax: 216-298-3405
**Specialties:** Traditional working/using knives of his design. **Patterns:** Bowies, hunters and utility/camp knives. **Technical:** Grinds ATS-34, D2 and customer requests. Does reverse etching; heat-treats; prefers natural handle materials; custom made sheath with each knife. **Prices:** $125 to $250. **Remarks:** Part-time maker. **Mark:** First and middle initials, last name, maker, city and state.

**MCGUANE IV, THOMAS F.,** 410 South 3rd Ave., Bozeman, MT 59715, Phone: 406-586-0248, Web: http://www.thomasmcguane.com
**Specialties:** Multi metal inlaid knives of handmade steel. **Patterns:** Lock back and liner lock folders, fancy straight knives. **Technical:** 1084/1SN20 Damascus and Mosaic steel by maker. **Prices:** $1,000 and up. **Mark:** Surname or name and city, state.

**MCHENRY, WILLIAM JAMES,** Box 67, Wyoming, RI 02898, Phone: 401-539-8353
**Specialties:** Fancy high-tech folders of his design. **Patterns:** Locking folders with various mechanisms. **Technical:** One-of-a-kind only, no duplicates. Inventor of the Axis Lock. Most pieces disassemble and feature top-shelf materials including gold, silver and gems. **Prices:** Upscale. **Remarks:** Full-time maker; first knife sold in 1988. Former goldsmith. **Mark:** Last name or first and last initials.

**MCINTOSH, DAVID L.,** PO Box 948, Haines, AK 99827, Phone: 907-766-3673
**Specialties:** Working straight knives and folders of all designs. **Patterns:** All styles, except swords. **Technical:** Grinds ATS-34 and top name maker Damascus. Engraves; offers tooling on sheaths. Uses fossil ivory. **Prices:** $60 to $800; some to $2,000. **Remarks:** Full-time maker; first knife sold in 1984. **Mark:** Last name, serial number, steel type, city and state.

**MCKENZIE, DAVID BRIAN,** 2311 B Ida Rd., Campbell River B, CANADA V9W-4V7

**MCKIERNAN, STAN,** 205 E. Park St., Vandalia, MO 63382, Phone: 573-594-6135, slmck@hotmailc.om
**Specialties:** Self-sheathed knives and miniatures. **Patterns:** Daggers, ethnic designs and individual styles. **Technical:** Grinds Damascus and 440C. **Prices:** $200 to $500; some to $1,500. **Mark:** "River's Bend" inside two concentric circles.

**MCLENDON, HUBERT W.,** 125 Thomas Rd., Waco, GA 30182, Phone: 770-574-9796
**Specialties:** Using knives; his design or customer's. **Patterns:** Bowies and hunters. **Technical:** Hand ground or forged ATS-34, 440C and D2. **Prices:** $100 to $300. **Remarks:** First knife sold in 1978. **Mark:** McLendon or Mc.

**MCLUIN, TOM,** 36 Fourth St., Dracut, MA 01826, Phone: 978-957-4899, tmcluin@comcast.net Web: http://home.comcast.net/~tmcluin/
**Specialties:** Working straight knives and folders of his design. **Patterns:** Boots, hunters and folders. **Technical:** Grinds ATS-34, 440C, O1 and Damascus; makes his own mokume. **Prices:** $100 to $400; some to $700. **Remarks:** Part-time maker; first knife sold in 1991. **Mark:** Last name.

**MCLURKIN, ANDREW,** 2112 Windy Woods Dr., Raleigh, NC 27607, Phone: 919-834-4693, mclurkincustomeknives.com
**Specialties:** Collector grade folders, working folders, fixed blades, and mini tures. Knives made to order and to his design. **Patterns:** Locking liner a lock back folders, hunter, working and tactical designs. **Technical:** Using pa terned Damascus, Mosaic Damascus, ATS-34, BG-42, and CPM steels. Pr fers natural handle materials such as pearl, ancient ivory and stabilized woo Also using synthetic materials such as carbon fiber, titanium, and G1 **Prices:** $250 and up. **Mark:** Last name. Mark is often on inside of folders.

**MCMANUS, DANNY,** 413 Fairhaven Drive., Taylors, SC 29687, Phone 864-268-9849, Fax: 864-268-9699, DannyMcManus@bigfoot.com
**Specialties:** High-tech and traditional working/using straight knives of h design, to customer specs and in standard patterns. **Patterns:** Boots, Bowie fighters, hunters and utility/camp knives. **Technical:** Forges stainless ste Damascus; grinds ATS-34. Offers engraving and scrimshaw. **Prices:** $300 $2,000; some to $3,000. **Remarks:** Full-time maker; first knife sold in 19 Doing business as Stamascus KnifeWorks Corp. **Mark:** Stamascus.

**MCNABB, TOMMY,** CAROLINA CUSTOM KNIVES, 4015 Brownsboro Rd., Winston-Salem, NC 27106, Phone: 336-924-6053, Fax: 336-924-4854, tommy@tmcnabb.com Web: carolinaknives.com

**MCNEIL, JIMMY,** 1175 Mt. Moriah Rd., Memphis, TN 38117, Phone: 901-544-0710 or 901-683-8133
**Specialties:** Fancy high-art straight knives of his design. **Patterns:** Bowi daggers and swords. **Technical:** Grinds O1 and Damascus. Engraves, carv and inlays. **Prices:** $50 to $300; some to $2,000. **Remarks:** Spare-ti maker; first knife sold in 1993. Doing business as McNeil's Minerals a Knives. **Mark:** Crossed mining picks and serial number.

**MCRAE, J. MICHAEL,** 6100 Lake Rd, Mint Hill, NC 28227, Phone: 70 545-2929, scotia@carolina.rr.com Web: www.scotiametalwork.com
**Specialties:** Scottish dirks and sgian dubhs. **Patterns:** Traditional bla styles with traditional and slightly non-traditional handle treatments. **Tech cal:** Forges 1095, 5160 and his own Damascus. Prefers Stag and exotic ha woods for handles, many intricately carved. **Prices:** Starting at $125; some $3,500. **Remarks:** Journeyman Smith in ABS, member of North Carolina C tom Knifemakers Guild and ABANA. Full-time maker, first knife sold in 19 Doing business as Scotia Metalwork. **Mark:** Last name underlined with a c more.

**MEERDINK, KURT,** 120 Split Rock Dr., Barryville, NY 12719, Phone: 845-557-0783
**Specialties:** Working straight knives. **Patterns:** Hunters, Bowies, tactical neck knives. **Technical:** Grinds ATS-34, 440C, D2, Damascus. **Prices:** $9 $1,100. **Remarks:** Full-time maker, first knife sold in 1994. **Mark:** Meero Maker, Rio NY.

**MEHR, FARID R,** 8 Sidney Close, Tunbridge Wells, Kent, ENGLAND TN2 5QQ, Phone: 011-44-1892 520345, farid@faridknives.com
**Specialties:** High-tech fixed blades and titanium folders. **Patterns:** Ch ground liner lock and integral mechanism folders. **Technical:** Grinds 44 CPM-T-440V, CPM-420V, CPM-15V, CPMS125V, and T-1 high speed s and Vasco-max alloy and tool steel. **Prices:** $550 to $15,000. **Remarks:** F time maker; first knife sold in 1991. **Mark:** First name and country.

**MEIER, DARYL,** 75 Forge Rd., Carbondale, IL 62901, Phone: 618-54 3234
**Specialties:** One-of-a-kind knives and swords. **Patterns:** Collaborates blades. **Technical:** Forges his own Damascus, W1 and A203E, 440C, nickel 200 and clad steel. **Prices:** $250 to $450; some to $6,000. **Remar** Full-time smith and researcher since 1974; first knife sold in 1974. **M** Name or circle/arrow symbol or SHAWNEE.

**MELIN, GORDON C.,** 11259 Gladhill Rd Unit 4, Whittier, CA 90604, Phone: 562-946-5753

**MELLARD, J. R.,** 17006 Highland Canyon Dr., Houston, TX 77095, Phone: 281-550-9464

**MELOY, SEAN,** 7148 Rosemary Lane, Lemon Grove, CA 91945-210 Phone: 619-465-7173
**Specialties:** Traditional working straight knives of his design. **Patterns:** B ies, fighters and utility/camp knives. **Technical:** Grinds 440C, ATS-34 and **Prices:** $125 to $300. **Remarks:** Part-time maker; first knife sold in 1 **Mark:** Broz Knives.

**MENSCH, LARRY C.,** 578 Madison Ave., Milton, PA 17847, Phone: 742-9554
**Specialties:** Custom orders. **Patterns:** Bowies, daggers, hunters, tar short swords and miniatures. **Technical:** Grinds ATS-34, carbon and stain steel Damascus; blade grinds hollow, flat and slack. Filework; bending gu and fluting handles with finger grooves. Offers engraving and scrims **Prices:** $200 and up. **Remarks:** Full-time maker; first knife sold in 1

Doing business as Larry's Knife Shop. **Mark:** Connected capital "L" and small "m" in script.

**MERCER, MIKE,** 149 N. Waynesville Rd., Lebanon, OH 45036, Phone: 513-932-2837
**Specialties:** Jeweled gold and ivory daggers; multi-blade folders. **Patterns:** 1-1/4" folders, hunters, axes, replicas. **Technical:** Uses O1 Damascus and mokume. **Prices:** $150 to $1,500. **Remarks:** Full-time maker since 1991. **Mark:** Last name in script.

**MERCHANT, TED,** 7 Old Garrett Ct., White Hall, MD 21161, Phone: 410-343-0380
**Specialties:** Traditional and classic working knives. **Patterns:** Bowies, hunters, camp knives, fighters, daggers and skinners. **Technical:** Forges W2 and 5160; makes own Damascus. Makes handles with wood, stag, horn, silver and gem stone inlay; fancy filework. **Prices:** $125 to $600; some to $1,500. **Remarks:** Full-time maker; first knife sold in 1985. **Mark:** Last name.

**MERZ III, ROBERT L.,** 1447 Winding Canyon, Katy, TX 77493, Phone: 281-391-2897
**Specialties:** Folders. **Technical:** Flat-grinds 440C, 154CM, ATS-34, 440V and commercial Damascus. **Prices:** $250 to $700. **Remarks:** Part-time maker; first knife sold in 1974. **Mark:** MERZ.

**MESHEJIAN, MARDI,** 33 Elm Dr., E. Northport, NY 11731, Phone: 631-757-4541
**Specialties:** One-of-a-kind fantasy and high-art straight knives of his design. **Patterns:** Swords, daggers, finger knives and other edged weapons. **Technical:** Forged Damascus and Chain Damascus. **Prices:** $150 to $2,500; some to $3,000. **Remarks:** Full-time maker; first knife sold in 1996. Doing business as Tooth and Nail Metalworks. **Mark:** Stamped Etched stylized "M".

**MESSER, DAVID T.,** 134 S. Torrence St., Dayton, OH 45403-2044, Phone: 513-228-6561
**Specialties:** Fantasy period pieces, straight and folding, of his design. **Patterns:** Bowies, daggers and swords. **Technical:** Grinds 440C, O1, 06 and commercial Damascus. Likes fancy guards and exotic handle materials. **Prices:** $100 to $225; some to $375. **Remarks:** Spare-time maker; first knife sold in 1991. **Mark:** Name stamp.

**METHENY, H.A. "WHITEY",** 7750 Waterford Dr., Spotsylvania, VA 22553, Phone: 540-582-3095, Fax: 540-582-3095, hamethen4@aol.com Web: www methenyknives.com
**Specialties:** Working and using straight knives of his design and to customer specs. **Patterns:** Hunters and kitchen knives. **Technical:** Grinds 440C and ATS-34. Offers filework; tooled custom sheaths. **Prices:** $200 to $350. **Remarks:** Spare-time maker; first knife sold in 1990. **Mark:** Initials/full name football logo.

**METZ, GREG T.,** c/o James Ranch HC 83, Cascade, ID 83611, Phone: 208-382-4336
**Specialties:** Hunting and utility knives. **Prices:** $300 and up. **Remarks:** Natural handle materials; hand forged blades; 1084 and 1095. **Mark:** METZ (last name).

**MICHINAKA, TOSHIAKI,** I-679 Koyamacho-nishi, Totton-shi, Tottori 680-0947, JAPAN, Phone: 0857-28-5911

**MICHO, KANDA,** 7-32-5 Shinzutsumi-cho, Shinnanyo-city, Yamaguchi, JAPAN, Phone: 0834-62-1910

**MICKLEY, TRACY,** 42112 Kerns Dr., North Mankato, MN 56003, Phone: 507-947-3760, tracy@mickleyknives.com Web: www.mickleyknives.com
**Specialties:** Working and collectable straight knives using mammoth ivory or burl woods, liner lock folders. **Patterns:** Custom and classic hunters, utility, fighters and Bowies. **Technical:** Grinding 154-CM, BG-42 forging 01 and 52100. **Prices:** Starting at $325. **Remarks:** Part-time since 1999. **Mark:** Last name.

**MILFORD, BRIAN A.,** RD 2 Box 294, Knox, PA 16232, Phone: 814-797-2595, Fax: 814-226-4351
**Specialties:** Traditional and working/using straight knives of his design or to customer specs. **Patterns:** Fighters, hunters and utility/camp knives. **Technical:** Forges Damascus and 52100; grinds 440C. **Prices:** $50 to $300; some to $750. **Remarks:** Part-time maker; first knife sold in 1991. Doing business as BAM Forge. **Mark:** Full name or initials.

**MILITANO, TOM,** CUSTOM KNIVES, 77 Jason Rd., Jacksonville, AL 36265-6655, Phone: 256-435-7132, jeffkin57@aol.com
**Specialties:** Fixed blade, one-of-a-kind knives. **Patterns:** Bowies, fighters, hunters and tactical knives. **Technical:** Grinds 440C, ATS-34, A2, and Damascus. Hollow grinds, flat grinds, and decorative filework. **Prices:** $150 plus. **Remarks:** Part-time maker. **Mark:** Name, city and state in oval with maker in the center. Sold first knives in the mid to late 1980s. Memberships: founding member-New England Custom Knife Association, Flint River Knife Club.

**MILLARD, FRED G.,** 27627 Kopezyk Ln., Richland Center, WI 53581, Phone: 608-647-5376
**Specialties:** Working/using straight knives of his design or to customer specs. **Patterns:** Bowies, hunters, utility/camp knives, kitchen/steak knives. **Technical:** Grinds ATS-34, O1, D2 and 440C. Makes sheaths. **Prices:** $110 to $300. **Remarks:** Full-time maker; first knife sold in 1993. Doing business as Millard Knives. **Mark:** Mallard duck in flight with serial number.

**MILLER, MICHAEL,** 2960 E Carver Ave, Kingman, AZ 86401, Phone: 928-757-1359
**Specialties:**Hunters, bowies, and skinners with exotic burl wood, stag, ivory and gemstone handles. **Patterns:** 01 and I-6 Damascus 1084 and 1095 and 01 steel knives. **Technical:** L-6 and 01 patterned Damascus. **Prices:** $150 to $1,000. **Remarks:** Full-time maker since 2002, first knife sold 2000; doing business as M Miller Originals. **Mark:** First initial and last name with 'handmade' underneath.

**MILLER, R.D.,** 10526 Estate Lane, Dallas, TX 75238, Phone: 214-348-3496
**Specialties:** One-of-a-kind collector-grade knives. **Patterns:** Boots, hunters, Bowies, camp and utility knives, fishing and bird knives, miniatures. **Technical:** Grinds a variety of steels to include O1, D2, 440C, 154CM and 1095. **Prices:** $65 to $300; some to $900. **Remarks:** Full-time maker; first knife sold in 1984. **Mark:** R.D. Custom Knives with date or bow and arrow logo.

**MILLER, MICHAEL K.,** 28510 Santiam Hwy., Sweet Home, OR 97386, Phone: 541-367-4927, miller@ptlnet.net
**Specialties:** Specializes in kitchen cutlery of his design or made to customer specs. **Patterns:** Hunters, utility/camp knives and kitchen cutlery. **Technical:** Grinds ATS-34, AEBL and 440-C. Wife does scrimshaw as well. Makes custom sheaths and holsters. **Prices:** $200. **Remarks:** Full-time maker; first knife sold in 1989. **Mark:** MandM Kustom Krafts.

**MILLER, BOB,** 7659 Fine Oaks Pl., Oakville, MO 63129, Phone: 314-846-8934
**Specialties:** Mosaic Damascus; collector using straight knives and folders. **Patterns:** Hunters, Bowies, utility/camp knives, daggers. **Technical:** Forges own Damascus, mosaic-Damascus and 52100. **Prices:** $125 to $500. **Remarks:** Part-time maker; first knife sold in 1983. **Mark:** First and middle initials and last name, or initials.

**MILLER, DON,** 1604 Harrodsburg Rd., Lexington, KY 40503, Phone: 606-276-3299

**MILLER, HANFORD J.,** Box 97, Cowdrey, CO 80434, Phone: 970-723-4708
**Specialties:** Working knives in Moran-style; period pieces. **Patterns:** Bowies, fighters, camp knives and other large straight knives. **Technical:** Forges W2, 1095, 5160 and his own Damascus; differential tempers; offers wire inlay. **Prices:** $300 to $800; some to $3,000. **Remarks:** Full-time maker; first knife sold in 1968. **Mark:** Initials or name within Bowie logo.

**MILLER, JAMES P.,** 9024 Goeller Rd., RR 2, Box 28, Fairbank, IA 50629, Phone: 319-635-2294, Web: www.damascusknives.biz
**Specialties:** All tool steel Damascus; working knives and period pieces. **Patterns:** Hunters, Bowies, camp knives and daggers. **Technical:** Forges and grinds 1095, 52100, 440C and his own Damascus. **Prices:** $100 to $350; some to $1,500. **Remarks:** Full-time maker; first knife sold in 1970. **Mark:** First and middle initials, last name with knife logo.

**MILLER, M.A.,** 11625 Community Center Dr., Unit #1531, Northglenn, CO 80233, Phone: 303-280-3816
**Specialties:** Using knives for hunting. 3-1/2"-4" Loveless drop-point. Made to customer specs. **Patterns:** Skinners and camp knives. **Technical:** Grinds 440C, D2, O1 and ATS-34 Damascus miniatures. **Prices:** $225 to $350; miniatures $75 to $150. **Remarks:** Part-time maker; first knife sold in 1988. **Mark:** Last name stamped in block letters or first and middle initials, last name, maker, city and state with triangles on either side etched.

**MILLER, RONALD T.,** 12922 127th Ave. N., Largo, FL 34644, Phone: 813-595-0378 (after 5 p.m.)
**Specialties:** Working straight knives in standard patterns. **Patterns:** Combat knives, camp knives, kitchen cutlery, fillet knives, locking folders and butterflies. **Technical:** Grinds D2, 440C and ATS-34; offers brass inlays and scrimshaw. **Prices:** $45 to $325; some to $750. **Remarks:** Part-time maker; first knife sold in 1984. **Mark:** Name, city and state in palm tree logo.

**MILLER, MICHAEL E.,** 1400 Skyview Dr., El Reno, OK 73036, Phone: 405-422-3602
**Specialties:** Traditional working/using knives of his design. **Patterns:** Bowies, hunters and kitchen knives. **Technical:** Grinds ATS-34, CPM 440V; forges Damascus and cable Damascus and 52100. Prefers scrimshaw, fancy pins, basket weave and embellished sheaths. **Prices:** $80 to $300; some to $500. **Remarks:** Part-time maker; first knife sold in 1984. Doing business as Miller Custom Knives. **Mark:** First and middle initials, last name, maker, city and

state. **Other:** Member of KG A of Oklahoma and Salt Fork Blacksmith Association.

**MILLER, RICK,** 516 Kanaul Rd., Rockwood, PA 15557, Phone: 814-926-2059
**Specialties:** Working/using straight knives of his design and in standard patterns. **Patterns:** Bowies, daggers, hunters and friction folders. **Technical:** Grinds L6. Forges 5160, L6 and Damascus. Patterns for Damascus are random, twist, rose or ladder. **Prices:** $75 to $250; some to $400. **Remarks:** Part-time maker; first knife sold in 1982. **Mark:** Script stamp "R.D.M.".

**MILLS, LOUIS G.,** 9450 Waters Rd., Ann Arbor, MI 48103, Phone: 734-668-1839
**Specialties:** High-art Japanese-style period pieces. **Patterns:** Traditional tantos, daggers and swords. **Technical:** Makes steel from iron; makes his own Damascus by traditional Japanese techniques. **Prices:** $900 to $2,000; some to $8,000. **Remarks:** Spare-time maker. **Mark:** Yasutomo in Japanese Kanji.

**MILLS, MICHAEL,** 5604 Lanham Station Rd., Lanham, MD 20706-2531, Phone: 301-459-7226
**Specialties:** Working knives, Hunters, Skinners, Utility and Bowies. **Technical:** Forge 5160 Differential Heat-Treats. **Prices:** $200 and up. **Remarks:** Part-time maker, ABS Journeyman. **Mark:** Last name in script.

**MINK, DAN,** PO Box 861, 196 Sage Circle, Crystal Beach, FL 34681, Phone: 727-786-5408, DBMink@ij.net
**Specialties:** Traditional and working knives of his design. **Patterns:** Bowies, fighters, folders and hunters. **Technical:** Grinds ATS-34, 440C and D2. Blades and tanges embellished with fancy filework. Uses natural and rare handle materials. **Prices:** $125 to $450. **Remarks:** Part-time maker; first knife sold in 1985. **Mark:** Name and star encircled by custom made, city, state.

**MINNICK, JIM,** 144 North 7th St., Middletown, IN 47356, Phone: 765-354-4108
**Specialties:** Lever-lock folding art knives, liner-locks. **Patterns:** Stilettos, Persian and one-of-a-kind folders. **Technical:** Grinds and carves Damascus, stainless, and high-carbon. **Prices:** $950 to $7,000. **Remarks:** Part-time maker; first knife sold in 1976. **Mark:** Minnick and JMJ. **Other:** Husband and wife team.

**MIRABILE, DAVID,** 1715 Glacier Ave., Juneau, AK 99801, Phone: 907-463-3404
**Specialties:** Elegant edged weapons. **Patterns:** Fighters, Bowies, claws, tklinget daggers, executive desk knives. **Technical:** Forged high-carbon steels, his own Damascus; uses ancient walrus ivory and prehistoric bone extensively, very rarely uses wood. **Prices:** $350 to $7,000. **Remarks:** Full-time maker. Knives sold through art gallery in Juneau, AK. **Mark:** Last name etched or engraved.

**MITCHELL, MAX, DEAN AND BEN,** 3803 V.F.W. Rd., Leesville, LA 71440, Phone: 318-239-6416
**Specialties:** Hatchet and knife sets with folder and belt and holster all match. **Patterns:** Hunters, 200 L6 steel. **Technical:** L6 steel; soft back, hand edge. **Prices:** $300 to $500. **Remarks:** Part-time makers; first knife sold in 1965. Custom orders only; no stock. **Mark:** First names.

**MITCHELL, JAMES A.,** PO Box 4646, Columbus, GA 31904, Phone: 404-322-8582
**Specialties:** Fancy working knives. **Patterns:** Hunters, fighters, Bowies and locking folders. **Technical:** Grinds D2, 440C and commercial Damascus. **Prices:** $100 to $400; some to $900. **Remarks:** Part-time maker; first knife sold in 1976. Sells knives in sets. **Mark:** Signature and city.

**MITCHELL, WM. DEAN,** PO Box 2, Warren, TX 77664, Phone: 409-547-2213, bebo@cminet.net
**Specialties:** Classic and period knives. **Patterns:** Bowies, hunters, daggers and swords. **Technical:** Forged carbon steel and Damascus 52100, 1095, 5160; makes pattern, composite and mosiac Damascus; offers filework. Makes wooden display cases. **Prices:** Mid-scale. **Remarks:** Hobbist maker since 1986. First knife sold in 1986.D.B.A. The Thicket Smithy. **Mark:** Full name with anvil, MS.

**MITSUYUKI, ROSS,** 94-1071 Kepakepa St, C-3, Waipahu, Hawaii 96797, Phone: 808-671-3335, Fax: 808-671-3335, www.hawaiian-grinds.net
**Specialties:** Working straight knives and folders. **Patterns:** Hunting, fighters, utility knives and boot knives. **Technical:** 440C, BG-42, ATS-34, 530V, and Damascus. **Prices:** $100 to $500. **Remarks:** Spare-time maker, first knife sold in 1998. **Mark:** Name, state, Hawaiian sea turtle.

**MIVILLE-DESCHENES, ALAIN,** 1952 Charles A Parent, Quebec, CANADA G2B 4B2, Phone: 418-845-0950, Fax: 418-845-0950, amd@miville-deschenes.com Web: www.miville-deschenes.com
**Specialties:** Working knives of his design or to customer specs and art knives. **Patterns:** Bowies, skinner, hunter, utility, camp knives, fighters, art knives. **Technical:** Grinds ATS-34, 440C, CPM S30V, 0-1, etc. **Prices:** $175 to $500; some higher. **Remarks:** Part-time maker; first knife sold in 2001 **Mark:** Logo (small hand) and initials (AMD).

**MIZE, RICHARD,** FOX CREEK FORGE, 2038 Fox Creek Rd., Lawrenceburg, KY 40342, Phone: 502-859-0602, foxcreek@kih.net Web: www.foxcreekforge.com
**Specialties:** Forges spring steel, 5160, 10xx steels, natural handle materials **Patterns:** Traditional working knives, period flavor Bowies, rifle knives. **Technical:** Does own heat treating, differential temper. **Prices:** $100 to $400 **Remarks:** Strongly advocates sole authorship. **Mark:** Initial M hot stamped.

**MOJZIS, JULIUS,** B. S. Timravy 6,, 98511 Halic, Slovakia, Web: www.m-art.sk
**Specialties:** Art Knives. **Prices:** USD $2,000. **Mark:** MOJZIS

**MOMCILOVIC, GUNNAR,** Nordlysv, 16, Waipahu, NORWAY, Phone: 0111-47-3287-3586

**MONCUS, MICHAEL STEVEN,** 1803 US 19 N, Smithville, GA 31787, Phone: 912-846-2408

**MONK, NATHAN P.,** 721 County Rd 1462, Cullman, AL 35055-0602, Phone: 256-737-0463
**Specialties:** Traditional working and using straight knives of his design and t customer specs; fancy knives. **Patterns:** Bowies, daggers, fighters, hunters utility/camp knives, bird knives and one-of-a-kinds. **Technical:** Grinds ATS 34, 440C and A2. **Prices:** $50 to $175. **Remarks:** Spare-time maker; firs knife sold in 1990. **Mark:** First and middle initials, last name, city, state.

**MONTANO, GUS A.,** 11217 Westonhill Dr., San Diego, CA 92126-1447, Phone: 619-273-5357
**Specialties:** Traditional working/using straight knives of his design. **Patterns** Boots, Bowies and fighters. **Technical:** Grinds 1095 and 5160; grinds an forges cable. Double or triple hardened and triple drawn; hand-rubbed finish Prefers natural handle materials. **Prices:** $200 to $400; some to $60 **Remarks:** Spare-time maker; first knife sold in 1997. **Mark:** First initial an last name.

**MONTEIRO, VICTOR,** 31, Rue D'Opprebais, 1360 Maleves Ste Marie, BELGIUM, Phone: 010 88 0441
**Specialties:** Working and fancy straight knives, folders and integrals of h design. **Patterns:** Fighters, hunters and kitchen knives. **Technical:** Grinc ATS-34, 440C, D2, Damasteel and other commercial Damascus, embellish ment, filework and domed pins. **Prices:** $300 to $1,000; some highe **Remarks:** Part-time maker; first knife sold in 1989. **Mark:** Logo with initia connected.

**MONTJOY, CLAUDE,** 706 Indian Creek Rd., Clinton, SC 29325, Phone 864-697-6160
**Specialties:** Folders, slip joint, lock, lock liner and inter frame. **Pattern** Hunters, boots, fighters, some art knives and folders. **Technical:** Grinds AT 34 and Damascus. Offers inlaid handle scales. **Prices:** $100 to $50 **Remarks:** Full-time maker; first knife sold in 1982. **Mark:** Montjoy. **Othe** Custom orders, no catalog.

**MOONEY, MIKE,** 19432 E Cloud Rd, Queen Creek, AZ 85242, Phone: 480-987-3576, mike@moonblades.com
**Specialties:** Fancy working straight knives of his design or customers. **Tec nical:** Flat-grind, S30V, ATS-34, O1, commercial Damascus. **Patterns:** Fig ers, bowies, daggers, hunters, kitchen, camp. **Remarks:** Doing business moonblades.com. **Mark:** M. Mooney followed by crescent moon.

**MOORE, TED,** 340 E Willow St., Elizabethtown, PA 17022, Phone: 717 367-3939, tedmoore@supernet.com Web: www.tedmooreknives.com
**Specialties:** Damascus folders, cigar cutters. **Patterns:** Locking folders a slip joint. **Technical:** Grinds Damascus, high-carbon and stainless; also AT 34 and D2. **Prices:** $250 to $1,500. **Remarks:** Part-time maker; first knife sc 1993. Knife and gun leather also. **Mark:** Moore U.S.A.

**MOORE, MARVE,** HC 89 Box 393, Willow, AK 99688, Phone: 907-232 0478, marvemoore@aol.com
**Specialties:** Fixed blades forged and stock removal. **Patterns:** Gunter, sk ners, fighter, short swords. **Technical:** 100% of his work is done by har **Prices:** $100 to $500. **Remarks:** Also makes his own sheaths. **Mark:** -MM-

**MOORE, MICHAEL ROBERT,** 70 Beauliew St., Lowell, MA 01850, Phone: 978-479-0589, Fax: 978-441-1819

**MOORE, JAMES B.,** 1707 N. Gillis, Ft. Stockton, TX 79735, Phone: 91 336-2113
**Specialties:** Classic working straight knives and folders of his design. **P terns:** Hunters, Bowies, daggers, fighters, boots, utility/camp knives, locki folders and slip-joint folders. **Technical:** Grinds 440C, ATS-34, D2, L6, CI and commercial Damascus. **Prices:** $85 to $700; exceptional knives $1,500. **Remarks:** Full-time maker; first knife sold in 1972. **Mark:** Name, c and state.

**MORAN JR., WM. F.,** PO Box 68, Braddock Heights, MD 21714, Phone: 301-371-7543
**Specialties:** High-art working knives of his design. **Patterns:** Fighters, camp knives, Bowies, daggers, axes, tomahawks, push knives and miniatures. **Technical:** Forges W2, 5160 and his own Damascus; puts silver wire inlay on most handles; uses only natural handle materials. **Prices:** $400 to $7,500; some to $9,000. **Remarks:** Full-time maker. **Mark:** W. F. Moran Jr. Master Smith MS.

**MORETT, DONALD,** 116 Woodcrest Dr., Lancaster, PA 17602-1300, Phone: 717-746-4888

**MORGAN, TOM,** 14689 Ellett Rd., Beloit, OH 44609, Phone: 330-537-2023
**Specialties:** Working straight knives and period pieces. **Patterns:** Hunters, boots and presentation tomahawks. **Technical:** Grinds O1, 440C and 154CM. **Prices:** Knives, $65 to $200; tomahawks, $100 to $325. **Remarks:** Full-time maker; first knife sold in 1977. **Mark:** Last name and type of steel used.

**MORGAN, JEFF,** 9200 Arnaz Way, Santee, CA 92071, Phone: 619-448-8430
**Specialties:** Fancy working straight knives. **Patterns:** Hunters, fighters, boots, miniatures. **Technical:** Grinds D2, 440C and ATS-34; likes exotic handles. **Prices:** $60 to $300; some to $800. **Remarks:** Full-time maker; first knife sold in 1977. **Mark:** Initials connected.

**MORRIS, C.H.,** 1590 Old Salem Rd., Frisco City, AL 36445, Phone: 334-575-7425
**Specialties:** Liner lock folders. **Patterns:** Interframe liner locks. **Technical:** Grinds 440C and ATS-34. **Prices:** Start at $350. **Remarks:** Full-time maker; first knife sold in 1973. Doing business as Custom Knives. **Mark:** First and middle initials, last name.

**MORRIS, DARRELL PRICE,** 92 Union, St. Plymouth, Devon, ENGLAND PL1 3EZ, Phone: 0752 223546
**Specialties:** Traditional Japanese knives, Bowies and high-art knives. **Technical:** Nickel Damascus and mokamame. **Prices:** $1,000 to $4,000. **Remarks:** Part-time maker; first knife sold in 1990. **Mark:** Initials and Japanese name—Kuni Shigae.

**MORRIS, ERIC,** 306 Ewart Ave., Beckley, WV 25801, Phone: 304-255-3951

**MORTENSON, ED,** 2742 Hwy. 93 N, Darby, MT 59829, Phone: 406-821-3146, Fax: 406-821-3146
**Specialties:** Period pieces and working/using straight knives of his design, to customer specs and in standard patterns. **Patterns:** Bowies, hunters and kitchen knives. **Technical:** Grinds ATS-34, 5160 and 1095. Sheath combinations - flashlight/knife, hatchet/knife, etc. **Prices:** $60 to $140; some to $300. **Remarks:** Full-time maker; first knife sold in 1993. Doing business as The Blade Lair. **Mark:** M with attached O.

**MOSES, STEVEN,** 1610 W Hemlock Way, Santa Ana, CA 92704

**MOSIER, JOSHUA J.,** SPRING CREEK KNIFE WORKS, PO Box 476/ 608 7th St, Deshler, NE 68340, scknifeworks@mail.com
**Specialties:** Working straight and folding knives of his designs with customer specs. **Patterns:** Hunters, utilities, locking liner folders, kitchen and camp knives. **Technical:** Forges and grinds 5160, W2, L6, simple carbon steels and his own Damascus, uses some antique materials, provides a history of the materials used in each knife. **Prices:** $55 and up. **Remarks:** Part-time maker, sold first knife in 1986. **Mark:** SCKW.

**MOSSER, GARY E.,** 11827 NE 102nd Place, Kirkland, WA 98033-5170, Phone: 425-827-2279, themossers@msn.com
**Specialties:** Working knives. **Patterns:** Hunters, skinners, camp knives, some art knives. **Technical:** Stock removal method; prefers ATS-34. **Prices:** $100 to $250; special orders and art knives are higher. **Remarks:** Part-time maker; first knife sold in 1976. **Mark:** Name.

**MOULTON, DUSTY,** 135 Hillview Lane, Loudon, TN 37774, Phone: 865-408-9779, Web: www.moultonknives.com
**Specialties:** Fancy and working straight knives. **Patterns:** Hunters, fighters, fantasy and miniatures. **Technical:** Grinds ATS-34 and Damascus. **Prices:** $300 to $2,000. **Remarks:** Full-time maker; first knife sold in 1991. **Mark:** Last name. **Other:** Now doing engraving on own knives as well as other makers.

**MOUNT, DON,** 4574 Little Finch Ln., Las Vegas, NV 89115, Phone: 702-531-2925
**Specialties:** High-tech working and using straight knives of his design. **Patterns:** Bowies, fighters and utility/camp knives. **Technical:** Uses 440C and ATS-34. **Prices:** $150 to $300; some to $1,000. **Remarks:** Part-time maker; first knife sold in 1985. **Mark:** Name below a woodpecker.

**MOUNTAIN HOME KNIVES, ,** PO Box 167, Jamul, CA 91935, Phone: 619-669-0833
**Specialties:** High-quality working straight knives. **Patterns:** Hunters, fighters, skinners, tantos, utility and fillet knives, Bowies and *san-mai* Damascus Bowies. **Technical:** Hollow-grind 440C by hand. Feature linen Micarta handles, nickel-silver handle bolts and handmade sheaths. **Prices:** $65 to $270. **Remarks:** Company owned by Jim English. **Mark:** Mountain Home Knives.

**MOYER, RUSS,** 1266 RD 425 So, Havre, MT 59501, Phone: 406-395-4423
**Specialties:** Working knives to customer specs. **Patterns:** Hunters, Bowies and survival knives. **Technical:** Forges W2 & 5160. **Prices:** $150 to $350. **Remarks:** Part-time maker; first knife sold in 1976. **Mark:** Initials in logo.

**MULLER, JODY,** PO Box 35, Pittsburg, MO 65724, Phone: 417-852-4306/417-752-3260, Web: www.mullerforge.com
**Specialties:** Hand engraving, carving and inlays, fancy folders. One-of-a-kind personal carry knives with billfold cases, cleavers and oriental styles. **Patterns:** One-of-a-kind fixed blades and folders in all styles. **Technical:** Forges patterned Damascus and high carbon steel. **Prices:** $200 and up. **Remarks:** Son and father team of part-time makers. Jody made first knife at age 12. Now does fine hand-engraving, carving and inlay. **Mark:** 4 Muller J.S.**Other:** Cross reference Muller Forge. Journeyman Smith Full Time kifemaker.

**MULLIN, STEVE,** 500 Snowberry Lane, Sandpoint, ID 83864, Phone: 208-263-7492, knives@packriver.com Web: www.packriver.com
**Specialties:** Damascus period pieces and folders. **Patterns:** Full range of folders, hunters and Bowies. **Technical:** Forges and grinds O1, D2, 154CM and his own Damascus. Engraves. **Prices:** $100 to $2,000. **Remarks:** Full-time maker; first knife sold in 1975. Sells line of using knives under Pack River Knife Co. **Mark:** Full name, city and state.

**MUNROE, DERYK C.,** PO Box 3454, Bozeman, MT 59772

**MURRAY, BILL,** 1632 Rio Mayo, Green Valley, AZ 85614

**MURSKI, RAY,** 12129 Captiva Ct., Reston, VA 22091-1204, Phone: 703-264-1102
**Specialties:** Fancy working/using folders of his design. **Patterns:** Hunters, slip-joint folders and utility/camp knives. **Technical:** Grinds CPM-3V **Prices:** $125 to $500. **Remarks:** Spare-time maker; first knife sold in 1996. **Mark:** Etched name with serial number under name.

**MYERS, PAUL,** 644 Maurice St., Wood River, IL 62095, Phone: 618-258-1707
**Specialties:** Fancy working straight knives and folders. **Patterns:** Full range of folders, straight hunters and Bowies; tie tacks; knife and fork sets. **Technical:** Grinds D2, 440C, ATS-34 and 154CM. **Prices:** $100 to $350; some to $3,000. **Remarks:** Full-time maker; first knife sold in 1974. **Mark:** Initials with setting sun on front; name and number on back.

**MYERS, STEVE,** 9034 Hickory Rd., Virginia, IL 62691-8716, Phone: 217-452-3157
**Specialties:** Working straight knives. **Patterns:** Camp knives, huntes, skinners, Bowies and boot. **Technical:** Grinds high carbon and Damascus. **Prices:** $250 to $1,000. **Remarks:** Full-time maker; first knife sold in 1985. **Mark:** First name logo.

# N

**NATEN, GREG,** 1804 Shamrock Way, Bakersfield, CA 93304-3921
**Specialties:** Fancy and working/using folders of his design. **Patterns:** Fighters, hunters and locking folders. **Technical:** Grinds 440C, ATS-34 and CPM440V. Heat-treats; prefers desert ironwood, stag and mother-of-pearl. Designs and sews leather sheaths for straight knives. **Prices:** $175 to $600; some to $950. **Remarks:** Spare-time maker; first knife sold in 1992. **Mark:** Last name above battle-ax, handmade.

**NAVAGATO, ANGELO,** 5 Commercial Apt 2, Camp Hill, PA 17011

**NEALEY, IVAN F. (FRANK),** Anderson Dam Rd., Box 65, HC #87, Mt. Home, ID 83647, Phone: 208-587-4060
**Specialties:** Working straight knives in standard patterns. **Patterns:** Hunters, skinners and utility knives. **Technical:** Grinds D2, 440C and 154CM. **Prices:** $90 to $135; some higher. **Remarks:** Part-time maker; first knife sold in 1975. **Mark:** Name.

**NEALY, BUD,** 1439 Poplar Valley Rd., Stroudsburg, PA 18360, Phone: 570-402-1018, Fax: 570-402-1019, budnealy@ptd.net Web: www.budnealyknifemaker.com
**Specialties:** Original design concealment knives with designer multi-concealment sheath system. **Patterns:** Concealment knives, boots, combat and collector pieces. **Technical:** Grinds ATS-34; uses Damascus. **Prices:** $200 to $2,500. **Remarks:** Full-time maker; first knife sold in 1980. **Mark:** Name, city, state or signature.

**NEDVED, DAN,** 206 Park Dr., Kalispell, MT 59901, Phone: 406-752-5060
**Specialties:** Slip joint folders, liner locks, straight knives. **Patterns:** Mostly traditional or modern blend with traditional lines. **Technical:** Grinds ATS-34, 440C, 1095 and uses other makers Damascus. **Prices:** $95 and up. Mostly in the $150 to $200 range. **Remarks:** Part-time maker, averages 2 a month. **Mark:** Dan Nedved or Nedved with serial # on opposite side.

**NEELY, GREG,** 5419 Pine St., Bellaire, TX 77401, Phone: 713-991-2677, ediiorio@houston.rr.com
**Specialties:** Traditional patterns and his own patterns for work and/or collecting. **Patterns:** Hunters, Bowies and utility/camp knives. **Technical:** Forges own Damascus, 1084, 5160 and some tool steels. Differentially tempers. **Prices:** $225 to $5,000. **Remarks:** Part-time maker; first knife sold in 1987. **Mark:** Last name or interlocked initials, MS.

**NEILSON, J.,** RR 2 Box 16, Wyalusing, PA 18853, Phone: 570-746-4944, mountainhollow@emcs.net Web: www.mountainhollow.net
**Specialties:** Working and collectable fixed blade knives. **Patterns:** Hunter/fighters, Bowies, neck knives and daggers. **Technical:** Flat and convex grinds, 1084, 5160, maker's own Damascus. **Prices:** $200 to $1,500. **Remarks:** Full-time maker, first knife sold in 2000. Doing business as Neilson's Mountain Hollow. **Mark:** J. Neilson. **Other:** Each knife comes with a sheath by Tess.

**NELSON, BOB,** 21 Glen Rd., Sparta, NJ 07871

**NELSON, KEN,** 11059 Hwy 73, Pittsville, WI 54466, Phone: 715-323-0538 or 715-884-6448, Email:dwarveniron@yahoo.com
**Specialties:** Working straight knives, period pieces. **Patterns:** Utility, hunters, dirks, daggers, throwers, hawks, axes, swords, pole arms and blade blanks as well. **Technical:** Forges 5160, 52100, W2, 10xx, L6, carbon steels and own Damascus. Do my own heat treating. **Prices:** $50 to $350; some to $3,000. **Remarks:** Part-time maker. First knife sold in 1995. Doing business as Iron Wolf Forge. **Mark:** Stylized wolf paw print.

**NELSON, TOM,** PO Box 2298, Wilropark 1731, Gauteng, SOUTH AFRICA, Phone: 27 11 7663991, Fax: 27 11 7687161, tom.nelson@telkomsa.net
**Specialties:** Own Damascus (Hosaic etc.) **Patterns:** One of akind art knives, swords and axes. **Prices:** $500 to $1,000.

**NELSON, DR. CARL,** 2500 N Robison Rd., Texarkana, TX 75501

**NETO JR., NELSON AND DE CARVALHO, HENRIQUE M.,** R. Joao Margarido, No. 20-V, Guerra, Braganca Paulista, SP-12900-000, BRAZIL, Phone: 011-7843-6889, Fax: 011-7843-6889
**Specialties:** Straight knives and folders. **Patterns:** Bowies, katanas, jambyias and others. **Technical:** Forges high-carbon steels. **Prices:** $70 to $3,000. **Remarks:** Full-time makers; first knife sold in 1990. **Mark:** HandN.

**NEUHAEUSLER, ERWIN,** Heiligenangerstrasse 15, 86179 Augsburg, GERMANY, Phone: 0821/81 49 97, eneuhaeusl@aol.com
**Specialties:** Using straight knives of his design. **Patterns:** Hunters, boots, bowies and folders. **Technical:** Grinds ATS-34, RWL-34 and Damascus. **Prices:** $200 to $750. **Remarks:** Spare-time maker; first knife sold in 1991. **Mark:** Etched logo, last name and city.

**NEVLING, MARK,** BURR OAK KNIVES, PO Box 9, Hume, IL 61932, Phone: 217-887-2522
**Specialties:** Straight knives and folders of his own design. **Patterns:** Hunters, fighters, Bowies, folders, and small executive knives. **Technical:** Convex grinds, Forges, uses only high-carbon and Damascus. **Prices:** $200 to $,2000. **Remarks:** Full-time maker, first knife sold 1988.

**NEWCOMB, CORBIN,** 628 Woodland Ave., Moberly, MO 65270, Phone: 660-263-4639
**Specialties:** Working straight knives and folders; period pieces. **Patterns:** Hunters, axes, Bowies, folders, buckskinned blades and boots. **Technical:** Hollow-grinds D2, 440C and 154CM; prefers natural handle materials. Makes own Damascus; offers cable Damascus. **Prices:** $100 to $500. **Remarks:** Full-time maker; first knife sold in 1982. Doing business as Corbin Knives. **Mark:** First name and serial number.

**NEWHALL, TOM,** 3602 E 42nd Stravenue, Tucson, AZ 85713, Phone: 520-721-0562, gggaz@aol.com

**NEWTON, LARRY,** 1758 Pronghorn Ct., Jacksonville, FL 32225, Phone: 904-221-2340, Fax: 904-220-4098, CNewton1234@aol.com
**Specialties:** Traditional and slender high-grade gentlemen's automatic folders, locking liner type tactical, and working straight knives. **Patterns:** Front release locking folders, interframes, hunters, and skinners. **Technical:** Grinds Damascus, ATS-34, 440C and D2. **Prices:** Folders start at $350, straights start at $150. **Remarks:** Spare-time maker; first knife sold in 1989. **Mark:** Last name.

**NEWTON, RON,** 223 Ridge Ln., London, AR 72847, Phone: 479-293-3001, rnewton@cei.net
**Specialties:** Mosaic Damascus folders with accelerated actions. **Patter** One-of-a-kind. **Technical:** 1084-15N20 steels used in his mosaic Damasc steels. **Prices:** $1,000 to $5,000. **Remarks:** Also making antique Bo repros and various fixed blades. **Mark:** All capital letters in NEWTON "We ern Invitation" font.

**NICHOLSON, R. KENT,** PO Box 204, Phoenix, MD 21131, Phone: 41 323-6925
**Specialties:** Large using knives. **Patterns:** Bowies and camp knives in Moran-style. **Technical:** Forges W2, 9260, 5160; makes Damascus. **Pric** $150 to $995. **Remarks:** Part-time maker; first knife sold in 1984. **Ma** Name.

**NIELSON, JEFF V.,** PO Box 365, Monroe, UT 84754, Phone: 801-527 4242, jun1u205@hotmail.com
**Specialties:** Classic knives of his design and to customer specs. **Patter** Fighters, hunters, locking folders; miniatures. **Technical:** Grinds 440C st less and Damascus. **Prices:** $100 to $1,200. **Remarks:** Part-time maker; knife sold in 1991. **Mark:** Name, location.

**NIEMUTH, TROY,** 3143 North Ave., Sheboygan, WI 53083, Phone: 4 452-2927
**Specialties:** Period pieces and working/using straight knives of his des and to customer specs. **Patterns:** Hunters and utility/camp knives. **Techni** Grinds 440C, 1095 and A2. **Prices:** $85 to $350; some to $500. **Remar** Full-time maker; first knife sold in 1995. **Mark:** Etched last name.

**NILSSON, JOHNNY WALKER,** Tingsstigen 11, SE Arvidsjaur, SWEDEN, Phone: 46-960-130-48, 0960.13048@telia.com Web: www.jwnknives.com
**Specialties:** High-end hand-carved and engraved Sami-style horn knives sheaths. **Patterns:** Traditional Sami and own design. **Technical:** For shapes and grinds carbon and Damascus, unique horn applications sculpted and bent horn plates. **Prices:** $800 to $6,000. **Remarks:** Ma since 1988. Nordic (5 countries) champion many times. Knives inspired 10,000 year old indigenous Sami culture, combines traditional techniques designs with hi sown innovations. Handles in reindeer horn, birch burl. Pe and bark spaces, bark coloring. Sheaths in reindeer horn and leather openings, file work, and engraved inlays. Hand stitches and hand t leather. Yearly award in his name at Nordic Championship. **Mark:** JN sheaths, handle, and wood custom boxes. JWN on blades.

**NISHIUCHI, MELVIN S.,** 6121 Forest Park Dr., Las Vegas, NV 8915 Phone: 702-438-2327
**Specialties:** Collectable quality using/working knives. **Patterns:** Locking folders, fighters, hunters and fancy personal knives. **Technical:** Grinds A 34 and Devin Thomas Damascus; prefers semi-precious stone and exotic ural handle materials. **Prices:** $375 to $2,000. **Remarks:** Part-time ma first knife sold in 1985. **Mark:** Circle with a line above it.

**NIX, ROBERT T.,** 4194 Cadillac, Wayne, MI 48184, Phone: 734-729-6468, merlin1215@wideopenwest.com
**Specialties:** Hunters, skinners, art, Bowie, camp/survival/boot folders. are file worked. Custom leather work available also, mainly sheaths/overl inlays, tooling, combinations of material/leather, micarta, wood, kydex, n **Technical:** Stock removal, ATS-34, stainless Damascus, 440C, 420V, 4 BG42, D2, 01, carbon Damascus. Every blade gets Rockwelled. Likes the ural handle materials best, but will use anything available; ivory, bone, h pearl, stabilized woods, micarta. **Prices:** Knives from $125 to $2,500. She from $40 to $400. **Remarks:** Part-time maker, first knife sold in 1993. M each piece as if it were for me. **Mark:** R.T. Nix in script or Nix in bold face.

**NOLEN, R.D. AND STEVE,** 105 Flowingwells Rd, Pottsboro, TX 750 Phone: 903-786-2454, blademaster@nolenkinves.com Web: www.no knives.com
**Specialties:** Working knives; display pieces. **Patterns:** Wide variet straight knives, butterflies and buckles. **Technical:** Grind D2, 440C 154CM. Offer filework; make exotic handles. **Prices:** $150 to $800; s higher. **Remarks:** Full-time makers; first knife sold in 1968. Steve is third eration maker. **Mark:** NK in oval logo.

**NORDELL, INGEMAR,** Skarpå 2103, 82041 Färila, SWEDEN, Phone 0651-23347
**Specialties:** Classic working and using straight knives. **Patterns:** Hun Bowies and fighters. **Technical:** Forges and grinds ATS-34, D2 and San **Prices:** $120 to $1,500. **Remarks:** Part-time maker; first knife sold in 1 **Mark:** Initials or name.

**NOREN, DOUGLAS E.,** 14676 Boom Rd., Springlake, MI 49456, Ph 616-842-4247, gwenhoren@novagate.com
**Specialties:** Hand forged blades, custom built and made to order. Han work, carving and casting. Stag and stacked handles. Replicas of Scagel

Joseph Rogers. Hand tooled custom made sheaths. **Technical:** 5160, 52100 and 1084 steel. **Prices:** Start at $250. **Remarks:** Sole authorship, works in all mediums, ABS Journey man msn., all knives come with a custom hand-tooled sheath. Also makes anvils. **Other:** Enjoy the challenge and meeting people.

**NORFLEET, ROSS W.,** 3947 Tanbark Rd., Richmond, VA 23235, Phone: 804-276-4169, rossknife@aol.com
**Specialties:** Classic, traditional and working/using knives of his design or in standard patterns. **Patterns:** Hunters and folders. **Technical:** Hollow-grinds 440C and ATS-34. **Prices:** $150 to $550. **Remarks:** Part-time maker; first knife sold in 1992. **Mark:** Last name.

**NORRIS, DON,** 8710 N Hollybrook, Tucson, AZ 85742, Phone: 520-744-2494
**Specialties:** Classic and traditional working/using straight knives and folders of his design, or to customer specs etc. **Patterns:** Bowies, daggers, fighters, hunters and utility/camp knives. **Technical:** Grinds and forges Damascus; grinds ATS-34 and 440C. Cast sterling guards and bolsters on Bowies. **Prices:** $350 to $2,000; some to $3,500. **Remarks:** Full-time maker; first knife sold in 1990. Doing business as Norris Custom Knives. **Mark:** Last name.

**NORTON, DON,** 95N Wilkison Ave, Port Townsend, WA 98368-2534, Phone: 306-385-1978
**Specialties:** Fancy and plain straight knives. **Patterns:** Hunters, small Bowies, tantos, boot knives, fillets. **Technical:** Prefers 440C, Micarta, exotic woods and other natural handle materials. Hollow-grinds all knives except fillet knives. **Prices:** $185 to $2800; average is $200. **Remarks:** Full-time maker; first knife sold in 1980. **Mark:** Full name, Hsi Shuai, city, state.

**NOTT, RON P.,** PO Box 281, Summerdale, PA 17093, Phone: 717-732-2763, neitznott@aol.com
**Specialties:** High-art folders and some straight knives. **Patterns:** Scale release folders. **Technical:** Grinds ATS-34, 416 and nickel-silver. Engraves, inlays gold. **Prices:** $250 to $3,000. **Remarks:** Full-time maker; first knife sold in 1993. Doing business as Knives By Nott, customer engraving. **Mark:** First initial, last name and serial number.

**NOWLAND, RICK,** 3677 E Bonnie Rd., Waltonville, IL 62894, Phone: 618-279-3170, ricknowland@frontiernet.net
**Specialties:** Slip joint folders in traditional patterns. **Patterns:** Trapper, whittler, sowbelly, toothpick and copperhead. **Technical:** Uses ATS-34, bolsters and liners have integral construction. **Prices:** $225 to $1,000. **Remarks:** Part-time maker. **Mark:** Last name.

**NUNN, GREGORY,** HC64 Box 2107, Castle Valley, UT 84532, Phone: 435-259-8607
**Specialties:** High-art working and using knives of his design; new edition knife with handle made from anatomized dinosaur bone - first ever made. **Patterns:** Flaked stone knives. **Technical:** Uses gem-quality agates, jaspers and obsidians for blades. **Prices:** $250 to $2300. **Remarks:** Full-time maker; first knife sold in 1989. **Mark:** Name, knife and edition numbers, year made.

# O

**OBRIEN, GEORGE,** 22511 Tullis Trails Ct., Katy, TX 77494-8265

**OCHS, CHARLES F.,** 124 Emerald Lane, Largo, FL 33771, Phone: 727-536-3827, Fax: 727-536-3827, chuckandbelle@juno.com
**Specialties:** Working knives; period pieces. **Patterns:** Hunters, fighters, Bowies, buck skinners and folders. **Technical:** Forges 52100, 5160 and his own Damascus. **Prices:** $150 to $1,800; some to $2,500. **Remarks:** Full-time maker; first knife sold in 1978. **Mark:** OX Forge.

**O'DELL, CLYDE,** 176 Ouachita 404, Camden, AR 71701, Phone: 870-574-2754, abcodell@arkansas.net
**Specialties:** Working knives. **Patterns:** Hunters, camp knives, Bowies, daggers, tomahawks. **Technical:** Forges 5160 and 1084. **Prices:** Starting at $125. **Remarks:** Spare-time maker. **Mark:** Last name.

**ODGEN, RANDY W.,** 10822 Sage Orchard, Houston, TX 77089, Phone: 713-481-3601

**ODOM JR, VICTOR L.,** PO Box 572, North, SC 29112, Phone: 803-247-5614, vlodom@joimail.com
**Specialties:** Forged knives and tomahawks; stock removal knives. **Patterns:** Hunters, Bowies and folders. **Technical:**Use 1095, 5160, 52100 high carbon and alloy steels, ATS-34, and 55. **Prices:** Straight knives $60.00 and up.Folders @250.00 and up. **Remarks:**Student of Mr. George Henron. **Mark:** Steel stamp "ODOM" and etched "Odom Forge North, SC" plus a serial number. **Other:**SCAK.ORG

**OGDEN, BILL,** OGDEN KNIVES, PO Box 52, Avis, PA 17721, Phone: 570-753-5568
**Specialties:** One-of-a-kind, liner-lock folders, hunters, skinners, minis. **Technical:** Grinds ATS-34, 440-C, D2, 52100, Damascus, natural and unnatural handle materials, hand-stitched custom sheaths. **Prices:** $50 and up. **Remarks:** Part-time maker since 1992. **Marks:** Last name or "OK" stamp (Ogden Knives).

**OGLETREE JR., BEN R.,** 2815 Israel Rd., Livingston, TX 77351, Phone: 409-327-8315
**Specialties:** Working/using straight knives of his design. **Patterns:** Hunters, kitchen and utility/camp knives. **Technical:** Grinds ATS-34, W1 and 1075; heat-treats. **Prices:** $200 to $400. **Remarks:** Part-time maker; first knife sold in 1955. **Mark:** Last name, city and state in oval with a tree on either side.

**O'HARE, SEAN,** PO Box 374, Fort Simpson, NT, CANADA X0E 0N0, Phone: 867-695-2619, sean@ohareknives.ca Web: www.ohareknives.ca
**Specialties:** Fixed blade hunters and tactical knives. **Patterns:** Neck knives to larger hunter and tactical knives. **Technical:** Stock removal, full and hidden tang knives. **Prices:** $115 USD to $300 USD. **Remarks:** Strives to balance aesthetics, functionality and durability. **Mark:** 1st is "OHARE KNIVES", 2nd is "NWT CANADA".

**OLIVE, MICHAEL E.,** HC 78 Box 442, Leslie, AR 72645, Phone: 870-363-4452

**OLIVER, TODD D.,** 894 Beaver Hollow, Spencer, IN 47460, Phone: 812-829-1762
**Specialties:** Damascus hunters and daggers. High-carbon as well. **Patterns:** Ladder, twist random. **Technical:** Sole author of all his blades. **Prices:** $350 and up. **Remarks:** Learned bladesmithing from Jim Batson at the ABS school and Damascus from Billy Merritt in Indiana. **Mark:** T.D. Oliver Spencer IN. **Other:** Two crossed swords and a battle ax.

**OLOFSON, CHRIS,** 29 KNIVES, 1 Kendall SQ Bldg. 600, Cambridge, MA 02139, Phone: 617-492-0451, artistacie@earthlink.net

**OLSON, ROD,** Box 5973, High River, AB, CANADA T1V 1P6, Phone: 403-652-2744, Fax: 403-646-5838
**Specialties:** Lockback folders with gold toothpicks. **Patterns:** Locking folders. **Technical:** Grinds ATS-34 blades and spring - filework- 14kt bolsters and liners. **Prices:** Mid range. **Remarks:** Part-time maker; first knife sold in 1979. **Mark:** Last name on blade.

**OLSON, WAYNE C.,** 890 Royal Ridge Dr., Bailey, CO 80421, Phone: 303-816-9486
**Specialties:** High-tech working knives. **Patterns:** Hunters to folding lockers; some integral designs. **Technical:** Grinds 440C, 154CM and ATS-34; likes hand-finishes; precision-fits stainless steel fittings—no solder, no nickel silver. **Prices:** $275 to $600; some to $3,000. **Remarks:** Part-time maker; first knife sold in 1979. **Mark:** Name, maker.

**OLSON, DARROLD E.,** PO Box 1539, Springfield, OR 97477, Phone: 541-726-8300/541-914-7238
**Specialties:** Straight knives and folders of his design and to customer specs. **Patterns:** Hunters, liner locks and locking folders. **Technical:** Grinds 440C, ATS-34 and 154CM. Uses anodized titanium; sheaths wet-molded. **Prices:** $150 to $350. **Remarks:** Part-time maker; first knife sold in 1989. **Mark:** Etched logo, year, type of steel and name.

**OLSZEWSKI, STEPHEN,** 1820 Harkney Hill Rd., Coventry, RI 02816, Phone: 401-397-4774, antlers53@msn.com Web: www.olszewskiknives.com
**Specialties:** Lock back, liner locks, automatics (art knives). **Patterns:** One-of-a-kind art knives specializing in figurals. **Technical:** Damascus steel, titanium file worked liners, fossil ivory and pearl. **Prices:** $1,800 to $6,500. **Remarks:** Will custom build to your specifications. **Other:** Quality work with guarantee. **Mark:** SCO inside fish symbol. Also "Olszewski".

**O'MALLEY, DANIEL,** 4338 Evanston Ave. N, Seattle, WA 98103, Phone: 206-527-0315
**Specialties:** Custom chef's knives. **Remarks:** Making knives since 1997.

**ONION, KENNETH J.,** 47-501 Hui Kelu St., Kaneohe, HI 96744, Phone: 808-239-1300, Fax: 808-289-1301, shopjunky@aol.com Web: www.kenonionknives.com
**Specialties:** Mostly folders featuring "speed safe", some fixed blades and miscellany. **Patterns:** Hybrid, art, fighter, utility. **Technical:** S-30X, BG-42, cowey Y, Damascus. **Prices:** $500 to $15,000. **Remarks:** Full-time maker; designer, first knife sold in 1991. **Mark:** Name and state.

**ORTEGA, BEN M.,** 165 Dug Rd., Wyoming, PA 18644, Phone: 717-696-3234

**ORTON, RICH,** 3625 Fleming St., Riverside, CA 92509, Phone: 909-685-3019, ortonknifeworks@earthlink.net Web: www.ortonknifeworks.com
**Specialties:** Collectible folders, using and collectible straight knives. **Patterns:** Wharncliffe, gents, tactical, boot, neck knives, bird and trout, hunters, camp, Bowie. **Technical:** Grinds ATS-34, Jim Fergeson Damascus titanium liners, bolsters, anodize, lots of filework, jigged and picked bone, giraffe bone.

Scrimshaw on some. **Prices:** Folders $300 to $600; straight $100 to $750. **Remarks:** Full-time maker; first knife sold in 1992. Doing business as Orton Knife Works. Now making folders. **Mark:** Rich Orton (maker) Riverside, CA.

**OSBORNE, WARREN,** 215 Edgefield, Waxahachie, TX 75165, Phone: 972-935-0899, Fax: 972-937-9004
**Specialties:** Investment grade collectible, interframes, one-of-a-kinds; unique locking mechanisms. **Patterns:** Folders; bolstered and interframes; conventional lockers, front lockers and back lockers; some slip-joints; some high-art pieces; fighters. **Technical:** Grinds ATS-34, 440 and 154; some Damascus and CPM400V. **Prices:** $400 to $2,000; some to $4,000. Interframes $650 to $1,500. **Remarks:** Full-time maker; first knife sold in 1980. **Mark:** Last name in boomerang logo.

**OSBORNE, DONALD H.,** 5840 N McCall, Clovis, CA 93611, Phone: 559-299-9483, Fax: 559-298-1751, oforge@sbcglobal.net
**Specialties:** Traditional working using straight knives and folder of his design. **Patterns:** Working straight knives, Bowies, hunters, camp knives and folders. **Technical:** Forges carbon steels and makes Damascus. Grinds ATS-34, 154CM, and 440C. **Prices:** $150 and up. **Remarks:** Part-time maker. **Mark:** Last name logo and J.S.

**OTT, FRED,** 1257 Rancho Durango Rd., Durango, CO 81303, Phone: 970-375-9669
**Patterns:** Bowies,hunters and daggers. **Technical:** Forges 1084-5160 and Damascus **Prices:** $250 to $1,000. **Remarks:** Full-time maker. **Mark:** Last name.

**OVEREYNDER, T.R.,** 1800 S. Davis Dr., Arlington, TX 76013, Phone: 817-277-4812, Fax: 817-277-4812, trovereynderknives@sbcglobal.net
**Specialties:** Highly finished collector-grade knives. Multi- Blades **Patterns:** Fighters, Bowies, daggers, locking folders, slip-joints and 90 percent collector-grade interframe folders. **Technical:** Grinds D2, BG-42, S-60V, S-30V, 154CM, RWL-34 vendor supplied Damascus. Has been making titanium-frame folders since 1977. **Prices:** $500 to $1,500; some to $7,000. **Remarks:** Full-time maker; first knife sold in 1977. Doing business as TRO Knives. **Mark:** T.R. OVEREYNDER KNIVES, city and state.

**OWENS, JOHN,** 14500 CR 270, Nathrop, CO 81236, Phone: 719-395-0870
**Specialties:** Hunters. **Prices:** $200 to $275; some to $650. **Remarks:** Spare-time maker. **Mark:** Last name.

**OWENS, DONALD,** 2274 Lucille Ln., Melbourne, FL 32935, Phone: 321-254-9765

**OWNBY, JOHN C.,** 3316 Springbridge Ln., Plano, TX 75025, john@johnownby.com Web: www.johnownby.com
**Specialties:** Hunters, utility/camp knives. **Patterns:** Hunters, locking folders and utility/camp knives. **Technical:** 440C, D2 and ATS-34. All blades are flat ground. Prefers natural materials for handles—exotic woods, horn and antler. **Prices:** $150 to $350; some to $500. **Remarks:** Part-time maker; first knife sold in 1993. **Mark:** Name, city, state. **Other:** Doing business as John C. Ownby Handmade Knives.

**OYSTER, LOWELL R.,** 543 Grant Rd., Corinth, ME 04427, Phone: 207-884-8663
**Specialties:** Traditional and original designed multi-blade slip-joint folders. **Patterns:** Hunters, minis, camp and fishing knives. **Technical:** Grinds O1; heat-treats. **Prices:** $55 to $450; some to $750. **Remarks:** Full-time maker; first knife sold in 1981. **Mark:** A scallop shell.

# P

**PACHI, FRANCESCO,** Via Pometta, 1, 17046 Sassello (SV), ITALY, Phone: 019 720086, Fax: 019 720086, Web: www.pachi-knives.com
**Specialties:** Folders and straight knives of his design. **Patterns:** Utility, hunters and skinners. **Technical:** Grinds RWL-34, CPM S30V and Damascus. **Prices:** $800 to $3,500. **Remarks:** Full-time maker; first knife sold in 1991. **Mark:** Logo with last name.

**PACKARD, BOB,** PO Box 311, Elverta, CA 95626, Phone: 916-991-5218
**Specialties:** Traditional working/using straight knives of his design and to customer specs. **Patterns:** Hunters, fishing knives, utility/camp knives. **Technical:** Grinds ATS-34, 440C; Forges 52100, 5168 and cable Damascus. **Prices:** $75 to $225. **Mark:** Engraved name and year.

**PADGETT JR., EDWIN L.,** 340 Vauxhall St., New London, CT 06320-3838, Phone: 860-443-2938
**Specialties:** Skinners and working knives of any design. **Patterns:** Straight and folding knives. **Technical:** Grinds ATS-34 or any tool steel upon request. **Prices:** $50 to $300. **Mark:** Name.

**PADILLA, GARY,** PO Box 6928, Auburn, CA 95604, Phone: 530-888-6992, gkpadilla@yahoo.com
**Specialties:** Unique knives of all designs and uses. **Patterns:** Hunter kitchen knives, utility/camp knives and obsidian ceremonial knives. **Techn cal:** Grinds 440C, ATS-34, O1 and Damascus. **Prices:** Generally $100 $200. **Remarks:** Part-time maker; first knife sold in 1977. Doing business Bighorn Knifeworks. **Mark:** Stylized initials or name over company name.

**PAGE, LARRY,** 1200 Mackey Scott Rd., Aiken, SC 29801-7620, Phone 803-648-0001
**Specialties:** Working knives of his design. **Patterns:** Hunters, boots and figh ers. **Technical:** Grinds ATS-34. **Prices:** Start at $85. **Remarks:** Part-tin maker; first knife sold in 1983. **Mark:** Name, city and state in oval.

**PAGE, REGINALD,** 6587 Groveland Hill Rd., Groveland, NY 14462, Phone: 716-243-1643
**Specialties:** High-art straight knives and one-of-a-kind folders of his desig **Patterns:** Hunters, locking folders and slip-joint folders. **Technical:** Forg O1, 5160 and his own Damascus. Prefers natural handle materials but w work with Micarta. **Remarks:** Spare-time maker; first knife sold in 1985. **Mar** First initial, last name.

**PAINTER, TONY,** 87 Fireweed Dr, Whitehorse Yukon, CANADA Y1A 5T8, Phone: 867-633-3323, jimmies@klondiker.com Web: www.tony-painterdesigns.com
**Specialties:** One-of-a-kind using knives, some fancy , fixed and folders. **Pa terns:**No fixed patterns.**Technical:**Grinds ATS-34, D2, O1, S30V, Damasc stain finish. Prefers to use exotic woods and other natural materials. Mica and G10 on working knives. **Prices:**Starting at $200.**Remarks:**Full-time kn maker and carver. First knife sol in 1996.**Mark:**Two stamps used: initials TP a circle and painter.

**PALAZZO, TOM,** 207-30 Jordon Dr., Bayside, NY 11360, Phone: 718-352-2170, tpknives@aol.com
**Specialties:** Fixed blades, custom sheaths, neck knives. **Patterns:** No fix patterns. **Prices:** $150 and up.

**PALMER, TAYLOR,** TAYLOR-MADE SCENIC KNIVES INC., Box 97, Blanding, UT 84511, Phone: 435-678-2523, taylormadewoodeu@cit-link.net
**Specialties:** Bronze carvings inside of blade area. **Prices:** $250 and **Mark:** Taylor Palmer Utah.

**PANAK, PAUL S.,** 9000 Stanhope Kellogsville Rd., Kinsman, OH 4442 Phone: 330-876-8473, burn@burnknives.com Web: www.burnknives.com
**Specialties:** Italian-styled knives. **Patterns:** Vintage-styled Italians, fight folders and high art gothic-styles all with various mechanisms. **Technic** Grinds ATS-34, 154 CM, 440C and Damascus. **Prices:** $800 to $3,0 **Remarks:** Full-time maker, first knife sold in 1998. **Mark:** "Burn".

**PANKIEWICZ, PHILIP R.,** RFD #1, Waterman Rd., Lebanon, CT 0624
**Specialties:** Working straight knives. **Patterns:** Hunters, daggers, minis a fishing knives. **Technical:** Grinds D2, 440C and 154CM. **Prices:** $60 to $1 some to $250. **Remarks:** Spare-time maker; first knife sold in 1975. **Ma** First initial in star.

**PARDUE, JOE,** PO Box 693, Spurger, TX 77660, Phone: 409-429-707 Fax: 409-429-5657

**PARDUE, MELVIN M.,** Rt. 1, Box 130, Repton, AL 36475, Phone: 334 248-2447, mpardue@frontiernet.net Web: www.melpardueknives.com
**Specialties:** Folders, collectable, combat, utility and tactical. **Patterns:** Lo back, liner lock, pushbutton; all blade and handle patterns. **Technical:** Gri 154-CM, 440-C, 12-C-27. Forges Mokume and Damascus. Uses Titani **Prices:** $400 to $1,600. **Remarks:** Full-time maker; Guild member, A member, AFC member. **Mark:** Mel Pardue or Pardue. **Other:** First knife ma 1957; first knife sold professionally 1974.

**PARKER, J.E.,** 11 Domenica Cir., Clarion, PA 16214, Phone: 814-226 4837, Web: www.jimparker.knives.com
**Specialties:** Fancy/embellished, traditional and working straight knives of design and to customer specs. Engraving and scrimshaw by the best in business. **Patterns:** Bowies, hunters and liner lock folders. **Technical:** Gri 440C, 440V, ATS-34 and nickel Damascus. Prefers mastodon, oosik, am and malachite handle material. **Prices:** $75 to $5200. **Remarks:** Full-t maker; first knife sold in 1991. Doing business as Custom Knife. **Mark:** Parker and Clarion PA stamped or etched in Blade.

**PARKER, ROBERT NELSON,** 5223 Wilhelm Rd. N.W., Rapid City, M 49676, Fax: 248-545-8211, rnparkerknives@wowway.com
**Specialties:** Traditional working and using straight knives of his design. **P terns:** Hunters, fighters, utility/camp knives; some Bowies. **Technical:** Gri ATS-34;GB-42,S-30V forges 01, 530V, 5160, L6 hollow and flat grinds, full hidden tangs. Hand-stitched leather sheaths. **Prices:** $350 to $500; some $1,500. **Remarks:** Full-time maker; first knife sold in 1986. **Mark:** Full name.

**PARKER, CLIFF,** 6350 Tulip Dr., Zephyrhills, FL 33544, Phone: 813-973-1682

**Specialties:** Damascus gent knives. **Patterns:** Locking liners, some straight knives. **Technical:** Mostly use 1095, 1084, 15N20, 203E and powdered steel. **Prices:** $700 to $1,800. **Remarks:** Making own Damascus and specializing in mosaics; first knife sold in 1996. **Mark:** CP. **Other:** Full-time beginning in 2000.

**PARKS, BLANE C.,** 15908 Crest Dr., Woodbridge, VA 22191, Phone: 703-221-4680

**Specialties:** Knives of his design. **Patterns:** Boots, Bowies, daggers, fighters, hunters, kitchen knives, locking and slip-joint folders, utility/camp knives, letter openers and friction folders. **Technical:** Grinds ATS-34, 440C, D2 and other carbon steels. Offers filework, silver wire inlay and wooden sheaths. **Prices:** Start at $250 and up. **Remarks:** Part-time maker; first knife sold in 1993. Doing business as B.C. Parks Knives. **Mark:** First and middle initials, last name.

**PARKS, JOHN,** 3539 Galilee Church Rd., Jefferson, GA 30549, Phone: 706-367-4916

**Specialties:** Traditional working and using straight knives of his design. **Patterns:** Trout knives, hunters and integral bolsters. **Technical:** Forges 1095 and 5168. **Prices:** $175 to $450; some to $650. **Remarks:** Part-time maker; first knife sold in 1989. **Mark:** Initials.

**PARLER, THOMAS O.,** 11 Franklin St., Charleston, SC 29401, Phone: 803-723-9433

**PARRISH, ROBERT,** 271 Allman Hill Rd., Weaverville, NC 28787, Phone: 828-645-2864

**Specialties:** Heavy-duty working knives of his design or to customer specs. **Patterns:** Survival and duty knives; hunters and fighters. **Technical:** Grinds 440C, D2, O1 and commercial Damascus. **Prices:** $200 to $300; some to $6,000. **Remarks:** Part-time maker; first knife sold in 1970. **Mark:** Initials connected, sometimes with city and state.

**PARRISH III, GORDON A.,** 940 Lakloey Dr., North Pole, AK 99705, Phone: 907-488-0357

**Specialties:** Classic and high-art straight knives of his design and to customer specs; working and using knives. **Patterns:** Bowies and hunters. **Technical:** Grinds tool steel and ATS-34. Uses mostly Alaskan handle materials. **Prices:** $150 to $1,000. **Remarks:** Spare-time maker; first knife sold in 1980. **Mark:** Last name, state.

**PARSONS, MICHAEL R.,** MCKEE KNIVES, 7042 McFarland Rd., Indianapolis, IN 46227, Phone: 317-784-7943, clparsons@aol.com

**Specialties:** Hand-forged fixed-blade knives, all fancy but all are useable knives. **Patterns:** Engraves, carves, wire inlay, and leather work. All knives one-of-a-kind. **Technical:** Blades forged from files, all work hand done. **Prices:** $350 to $2,000. **Mark:** McKee.

**PASSMORE, JIMMY D.,** 316 SE Elm, Hoxie, AR 72433, Phone: 870-886-1922

**PATRICK, WILLARD C.,** PO Box 5716, Helena,, MT 59604, Phone: 406-458-6552, Fax: 406-458-7068, wkamar2@onewest.net

**Specialties:** Working straight knives and one-of-a-kind art knives of his design or to customer specs. **Patterns:** Hunters, Bowies, fish, patch and kitchen knives. **Technical:** Grinds ATS-34, 1095, O1, A2 and Damascus. **Prices:** $100 to $2,000. **Remarks:** Full-time maker; first knife sold in 1989. Doing business as Wil-A-Mar Cutlery. **Mark:** Shield with last name and a dagger.

**PATRICK, PEGGY,** PO Box 127, Brasstown, NC 28902, Phone: 828-837-7627

**Specialties:** Authentic period and Indian sheaths, braintan, rawhide, beads and quill work. **Technical:** Does own braintan, rawhide; uses only natural dyes for quills, old color beads.

**PATRICK, CHUCK,** PO Box 127, Brasstown, NC 28902, Phone: 828-837-7627

**Specialties:** Period pieces. **Patterns:** Hunters, daggers, tomahawks, pre-Civil War folders. **Technical:** Forges hardware, his own cable and Damascus, available in fancy pattern and mosaic. **Prices:** $150 to $1,000; some higher. **Remarks:** Full-time maker. **Mark:** Hand-engraved name or flying owl.

**PATRICK, BOB,** 12642 24A Ave., S. Surrey, B.C., CANADA V4A 8H9, Phone: 604-538-6214, Fax: 604-888-2683, bob@knivesonnet.com Web: www.knivesonnet.com

**Specialties:** Presentation pieces of his design only. **Patterns:** Bowies, push daggers, art pieces. **Technical:** D2, 5160, Damascus. **Prices:** Fair. **Remarks:** Full-time maker; first knife sold in 1987. Doing business as Crescent Knife Works. **Mark:** Logo with name and province or Crescent Knife Works.

**PATTAY, RUDY,** 510 E. Harrison St., Long Beach, NY 11561, Phone: 516-431-0847, dolphinp@optonline.net

**Specialties:** Fancy and working straight knives of his design. **Patterns:** Bowies, hunters, utility/camp knives. **Technical:** Hollow-grinds ATS-34, 440C, O1. Offers commercial Damascus, stainless steel soldered guards; fabricates guard and butt cap on lathe and milling machine. Heat-treats. Prefers synthetic handle materials. Offers hand-sewn sheaths. **Prices:** $100 to $350; some to $500. **Remarks:** Part-time maker; first knife sold in 1990. **Mark:** First initial, last name in sorcerer logo.

**PATTERSON, PAT,** Box 246, Barksdale, TX 78828, Phone: 830-234-3586, pat@pattersonknives.com

**Specialties:** Traditional fixed blades and liner lock folders. **Patterns:** Hunters and folders. **Technical:** Grinds 440C, ATS-34, D2, 01 and Damascus. **Prices:** $250 to $1,000. **Remarks:** Full-time maker. First knife sold in 1991. **Mark:** Name and city.

**PATTON, DICK AND ROB,** 6803 View Ln., Nampa, ID 83687, Phone: 208-468-4123, grpatton@pattonknives.com Web: www.pattonknives.com

**Specialties:** Custom Damascus, hand forged, fighting knives-Bowie and tactical. **Patterns:** Mini Bowie, Merlin Fighter, Mandrita Fighting Bowie. **Prices:** $100 to $2,000.

**PAULO, FERNANDES R.,** Raposo Tavares, No. 213, Lencois Paulista, 18680, Sao Paulo, BRAZIL, Phone: 014-263-4281

**Specialties:** An apprentice of Jose Alberto Paschoarelli, his designs are heavily based on the later designs. **Technical:** Grinds tool steels and stainless steels. Part-time knife maker. **Prices:** Start from $100. **Mark:** P.R.F.

**PAWLOWSKI, JOHN R.,** 4349 William Styron Sq N, Newport News, VA 23606, Phone: 757-223-0613, www.virginiacustomcutlery.com

**Specialties:** Traditional working and using straight knives and folders. **Patterns:** Hunters, Bowies, fighters and camp knives. **Technical:** Stock removal, grinds 440C, ATS-34, 154CM and buys Damascus. **Prices:** $150 to $500; some higher. **Remarks:** Part-time maker, first knife sold in 1983. **Mark:** Early mark, name over attacking Eagle and Alaska. Current mark, name over attacking Eagle and Virginia.

**PEAGLER, RUSS,** PO Box 1314, Moncks Corner, SC 29461, Phone: 803-761-1008

**Specialties:** Traditional working straight knives of his design and to customer specs. **Patterns:** Hunters, fighters, boots. **Technical:** Hollow-grinds 440C, ATS-34 and O1; uses Damascus steel. Prefers bone handles. **Prices:** $85 to $300; some to $500. **Remarks:** Spare-time maker; first knife sold in 1983. **Mark:** Initials.

**PEASE, W.D.,** 657 Cassidy Pike, Ewing, KY 41039, Phone: 606-845-0387, Web: www.wdpeaseknives.com

**Specialties:** Display-quality working folders. **Patterns:** Fighters, tantos and boots; locking folders and interframes. **Technical:** Grinds ATS-34 and commercial Damascus; has own side-release lock system. **Prices:** $500 to $1,000; some to $3,000. **Remarks:** Full-time maker; first knife sold in 1970. **Mark** First and middle initials, last name and state. W. D. Pease Kentucky.

**PEELE, BRYAN,** 219 Ferry St., PO Box 1363, Thompson Falls, MT 59873, Phone: 406-827-4633

**Specialties:** Fancy working and using knives of his design. **Patterns:** Hunters, Bowies and fighters. **Technical:** Grinds 440C, ATS-34, D2, O1 and commercial Damascus. **Prices:** $110 to $300; some to $900. **Remarks:** Part-time maker; first knife sold in 1985. **Mark:** The Elk Rack, full name, city, state.

**PENDLETON, LLOYD,** 24581 Shake Ridge Rd., Volcano, CA 95689, Phone: 209-296-3353, Fax: 209-296-3353

**Specialties:** Contemporary working knives in standard patterns. **Patterns:** Hunters, fighters and boots. **Technical:** Grinds 154CM and ATS-34; mirror finishes. **Prices:** $400 to $725; some to $2,500. **Remarks:** Full-time maker; first knife sold in 1973. **Mark:** First initial, last name logo, city and state.

**PENDRAY, ALFRED H.,** 13950 NE 20th St., Williston, FL 32696, Phone: 352-528-6124

**Specialties:** Working straight knives and folders; period pieces. **Patterns:** Fighters and hunters, axes, camp knives and tomahawks. **Technical:** Forges Wootz steel; makes his own Damascus; makes traditional knives from old files and rasps. **Prices:** $125 to $1,000; some to $3,500. **Remarks:** Part-time maker; first knife sold in 1954. **Mark:** Last initial in horseshoe logo.

**PENFOLD, MICK,** PENFOLD KNIVES, 5 Highview Close, Tremar, Cornwall PL14 5SJ, ENGLAND, Phone: 01579-345783, mickpenfold@btinternet.com Web: www.penfoldknives.co.uk

**Specialties:** Hunters, fighters, Bowies. **Technical:** Grinds 440C, ATS-34, and Damascus. **Prices:** $150 to $1,200. **Remarks:** Part-time maker. First knives sold in 1999. **Mark:** Last name.

**PENNINGTON, C.A.,** 163 Kainga Rd., Kainga Christchurch 8009, NEW ZEALAND, Phone: 03-3237292, capennington@xtra.co.nz
**Specialties:** Classic working and collectors knives. Folders a specialty. **Patterns:** Classical styling for hunters and collectors. **Technical:** Forges his own all tool steel Damascus. Grinds D2 when requested. **Prices:** $240 to $2,000. **Remarks:** Full-time maker; first knife sold in 1988. **Mark:** Name, country. **Other:** Color brochure $3.

**PEPIOT, STEPHAN,** 73 Cornwall Blvd., Winnipeg, Man., CANADA R3J-1E9, Phone: 204-888-1499
**Specialties:** Working straight knives in standard patterns. **Patterns:** Hunters and camp knives. **Technical:** Grinds 440C and industrial hack-saw blades. **Prices:** $75 to $125. **Remarks:** Spare-time maker; first knife sold in 1982. Not currently taking orders. **Mark:** PEP.

**PERRY, CHRIS,** 1654 W. Birch, Fresno, CA 93711, Phone: 209-498-2342
**Specialties:** Traditional working/using straight knives of his design. **Patterns:** Boots, hunters and utility/camp knives. **Technical:** Grinds ATS-34 and 416 ss fittings. **Prices:** $190 to $225. **Remarks:** Spare-time maker. **Mark:** Name above city and state.

**PERRY, JOHN,** 9 South Harrell Rd., Mayflower, AR 72106, Phone: 501-470-3043
**Specialties:** Investment grade and working folders; some straight knives. **Patterns:** Front and rear lock folders, liner locks and hunters. **Technical:** Grinds CPM440V, D2 and making own Damascus. Offers filework. **Prices:** $375 to $950; some to $2,500. **Remarks:** Part-time maker; first knife sold in 1990. Doing business as Perry Custom Knives. **Mark:** Initials or last name in high relief set in a diamond shape.

**PERRY, JIM,** Hope Star, PO Box 648, Hope, AR 71801, jenn@comfab-inc.com

**PERRY, JOHNNY,** PO Box 4666, Spartanburg, SC 29305-4666, Phone: 803-578-3533, comfabinc@mindspring.com

**PERSSON, CONNY,** PL 588, 820 50 Loos, SWEDEN, Phone: +46 657 10305, Fax: +46 657 413 435, connyknives@swipnet.se Web: www.connyknives.com
**Specialties:** Mosaic Damascus. **Patterns:** Mosaic Damascus. **Technical:** Straight knives and folders. **Prices:** $1,000 and up. **Mark:** C. Persson.

**PETEAN, FRANCISCO AND MAURICIO,** R. Dr.Carlos de Carvalho Rosa, 52, Centro, Birigui, SP-16200-000, BRAZIL, Phone: 0186-424786
**Specialties:** Classic knives to customer specs. **Patterns:** Bowies, boots, fighters, hunters and utility knives. **Technical:** Grinds D6, 440C and high-carbon steels. Prefers natural handle material. **Prices:** $70 to $500. **Remarks:** Full-time maker; first knife sold in 1985. **Mark:** Last name, hand made.

**PETERSEN, DAN L.,** 10610 SW 81st, Auburn, KS 66402, Phone: 785-256-2640
**Specialties:** Period pieces and forged integral hilts on hunters and fighters. **Patterns:** Texas-style Bowies, boots and hunters in high-carbon and Damascus steel. **Technical:** Austempers forged high-carbon blades. Precisin heat treating using salt takns. **Prices:** $400 to $5,000. **Remarks:** First knife sold in 1978. **Mark:** Stylized initials, MS.

**PETERSON, LLOYD (PETE) C.,** 64 Halbrook Rd., Clinton, AR 72031, Phone: 501-893-0000, wmblade@cyberback.com
**Specialties:** Miniatures, and mosaic folders. **Prices:** $250 and up. **Remarks:** Lead time is 6-8 months. **Mark:** Pete.

**PETERSON, CHRIS,** Box 143, 2175 W. Rockyford, Salina, UT 84654, Phone: 801-529-7194
**Specialties:** Working straight knives of his design. **Patterns:** Large fighters, boots, hunters and some display pieces. **Technical:** Forges O1 and meteor. Makes and sells his own Damascus. Engraves, scrimshaws and inlays. **Prices:** $150 to $600; some to $1,500. **Remarks:** Full-time maker; first knife sold in 1986. **Mark:** A drop in a circle with a line through it.

**PETERSON, KAREN,** THE PEN AND THE SWORD LTD., PO Box 290741, Brooklyn, NY 11229-0741, Phone: 718-382-4847, Fax: 718-376-5745, info@pensword.com Web: www.pensword.com

**PETERSON, ELDON G.,** 260 Haugen Heights Rd., Whitefish, MT 59937, Phone: 406-862-2204, draino@digisys.net Web: http://www.kmg.org/egpeterson
**Specialties:** Fancy and working folders, any size. **Patterns:** Lockback interframes, integral bolster folders, liner locks, and two-blades. **Technical:** Grinds 440C and ATS-34. Offers gold inlay work, gem stone inlays and engraving. **Prices:** $285 to $5,000. **Remarks:** Full-time maker; first knife sold in 1974. **Mark:** Name, city and state.

**PFANENSTIEL, DAN,** 1824 Lafayette Ave., Modesto, CA 95355, Phone 209-575-5937, dpfan@sbcglobal.net
**Specialties:** Japanese tanto, swords. One-of-a-kind knives. **Technical:** Forges simple carbon steels, some Damascus. **Prices:** $200 to $1,000. **Mark:** Circle with wave inside.

**PHILIPPE, D. A.,** PO Box 306, Cornish, NH 03746, Phone: 603-543-0662
**Specialties:** Traditional working straight knives. **Patterns:** Hunters, trout and bird, camp knives etc. **Technical:** Grinds ATS-34, 440c, A-2, Damascus, fla and hollow ground. Exotic woods and antler handles. Brass, nickel silver and stainless components. **Prices:** $125 to $800. **Remarks:** Full-time maker, first knife sold in 1984. **Mark:** First initial, last name.

**PHILLIPS, JIM,** PO Box 168, Williamstown, NJ 08094, Phone: 609-567-0695

**PHILLIPS, SCOTT C.,** 671 California Rd., Gouverneur, NY 13642, Phone: 315-287-1280, Web: www.mangusknives.com
**Specialties:** Sheaths in leather. Fixed blade hunters, boot knives, Bowie buck skinners (hand forged and stock removal). **Technical:** 440C, 5160, 109 and 52100. **Prices:** Start at $125. **Remarks:** Part-time maker; first knife so in 1993. **Mark:** Before "2000" as above after S Mangus.

**PHILLIPS, DENNIS,** 16411 West Bennet Rd., Independence, LA 7044 Phone: 985-878-8275
**Specialties:** Specializes in fixed blade military combat tacticals.

**PHILLIPS, RANDY,** 759 E. Francis St., Ontario, CA 91761, Phone: 909-923-4381
**Specialties:** Hunters, collector-grade liner locks and high-art daggers. **Technical:** Grinds D2, 440C and 154CM; embellishes. **Prices:** Start at $20 **Remarks:** Part-time maker; first knife sold in 1981. Not currently taki orders. **Mark:** Name, city and state in eagle head.

**PICKENS, SELBERT,** Rt. 1, Box 216, Liberty, WV 25124, Phone: 304-586-2190
**Specialties:** Using knives. **Patterns:** Standard sporting knives. **Technical:** Stainless steels; stock removal method. **Prices:** Moderate. **Remarks:** Pa time maker. **Mark:** Name.

**PIENAAR, CONRAD,** 19A Milner Rd., Bloemfontein 9300, SOUTH AFRICA, Phone: 027 514364180, Fax: 027 514364180
**Specialties:** Fancy working and using straight knives and folders of his design, to customer specs and in standard patterns. **Patterns:** Hunters, loc ing folders, cleavers, kitchen and utility/camp knives. **Technical:** Grin 12C27, D2 and ATS-34. Uses some Damascus. Scrimshaws; inlays go Knives come with wooden box and custom-made leather sheath. **Prices:** $300 to $1,000. **Remarks:** Part-time maker; first knife sold in 1981. Doi business as C.P. Knife maker. **Mark:** Initials and serial number. **Other:** Mak slip joint folders and liner locking folders.

**PIERCE, HAROLD L.,** 106 Lyndon Lane, Louisville, KY 40222, Phone: 502-429-5136
**Specialties:** Working straight knives, some fancy. **Patterns:** Big fighters a Bowies. **Technical:** Grinds D2, 440C, 154CM; likes sub-hilts. **Prices:** $150 $450; some to $1,200. **Remarks:** Full-time maker; first knife sold in 19 **Mark:** Last name with knife through the last initial.

**PIERCE, RANDALL,** 903 Wyndam, Arlington, TX 76017, Phone: 817-468-0138

**PIERGALLINI, DANIEL E.,** 4011 N. Forbes Rd., Plant City, FL 33565, Phone: 813-754-3908, Fax: 8137543908, coolnifedad@earthlink.net
**Specialties:** Traditional and fancy straight knives and folders of his design to customer's specs. **Patterns:** Hunters, fighters, three-fingered skinners, let, working and camp knives. **Technical:** Grinds 440C, O1, D2, ATS- some Damascus; forges his own mokume. Uses natural handle mater **Prices:** $450 to $800; some to $1,800. **Remarks:** Part-time maker; sold f knife in 1994. **Mark:** Last name, city, state or last name in script.

**PIESNER, DEAN,** 1786 Sawmill Rd, Conestogo ON, CANADA N0B 1N Phone: 519-699-4319, Fax: 519-699-5452, dpey@kw.lgs.net Web: www.forgeandanvil.com
**Specialties:** Classic and period pieces of his design and to customer spe **Patterns:** Bowies, skinners, fighters and swords. **Technical:** Forges 51 52100, steel Damascus and nickel-steel Damascus. Makes own moku gane with copper, brass and nickel silver. Silver wire inlays in wood. **Prices:** Start at $150. **Remarks:** Full-time maker; first knife sold in 1990. **Mark:** F initial, last name, JS.

**PIOREK, JAMES S.,** PO Box 335, Rexford, MT 59930, Phone: 406-8 5510, jsp@bladerigger.com; Web: http://www.bladerigger.com
**Specialties:** True custom and semi-custom production (SCP), speciali concealment blades; advanced sheaths and tailored body harnessing s tems. **Patterns:** Tactical/personal defense fighters, swords, utility and cus patterns. **Technical:** Grinds A2 and Talonite®; heat-treats. Sheaths: Kyde

ydex-lined leather laminated or Kydex-lined with Rigger Coat™. Exotic mate-als available. **Prices:** $50 to $10,000. **Remarks:** Full-time maker. Doing usiness as Blade Rigger L.L.C. **Mark:** For true custom: Initials with abstract utting edge and for SCP: Blade Rigger. **Other:** Martial artist and unique efense industry tools and equipment.

**ITMAN, DAVID,** PO Drawer 2566, Williston, ND 58802, Phone: 701-72-3325

**ITT, DAVID F.,** 6812 Digger Pine Ln., Anderson, CA 96007, Phone: 30-357-2393
**pecialties:** Fixed blade, hunters and hatchets. Flat ground mirror finish. **Pat-rns:** Hatchets with gut hook, small gut hooks, guards, bolsters or guard less. **echnical:** Grinds A2, 440C, 154CM, ATS-34, D2. **Prices:** $150 to $750. **emarks:** Guild member since 1982. **Mark:** Bear paw with name David F. itt.

**LUNKETT, RICHARD,** 29 Kirk Rd., West Cornwall, CT 06796, Phone: 30-672-3419; Toll free: 888-KNIVES-8
**pecialties:** Traditional, fancy folders and straight knives of his design. **Pat-rns:** Slip-joint folders and small straight knives. **Technical:** Grinds O1 and ainless steel. Offers many different file patterns. **Prices:** $150 to $450. **emarks:** Full-time maker; first knife sold in 1994. **Mark:** Signature and date nder handle scales.

**OLK, CLIFTON,** 4625 Webber Creek Rd, Van Buren, AR 72956, hone: 479-474-3828, cliffpolkknives@aol.com Web: ww.polkknives.com
**ecialties:** Fancy working folders. **Patterns:** One blades spring backs in five zes, Liner Lock, Automatics, Double blades spring back folder with standard op & clip blade or bird knife with drop and vent hook or cow boy's knives with op and hoof pick and straight knives. **Technical:** I use D2 & ATS-34. I make my own Damascus using 1084, 1095, 01, 15N20, 5160. Using all kinds of otic woods. Stage, pearls, ivory, mastodon ivory and other boon and horns. **ices:** $200 to $3,000. **Remarks:** Retired fire fighter - made knives since 74. **Mark:** Polk.

**OLK, RUSTY,** 5900 Wildwood Dr., Van Buren, AR 72956, Phone: 479-0-3661, polkknives@aol.com Web: www.polkknives.com
**ecialties:** Skinner's, hunter's, Bowie's, fighter's and forging working knives cy Damascus, hunting, Bowies, fighters daggers, boot knives and survival ives. **Patterns:** Drop point, and forge to shape. **Technical:** ATS-34, 440C, mascus, D2, 51/60, 1084, 15N20, Damascus and do all his forging. **Prices:** 00 to $1,000. **Remarks:** R. Polk all hand made. **Mark:** R. Polk.

**OLKOWSKI, AL,** 8 Cathy Ct., Chester, NJ 07930, Phone: 908-879-30
**ecialties:** High-tech straight knives and folders for adventurers and profes-nals. **Patterns:** Fighters, side-lock folders, boots and concealment knives. **chnical:** Grinds D2 and ATS-34; features satin and bead-blast finishes; dex sheaths. **Prices:** Start at $100. **Remarks:** Full-time maker; first knife d in 1985. **Mark:** Full name, Handmade.

**OLLOCK, WALLACE J.,** 806 Russet Vly Dr., Cedar Park, TX 78613, ollock@austin.rr.com wjpollock@pollockn.feworks.com
**ecialties:** Using knives, skinner, hunter, fighting, camp knives. **Patterns:** e his own patterns or your. Traditional hunters, daggers, fighters, camp ves. **Technical:** Grinds ATS-34, D-2, BG-42, makes own Damascus, D-2, , ATS-34, prefer D-2, handles exotic wood, horn, bone, ivory. **Remarks:** l-time maker, sold first knife 1973. **Prices:** $250 to $2,500. **Mark:** Last ne, maker, city/state.

**OLZIEN, DON,** 1912 Inler Suite-L, Lubbock, TX 79407, Phone: 806-1-0766, blindinglightknives.com
**ecialties:** Traditional Japanese-style blades; restores antique Japanese ords, scabbards and fittings. **Patterns:** Hunters, fighters, one-of-a-kind art ves. **Technical:** 1045-1050 carbon steels, 440C, D2, ATS 34, standard d cable Damascus. **Prices:** $150 to $2,500. **Remarks:** Full-time maker. st knife sold in 1990. **Mark:** Oriental characters inside square border.

**NZIO, DOUG,** 3212 93rd St., Pleasant Prairie, WI 53158, Phone: 262-4-3188, prfgdough@aol.com Web: www.prairie-forge.com
**ecialties:** Damascus - Gem stone handles. **Mark:** P.F.

**OLE, MARVIN O.,** PO Box 552, Commerce, GA 30529, Phone: 803-5-5970
**ecialties:** Traditional working/using straight knives and folders of his ign and in standard patterns. **Patterns:** Bowies, fighters, hunters, locking ders, bird and trout knives. **Technical:** Grinds 440C, D2, ATS-34. **Prices:** to $150; some to $750. **Remarks:** Part-time maker; first knife sold in 0. **Mark:** First initial, last name, year, serial number.

**SKOCIL, HELMUT,** Oskar Czeijastrasse 2, A-3340 Waidhofen/Ybbs, STRIA, Phone: 0043-7442-54519, Fax: 0043-7442-54519
**ecialties:** High-art and classic straight knives and folders of his design. **terns:** Bowies, daggers, hunters and locking folders. **Technical:** Grinds ATS-34 and stainless and carbon Damascus. Hardwoods, fossil ivory, horn and amber for handle material; silver wire and gold inlays; silver butt caps. Offers engraving and scrimshaw. **Prices:** $350 to $850; some to $3,500. **Remarks:** Part-time maker; first knife sold in 1991. **Mark:** Name.

**POSNER, BARRY E.,** 12501 Chandler Blvd., Suite 104, N. Hollywood, CA 91607, Phone: 818-752-8005, Fax: 818-752-8006
**Specialties:** Working/using straight knives. **Patterns:** Hunters, kitchen and utility/camp knives. **Technical:** Grinds ATS-34; forges 1095 and nickel. **Prices:** $95 to $400. **Remarks:** Part-time maker; first knife sold in 1987. Doing business as Posner Knives. Supplier of finished mosaic handle pin stock. **Mark:** First and middle initials, last name.

**POTIER, TIMOTHY F.,** PO Box 711, Oberlin, LA 70655, Phone: 337-639-2229, tpotier@hotmail.com
**Specialties:** Classic working and using straight knives to customer specs; some collectible. **Patterns:** Hunters, Bowies, utility/camp knives and belt axes. **Technical:** Forges carbon steel and his own Damascus; offers filework. **Prices:** $300 to $1,800; some to $4,000. **Remarks:** Part-time maker; first knife sold in 1981. **Mark:** Last name, MS.

**POTOCKI, ROGER,** Route 1, Box 333A, Goreville, IL 62939, Phone: 618-995-9502

**POTTER, BILLY,** 6280 Virginia Rd., Nashport, OH 43830, Phone: 740-454-7412, bwp@potterknives.com potterknives@voyager.net
**Specialties:** Working straight knives; his design or to customers patterns. **Patterns:** Bowie, fighters, utilities, skinners, hunters, folding lock blade, miniatures and tomahawks. **Technical:** Grinds and forges, carbon steel, L-6, 0-1, 1095, 5160, 1084 and 52000. Grinds 440C stainless. Forges own Damascus. Handles: prefers exotic hardwood, curly and birdseye maples. Bone, ivory, antler, pearl and horn. Some scrimshaw. **Prices:** Start at $100 up to $800. **Remarks:** Part-time maker; first knife sold 1996. **Mark: Last name.**

**POWELL, JAMES,** 2500 North Robinson Rd., Texarkana, TX 75501

**POWELL, ROBERT CLARK,** PO Box 321, 93 Gose Rd., Smarr, GA 31086, Phone: 478-994-5418
**Specialties:** Composite bar Damascus blades. **Patterns:** Art knives, hunters, combat, tomahawks. **Patterns:** Hand forge all blades. **Prices:** $300 and up. **Remarks:** Member ABS. **Mark:** Powell.

**PRATER, MIKE,** PRATER AND COMPANY, 81 Sanford Ln., Flintstone, GA 30725, cmprater@aol.com Web: www.casecustomknives.com
**Specialties:** Customizing factory knives. **Patterns:** Buck knives, case knives, hen and rooster knives. **Technical:** Manufacture of mica pearl. **Prices:** Varied. **Remarks:** First knife sold in 1980. **Mark:** Mica pearl.

**PRESSBURGER, RAMON,** 59 Driftway Rd., Howell, NJ 07731, Phone: 732-363-0816
**Specialties:** BG-42. Only knife maker in U.S.A. that has complete line of affordable hunting knives made from BG-42. **Patterns:** All types hunting styles. **Technical:** Uses all steels; main steels are D-2 and BG-42. **Prices:** $75 to $500. **Remarks:** Full-time maker; has been making hunting knives for 30 years. **Mark:** NA. **Other:** Makes knives to your patterning.

**PRICE, TIMMY,** PO Box 906, Blairsville, GA 30514, Phone: 706-745-5111

**PRIMOS, TERRY,** 932 Francis Dr., Shreveport, LA 71118, Phone: 318-686-6625, tprimos@sport.rr.com or terry@primosknives.com Web: www.primosknives.com
**Specialties:** Traditional forged straight knives. **Patterns:** Hunters, Bowies, camp knives, and fighters. **Technical:** Forges primarily 1084 and 5160; also forges Damascus. **Prices:** $250 to $600. **Remarks:** Full-time maker; first knife sold in 1993. **Mark:** Last name.

**PRINSLOO, THEUNS,** PO Box 2263, Bethlehem, 9700, SOUTH AFRICA, Phone: 27821663885, theunmesa@telkomsa.net Web: www.theunsprinsloo.com
**Specialties:** Fancy folders. **Technical:** Own Damascus and Mokume. **Prices:** $450 to $1,500.

**PRITCHARD, RON,** 613 Crawford Ave., Dixon, IL 61021, Phone: 815-284-6005
**Specialties:** Plain and fancy working knives. **Patterns:** Variety of straight knives, locking folders, interframes and miniatures. **Technical:** Grinds 440C, 154CM and commercial Damascus. **Prices:** $100 to $200; some to $1,500. **Remarks:** Part-time maker; first knife sold in 1979. **Mark:** Name and city.

**PROVENZANO, JOSEPH D.,** 3024 Ivy Place, Chalmette, LA 70043, Phone: 504-279-3154
**Specialties:** Working straight knives and folders in standard patterns. **Patterns:** Hunters, Bowies, folders, camp and fishing knives. **Technical:** Grinds ATS-34, 440C, 154CM, CPM 4400V, CPM420V and Damascus. Hollow grinds hunters. **Prices:** $110 to $300; some to $1,000. **Remarks:** Part-time maker; first knife sold in 1980. **Mark:** Joe-Pro.

**PRYOR, STEPHEN L.,** HC Rt. 1, Box 1445, Boss, MO 65440, Phone: 573-626-4838, Fax: same, Knives4U3@juno.com Web: www.stevescutler.com
**Specialties:** Working and fancy straight knives, some to customer specs. **Patterns:** Bowies, hunting/fishing, utility/camp, fantasy/art. **Technical:** Grinds 440C, ATS-34, 1085, some Damascus, and does filework. Stag and exotic hardwood handles. **Prices:** $250 and up. **Remarks:** Full-time maker; first knife sold in 1991. **Mark:** Stylized first initial and last name over city and state.

**PUDDU, SALVATORE,** Via Lago Bunnari, 11 Localita Flumini, Quartu s Elena (CA), ITALY 09046, Phone: 0039070892208, salvatorepuddu@tin.it
**Specialties:** Collector-quality folders, straight. **Patterns:** Multi blade, folders, automatics. **Technical:** Grinds ATS-34. **Prices:** Start $1,300 to $3,800. **Remarks:** Full-time maker. **Mark:** Name.

**PUGH, JIM,** PO Box 711, Azle, TX 76020, Phone: 817-444-2679, Fax: 817-444-5455
**Specialties:** Fancy/embellished limited editions by request. **Patterns:** 5- to 7-inch Bowies, wildlife art pieces, hunters, daggers and fighters; some commemoratives. **Technical:** Multi color transplanting in solid 18K gold, fine gems; grinds 440C and ATS-34. Offers engraving, fancy file etching and leather sheaths for wildlife art pieces. Ivory and coco bolo handle material on limited editions. Designs animal head butt caps and paws or bear claw guards; sterling silver heads and guards. **Prices:** $60,000 to $80,000 each in the Big Five 2000 edition. **Remarks:** Full-time maker; first knife sold in 1970. **Mark:** Pugh (old English).

**PULIS, VLADIMIR,** Horna Ves 43/B/25, 96 701 Kremnica, SLOVAKIA, Phone: 00427 45 67 57 214, Fax: 00427 903 390076, vpulis@host.sk Web: www.upulis.host.sk
**Specialties:** Fancy and high-art straight knives of his design. **Patterns:** Daggers and hunters. **Technical:** Forges Damascus steel. All work done by hand. **Prices:** $250 to $3,000; some to $10,000. **Remarks:** Full-time maker; first knife sold in 1990. **Mark:** Initials in sixtagon.

**PULLIAM, MORRIS C.,** 560 Jeptha Knob Rd., Shelbyville, KY 40065, Phone: 502-633-2261, mcpulliam@fastballinternet.com
**Specialties:** Working knives; classic Bowies. Cherokee River pattern Damascus. **Patterns:** Bowies, hunters, and tomahawks. **Technical:** Forges L6, W2, 1095, Damascus and bar 320 layer Damascus. **Prices:** $165 to $1,200. **Remarks:** Full-time maker; first knife sold in 1974. Makes knives for Native American festivals. Doing business as Knob Hill Forge. Member of Piqua Sept Shawnee of Ohio. Indian name Weshe Wapebe (The Elk) **Mark:** Small and large - Pulliam **Other:** As a member of a state tribe,is an American Indian artist and craftsman by federal law.

**PURSLEY, AARON,** 8885 Coal Mine Rd., Big Sandy, MT 59520, Phone: 406-378-3200
**Specialties:** Fancy working knives. **Patterns:** Locking folders, straight hunters and daggers, personal wedding knives and letter openers. **Technical:** Grinds O1 and 440C; engraves. **Prices:** $900 to $2,500. **Remarks:** Full-time maker; first knife sold in 1975. **Mark:** Initials connected with year.

**PURVIS, BOB AND ELLEN,** 2416 N Loretta Dr., Tucson, AZ 85716, Phone: 520-795-8290, repknives2@cox.net
**Specialties:** Hunter, skinners, Bowies, using knives, gentlemen's folders and collectible knives. **Technical:** Grinds ATS-34, 440C, Damascus, Dama steel, heat-treats and cryogenically quenches. We do gold-plating, salt bluing, scrimshawing, filework and fashion hand made leather sheaths. Materials used for handles include exotic woods, mammoth ivory, mother-of-pearl, G-10 and micarta. **Prices:** $165 to $800. **Remarks:** Knifemaker since retirement in 1984. Selling them since 1993. **Mark:** Script or print R.E. Purvis ~ Tucson, AZ or last name only.

**PUTNAM, DONALD S.,** 590 Wolcott Hill Rd., Wethersfield, CT 06109, Phone: 860-563-9718, Fax: 860-563-9718, dpknives@cox.net
**Specialties:** Working knives for the hunter and fisherman. **Patterns:** His design or to customer specs. **Technical:** Uses stock removal method, O1, W2, D2, ATS-34, 154CM, 440C and CPM REX 20; stainless steel Damascus on request. **Prices:** $250 and up. **Remarks:** Full-time maker; first knife sold in 1985. **Mark:** Last name with a knife outline.

**QUAKENBUSH, THOMAS C.,** 2426 Butler Rd., Ft Wayne, IN 46808, Phone: 219-483-0749

**QUARTON, BARR,** PO Box 4335, McCall, ID 83638, Phone: 208-634-3641
**Specialties:** Plain and fancy working knives; period pieces. **Patterns:** Hunters, tantos and swords. **Technical:** Forges and grinds 154CM, ATS-34 and his own Damascus. **Prices:** $180 to $450; some to $4,500. **Remarks:** P time maker; first knife sold in 1978. Doing business as Barr Custom Kniv **Mark:** First name with bear logo.

**QUATTLEBAUM, CRAIG,** 2 Ridgewood Ln., Searcy, AR 72143
**Specialties:** Traditional straight knives and one-of-a-kind knives of his desi period pieces. **Patterns:** Bowies and fighters. **Technical:** Forges 5168, 52 and own Damascus. **Prices:** $100 to $1,200. **Remarks:** Part-time maker; knife sold in 1988. **Mark:** Stylized initials.

**QUICK, MIKE,** 23 Locust Ave., Kearny, NJ 07032, Phone: 201-991-65
**Specialties:** Traditional working/using straight knives. **Patterns:** Bow **Technical:** 440C and ATS-34 for blades; Micarta, wood and stag for handl

**R. BOYES KNIVES, ,** N81 W16140 Robin Hood Dr., Menomonee Fal WI 53051, Phone: 262-255-7341, tomboyes@earthlink.net or tomboyes5@hotmail.com
**Specialties:** Hunters, working knives. **Technical:** Grinds ATS-34, 440C, tool steel and Damascus. **Prices:** $60 to $700. **Remarks:** First knife sol 1998. Tom Boyes changed to R. Boyes Knives.

**RACHLIN, LESLIE S.,** 1200 W. Church St., Elmira, NY 14905, Phone 607-733-6889
**Specialties:** Classic and working/using straight knives and folders of design. **Patterns:** Hunters, locking folders and utility/camp knives. **Techni** Grinds 440C and Damascus. **Prices:** $110 to $200; some to $450. **Rema** Spare-time maker; first knife sold in 1989. Doing business as Tinkerm Knives. **Mark:** Stamped initials or Tinkermade, city and state.

**RADOS, JERRY F.,** 7523 E 5000 N Rd., Grant Park, IL 60940, Phon 815-472-3350, Fax: 815-472-3944
**Specialties:** Deluxe period pieces. **Patterns:** Hunters, fighters, locking ers, daggers and camp knives. **Technical:** Forges and grinds his own D ascus which he sells commercially; makes pattern-welded Turkish Damas **Prices:** Start at $900. **Remarks:** Full-time maker; first knife sold in 1 **Mark:** Last name.

**RAGSDALE, JAMES D.,** 3002 Arabian Woods Dr., Lithonia, GA 300 Phone: 770-482-6739
**Specialties:** Fancy and embellished working knives of his design or to tomer specs. **Patterns:** Hunters, folders and fighters. **Technical:** Gr 440C, ATS-34 and A2. **Prices:** $150 and up. **Remarks:** Full-time maker; knife sold in 1984. **Mark:** Fish symbol with name above, town below.

**RAINVILLE, RICHARD,** 126 Cockle Hill Rd., Salem, CT 06420, Pho 860-859-2776, w1jo@snet.net
**Specialties:** Traditional working straight knives. **Patterns:** Outdoor kn including fishing knives. **Technical:** L6, 400C, ATS-34. **Prices:** $100 to $ **Remarks:** Full-time maker; first knife sold in 1982. **Mark:** Name, city, sta oval logo.

**RALEY, R. WAYNE,** 825 Poplar Acres Rd., Collierville, TN 38017, Phone: 901-853-2026

**RALPH, DARREL,** BRIAR KNIVES, 4185 S St. Rt. 605, Galena, OH 43021, Phone: 740-965-9970, dr@darrelralph.com Web: www.darrelralph.com
**Specialties:** Fancy, high-art, high-tech, collectible straight knives and fo of his design and to customer specs; unique mechanisms, some disasser **Patterns:** Daggers, fighters and swords. **Technical:** Forges his own D ascus, nickel and high-carbon. Uses mokume and Damascus; mosaics special patterns. Engraves and heat-treats. Prefers pearl, ivory and aba handle material; uses stones and jewels. **Prices:** $250 to six fig **Remarks:** Full-time maker; first knife sold in 1987. Doing business as Knives. **Mark:** DDR.

**RAMEY, LARRY,** 1315 Porter Morris Rd., Chapmansboro, TN 3703 5120, Phone: 615-307-4233, larryrameyknives@hotmail.com Web: www.larryrameyknives.com
**Specialties:** Titanium knives. **Technical:** Pictures taken by Hawkinson tography.

**RAMEY, MARSHALL F.,** PO Box 2589, West Helena, AR 72390, Phone: 501-572-7436, Fax: 501-572-6245
**Specialties:** Traditional working knives. **Patterns:** Designs military cc knives; makes butterfly folders, camp knives and miniatures. **Techr** Grinds D2 and 440C. **Prices:** $100 to $500. **Remarks:** Full-time maker knife sold in 1978. **Mark:** Name with ram's head.

**RAMSEY, RICHARD A.,** 8525 Trout Farm Rd., Neosho, MO 64850, Phone: 417-451-1493, rams@direcway.com Web: www.ramseyknives.com
**Specialties:** Drop point hunters. **Patterns:** Various Damascus. **Prices:** $125 to $1,500. **Mark:** RR double R also last name-RAMSEY.

**RANDALL JR., JAMES W.,** 11606 Keith Hall Rd., Keithville, LA 71047, Phone: 318-925-6480, Fax: 318-925-1709, jw@jwrandall-knives.com
**Specialties:** Collectible and functional knives. **Patterns:** Bowies, hunters, daggers, swords, folders and combat knives. **Technical:** Forges 5160, 1084, 01 and his Damascus. **Prices:** $400 to $8,000. **Remarks:** Part-time. First knive sold in 1998. **Mark:** J.W Randall M.S.

**RANDALL MADE KNIVES, ,** PO Box 1988, Orlando, FL 32802, Phone: 407-855-8075, Fax: 407-855-9054, Web: http://www.randallknives.com
**Specialties:** Working straight knives. **Patterns:** Hunters, fighters and Bowies. **Technical:** Forges and grinds O1 and 440B. **Prices:** $170 to $550; some to $450. **Remarks:** Full-time maker; first knife sold in 1937. **Mark:** Randall made, city and state in scimitar logo.

**RANDOW, RALPH,** 4214 Blalock Rd., Pineville, LA 71360, Phone: 318-640-3369

**RANKL, CHRISTIAN,** Possenhofenerstr. 33, 81476 Munchen, GERMANY, Phone: 0049 01 71 3 66 26 79, Fax: 0049 8975967265, christian@crankl.de.
**Specialties:** Tail-lock knives. **Patterns:** Fighters, hunters and locking folders. **Technical:** Grinds ATS-34, D2, CPM1440V, RWL 34 also stainless Damascus. **Prices:** $450 to $950; some to $2,000. **Remarks:** Full-time maker; first knife sold in 1989. **Mark:** Electrochemical etching on blade.

**RAPP, STEVEN J.,** 7273 South 245 East, Midvale, UT 84047, Phone: 801-567-9553
**Specialties:** Gold quartz; mosaic handles. **Patterns:** Daggers, Bowies, fighters and San Francisco knives. **Technical:** Hollow- and flat-grinds 440C and Damascus. **Prices:** Start at $500. **Remarks:** Full-time maker; first knife sold in 1981. **Mark:** Name and state.

**RAPPAZZO, RICHARD,** 142 Dunsbach Ferry Rd., Cohoes, NY 12047, Phone: 518-783-6843
**Specialties:** Damascus locking folders and straight knives. **Patterns:** Folders, dirks, fighters and tantos in original and traditional designs. **Technical:** Hand-forges all blades; specializes in Damascus; uses only natural handle materials. **Prices:** $400 to $1,500. **Remarks:** Part-time maker; first knife sold in 1985. **Mark:** Name, date, serial number.

**RARDON, ARCHIE F.,** 1589 SE Price Dr., Polo, MO 64671, Phone: 660-354-2330
**Specialties:** Working knives. **Patterns:** Hunters, Bowies and miniatures. **Technical:** Grinds O1, D2, 440C, ATS-34, cable and Damascus. **Prices:** $50 to $500. **Remarks:** Part-time maker. **Mark:** Boar hog.

**RARDON, A.D.,** 1589 SE Price Dr., Polo, MO 64671, Phone: 660-354-2330
**Specialties:** Folders, miniatures. **Patterns:** Hunters, buck skinners, Bowies, miniatures and daggers. **Technical:** Grinds O1, D2, 440C and ATS-34. **Prices:** $150 to $2,000; some higher. **Remarks:** Full-time maker; first knife sold in 1954. **Mark:** Fox logo.

**RAY, ALAN W.,** PO Box 479, Lovelady, TX 75851, Phone: 936-636-2350, Fax: 936-636-2931, awray@raysmfg.com Web: www.raysmfg.com
**Specialties:** Working straight knives of his design. **Patterns:** Hunters, camp knives, steak knives and carving sets. **Technical:** Forges L6 and 5160 for straight knives; grinds D2 and 440C for folders and kitchen cutlery. **Prices:** $200 to $1,000. **Remarks:** Full-time maker; first knife sold in 1979. **Mark:** Stylized initials.

**REBELLO, INDIAN GEORGE,** 358 Elm St., New Bedford, MA 02740-4837, Phone: 508-999-7090, indgeo@juno.com Web: www.indiangeorgesknives.com
**Specialties:** One-of-a-kind fighters and Bowies. **Patterns:** To customer's specs, hunters and utilities. **Technical:** Forges his own Damascus, 5160, 52100, 1084, 1095, cable and O-1. Grinds S30V, ATS-34, 154CM, 440C, D2 and A2. Makes own Mokumme. **Prices:** Starting at $250. **Remarks:** Full-time maker, first knife sold in 1991. Doing business as Indian George's Knives. President and founding father of the New England Custom Knives Association. **Mark:** Indian George's Knives.

**RED, VERNON,** 2020 Benton Cove, Conway, AR 72032, Phone: 501-450-7284, knivesvr@conwaycorp.net
**Specialties:** Custom design straight knives or folders of your design or mine. Love one-of-a-kind. **Patterns:** Hunters, fighters, Bowies, fillet, folders and lock-blades. **Technical:** Hollow Grind or flat grind; use 440C, D-2, ATS-34, Damascus. **Prices:** $180 and up. **Remarks:** Made first skinner in 1982, first lock blade folder in 1992. Make about 50/50. Part-time maker. Do scrimshaw on ivory and micarta. **Mark:** Last name. **Other:** Member of (AKA) Arkansas Knives Assoc., attend annual show in Feb. at Little Rock, AR. Custom Made Knives by Vernon Red.

**REDDIEX, BILL,** 27 Galway Ave., Palmerston North, NEW ZEALAND, Phone: 06-357-0383, Fax: 06-358-2910
**Specialties:** Collector-grade working straight knives. **Patterns:** Traditional-style Bowies and drop-point hunters. **Technical:** Grinds 440C, D2 and O1; offers variety of grinds and finishes. **Prices:** $130 to $750. **Remarks:** Full-time maker; first knife sold in 1980. **Mark:** Last name around kiwi bird logo.

**REED, DAVE,** Box 132, Brimfield, MA 01010, Phone: 413-245-3661
**Specialties:** Traditional styles. Makes knives from chains, rasps, gears, etc. **Patterns:** Bush swords, hunters, working minis, camp and utility knives. **Technical:** Forges 1075 and his own Damascus. **Prices:** Start at $50. **Remarks:** Part-time maker; first knife sold in 1970. **Mark:** Initials.

**REED, JOHN M.,** 257 Navajo Dr., Oak Hill, FL 32759, Phone: 386-345-4763
**Specialties:** Hunter, utility, some survival knives. **Patterns:** Trailing Point, and drop point sheath knives. **Technical:** ATS-34, rockwell 60 exotic wood or natural material handles. **Prices:** $135 to $300. Depending on handle material. **Remarks:** Likes the stock removal method. "Old Fashioned trainling point blades". **Mark:** "Reed" acid etched on left side of blade. **Other:** Hand made and sewn leather sheaths.

**REEVE, CHRIS,** 11624 W. President Dr., Ste. B, Boise, ID 83713, Phone: 208-375-0367, Fax: 208-375-0368, crkinfo@chrisreeve.com
**Specialties:** Originator and designer of the One Piece range of fixed blade utility knives and of the Sebenza Integral Lock folding knives made by Chris Reeve Knives. Currently makes only one or two pieces per year himself. **Patterns:** Art folders and fixed blades; one-of-a-kind. **Technical:** Grinds specialty stainless steels, Damascus and other materials to his own design. **Prices:** $1,000 and upwards. **Remarks:** Full-time in knife business; first knife sold in 1982. **Mark:** Signature and date.

**REGGIO JR., SIDNEY J.,** PO Box 851, Sun, LA 70463, Phone: 504-886-5886
**Specialties:** Miniature classic and fancy straight knives of his design or in standard patterns. **Patterns:** Fighters, hunters and utility/camp knives. **Technical:** Grinds 440C, ATS-34 and commercial Damascus. Engraves; scrimshaws; offers filework. Hollow grinds most blades. Prefers natural handle material. Offers handmade sheaths. **Prices:** $85 to $250; some to $500. **Remarks:** Part-time maker; first knife sold in 1988. Doing business as Sterling Workshop. **Mark:** Initials.

**REPKE, MIKE,** 4191 N. Euclid Ave., Bay City, MI 48706, Phone: 517-684-3111
**Specialties:** Traditional working and using straight knives of their design or to customer specs; classic knives; display knives. **Patterns:** Hunters, Bowies, skinners, fighters boots, axes and swords. **Technical:** Grind 440C. Offer variety of handle materials. **Prices:** $99 to $1,500. **Remarks:** Full-time makers. Doing business as Black Forest Blades. **Mark:** Knife logo.

**REVERDY, PIERRE,** 5 Rue de L'egalite', 26100 Romans, FRANCE, Phone: 334 75 05 10 15, Fax: 334 75 02 28 40, Web: http://www.reverdy.com
**Specialties:** Art knives; legend pieces. **Patterns:** Daggers, Bowies, hunters and other large patterns. **Technical:** Forges his Damascus and "poetique Damascus"; works with his own EDM machine to create any kind of pattern inside the steel with his own touch. **Prices:** $2,000 and up. **Remarks:** Full-time maker; first knife sold in 1986. Nicole (wife) collaborates with enamels. **Mark:** Initials connected.

**REVISHVILI, ZAZA,** 2102 Linden Ave., Madison, WI 53704, Phone: 608-243-7927
**Specialties:** Fancy/embellished and high-art straight knives and folders of his design. **Patterns:** Daggers, swords and locking folders. **Technical:** Uses Damascus; silver filigree, silver inlay in wood; enameling. **Prices:** $1,000 to $9,000; some to $15,000. **Remarks:** Full-time maker; first knife sold in 1987. **Mark:** Initials, city.

**REXROAT, KIRK,** 527 Sweetwater Circle, Box 224, Wright, WY 82732, Phone: 307-464-0166, rexknives@vcn.com Web: www.rexroatknives.com
**Specialties:** Using and collectible straight knives and folders of his design or to customer specs. **Patterns:** Bowies, hunters, folders. **Technical:** Forges Damascus patterns, mosaic and 52100. **Prices:** $400 and up. **Remarks:** Part-time maker, Master Smith in the ABS; first knife sold in 1984. Doing business as Rexroat Knives. **Mark:** Last name.

**REYNOLDS, JOHN C.,** #2 Andover, HC77, Gillette, WY 82716, Phone: 307-682-6076
**Specialties:** Working knives, some fancy. **Patterns:** Hunters, Bowies, tomahawks and buck skinners; some folders. **Technical:** Grinds D2, ATS-34, 440C and forges own Damascus and Knifes now. Scrimshaws. **Prices:** $200 to

$3,000. **Remarks:** Spare-time maker; first knife sold in 1969. **Mark:** On ground blades JC Reynolds Gillette,WY, on forged blades, initials make the mark-JCR.

**REYNOLDS, LEE,** 5552 Dwight Ave, San Jose, CA 95118, leecreynolds@comcast.net

**REYNOLDS, DAVE,** Rt. 2, Box 36, Harrisville, WV 26362, Phone: 304-643-2889, wvreynolds@hotmail.com
**Specialties:** Working straight knives of his design. **Patterns:** Bowies, kitchen and utility knives. **Technical:** Grinds and forges L6, 1095 and 440C. Heat-treats. **Prices:** $50 to $85; some to $175. **Remarks:** Full-time maker; first knife sold in 1980. Doing business as Terra-Gladius Knives. **Mark:** Mark on special orders only; serial number on all knives.

**RHO, NESTOR LORENZO,** Primera Junta 589, (6000) Junin, Buenos Aires, ARGENTINA, Phone: (02362) 15670686
**Specialties:** Classic and fancy straight knives of his design. **Patterns:** Bowies, fighters and hunters. **Technical:** Grinds 420C, 440C and 1050. Offers semi-precious stones on handles, acid etching on blades and blade engraving. **Prices:** $60 to $300 some to $1,200. **Remarks:** Full-time maker; first knife sold in 1975. **Mark:** Name.

**RHODES, JAMES D.,** 205 Woodpoint Ave., Hagerstown, MD 21740, Phone: 301-739-2657
**Specialties:** Traditional working and using straight knives of his design. **Patterns:** Bowies, fighters, hunters and kitchen knives. **Technical:** Forges 5160, 1085, and 9260; makes own Damascus. Hard edges, soft backs, dead soft tangs. Heat-treats. **Prices:** $150 to $350. **Remarks:** Part-time maker. **Mark:** Last name, JS.

**RIBONI, CLAUDIO,** Via L Da Vinci, Truccazzano (MI), ITALY, Phone: 02 95309010, Web: www.riboni-knives.com

**RICARDO ROMANO, BERNARDES,** Ruai Coronel Rennò, 1261, Itajuba MG, BRAZIL 37500, Phone: 0055-2135-622-5896
**Specialties:** Hunters, fighters, Bowies. **Technical:** Grinds blades of stainless and tools steels. **Patterns:** Hunters. **Prices:** $100 to $700. **Mark:** Romano.

**RICHARD, RON,** 4875 Calaveras Ave., Fremont, CA 94538, Phone: 510-796-9767
**Specialties:** High-tech working straight knives of his design. **Patterns:** Bowies, swords and locking folders. **Technical:** Forges and grinds ATS-34, 154CM and 440V. All folders have dead-bolt button locks. **Prices:** $650 to $850; some to $1,400. **Remarks:** Full-time maker; first knife sold in 1968. **Mark:** Full name.

**RICHARDS JR., ALVIN C.,** 2889 Shields Ln., Fortuna, CA 95540-3241, Phone: 707-725-2526, bldsmith@cox.net
**Specialties:** Fixed blade Damascus. One-of-a-kind. **Patterns:** Hunters, fighters. **Prices:** $125 to $500. **Remarks:** Like to work with customers on a truly custom knife. **Mark:** A C Richards or ACR.

**RICHTER, JOHN C.,** 932 Bowling Green Trail, Chesapeake, VA 23320
**Specialties:** Hand-forged knives in original patterns. **Patterns:** Hunters, fighters, utility knives and other belt knives, folders, swords. **Technical:** Hand-forges high-carbon and his own Damascus; makes mokume gane. **Prices:** $75 to $1,500. **Remarks:** Part-time maker. **Mark:** Richter Forge.

**RICHTER, SCOTT,** 516 E. 2nd St., S. Boston, MA 02127, Phone: 617-269-4855
**Specialties:** Traditional working/using folders. **Patterns:** Locking folders, swords and kitchen knives. **Technical:** Grinds ATS-34, 5160 and A2. High-tech materials. **Prices:** $150 to $650; some to $1,500. **Remarks:** Full-time maker; first knife sold in 1991. Doing business as Richter Made. **Mark:** Last name, Made.

**RICKE, DAVE,** 1209 Adams, West Bend, WI 53090, Phone: 262-334-5739, R.L5710@sbcglobal.net
**Specialties:** Working knives; period pieces. **Patterns:** Hunters, boots, Bowies; locking folders and slip-joints. **Technical:** Grinds ATS-34, A2, 440C and 154CM. **Prices:** $125 to $1,600. **Remarks:** Full-time maker; first knife sold in 1976. **Mark:** Last name.

**RIDER, DAVID M.,** PO Box 5946, Eugene, OR 97405-0911, Phone: 541-343-8747

**RIEPE, RICHARD A.,** 17604 E 296 St., Harrisonville, MO 64701

**RIETVELD, BERTIE,** PO Box 53, Magaliesburg 1791, SOUTH AFRICA, Phone: +2714 5771294, Fax: +2714 5771294, bertie@batavia.co.za Web: www.batavia.co.za
**Specialties:** Art daggers, Bolster lock folders, persian designs, Embraces elegant designs.**Patterns:** Mostly one off's. **Technical:** Work only in own damascus, gold inlay, blued stainless fittings logo in stanhope lens - sole authorship. **Remarks:** First knife made in 1979. Annual Shows attended: ECCKS - March Blade Show, Guild Show, Milan Show, South African Guild Show.

**RIGNEY JR., WILLIE,** 191 Colson Dr., Bronston, KY 42518, Phone: 606-679-4227
**Specialties:** High-tech period pieces and fancy working knives. **Patterns:** Fighters, boots, daggers and push knives. **Technical:** Grinds 440C and 154CM; buys Damascus. Most knives are embellished. **Prices:** $150 to $1,500; some to $10,000. **Remarks:** Full-time maker; first knife sold in 1978. **Mark:** First initial, last name.

**RINALDI, T.H.,** RINALDI CUSTOM BLADES, PO Box 718, Winchester, CA 92596, Phone: 909-926-5422, Trace@thrblades.com Web: www.thrblades.com
**Technical:** Grinds S30V, 3V, A2 and talonite fixed blades. **Prices:** $175-600 **Remarks:** Tactical and utility for the most part.

**RINKES, SIEGFRIED,** Am Sportpl 2, D 91459, Markterlbach, GERMANY

**RIZZI, RUSSELL J.,** 37 March Rd., Ashfield, MA 01330, Phone: 413-625-2842
**Specialties:** Fancy working and using straight knives and folders of his design or to customer specs. **Patterns:** Hunters, locking folders and fighters. **Technical:** Grinds 440C, D2 and commercial Damascus. **Prices:** $150 to $750 some to $2,500. **Remarks:** Part-time maker; first knife sold in 1990. **Mark:** Last name, Ashfield, MA.

**ROATH, DEAN,** 3050 Winnipeg Dr., Baton Rouge, LA 70819, Phone: 225-272-5562
**Specialties:** Classic working knives; focusing on fillet knives for salt water fishermen. **Patterns:** Hunters, filets, canoe/trail, and boating/sailing knives. **Technical:** Grinds 440C. **Prices:** $85 to $500; some to $1,500. **Remarks:** Part-time maker; first knife sold in 1978. **Mark:** Name, city and state.

**ROBBINS, HOWARD P.,** 1407 S. 217th Ave., Elkhorn, NE 68022, Phone: 402-289-4121, ARobb1407@aol.com
**Specialties:** High-tech working knives with clean designs, some fancy. **Patterns:** Folders, hunters and camp knives. **Technical:** Grinds 440C. Heat-treats; likes mirror finishes. Offers leatherwork. **Prices:** $100 to $500; some to $1,000. **Remarks:** Full-time maker; first knife sold in 1982. **Mark:** Name, city and state.

**ROBBINS, BILL,** 299 Fairview St, Globe, AZ 85501, Phone: 928-402-0052, billrknifemaker@aol.com
**Specialties:**Plain and fancy working straight knives. I will make to my design and most anything you can draw. **Patterns:**Hunting knives, utility knives, and bowies. **Technical:**Grinds ATS-34, 440C, tool steel, high carbon, buys Damascus. **Prices:**$70.00 to $450.00. **Remarks:**Part-time maker, first knife sold 2001.**Mark:**Last name or desert scene with name.

**ROBERTS, MIKE,** 601 Oakwood Dr., Clinton, MS 39056-4332, Phone: 601-924-3154

**ROBERTS, CHUCK,** PO Box 7174, Golden, CO 80403, Phone: 303-642-0512, robertsart@juno.com
**Specialties:** Sheffield Bowies; historic-styles only. **Patterns:** Bowies and California knives. **Technical:** Grinds 440C, 5160 and ATS-34. Handles made of stag, ivory or mother-of-pearl. **Prices:** Start at $750. **Remarks:** Full-time maker. **Mark:** Last initial or last name.

**ROBERTS, E. RAY,** 191 Nursery Rd., Monticello, FL 32344, Phone: 850-997-4403
**Specialties:** High-Carbon Damascus knives and tomahawks.

**ROBERTS, GEORGE A.,** PO Box 31228, 211 Main St., Whitehorse, YT CANADA Y1A 5P7, Phone: 867-667-7099, Fax: 867-667-7099, Web: www.yuk-biz.com/bandit blades
**Specialties:** Mastadon ivory, fossil walrus ivory handled knives, scrimshawed or carved. **Patterns:** Side lockers, fancy bird and trout knives, hunters, fillet blades. **Technical:** Grinds stainless Damascus, all surgical steels. **Prices:** $ to $3,500 U.S. **Remarks:** Full-time maker; first knives sold in 1986. Doing business as Bandit Blades. **Mark:** Bandit Yukon with pick and shovel crossed. **Other:** Most recent works have gold nuggets in fossilized Mastodon ivory. Something new using mosaic pins in mokume bolster and in mosaic Damascus, it creates a new look.

**ROBERTS, JACK,** 10811 Sagebluff Dr., Houston, TX 77089, Phone: 281-481-1784, jroberts59@houston.rr.com
**Specialties:** Hunting knives and folders, offers scrimshaw by wife Barba **Patterns:** Drop point hunters and liner lock folders. **Technical:** Grinds 440 offers file work, texturing, natural handle materials and micarta. **Prices:** $2 to $800 some higher. **Remarks:** Part-time maker, sold first knife in 19 **Mark:** Name, city, state.

**ROBERTS, MICHAEL,** 601 Oakwood Dr., Clinton, MS 39056, Phone: 601-924-3154; Pager 601-978-8180
**Specialties:** Working and using knives in standard patterns and to custom specs. **Patterns:** Hunters, Bowies, tomahawks and fighters. **Technical:** Forges 5160, O1, 1095 and his own Damascus. Uses only natural han

materials. **Prices:** $145 to $500; some to $1,100. **Remarks:** Part-time maker; first knife sold in 1988. **Mark:** Last name or first and last name in Celtic script.

**ROBERTSON, LEO D.,** 3728 Pleasant Lake Dr., Indianpolis, IN 46227, Phone: 317-882-9899, ldr52@juno.com
**Specialties:** Hunting and folders. **Patterns:** Hunting, fillet, Bowie, utility, folders and tantos. **Technical:** Uses ATS-34, 154CM, 440C, 1095, D2 and Damascus steels. **Prices:** Fixed knives $75 to $350, folders $350 to $600. **Remarks:** Handles made with stag, wildwoods, laminates, mother-of-pearl. **Mark:** Logo with full name in oval around logo. **Other:** Made first knife in 1990. Member of American bladesmith society.

**ROBINSON, CHARLES (DICKIE),** PO Box 221, Vega, TX 79092, Phone: 806-267-2629, dickie@amaonline.com
**Specialties:** Classic and working/using knives. **Patterns:** Bowies, daggers, fighters, hunters and camp knives. **Technical:** Forges O1, 5160, 52100 and his own Damascus. **Prices:** $350 to $850; some to $5,000. **Remarks:** Part-time maker; first knife sold in 1988. Doing business as Robinson Knives. ABS Master Smith. **Mark:** Robinson MS.

**ROBINSON, CHUCK,** Sea Robin Forge, 1423 Third Ave., Picayune, MS 39466, Phone: 601-798-0060, crobin@datastar.net
**Specialties:** Deluxe period pieces and working / using knives of his design and to customer specs. **Patterns:** Bowies, fighters, hunters, folders, utility knives and original designs. **Technical:** Forges own Damascus, 52100, 01, L6 and 1070 thru 1095. **Prices:** Start At $225. **Remarks:** First knife 1958. Recently transitioned to full-time maker. **Mark:** Fish logo, anchor and initials C.R.

**ROBINSON, ROBERT W.,** 1569 N. Finley Pt., Polson, MT 59860, Phone: 406-887-2259, Fax: 406-887-2259
**Specialties:** High-art straight knives, folders and automatics of his design. **Patterns:** Hunters and locking folders. **Technical:** Grinds ATS-34, 154CM and 440V. Inlays pearl and gold; engraves sheep horn and ivory. **Prices:** $150 to $500; some to $2,000. **Remarks:** Full-time maker; first knife sold in 1983. Doing business as Robbie Knife. **Mark:** Name on left side of blade.

**ROBINSON III, REX R.,** 10531 Poe St., Leesburg, FL 34788, Phone: 352-787-4587
**Specialties:** One-of-a-kind high-art automatics of his design. **Patterns:** Automatics, liner locks and lock back folders. **Technical:** Uses tool steel and stainless Damascus and mokume; flat grinds. Hand carves folders. **Prices:** $1,800 to $7,500. **Remarks:** First knife sold in 1988. **Mark:** First name inside oval.

**ROCHFORD, MICHAEL R.,** PO Box 577, Dresser, WI 54009, Phone: 715-755-3520, mrrochford@centurytel.net
**Specialties:** Working straight knives and folders. Classic Bowies and Moran traditional. **Patterns:** Bowies, fighters, hunters: slip-joint, locking and liner locking folders. **Technical:** Grinds ATS-34, 440C, 154CM and D-2; forges W2, 5160, and his own Damascus. Offers metal and metal and leather sheaths. Filework and wire inlay. **Prices:** $150 to $1,000; some to $2,000. **Remarks:** Part-time maker; first knife sold in 1984. **Mark:** Name.

**RODEBAUGH, JAMES L.,** 9374 Joshua Rd., Oak Hills, CA 92345

**RODEWALD, GARY,** 447 Grouse Ct., Hamilton, MT 59840, Phone: 406-363-2192
**Specialties:** Bowies of his design as inspired from his torical pieces. **Patterns:** Hunters, Bowies and camp/combat. Forges 5160 1084 and his own Damascus of 1084, 15N20, field grade hunters AT-34 - 440C, 440V, and BG42. **Prices:** $200 to $1,500. **Remarks:** Sole author on knives - sheaths done by saddle maker. **Mark:** Rodewald.

**RODKEY, DAN,** 18336 Ozark Dr., Hudson, FL 34667, Phone: 727-863-8264
**Specialties:** Traditional straight knives of his design and in standard patterns. **Patterns:** Boots, fighters and hunters. **Technical:** Grinds 440C, D2 and ATS-34. **Prices:** Start at $200. **Remarks:** Full-time maker; first knife sold in 1985. Doing business as Rodkey Knives. **Mark:** Etched logo on blade.

**ROE JR., FRED D.,** 4005 Granada Dr., Huntsville, AL 35802, Phone: 205-881-6847
**Specialties:** Highly finished working knives of his design; period pieces. **Patterns:** Hunters, fighters and survival knives; locking folders; specialty designs like divers' knives. **Technical:** Grinds 154CM, ATS-34 and Damascus. Field-tests all blades. **Prices:** $125 to $250; some to $2,000. **Remarks:** Part-time maker; first knife sold in 1980. **Mark:** Last name.

**ROGERS, RICHARD,** PO Box 769, Magdalena, NM 87825, Phone: 505-854-2567, rsrogers1@yahoo.com
**Specialties:** Sheffield-style folders and multi-blade folders. **Patterns:** Folders: various traditional patterns. One-of-a-kind fixed blades. Fixed blades: Bowies, daggers, hunters, utility knives. **Technical:** Mainly use ATS-34 and prefer natural handle materials. **Prices:** $400 and up. **Mark:** Last name.

**ROGERS, RAY,** PO Box 126, Wauconda, WA 98859, Phone: 509-486-8069
**Specialties:**Liner lock folders. Asian and European professional chef's knives. **Patterns:**Rayzor folders, chef's knives and cleavers of my own and traditional designs, drop point hunters and fillet knives. **Technical:**Stock removal S30V, 440, 1095, O1 Damascus and other steels. I do all my own heat treating, clay tempering, some forging G-10, Micarta®, Carbon fiber on folders, stabilized burl woods on fixed blades. **Prices:** $200 to $450. **Remarks:**My knives are made one at a time to the customer's order. I am happy to consider customizing y knife designs to suit your preferences and sometimes create entirely new knives when necessary. As a full-time knifemaker I am willing to spend as much time as it takes (usually through email) discussing the options and refining details of a knife's design to insure that you get the knife you really want.

**ROGERS, RODNEY,** 602 Osceola St., Wildwood, FL 34785, Phone: 352-748-6114
**Specialties:** Traditional straight knives and folders. **Patterns:** Fighters, hunters, skinners. **Technical:** Flat-grinds ATS-34 and Damascus. Prefers natural materials. **Prices:** $150 to $1,400. **Remarks:** Full-time maker; first knife sold in 1986. **Mark:** Last name, Handmade.

**ROGERS, CHARLES W.,** Rt. 1 Box 1552, Douglas, TX 75943, Phone: 409-326-4496

**ROGERS JR., ROBERT P.,** 3979 South Main St., Acworth, GA 30101, Phone: 404-974-9982
**Specialties:** Traditional working knives. **Patterns:** Hunters, 4-inch trailing-points. **Technical:** Grinds D2, 154CM and ATS-34; likes ironwood and ivory Micarta. **Prices:** $125 to $175. **Remarks:** Spare-time maker; first knife sold in 1975. **Mark:** Name.

**ROGHMANS, MARK,** 607 Virginia Ave., LaGrange, GA 30240, Phone: 706-885-1273
**Specialties:** Classic and traditional knives of his design. **Patterns:** Bowies, daggers and fighters. **Technical:** Grinds ATS-34, D2 and 440C. **Prices:** $250 to $500. **Remarks:** Part-time maker; first knife sold in 1984. Doing business as LaGrange Knife. **Mark:** Last name and/or LaGrange Knife.

**ROHN, FRED,** 7675 W Happy Hill Rd., Coeur d'Alene, ID 83814, Phone: 208-667-0774
**Specialties:** Hunters, boot knives, custom patterns. **Patterns:** Drop points, double edge etc. **Technical:** Grinds 440 or 154CM. **Prices:** $85 and up. **Remarks:** Part-time maker. **Mark:** Logo on blade; serial numbered.

**ROLLERT, STEVE,** PO Box 65, Keenesburg, CO 80643-0065, Phone: 303-732-4858, steve@doveknives.com Web: www.doveknives.com
**Specialties:** Highly finished working knives. **Patterns:** Variety of straight knives; locking folders and slip-joints. **Technical:** Forges and grinds W2, 1095, ATS-34 and his pattern-welded, cable Damascus and nickel Damascus. **Prices:** $300 to $1,000; some to $3,000. **Remarks:** Full-time maker; first knife sold in 1980. Doing business as Dove Knives. **Mark:** Last name in script.

**ROLLICK, WALTER D.,** 2001 Cochran Rd., Maryville, TN 37803, Phone: 423-681-6105

**RONZIO, N. JACK,** PO Box 248, Fruita, CO 81521, Phone: 970-858-0921

**ROOT, GARY,** 644 East 14th St, Erie, PA 16503, Phone: 814-459-0196
**Specialties:** Damascus bowies with hand carved eagles, hawks and snakes for handles. Few folders made. **Patterns:** Daggers, fighters, hunter/field knives. **Technical:** Using handforged Damascus from Ray Bybar Jr (M.S.) and Robert Eggerling. Grinds D2, 440C, 1095 and 5160. Some 5160 is hand forged. **Prices:** $80 to $300; some to $1,000. **Remarks:** Part-time maker, first knife sold in 1976. **Mark:** Name over Erie, PA.

**ROSA, PEDRO GULLHERME TELES,** R. das Magnolias, 45 CECAP Presidente Prudente, SP-19065-410, BRAZIL, Phone: 0182-271769
**Specialties:** Using straight knives and folders to customer specs; some high-art. **Patterns:** Fighters, Bowies and daggers. **Technical:** Grinds and forges D6, 440C, high-carbon steels and Damascus. **Prices:** $60 to $400. **Remarks:** Full-time maker; first knife sold in 1991. **Mark:** A hammer over "Hammer."

**ROSE, DEREK W.,** 14 Willow Wood Rd., Gallipolis, OH 45631, Phone: 740-446-4627

**ROSENFELD, BOB,** 955 Freeman Johnson Rd., Hoschton, GA 30548, Phone: 770-867-2647, www.1bladesmith@msn.com
**Specialties:** Fancy and embellished working/using straight knives of his design and in standard patterns. **Patterns:** Daggers, hunters and utility/camp knives. **Technical:** Forges 52100, A203E, 1095 and L6 Damascus. Offers engraving. **Prices:** $125 to $650; some to $1,000. **Remarks:** Full-time maker; first knife sold in 1984. Also makes folders; ABS Journeyman. **Mark:** Last name or full name, Knifemaker.

**ROSS, STEPHEN,** 534 Remington Dr., Evanston, WY 82930, Phone: 307-789-7104
**Specialties:** One-of-a-kind collector-grade classic and contemporary straight knives and folders of his design and to customer specs; some fantasy pieces. **Patterns:** Combat and survival knives, hunters, boots and folders. **Technical:** Grinds stainless; forges spring and tool steel. Engraves, scrimshaws. Makes leather sheaths. **Prices:** $160 to $3,000. **Remarks:** Part-time-time maker; first knife sold in 1971. **Mark:** Last name in modified Roman; sometimes in script.

**ROSS, TIM,** 3239 Oliver Rd, Thunder Bay, ONT, CANADA P7G 1S9, Phone: 807-935-2667, Fax: 807-935-3179
**Specialties:** Fixed blades. **Patterns:** Hunting, fishing, collector. **Technical:** Uses D2, Stellite, 440C, Forges 52100, Damascus cable. **Prices:** $150 to $750 some to $5,000. **Mark:** Tang stamps Ross custom knives.

**ROSS, GREGG,** 4556 Wenhart Rd., Lake Worth, FL 33463, Phone: 407-439-4681
**Specialties:** Working/using straight knives. **Patterns:** Bowies, hunters and utility/camp knives. **Technical:** Forges and grinds ATS-34, Damascus and cable Damascus. Uses decorative pins. **Prices:** $125 to $250; some to $400. **Remarks:** Part-time maker; first knife sold in 1992. **Mark:** Name, city and state.

**ROSS, D.L.,** 27 Kinsman St., Dunedin, NEW ZEALAND, Phone: 64 3 464 0239, Fax: 64 3 464 0239
**Specialties:** Working straight knives of his design. **Patterns:** Hunters, various others. **Technical:** Grinds 440C. **Prices:** $100 to $450; some to $700 NZ dollars. **Remarks:** Part-time maker; first knife sold in 1988. **Mark:** Dave Ross, Maker, city and country.

**ROSSDEUTSCHER, ROBERT N.,** 133 S Vail Ave., Arlington Heights, IL 60005, Phone: 847-577-0404, Web: www.rnrknives.com
**Specialties:** Frontier-style and historically inspired knives. **Patterns:** Trade knives, Bowies, camp knives and hunting knives, tomahawks and lances. **Technical:** Most knives are hand forged, a few are stock removal. **Prices:** $135 to $1,500. **Remarks:** Journeyman Smith of the American Bladesmith Society and Neo-Tribal Bladesmiths. **Mark:** Back-to-back "R's", one upside down and backwards, one right side up and forward in an oval. Sometimes with name, town and state; depending on knife style.

**ROTELLA, RICHARD A.,** 643—75th St., Niagara Falls, NY 14304
**Specialties:** Working knives of his design. **Patterns:** Various fishing, hunting and utility knives; folders. **Technical:** Grinds ATS-34. Prefers hand-rubbed finishes. **Prices:** $65 to $450; some to $900. **Remarks:** Spare-time maker; first knife sold in 1977. Not taking orders at this time; only sells locally. **Mark:** Name and city in stylized waterfall logo.

**ROULIN, CHARLES,** 113 B Rt. de Soral, 1233 Geneva, SWITZERLAND, Phone: 022-757-4479, Fax: 022-757-4479, coutelier@coutelier-Roulin.com Web: www.coutelier-roulin.com
**Specialties:** Fancy high-art straight knives and folders of his design. **Patterns:** Bowies, locking folders, slip-joint folders and miniatures. **Technical:** Grinds 440C, ATS-34 and D2. Engraves; carves nature scenes and detailed animals in steel, ivory, on handles and blades. **Prices:** $500 to $3,000; some to $10,000. **Remarks:** Full-time maker; first knife sold in 1988. **Mark:** Symbol of fish with name or name engraved.

**ROWE, FRED,** BETHEL RIDGE FORGE, 3199 Roberts Rd., Amesville, OH 45711, Phone: 866-325-2164, fred.rowe@bethelridgeforge.com Web: www.bethelridgeforge.com
**Specialties:** Damascus and carbon steel sheath knives. **Patterns:** Bowies, hunters, fillet small kokris. **Technical:** My own Damascus, 52100, O1, L-6, 1095 carbon steels. **Prices:** $150 to $800. **Remarks:** All blades are clay hardened. **Mark:** Bethel Ridge Forge.

**ROZAS, CLARK D.,** 1436 W "G" St., Wilmington, CA 90744, Phone: 310-518-0488
**Specialties:** Hand forged blades. **Patterns:** Pig stickers, toad stabbers, whackers, choppers. **Technical:** Damascus, 52100, 1095, 1084, 5160. **Prices:** $200 to $600. **Remarks:** A.B.S. member; part-time maker since 1995. **Mark:** Name over dagger.

**RUANA KNIFE WORKS, ,** Box 520, Bonner, MT 59823, Phone: 406-258-5368, www.ruanaknives.com
**Specialties:** Working knives and period pieces. **Patterns:** Variety of straight knives. **Technical:** Forges 5160 chrome alloy for Bowies and 1095. **Prices:** $155 and up. **Remarks:** Full-time maker; first knife sold in 1938. Currently making knife honoring the lewis and clark expedition. **Mark:** Name.

**RUPERT, BOB,** 301 Harshaville Rd., Clinton, PA 15026, Phone: 724-573-4569, rbrupert@aol.com
**Specialties:** Wrought period pieces with natural elements. **Patterns:** Elegant straight blades - friction folders. **Technical:** Forges colonial 7; 1095; 5160; diffuse mokume-gane and form Damascus. **Prices:** $150 to $1,500; som higher. **Remarks:** Part-time maker; first knife sold in 1980. Evening hours studio since 1980. **Mark:** R etched in Old English. **Other:** Likes simplicity that dis assembles.

**RUPLE, WILLIAM H.,** PO Box 370, Charlotte, TX 78011, Phone: 830-277-1371
**Specialties:** Multi-blade folders, slip joints, some lock backs. **Patterns:** Lik to reproduce old patterns. **Technical:** Grinds 440C, ATS-34, D2 and commercial Damascus. Offers filework on back springs and liners. **Prices:** $300 t $500; some to $1,000. **Remarks:** Full-time maker; first knife sold in 198 **Mark:** Ruple.

**RUSS, RON,** 5351 NE 160th Ave., Williston, FL 32696, Phone: 352-528 2603, RussRs@aol.com
**Specialties:** Damascus and Mokume. **Patterns:** Ladder, rain drop and butte fly. **Technical:** Most knives, including Damascus, are forged from 52100-E **Prices:** $65 to $2,500. **Mark:** Russ.

**RUSSELL, MICK,** 4 Rossini Rd., Pari Park, Port Elizabeth 6070, SOUTH AFRICA
**Specialties:** Art knives. **Patterns:** Working and collectible bird, trout and hun ing knives, defense knives and folders. **Technical:** Grinds D2, 440C, ATS-3 and Damascus. Offers mirror or satin finishes. **Prices:** Start at $10 **Remarks:** Full-time maker; first knife sold in 1986. **Mark:** Stylized rhino inco porating initials.

**RUSSELL, TOM,** 6500 New Liberty Rd., Jacksonville, AL 36265, Phone 205-492-7866
**Specialties:** Straight working knives of his design or to customer specs. **Pa terns:** Hunters, folders, fighters, skinners, Bowies and utility knives. **Techn cal:** Grinds D2, 440C and ATS-34; offers filework. **Prices:** $75 to $22 **Remarks:** Part-time maker; first knife sold in 1987. Full-time tool and d maker. **Mark:** Last name with tulip stamp.

**RUTH, MICHAEL G,** 3101 New Boston Rd., Texarkana, TX 75501, Phone: 903-832-7166

**RYBAR JR., RAYMOND B.,** 726 W Lynwood St., Phoenix, AZ 85007, Phone: 605-523-0201
**Specialties:** Fancy/embellished, high-art and traditional working usi straight knives and folders of his design and in standard patterns; peri pieces. **Patterns:** Daggers, fighters and swords. **Technical:** Forges Da ascus. All blades have etched biblical scripture or biblical significance. **Price** $120 to $1,200; some to $4,500. **Remarks:** Full-time maker; first knife sold 1972. Doing business as Stone Church Forge. **Mark:** Last name or busine name.

**RYBERG, GOTE,** Faltgatan 2, S-562 00 Norrahammar, SWEDEN, Phone: 4636-61678

**RYDBOM, JEFF,** PO Box 548, Annandale, MN 55302, Phone: 320-27 9639, jry1890@hotmail.com
**Specialties:** Ring knives. **Patterns:** Hunters, fighters, Bowie and ca knives. **Technical:** Straight grinds 01, A2, 1566 and 5150 steels. **Price** $150 to $1,000. **Remarks:** No pinning of guards or pommels. All silver braz **Mark:** Capital "C" with J R inside.

**RYDER, BEN M.,** PO Box 133, Copperhill, TN 37317, Phone: 615-496 2750
**Specialties:** Working/using straight knives of his design and to custom specs. **Patterns:** Fighters, hunters, utility/camp knives. **Technical:** Grin 440C, ATS-34, D2, commercial Damascus. **Prices:** $75 to $400. **Remark** Part-time maker; first knife sold in 1992. **Mark:** Full name in double butte logo.

**RYUICHI, KUKI,** 504-7 Tokorozawa-Shinmachi, Tokorozawa-City, Saitama, JAPAN, Phone: 042-943-3451

**RZEWNICKI, GERALD,** 8833 S Massbach Rd., Elizabeth, IL 61028-9714, Phone: 815-598-3239

**SAINDON, R. BILL,** 233 Rand Pond Rd., Goshen, NH 03752, Phone: 603-863-1874, dayskiev71@aol.com
**Specialties:** Collector-quality folders of his design or to customer specs. **P terns:** Latch release, liner lock and lockback folders. **Technical:** Offers limi amount of own Damascus; also uses Damas makers steel. Prefers natu handle material, gold and gems. **Prices:** $500 to $4,000. **Remarks:** Full-ti maker; first knife sold in 1981. Doing business as Daynia Forge. **Mark:** S logo or engraved surname.

**SAKAKIBARA, MASAKI,** 20-8 Sakuragaoka, 2-Chome Setagaya-ku, Tokyo 156-0054, JAPAN, Phone: 81-3-3420-0375

**SAKMAR, MIKE,** 1451 Clovelly Ave., Rochester, MI 48307, Phone: 248-852-6775, Fax: 248-852-8544, mikesakmar@yahoo.com
**Specialties:** Mokume in various patterns and alloy combinations. **Patterns:** Bowies, fighters, hunters and integrals. **Technical:** Grinds ATS-34, Damascus and high-carbon tool steels. Uses mostly natural handle materials—elephant ivory, walrus ivory, stag, wildwood, oosic, etc. Makes mokume for resale. **Prices:** $250 to $2,500; some to $4,000. **Remarks:** Part-time maker; first knife sold in 1990. **Mark:** Last name. **Other:** Supplier of Mokume.

**SALLEY, JOHN D.,** 3965 Frederick-Ginghamsburg Rd., Tipp City, OH 45371, Phone: 937-698-4588, Fax: 937-698-4131
**Specialties:** Fancy working knives and art pieces. **Patterns:** Hunters, fighters, daggers and some swords. **Technical:** Grinds ATS-34, 12C27 and W2; buys Damascus. **Prices:** $85 to $1,000; some to $6,000. **Remarks:** Part-time maker; first knife sold in 1979. **Mark:** First initial, last name.

**SAMPSON, LYNN,** 381 Deakins Rd., Jonesborough, TN 37659, Phone: 423-348-8373
**Specialties:** Highly finished working knives, mostly folders. **Patterns:** Locking folders, slip-joints, interframes and two-blades. **Technical:** Grinds D2, 440C and ATS-34; offers extensive filework. **Prices:** Start at $300. **Remarks:** Full-time maker; first knife sold in 1982. **Mark:** Name and city in logo.

**SANDBERG, RONALD B.,** 24784 Shadowwood Ln., Browntown, MI 48134, Phone: 734-671-6866, msc@ili.net
**Specialties:** Good looking and functional hunting knives, filework, mixing of handle materials. **Patterns:** Hunters, skinners and Bowies. **Prices:** $120 and up. **Remarks:** Doing business as mighty Sharp Cuts. **Mark:** R.B. Sandberg.

**SANDERS, A.A.,** 3850 72 Ave. NE, Norman, OK 73071, Phone: 405-364-8660
**Specialties:** Working straight knives and folders. **Patterns:** Hunters, fighters, daggers and Bowies. **Technical:** Forges his own Damascus; offers stock removal with ATS-34, 440C, A2, D2, O1, 5160 and 1095. **Prices:** $85 to $1,500. **Remarks:** Full-time maker; first knife sold in 1985. Formerly known as Athern Forge. **Mark:** Name.

**SANDERS, MICHAEL M.,** PO Box 1106, Ponchatoula, LA 70454, Phone: 225-294-3601
**Specialties:** Working straight knives and folders, some deluxe. **Patterns:** Hunters, fighters, Bowies, daggers, large folders and deluxe Damascus miniatures. **Technical:** Grinds O1, D2, 440C, ATS-34 and Damascus. **Prices:** $75 to $650; some higher. **Remarks:** Full-time maker; first knife sold in 1967. **Mark:** Name and state.

**SANDERS, BILL,** 335 Bauer Ave., PO Box 957, Mancos, CO 81328, Phone: 970-533-7223, Fax: 970-533-7390, billsand@frontier.net Web: www.billsandershandmadeknives.com
**Specialties:** Survival knives, working straight knives, some fancy and some fantasy, of his design. **Patterns:** Hunters, boots, utility knives, using belt knives. **Technical:** Grinds 440C, ATS-34 and commercial Damascus. Provides wide variety of handle materials. **Prices:** $170 to $800. **Remarks:** Full-time maker. Formerly of Timberline knives. **Mark:** Name, city and state.

**SANDERSON, RAY,** 4403 Uplands Way, Yakima, WA 98908, Phone: 509-965-0128
**Specialties:** One-of-a-kind Buck knives; traditional working straight knives and folders of his design. **Patterns:** Bowies, hunters and fighters. **Technical:** Grinds 440C and ATS-34. **Prices:** $200 to $750. **Remarks:** Part-time maker; first knife sold in 1984. **Mark:** Sanderson Knives in shape of Bowie.

**SANDLIN, LARRY,** 4580 Sunday Dr., Adamsville, AL 35005, Phone: 205-674-1816
**Specialties:** High-art straight knives of his design. **Patterns:** Boots, daggers, hunters and fighters. **Technical:** Forges 1095, L6, O1, carbon steel and Damascus. **Prices:** $200 to $1,500; some to $5,000. **Remarks:** Part-time maker; first knife sold in 1990. **Mark:** Chiseled last name in Japanese.

**SANDOW, NORMAN E,** 20 Redcastle Dr, Howick, Auckland, NEW ZEALAND, Phone: 09 2770916, sanknife@ezysurf.co.nz
**Specialties**Quality liner lock folders. Working and fancy straight knives. Some one of a kind. Embellishments available. **Patterns:** Most patterns, hunters, boot, bird and trout etc. and to customers specs. **Technical:** Predominate knife steel ATS-34. Also in use 12C27, D2 and Damascus. High class handle material used on both folders and straight knives. All blades made via the stock removal method. **Prices:** $250 to $1,500. **Remarks:** Full-time maker. **Mark:** Norma E Sandow in semi - circular design.

**SANDS, SCOTT,** 2 Lindis Ln., New Brighton, Christchurch 9, NEW ZEALAND
**Specialties:** Classic working and fantasy swords. **Patterns:** Fantasy, medieval, celtic, viking, katana, some daggers. **Technical:** Forges own Damascus; 1080 and L6; 5160 and L6; 01 and L6. All hand-polished, does own heat-treating, forges non-Damascus on request. **Prices:** $1,500 to $15,000+. **Remarks:** Full-time maker; first blade sold in 1996. **Mark:** Stylized Moon.

**SARVIS, RANDALL J.,** 110 West Park Ave., Fort Pierre, SD 57532, Phone: 605-223-2772, rsarvis@sdln.net

**SASS, GARY N.,** 2048 Buckeye Dr, Sharpsville, PA 16150, Phone: 724-866-6165, gnsass@verizon.net
**Specialties:** Working straight knives of his design or to customer specifications. **Patterns:** Hunters, fighters, utility knives, push daggers. **Technical:** Grinds 440C, ATS-34 and Damascus. Uses exotic wood, buffalo horn, warthog tusk and semi-precious stones. **Prices:** $50 to $250; some higher. **Remarks:** Part-time maker. First knife sold in 2003. **Mark:** Initials G.S. formed into a diamond shape.

**SAWBY, SCOTT,** 480 Snowberry Ln., Sandpoint, ID 83864, Phone: 208-263-4171, scotmar@imbris.net Web: www.sawbycustomknives.com
**Specialties:** Folders, working and fancy. **Patterns:** Locking folders, patent locking systems and interframes. **Technical:** Grinds D2, 440C, 154CM, CPM-T-440V and ATS-34. **Prices:** $500 to $1,500. **Remarks:** Full-time maker; first knife sold in 1974. Engraving by wife Marian. **Mark:** Last name, city and state.

**SCARROW, WIL,** c/o LandW Mail Service, 919 E Hermosa Dr., San Gabriel, CA 91775, Phone: 626-286-6069, willsknife@earthlink.net
**Specialties:** Carving knives, also working straight knives in standard patterns or to customer specs. **Patterns:** Carving, fishing, hunting, skinning, utility, swords and Bowies. **Technical:** Forges and grinds: A2, L6, W1, D2, 5160, 1095, 440C, AEB-L, ATS-34 and others on request. Offers some filework. **Prices:** $105 to $850; some higher. Prices include sheath (carver's $40 and up). **Remarks:** Spare-time maker; first knife sold in 1983. Two to eight month construction time on custom orders. Doing business as Scarrow's Custom Stuff and Gold Hill Knife works (in Oregon). **Mark:** SC with arrow and date/year made. **Other:** Carving knives available at the 'Wild Duck' Woodcarvers Supply. Contact at duckstore@aol.com.

**SCHALLER, ANTHONY BRETT,** 5609 Flint Ct. NW, Albuquerque, NM 87120, Phone: 505-899-0155, brett@schallerknives.com Web: www.schallerknives.com
**Specialties:** Straight knives and locking-liner folders of his design and in standard patterns. **Patterns:** Boots, fighters, utility knives and folders. **Technical:** Grinds ATS-34, BG42 and stainless Damascus. Offers filework, hand-rubbed finishes and full and narrow tangs. Prefers exotic woods or Micarta for handle materials, G-10 and carbon fiber to handle materials. **Prices:** $60 to $350; some to $500. **Remarks:** Part-time maker; first knife sold in 1990. **Mark:** A.B. Schaller - Albuquerque NM - handmade.

**SCHEID, MAGGIE,** 124 Van Stallen St., Rochester, NY 14621-3557
**Specialties:** Simple working straight knives. **Patterns:** Kitchen and utility knives; some miniatures. **Technical:** Forges 5160 high-carbon steel. **Prices:** $100 to $200. **Remarks:** Part-time maker; first knife sold in 1986. **Mark:** Full name.

**SCHEMPP, MARTIN,** PO Box 1181, 5430 Baird Springs Rd. N.W., Ephrata, WA 98823, Phone: 509-754-2963, Fax: 509-754-3212
**Specialties:** Fantasy and traditional straight knives of his design, to customer specs and in standard patterns; Paleolithic-styles. **Patterns:** Fighters and Paleolithic designs. **Technical:** Uses opal, Mexican rainbow and obsidian. Offers scrimshaw. **Prices:** $15 to $100; some to $250. **Remarks:** Spare-time maker; first knife sold in 1995. **Mark:** Initials and date.

**SCHEMPP, ED,** PO Box 1181, Ephrata, WA 98823, Phone: 509-754-2963, Fax: 509-754-3212
**Specialties:** Mosaic Damascus and unique folder designs. **Patterns:** Primarily folders. **Technical:** Grinds CPM440V; forges many patterns of mosaic using powdered steel. **Prices:** $100 to $400; some to $2,000. **Remarks:** Part-time maker; first knife sold in 1991. Doing business as Ed Schempp Knives. **Mark:** Ed Schempp Knives over five heads of wheat, city and state.

**SCHEPERS, GEORGE B.,** PO Box 395, Shelton, NE 68876-0395
**Specialties:** Fancy period pieces of his design. **Patterns:** Bowies, swords, tomahawks; locking folders and miniatures. **Technical:** Grinds W1, W2 and his own Damascus; etches. **Prices:** $125 to $600; some higher. **Remarks:** Full-time maker; first knife sold in 1981. **Mark:** Schep.

**SCHEURER, ALFREDO E. FAES,** Av. Rincon de los Arcos 104, Col. Bosque Res. del Sur, C.P. 16010, MEXICO, Phone: 5676 47 63
**Specialties:** Fancy and fantasy knives of his design. **Patterns:** Daggers. **Technical:** Grinds stainless steel; casts and grinds silver. Sets stones in silver. **Prices:** $2,000 to $3,000. **Remarks:** Spare-time maker; first knife sold in 1989. **Mark:** Symbol.

**SCHILLING, ELLEN,** 95 Line Rd., Hamilton Square, NJ 08690, Phone: 609-448-0483

**SCHIPPNICK, JIM,** PO Box 326, Sanborn, NY 14132, Phone: 716-731-3715, ragnar@ragweedforge.com Web: www.ragweedforge.com
**Specialties:** Nordic, early American, rustic. **Mark:** Runic R. **Remarks:** Also import Nordic knives from Norway, Sweden and Finland.

**SCHIRMER, MIKE,** 312 E 6th St., Rosalia, WA 99170-9506, Phone: 208-523-3249, schirmer@3rivers.net
**Specialties:** Working straight knives of his design or to customer specs; mostly hunters and personal knives. **Patterns:** Hunters, camp, kitchen, Bowies and fighters. **Technical:** Grinds O1, D2, A2 and Damascus and Talonoite. **Prices:** Start at $150. **Remarks:** Full-time maker; first knife sold in 1992. Doing business as Ruby Mountain Knives. **Mark:** Name or name and location.

**SCHLOMER, JAMES E.,** 2543 Wyatt Pl., Kissimmee, FL 34741, Phone: 407-348-8044
**Specialties:** Working and show straight knives. **Patterns:** Hunters, Bowies and skinners. **Technical:** Stock removal method, 440C. Scrimshaws; carves sambar stag handles. Works on corean and Micarta. **Prices:** $150 to $750. **Remarks:** Full-time maker. **Mark:** Name and steel number.

**SCHLUETER, DAVID,** PO Box 463, Syracuse, NY 13209, Phone: 315-485-0829, david@oddfrogforge.com Web: http://www.oddfrogforge.com
**Specialties:** Japanese-style swords, handmade fittings, leather wraps. **Patterns:** Kozuka to Tach, blades with bo-hi and o-kissaki. **Technical:** Sole author, forges and grinds, high-carbon steels. Blades are tempered after clay-coated and water-quenched heat treatment. All fittings are handmade. **Prices:** $800 to $5,000 plus. **Remarks:** Full-time maker, doing business as Odd Frog Forge. **Mark:** Full name and date.

**SCHMITZ, RAYMOND E.,** PO Box 1787, Valley Center, CA 92082, Phone: 760-749-4318

**SCHMOKER, RANDY,** SPIRIT OF THE HAMMER, HC 63 Box 1085, Slana, AK 99586, Phone: 907-822-3371, spiritofthehammer@hotmail.com
**Specialties:** Hand carved, natural materials, mastodon ivory, moose antler. **Patterns:** Hunter, skinner, Bowie, fighter, artistic collectables. **Technical:** Hand forged. **Prices:** $300 to $600. **Remarks:** 01 tool steel, 1095, 5160, 52100. **Mark:** Sheep with an S. **Other:** Custom sheaths, display stands.

**SCHNEIDER, CRAIG M.,** 5380 N Amity Rd., Claremont, IL 62421, Phone: 217-377-5715
**Specialties:** Straight knives of his own design. **Patterns:** Bowies, hunters and miniatures. **Technical:** Forged high-carbon steel and Damascus. Flat grind and differential heat treatment use a wide selection of handle, guard and bolster material also offer leather sheaths. **Prices:** $85 to $2,500. **Remarks:** Part-time maker; first knife sold in 1985. **Mark:** Stylized initials.

**SCHNEIDER, KARL A.,** 209 N. Brownleaf Rd., Newark, DE 19713, Phone: 302-737-0277
**Specialties:** Traditional working and using straight knives of his design. **Patterns:** Hunters, kitchen and fillet knives. **Technical:** Grinds ATS-34. Shapes handles to fit hands; uses Micarta, Pakkawood and exotic woods. Makes hand-stitched leather cases. **Prices:** $95 to $225. **Remarks:** Part-time maker; first knife sold in 1984-85. **Mark:** Name, address; also name in shape of fish.

**SCHNEIDER, HERMAN,** 14084 Apple Valley Rd, Apple Valley, CA 92307, Phone: 760-946-9096
**Mark:** H.J. Schneider-Maker-

**SCHOEMAN, CORRIE,** Box 28596, Danhof 9310, SOUTH AFRICA, Phone: 027 51 4363528 Cell: 027 82-3750789, corries@intekom.co.za
**Specialties:** High-tech folders of his design or to customer's specs. **Patterns:** Linerlock folders and automatics. **Technical:** ATS-34, Damascus or stainless Damascus with titanium frames; prefers exotic materials for handles. **Prices:** $650 to $2,000. **Remarks:** Full-time maker; first knife sold in 1984. **Mark:** Logo in knife shape engraved on inside of back bar. **Other:** All folders come with filed liners and back and jewled inserts.

**SCHOENFELD, MATTHEW A.,** RR #1, Galiano Island, B.C., CANADA V0N 1P0, Phone: 250-539-2806
**Specialties:** Working knives of his design. **Patterns:** Kitchen cutlery, camp knives, hunters. **Technical:** Grinds 440C. **Prices:** $85 to $500. **Remarks:** Part-time maker; first knife sold in 1978. **Mark:** Signature, Galiano Is. B.C., and date.

**SCHOENINGH, MIKE,** 49850 Miller Rd, North Powder, OR 97867, Phone: 541-856-3239

**SCHOLL, TIM,** 1389 Langdon Rd., Angier, NC 27501, Phone: 910-897-2051, tscholl@surrealnet.net
**Specialties:** Fancy and working/using straight knives and folders of his design and to customer specs. **Patterns:** tomahawks, swords, tantos, hunters and fantasy knives. **Technical:** Grinds ATS-34 and D2; forges carbon and tool steel and Damascus. Offers filework, engraving and scrimshaw. **Prices:** $11[illegible] some to $4,000. **Remarks:** Part-time maker; first knife sold in 1990. Doin[illegible] business as Tim Scholl Custom Knives. **Mark:** S pierced by arrow.

**SCHRADER, ROBERT,** 55532 Gross De, Bend, OR 97707, Phone: 54[illegible] 598-7301
**Specialties:** Hunting, utility, Bowie. **Patterns:** Fixed blade. **Prices:** $150 [illegible] $600.

**SCHRAP, ROBERT G.,** CUSTOM LEATHER KNIFE SHEATH CO., 7024 W. Wells St., Wauwatosa, WI 53213-3717, Phone: 414-771-6472, Fax: 414-479-9765, knifesheaths@aol.com
**Specialties:** Leatherwork. **Prices:** $35 to $100. **Mark:** Schrap in oval.

**SCHROEN, KARL,** 4042 Bones Rd., Sebastopol, CA 95472, Phone: 707-823-4057, Fax: 707-823-2914
**Specialties:** Using knives made to fit. **Patterns:** Sgian dubhs, carving se[illegible] wood-carving knives, fishing knives, kitchen knives and new cleaver desig[illegible] **Technical:** Forges A2, ATS-34,D2 and L-6 cruwear S30V 590V. **Prices:** $1[illegible] to $6,000. **Remarks:** Full-time maker; first knife sold in 1968. Author of *T[illegible] Hand Forged Knife*. **Mark:** Last name.

**SCHUCHMANN, RICK,** 1500 Brandie Ln, New Richmond, OH 45157, Phone: 513-553-4316
**Specialties:** Replicas of antique and out of production Scagels and Randal[illegible] primarily miniatures. **Patterns:** All sheath knives, mostly miniatures, hunti[illegible] and fighting knives, some daggers and hatchets. **Technical:** Stock remov[illegible] 440 C and 01 steel. Most knives are flat ground, some convex. **Prices:** $1[illegible] to $600 and custom to $4,000. **Remarks:** Part-time maker, sold first knife [illegible] 1997. We have knives on display in the Randall Museum. Sheaths are ma[illegible] exclusively at Sullivan's Holster Shop, Tampa, FL **Mark:**SCAR

**SCHUCKMANN, RICK,** SCAR CUSTOM KNIVES, 1500 Brandie Ln, New Richmond, OH 45159, Phone: 513-553-4316

**SCHULTZ, ROBERT W.,** PO Box 70, Cocolalla, ID 83813-0070

**SCHWARZER, STEPHEN,** PO Box 4, Pomona Park, FL 32181, Phone 386-649-5026, Fax: 386-649-8585, steveschwarzer@gbso.net Web: www.steveschwarzer.com
**Specialties:** Mosaic Damascus and picture mosaic in folding knives. All Jap[illegible] nese blades are finished working with Wally Hostetter considered the top Ja[illegible] anese lacquer specialist in the USA. I am also producing a line of carbon st[illegible] skinning knives at $300 and a line of high end mosaic Damascus bar stock [illegible] the discriminating knife maker who wants to use the best. **Patterns:** Folde[illegible] axes and buckskinner knives. **Technical:** Specializes in picture mosaic Da[illegible] ascus and powder metal mosaic work. Sole authorship; all work includi[illegible] carving done in-house. Most knives have file work and carving. **Pric[illegible]** $1,500 to $5,000, some higher; carbon steel and primitive knives much le[illegible] **Remarks:** Full-time maker; first knife sold in 1976, considered by many to one of the top mosaic Damascus specialists in the world. Mosaic Master le[illegible] work. **Mark:** Schwarzer + anvil.

**SCIMIO, BILL,** HC 01 Box 24A, Spruce Creek, PA 16683, Phone: 814 632-3751, blackcrowforge@aol.com

**SCOFIELD, EVERETT,** 2873 Glass Mill Rd., Chickamauga, GA 30707 Phone: 706-375-2790
**Specialties:** Historic and fantasy miniatures. **Patterns:** All patterns. **Tech[illegible] cal:** Uses only the finest tool steels and other materials. Uses only natu[illegible] precious and semi-precious materials. **Prices:** $100 to $1,500. **Remar[illegible]** Full-time maker; first knife sold in 1971. Doing business as Three Crowns C[illegible] lery. **Mark:** Three Crowns logo.

**SCORDIA, PAOLO,** Via Terralba 143, 00050 Torrimpietra, Roma, ITALY, Phone: 06-61697231, pands@mail.nexus.it Web: www.scordia knives.com
**Specialties:** Working and fantasy knives of his own design. **Patterns:** [illegible] pattern. **Technical:** Forges own Damascus, welds own Mokume and gri[illegible] ATS-34, etc. use hardwoods and Micarta for handles, brass and nickel-sil[illegible] for fittings. Makes sheaths. **Prices:** $100 to $1,000. **Remarks:** Part-ti[illegible] maker; first knife sold in 1988. **Mark:** Initials with sun and moon logo.

**SCOTT, AL,** 2245 Harper Valley Rd., Harper, TX 78631, Phone: 830-864-4182
**Specialties:** High-art straight knives of his design. **Patterns:** Dagg[illegible] swords, early European, Middle East and Japanese knives. **Technical:** U[illegible] ATS-34, 440C and Damascus. Hand engraves; does file work cuts filigre[illegible] the blade; offers ivory carving and precious metal inlay. **Remarks:** Full-ti[illegible] maker; first knife sold in 1994. Doing business as Al Scott Maker of Fine Bl[illegible] Art. **Mark:** Name engraved in old English, sometime inlaid in 24K gold.

**SCROGGS, JAMES A.,** 108 Murray Hill Dr., Warrensburg, MO 64093 Phone: 660-747-2568
**Specialties:** Straight knives, prefers light weight. **Patterns:** Hunters, hideo[illegible] and fighters. **Technical:** Grinds CMP3V plus experiments in steels. Pre[illegible] handles of walnut in English, bastonge, American black Also uses my[illegible]

maple, Osage orange. **Prices:** $200 to $1,000. **Remarks:** 1st knife sold in 1985. Part-time maker, no orders taken. **Mark:** SCROGGS in block or script.

**SCULLEY, PETER E.,** 340 Sunset Dr., Rising Fawn, GA 30738, Phone: 706-398-0169

**SEARS, MICK,** 1697 Peach Orchard Rd. #302, Sumter, SC 29154, Phone: 803-499-5074
**Specialties:** Scots and confederate reproductions; Bowies and fighters. **Patterns:** Bowies, fighters. **Technical:** Grinds 440C and 1095. **Prices:** $50 to $150; some to $300. **Remarks:** Part-time maker; first knife sold in 1975. Doing business as Mick's Custom Knives. **Mark:** First name.

**SELENT, CHUCK,** PO Box 1207, Bonners Ferry, ID 83805-1207, Phone: 208-267-5807
**Specialties:** Period, art and fantasy miniatures; exotics; one-of-a-kinds. **Patterns:** Swords, daggers and others. **Technical:** Works in Damascus, meteorite, 440C and tool steel. Offers scrimshaw. Offers his own casting and leatherwork; uses jewelry techniques. Makes display cases for miniatures. **Prices:** $75 to $400. **Remarks:** Part-time maker; first knife sold in 1990. **Mark:** Last name and bear paw print logo scrimshawed on handles or leatherwork.

**SELF, ERNIE,** 950 O'Neill Ranch Rd., Dripping Springs, TX 78620-9760, Phone: 512-858-7133, ernieself@aol.com
**Specialties:** Traditional and working straight knives and folders of his design and in standard patterns. **Patterns:** Hunters, locking folders and slip-joints. **Technical:** Grinds 440C, D2, 440V, ATS-34 and Damascus. Offers fancy filework. **Prices:** $125 to $500; some to $1,500. **Remarks:** Full-time maker; first knife sold in 1982. **Mark:** In oval shape - Ernie Self Maker Dripping Springs TX. **Other:** Also customizes Buck 110's and 112's folding hunters.

**SELLEVOLD, HARALD,** S.Kleivesmau:2, PO Box 4134, N5835 Bergen, NORWAY, Phone: 55-310682, haraldsellevold@c2i.net; Web: http://euroedge.net/sellevold
**Specialties:** Norwegian-styles; collaborates with other Norse craftsmen. **Patterns:** Distinctive ferrules and other mild modifications of traditional patterns; Bowies and friction folders. **Technical:** Buys Damascus blades; blacksmiths his own blades. Semi-gemstones used in handles; gemstone inlay. **Prices:** $350 to $2,000. **Remarks:** Full-time maker; first knife sold in 1980. **Mark:** Name and country in logo.

**SELZAM, FRANK,** Martin Reinhard Str 23, 97631, Bad Koenigshofen, GERMANY, Phone: 09761-5980
**Specialties:** Hunters, working knives to customers specs, hand tooled and stitched leather sheaths large stock of wood and German stag horn. **Patterns:** Mostly own design. **Technical:** Forged blades, own Damascus, also stock removal stainless. **Prices:** $250 to $1,500. **Remark:** First knife sold in 1978. **Mark:** Last name stamped.

**SENTZ, MARK C.,** 4084 Baptist Rd., Taneytown, MD 21787, Phone: 410-756-2018
**Specialties:** Fancy straight working knives of his design. **Patterns:** Hunters, fighters, folders and utility/camp knives. **Technical:** Forges 1085, 1095, 5160, 5155 and his Damascus. Most knives come with wood-lined leather sheath or wooden presentation sheath. **Prices:** Start at $275. **Remarks:** Full-time maker; first knife sold in 1989. Doing business as M. Charles Sentz Gunsmithing, Inc. **Mark:** Last name.

**SERAFEN, STEVEN E.,** 24 Genesee St., New Berlin, NY 13411, Phone: 607-847-6903
**Specialties:** Traditional working/using straight knives of his design and to customer specs. **Patterns:** Bowies, fighters, hunters. **Technical:** Grinds ATS-34, 440C, high-carbon steel. **Prices:** $175 to $600; some to $1,200. **Remarks:** Part-time maker; first knife sold in 1990. **Mark:** First and middle initial, last name in script.

**SERVEN, JIM,** PO Box 1, Fostoria, MI 48435, Phone: 517-795-2255
**Specialties:** Highly finished unique folders. **Patterns:** Fancy working folders, axes, miniatures and razors; some straight knives. **Technical:** Grinds 440C; forges his own Damascus. **Prices:** $150 to $800; some to $1,500. **Remarks:** Full-time maker; first knife sold in 1971. **Mark:** Name in map logo.

**SEVEY CUSTOM KNIFE, ,** 94595 Chandler Rd., Gold Beach, OR 97444, Phone: 541-247-2649, sevey@charter.net Web: www.seveyknives.com
**Specialties:** Fixed blade hunters. **Patterns:** Drop point, trailing paint, clip paint, full tang, hidden tang. **Technical:** D-2, and ATS-34 blades, stock removal. Heat treatment by Paul Bos. **Prices:** $225 and up depending on overall length and grip material. **Mark:** Sevey Custom Knife.

**SFREDDO, RODRITO MENEZES,** Rua 15 De Novembro 2222, Nova Petropolis, RS, BRASIL 95150-000, Phone: 011-55-54-303-303-90, sfreddo@ig.com.br.
**Specialties:** Traditional Brazilian-style working and high-art knives of his design. **Patterns:** Fighters, Bowies, utility and camp knives, classic Mediterranean Dirk. Welcome customer design. **Technical:** Forges only with sledge hammers (no power hammer here) 100% to shape in 52100 and his own Damascus. Makes own sheaths in the true traditional Brazilian-style. **Remark:** Full-time maker. **Prices:** $250 to $1,100 for his elaborate Mediterranean Dirk. Uses only natural handle materials. Considered by many to be Brazil's best bladesmith.

**SHADLEY, EUGENE W.,** 26315 Norway Dr., Bovey, MN 55709, Phone: 218-245-3820, Fax: 218-245-1639, bses@uslink.net
**Specialties:** Classic multi-blade folders. **Patterns:** Whittlers, stockman, sowbelly, congress, trapper, etc. **Technical:** Grinds ATS-34, 416 frames. **Prices:** Start at $300. **Remarks:** Full-time maker; first knife sold in 1985. Doing business as Shadley Knives. **Mark:** Last name.

**SHADMOT, BOAZ,** MOSHAV PARAN D N, Arava, ISRAEL 86835, srb@arava.co.il

**SHARRIGAN, MUDD,** 111 Bradford Rd., Wiscasset, ME 04578-4457, Phone: 207-882-9820, Fax: 207-882-9835
**Specialties:** Custom designs; repair straight knives, custom leather sheaths. **Patterns:** Daggers, fighters, hunters, buckskinner, Indian crooked knives and seamen working knives; traditional Scandinavian-styles. **Technical:** Forges 1095, 52100, 5160, W2, O1. Laminates 1095 and mild steel. **Prices:** $50 to $325; some to $1,200. **Remarks:** Full-time maker; first knife sold in 1982. **Mark:** First name and swallow tail carving.

**SHAVER II, JAMES R.,** 1529 Spider Ridge Rd., Parkersburg, WV 26104, Phone: 304-422-2692, jrsknives@wirefree.com Web: www.spiderridgeforge.com
**Specialties:** Hunting and working straight knives in carbon and Damascus steel. **Patterns:** Bowies and daggers in Damascus and carbon steels. **Technical:** Forges 5160 carbon and Damascus in O101018 mild steel and pvee nickel. **Prices:** $85 to $225; some to $750. **Remarks:** Part-time maker; sold first knife in 1998. Believes in sole authorship. **Mark:** Last name.

**SHEEHY, THOMAS J.,** 4131 NE 24th Ave., Portland, OR 97211-6411, Phone: 503-493-2843
**Specialties:** Hunting knives and ULUs. **Patterns:** Own or customer designs. **Technical:** 1095/01 and ATS-34 steel. **Prices:** $35 to $200. **Remarks:** Do own heat treating; forged or ground blades. **Mark:** Name.

**SHEETS, STEVEN WILLIAM,** 6 Stonehouse Rd, Mendham, NJ 07945, Phone: 201-543-5882

**SHIFFER, STEVE,** PO Box 582, Leakesville, MS 39451, Phone: 601-394-4425, aiifish2@yahoo.com Web: wwwchoctawplantationforge.com
**Specialties:** Bowies, Fighters, Hard use knives. **Patterns:** Fighters, Hunters, Combat/Utility knives Walker pattern liner lock folders. Allen pattern scale and bolster release autos. **Technical:** Most work forged, stainless stock removal. Make own Damascus. O-1 and 5160 most used also 1084, 440c, 154cm, s30v. **Prices:** $125 to $1,000. **Remarks:** First knife sold in 2000, all heat treatment done by myself. Doing business as Choctaw Plantation Forge. **Mark:** Hot mark sunrise over creek.

**SHIKAYAMA, TOSHIAKI,** 259-2 Suka Yoshikawa City, Saitama 342-0057, JAPAN, Phone: 04-89-81-6605, Fax: 04-89-81-6605
**Specialties:** Folders in standard patterns. **Patterns:** Locking and multi-blade folders. **Technical:** Grinds ATS, carbon steel, high speed steel. **Prices:** $400 to $2,500; $4,500 with engraving. **Remarks:** Full-time maker; first knife sold in 1952. **Mark:** First initial, last name.

**SHINOSKY, ANDY,** 3117 Meanderwood Dr., Canfield, OH 44406, Phone: 330-702-0299, andy@shinosky.com Web: www.shinosky.com
**Specialties:** Collectible fancy folders and interframes. **Patterns:** Drop points, trailing points and daggers. **Technical:** Grinds ATS-34 and Damascus. Prefers natural handle materials. **Prices:** Start at $450. **Remarks:** Part-time maker; first knife sold in 1992. **Mark:** Name or bent folder logo.

**SHIPLEY, STEVEN A.,** 800 Campbell Rd. Ste 137, Richardson, TX 75081, Phone: 972-644-7981, Fax: 972-644-7985, steve@shipleysphotography
**Specialties:** Hunters, skinners and traditional straight knives. **Technical:** Hand grinds ATS-34, 440C and Damascus steels. Each knife is custom sheathed by his son, Dan. **Prices:** $175 to $2,000. **Remarks:** Part-time maker; like smooth lines and unusual handle materials. **Mark:** S A Shipley.

**SHOEMAKER, SCOTT,** 316 S. Main St., Miamisburg, OH 45342, Phone: 513-859-1935
**Specialties:** Twisted, wire-wrapped handles on swords, fighters and fantasy blades; new line of seven models with quick-draw, multi-carry Kydex sheaths. **Patterns:** Bowies, boots and one-of-a-kinds in his design or to customer specs. **Technical:** Grinds A6 and ATS-34; buys Damascus. Hand satin finish is standard. **Prices:** $100 to $1,500; swords to $8,000. **Remarks:** Part-time maker; first knife sold in 1984. **Mark:** Angel wings with last initial, or last name.

**SHOEMAKER, CARROLL,** 380 Yellowtown Rd., Northup, OH 45658, Phone: 740-446-6695
**Specialties:** Working/using straight knives of his design. **Patterns:** Hunters, utility/camp and early American backwoodsmen knives. **Technical:** Grinds ATS-34; forges old files, O1 and 1095. Uses some Damascus; offers scrimshaw and engraving. **Prices:** $100 to $175; some to $350. **Remarks:** Spare-time maker; first knife sold in 1977. **Mark:** Name and city or connected initials.

**SHOGER, MARK O.,** 14780 SW Osprey Dr., Suite 345, Beaverton, OR 97007, Phone: 503-579-2495
**Specialties:** Working and using straight knives and folders of his design; fancy and embellished knives. **Patterns:** Hunters, Bowies, daggers and locking folders. **Technical:** Forges O1, W2 and his own pattern-welded Damascus. **Remarks:** Spare-time maker. **Mark:** Last name or stamped last initial over anvil.

**SHORE, JOHN I.,** ALASKA KNIFEMAKER, 2901 Sheldon Jackson St., Anchorage, AK 99508, Phone: 907-272-2253, akknife@acsalaska.net Web: www.akknife.com
**Specialties:** Working straight knives, hatchets, and folders. **Patterns:** Hunters, skinners, Bowies, fighters, working using knives. **Technical:** Prefer using exotic steels, grinds most CPM's, Damasteel, RWL34, BG42, D2 and some ATS-34. Prefers exotic hardwoods, stabilized materials, Micarta, and Pearl. **Prices:** Start at $200. **Remarks:** Full-time maker; first knife sold in 1985. **Mark:** Name in script, Anchorage, AK.

**SHOSTLE, BEN,** 1121 Burlington, Muncie, IN 47302, Phone: 765-282-9073, Fax: 765-282-5270
**Specialties:** Fancy high-art straight knives of his design. **Patterns:** Bowies, daggers and fighters. **Technical:** Uses 440C, ATS-34 and commercial Damascus. All knives and engraved. **Prices:** $900 to $3,200; some to $4,000. **Remarks:** Full-time maker; first knife sold in 1987. Doing business as The Gun Room (T.G.R.). **Mark:** Last name.

**SIBRIAN, AARON,** 4308 Dean Dr., Ventura, CA 93003, Phone: 805-642-6950
**Specialties:** Tough working knives of his design and in standard patterns. **Patterns:** Makes a "Viper utility"—a kukri derivative and a variety of straight using knives. **Technical:** Grinds 440C and ATS-34. Offers traditional Japanese blades; soft backs, hard edges, temper lines. **Prices:** $60 to $100; some to $250. **Remarks:** Spare-time maker; first knife sold in 1989. **Mark:** Initials in diagonal line.

**SIGMAN, CORBET R.,** Rt. 1, Box 260, Liberty, WV 25124, Phone: 304-586-9131
**Specialties:** Collectible working straight knives and folders. **Patterns:** Hunters, fighters, boots, camp knives and exotics such as sgian dubhs—distinctly Sigman lines; folders. **Technical:** Grinds D2, 154CM, plain carbon tool steel and ATS-34. **Prices:** $60 to $800; some to $4,000. **Remarks:** Full-time maker; first knife sold in 1970. **Mark:** Name or initials.

**SIGMAN, JAMES P.,** 10391 Church Rd., North Adams, MI 49262, Phone: 517-523-3028
**Specialties:** High-tech working knives of his design. **Patterns:** Daggers, hunters, fighters and folders. **Technical:** Forges and grinds L6, O1, W2 and his Damascus. **Prices:** $150 to $750. **Remarks:** Part-time maker; first knife sold in 1982. **Mark:** Sig or Sig Forge.

**SIMMONS, H.R.,** 1100 Bay City Rd., Aurora, NC 27806, Phone: 252-322-5969
**Specialties:** Working/using straight knives of his design. **Patterns:** Fighters, hunters and utility/camp knives. **Technical:** Forges and grinds Damascus and L6; grinds ATS-34. **Prices:** $150 to $250; some to $400. **Remarks:** Part-time maker; first knife sold in 1987. Doing business as HRS Custom Knives, Royal Forge and Trading Company. **Mark:** Initials.

**SIMONELLA, GIANLUIGI,** 15, via Rosa Brustolo, 33085 Maniago, ITALY, Phone: 01139-427-730350
**Specialties:** Traditional and classic folding and working/using knives of his design and to customer specs. **Patterns:** Bowies, fighters, hunters, utility/camp knives. **Technical:** Forges ATS-34, D2, 440C. **Prices:** $250 to $400; some to $1,000. **Remarks:** Full-time maker; first knife sold in 1988. **Mark:** Wilson.

**SIMONS, BILL,** 6217 Michael Ln., Lakeland, FL 33811, Phone: 863-646-3783
**Specialties:** Working folders. **Patterns:** Locking folders, liner locks, hunters, slip joints most patterns; some straight camp knives. **Technical:** Grinds D2, ATS-34 and O1. **Prices:** Start at $100. **Remarks:** Full-time maker; first knife sold in 1970. **Mark:** Last name.

**SIMS, BOB,** PO Box 772, Meridian, TX 76665, Phone: 254-435-6240
**Specialties:** Traditional working straight knives and folders in standard patterns. **Patterns:** Locking folders, slip-joint folders and hunters. **Technical:** Grinds D2, ATS-34 and O1. Offers filework on some knives. **Prices:** $150 to $275; some to $600. **Remarks:** Full-time maker; first knife sold in 1975. **Mark** The division sign.

**SINCLAIR, J.E.,** 520 Francis Rd., Pittsburgh, PA 15239, Phone: 412-793-5778
**Specialties:** Fancy hunters and fighters, liner locking folders. **Patterns:** Figh ers, hunters and folders. **Technical:** Flat-grinds and hollow grind, prefer hand rubbed satin finish. Uses natural handle materials. **Prices:** $185 to $80 **Remarks:** Part-time maker; first knife sold in 1995. **Mark:** First and middle in tials, last name and maker.

**SINYARD, CLESTON S.,** 27522 Burkhardt Dr., Elberta, AL 36530, Phone: 334-987-1361, nimoforge1@gulftel.com Web: www.knifemakers guild
**Specialties:** Working straight knives and folders of his design. **Pattern** Hunters, buckskinners, Bowies, daggers, fighters and all-Damascus folder **Technical:** Makes Damascus from 440C, stainless steels, D2 and regul high-carbon steel; forges "forefinger pad" into hunters and skinners. **Prices:** Damascus $450 to $1,500; some $2,500. **Remarks:** Full-time maker; fir knife sold in 1980. Doing business as Nimo Forge. **Mark:** Last name, U.S.A. anvil.

**SISEMORE, CHARLES RUSSEL,** RR 2 Box 329AL, Mena, AR 71953, Phone: 918-383-1360

**SISKA, JIM,** 6 Highland Ave., Westfield, MA 01085, Phone: 413-568-9787, Fax: 413-568-6341
**Specialties:** Traditional working straight knives and folders. **Patterns:** Hur ers, fighters, Bowies and one-of-a-kinds; folders. **Technical:** Grinds D2 ar ATS-34; buys Damascus. Likes exotic woods. **Prices:** $195 to $2,50 **Remarks:** Part-time maker; first knife sold in 1983. **Mark:** Last name in O English.

**SJOSTRAND, KEVIN,** 1541 S. Cain St., Visalia, CA 93292, Phone: 20 625-5254
**Specialties:** Traditional and working/using straight knives and folders of h design or to customer specs. **Patterns:** Bowies, hunters, utility/camp knive lockback, springbuck and liner lock folders. **Technical:** Grinds ATS-34, 44 and 1095. Prefers high polished blades and full tang. Natural and stabiliz hardwoods, Micarta and stag handle material. **Prices:** $75 to $300. **Remark** Part-time maker; first knife sold in 1992. Doing business as Black Oak Blade **Mark:** Oak tree, Black Oak Blades, name, or just last name.

**SKIFF, STEVEN,** SKIFF MADE BLADES, PO Box 537, Broadalbin, NY 12025, Phone: 518-883-4875, skiffmadeblades@hotmail.com Web: www.skiffmadeblades.com
**Specialties:** Custom using/collector grade straight blades and liner lock fo ers of maker's design or customer specifications. **Patterns:** Hunters, utili camp knives - tactical/fancy art folders **Prices:** $180 to $395; and up. **Techn cal:** Stock removal hollow ground ATS-34, 154 CM, S30V, and tool ste Damascus-Devon Thomas, Robert Eggerling, Mike Norris and Delbert Ea Nickel silver and stainless in-house heat treating. Handle materials man ma and natural woods (stablilized). Horn shells sheaths for straight blades se own leather and uses sheaths by "Tree-Stump Leather". **Remarks:** First kn sold 1997. Started making folders in 2000. **Mark:** SKIFF on blade of straig blades and in inside of backspacer on folders.

**SKOW, H. A. "TEX",** TEX KNIVES, 3534 Gravel Springs Rd., Senatobia, MS 38668, Phone: 662-301-1568, texknives@bellsouth.net
**Specialties:** One-of-a-kind daggers, Bowies, boot knives and hunters. **Pa terns:** Different Damascus patterns (By Bob Eggerling). **Technical:** 440C, 60 Rockwell hardness. Engraving by Joe Mason. **Prices:** Negotiable. . **Ma** TEX.

**SLEE, FRED,** 9 John St., Morganville, NJ 07751, Phone: 908-591-904
**Specialties:** Working straight knives, some fancy, to customer specs. **P terns:** Hunters, fighters, boots, fancy daggers and folders. **Technical:** Grin D2, 440C and ATS-34. **Prices:** $285 to $1,100. **Remarks:** Part-time mak first knife sold in 1980. **Mark:** Last name in old English.

**SLOAN, SHANE,** 4226 FM 61, Newcastle, TX 76372, Phone: 940-846 3290
**Specialties:** Collector-grade straight knives and folders. **Patterns:** Us stainless Damascus, ATS-34 and 12-C-27. Bowies, lockers, slip-joints, fa folders, fighters and period pieces. **Technical:** Grinds D2 and ATS-34. Us hand-rubbed satin finish. Prefers rare natural handle materials. **Prices:** $2 to $6,500. **Remarks:** Full-time maker; first knife sold in 1985. **Mark:** Na and city.

**SLOBODIAN, SCOTT,** 4101 River Ridge Dr., PO Box 1498, San Andreas, CA 95249, Phone: 209-286-1980, Fax: 209-286-1982, scott@slobodianswords.com Web: www.slobodianswords.com
**Specialties:** Japanese-style knives and swords, period pieces, fantasy pie and miniatures. **Patterns:** Small kweikens, tantos, wakazashis, katanas, tr tional samurai swords. **Technical:** Flat-grinds 1050, commercial Damasc

**Prices:** $800 to $3,500; some to $7,500. **Remarks:** Full-time maker; first knife sold in 1987. **Mark:** Blade signed in Japanese characters and various scripts.

**SMALE, CHARLES J.,** 509 Grove Ave., Waukegan, IL 60085, Phone: 847-244-8013

**SMALL, ED,** Rt. 1, Box 178-A, Keyser, WV 26726, Phone: 304-298-4254
**Specialties:** Working knives of his design; period pieces. **Patterns:** Hunters, daggers, buckskinners and camp knives; likes one-of-a-kinds. **Technical:** Forges and grinds W2, L6 and his own Damascus. **Prices:** $150 to $1,500. **Remarks:** Full-time maker; first knife sold in 1978. Doing business as Iron Mountain Forge Works. **Mark:** Script initials connected.

**SMALLWOOD, WAYNE,** 146 Poplar Dr., Kalispell, MT 59901

**SMART, STEATEN,** 15815 Acorn Cir., Tavares, FL 32778, Phone: 352-343-8423

**SMART, STEVE,** 907 Park Row Cir., McKinney, TX 75070-3847, Phone: 214-837-4216, Fax: 214-837-4111
**Specialties:** Working/using straight knives and folders of his design, to customer specs and in standard patterns. **Patterns:** Bowies, hunters, kitchen knives, locking folders, utility/camp, fishing and bird knives. **Technical:** Grinds ATS-34, D2, 440C and O1. Prefers mirror polish or satin finish; hollow-grinds all blades. All knives come with sheath. Offers some filework. **Prices:** $95 to $225; some to $500. **Remarks:** Spare-time maker; first knife sold in 1983. **Mark:** Name, Custom, city and state in oval.

**SMIT, GLENN,** 627 Cindy Ct., Aberdeen, MD 21001, Phone: 410-272-2959, wolfsknife@msn.com
**Specialties:** Working and using straight and folding knives of his design or to customer specs. Customizes and repairs all types of cutlery. Exclusive maker of Dave Murphy Style knives. **Patterns:** Hunters, Bowies, daggers, fighters, utility/camp, folders, kitchen knives and miniatures, Murphy combat, C.H.A.I.K., Little 88 and Tiny 90-styles. **Technical:** Grinds 440C, ATS-34, O1, A2 also grinds 6AL4V titanium allox for blades. Reforges commercial Damascus and makes own Damascus, cast aluminum handles. **Prices:** Miniatures start at $30; full-size knives start at $50. **Remarks:** Spare-time maker; first knife sold in 1986. Doing business as Wolf's Knives. **Mark:** G.P. SMIT, with year on reverse side, Wolf's knives-Murphy's way with date.

**SMITH, D. NOEL,** 12018 NE Lonetree Ct., Poulsbo, WA 98370, Phone: 360-697-6992, blademan2@attbi.com
**Specialties:** Fantasy art knives of his own design or to standard patterns. **Patterns:** Daggers, hunters and art knives. **Technical:** Grinds O1, D2, 440C stainless and Damascus. Offers natural and synthetic carved handles, engraved and acid etched blades, sculptured guards, butt caps and bases. **Prices:** Start at $250. **Remarks:** Full-time maker; first knife sold in 1990. Doing business as Minds' Eye Metal master. **Mark:** Signature.

**SMITH, GREGORY H.,** 8607 Coddington Ct., Louisville, KY 40299, Phone: 502-491-7439
**Specialties:** Traditional working straight knives and fantasy knives to customer specs. **Patterns:** Fighters and modified Bowies; camp knives and swords. **Technical:** Grinds O1, 440C and commercial Damascus bars. **Prices:** $55 to $300. **Remarks:** Part-time maker; first knife sold in 1985. **Mark:** JAGED, plus signature.

**SMITH, J.D.,** 69 Highland, Roxbury, MA 02119, Phone: 617-989-0723, jdsmith02119@yahoo.com
**Specialties:** Fighters, Bowies, Persian, locking folders and swords. **Patterns:** Bowies, fighters and locking folders. **Technical:** Forges and grinds D2, his Damascus, O1, 52100 etc. and wootz-pattern hammer steel. **Prices:** $500 to $2,000; some to $5,000. **Remarks:** Full-time maker; first knife sold in 1987. Doing business as Hammersmith. **Mark:** Last initial alone or in cartouche.

**SMITH, JOSH,** Box 753, Frenchtown, MT 59834, Phone: 406-626-5775, josh@joshsmithknives.com Web: www.joshsmithknives.com
**Specialties:** Mosaic, Damascus, liner lock folders, automatics, bowies, fighters, etc. **Patterns:** All kinds. **Technical:** Advanced Mosaic and Damascus. **Prices:** $450 and up. **Mark:** JOSH. **Other:** A.B.S. Master Smith.

**SMITH, JOHN M.,** 3450 E Beguelin Rd., Centralia, IL 62801, Phone: 618-249-6444, Fax: 618-249-6444, jknife@accessus.net
**Specialties:** Traditional work knives, art knives. **Patterns:** daggers, Bowies, folders. **Technical:** Forges Damascus and hi-carbon. Also uses stainless. **Prices:** $250 to $2,500. **Remarks:** Full-time maker; first knife sold in 1980. **Mark:** Etched signature or logo.

**SMITH, JOHN W.,** 1322 Cow Branch Rd., West Liberty, KY 41472, Phone: 606-743-3599, jwsknive@mrtc.com; Web: www.jwsmith-knives.com
**Specialties:** Fancy and working locking folders of his design or to customer specs. **Patterns:** Interframes, traditional and daggers. **Technical:** Grinds 530V and his own Damascus. Offers gold inlay, engraving with gold inlay, hand-fitted mosaic pearl inlay and filework. Prefers hand-rubbed finish. Pearl and ivory available. **Prices:** Utility pieces $375 to $650. Art knives $1,200 to $10,000 **Remarks:** Full-time maker. **Mark:** Initials engraved inside diamond.

**SMITH, LENARD C.,** PO Box D68, Valley Cottage, NY 10989, Phone: 914-268-7359

**SMITH, MICHAEL J.,** 1418 Saddle Gold Ct., Brandon, FL 33511, Phone: 813-431-3790, smithknife@hotmail.com Web: www.smithknife.com
**Specialties:** Fancy high art folders of his design. **Patterns:** Locking locks and automatics. **Technical:** Uses ATS-34, non-stainless and stainless Damascus; hand carves folders, prefers ivory and pearl. Hand-rubbed satin finish. Liners are 6AL4V titanium. **Prices:** $500 to $3,000. **Remarks:** Full-time maker; first knife sold in 1989. **Mark:** Name, city, state.

**SMITH, NEWMAN L.,** 676 Glades Rd., Shop #3, Gatlinburg, TN 37738, Phone: 865-436-3322; thesmithshop@aol.com; Web: thesmithshop.com
**Specialties:** Collector-grade and working knives. **Patterns:** Hunters, slip-joint and lock-back folders, some miniatures. **Technical:** Grinds O1 and ATS-34; makes fancy sheaths. **Prices:** $165 to 750. **Remarks:** Full-time maker; first knife sold in 1984. Partners part-time to handle Damascus blades by Jeff Hurst; marks these with SH connected. **Mark:** First and middle initials, last name.

**SMITH, RAYMOND L.,** 217 Red Chalk Rd., Erin, NY 14838, Phone: 607-795-5257, Web: www.theanvilsedge.com
**Specialties:** Working/using straight knives and folders to customer specs and in standard patterns; period pieces. **Patterns:** Bowies, hunters, skip-joints. **Technical:** Forges 5160, 52100, 1018, 15N20, 1084 Damascus and wire cable Damascus. Filework. **Prices:** $100 to $1,500; estimates for custom orders. **Remarks:** Full-time maker; first knife sold in 1991. ABS Master Smith. Doing business as The Anvils Edge. **Mark:** Initials in script.

**SMITH, RICK,** BEAR BONE KNIVES, 1843 W Evans Creek Rd., Rogue River, OR 97537, Phone: 541-582-4144, BearBoneSmith@msn.com Web: www.bearbone.com
**Specialties:** Classic, historical-style Bowies for re-enactors and custom sheaths. **Patterns:** Historical-style Bowies, varied contemporary knife styles. **Technical:** Made by stock removal method; also forge weld tri-cable Damascus blades. Do own heat treating and tempering using an even heat digital kiln. Preferred steels are ATS-34, 154CM, 5160, D-2, 1095 and 01 tool and various carbon Damascus. **Prices:** $350 to $1,100. **Remarks:** Full-time maker since 1997 Now forging random pattern Damascus up to 600 layers. Discontinued using BG42 steel. Serial numbers now appear under log. Damascus knives are not given a serial number. Official business name is Bear Bone Knives. Stainless steel blades sent our for cryogenic "freeze treat."**Mark:** "Bear Bone" over initials "R S" (separated by downward arrow) on blade; initials R S (separated by downward arrow) within a 3/8" circle; 2 shooting stars and a Bowie. Serial numbers appear on ricasso area of blade unless otherwise requested.

**SMITH JR., JAMES B. "RED",** Rt. 2, Box 1525, Morven, GA 31638, Phone: 912-775-2844
**Specialties:** Folders. **Patterns:** Rotating rear-lock folders. **Technical:** Grinds ATS-34, D2 and Vascomax 350. **Prices:** Start at $350. **Remarks:** Full-time maker; first knife sold in 1985. **Mark:** GA RED in cowboy hat.

**SMOCK, TIMOTHY E.,** 1105 N Sherwood Dr., Marion, IN 46952, Phone: 765-664-0123

**SMOKER, RAY,** 113 Church Rd., Searcy, AR 72143, Phone: 501-796-2712
**Specialties:** Rugged, no nonsense working knives of his design only. **Patterns:** Hunters, skinners, utility/camp and flat-ground knives. **Technical:** Forges his own Damascus and 52100; makes sheaths. Uses improved multiple edge quench he developed. **Prices:** $450 and up; price includes sheath. **Remarks:** Semi-retired; first knife sold in 1992. **Mark:** Last name.

**SNARE, MICHAEL,** 3352 E. Mescal St., Phoenix, AZ 85028

**SNELL, JERRY L.,** 539 Turkey Trl, Fortson, GA 31808, Phone: 706-324-4922
**Specialties:** Working straight knives of his design and in standard patterns. **Patterns:** Hunters, boots, fighters, daggers and a few folders. **Technical:** Grinds 440C, ATS-34; buys Damascus. **Prices:** $175 to $1,000. **Remarks:** Part-time maker. **Mark:** Last name, or name, city and state.

**SNODY, MIKE,** 7169 Silk Hope Rd., Liberty, NC 27298, Phone: 888-393-9534, mnmsnody@juno.com
**Specialties:** High performance straight knives in traditional and Japanese-styles. **Patterns:** Skinners, hunters, tactical, Kwaiken andTantos. **Technical:** Grinds BG-42, ATS-34, 440C and A-2. Offers full or tapered tangs, upgraded handle materials such as fossil ivory, coral and exotic woods. Traditional diamond wrap over stingray on Japanese-style knives. Sheaths available in leather or Kydex. **Prices:** $100 to $1,000. **Remarks:** Part-time maker; first knife sold in 1999. **Mark:** Name over knife maker.

**SNOW, BILL,** 4824 18th Ave., Columbus, GA 31904, Phone: 706-576-4390, tipikw@knology.net
**Specialties:** Traditional working/using straight knives and folders of his design and to customer specs. Offers engraving and scrimshaw. **Patterns:** Bowies, fighters, hunters and folders. **Technical:** Grinds ATS-34, 440V, 440C, 420V, CPM350, BG42, A2, D2, 5160, 52100 and O1; forges if needed. Cryogenically quenches all steels; inlaid handles; some integrals; leather or Kydex sheaths. **Prices:** $125 to $700; some to $3,500. **Remarks:** Now also have 530V, 10V and 3V steels in use. Full-time maker; first knife sold in 1958. Doing business as Tipi Knife works. **Mark:** Old English scroll "S" inside a tipi.

**SNYDER, MICHAEL TOM,** PO Box 522, Zionsville, IN 46077-0522, Phone: 317-873-6807, wildcatcreek@indy.pr.com

**SOLOMON, MARVIN,** 23750 Cold Springs Rd., Paron, AR 72122, Phone: 501-821-3170, Fax: 501-821-6541, mardot@swbell.net Web: www.coldspringsforge.com
**Specialties:** Traditional working and using straight knives of his design and to customer specs also lock back 7 liner lock folders. **Patterns:** Single blade folders. **Technical:** Forges 5160, 1095, O1 and random Damascus. **Prices:** $125 to $1,000. **Remarks:** Part-time maker; first knife sold in 1990. Doing business as Cold Springs Forge. **Mark:** Last name.

**SONNTAG, DOUGLAS W.,** 906 N 39 ST, Nixa, MO 65714, Phone: 417-693-1640, Fax: 417-582-1392, dougsonntag@aol.com
**Specialties:** Working knives; art knives. **Patterns:** Hunters, boots, straight working knives; Bowies, some folders, camp/axe sets. **Technical:** Grinds D-2, ATS-34, forges own Damascus; does own heat treating. **Prices:** $225 and up. **Remarks:** Part-time maker; first knife sold in 1986. **Mark:** Etched name in arch.

**SONTHEIMER, G. DOUGLAS,** 12604 Bridgeton Dr., Potomac, MD 20854, Phone: 301-948-5227
**Specialties:** Fixed blade knives. **Patterns:** Whitetail deer, backpackers, camp, claws, filet, fighters. **Technical:** Hollow Grinds. **Price:** $500 and up. **Remarks:** Spare-time maker; first knife sold in 1976. **Mark:** LORD.

**SOPPERA, ARTHUR,** "Pilatusblick", Oberer Schmidberg, CH-9631 Ulisbach, SWITZERLAND, Phone: 71-988 23 27, Fax: 71-988 47 57, doublelock@hotmail.com Web: www.customknives.com/arthur.soppera
**Specialties:** High-art, high-tech knives of his design. **Patterns:** Mostly locking folders, some straight knives. **Technical:** Grinds ATS-34 and commercial Damascus. Folders have button lock of his own design; some are fancy folders in jeweler's fashion. Also makes jewelry with integrated small knives. **Prices:** $200 to $1,000; some $2,000 and higher. **Remarks:** Full-time maker; first knife sold in 1986. **Mark:** Stylized initials, name, country.

**SORNBERGER, JIM,** 25126 Overland Dr., Volcano, CA 95689, Phone: 209-295-7819
**Specialties:** Classic San Francisco-style knives. Collectible straight knives. **Patterns:** Forges 1095-1084/15W2. Makes own Damascus and powder metal. Fighters, daggers, Bowies; miniatures; hunters, custom canes, liner locks folders. **Technical:** Grinds 440C, 154CM and ATS-34; engraves, carves and embellishes. **Prices:** $500 to $20,000 in gold with gold quartz inlays. **Remarks:** Full-time maker; first knife sold in 1970. **Mark:** First initial, last name, city and state.

**SOWELL, BILL,** 100 Loraine Forest Ct., Macon, GA 31210, Phone: 478-994-9863, billsowell@reynoldscable.net
**Specialties:** Antique reproduction Bowies, forging Bowies, hunters, fighters, and most others. Also folders. **Technical:** Makes own Damascus, using 1084/15N20, also making own designs in powder metals, forges 5160-1095-1084, and other carbon steels, grinds ATS-34. **Prices:** Starting at $150 and up. **Remarks:** Part-time maker. Sold first knife in 1998. **Mark:** Iron Horse Knives; Iron Horse Forge. **Other:** Does own leather work.

**SPARKS, BERNARD,** PO Box 73, Dingle, ID 83233, Phone: 208-847-1883, dogknifeii@juno.com Web: www.sparksknives.com
**Specialties:** Maker engraved, working and art knives. Straight knives and folders of his own design. **Patterns:** Locking inner-frame folders, hunters, fighters, one-of-a-kind art knives. **Technical:** Grinds 530V steel, 440-C, 154CM, ATS-34, D-2 and forges by special order; triple temper, cryogenic soak. Mirror or hand finish. New Liquid metal steel. **Prices:** $300 to $2,000. **Remarks:** Full-time maker, first knife sold in 1967. **Mark:** Last name over state with a knife logo on each end of name. Prior 1980, stamp of last name.

**SPENCER, KEITH,** PO Box 149, Chidlow WA, Western Australia 6556, Phone: 61 8 95727255, Fax: 61 8 95727266, spencer@knivesaustralia.com.au
**Specialties:** Survival & bushcraft bladeware. **Patterns:** Best known for Kakadu Bushcraft knife (since 1989). Lekira mini survival knife. (since 1993). **Prices:** $100 to $400 AV. **Mark:** Spencer Australia.

**SPICKLER, GREGORY NOBLE,** 5614 Mose Cir., Sharpsburg, MD 21782, Phone: 301-432-2746

**SPINALE, RICHARD,** 4021 Canterbury Ct., Lorain, OH 44053, Phone: 440-282-1565
**Specialties:** High-art working knives of his design. **Patterns:** Hunters, figh ers, daggers and locking folders. **Technical:** Grinds 440C, ATS-34 and C engraves. Offers gold bolsters and other deluxe treatments. **Prices:** $300 $1,000; some to $3,000. **Remarks:** Spare-time maker; first knife sold in 197 **Mark:** Name, address, year and model number.

**SPIVEY, JEFFERSON,** 9244 W. Wilshire, Yukon, OK 73099, Phone: 405-721-4442
**Specialties:** The Saber tooth: a combination hatchet, saw and knife. **Pa terns:** Built for the wilderness, all are one-of-a-kind. **Technical:** Grin chromemoly steel. The saw tooth spine curves with a double row of biangu teeth. **Prices:** Start at $300. **Remarks:** First knife sold in 1977. The abo Saber tooth knives are no longer in production as of Jan 1 2004. **Mark:** Nar and serial number.

**SPRAGG, WAYNE E.,** 252 Oregon Ave, 1314 3675 East Rd., Lovell, W 82431, Phone: 307-548-7212
**Specialties:** Working straight knives, some fancy. **Patterns:** Folders. **Techni cal:** Forges carbon steel and makes Damascus. **Prices:** $110 to $400; sor higher. **Remarks:** All stainless heat-treated by Paul Bos. Carbon steel in sh heat treat. **Mark:** Name, city and state with bucking horse logo.

**SPROKHOLT (GATHERWOOD), ROB,** Werkendelslaan 108, 1851VE Heiloo, Nederland, Europe, Phone: 0031-72-5336097, buckx@gatherwood.nl Web: www.gatherwood.nl
**Specialties:** One-of-a-kind stiff knives. Top materials collector grade made use. Oiled realwood handles, intarsia mostly wood. Characteristic one row massive silver pins or tubes. **Patterns:** Outdoor knives (hunting, sailing, h ing), Bowies, Mans Surviving Companions MSC, big tantos. **Technic** Stockremoval grinder; flat, hollow or confex steel; 440, RWL-34, ATS-34 po der steel Damascener, D-2, stiff knives, mostly full tang, home made mokun gane. **Prices:** Starts at Euro 260. **Remarks:** Part-time knifemaker. Writer first Dutch knifemaking book. **Mark:** Gatherwood in an elipse etched in blade or stamped in an intarsia of silver in the spine. **Other:** Wife is his worker and goldsmith. Do everything themselves. Supply shop for knife ent siastics. First knife sold in 2000.

**SPROUSE, TERRY,** 1633 Newfound Rd., Asheville, NC 28806, Phone 704-683-3400
**Specialties:** Traditional and working straight knives of his design. **Patter** Bowies and hunters. **Technical:** Grinds ATS-34, 440C and D2. Mak sheaths. **Prices:** $85 to $125; some to $225. **Remarks:** Part-time maker; knife sold in 1989. **Mark:** NA.

**ST. AMOUR, MURRAY,** RR 3, 222 Dicks Rd., Pembroke ON, CANAD K8A 6W4, Phone: 613-735-1061, knives@webhart.net Web: www.web hart.net/knives
**Specialties:** Working fixed blades. **Patterns:** Hunters, fish, fighters, Bow and utility knives. **Technical:** Grinds ATS-34, 154-CM, CPM-440V and Da ascus. **Prices:** $75 and up. **Remarks:** Full-time maker; sold first knife in 19 **Mark:** Last name over Canada.

**ST. CLAIR, THOMAS K.,** 12608 Fingerboard Rd., Monrovia, MD 217 Phone: 301-482-0264

**ST. CYR, H. RED,** 1218 N Cary Ave., Wilmington, CA 90744, Phone: 310-518-9525

**STAFFORD, RICHARD,** 104 Marcia Ct., Warner Robins, GA 31088, Phone: 912-923-6372
**Specialties:** High-tech straight knives and some folders. **Patterns:** Hunter several patterns, fighters, boots, camp knives, combat knives and pe pieces. **Technical:** Grinds ATS-34 and 440C; satin finish is standard. **Pric** Starting at $75. **Remarks:** Part-time maker; first knife sold in 1983. **Mark:** L name.

**STALCUP, EDDIE,** PO Box 2200, Gallup, New Mexico 87305, Phone 505-863-3107, sstalcup@cnetco.com
**Specialties:** Working and fancy hunters, bird and trout. Special cus orders. **Patterns:** Drop point hunters, locking liner and multi blade fold **Technical:** ATS-34, 154 CM and 440C. **Prices:** $150 to $500. **Mark:** Stalcup, Gallup, NM. **Other:** Scrimshaw, Exotic handle material, wet forr sheaths. Membership Arizona Knife Collectors Association.

**STANCER, CHUCK,** 62 Hidden Ranch Rd. NW, Calgary AB, CANAD T3A 5S5, Phone: 403-295-7370, stancere@teluspianet.net
**Specialties:** Traditional and working straight knives. **Patterns:** Bowies, h ers and utility knives. **Technical:** Forges and grinds most steels. **Prices:** $ and up. **Remarks:** Part-time maker. **Mark:** Last name.

**STANLEY, JOHN,** 604 Elm St., Crossett, AR 71635, Phone: 970-304-3005
**Specialties:** Hand forged fixed blades with engraving and carving. **Patterns:** Scottish dirks, skeans and fantasy blades. **Technical:** Forge high-carbon steel, own Damascus. Prices $70 to $500. **Remarks:** All work is sole authorship. **Mark:** Varies. **Other:** Offer engraving and carving services on other knives and handles.

**STAPEL, CHUCK,** Box 1617, Glendale, CA 91209, Phone: 213-66-KNIFE, Fax: 213-669-1577, www.stapelknives.com
**Specialties:** Working knives of his design. **Patterns:** Variety of straight knives tantos, hunters, folders and utility knives. **Technical:** Grinds D2, 440C and AEB-L. **Prices:** $185 to $12,000. **Remarks:** Full-time maker; first knife sold in 1974. **Mark:** Last name or last name, U.S.A.

**STAPLETON, WILLIAM E.,** BUFFALO 'B' FORGE, 5425 Country Ln., Merritt Island, FL 32953
**Specialties:** Classic and traditional knives of his design and customer spec. **Patterns:** Hunters and using knives. **Technical:** Forges, 01 and L-6 Damascus, cable Damascus and 5160; stock removal on request. **Prices:** $150 to $1,000. **Remarks:** Part-time maker, first knife sold 1990. Doing business as Buffalo "B" Forge. **Mark:** Anvil with S initial in center of anvil.

**STAPLETON, WILLIAM E.,** 5425 Country Ln., Merritt Island, FL 32953, Phone: 407-452-8946, staplewe@brevard.net

**STECK, VAN R.,** 260 W Dogwood Ave., Orange City, FL 32763, Phone: 386-775-7303
**Specialties:** Frame lock folders with my own lock design. Fighters, hunting & fillet, spike hawks and Asian influence on swords, sickles, spears, also traditional bowies. **Technical:** Stock removal ATS-34, D-2, forges 5160, 1050 & 1084. **Prices:** $75 to $750. **Remarks:** Free hand grinds, distal taper, hollow and chisel. Specialize in filework and Japanese handle wrapping. **Mark:** GEISHA with sword & my initials and T.H.U.D. knives

**STEFFAN, ALBERT,** U Lucenecka 434/4, Filakovo 98604, Slovak Rebublic, svidi@naex.sk
**Specialties:**Art Knives, miniatures, Scrimshaw. **Prices:** From USD $300 to USD $2,000. **Mark:** A.

**STEFFEN, CHUCK,** 504 Dogwood Ave. NW, St. Michael, MN, Phone: 763-497-3615
**Specialties:** Custom hunting knives, fixed blades folders. Specializing in exotic materials. Damascus excellent fit form and finishes.

**STEGALL, KEITH,** 2101 W. 32nd, Anchorage, AK 99517, Phone: 907-276-6002
**Specialties:** Traditional working straight knives. **Patterns:** Most patterns. **Technical:** Grinds 440C and 154CM. **Prices:** $100 to $300. **Remarks:** Spare-time maker; first knife sold in 1987. **Mark:** Name and state with anchor.

**STEGNER, WILBUR G.,** 9242 173rd Ave. SW, Rochester, WA 98579, Phone: 360-273-0937, stegner@myhome.net, Web: landru.myhome.net/stegner/
**Specialties:** Working/using straight knives and folders of his design. **Patterns:** Hunters and locking folders. **Technical:** Grinds ATS-34 and other tool steels. Quenches, tempers and hardness tests each blade. **Prices:** $100 to $1,000; some to $5,000. **Remarks:** Full-time maker; first knife sold in 1979. **Other:** Google search key words-"STEGNER KNIVES". **Mark:** First and middle initials, last name in bar over shield logo.

**STEIGER, MONTE L.,** Box 186, Genesee, ID 83832, Phone: 208-285-1769
**Specialties:** Traditional working/using straight knives of all designs. **Patterns:** Hunters, utility/camp knives, filet and chefs. **Technical:** Grinds 1095, O1, 440C, ATS-34. Handles of stacked leather, natural wood, Micarta or Pakkawood. Each knife comes with right- or left-handed sheath. **Prices:** $70 to $220. **Remarks:** Spare-time maker; first knife sold in 1988. **Mark:** First initial, last name, city and state.

**STEIGERWALT, KEN,** 507 Savagehill Rd, Orangeville, PA 17859, Phone: 570-683-5156, Web: www.steigerwaltknives.com
**Specialties:** Carving on bolsters and handle material. **Patterns:** Folders, button locks and rear locks. **Technical:** Grinds ATS-34, 440C and commercial Damascus. Experiments with unique filework. **Prices:** $500 to $5,000. **Remarks:** Full-time maker; first knife sold in 1981. **Mark:** Kasteigerwalt

**STEINAU, JURGEN,** Julius-Hart Strasse 44, Berlin 0-1162, GERMANY, Phone: 372-6452512, Fax: 372-645-2512
**Specialties:** Fantasy and high-art straight knives of his design. **Patterns:** Boots, daggers and switch-blade folders. **Technical:** Grinds 440B, 2379 and 4190 Cr.Mo.V. 78. **Prices:** $1,500 to $2,500; some to $3,500. **Remarks:** Full-time maker; first knife sold in 1984. **Mark:** Symbol, plus year, month day and serial number.

**STEINBERG, AL,** 5244 Duenas, Laguna Woods, CA 92653, Phone: 949-951-2889, lagknife@fsa.net
**Specialties:** Fancy working straight knives to customer specs. **Patterns:** Hunters, Bowies, fishing, camp knives, push knives and high end kitchen knives. **Technical:** Grinds O1, 440C and 154CM. **Prices:** $60 to $2,500. **Remarks:** Full-time maker; first knife sold in 1972. **Mark:** Signature, city and state.

**STEINBRECHER, MARK W.,** 4725 Locust Ave., Glenview, IL 60025, Phone: 847-298-5721
**Specialties:** Working and fancy folders. **Patterns:** Daggers, pocket knives, fighters and gents of his own design or to customer specs. **Technical:** Hollow grinds ATS-34, O-1 other makers Damascus. Uses natural handle materials: stag, ivories, mother-of-pearl. File work and some inlays. **Prices:** $500 to $1,200; some to $2,500. **Remarks:** Part-time maker, first folder sold in 1989. **Mark:** Name etched or handwritten on ATS-34; stamped on Damascus.

**STEKETEE, CRAIG A.,** 871 N. Hwy. 60, Billings, MO 65610, Phone: 417-744-2770, stekknives@earthlink.net
**Specialties:** Classic and working straight knives and swords of his design. **Patterns:** Bowies, hunters, and Japanese-style swords. **Technical:** Forges his own Damascus; bronze, silver and Damascus fittings, offers filework. Prefers exotic and natural handle materials. **Prices:** $200 to $4,000. **Remarks:** Full-time maker. **Mark:** STEK.

**STEPHAN, DANIEL,** 2201 S. Miller Rd., Valrico, FL 33594, Phone: 813-684-2781

**STERLING, MURRAY,** 693 Round Peak Church Rd., Mount Airy, NC 27030, Phone: 336-352-5110, Fax: Fax: 336-352-5105, sterck@surry.net; Web: www.sterlingcustomknives.com
**Specialties:** Single and dual blade folders. Interframes and integral dovetail frames. **Technical:** Grinds ATS-34 or Damascus by Mike Norris and/or Devin Thomas. **Prices:** $300 and up. **Remarks:** Full-time maker; first knife sold in 1991. **Mark:** Last name stamped.

**STEWART, EDWARD L.,** 4297 Audrain Rd. 335, Mexico, MO 65265, Phone: 573-581-3883
**Specialties:** Fixed blades, working knives some art. **Patterns:** Hunters, Bowies, Utility/camp knives. **Technical:** Forging 1095-W-2-I-6-52100 makes own Damascus. **Prices:** $85 to $500. **Remarks:** Part-time maker first knife sold in 1993. **Mark:** First and last initials-last name.

**STIMPS, JASON M.,** 374 S Shaffer St., Orange, CA 92866, Phone: 714-744-5866

**STIPES, DWIGHT,** 2651 SW Buena Vista Dr., Palm City, FL 34990, Phone: 772-597-0550, dwightstipes@adelphia.net
**Specialties:** Traditional and working straight knives in standard patterns. **Patterns:** Boots, Bowies, daggers, hunters and fighters. **Technical:** Grinds 440C, D2 and D3 tool steel. Handles of natural materials, animal, bone or horn. **Prices:** $75 to $150. **Remarks:** Full-time maker; first knife sold in 1972. **Mark:** Stipes.

**STOCKWELL, WALTER,** 368 San Carlos Ave., Redwood City, CA 94061, Phone: 650-363-6069, walter@stockwellknives.com Web: www.stockwellknives.com
**Specialties:** Scottish dirks,sgian dubhs. **Patterns:** All knives one-of-a-kind. **Technical:** Grinds ATS-34, forges 5160, 52100, L6. **Prices:** $125 to $500. **Remarks:** Part-time maker since 1992; graduate of ABS bladesmithing school. **Mark:** Shooting star over "STOCKWELL". Pre-2000, "WKS".

**STODDARD'S, INC., COPLEY PLACE,** 100 Huntington Ave., Boston, MA 02116, Phone: 617-536-8688, Fax: 617-536-8689
**Specialties:** Cutlery (kitchen, pocket knives, Randall-made Knives, custom knives, scissors, and manicure tools), binoculars, low vision aids, personal care items (hair brushes, manicure sets, mirrors).

**STODDART, W.B. BILL,** 917 Smiley, Forest Park, OH 45240, Phone: 513-851-1543
**Specialties:** Sportsmen's working knives and multi-blade folders. **Patterns:** Hunters, camp and fish knives; multi-blade reproductions of old standards. **Technical:** Grinds A2, 440C and ATS-34; makes sheaths to match handle materials. **Prices:** $80 to $300; some to $850. **Remarks:** Part-time maker; first knife sold in 1976. **Mark:** Name, Cincinnati, state.

**STOKES, ED,** 22614 Cardinal Dr., Hockley, TX 77447, Phone: 713-351-1319
**Specialties:** Working straight knives and folders of all designs. **Patterns:** Boots, Bowies, daggers, fighters, hunters and miniatures. **Technical:** Grinds ATS-34, 440C and D2. Offers decorative butt caps, tapered spacers on handles and finger grooves, nickel-silver inlays, hand-made sheaths. **Prices:** $185 to $290; some to $350. **Remarks:** Full-time maker; first knife sold in 1973. **Mark:** First and last name, Custom Knives with Apache logo.

**STONE, JERRY,** PO Box 1027, Lytle, TX 78052, Phone: 512-772-4502
**Specialties:** Traditional working and using folders of his design and to customer specs; fancy knives. **Patterns:** Fighters, hunters, locking folders and slip-joints. **Technical:** Grinds 440C and ATS-34. Offers filework. **Prices:** $125 to $375; some to $700. **Remarks:** Full-time maker; first knife sold in 1973. **Mark:** Initials.

**STORCH, ED,** R.R. 4 Mannville, Alberta T0B 2W0, CANADA, Phone: 780-763-2214, storchkn@agt.net Web: www.storchknives.com
**Specialties:** Working knives, fancy fighting knives, kitchen cutlery and art knives. Knifemaking classes. **Patterns:** Working patterns, Bowies and folders. **Technical:** Forges his own Damascus. Grinds ATS-34. Builds friction folders. Salt heat treating. **Prices:** $45 to $750 (U.S.). **Remarks:** Part-time maker; first knife sold in 1984. Hosts annual northwest canadian knifemakers symposium 60 to 80 knife makers and families. **Mark:** Last name.

**STORMER, BOB,** 10 Karabair Rd., St. Peters, MO 63376, Phone: 636-441-6807, bobstormer@sbcglobal.net
**Specialties:** Straight knives - Using collector grade. **Patterns:** Bowies, skinners, hunters, camp knives. **Technical:** Forges 5160, 1095. **Prices:** $150 to $400. **Remarks:** Part-time maker ABS JourneymanSmith 2001. **Mark:** Setting Sun/Fall trees/Initials.

**STOUT, CHARLES,** RT3 178 Stout Rd., Gillham, AR 71841, Phone: 870-386-5521

**STOUT, JOHNNY,** 1205 Forest Trail, New Braunfels, TX 78132, Phone: 830-606-4067, johnny@stoutknives.com Web: www.stoutknives.com
**Specialties:** Folders, some fixed blades. Working knives, some fancy. **Patterns:** Hunters, tactical, Bowies, automatics, liner locks and slip-joints. **Technical:** Grinds stainless and carbon steels; forges own Damascus. **Prices:** $450 to $895; some to $3,500. **Remarks:** Full-time maker; first knife sold in 1983. **Mark:** Name and city in logo with serial number. **Other:** Hosts semi-annual Guadalupe forge hammer-in and knifemakers rendezvous.

**STOVER, HOWARD,** 100 Palmetto Dr. Apt. 7, Pasadena, CA 91105, Phone: 765-452-3928

**STOVER, TERRY "LEE",** 1809 N. 300 E., Kokomo, IN 46901, Phone: 765-452-3928
**Specialties:** Damascus folders with filework; Damascus Bowies of his design or to customer specs. **Patterns:** Lockback folders and Sheffield-style Bowies. **Technical:** Forges 1095, Damascus using O2, 203E or O2, pure nickel. Makes mokume. Uses only natural handle material. **Prices:** $300 to $1,700; some to $2,000. **Remarks:** Part-time maker; first knife sold in 1984. **Mark:** First and middle initials, last name in knife logo; Damascus blades marked in Old English.

**STRAIGHT, DON,** PO Box 12, Points, WV 25437, Phone: 304-492-5471
**Specialties:** Traditional working straight knives of his design. **Patterns:** Hunters, Bowies and fighters. **Technical:** Grinds 440C, ATS-34 and D2. **Prices:** $75 to $125; some to $225. **Remarks:** Spare-time maker; first knife sold in 1978. **Mark:** Last name.

**STRAIGHT, KENNETH J.,** 11311 103 Lane N., Largo, FL 33773, Phone: 813-397-9817

**STRANDE, POUL,** Soster Svenstrup Byvej 16, Dastrup 4130 Viby Sj., DENMARK, Phone: 46 19 43 05, Fax: 46 19 53 19, Web: www.poul-strande.com
**Specialties:** Classic fantasy working knives; Damasceret blade, Nikkel Damasceret blade, Lamineret - Lamineret blade with Nikkel. **Patterns:** Bowies, daggers, fighters, hunters and swords. **Technical:** Uses carbon steel and 15C20 steel. **Prices:** NA. **Remarks:** Full-time maker; first knife sold in 1985. **Mark:** First and last initials.

**STRICKLAND, DALE,** 1440 E. Thompson View, Monroe, UT 84754, Phone: 435-896-8362
**Specialties:** Traditional and working straight knives and folders of his design and to customer specs. **Patterns:** Hunters, folders, miniatures and utility knives. **Technical:** Grinds Damascus and 440C. **Prices:** $120 to $350; some to $500. **Remarks:** Part-time maker; first knife sold in 1991. **Mark:** Oval stamp of name, Maker.

**STRIDER, MICK,** STRIDER KNIVES, 120 N Pacific Unit L-7, San Marcos, CA 92069, Phone: 760-471-8275, Fax: 503-218-7069, striderguys@striderknives.com Web: www.striderknives.com

**STRONG, SCOTT,** 2138 Oxmoor Dr., Beavercreek, OH 45431, Phone: 937-426-9290
**Specialties:** Working knives, some deluxe. **Patterns:** Hunters, fighters, survival and military-style knives, art knives. **Technical:** Forges and grinds O1, A2, D2, 440C and ATS-34. Uses no solder; most knives disassemble. **Prices:** $75 to $450; some to $1,500. **Remarks:** Spare-time maker; first knife sold in 1983. **Mark:** Strong Knives.

**STROYAN, ERIC,** Box 218, Dalton, PA 18414, Phone: 717-563-2603
**Specialties:** Classic and working/using straight knives and folders of h design. **Patterns:** Hunters, locking folders, slip-joints. **Technical:** Forg Damascus; grinds ATS-34, D2. **Prices:** $200 to $600; some to $2,00 **Remarks:** Part-time maker; first knife sold in 1968. **Mark:** Signature or initia stamp.

**STUART, STEVE,** Box 168, Gores Landing, Ont., CANADA K0K 2E0, Phone: 905-342-5617
**Specialties:** Straight knives. **Patterns:** Tantos, fighters, skinners, file a rasp knives. **Technical:** Uses 440C, files, Micarta and natural handle mate als. **Prices:** $60 to $400. **Remarks:** Part-time maker. **Mark:** Interlocking S with last name.

**STYREFORS, MATTIAS,** Unbyn 23, SE-96193 Boden, SWEDEN, infor@styrefors.com
**Specialties:** Damascus and mosaic Damascus. Fixed blade Nordic hunte folders and swords. **Technical:** Forges, shapes and grinds Damascus a mosaic Damascus from mostly UHB 15N20 and 20C with contrasts in nick and 15N20. Hardness HR 58. **Prices:** $800 to $3,000. **Remarks:** Fulltin maker since 1999. International reputation for high end Damascus blade Uses stabilized Arctic birch and willow burl, horn, fossils, exotic materials, a scrimshaw by Viveca Sahlin for knife handles. Hand tools and hand stitch leather sheaths in cow raw hide. Works in well equipped former military fo ery in northern Sweden. **Mark:** MS.

**SUEDMEIER, HARLAN,** 754 N 60th Rd, Nebraska City, NE 68410, Phone: 402-873-4372
**Patterns:**Straigt knives.**Technical:** Forging hi carbon Damascus. **Price** Starting at $175. **Remarks:** Does not take orders. **Mark:** First initials & la name.

**SUGIHARA, KEIDOH,** 4-16-1 Kamori-Cho, Kishiwada City, Osaka, F596-0042, JAPAN, Fax: 0724-44-2677
**Specialties:** High-tech working straight knives and folders of his design. **Pa terns:** Bowies, hunters, fighters, fishing, boots, some pocket knives and lin lock folders. **Technical:** Grinds ATS-34, COS-25, buys Damascus and hig carbon steels. Prices $60 to $4,000. **Remarks:** Full-time maker, first knife s in 1980. **Mark:** Initial logo with fish design.

**SUGIYAMA, EDDY K.,** 2361 Nagayu, Naoirimachi Naoirigun, Ohita, JAPAN, Phone: 0974-75-2050
**Specialties:** One of kind, exotic-style knives. **Patterns:** Working, utility a miniatures. **Technical:** CT rind, ATS-34 and D2. **Prices:** $400 to $1,2 **Remarks:** Full-time maker. **Mark:** Name or cedar mark.

**SUMMERS, ARTHUR L.,** 1310 Hess Rd., Concord, NC 28025, Phone 704-795-2863, arthursummers88@hotmail.com
**Specialties:** Collector-grade knives in drop points, clip points or strai blades. **Patterns:** Fighters, hunters, Bowies and personal knives. **Technic** Grinds 440C, ATS-34, D2 and Damascus. **Prices:** $150 to $650; some $2,000. **Remarks:** Full-time maker; first knife sold in 1987. **Mark:** Last na and serial number.

**SUMMERS, DAN,** 2675 NY Rt. 11, Whitney Pt., NY 13862, Phone: 60 692-2391, dansumm11@msn.com
**Specialties:** Period knives and tomahawks. **Technical:** All hand forgi **Prices:** Most $100 to $400.

**SUMMERS, DENNIS K.,** 827 E. Cecil St., Springfield, OH 45503, Phor 513-324-0624
**Specialties:** Working/using knives. **Patterns:** Fighters and personal kniv **Technical:** Grinds 440C, A2 and D2. Makes drop and clip point. **Prices:** $ to $200. **Remarks:** Part-time maker; first knife sold in 1995. **Mark:** First a middle initials, last name, serial number.

**SUNDERLAND, RICHARD,** Av Infraganti 23, Col Lazaro Cardenas, Puerto Escondido Oaxaca, Mexico 71980, Phone: 011 52 94 582 145 sunamerica@prodigy.net.mx7
**Specialties:** Personal and hunting knives with carved handles in oosic ivory. **Patterns:** Hunters, Bowies, daggers, camp and personal knives. **Te nical:** Grinds 440C, ATS-34 and O1. Handle materials of rosewoods, fo mammoth ivory and oosic. **Prices:** $150 to $1,000. **Remarks:** Part-t maker; first knife sold in 1983. Doing business as Sun Knife Co. **Mark:** SU

**SUTTON, S. RUSSELL,** 4900 Cypress Shores Dr., New Bern, NC 28562, Phone: 252-637-3963, srsutton@cox.net Web: www.suttoncus tomknives.com
**Specialties:** Straight knives and folders to customer specs and in stanc patterns. **Patterns:** Boots, hunters, interframes, slip joints and locking lin **Technical:** Grinds ATS-34, 440C and stainless Damascus. **Prices:** $18 $650; some to $950. **Remarks:** Full-time maker; first knife sold in 1992. **M** Etched last name.

**SWEAZA, DENNIS,** 4052 Hwy 321 E, Austin, AR 72007, Phone: 501-941-1886, knives4den@aol.com

**SWEDER, JORAM,** TILARU METALSMITHING, PO Box 4175, Ocala, FL 34470, Phone: 352-546-4438, tilaru@tilaru.com Web: www.tilaru.com **Specialties:** Hand forged one-of-a-kind and custom pieces. **Prices:** $100 and up.

**SWEENEY, COLTIN D.,** 1216 S 3 St. W, Missoula, MT 59801, Phone: 406-721-6782

**SWYHART, ART,** 509 Main St., PO Box 267, Klickitat, WA 98628, Phone: 509-369-3451, swyhart@gorge.net, Web: www.knifeoutlet.com/swyhart.htm **Specialties:** Traditional working and using knives of his design. **Patterns:** Bowies, hunters and utility/camp knives. **Technical:** Forges 52100, 5160 and Damascus 1084 mixed with either 15N20 or 0186. Blades differentially heat-treated with visible temper line. **Prices:** $75 to $250; some to $350. **Remarks:** Part-time maker; first knife sold in 1983. **Mark:** First name, last initial in script.

**SYMONDS, ALBERTO E.,** Rambla M Gandhi 485, Apt 901, Montevideo 11300, URUGUAY, Phone: 011 598 5608207, Fax: 011 598 2 7103201, albertosymonds@hotmail.com **Specialties:** All sorts-including puukos, nice sheaths, leather and wood. **Prices:** $140 to $900. **Mark:** AESH and year (2005).

**SYSLO, CHUCK,** 3418 South 116 Ave., Omaha, NE 68144, Phone: 402-333-0647, ciscoknives@cox.net **Specialties:** Hunters, working knives, daggers & misc. **Patterns:** Hunters, daggers and survival knives; locking folders. **Technical:** Flat-grinds D2, 440C and 154CM; hand polishes only. **Prices:** $250 to $1,000; some to $3,000. **Remarks:** Part-time maker; first knife sold in 1978. Uses many matural materials. **Mark:** CISCO in logo.

**SZAREK, MARK G.,** 94 Oakwood Ave., Revere, MA 02151, Phone: 781-289-7102 **Specialties:** Classic period working and using straight knives and tools. **Patterns:** Hunting knives, American and Japanese woodworking tools. **Technical:** Forges 5160, 1050, Damascus; differentially hardens blades with fireclay. **Prices:** $50 to $750. **Remarks:** Part-time maker; first knife sold in 1989. **Mark:** Last name. **Other:** Produces Japanese alloys for sword fittings and accessories. Custom builds knife presentation boxes and cabinets.

**SZILASKI, JOSEPH,** 29 Carroll Dr., Wappingers Falls, NY 12590, Phone: 845-297-5397, Web: www.szilaski.com **Specialties:** Straight knives, folders and tomahawks of his design, to customer specs and in standard patterns. Many pieces are one-of-a-kind. **Patterns:** Bowies, daggers, fighters, hunters, art knives and early American-styles. **Technical:** Forges A2, D2, O1 and Damascus. **Prices:** $450 to $4,000; some to $10,000. **Remarks:** Full-time maker; first knife sold in 1990. **Mark:** Snake logo. **Other:** ABS Master Smith and voting member KMG.

## T

**TAKAHASHI, KAORU,** 2506 TOYO OKA YADO UEKI, Kamoto Kumamoto, JAPAN 861-01, Phone: (8196) 272-6759

**TAKAHASHI, MASAO,** 39-3 Sekine-machi, Maebashi-shi, Gunma 371 0047, JAPAN, Phone: 81 27 234 2223, Fax: 81 27 234 2223 **Specialties:** Working straight knives. **Patterns:** Daggers, fighters, hunters, fishing knives, boots. **Technical:** Grinds ATS-34 and Damascus. **Prices:** $350 to $1,000 and up. **Remarks:** Full-time maker; first knife sold in 1982. **Mark:** M. Takahashi.

**TALLY, GRANT,** 26961 James Ave., Flat Rock, MI 48134, Phone: 734-789-8961 **Specialties:** Straight knives and folders of his design. **Patterns:** Bowies, daggers, fighters. **Technical:** Grinds ATS-34, 440C and D2. Offers filework. **Prices:** $250 to $1,000. **Remarks:** Part-time maker; first knife sold in 1985. Doing business as Tally Knives. **Mark:** Tally (last name).

**TAMBOLI, MICHAEL,** 12447 N. 49 Ave., Glendale, AZ 85304, Phone: 602-978-4308 **Specialties:** Miniatures, some full size. **Patterns:** Miniature hunting knives to fantasy art knives. **Technical:** Grinds ATS-34. **Prices:** $75 to $500; some to $1,000. **Remarks:** Part-time maker; first knife sold in 1978. **Mark:** Initials or last name, city and state, also M.T. Custom Knives.

**TASMAN, KERLEY,** 9 Avignon Retreat, Pt. Kennedy, 6172, Western Australia, AUSTRALIA, Phone: 61 8 9593 0554, Fax: 61 8 9593 0554, taskerley@optusnet.com.au **Specialties:** Knife/harness/sheath systems for elite military personnel and body guards. **Patterns:** Utility/tactical knives, hunters small game and presentation grade knives. **Technical:** ATS-34 and 440C, Damascus, flat and hollow grinds. **Prices:** US $200 to $1,800. **Remarks:** Will take presentation grade commissions. **Mark:** Makers Initials. **Other:** Multi award winning maker and custom jeweler.

**TAY, LARRY C-G.,** Siglap PO Box 315, Singapore 9145, SINGAPORE, Phone: 65-2419421, Fax: 65-2434879 **Specialties:** Push knives, working and using straight knives and folders of his design; Marble's Safety Knife with stained or albino Asian buffalo horn and bone or rosewood handles. **Patterns:** Fighters and utility/camp knives. **Technical:** Forges and grinds D2, truck leaf springs. **Prices:** $200 to $1,000. **Remarks:** Spare-time maker; first knife sold in 1957. **Mark:** LDA/LAKELL, from 1999 initials L.T.

**TAYLOR, SHANE,** 18 Broken Bow Ln., Miles City, MT 59301, Phone: 406-234-7175, shane@taylorknives.com Web: www.taylorknives.com **Specialties:** One-of-a-kind fancy Damascus straight knives and folders. **Patterns:** Bowies, folders and fighters. **Technical:** Forges own mosaic and pattern welded Damascus. **Prices:** $450 and up. **Remarks:** ABS Master Smith, full-time maker; first knife sold in 1982. **Mark:** First name.

**TAYLOR, C. GRAY,** 560 Poteat Ln., Fall Branch, TN 37656, Phone: 423-348-8304, grayknives@aol.com or graysknives@hotmail.com Web: www.cgraytaylor.com **Specialties:** High-art display knives; period pieces. **Patterns:** Fighters, Bowies, daggers, locking folders and interframes. **Technical:** Grinds 440C, 154CM and ATS-34. **Prices:** $350 and up. **Remarks:** Full-time maker; first knife sold in 1975. **Mark:** Name, city and state.

**TAYLOR, BILLY,** 10 Temple Rd., Petal, MS 39465, Phone: 601-544-0041 **Specialties:** Straight knives of his design. **Patterns:** Bowies, skinners, hunters and utility knives. **Technical:** Flat-grinds 440C, ATS-34 and 154CM. **Prices:** $60 to $300. **Remarks:** Part-time maker; first knife sold in 1991. **Mark:** Full name, city and state.

**TERAUCHI, TOSHIYUKI,** 7649-13 219-11 Yoshida, Fujita-Cho Gobo-Shi, JAPAN

**TERRILL, STEPHEN,** 21363 Rd. 196, Lindsay, CA 93247, Phone: 559-562-1966, sterrill@yahoo.com **Specialties:** Deluxe working straight knives and folders. **Patterns:** Fighters, tantos, boots, locking folders and axes; traditional oriental patterns. **Technical:** Forges 1095, 5160, Damascus, stock removal ATS-34. **Prices:** $250 to $1,000, some $8,000. **Remarks:** Full-time maker; first knife sold in 1972. **Mark:** Name, city, state in logo.

**TERZUOLA, ROBERT,** 3933 Agua Fria St., Santa Fe, NM 87507, Phone: 505-473-1002, Fax: 505-438-8018 **Specialties:** Working folders of his design; period pieces. **Patterns:** High-tech utility, defense and gentleman's folders. **Technical:** Grinds 154CM and CPM S30V. Offers titanium, carbon fiber and G10 composite for side-lock folders and tactical folders. **Prices:** $400 to $1,200. **Remarks:** Full-time maker; first knife sold in 1980. **Mark:** Mayan dragon head, name.

**THAYER, DANNY O.,** 8908S 100W, Romney, IN 47981, Phone: 765-538-3105, dot61h@juno.com **Specialties:** Hunters, fighters, Bowies. **Prices:** $250 and up.

**THEIS, TERRY,** 21452 FM 2093, Harper, TX 78631, Phone: 830-864-4438 **Specialties:** All European and American engraving styles. **Prices:** $200 to $2,000. **Remarks:** Engraver only.

**THEVENOT, JEAN-PAUL,** 16 Rue De La Prefecture, Dijon, FRANCE 21000

**THIE, BRIAN,** 13250 150th St, Burlington, IA 52601, Phone: 319-985-2276, bkthie@mepotelco.net Web: www.mepotelco.net/web/tknives **Specialties:** Working using knives from basic to fancy. **Patterns:** Hunters, fighters, camp and folders. **Technical:** Forges blades and own Damascus. **Prices:** $100 and up. **Remarks:** Member of ABS, part-time maker. Sole author of blades including forging, heat treat, engraving and sheath making. **Mark:** Last name, anvil with last name initial inside, serial number all hand engraved into the blade.

**THILL, JIM,** 10242 Bear Run, Missoula, MT 59803, Phone: 406-251-5475 **Specialties:** Traditional and working/using knives of his design. **Patterns:** Fighters, hunters and utility/camp knives. **Technical:** Grinds D2 and ATS-34; forges 10-95-85, 52100, 5160, 10 series, reg. Damascus-mosaic. Offers hand cut sheaths with rawhide lace. **Prices:** $145 to $350; some to $1,250. **Remarks:** Full-time maker; first knife sold in 1962. **Mark:** Running bear in triangle.

**THOMAS, ROCKY,** 1716 Waterside Blvd., Moncks Corner, SC 29461, Phone: 843-761-7761 **Specialties:** Traditional working and using straight knives in standard patterns. **Patterns:** Hunters and utility/camp knives. **Technical:** Grinds 440C,

ATS-34 and commercial Damascus. **Prices:** $85 to $150. **Remarks:** Spare-time maker; first knife sold in 1986. **Mark:** First name in script and/or block.

**THOMAS, BOB G.,** RR 1 Box 121, Thebes, IL 62990-9718

**THOMAS, DAVID E.,** 8502 Hwy 91, Lillian, AL 36549, Phone: 251-961-7574, redbluff@gulftel.com
**Specialties:** Bowies and hunters. **Technical:** Hand forged blades in 5160, 1095 and own Damascus. **Prices:** $400 and up. **Mark:** Stylized DT, maker's last name, serial number.

**THOMAS, DEVIN,** 90 N. 5th St., Panaca, NV 89042, Phone: 775-728-4363, hoss@devinthomas.com Web: www.devinthomas.com
**Specialties:** Traditional straight knives and folders in standard patterns. **Patterns:** Bowies, fighters, hunters. **Technical:** Forges stainless Damascus, nickel and 1095. Uses, makes and sells Mokume with brass, copper and nickel-silver. **Prices:** $300 to $1,200. **Remarks:** Full-time maker; first knife sold in 1979. **Mark:** First and last name, city and state with anvil, or first name only.

**THOMAS, KIM,** PO Box 531, Seville, OH 44273, Phone: 330-769-9906
**Specialties:** Fancy and traditional straight knives of his design and to customer specs; period pieces. **Patterns:** Boots, daggers, fighters, swords. **Technical:** Forges own Damascus from 5160, 1010 and nickel. **Prices:** $135 to $1,500; some to $3,000. **Remarks:** Part-time maker; first knife sold in 1986. Doing business as Thomas Iron Works. **Mark:** KT.

**THOMPSON, TOMMY,** 4015 NE Hassalo, Portland, OR 97232-2607, Phone: 503-235-5762
**Specialties:** Fancy and working knives; mostly liner-lock folders. **Patterns:** Fighters, hunters and liner locks. **Technical:** Grinds D2, ATS-34, CPM440V and T15. Handles are either hardwood inlaid with wood banding and stone or shell, or made of agate, jasper, petrified woods, etc. **Prices:** $75 to $500; some to $1,000. **Remarks:** Part-time maker; first knife sold in 1987. Doing business as Stone Birds. **Mark:** First and last name, city and state. **Other:** Knife making temporarily stopped due to family obligations.

**THOMPSON, LEON,** 45723 S.W. Saddleback Dr., Gaston, OR 97119, Phone: 503-357-2573
**Specialties:** Working knives. **Patterns:** Locking folders, slip-joints and liner locks. **Technical:** Grinds ATS-34, D2 and 440C. **Prices:** $200 to $600. **Remarks:** Full-time maker; first knife sold in 1976. **Mark:** First and middle initials, last name, city and state.

**THOMPSON, LLOYD,** PO Box 1664, Pagosa Springs, CO 81147, Phone: 970-264-5837
**Specialties:** Working and collectible straight knives and folders of his design. **Patterns:** Straight blades, lock back folders and slip joint folders. **Technical:** Hollow-grinds ATS-34, D2 and O1. Uses sambar stag and exotic woods. **Prices:** $150 to upscale. **Remarks:** Full-time maker; first knife sold in 1985. Doing business as Trapper Creek Knife Co. **Remarks:** Offers three-day knife-making classes. **Mark:** Name.

**THOMPSON, KENNETH,** 4887 Glenwhite Dr., Duluth, GA 30136, Phone: 770-446-6730
**Specialties:** Traditional working and using knives of his design. **Patterns:** Hunters, Bowies and utility/camp knives. **Technical:** Forges 5168, O1, 1095 and 52100. **Prices:** $75 to $1,500; some to $2,500. **Remarks:** Part-time maker; first knife sold in 1990. **Mark:** P/W; or name, P/W, city and state.

**THOMSEN, LOYD W.,** HCR-46, Box 19, Oelrichs, SD 57763, Phone: 605-535-6162, Web: horseheadcreekknives.com
**Specialties:** High-art and traditional working/using straight knives and presentation pieces of his design and to customer specs; period pieces. Hand carved animals in crown of stag on handles and carved display stands. **Patterns:** Bowies, hunters, daggers and utility/camp knives. **Technical:** Forges and grinds 1095HC, 1084, L6, 15N20, 440C stainless steel, nickel 200; special restoration process on period pieces. Makes sheaths. Uses natural materials for handles. **Prices:** $350 to $1,000. **Remarks:** Full-time maker; first knife sold in 1995. Doing business as Horsehead Creek Knives. **Mark:** Initials and last name over a horse's head.

**THOUROT, MICHAEL W.,** T-814 Co. Rd. 11, Napoleon, OH 43545, Phone: 419-533-6832, Fax: 419-533-3516, mwtknives@yahoo.com Web: wwwsafariknives.com
**Specialties:** Working straight knives to customer specs. Designed two-handled skinning ax and limited edition engraved knife and art print set. **Patterns:** Fishing and fillet knives, Bowies, tantos and hunters. **Technical:** Grinds O1, D2, 440C and Damascus. **Prices:** $200 to $5,000. **Remarks:** Part-time maker; first knife sold in 1968. **Mark:** Initials.

**THUESEN, ED,** 21211 Knolle Rd., Damon, TX 77430, Phone: 979-553-1211, Fax: 979-553-1211
**Specialties:** Working straight knives. **Patterns:** Hunters, fighters and survival knives. **Technical:** Grinds D2, 440C, ATS-34 and Vascowear. **Prices:** $150 to $275; some to $600. **Remarks:** Part-time maker; first knife sold in 1979. Rur knife maker supply business. **Mark:** Last name in script.

**TICHBOURNE, GEORGE,** 7035 Maxwell Rd. #5, Mississauga, Ont., CANADA L5S 1R5, Phone: 905-670-0200, sales @tichbourneknives.com Web: www.tichbourneknives.com
**Specialties:** Traditional working and using knives as well as unique collec bles. **Patterns:** Bowies, hunters, outdoor, kitchen, integrals, art, military, Scc tish dirks, folders, kosher knives. **Technical:** Stock removal 440C, Stellite 6 stainless Damascus, liquid metal. Handle materials include mammoth, mete orite, mother-of-pearl, Precious gems, Mosiac, Abalone, Stag, Micarta, Exo High Resin Woods and Corian scrimshawed by George. Leather sheaths a hand stitched and tooled by George as well as the silver adornments for t Dirk Sheaths. **Prices:** $60 U.S. up to $5,000 U.S. **Remarks:** Full-time mak with his OWN STORE. First knife sold in 1990. **Mark:** Full name over Map Leaf.

**TIENSVOLD, ALAN L.,** PO Box 355, Rushville, NE 69360, Phone: 308-327-2046
**Specialties:** Working knives, tomahawks and period pieces, high end Da ascus knives. **Patterns:** Random, ladder, twist and many more. **Technic** Hand forged blades, we forge our own Damascus. **Prices:** Working kniv start at $300. **Remarks:** Feceived Journeyman rating with the ABS in 20C **Mark:** Tiensvold hand made U.S.A. on left side, JS on right. **Other:** Does o engraving and fine work.

**TIENSVOLD, JASON,** PO Box 795, Rushville, NE 69360, Phone: 308-327-2046, ironprik@gpcom.net
**Specialties:** Working and using straight knives of his design; period piec Gentlemans folders, art folders. **Patterns:** Hunters, skinners, Bowies, fighte daggers, linder locks. **Technical:** Forges own Damascus using 15N20 a 1084, 1095, nickle, custom file work. **Prices:** $200 to $4,000. **Remarks:** Fu time maker, first knife sold in 1994; doing business under Tiensvold Custo Knives. **Mark:** Tiensvold USA Handmade in a circle.

**TIGHE, BRIAN,** 12-111 Fourth Ave, Suite 376 Ridley Square, St Catharines ON, CANADA L0S 1M0, Phone: 905-892-2734, Fax: 905-892-2734, Web: www.tigheknives.com
**Specialties:** High tech tactical folders. **Patterns:** Boots, daggers, locking a slip-joint folders. **Technical:** CPM 440V and CPM 420V. Prefers natural h dle material inlay; hand finishes. **Prices:** $450 to $2,000. **Remarks:** Part-ti maker; first knife sold in 1989. **Mark:** Etched signature.

**TILL, CALVIN E. AND RUTH,** 211 Chaping, Chadron, NE 69337
**Specialties:** Straight knives, hunters, Bowies; no folders **Patterns:** Train point, drop point hunters, Bowies. **Technical:** ATS-34 sub zero quench F 59, 61. **Prices:** $700 to $1,200. **Remarks:** Sells only the absolute best kni they can make. **Mark:** RC Till. The R is for Ruth. **Other:** Manufactures ev part in their knives.

**TILTON, JOHN,** 24041 HWY 383, Iowa, LA 70647, Phone: 337-582-6785, jetknives@netscape.net
**Specialties:** Camp knives and skinners. **Technical:** All forged blad **Prices:** $125 and up. **Mark:** Initials J.E.T. **Other:** ABS Journeyman Smith.

**TINDERA, GEORGE,** BURNING RIVER FORGE, 751 Hadcock Rd., Brunswick, OH 44212-2648, Phone: 330-220-6212
**Specialties:** Straight knives; his designs. **Patterns:** Personal knives; clas Bowies and fighters. **Technical:** Hand-forged high-carbon; his own cable pattern welded Damascus. **Prices:** $100 to $400. **Remarks:** Spare-ti maker; sold first knife in 1995. **Other:** Natural handle materials.

**TINGLE, DENNIS P.,** 19390 E Clinton Rd., Jackson, CA 95642, Phon 209-223-4586, dtknives@webtv.net
**Specialties:** Fixed-blade hunting, using knives w/guards and natural har materials.

**TIPPETTS, COLTEN,** , PO Box 1436, Ketchum, ID 83340, Phone: 20 853-7779, colten@interstate-electric.com
**Specialties:** Fancy and working straight knives and fancy locking folder his own design or to customer specifications. **Patterns:** Hunters and skinn fighters and utility. **Technical:** Grinds BG-42, high-carbon 1095 and D ascus. **Prices:** $200 to $1,000. **Remarks:** Part-time maker; first knife sol 1996. **Mark:** Fused initials.

**TODD, RICHARD C.,** RR 1, Chambersburg, IL 62323, Phone: 217-32 4380, ktodd45@yahoo.com
**Specialties:** Multi blade folders and silver sheaths. **Patterns:** Blacksmit and tool making. **Mark:** RT with letter R crossing the T.

**TOICH, NEVIO,** Via Pisacane 9, Rettorgole di Caldogna, Vincenza, ITALY 36030, Phone: 0444-985065, Fax: 0444-301254
**Specialties:** Working/using straight knives of his design or to customer sp **Patterns:** Bowies, hunters, skinners and utility/camp knives. **Techni** Grinds 440C, D2 and ATS-34. Hollow-grinds all blades and uses mirror po Offers hand-sewn sheaths. Uses wood and horn. **Prices:** $120 to $300; s

o $450. **Remarks:** Spare-time maker; first knife sold in 1989. Doing business ıs Custom Toich. **Mark:** Initials and model number punched.

**TOKAR, DANIEL,** Box 1776, Shepherdstown, WV 25443
**Specialties:** Working knives; period pieces. **Patterns:** Hunters, camp knives, uckskinners, axes, swords and battle gear. **Technical:** Forges L6, 1095 and ıis Damascus; makes mokume, Japanese alloys and bronze daggers; estores old edged weapons. **Prices:** $25 to $800; some to $3,000. **Remarks:** Part-time maker; first knife sold in 1979. Doing business as The Willow Forge. **Mark:** Arrow over rune and date.

**TOLLEFSON,, BARRY A.,** 177 Blackfoot Trail, Gunnison, CO 81230-720, Phone: 970-641-0752
**Specialties:** Working straight knives, some fancy. **Patterns:** Hunters, skin-ers, fighters and camp knives. **Technical:** Grinds 440C, ATS-34 and D2. ikes mirror-finishes; offers some fancy filework. Handles made from elk, deer nd exotic hardwoods. **Prices:** $75 to $300; some higher. **Remarks:** Part-time naker; first knife sold in 1990. **Mark:** Stylized initials.

**OMBERLIN, BRION R.,** ANVIL TOP CUSTOM KNIVES, 825 W Tim-erdell, Norman, OK 73072, Phone: 405-202-6832, anviltopp@aol.com
**Specialties:** Hand forged blades, working pieces, standard classic patterns, ome swords, and customer designs. **Patterns:** Bowies, hunters, fighters, ersian and eastern-styles. Likes Japanese blades. **Technical:** Forge 050,1075,1084,1095,5160, some forged stainless, also do some stock emoval in stainless. **Prices:** Start at $150 up to $800 or higher for swords and ustom pieces. **Remarks:** Part-time maker, first knife sold in 1984, member merica Bladesmith Society, member Japanese Sword Society. **Mark:** BRION" on forged blades, :ATCK" on stock removal, stainless ad early forged lades. **Other:** Prefer natural handle materials, hand rubbed finishes. Like mperlines.

**OMES, P.J.,** 594 High Peak Ln., Shipman, VA 22971, Phone: 434-263-662, tomgsknives@juno.com Web: www.tomesknives.com
**pecialties:** Scagel reproductions. **Patterns:** Front-lock folders. **Technical:** orges 52100. **Prices:** $150 to $750. **Mark:** Last name, USA, MS, stamped in rged blades.

**OMEY, KATHLEEN,** 146 Buford Pl., Macon, GA 31204, Phone: 478-46-8454, ktomey@tomeycustomknives.com Web: www.tomeycus-mknives.com
**pecialties:** Working hunters, skinners, daily users in fixed blades, plain and nbellished. Tactical neck and tanto. Bowies. **Technical:** Grinds 01, ATS-34, t or hollow grind, filework, satin and mirror polish finishes. High quality eaths with tooling. Kydex with tactical. **Prices:** $150 to $500. **Remarks:** most full-time maker. **Mark:** Last name in diamond.

**OMPKINS, DAN,** PO Box 398, Peotone, IL 60468, Phone: 708-258-520
**ecialties:** Working knives, some deluxe, some folders. **Patterns:** Hunters, ots, daggers and push knives. **Technical:** Grinds D2, 440C, ATS-34 and 4CM. **Prices:** $85 to $150; some to $400. **Remarks:** Part-time maker; first ife sold in 1975. **Mark:** Last name, city, state.

**ONER, ROGER,** 531 Lightfoot Place, Pickering, Ont., CANADA L1V 8, Phone: 905-420-5555
**ecialties:** Exotic Sword canes. **Patterns:** Bowies, daggers and fighters. **chnical:** Grinds 440C, D2 and Damascus. Scrimshaws and engraves. Sil-r cast pommels and guards in animal shapes; twisted silver wire inlays. es semi-precious stones. **Prices:** $200 to $2,000; some to $3,000. **marks:** Part-time maker; first knife sold in 1982. **Mark:** Last name.

**OPLISS, M.W. "IKE",** 1668 Hermosa Ct., Montrose, CO 81401, Phone: 0-249-4703
**ecialties:** Working/using straight knives of his design and to customer ecs. **Patterns:** Boots, hunters, utility/camp knives. **Technical:** Prefers ATS-. Other steels available on request. Likes stabilized wood, natural hard-ods, antler and Micarta. **Prices:** $175 to $300; some to $800. **Remarks:** rt-time maker; first knife sold in 1984. **Mark:** Name, city, state.

**RGESON, SAMUEL L.,** 25 Alpine Ln., Sedona, AZ 86336-6809

**OSHIFUMI, KURAMOTO,** 3435 Higashioda, Asakura-gun, Fukuoka, PAN, Phone: 0946-42-4470

**OWELL, DWIGHT L.,** 2375 Towell Rd., Midvale, ID 83645, Phone: 208-5-2419
**ecialties:** Solid, elegant working knives; art knives. **Patterns:** Hunters, wies, daggers; folders in several weights. **Technical:** Grinds 154CM; some graving. **Prices:** $250 to $800; some $3,500 and higher. **Remarks:** Part-e maker; first knife sold in 1970. **Mark:** Last name.

**TOWNSEND, ALLEN MARK,** 6 Pine Trail, Texarkana, AR 71854, Phone: 870-772-8945

**TRACY, BUD,** 495 Flanders Rd., Reno, NV 8951-4784

**TREIBER, LEON,** PO Box 342, Ingram, TX 78025, Phone: 830-367-2246, Web: www.treiberknives.com
**Specialties:** Folders of his design and to customer specs. **Patterns:** Locking folders. **Technical:** Grinds CPM-T-440V, D2, 440C, Damascus, 420v and ATS-34. **Prices:** $350 to $3,500. **Remarks:** Part-time maker; first knife sold in 1992. Doing business as Treiber Knives. **Mark:** First initial, last name, city, state.

**TREML, GLENN,** RR #14, Site 11-10, Thunder Bay, Ont., CANADA P7B 5E5, Phone: 807-767-1977
**Specialties:** Working straight knives of his design and to customer specs. **Patterns:** Hunters, kitchen knives and double-edged survival knives. Technical Grinds 440C, ATS-34 and O1; stock removal method. Uses various woods and Micarta for handle material. **Prices:** $60 to $400; some higher. **Mark:** Stamped last name.

**TRINDLE, BARRY,** 1660 Ironwood Trail, Earlham, IA 50072-8611, Phone: 515-462-1237
**Specialties:** Engraved folders. **Patterns:** Mostly small folders, classical-styles and pocket knives. **Technical:** 440 only. Engraves. Handles of wood or mineral material. **Prices:** Start at $1,000. **Mark:** Name on tang.

**TRISLER, KENNETH W.,** 6256 Federal 80, Rayville, LA 71269, Phone: 318-728-5541

**TRITZ, JEAN JOSE,** Schopstrasse 23, 20255 Hamburg, GERMANY, Phone: 040-49 78 21
**Specialties:** Scandinavian knives, Japanese kitchen knives, friction folders, swords. **Patterns:** Puukkos, Tollekniven, Hocho, friction folders, swords. **Technical:** Forges tool steels, carbon steels, 52100 Damascus Mokume, San Maj. **Prices:** $200 to $2,000; some higher. **Remarks:** Full-time maker; first knife sold in 1989. **Mark:** Initials in monogram. **Other:** Does own leatherwork, prefers natural materials. Sole authorship. Speaks French, German, English, Norwegian.

**TRUDEL, PAUL,** 525 Braydon Ave., Ottawa ON, CANADA K1G 0W7
**Remarks:** Part-time knife maker.

**TRUJILLO, ALBERT M.B.,** 2035 Wasmer Cir., Bosque Farms, NM 87068, Phone: 505-869-0428
**Specialties:** Working/using straight knives of his design or to customer specs. **Patterns:** Hunters, skinners, fighters, working/using knives. File work offered. **Technical:** Grinds ATS-34, D2, 440C. Tapers tangs, all blades cryogenically treated. **Prices:** $75 to $500. **Remarks:** Part-time maker; first knife sold in 1997. **Mark:** First and last name under logo.

**TRUJILLO, ADAM,** 3001 Tanglewood Dr., Anchorage, AK 99517, Phone: 907-243-6093
**Specialties:** Working/using straight knives of his design. **Patterns:** Hunters and utility/camp knives. **Technical:** Grinds 440C, ATS-34 and O1; ice tempers blades. Sheaths are dipped in wax and oil base. **Prices:** $200 to $500; some to $1,000. **Remarks:** Spare-time maker; first knife sold in 1995. Doing business as Alaska Knife and Service Co. **Mark:** NA.

**TRUJILLO, MIRANDA,** 3001 Tanglewood Dr., Anchorage, AK 99517, Phone: 907-243-6093
**Specialties:** Working/using straight knives of her design. **Patterns:** Hunters and utility/camp knives. **Technical:** Grinds ATS-34 and 440C. Sheaths are water resistant. **Prices:** $145 to $400; some to $600. **Remarks:** Spare-time maker; first knife sold in 1989. Doing business as Alaska Knife and Service Co. **Mark:** NA.

**TRUJILLO, THOMAS A.,** 3001 Tanglewood Dr., Anchorage, AK 99517, Phone: 907-243-6093
**Specialties:** High-end art knives. **Patterns:** Hunters, Bowies, daggers and locking folders. **Technical:** Grinds to customer choice, including rock and commercial Damascus. Inlays jewels and carves handles. **Prices:** $150 to $900; some to $6,000. **Remarks:** Full-time maker; first knife sold in 1976. Doing business as Alaska Knife and Service Co. **Mark:** Alaska Knife and/or Thomas Anthony.

**TSCHAGER, REINHARD,** Piazza Parrocchia 7, I-39100 Bolzano, ITALY, Phone: 0471-970642, Fax: 0471-970642, goldtschager@dnet.it
**Specialties:** Classic, high-art, collector-grade straight knives of his design. **Patterns:** Hunters. **Technical:** Grinds ATS-34, D2 and Damascus. Oval pins. Gold inlay. Offers engraving. **Prices:** $500 to $1,200; some to $4,000. **Remarks:** Spare-time maker; first knife sold in 1979. **Mark:** Gold inlay stamped with initials.

**TURCOTTE, LARRY,** 1707 Evergreen, Pampa, TX 79065, Phone: 806-665-9369, 806-669-0435
**Specialties:** Fancy and working/using knives of his design and to customer specs. **Patterns:** Hunters, kitchen knives, utility/camp knives. **Technical:** Grinds 440C, D2, ATS-34. Engraves, scrimshaws, silver inlays. **Prices:** $150 to $350; some to $1,000. **Remarks:** Part-time maker; first knife sold in 1977. Doing business as Knives by Turcotte. **Mark:** Last name.

**TURECEK, JIM,** 12 Elliott Rd., Ansonia, CT 06401, Phone: 203-734-8406
**Specialties:** Exotic folders, art knives and some miniatures. **Patterns:** Trout and bird knives with split bamboo handles and one-of-a-kind folders. **Technical:** Grinds and forges stainless and carbon Damascus. **Prices:** $750 to $1,500; some to $3,000. **Remarks:** Full-time maker; first knife sold in 1983. **Mark:** Last initial in script, or last name.

**TURNBULL, RALPH A.,** 14464 Linden Dr., Spring Hill, FL 34609, Phone: 352-688-7089, tbull2000@aol.com Web: www.turnbullknives.com
**Specialties:** Fancy folders. **Patterns:** Primarily gents pocket knives. **Technical:** Wire EDM work on bolsters. **Prices:** $300 and up. **Remarks:** Full-time maker; first knife sold in 1973. **Mark:** Signature or initials.

**TURNER, KEVIN,** 17 Hunt Ave., Montrose, NY 10548, Phone: 914-739-0535
**Specialties:** Working straight knives of his design and to customer specs; period pieces. **Patterns:** Daggers, fighters and utility knives. **Technical:** Forges 5160 and 52100. **Prices:** $90 to $500. **Remarks:** Part-time maker; first knife sold in 1991. **Mark:** Acid-etched signed last name and year.

**TYCER, ART,** 23820 N Cold Springs Rd., Paron, AR 72122, Phone: 501-821-4487, blades1@tycerknives.com Web: www.tycerknives.com
**Specialties:** Fancy working/using straight knives of his design, to customer specs and standard patterns. **Patterns:** Boots, Bowies, daggers, fighters, hunters, kitchen and utility knives. **Technical:** Grinds ATS-34, 440C and a variety of carbon steels. Uses exotic woods with spacer material, stag and water buffalo. Offers filework. **Prices:** $150 and up depending on size and embellishments or Damascus. **Remarks:** Making and using his own Damascus and other Damascus also. **Mark:** Flying "T" over first initial inside an oval. **Other:** Full-time maker.

**TYSER, ROSS,** 1015 Hardee Court, Spartanburg, SC 29303, Phone: 864-585-7616
**Specialties:** Traditional working and using straight knives and folders of his design and in standard patterns. **Patterns:** Bowies, hunters and slip-joint folders. **Technical:** Grinds 440C and commercial Damascus. Mosaic pins; stone inlay. Does filework and scrimshaw. Offers engraving and cut-work and some inlay on sheaths. **Prices:** $45 to $125; some to $400. **Remarks:** Part-time maker; first knife sold in 1995. Doing business as RT Custom Knives. **Mark:** Stylized initials.

## U

**UCHIDA, CHIMATA,** 977-2 Oaza Naga Shisui Ki, Kumamoto, JAPAN 861-1204

**UEKAMA, NOBUYUKI,** 3-2-8-302 Ochiai, Tama City, Tokyo, JAPAN

## V

**VAGNINO, MICHAEL,** PO Box 67, Visalia, CA 93279, Phone: 559-528-2800, mvknives@lightspeed.net Web: www.mvknives.com
**Specialties:** Working and fancy straight knives and folders of his design and to customer specs. **Patterns:** Hunters, Bowies, camp, kitchen and folders: locking liners, slip-joint, lock-back and double-action autos. **Technical:** Forges 52100, A2, 1084 and 15N20 Damascus and grinds stainless. **Prices:** $275 to $2,000 plus. **Remarks:** Full-time maker, ABS Master Smith. **Mark:** Logo, last name.

**VAIL, DAVE,** 554 Sloop Point Rd., Hampstead, NC 28443, Phone: 910-270-4456
**Specialties:** Working/using straight knives of his own design or to the customer's specs. **Patterns:** Hunters/skinners, camp/utility, fillet, Bowies. **Technical:** Grinds ATS-34, 440c, 154 CM and 1095 carbon steel. **Prices:** $90 to $450. **Remarks:** Part-time maker. Member of NC Custom Knifemakers Guild. **Mark:** Etched oval with "Dave Vail Hampstead NC" inside.

**VALLOTTON, THOMAS,** 621 Fawn Ridge Dr., Oakland, OR 97462, Phone: 541-459-2216
**Specialties:** Custom autos. **Patterns:** Tactical, fancy. **Technical:** File work, uses Damascus, uses Spectrum Metal. **Prices:** From $350 to $700. **Remarks:** Full-time maker. **Mark:** T and a V mingled. **Other:** Maker of Pr tégé 3 canoe.

**VALLOTTON, SHAWN,** 621 Fawn Ridge Dr., Oakland, OR 97462, Phone: 503-459-2216
**Specialties:** Left-hand knives. **Patterns:** All styles. **Technical:** Grinds 440 ATS-34 and Damascus. Uses titanium. Prefers bead-blasted or anodized f ishes. **Prices:** $250 to $1,400. **Remarks:** Full-time maker. **Mark:** Name a specialty.

**VALLOTTON, RAINY D.,** 1295 Wolf Valley Dr., Umpqua, OR 97486, Phone: 541-459-0465
**Specialties:** Folders, one-handed openers and art pieces. **Patterns:** All p terns. **Technical:** Stock removal all steels; uses titanium liners and bolste uses all finishes. **Prices:** $350 to $3,500. **Remarks:** Full-time maker. **Ma** Name.

**VALLOTTON, BUTCH AND AREY,** 621 Fawn Ridge Dr., Oakland, OF 97462, Phone: 541-459-2216, Fax: 541-459-7473
**Specialties:** Quick opening knives w/complicated mechanisms. **Patter** Tactical, fancy, working, and some art knives. **Technical:** Grinds all stee uses others' Damascus. Uses Spectrum Metal. **Prices:** From $350 to $4,5 **Remarks:** Full-time maker since 1984; first knife sold in 1981. **Mark:** Name viper head in the "V". **Other:** Co/designer, Appelgate Fairbarn folding w/ Harsey.

**VALOIS, A. DANIEL,** 3552 W. Lizard Ck. Rd., Lehighton, PA 18235, Phone: 717-386-3636
**Specialties:** Big working knives; various sized lock-back folders with n safety releases. **Patterns:** Fighters in survival packs, sturdy working kniv belt buckle knives, military-style knives, swords. **Technical:** Forges a grinds A2, O1 and 440C; likes full tangs. **Prices:** $65 to $240; some to $6 **Remarks:** Full-time maker; first knife sold in 1969. **Mark:** Anvil logo with name inside.

**VAN CLEVE, STEVE,** Box 372, Sutton, AK 99674, Phone: 907-745-3038

**VAN DE MANAKKER, THIJS,** Koolweg 34, 5759 px Helenaveen, HO LAND, Phone: 0493539369
**Specialties:** Classic high-art knives. **Patterns:** Swords, utility/camp kni and period pieces. **Technical:** Forges soft iron, carbon steel and Bloom Iron. Makes own Damascus, Bloomery Iron and patterns. **Prices:** $2C $2,000; some higher. **Remarks:** Full-time maker; first knife sold in 19 **Mark:** Stylized "V".

**VAN DEN ELSEN, GERT,** Purcelldreef 83, 5012 AJ Tilburg, NETHEF LANDS, Phone: 013-4563200, gvdelsen@home.nl Web: www.7knifedwarfs.com
**Specialties:** Fancy, working/using, miniatures and integral straight knive the maker's design or to customer specs. **Patterns:** Bowies, fighters, hur and Japanese-style blades. **Technical:** Grinds ATS-34 and 440C; for Damascus. Offers filework, differentially tempered blades and some moku gane fittings. **Prices:** $350 to $1,000; some to $4,000. **Remarks:** Part-t maker; first knife sold in 1982. Doing business as G-E Knives. **Mark:** Ini GE in lozenge shape.

**VAN DIJK, RICHARD,** 76 Stepney Ave RD 2, Harwood Dunedin, Ne Zealand, Phone: 0064-3-4780401, Web: www.hoihoknives.com
**Specialties:**Damascus, Fantasy knives, Sigian Dubh's. **Patterns:**Mostly ofs, anything from bird and trout to swords, no folders. **Technical:** Fo mainly won made Damascus, some 5160, O1, 1095, L6. Prefers natural dle materials with 30 years experience as goldsmith, handle fittings are c made from sterling silver and sometimes gold, manufactured to cap the dle, use gemstones if required. Makes own sheaths. **Prices:** $300 and **Remarks:** Full-time maker, first knife sold in 1980. Doing business as HC KNIVES. **Mark:** Stylized initials RvD in triangle.

**VAN EIZENGA, JERRY W.,** 14227 Cleveland, Nunica, MI 49448, Phone: 616-842-2699
**Specialties:** Hand forged blades, Scagel patterns and other styles. **Patte** Camp, hunting, bird, trout, folders, axes, miniatures. **Technical:** 5160, 52 1084. **Prices:** Start at $250. **Remarks:** Part-time maker, sole author of and sheath. **Mark:** Interconnecting letters spelling VAN, city and state. **O** First knife made early 1970s. ABS member who believes in the beauty of plicity.

**VAN ELDIK, FRANS,** Ho Flaan 3, 3632BT Loenen, NETHERLANDS Phone: 0031 294 233 095, Fax: 0031 294 233 095
**Specialties:** Fancy collector-grade straight knives and folders of his de **Patterns:** Hunters, fighters, boots and folders. **Technical:** Forges and g D2, 154CM, ATS-34 and stainless Damascus. **Prices:** Start at $ **Remarks:** Spare-time maker; first knife sold in 1979. Knivemaker 25 y **Mark:** Lion with name and Amsterdam.

**VAN RIJSWIJK, AAD,** AVR KNIVES, Arij Koplaan 16B, 3132 AA Vlaardingen, THE NETHERLANDS, Phone: +31 10 2343227, Fax: +31 10 2343648, info@avrknives.com Web: www.avrknives.com
**Specialties:** High-art interframe folders of his design and in shaving sets. **Patterns:** Hunters and locking folders. **Technical:** Uses semi-precious stones, mammoth, ivory, walrus ivory, iron wood. **Prices:** $550 to $3800. **Remarks:** Full-time maker; first knife sold in 1993. **Mark:** NA.

**VAN RIPER, JAMES N.,** PO Box 7045, Citrus Heights, CA 95621-7045, Phone: 916-721-0892

**VANDERFORD, CARL G.,** Rt. 9, Box 238B, Columbia, TN 38401, Phone: 615-381-1488
**Specialties:** Traditional working straight knives and folders of his design. **Patterns:** Hunters, Bowies and locking folders. **Technical:** Forges and grinds 440C, O1 and wire Damascus. **Prices:** $60 to $125. **Remarks:** Part-time maker; first knife sold in 1987. **Mark:** Last name.

**VANDEVENTER, TERRY L.,** 3274 Davis Rd., Terry, MS 39170-9750, Phone: 601-371-7414, tvandeventer@jam.rr.com
**Specialties:** Camp knives, Bowies, friction folders. **Technical:** 1095, 1084, L-6, Damascus and Mokume; natural handles. **Prices:** $250 to $1,200. **Remarks:** Sole author; makes everything here. **Mark:** T L Vandeventer (with silhouette of snake), handcrafted knives. **Other:** Part-time since 1994. ABS Journeyman Smith.

**VANHOY, ED AND TANYA,** 24255 N Fork River Rd., Abingdon, VA 24210, Phone: 276-944-4885, vanhoyknives@direcway.com
**Specialties:** Traditional and working/using straight knives of his design, make folders. **Patterns:** Fighters, straight knives, folders, hunters and art knives. **Technical:** Grinds ATS-34 and 440V; forges D2. Offers filework, engraves, acid etching, mosaic pins, decorative bolsters and custom fitted English bridle leather sheaths. **Prices:** $250 to $3,000. **Remarks:** Full-time maker; first knife sold in 1977. Wife also engraves. Doing business as Van Hoy Custom Knives. **Mark:** Acid etched last name.

**VASQUEZ, JOHNNY DAVID,** 1552 7th St., Wyandotte, MI 48192, Phone: 734-281-2455

**VAUGHAN, IAN,** 351 Doe Run Rd., Manheim, PA 17545-9368, Phone: 717-665-6949

**VEATCH, RICHARD,** 2580 N. 35th Pl., Springfield, OR 97477, Phone: 541-747-3910
**Specialties:** Traditional working and using straight knives of his design and in standard patterns; period pieces. **Patterns:** Daggers, hunters, swords, utility/camp knives and minis. **Technical:** Forges and grinds his own Damascus; uses L6 and O1. Prefers natural handle materials; offers leatherwork. **Prices:** $50 to $300; some to $500. **Remarks:** Full-time maker; first knife sold in 1991. **Mark:** Stylized initials.

**VEIT, MICHAEL,** 3289 E. Fifth Rd., LaSalle, IL 61301, Phone: 815-223-3538, whitebear@starband.net
**Specialties:** Damascus folders. **Technical:** Engraver-Sole author. **Prices:** $2,500 to $6,500. **Remarks:** Part-time maker; first knife sold in 1985. **Mark:** Name in script.

**VELARDE, RICARDO,** 7240 N Greefield Dr., Park City, UT 84098, Phone: 435-940-1378/Cell 801-360-1413/801-361-0204, velardeknives.com
**Specialties:** Investment grade integrals and interframs. **Patterns:** Boots, fighters and hunters; hollow grind. **Technical:** BG on Integrals. **Prices:** $850 to $4,500. **Remarks:** First knife sold in 1992. **Mark:** First initial, last name on blade; city, state, U.S.A. at bottom of tang.

**VENSILD, HENRIK,** Gl Estrup, Randersvei 4, DK-8963 Auning, DENMARK, Phone: +45 86 48 44 48
**Specialties:** Classic and traditional working and using knives of his design; Scandinavian influence. **Patterns:** hunters and using knives. **Technical:** Forges Damascus. Hand makes handles, sheaths and blades. **Prices:** $350 to $1,000. **Remarks:** Part-time maker; first knife sold in 1967. **Mark:** Initials.

**VIALLON, HENRI,** Les Belins, 63300 Thiers, FRANCE, Phone: 04-73-80-24-03, Fax: 04 73-51-02-02
**Specialties:** Folders and complex Damascus **Patterns:** My draws. **Technical:** Forge **Prices:** $1,000 to $5,000. **Mark:** H. Viallon.

**VIELE, H.J.,** 88 Lexington Ave., Westwood, NJ 07675, Phone: 201-666-2906
**Specialties:** Folding knives of distinctive shapes. **Patterns:** High-tech folders. **Technical:** Grinds 440C and ATS-34. **Prices:** Start at $475. **Remarks:** Full-time maker; first knife sold in 1973. **Mark:** Last name with stylized throwing star.

**VIKING KNIVES (SEE JAMES THORLIEF ERIKSEN)**

**VILAR, RICARDO AUGUSTO FERREIRA,** Rua Alemada Dos Jasmins, NO 243, Parque Petropolis, Mairipora Sao Paulo, BRASIL 07600-000, Phone: 011-55-11-44-85-43-46, ricardovilar@ig.com.br.
**Specialties:** Traditional Brazilian-style working knives of the Sao Paulo state. **Patterns:** Fighters, hunters, utility, and camp knives, welcome customer design. Specialize in the "true" Brazilian camp knife "Soracabana." **Technical:** Forges only with sledge hammer to 100% shape in 5160 and 52100 and his own Damascus steels. Makes own sheaths in the "true" traditional "Paulista"-style of the state of Sao Paulo. **Remark:** Full-time maker. **Prices:** $250 to $600. Uses only natural handle materials. **Mark:** Special designed signature styled name R. Vilar.

**VILLA, LUIZ,** R. Com. Miguel Calfat, 398 Itaim Bibi, Sao Paulo, SP-04537-081, BRAZIL, Phone: 011-8290649
**Specialties:** One-of-a-kind straight knives and jewel knives of all designs. **Patterns:** Bowies, hunters, utility/camp knives and jewel knives. **Technical:** Grinds D6, Damascus and 440C; forges 5160. Prefers natural handle material. **Prices:** $70 to $200. **Remarks:** Part-time maker; first knife sold in 1990. **Mark:** Last name and serial number.

**VILLAR, RICARDO,** Al. dos Jasmins, 243, Mairipora, S.P. 07600-000, BRAZIL, Phone: 011-4851649
**Specialties:** Straight working knives to customer specs. **Patterns:** Bowies, fighters and utility/camp knives. **Technical:** Grinds D6, ATS-34 and 440C stainless. **Prices:** $80 to $200. **Remarks:** Part-time maker; first knife sold in 1993. **Mark:** Percor over sword and circle.

**VISTE, JAMES,** Edgewize Forge, 13401 Mt Elliot, Detroit, MI 48212, Phone: 313-664-7455, grumblejunky@hotmail.com
**Mark:** EWF touch mark.

**VISTNES, TOR,** N-6930 Svelgen, NORWAY, Phone: 047-57795572
**Specialties:** Traditional and working knives of his design. **Patterns:** Hunters and utility knives. **Technical:** Grinds Uddeholm Elmax. Handles made of rear burls of different Nordic stabilized woods. **Prices:** $300 to $1,100. **Remarks:** Part-time maker; first knife sold in 1988. **Mark:** Etched name and deer head.

**VITALE, MACE,** 925 Rt 80, Guilford, CT 06437, Phone: 203-457-5591
**Specialties:** Hand forged blades. **Patterns:** Hunters, utility, chef, Bowies and fighters. **Technical:** 5160, 1095, 1084, L-6. Hand forged and finished. **Prices:** $50 to $500. **Remarks:** Full-time maker; first knife sold 2001. **Mark:** MACE.

**VOGT, DONALD J.,** 9007 Hogans Bend, Tampa, FL 33647, Phone: 813 973-3245, vogtknives@aol.com
**Specialties:** Art knives, folders, automatics, large fixed blades. **Technical:** Uses Damascus steels for blade and bolsters, filework, hand carving on blade bolsters and handles. Other materials used - jewels, gold, stainless steel, mokume. Prefers to use natural handle materials. **Prices:** $800 to $7,000. **Remarks:** Part-time maker; first knife sold in 1997. **Mark:** Last name.

**VOGT, PATRIK,** KUNGSVAGEN 83, S-30270 Halmstad, SWEDEN, Phone: 46-35-30977
**Specialties:** Working straight knives. **Patterns:** Bowies, hunters and fighters. **Technical:** Forges carbon steel and own Damascus. **Prices:** From $100. **Remarks:** Not currently making knives. **Mark:** Initials or last name.

**VOORHIES, LES,** 14511 Lk. Mazaska Tr., Faribault, MN 55021, Phone: 507-332-0736
**Specialties:** Steels. **Technical:** ATS-34 Damascus. **Prices:** $75 to $450.

**VOSS, BEN,** 362 Clark St., Galesburg, IL 61401, Phone: 309-342-6994
**Specialties:** Fancy working knives of his design. **Patterns:** Bowies, fighters, hunters, boots and folders. **Technical:** Grinds 440C, ATS-34 and D2. **Prices:** $35 to $1,200. **Remarks:** Part-time maker; first knife sold in 1986. **Mark:** Name, city and state.

**VOTAW, DAVID P.,** Box 327, Pioneer, OH 43554, Phone: 419-737-2774
**Specialties:** Working knives; period pieces. **Patterns:** Hunters, Bowies, camp knives, buckskinners and tomahawks. **Technical:** Grinds O1 and D2. **Prices:** $100 to $200; some to $500. **Remarks:** Part-time maker; took over for the late W.K. Kneubuhler. Doing business as W-K Knives. **Mark:** WK with V inside anvil.

**VOWELL, DONALD J.,** 815 Berry Dr., Mayfield, KY 42066, Phone: 270-247-2157

# W

**WADA, YASUTAKA,** Fujinokidai 2-6-22, Nara City, Nara prefect 631-0044, JAPAN, Phone: 0742 46-0689
**Specialties:** Fancy and embellished one-of-a-kind straight knives of his design. **Patterns:** Bowies, daggers and hunters. **Technical:** Grinds ATS-34, Cowry X and Cowry X L-30 laminate. **Prices:** $400 to $2,500; some higher. **Remarks:** Part-time maker; first knife sold in 1990. **Mark:** Owl eyes with initial and last name underneath.

**WAGAMAN, JOHN K.,** 107 E Railroad St., Selma, NC 27576, Phone: 919-965-9659, Fax: 919-965-9901
**Specialties:** Fancy working knives. **Patterns:** Bowies, miniatures, hunters, fighters and boots. **Technical:** Grinds D2, 440C, 154CM and commercial Damascus; inlays mother-of-pearl. **Prices:** $110 to $2,000. **Remarks:** Part-time maker; first knife sold in 1975. **Mark:** Last name.

**WALDROP, MARK,** 14562 SE 1st Ave. Rd., Summerfield, FL 34491, Phone: 352-347-9034
**Specialties:** Period pieces. **Patterns:** Bowies and daggers. **Technical:** Uses stock removal. Engraves. **Prices:** Moderate to upscale. **Remarks:** Part-time maker; first knife sold in 1978. **Mark:** Last name.

**WALKER, DON,** 645 Halls Chapel Rd., Burnsville, NC 28714, Phone: 828-675-9716, dlwalkernc@aol.com

**WALKER, JIM,** 22 Walker Lane, Morrilton, AR 72110, Phone: 501-354-3175, jwalker@mail.cswnet.com
**Specialties:** Period pieces and working/using knives of his design and to customer specs. **Patterns:** Bowies, fighters, hunters, camp knives. **Technical:** Forges 5160, O1, L6, 52100, 1084, 1095. **Prices:** Start at $425. **Remarks:** Full-time maker; first knife sold in 1993. **Mark:** Three arrows with last name/ MS.

**WALKER, BILL,** 431 Walker Rd., Stevensville, MD 21666, Phone: 410-643-5041

**WALKER, JOHN W.,** 10620 Moss Branch Rd., Bon Aqua, TN 37025, Phone: 931-670-4754
**Specialties:** Straight knives, daggers and folders; sterling rings, 14K gold wire wrap; some stone setting. **Patterns:** Hunters, boot knives, others. **Technical:** Grinds 440C, ATS-34, L6, etc. Buys Damascus. **Prices:** $150 to $500; some to $1,500. **Remarks:** Part-time maker; first knife sold in 1982. **Mark:** Hohenzollern Eagle with name, or last name.

**WALKER, GEORGE A.,** PO Box 3272, 483 Aspen Hills, Alpine, WY 83128-0272, Phone: 307-883-2372, Fax: 307-883-2372, GWKNIVES@SILVERSTAR.COM
**Specialties:** Deluxe working knives. **Patterns:** Hunters, boots, fighters, Bowies and folders. **Technical:** Forges his own Damascus and cable; engraves, carves, scrimshaws. Makes sheaths. **Prices:** $125 to $750; some to $1,000. **Remarks:** Full-time maker; first knife sold in 1979. Partners with wife. **Mark:** Name, city and state.

**WALKER, MICHAEL L.,** PO Box 1924, Rancho de Taos, NM 87571, Phone: 505-737-3086, Fax: 505-751-0284, lockers@newmex.com
**Specialties:** Innovative knife designs and locking systems; Titanium and SS furniture and art. **Patterns:** Folders from utility grade to museum quality art; others upon request. **Technical:** State-of-the-art materials: titanium, stainless Damascus, gold, etc. **Prices:** $3,500 and above. **Remarks:** Designer/Metal-Crafts; Full-time professional knife maker since 1980; Four U.S. Patents; Invented Liner Lock® and was awarded Registered U.S. Trademark No. 1,585,333. **Mark:** Early mark MW, Walker's Lockers by M.L. Walker; current M.L. Walker or Michael Walker.

**WALKER III, JOHN WADE,** 2595 HWY 1647, Paintlick, KY 40461, Phone: 606-792-3498

**WALLACE, ROGER L.,** 4902 Collins Lane, Tampa, FL 33603, Phone: 813-239-3261
**Specialties:** Working straight knives, Bowies and camp knives to customer specs. **Patterns:** Hunters, skinners and utility knives. **Technical:** Forges high-carbon steel. **Prices:** Start at $75. **Remarks:** Part-time maker; first knife sold in 1985. **Mark:** First initial, last name.

**WALLINGFORD JR., CHARLES W.,** 9027 Old Union Rd, Union, KY 41091, Phone: 859-384-4141
**Specialties:** 18th and 19th century styles - Patch knives, Rifleman knives. **Technical:** 1084 and 5160 forged blades. **Prices:** $125 to $300. **Mark:** CW.

**WALTERS, A.F.,** PO Box 523, 275 Crawley Rd., TyTy, GA 31795, Phone: 229-528-6207
**Specialties:** Working knives, some to customer specs. **Patterns:** Locking folders, straight hunters, fishing and survival knives. **Technical:** Grinds D2, 154CM and 13C26. **Prices:** Start at $200. **Remarks:** Part-time maker. Label: "The jewel knife" **Mark:** "J" in diamond and knife logo.

**WARD, KEN,** 5122 Lake Shastina Blvd., Weed, CA 96094, Phone: 530-938-9720
**Specialties:** Working knives, some to customer specs. **Patterns:** Straight and folding hunters, axes, Bowies, buckskinners and miniatures. **Technical:** Grinds ATS-34, Damascus and Stellite 6K. **Prices:** $100 to $700. **Remarks:** Part-time maker; first knife sold in 1977. **Mark:** Name.

**WARD, J.J.,** 7501 S.R. 220, Waverly, OH 45690, Phone: 614-947-5328
**Specialties:** Traditional and working/using straight knives and folders of h design. **Patterns:** Hunters and locking folders. **Technical:** Grinds ATS-3 440C and Damascus. Offers handmade sheaths. **Prices:** $125 to $250; som to $500. **Remarks:** Spare-time maker; first knife sold in 1980. **Mark:** Etche name.

**WARD, W.C.,** 817 Glenn St., Clinton, TN 37716, Phone: 615-457-3568
**Specialties:** Working straight knives; period pieces. **Patterns:** Hunters, Bow ies, swords and kitchen cutlery. **Technical:** Grinds O1. **Prices:** $85 to $15 some to $500. **Remarks:** Part-time maker; first knife sold in 1969. He style the Tennessee Knife Maker. **Mark:** TKM.

**WARD, RON,** 1363 Nicholas Dr., Loveland, OH 45140, Phone: 513-72 0602
**Specialties:** Classic working and using straight knives, fantasy knives. **Pa terns:** Bowies, hunter, fighters, and utility/camp knives. **Technical:** Grin 440C, 154CM, ATS-34, uses composite and natural handle materials. **Price** $50 to $750. **Remarks:** Part-time maker, first knife sold in 1992. Doing bus ness as Ron Ward Blades. **Mark:** Ron Ward Blades, Loveland OH.

**WARD, CHUCK,** PO Box 2272, 1010 E North St, Benton, AR 72018-2272, Phone: 501-778-4329, chuckbop@aol.com
**Specialties:** Traditional working and using straight knives and folders of h design. **Technical:** Grinds 440C, D2, A2, ATS-34 and O1; uses natural a composite handle materials. **Prices:** $90 to $400, some higher. **Remark** Part-time maker; first knife sold in 1990. **Mark:** First initial, last name.

**WARDELL, MICK,** 20, Clovelly Rd., Bideford, N Devon EX39 3BU, ENGLAND, Phone: 01237 475312, Fax: 01237 475312, Web: www.wardellscustomknives.com
**Specialties:** Folders of his design. **Patterns:** Locking and slip-joint folde Bowies. **Technical:** Grinds stainless Damascus and RWL34. Heat-trea **Prices:** $200 to $2,000. **Remarks:** Full-time maker; first knife sold in 19 **Mark:** M. Wardell - England.

**WARDEN, ROY A.,** 275 Tanglewood Rd., Union, MO 63084, Phone: 314-583-8813, rwarden@mail.usmo.com
**Specialties:** Complex mosaic designs of "EDM wired figures" and " Stack patterns and "Lazer Cut" and "Torch cut" and "Sawed" patterns combin **Patterns:** Mostly "all mosaic" folders, automatics, fixed blades. **Technic** Mosaic Damascus with all tool steel edges. **Prices:** $500 to $2,000 and **Remarks:** Part-time maker; first knife sold in 1987. **Mark:** WARDEN stamp or initials connected.

**WARE, TOMMY,** PO Box 488, Datil, NM 87821, Phone: 505-772-5817
**Specialties:** Traditional working and using straight knives, folders and au matics of his design and to customer specs. **Patterns:** Hunters, automat and locking folders. **Technical:** Grinds ATS-34, 440C and D2. Offers engr ing and scrimshaw. **Prices:** $275 to $575; some to $1,000. **Remarks:** F time maker; first knife sold in 1990. Doing business as Wano Knives. **Ma** Last name inside oval, business name above, city and state below, year side.

**WARENSKI, BUSTER,** PO Box 214, Richfield, UT 84701, Phone: 435 896-5319, Fax: 435-896-8333, buster@warenskiknives.com Web: www.warenskiknives.com
**Specialties:** Investor-class straight knives. **Patterns:** Daggers, swords. **Te nical:** Grinds, engraves and inlays; offers surface treatments. All engraved Julie Warenski. **Prices:** Upscale. **Remarks:** Full-time maker. **Mark:** Warer (hand engraved on blade).

**WARREN, DANIEL,** 571 Lovejoy Rd., Canton, NC 28716, Phone: 828 648-7351
**Specialties:** Using knives. **Patterns:** Drop point hunters. **Prices:** $200 $500. **Mark:** Warren-Bethel NC.

**WARREN, AL,** 1423 Sante Fe Circle, Roseville, CA 95678, Phone: 91 784-3217/Cell Phone 916-257-5904, al@warrenknives.com Web: www.warrenknives.com
**Specialties:** Working straight knives and folders, some fancy. **Patter** Hunters, Bowies, daggers, short swords, fillets, folders and kitchen kni **Technical:** Grinds D2, ATS-34 and 440C, 440V. **Prices:** $110 to $1, some to $3,700. **Remarks:** Part-time maker; first knife sold in 1978. **Ma** First and middle initials, last name.

**WARREN DELLANA, SEE DELLANA**

**WARTHER, DALE,** 331 Karl Ave., Dover, OH 44622, Phone: 216-34 7513
**Specialties:** Working knives; period pieces. **Patterns:** Kitchen cutlery, d gers, hunters and some folders. **Technical:** Forges and grinds O1, D2 440C. **Prices:** $250 to $7,000. **Remarks:** Full-time maker; first knife sol 1967. Takes orders only at shows or by personal interviews at his shop. **Ma** Warther Originals.

**WASHBURN, ARTHUR D.,** ADW CUSTOM KNIVES, 10 Hinman St/ POB 625, Pioche, NV 89043, Phone: 775-962-5463, awashburn@adw-customknives.com; Web: www.adwcustomknives.com
**Specialties:** Locking liner folders. **Patterns:** Slip joint folders (single and multiplied), lock-back folders, some fixed blades. Do own heat-treating; Rockwell test each blade. **Technical:** Carbon and stainless Damascus, some 1084, 1095, ATS-34. **Prices:** $200 to $1,000 and up. **Remarks:** Sold first knife in 1997. Part-time maker. **Mark:** ADW enclosed in an oval or ADW.

**WASHBURN JR., ROBERT LEE,** 244 Lovett Scott Rd., Adrian, GA 31002, Phone: 475-275-7926, Fax: 475-272-6849, washburn@nlamer-ica.com Web: www.washburnknives.com
**Specialties:** Hand-forged period, Bowies, tactical, boot and hunters. **Patterns:** Bowies, tantos, loot hunters, tactical and folders. **Prices:** $100 to $2,500. **Remarks:** All hand forged. 52100 being his favorite steel. **Mark:** Washburn Knives W of Dublin GA.

**WATANABE, WAYNE,** PO Box 3563, Montebello, CA 90640, wwknives@earthlink.net Web: www.geocities.com/ww-knives
**Specialties:** Straight knives in Japanese-styles. One-of-a-kind designs; welcomes customer designs. **Patterns:** Tantos to katanas, Bowies. **Technical:** Flat grinds A2, O1 and ATS-34. Offers hand-rubbed finishes and wrapped handles. **Prices:** Start at $200. **Remarks:** Part-time maker. **Mark:** Name in characters with flower.

**WATERS, GLENN,** 11 Shinakawa Machi, Hirosaki City 036-8183, JAPAN, Phone: 172-33-8881, gwaters@luck.ocn.ne.jp Web: www.glen-nwaters.com
**Specialties:** One-of-a-kind collector-grade highly embellished art knives. Folders, fixed blades, and automatics. **Patterns:** Locking liner folders, automatics and fixed art knives. **Technical:** Grinds blades from Damasteel, and selected Damascus makers, mostly stainless. Does own engraving, gold inlaying and stone setting, filework, and carving. Gold and Japanese precious metal fabrication. Prefers exotic material, high karat gold, silver, Shyaku Dou, Shibu Ichi Gin, precious gemstones. **Prices:** Upscale. **Remarks:** Designs and makes some-of-a-kind highly embellished art knives often with fully engraved handles and blades. A jeweler by trade for 20 years before starting to make knives. Full-time since 1999, first knife sold in 1994. **Mark:** Glenn Waters maker Japan, G. Waters or Glen in Japanese writing.

**WATERS, HERMAN HAROLD,** 2516 Regency, Magnolia, AR 71753, Phone: 870-234-5409

**WATERS, LU,** 2516 Regency, Magnolia, AR 71753, Phone: 870-234-5409

**WATSON, BERT,** PO Box 26, Westminster, CO 80036-0026, Phone: 303-426-7577
**Specialties:** Working/using straight knives of his design and to customer specs. **Patterns:** Hunters, utility/camp knives. **Technical:** Grinds O1, ATS-34, 440C, D2, A2 and others. **Prices:** $50 to $250. **Remarks:** Part-time maker; first knife sold in 1974. Doing business as Game Trail Knives. **Mark:** GTK stamped or etched, sometimes with first or last name.

**WATSON, BILLY,** 440 Forge Rd., Deatsville, AL 36022, Phone: 334-265-1482, billy@watsonknives.com Web: www.watsonknives.com
**Specialties:** Working and using straight knives and folders of his design; period pieces. **Patterns:** Hunters, Bowies and utility/camp knives. **Technical:** Forges and grinds his own Damascus, 1095, 5160 and 52100. **Prices:** $40 to $1,500. **Remarks:** Full-time maker; first knife sold in 1970. Doing business as Billy's Blacksmith Shop. **Mark:** Last name.

**WATSON, DANIEL,** 350 Jennifer Ln., Driftwood, TX 78619, Phone: 512-847-9679, info@angelsword.com Web: http://www.angelsword.com
**Specialties:** One-of-a-kind knives and swords. **Patterns:** Hunters, daggers, swords. **Technical:** Hand-purify and carbonize his own high-carbon steel, pattern-welded Damascus, cable and carbon-induced crystalline Damascus. Techno-Wootz ™Damascus steel, heat treats including cryogenic processing. European and Japanese tempering. **Prices:** $125 to $25,000. **Remarks:** Full-time maker; first knife sold in 1979. **Mark:** "Angel Sword" on forged pieces; "Bright Knight" for stock removal. Avatar on Techno-Wootz ™ Damascus. Kumon on traditional Japanese blades.

**WATSON, PETER,** 66 Kielblock St., La Hoff 2570, SOUTH AFRICA, Phone: 018-84942
**Specialties:** Traditional working and using straight knives and folders of his design. **Patterns:** Hunters, locking folders and utility/camp knives. **Technical:** Sandvik and 440C. **Prices:** $120 to $250; some to $1,500. **Remarks:** Part-time maker; first knife sold in 1989. **Mark:** Buffalo head with name.

**WATSON, TOM,** 1103 Brenau Terrace, Panama City, FL 32405, Phone: 850-785-9209, tomwatsonknives@aol.com Web: www.tomwat-sonknives.com
**Specialties:** Liner-lock folders. **Patterns:** Tactical, utility and art investment pieces. **Technical:** Flat-grinds ATS-34, 440-V, Damascus. **Prices:** Tactical start at $250, investment pieces $500 and up. **Remarks:** In business since 1978. **Mark:** Name and city.

**WATT III, FREDDIE,** PO Box 1372, Big Spring, TX 79721, Phone: 915-263-6629
**Specialties:** Working straight knives, some fancy. **Patterns:** Hunters, fighters and Bowies. **Technical:** Grinds A2, D2, 440C and ATS-34; prefers mirror finishes. **Prices:** $150 to $350; some to $750. **Remarks:** Full-time maker; first knife sold in 1979. **Mark:** Last name, city and state.

**WATTELET, MICHAEL A.,** PO Box 649, 125 Front, Minocqua, WI 54548, Phone: 715-356-3069, redtroll@nnex.net
**Specialties:** Working and using straight knives of his design and to customer specs; fantasy knives. **Patterns:** Daggers, fighters and swords. **Technical:** Grinds 440C and L6; forges and grinds O1. Silversmith. **Prices:** $75 to $1,000; some to $5,000. **Remarks:** Full-time maker; first knife sold in 1966. Doing business as M and N Arts Ltd. **Mark:** First initial, last name.

**WATTS, WALLY,** 9560 S. Hwy. 36, Gatesville, TX 76528, Phone: 254-487-2866
**Specialties:** Unique traditional folders of his design. **Patterns:** One- to five-blade folders and single-blade gents in various blade shapes. **Technical:** Grinds ATS-34; Damascus on request. **Prices:** $165 to $500. **Remarks:** Full-time maker; first knife sold in 1986. **Mark:** Last name.

**WATTS, JOHNATHAN,** 9560 S State Hwy 36, Gatesville, TX 76528, Phone: 254-487-2866
**Specialties:** Traditional folders. **Patterns:** One and two blade folders in various blade shapes. **Technical:** Grinds ATS-34 and Damascus on request. **Prices:** $120 to $400. **Remarks:** Part-time maker; first knife sold in 1997. **Mark:** J Watts.

**WEDDLE JR., DEL,** 2703 Green Valley Rd., St. Joseph, MO 64505, Phone: 816-364-1981
**Specialties:** Working knives; some period pieces. **Patterns:** Hunters, fighters, locking folders, push knives. **Technical:** Grinds D2 and 440C; can provide precious metals and set gems. Offers his own forged wire-cable Damascus in his finished knives. **Prices:** $80 to $250; some to $2,000. **Remarks:** Full-time maker; first knife sold in 1972. **Mark:** Signature with last name and date.

**WEHNER, RUDY,** 297 William Warren Rd, Collins, MS 39428, Phone: 601-765-4997
**Specialties:** Reproduction antique Bowies and contemporary Bowies in full and miniature. **Patterns:** Skinners, camp knives, fighters, axes and Bowies. **Technical:** Grinds 440C, ATS-34, 154CM and Damascus. **Prices:** $100 to $500; some to $850. **Remarks:** Full-time maker; first knife sold in 1975. **Mark:** Last name on Bowies and antiques; full name, city and state on skinners.

**WEILAND JR., J. REESE,** PO Box 2337, Riverview, FL 33568, Phone: 813-671-0661, RWPHIL413@earthlink.net Web: www.rwcus-tomknive.som
**Specialties:** Hawk bills; tactical to fancy folders. **Patterns:** Hunters, tantos, Bowies, fantasy knives, spears and some swords. **Technical:** Grinds ATS-34, 154CM, 440C, D2, 01, A2, Damascus. Titanium hardware on locking liners and button locks. **Prices:** $150 to $4,000. **Other:** Full-time maker, first knife sold in 1978. Knifemakers Guild member since 1988.

**WEILER, DONALD E.,** PO Box 1576, Yuma, AZ 85366-9576, Phone: 928-782-1159
**Specialties:** Working straight knives; period pieces. **Patterns:** Strong spring-buck folders, blade and spring ATS-34. **Technical:** Forges O1, W2, 5160, ATS-34, D2, 52100, L6 and cable Damascus. Makes his own high-carbon steel Damascus. **Prices:** $150 to $1,000. **Remarks:** Full-time maker; first knife sold in 1952. **Mark:** Last name, city.

**WEINAND, GEROME M.,** 14440 Harpers Bridge Rd., Missoula, MT 59808, Phone: 406-543-0845
**Specialties:** Working straight knives. **Patterns:** Bowies, fishing and camp knives, large special hunters. **Technical:** Grinds O1, 440C, ATS-34, 1084, L6, also stainless Damascus, Aebl and 304; makes all-tool steel Damascus; Dendritic D2 from powdered steel. Heat-treats. **Prices:** $30 to $100; some to $500. **Remarks:** Full-time maker; first knife sold in 1982. **Mark:** Last name.

**WEINSTOCK, ROBERT,** PO Box 170028, San Francisco, CA 94117-0028, Phone: 415-731-5968, weinstock_r@msn.com
**Specialties:** Fancy and high-art straight knives of his design. **Patterns:** Daggers, folders, poignards and miniatures. **Technical:** Grinds A2, O1 and 440C. Chased and hand-carved blades and handles. Also using various Damascus steels from other makers. **Prices:** $3,000 to 7,000+. **Remarks:** Full-time maker; first knife sold in1994. **Mark:** Last name carved.

**WEISS, CHARLES L.,** 18847 N. 13th Ave., Phoenix, AZ 85027, Phone: 623-582-6147, weissknife@juno.com Web: www.weissknives.com
**Specialties:** High-art straight knives and folders; deluxe period pieces. **Patterns:** Daggers, fighters, boots, push knives and miniatures. **Technical:**

Grinds 440C, 154CM and ATS-34. **Prices:** $300 to $1,200; some to $2,000. **Remarks:** Full-time maker; first knife sold in 1975. **Mark:** Name and city.

**WERNER JR., WILLIAM A.,** 336 Lands Mill, Marietta, GA 30067, Phone: 404-988-0074
**Specialties:** Fantasy and working/using straight knives. **Patterns:** Bowies, daggers, fighters. **Technical:** Grinds 440C stainless, 10 series carbon and Damascus. **Prices:** $150 to $400; some to $750. **Remarks:** Part-time maker. Doing business as Werner Knives. **Mark:** Last name.

**WERTH, GEORGE W.,** 5223 Woodstock Rd., Poplar Grove, IL 61065, Phone: 815-544-4408
**Specialties:** Period pieces, some fancy. **Patterns:** Straight fighters, daggers and Bowies. **Technical:** Forges and grinds O1, 1095 and his Damascus, including mosaic patterns. **Prices:** $200 to $650; some higher. **Remarks:** Full-time maker. Doing business as Fox Valley Forge. **Mark:** Name in logo or initials connected.

**WESCOTT, CODY,** 5330 White Wing Rd., Las Cruces, NM 88012, Phone: 505-382-5008
**Specialties:** Fancy and presentation-grade working knives. **Patterns:** Hunters, locking folders and Bowies. **Technical:** Hollow-grinds D2 and ATS-34; all knives file worked. Offers some engraving. Makes sheaths. **Prices:** $80 to $300; some to $950. **Remarks:** Full-time maker; first knife sold in 1982. **Mark:** First initial, last name.

**WEST, CHARLES A.,** 1315 S. Pine St., Centralia, IL 62801, Phone: 618-532-2777
**Specialties:** Classic, fancy, high tech, period pieces, traditional and working/using straight knives and folders. **Patterns:** Bowies, fighters and locking folders. **Technical:** Grinds ATS-34, O1 and Damascus. Prefers hot blued finishes. **Prices:** $100 to $1,000; some to $2,000. **Remarks:** Full-time maker; first knife sold in 1963. Doing business as West Custom Knives. **Mark:** Name or name, city and state.

**WEST, PAT,** PO Box 9, Charlotte, TX 78011, Phone: 830-277-1290
**Specialties:** Classic working and using straight knives and folders. **Patterns:** Hunters, kitchen knives, slip-joint folders. **Technical:** Grinds ATS-34, D2 and Vascowear. Offers filework and decorates liners on folders. **Prices:** $300 to $600. **Remarks:** Spare-time maker; first knife sold in 1984. **Mark:** Name.

**WESTBERG, LARRY,** 305 S. Western Hills Dr., Algona, IA 50511, Phone: 515-295-9276
**Specialties:** Traditional and working straight knives of his design and in standard patterns. **Patterns:** Bowies, hunters, fillets and folders. **Technical:** Grinds 440C, D2 and 1095. Heat-treats. Uses natural handle materials. **Prices:** $85 to $600; some to $1,000. **Remarks:** Part-time maker; first knife sold in 1987. **Mark:** Last name-town and state.

**WHEELER, ROBERT,** 289 S Jefferson, Bradley, IL 60915, Phone: 815-932-5854

**WHEELER, GARY,** 351 Old Hwy 48, Clarksville, TN 37040, Phone: 931-552-3092, ir22shtr@charter.net
**Specialties:** Working to high end fixed blades. **Patterns:** Bowies, Hunters, combat knives, daggers and a few folders. **Technical:** Forges 5160, 1080, 52100 and his own Damascus, will use stainless steels on request. **Prices:** $125 to $2,000. **Remarks:** Full-time maker since 2001, first knife sold in 1985 collaborates/works at B&W blade works. **Mark:** Stamped last name.

**WHETSELL, ALEX,** 1600 Palmetto Tyrone Rd., Sharpsburg, GA 30277, Phone: 770-463-4881
**Specialties:** Knifekits.com, a source for fold locking liner type and straight knife kits. Our kits are industry standard for folding knife kits. **Technical:** Many selections of colored G10 carbon fiber and wood handle material for our kits as well as bulk sizes for the custom knife maker, heat treated folding knife pivots, screws, bushings, etc.

**WHIPPLE, WESLEY A.,** PO Box 3771, Kodiak, AK 99615, Phone: 907-486-6737
**Specialties:** Working straight knives, some fancy. **Patterns:** Hunters, Bowies, camp knives, fighters. **Technical:** Forges high-carbon steels, Damascus, offers relief carving and silver wire inlay checkering. **Prices:** $200 to $1,400; some higher. **Remarks:** Part-time maker; first knife sold in 1989. **Mark:** Last name/JS. **Other:** A.K.A. Wilderness Knife and Forge.

**WHITE, ROBERT J.,** RR 1, 641 Knox Rd. 900 N., Gilson, IL 61436, Phone: 309-289-4487
**Specialties:** Working knives, some deluxe. **Patterns:** Bird and trout knives, hunters, survival knives and locking folders. **Technical:** Grinds A2, D2 and 440C; commercial Damascus. Heat-treats. **Prices:** $125 to $250; some to $600. **Remarks:** Full-time maker; first knife sold in 1976. **Mark:** Last name in script.

**WHITE, DALE,** 525 CR 212, Sweetwater, TX 79556, Phone: 325-798-4178, dalew@taylortel.net
**Specialties:** Working and using knives. **Patterns:** Hunters, skinners, utilitie and Bowies. **Technical:** Grinds 440C, offers file work, fancy pins and scrim shaw by Sherry Sellers. **Prices:** From $45 to $300. **Remarks:** Sold first knif in 1975. **Mark:** Full name, city and state.

**WHITE, GENE E.,** 6620 Briarleigh Way, Alexandria, VA 22315, Phone: 703-924-1268
**Specialties:** Small utility/gents knives. **Patterns:** Eight standard hunter most other patterns on commission basis. Currently no swords, axes and fan tasy knives. **Technical:** Stock removal 440C and D2; others on reques Mostly hollow grinds; some flat grinds. Prefers natural handle material Makes own sheaths. **Prices:** Start at $85. **Remarks:** Part-time maker; fir knife sold in 1971. **Mark:** First and middle initials, last name.

**WHITE, LOU,** 7385 Red Bud Rd. NE, Ranger, GA 30734, Phone: 706-334-2273

**WHITE, BRYCE,** 1415 W Col. Glenn Rd., Little Rock, AR 72210, Phone 501-821-2956
**Specialties:** Hunters, fighters, makes Damascus, file work, handmade onl **Technical:** L6, 1075, 1095, 01 steels used most. **Patterns:** Will do any pa tern or use his own. **Prices:** $200 to $300. Sold first knife in 1995. **Mar** White.

**WHITE, RICHARD T.,** 359 Carver St, Grosse Pointe Farms, MI 48236, Phone: 313-881-4690

**WHITE JR., ROBERT J. BUTCH,** RR 1, Gilson, IL 61436, Phone: 309-289-4487
**Specialties:** Folders of all sizes. **Patterns:** Hunters, fighters, boots and fol ers. **Technical:** Forges Damascus; grinds tool and stainless steels. **Price** $500 to $1,800. **Remarks:** Spare-time maker; first knife sold in 1980. **Mar** Last name in block letters.

**WHITENECT, JODY,** Elderbank, Halifax County, Nova Scotia, CANAD B0N 1K0, Phone: 902-384-2511
**Specialties:** Fancy and embellished working/using straight knives of h design and to customer specs. **Patterns:** Bowies, fighters and hunters. **Tec nical:** Forges 1095 and O1; forges and grinds ATS-34. Various filework blades and bolsters. **Prices:** $200 to $400; some to $800. **Remarks:** Pa time maker; first knife sold in 1996. **Mark:** Longhorn stamp or engraved.

**WHITLEY, WELDON G.,** 1308 N Robin Ave., Odessa, TX 79764, Phon 915-584-2274
**Specialties:** Working knives of his design or to customer specs. **Pattern** Hunters, folders and various double-edged knives. **Technical:** Grinds 440 154CM and ATS-34. **Prices:** $150 to $1,250. **Mark:** Name, address, road-ru ner logo.

**WHITLEY, L. WAYNE,** 1675 Carrow Rd., Chocowinity, NC 27817-949 Phone: 252-946-5648

**WHITMAN, JIM,** 21044 Salem St., Chugiak, AK 99567, Phone: 907-68 4575, Fax: 907-688-4278, Web: www.whitmanknives.com
**Specialties:** Working straight knives and folders; some art pieces. **Patterr** Hunters, skinners, Bowies, camp knives, working fighters, swords and hat ets. **Technical:** Grinds AEB-L Swedish, 440C, 154CM, ATS-34, and Da ascus in full convex. Prefers exotic hardwoods, natural and native han materials—whale bone, antler, ivory and horn. **Prices:** Start at $1 **Remarks:** Full-time maker; first knife sold in 1983. **Mark:** Name, city, state.

**WHITMIRE, EARL T.,** 725 Colonial Dr., Rock Hill, SC 29730, Phone: 803-324-8384
**Specialties:** Working straight knives, some to customer specs; some fant pieces. **Patterns:** Hunters, fighters and fishing knives. **Technical:** Grinds D 440C and 154CM. **Prices:** $40 to $200; some to $250. **Remarks:** Full-ti maker; first knife sold in 1967. **Mark:** Name, city, state in oval logo.

**WHITTAKER, WAYNE,** 2900 Woodland Ct., Metamore, MI 48455, Phone: 810-797-5315
**Specialties:** Folders, hunters on request. **Patterns:** Bowies, daggers a hunters. **Technical:** ATS-34 S.S. and Damascus **Prices:** $300 to $500; so to $2,000. **Remarks:** Full-time maker; first knife sold in 1985. **Mark:** Etc name on one side.

**WHITTAKER, ROBERT E.,** PO Box 204, Mill Creek, PA 17060
**Specialties:** Using straight knives. Has a line of knives for buckskinners. **P terns:** Hunters, skinners and Bowies. **Technical:** Grinds O1, A2 and Offers filework. **Prices:** $35 to $100. **Remarks:** Part-time maker; first kn sold in 1980. **Mark:** Last initial or full initials.

**WHITWORTH, KEN J.,** 41667 Tetley Ave., Sterling Heights, MI 4807 Phone: 313-739-5720
**Specialties:** Working straight knives and folders. **Patterns:** Locking fold slip-joints and boot knives. **Technical:** Grinds 440C, 154CM and D2. **Pric**

$100 to $225; some to $450. **Remarks:** Part-time maker; first knife sold in 1976. **Mark:** Last name.

**WICKER, DONNIE R.,** 2544 E. 40th Ct., Panama City, FL 32405, Phone: 904-785-9158
**Specialties:** Traditional working and using straight knives of his design or to customer specs. **Patterns:** Hunters, fighters and slip-joint folders. **Technical:** Grinds 440C, ATS-34, D2 and 154CM. Heat-treats and does hardness testing. **Prices:** $90 to $200; some to $400. **Remarks:** Part-time maker; first knife sold in 1975. **Mark:** First and middle initials, last name.

**WIGGINS, HORACE,** 203 Herndon, Box 152, Mansfield, LA 71502, Phone: 318-872-4471
**Specialties:** Fancy working knives. **Patterns:** Straight and folding hunters. **Technical:** Grinds O1, D2 and 440C. **Prices:** $90 to $275. **Remarks:** Part-time maker; first knife sold in 1970. **Mark:** Name, city and state in diamond logo.

**WILCHER, WENDELL L.,** RR 6 Box 6573, Palestine, TX 75801, Phone: 903-549-2530
**Specialties:** Fantasy, miniatures and working/using straight knives and folders of his design and to customer specs. **Patterns:** Fighters, hunters, locking folders. **Technical:** Hand works (hand file and hand sand knives), not grind. **Prices:** $75 to $250; some to $600. **Remarks:** Part-time maker; first knife sold in 1987. **Mark:** Initials, year, serial number.

**WILE, PETER,** RR 3, Bridgewater, Nova Scotia, CANADA B4V 2W2, Phone: 902-543-1373, peterwile@ns.sympatico.ca
**Specialties:** Collector-grade one-of-a-kind file-worked folders. **Patterns:** Folders or fixed blades of his design or to customers specs. **Technical:** Grinds ATS-34, carbon and stainless Damascus. Does intricate filework on blades, spines and liners. Carves. Prefers natural handle materials. Does own heat treating. **Prices:** $350 to $2,000; some to $4,000. **Remarks:** Part-time maker; sold first knife in 1985; doing business as Wile Knives. **Mark:** Wile.

**WILKINS, MITCHELL,** 15523 Rabon Chapel Rd., Montgomery, TX 77316, Phone: 936-588-2696, mwilkins@consolidated.net

**WILLEY, W.G.,** 14210 Sugar Hill Rd, Greenwood, DE 19950, Phone: 302-349-4070, Web: www.willeyknives.com
**Specialties:** Fancy working straight knives. **Patterns:** Small game knives, Bowies and throwing knives. **Technical:** Grinds 440C and 154CM. **Prices:** $350 to $600; some to $1,500. **Remarks:** Part-time maker; first knife sold in 1975. Owns retail store. **Mark:** Last name inside map logo.

**WILLIAMS, MICHAEL L.,** Rt. 4, PO Box 64-1, Broken Bow, OK 74728, Phone: 405-494-6326, hforge@pine-net.com
**Specialties:** Plain to fancy working and dress knives. **Patterns:** Hunters, Bowies, camp knives and others. **Technical:** Forges 1084, L6, 52100 and pattern-welded steel. **Prices:** $295 and up. **Remarks:** Part-time maker; first knife sold in 1989. ABS Master Smith. **Mark:** Williams.

**WILLIAMS, JASON L.,** PO Box 67, Wyoming, RI 02898, Phone: 401-539-8353, Fax: 401-539-0252
**Specialties:** Fancy and high tech folders of his design, co-inventor of the Axis Lock. **Patterns:** Fighters, locking folders, automatics and fancy pocket knives. **Technical:** Forges Damascus and other steels by request. Uses exotic handle materials and precious metals. Offers inlaid spines and gemstone thumb knobs. **Prices:** $1,000 and up. **Remarks:** Full-time maker; first knife sold in 1989. **Mark:** First and last initials on pivot.

**WILLIAMS JR., RICHARD,** 1440 Nancy Circle, Morristown, TN 37814, Phone: 615-581-0059
**Specialties:** Working and using straight knives of his design or to customer specs. **Patterns:** Hunters, dirks and utility/camp knives. **Technical:** Forges 5160 and uses file steel. Hand-finish is standard; offers filework. **Prices:** $80 to $180; some to $250. **Remarks:** Spare-time maker; first knife sold in 1985. **Mark:** Last initial or full initials.

**WILLIAMSON, TONY,** Rt. 3, Box 503, Siler City, NC 27344, Phone: 919-663-3551
**Specialties:** Flint knapping—knives made of obsidian flakes and flint with wood, antler or bone for handles. **Patterns:** Skinners, daggers and flake knives. **Technical:** Blades have width/thickness ratio of at least 4 to 1. Hafts with methods available to prehistoric man. **Prices:** $58 to $160. **Remarks:** Student of Errett Callahan. **Mark:** Initials and number code to identify year and number of knives made.

**WILLIS, BILL,** RT 7 Box 7549, Ava, MO 65608, Phone: 417-683-4326
**Specialties:** Forged blades, Damascus and carbon steel. **Patterns:** Cable, random or ladder lamented. **Technical:** Professionally heat treated blades. **Prices:** $75 to $600. **Remarks:** Lifetime guarantee on all blades against breakage. **Mark:** WF. **Other:** All work done by myself; including leather work.

**WILSON, JON J.,** 1826 Ruby St., Johnstown, PA 15902, Phone: 814-266-6410
**Specialties:** Miniatures and full size. **Patterns:** Bowies, daggers and hunters. **Technical:** Grinds Damascus, 440C and O1. Scrimshaws and carves. **Prices:** $75 to $500; some higher. **Remarks:** Full-time maker; first knife sold in 1988. **Mark:** First and middle initials, last name.

**WILSON, RON,** 2639 Greenwood Ave., Morro Bay, CA 93442, Phone: 805-772-3381
**Specialties:** Classic and fantasy straight knives of his design. **Patterns:** Daggers, fighters, swords and axes-mostly all miniatures. **Technical:** Forges and grinds Damascus and various tool steels; grinds meteorite. Uses gold, precious stones and exotic wood. **Prices:** Vary. **Remarks:** Part-time maker; first knives sold in 1995. **Mark:** Stamped first and last initials.

**WILSON, PHILIP C.,** SEAMOUNT KNIFEWORKS, PO Box 846, Mountain Ranch, CA 95246, Phone: 209-754-1990, SEAMOUNT@BIGPLANET.COM
**Specialties:** Working knives; emphasis on salt water fillet knives and utility hunters of his design. **Patterns:** Fishing knives, hunters, kitchen knives. **Technical:** Grinds CPM S-30V, CPM10V, S-90V and 154CM. Heat-treats and Rockwell tests all blades. **Prices:** Start at $280. **Remarks:** First knife sold in 1985. Doing business as Sea-Mount Knife Works. **Mark:** Signature.

**WILSON, JAMES G.,** PO Box 4024, Estes Park, CO 80517, Phone: 303-586-3944
**Specialties:** Bronze Age knives; Medieval and Scottish-styles; tomahawks. **Patterns:** Bronze knives, daggers, swords, spears and battle axes; 12-inch steel Misericorde daggers, sgian dubhs, "his and her" skinners, bird and fish knives, capers, boots and daggers. **Technical:** Casts bronze; grinds D2, 440C and ATS-34. **Prices:** $49 to $400; some to $1,300. **Remarks:** Part-time maker; first knife sold in 1975. **Mark:** WilsonHawk.

**WILSON, R.W.,** PO Box 2012, Weirton, WV 26062, Phone: 304-723-2771
**Specialties:** Working straight knives; period pieces. **Patterns:** Bowies, tomahawks and patch knives. **Prices:** $85 to $175; some to $1,000. **Technical:** Grinds 440C; scrimshaws. **Remarks:** Part-time maker; first knife sold in 1966. Knife maker supplier. Offers free knife-making lessons. **Mark:** Name in tomahawk.

**WILSON, MIKE,** 1416 McDonald Rd., Hayesville, NC 28904, Phone: 828-389-8145
**Specialties:** Fancy working and using straight knives of his design or to customer specs, folders. **Patterns:** Hunters, Bowies, utility knives, gut hooks, skinners, fighters and miniatures. **Technical:** Hollow-grinds 440C, L-6, 01 and D2. Mirror finishes are standard. Offers filework. **Prices:** $50 to $600. **Remarks:** Full-time maker; first knife sold in 1985. **Mark:** Last name.

**WILSON (SEE SIMONELLA, GIANLUIGI), ,**

**WIMPFF, CHRISTIAN,** PO Box 700526, 70574 Stuttgart 70, GERMANY, Phone: 711 7260 749, Fax: 711 7260 749
**Specialties:** High-tech folders of his design. **Patterns:** Boots, locking folders and liners locks. **Technical:** Offers meteorite, bolsters and blades. **Prices:** $1,000 to $2,800; some to $4,000. **Remarks:** Full-time maker; first knife sold in 1984. **Mark:** First initial, last name.

**WINBERG, DOUGLAS R.,** 19720 Hwy 78, Ramona, CA 92076, Phone: 760-788-8304

**WINGO, GARY,** 240 Ogeechee, Ramona, OK 74061, Phone: 918-536-1067, wingg_2000@yahoo.com Web: www.geocities.com/wings_2000/gary.html
**Specialties:** Folder specialist. Steel 44OC, D2, others on request. Handle bone-stag, others on request. **Patterns:** Trapper three-blade stockman, four-blade congress, single- and two-blade barlows. **Prices:** 150 to $400. **Mark:** First knife sold 1994. Steer head with Wingo Knives or Straight line Wingo Knives.

**WINGO, PERRY,** 22 55th St., Gulfport, MS 39507, Phone: 228-863-3193
**Specialties:** Traditional working straight knives. **Patterns:** Hunters, skinners, Bowies and fishing knives. **Technical:** Grinds 440C. **Prices:** $75 to $1,000. **Remarks:** Full-time maker; first knife sold in 1988. **Mark:** Last name.

**WINKLER, DANIEL,** PO Box 2166, Blowing Rock, NC 28605, Phone: 828-295-9156, daniel@winklerknives.com Web: www.winklerknives.com
**Specialties:** Forged cutlery styled in the tradition of an era past. **Patterns:** Fixed blades, friction folders, axes/tomahawks and war clubs. **Technical:** Forges and grinds carbon steels and his own Damascus. **Prices:** $200 to $4,000. **Remarks:** Full-time maker since 1988. Exclusively offers leatherwork by Karen Shook. **Mark:** Initials connected. **Other:** ABS Master Smith; Knifemakers Guild voting member.

**WINN, TRAVIS A.,** 558 E. 3065 S., Salt Lake City, UT 84106, Phone: 801-467-5957
**Specialties:** Fancy working knives and knives to customer specs. **Patterns:** Hunters, fighters, boots, Bowies and fancy daggers, some miniatures, tantos and fantasy knives. **Technical:** Grinds D2 and 440C. Embellishes. **Prices:** $125 to $500; some higher. **Remarks:** Part-time maker; first knife sold in 1976. **Mark:** TRAV stylized.

**WINSTON, DAVID,** 1671 Red Holly St., Starkville, MS 39759, Phone: 601-323-1028
**Specialties:** Fancy and traditional knives of his design and to customer specs. **Patterns:** Bowies, daggers, hunters, boot knives and folders. **Technical:** Grinds 440C, ATS-34 and D2. Offers filework; heat-treats. **Prices:** $40 to $750; some higher. **Remarks:** Part-time maker; first knife sold in 1984. Offers lifetime sharpening for original owner. **Mark:** Last name.

**WINTER, GEORGE,** 5940 Martin Hwy., Union City, TN 38261

**WIRTZ, ACHIM,** Mittelstrasse 58, WUERSELEN, D -52146, GERMANY, Phone: 0049-2405-462-486, wootz@web.de Web: www.7knifedwarfs.com
**Specialties:** Period pieces, Scandinavian and middle east-style knives. **Technical:** Forged blades, makes Damascus, Mossic, Woots. Stainless Woots. Mokume. **Prices:** Start at $50. **Remarks:** Spare-time maker. First knife sold in 1997. **Mark:** Stylized initials.

**WISE, DONALD,** 304 Bexhill Rd., St. Leonardo-On-Sea, East Sussex, TN3 8AL, ENGLAND
**Specialties:** Fancy and embellished working straight knives to customer specs. **Patterns:** Hunters, Bowies and daggers. **Technical:** Grinds Sandvik 12C27, D2 D3 and O1. Scrimshaws. **Prices:** $110 to $300; some to $500. **Remarks:** Full-time maker; first knife sold in 1983. **Mark:** KNIFECRAFT.

**WITSAMAN, EARL,** 3957 Redwing Circle, Stow, OH 44224, Phone: 330-688-4208, eawits@aol.com Web: http://hometown.aol.com//eawits/index.html
**Specialties:** Straight and fantasy miniatures. **Patterns:** Wide variety—Randalls to D-guard Bowies. **Technical:** Grinds O1, 440C and 300 stainless; buys Damascus; highly detailed work. **Prices:** $85 to $300. **Remarks:** Part-time maker; first knife sold in1974. **Mark:** Initials.

**WOLF, BILL,** 4618 N. 79th Ave., Phoenix, AZ 85033, Phone: 623-846-3585, Fax: 623-846-3585, bwolf@cox.net
**Specialties:** Investor-grade folders and straight knives. **Patterns:** Lockback, slip joint and side lock interframes. **Technical:** Grinds ATS-34 and 440C. **Prices:** $400 to $10,000. **Remarks:** Full-time maker; first knife sold in 1989. **Mark:** Name.

**WOLF JR., WILLIAM LYNN,** 4006 Frank Rd., Lagrange, TX 78945, Phone: 409-247-4626

**WOOD, WILLIAM W.,** PO Box 606, Seymour, TX 76380, Phone: 817-888-5832
**Specialties:** Exotic working knives with Middle-East flavor. **Patterns:** Fighters, boots and some utility knives. **Technical:** Grinds D2 and 440C; buys Damascus. Prefers hand-rubbed satin finishes; uses only natural handle materials. **Prices:** $300 to $600; some to $2,000. **Remarks:** Full-time maker; first knife sold in 1977. **Mark:** Name, city and state.

**WOOD, WEBSTER,** 22041 Shelton Trail, Atlanta, MI 49709, Phone: 989-785-2996, littlewolf@racc2000.com
**Specialties:** Work mainly in stainless; art knives, Bowies, hunters and folders. **Remarks:** Full-time maker; first knife sold in 1980. Guild member since 1984. All engraving done by maker. **Mark:** Initials inside shield and name.

**WOOD, OWEN DALE,** 6492 Garrison St., Arvada, CO 80004-3157, Phone: 303-466-2748, ow2knives@cs.com
**Specialties:** Folding, knives and daggers. **Patterns:** Own Damascus, specialties in 456 composite blades. **Technical:** Materials: Damascus stainless steel, exotic metals, gold, rare handle materials. **Prices:** $1,000 to $,9000. **Remarks:** Folding knives in art deco and art noveau themes. **Other:** Full-time maker from 1981. **Mark:** OWEN WOOD.

**WOOD, LARRY B.,** 6945 Fishburg Rd., Huber Heights, OH 45424, Phone: 513-233-6751
**Specialties:** Fancy working knives of his design. **Patterns:** Hunters, buckskinners, Bowies, tomahawks, locking folders and Damascus miniatures. **Technical:** Forges 1095, file steel and his own Damascus. **Prices:** $125 to $500; some to $2,000. **Remarks:** Full-time maker; first knife sold in 1974. Doing business as Wood's Metal Studios. **Mark:** Variations of last name, sometimes with blacksmith logo.

**WOOD, ALAN,** Greenfield Villa, Greenhead, Brampton CA8 7HH, ENGLAND, Phone: 016977-47303, a.wood@kivesfreeserve.co.uk Web: www.alanwoodknives.co.uk
**Specialties:** High-tech working straight knives of his design. **Patterns:** Hunters, utility/camp and woodcraft knives. **Technical:** Grinds 12027, RWL-34, stainless Damascus and 01. Blades are cryogenic treated. **Prices:** $200 t $800; some to $750. **Remarks:** Full-time maker; first knife sold in 1979. N currently taking orders **Mark:** Full name and state motif.

**WOODARD, WILEY,** 4527 Jim Mitchell W, Colleyville, TX 76034
**Specialties:** Straight knives, Damascus carbon and stainless, all natur material.

**WOODIWISS, DORREN,** PO Box 396, Thompson Falls, MT 59873-0396, Phone: 406-827-0079

**WOODWARD, WILEY,** 4517 Jim Mitchell W, Colleyville, TX 76034, Phone: 817-267-3277

**WOOTTON, RANDY,** 83 Lafayett 254, Stamps, AR 71860, Phone: 870-533-2472

**WORTHEN, BILL,** 200 E 3rd, Little Rock, AR 72201-1608, Phone: 501-324-9351

**WRIGHT, L.T.,** 1523 Pershing Ave., Steubenville, OH 43952, Phone: 740-282-4947
**Specialties:** Filework, hunting knives. **Patterns:** Drop point hunters, straigh back hunter, small game, bird & trout. **Technical:** Grinds 440C. **Prices:** $60 $500. **Remarks:** Part-time maker. **Mark:** First, middle initials and last name house logo.

**WRIGHT, TIMOTHY,** PO Box 3746, Sedona, AZ 86340, Phone: 928-282-4180
**Specialties:** High-tech folders and working knives. **Patterns:** Interframe loc ing folders, non-inlaid folders, straight hunters and kitchen knives. **Technic** Grinds BG-42, AEB-L, K190 and Cowry X; works with new steels. All folde can disassemble and are furnished with tools. **Prices:** $150 to $1,800; son to $3,000. **Remarks:** Full-time maker; first knife sold in 1975. **Mark:** La name and type of steel used.

**WRIGHT, RICHARD S.,** PO Box 201, 111 Hilltop Dr., Carolina, RI 02812, Phone: 401-364-3579, rswswitchblades@hotmail.com Web: www.richards.wright.com
**Specialties:** Bolster release switchblades. **Patterns:** Folding fighters, ger pocket knives, one-of-a-kind high-grade automatics. **Technical:** Reforges a grinds various makers Damascus. Uses a variety of tool steels. Uses natu handle material such as ivory and pearl, extensive file-work on most knive **Prices:** $2,000 and up. **Remarks:** Part-time knife maker with background a gunsmith. Made first folder in 1991. **Mark:** RSW on blade, all folders are ser numbered.

**WRIGHT, KEVIN,** 671 Leland Valley Rd. W, Quilcene, WA 98376-951 Phone: 360-765-3589
**Specialties:** Fancy working or collector knives to customer specs. **Pattern** Hunters, boots, buckskinners, miniatures. **Technical:** Forges and grinds L 1095, 440C and his own Damascus. **Prices:** $75 to $500; some to $2,0 **Remarks:** Part-time maker; first knife sold in 1978. **Mark:** Last initial in anvi

**WUERTZ, TRAVIS,** 2487 E. Hwy. 287, Casa Grande, AZ 85222, Phon 520-723-4432

**WYATT, WILLIAM R.,** Box 237, Rainelle, WV 25962, Phone: 304-438-5494
**Specialties:** Classic and working knives of all designs. **Patterns:** Hunters a utility knives. **Technical:** Forges and grinds saw blades, files and rasps. P fers stag handles. **Prices:** $45 to $95; some to $350. **Remarks:** Part-ti maker; first knife sold in 1990. **Mark:** Last name in star with knife logo.

**WYMAN, MARC L.,** 3325 Griffin Rd. Ste. 124, Ft. Lauderdale, FL 3331 Phone: 754-234-5111, Fax: 954-964-4418
**Specialties:** Custom pattern welded Damascus for stock removal. **Patter** Tactical fighters, combat and hunting knives. **Technical:** High-carbon ste **Prices:** Upon request. **Remarks:** Part-time maker. **Mark:** MLW over skull a cross bones. **Other:** Florida fish and wildlife hunter safety education instruc

## Y

**YASHINSKI, JOHN L.,** 207 N Platt, PO Box 1284, Red Lodge, MT 59068, Phone: 406-446-3916
**Specialties:** Native American Beaded sheathes. **Prices:** Vary.

**YEATES, JOE A.,** 730 Saddlewood Circle, Spring, TX 77381, Phone: 281-367-2765, joeyeates291@cs.com Web: www.yeatesbowies.com
**Specialties:** Bowies and period pieces. **Patterns:** Bowies, toothpicks a combat knives. **Technical:** Grinds 440C, D2 and ATS-34. **Prices:** $600 $2,500. **Remarks:** Full-time maker; first knife sold in 1975. **Mark:** Last in within outline of Texas; or last initial.

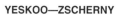

**YESKOO, RICHARD C.,** 76 Beekman Rd., Summit, NJ 07901

**YORK, DAVID C.,** PO Box 3166, Chino Valley, AZ 86323, Phone: 928-636-1709
**Specialties:** Working straight knives and folders. **Patterns:** Prefers small hunters and skinners; locking folders. **Technical:** Grinds D2 and 440C; buys Damascus. **Prices:** $75 to $300; some to $600. **Remarks:** Part-time maker; first knife sold in 1975. **Mark:** Last name.

**YOSHIHARA, YOSHINDO,** 8-17-11 TAKASAGO, KATSUSHI, Tokyo, JAPAN

**YOSHIKAZU, KAMADA,** , 540-3 Kaisaki Niuta-cho, Tokushima, JAPAN, Phone: 0886-44-2319

**YOSHIO, MAEDA,** , 3-12-11 Chuo-cho tamashima Kurashiki-city, Okayama, JAPAN, Phone: 086-525-2375

**YOUNG, GEORGE,** 713 Pinoak Dr., Kokomo, IN 46901, Phone: 765-457-8893
**Specialties:** Fancy/embellished and traditional straight knives and folders of his design and to customer specs. **Patterns:** Hunters, fillet/camp knives and locking folders. **Technical:** Grinds 440C, CPM440V, and Stellite 6K. Fancy ivory, black pearl and stag for handles. Filework—all Stellite construction (6K and 25 alloys). Offers engraving. **Prices:** $350 to $750; some $1,500 to $3,000. **Remarks:** Full-time maker; first knife sold in 1954. Doing business as Young's Knives. **Mark:** Last name integral inside Bowie.

**YOUNG, PAUL A.,** 168 Elk Ridge Rd., Boone, NC 28607, Phone: 704-264-7048
**Specialties:** Working straight knives and folders of his design or to customer specs; some art knives. **Patterns:** Small boot knives, skinners, 18th-century period pieces and folders. **Technical:** Forges O1 and file steels. Full-time embellisher—engraves and scrimshaws. Prefers floral designs; any design accepted. Does not engrave hardened metals. **Prices:** Determined by type and design. **Remarks:** Full-time maker; first knife sold in 1978. **Mark:** Initials in logo.

**YOUNG, BUD,** Box 336, Port Hardy, BC, CANADA V0N 2P0, Phone: 250-949-6478
**Specialties:** Fixed blade, working knives, some fancy. **Patterns:** Drop-points to skinners. **Technical:** Hollow or flat grind, 5160, 440-C, mostly ATS-34, satin finish. **Prices:** $150 to $500 CDN. **Remarks:** Spare-time maker; making knives since 1962; first knife sold in 1985. **Mark:** Name. **Other:** Not taking orders at this time, sell as produced.

**YOUNG, CLIFF,** Fuente De La Cibeles No. 5, Atascadero, San Miguel De Allende, GTO., MEXICO, Phone: 37700, Fax: 011-52-415-2-57-11
**Specialties:** Working knives. **Patterns:** Hunters, fighters and fishing knives. **Technical:** Grinds all; offers D2, 440C and 154CM. **Prices:** Start at $250. **Remarks:** Part-time maker; first knife sold in 1980. **Mark:** Name.

**YOUNG, ERROL,** 4826 Storey Land, Alton, IL 62002, Phone: 618-466-4707
**Specialties:** Traditional working straight knives and folders. **Patterns:** Wide range, including tantos, Bowies, miniatures and multi-blade folders. **Technical:** Grinds D2, 440C and ATS-34. **Prices:** $75 to $650; some to $800. **Remarks:** Part-time maker; first knife sold in 1987. **Mark:** Last name with arrow.

**YOUNG, RAYMOND L.,** Cutler/Bladesmith, 2922 Hwy 188E, Mt Ida, AR 71957, Phone: 870-867-3947
**Specialties:** Cutler-Bladesmith, Sharpening service. **Patterns:** Hunter, skinners, fighters, no guard, no ricasso, chef tools. **Technical:** Edge tempered 1095, 516C, Mosiac handles, water buffalo and exotic woods. **Prices:** $100 and up. **Remarks:** Federal contractor since 1995. Surgical steel sharpening. **Mark:** R.

**YURCO, MIKE,** PO Box 712, Canfield, OH 44406, Phone: 330-533-4928, shorinki@aol.com
**Specialties:** Working straight knives. **Patterns:** Hunters, utility knives, Bowies and fighters, push knives, claws and other hideouts. **Technical:** Grinds 440C, ATS-34 and 154CM; likes mirror and satin finishes. **Prices:** $20 to $500. **Remarks:** Part-time maker; first knife sold in 1983. **Mark:** Name, steel, serial number.

# Z

**ZACCAGNINO JR., DON,** 2256 Bacom Point Rd., Pahokee, FL 33476-2622, Phone: 561-924-7032, zackknife@aol.com
**Specialties:** Working knives and some period pieces of their designs. **Patterns:** Heavy-duty hunters, axes and Bowies, a line of light-weight hunters, fillets and personal knives. **Technical:** Grinds 440C and 17-4 PH—highly finished in complex handle and blade treatments. **Prices:** $165 to $500; some to $2,500. **Remarks:** Part-time maker; first knife sold in 1969 by Don Zaccagnino Sr. **Mark:** ZACK, city and state inside oval.

**ZAHM, KURT,** 488 Rio Casa, Indialantic, FL 32903, Phone: 407-777-4860
**Specialties:** Working straight knives of his design or to customer specs. **Patterns:** Daggers, fancy fighters, Bowies, hunters and utility knives. **Technical:** Grinds D2, 440C; likes filework. **Prices:** $75 to $1,000. **Remarks:** Part-time maker; first knife sold in 1985. **Mark:** Last name.

**ZAKABI, CARL S.,** PO Box 893161, Mililani Town, HI 96789-0161, Phone: 808-626-2181
**Specialties:** Working and using straight knives of his design. **Patterns:** Fighters, hunters and utility/camp knives. **Technical:** Grinds 440C and ATS-34. **Prices:** $90 to $400. **Remarks:** Spare-time maker; first knife sold in 1988. Doing business as Zakabi's Knifeworks LLC. **Mark:** Last name and state inside a Hawaiian sharktooth dagger.

**ZAKHAROV, GLADISTON,** Bairro Rio Comprido, Rio Comprido Jacarei, Jacaret SP, BRAZIL 12302-070, Phone: 55 12 3958 4021, Fax: 55 12 3958 4103, arkhip@terra.com.br; Web: www.arkhip.com.br
**Specialties:** Using straight knives of his design. **Patterns:** Hunters, kitchen, utility/camp and barbecue knives. **Technical:** Grinds his own "secret steel." **Prices:** $30 to $200. **Remarks:** Full-time maker. **Mark:** Arkhip Special Knives.

**ZBORIL, TERRY,** 5320 CR 130, Caldwell, TX 77836, Phone: 979-535-4157, terry.zboril@worldnet.att.net
**Specialties:** ABS Journeyman Smith.

**ZEMBKO III, JOHN,** 140 Wilks Pond Rd., Berlin, CT 06037, Phone: 860-828-3503, zemknives@aol.com
**Specialties:** Working knives of his design or to customer specs. **Patterns:** Likes to use stabilized high-figured woods. **Technical:** Grinds ATS-34, A-2, D-2; forges O-1, 1095; grinds Damasteel. **Prices:** $50 to $400; some higher. **Remarks:** First knife sold in 1987. **Mark:** Name.

**ZEMITIS, JOE,** 14 Currawong Rd., Cardiff Hts., 2285 Newcastle, AUSTRALIA, Phone: 0249549907, jjvzem@optusnet.com.au Web: www.unitedbladeworx.com.au
**Specialties:** Traditional working straight knives. **Patterns:** Hunters, Bowies, tantos, fighters and camp knives. **Technical:** Grinds O1, D2, W2 and 440C; makes his own Damascus. Embellishes; offers engraving and scrimshaw. **Prices:** $150 to $3,000. **Remarks:** Full-time maker; first knife sold in 1983. **Mark:** First initial, last name and country, or last name.

**ZIMA, MICHAEL F.,** 732 State St., Ft. Morgan, CO 80701, Phone: 970-867-6078, Web: http://www.zimaknives.com
**Specialties:** Working straight knives and folders. **Patterns:** Hunters; utility, locking and slip-joint folders. **Technical:** Grinds D-2, 440C, ATS-34, and Specialty Damascus. **Prices:** $150 to $300; some higher. **Remarks:** Full-time maker; first knife sold in 1982. **Mark:** Last name.

**ZINKER, BRAD,** BZ KNIVES, 1591 NW 17 St., Homestead, FL 33030, Phone: 305-216-0404, bzknives@aol.com
**Specialties:** Fillets, folders and hunters. **Technical:** Uses ATS-34 and stainless Damascus. **Prices:** $200 to $600. **Remarks:** Voting member of Knifemakers Guild and Florida Knifemakers Association. **Mark:** Offset connected initials BZ.

**ZIRBES, RICHARD,** Neustrasse 15, D-54526 Niederkail, GERMANY, Phone: 0049 6575 1371
**Specialties:** Fancy embellished knives with engraving and self-made scrimshaw (scrimshaw made by maker). High-tech working knives and high-tech hunters, boots, fighters and folders. All knives made by hand. **Patterns:** Boots, fighters, folders, hunters. **Technical:** Uses only the best steels for blade material like CPM-T 440V, CPM-T 420V, ATS-34, D2, C440, stainless Damascus or steel according to customer's desire. **Prices:** Working knives and hunters: $200 to $600. Fancy embellished knives with engraving and/or scrimshaw: $800 to $3,000. **Remarks:** Part-time maker; first knife sold in 1991. Member of the German Knife Maker Guild. **Mark:** Zirbes or R. Zirbes.

**ZOWADA, TIM,** 4509 E. Bear River Rd., Boyne Falls, MI 49713, Phone: 231-348-5446, knifeguy@nmo.net
**Specialties:** Working knives, some fancy. **Patterns:** Hunters, camp knives, boots, swords, fighters, tantos and locking folders. **Technical:** Forges O2, L6, W2 and his own Damascus. **Prices:** $150 to $1,000; some to $5,000. **Remarks:** Full-time maker; first knife sold in 1980.

**ZSCHERNY, MICHAEL,** 1840 Rock Island Dr., Ely, IA 52227, Phone: 319-848-3629
**Specialties:** Quality folding knives. **Patterns:** Liner-lock and lock-back folders in titanium, working straight knives. **Technical:** Grinds 440 and commercial Damascus, prefers natural materials such as pearls and ivory. **Prices:** Starting at $200. **Remarks:** Full-time maker, first knife sold in 1978. **Mark:** Last name, city and state; folders, last name with stars inside folding knife.

# knifemakers state-by-state

## AK

| | |
|---|---|
| Barlow, Jana Poirier | Anchorage |
| Brennan, Judson | Delta Junction |
| Breuer, Lonnie | Wasilla |
| Broome, Thomas A. | Kenai |
| Cannon, Raymond W. | Homer |
| Cawthorne, Christopher A. | Wrangell |
| Chamberlin, John A. | Anchorage |
| Dempsey, Gordon S. | N. Kenai |
| Dufour, Arthur J. | Anchorage |
| England, Virgil | Anchorage |
| Flint, Robert | Anchorage |
| Gouker, Gary B. | Sitka |
| Grebe, Gordon S. | Anchor Point |
| Hibben, Westley G. | Anchorage |
| Kommer, Russ | Anchorage |
| Lance, Bill | Eagle River |
| Little, Jimmy L. | Wasilla |
| Malaby, Raymond J. | Juneau |
| McFarlin, Eric E. | Kodiak |
| McIntosh, David L. | Haines |
| Mirabile, David | Juneau |
| Moore, Marve | Willow |
| Parrish III, Gordon A. | North Pole |
| Schmoker, Randy | Slana |
| Shore, John I. | Anchorage |
| Stegall, Keith | Anchorage |
| Trujillo, Adam | Anchorage |
| Trujillo, Miranda | Anchorage |
| Trujillo, Thomas A. | Anchorage |
| Van Cleve, Steve | Sutton |
| Whipple, Wesley A. | Kodiak |
| Whitman, Jim | Chugiak |

## AL

| | |
|---|---|
| Andress, Ronnie | Satsuma |
| Batson, James | Madison |
| Baxter, Dale | Trinity |
| Bowles, Chris | Reform |
| Brend, Walter | Vinemont |
| Bullard, Bill | Andalusia |
| Coffman, Danny | Jacksonville |
| Conn Jr., C.T. | Attalla |
| Cutchin, Roy D. | Seale |
| Daniels, Alex | Town Creek |
| Dark, Robert | Oxford |
| Di Marzo, Richard | Birmingham |
| Durham, Kenneth | Cherokee |
| Elrod, Roger R. | Enterprise |
| Fikes, Jimmy L. | Jasper |
| Fogg, Don | Jasper |
| Fowler, Ricky and Susan | Robertsdale |
| Fronefield, Daniel | Hampton Cove |
| Gilbreath, Randall | Dora |
| Green, Mark | Graysville |
| Hammond, Jim | Arab |
| Hodge, J.B. | Huntsville |
| Howard, Durvyn M. | Hokes Bluff |
| Howell, Len | Opelika |
| Howell, Ted | Wetumpka |
| Huckabee, Dale | Maylene |
| Hulsey, Hoyt | Attalla |
| Madison II, Billy D. | Remlap |
| McCullough, Jerry | Georgiana |
| Militano, Tom | Jacksonville |
| Monk, Nathan P. | Cullman |
| Morris, C.H. | Frisco City |
| Pardue, Melvin M. | Repton |
| Roe Jr., Fred D. | Huntsville |
| Russell, Tom | Jacksonville |
| Sandlin, Larry | Adamsville |
| Sinyard, Cleston S. | Elberta |
| Thomas, David E. | Lillian |
| Watson, Billy | Deatsville |

## AR

| | |
|---|---|
| Alexander, Jered | Dierks |
| Anders, David | Center Ridge |
| Anders, Jerome | Center Ridge |
| Ardwin, Corey | North Little Rock |
| Barnes, Eric | Mountain View |
| Barnes Jr., Cecil C. | Center Ridge |
| Brown, Jim | Little Rock |
| Browning, Steven W. | Benton |
| Bullard, Tom | Flippin |
| Burnett, Max | Paris |
| Cabe, Jerry (Buddy) | Hattieville |
| Cook, James R. | Nashville |
| Copeland, Thom | Nashville |
| Crawford, Pat and Wes | West Memphis |
| Crowell, James L. | Mtn. View |
| Dozier, Bob | Springdale |
| Duvall, Fred | Benton |
| Echols, Roger | Nashville |
| Edge, Tommy | Cash |
| Ferguson, Lee | Hindsville |
| Fisk, Jerry | Nashville |
| Fitch, John S. | Clinton |
| Flournoy, Joe | El Dorado |
| Foster, Ronnie E. | Morrilton |
| Foster, Timothy L. | El Dorado |
| Frizzell, Ted | West Fork |
| Gadberry, Emmet | Hattieville |
| Greenaway, Don | Fayetteville |
| Herring, Morris | Dyer |
| Kelsey, Nate | Springdale |
| Lane, Ben | North Little Rock |
| Lawrence, Alton | De Queen |
| Livesay, Newt | Siloam Springs |
| Martin, Bruce E. | Prescott |
| Martin, Hal W. | Morrilton |
| Massey, Roger | Texarkana |
| Newton, Ron | London |
| O'Dell, Clyde | Camden |
| Olive, Michael E. | Leslie |
| Passmore, Jimmy D. | Hoxie |
| Perry, Jim | Hope |
| Perry, John | Mayflower |
| Peterson, Lloyd (Pete) C. | Clinton |
| Polk, Clifton | Van Buren |
| Polk, Rusty | Van Buren |
| Quattlebaum, Craig | Searcy |
| Ramey, Marshall F. | West Helena |
| Red, Vernon | Conway |
| Sisemore, Charles Russel | Mena |
| Smoker, Ray | Searcy |
| Solomon, Marvin | Paron |
| Stanley, John | Crossett |
| Stout, Charles | Gillham |
| Sweaza, Dennis | Austin |
| Townsend, Allen Mark | Texarkana |
| Tycer, Art | Paron |
| Walker, Jim | Morrilton |
| Ward, Chuck | Benton |
| Waters, Herman Harold | Magnolia |
| Waters, Lu | Magnolia |
| White, Bryce | Little Rock |
| Wootton, Randy | Stamps |
| Worthen, Bill | Little Rock |
| Young, Raymond L. | Mt Ida |

## AZ

| | |
|---|---|
| Ammons, David C. | Tucso |
| Amos, Chris | Tucso |
| Bennett, Glen C. | Tucso |
| Birdwell, Ira Lee | Bagda |
| Boye, David | Dolan Sprin |
| Bryan, Tom | Gilbe |
| Cheatham, Bill | Lave |
| Choate, Milton | Somert |
| Dodd, Robert F. | Camp Ver |
| Fuegen, Larry | Presc |
| Goo, Tai | Tucs |
| Guignard, Gib | Quartzs |
| Hancock, Tim | Scottsda |
| Hankins, R. | Tem |
| Hoel, Steve | Pi |
| Holder, D'Alton | Peo |
| Hull, Michael J. | Cottonwo |
| Karp, Bob | Phoen |
| Kelley, Thomas P. | Cave Cre |
| Kopp, Todd M. | Apache J |
| Lampson, Frank G. | Rimro |
| Lee, Randy | St. Joh |
| McFall, Ken | Lakesi |
| McFarlin, J.W. | Lake Havasu C |
| Miller, Michael | Kingm |
| Mooney, Mike | Queen Cre |
| Murray, Bill | Green Val |
| Newhall, Tom | Tucs |
| Norris, Don | Tucs |
| Purvis, Bob and Ellen | Tucs |
| Robbins, Bill | Glo |
| Rybar Jr., Raymond B. | Phoe |
| Snare, Michael | Phoe |
| Tamboli, Michael | Glend |
| Torgeson, Samuel L. | Sedo |
| Weiler, Donald E. | Yu |
| Weiss, Charles L. | Phoe |
| Wolf, Bill | Phoe |
| Wright, Timothy | Sedo |
| Wuertz, Travis | Casa Gran |
| York, David C. | Chino Val |

## CA

| | |
|---|---|
| Abegg, Arnie | Huntington Bea |
| Abernathy, Paul J. | Eure |
| Adkins, Richard L. | Mission V |
| Aldrete, Bob | Lom |
| Barnes, Gregory | Altade |
| Barron, Brian | San Ma |
| Benson, Don | Esca |
| Berger, Max A. | Carmich |
| Biggers, Gary | Vent |
| Blum, Chuck | B |
| Bost, Roger E. | Palos Ver |
| Boyd, Francis | Berke |
| Brack, Douglas D. | Cami |
| Breshears, Clint | Manhattan Bea |
| Brooks, Buzz | Los Ange |
| Browne, Rick | Upla |
| Brunetta, David | Laguna Be |
| Butler, Bart | Ram |
| Cabrera, Sergio B. | Harbor |
| Cantrell, Kitty D. | Ram |
| Caston, Darriel | Sacrame |
| Chelquist, Cliff | Arroyo Gra |
| Clark, R.W. | Cor |
| Coffey, Bill | Clo |
| Coffey, Bill | Cl |
| Cohen, Terry A. | Layton |

| | |
|---|---|
| Coleman, John A. | Citrus Heights |
| Comus, Steve | Anaheim |
| Connolly, James | Oroville |
| Davis, Charlie | Santee |
| Davisson, Cole | Hemet |
| De Maria Jr., Angelo | Carmel Valley |
| Dion, Greg | Oxnard |
| Dixon Jr., Ira E. | Ventura |
| Doolittle, Mike | Novato |
| Driscoll, Mark | La Mesa |
| Dugan, Brad M. | San Marcos |
| Ellis, Dave/Abs Mastersmith | Vista |
| Ellis, William Dean | Fresno |
| Emerson, Ernest R. | Torrance |
| English, Jim | Jamul |
| Essegian, Richard | Fresno |
| Felix, Alexander | Torrance |
| Ferguson, Jim | Temecula |
| Fisher, Theo (Ted) | Montague |
| Forrest, Brian | Descanso |
| Fox, Jack L. | Citrus Heights |
| Fraley, D.B. | Dixon |
| Francis, Vance | Alpine |
| Fred, Reed Wyle | Sacramento |
| Freer, Ralph | Seal Beach |
| Fulton, Mickey | Willows |
| Gamble, Frank | Fremont |
| Girtner, Joe | Brea |
| Gofourth, Jim | Santa Paula |
| Golding, Robin | Lathrop |
| Green, Russ | Lakewood |
| Guarnera, Anthony R. | Quartzhill |
| Guidry, Bruce | Murrieta |
| Hall, Jeff | Los Alamitos |
| Hardy, Scott | Placerville |
| Harris, Jay | Redwood City |
| Harris, John | Riverside |
| Hartsfield, Phill | Newport Beach |
| Hayes, Dolores | Los Angeles |
| Helton, Roy | San Diego |
| Herndon, Wm. R. "Bill" | Acton |
| Hink III, Les | Stockton |
| Hockenbary, Warren E. | San Pedro |
| Hoy, Ken | North Fork |
| Humenick, Roy | Rescue |
| Jacks, Jim | Covina |
| Jackson, David | Lemoore |
| Jensen, John Lewis | Pasadena |
| Johnson, Randy | Turlock |
| Jones, Curtis J. | Palmdale |
| Kazsuk, David | Perris |
| Keyes, Dan | Chino |
| Koster, Steven C. | Huntington Beach |
| Laner, Dean | Susanville |
| Larson, Richard | Turlock |
| Leland, Steve | Fairfax |
| Likarich, Steve | Colfax |
| Lockett, Sterling | Burbank |
| Loveless, R.W. | Riverside |
| Luchini, Bob | Palo Alto |
| Mackie, John | Whittier |
| Mallett, John | Ontario |
| Manabe, Michael K. | San Diego |
| Martin, Jim | Oxnard |
| Massey, Ron | Joshua Tree |
| Mata, Leonard | San Diego |
| Maxwell, Don | Clovis |
| McAbee, William | Colfax |
| McClure, Michael | Menlo Park |
| McGrath, Patrick T. | Westchester |
| Melin, Gordon C. | Whittier |
| Meloy, Sean | Lemon Grove |
| Montano, Gus A. | San Diego |
| Morgan, Jeff | Santee |
| Moses, Steven | Santa Ana |
| Mountain Home Knives, | Jamul |
| Naten, Greg | Bakersfield |
| Orton, Rich | Riverside |
| Osborne, Donald H. | Clovis |
| Packard, Bob | Elverta |
| Padilla, Gary | Auburn |
| Pendleton, Lloyd | Volcano |
| Perry, Chris | Fresno |
| Pfanenstiel, Dan | Modesto |
| Phillips, Randy | Ontario |
| Pitt, David F. | Anderson |
| Posner, Barry E. | N. Hollywood |
| Reynolds, Lee | San Jose |
| Richard, Ron | Fremont |
| Richards Jr., Alvin C. | Fortuna |
| Rinaldi, T.H. | Winchester |
| Rodebaugh, James L. | Oak Hills |
| Rozas, Clark D. | Wilmington |
| Scarrow, Wil | San Gabriel |
| Schmitz, Raymond E. | Valley Center |
| Schneider, Herman | Apple Valley |
| Schroen, Karl | Sebastopol |
| Sibrian, Aaron | Ventura |
| Sjostrand, Kevin | Visalia |
| Slobodian, Scott | San Andreas |
| Sornberger, Jim | Volcano |
| St. Cyr, H. Red | Wilmington |
| Stapel, Chuck | Glendale |
| Steinberg, Al | Laguna Woods |
| Stimps, Jason M. | Orange |
| Stockwell, Walter | Redwood City |
| Stover, Howard | Pasadena |
| Strider, Mick | San Marcos |
| Terrill, Stephen | Lindsay |
| Tingle, Dennis P. | Jackson |
| Vagnino, Michael | Visalia |
| Van Riper, James N. | Citrus Heights |
| Ward, Ken | Weed |
| Warren, Al | Roseville |
| Watanabe, Wayne | Montebello |
| Weinstock, Robert | San Francisco |
| Wilson, Philip C. | Mountain Ranch |
| Wilson, Ron | Morro Bay |
| Winberg, Douglas R. | Ramona |

## CO

| | |
|---|---|
| Anderson, Mark Alan | Denver |
| Anderson, Mel | Cedaredge |
| Appleton, Ray | Byers |
| Barrett, Cecil Terry | Colorado Springs |
| Booco, Gordon | Hayden |
| Brandon, Matthew | Denver |
| Brock, Kenneth L. | Allenspark |
| Burrows, Chuck | Durango |
| Davis, Don | Loveland |
| Dawson, Barry | Durango |
| Dawson, Lynn | Durango |
| Delong, Dick | Aurora |
| Dennehy, Dan | Del Norte |
| Dennehy, John D | Wellington |
| Dill, Robert | Loveland |
| Hatch, Ken | Dinosaur |
| High, Tom | Alamosa |
| Hockensmith, Dan | Crook |
| Hodgson, Richard J. | Boulder |
| Hughes, Ed | Grand Junction |
| Irie, Michael L. | Colorado Springs |
| Kitsmiller, Jerry | Montrose |
| Leck, Dal | Hayden |
| Lewis, Steve | Woodland Park |
| Magruder, Jason | Colorado Springs |
| Miller, Hanford J. | Cowdrey |
| Miller, M.A. | Northglenn |
| Olson, Wayne C. | Bailey |
| Ott, Fred | Durango |
| Owens, John | Nathrop |
| Roberts, Chuck | Golden |
| Rollert, Steve | Keenesburg |
| Ronzio, N. Jack | Fruita |
| Sanders, Bill | Mancos |
| Thompson, Lloyd | Pagosa Springs |
| Tollefson,, Barry A. | Gunnison |
| Topliss, M.W. "Ike" | Montrose |
| Watson, Bert | Westminster |
| Wilson, James G. | Estes Park |
| Wood, Owen Dale | Arvada |
| Zima, Michael F. | Ft. Morgan |

## CT

| | |
|---|---|
| Barnes, William | Wallingford |
| Buebendorf, Robert E. | Monroe |
| Chapo, William G. | Wilton |
| Framski, Walter P. | Prospect |
| Jean, Gerry | Manchester |
| Lepore, Michael J. | Bethany |
| Padgett Jr., Edwin L. | New London |
| Pankiewicz, Philip R. | Lebanon |
| Plunkett, Richard | West Cornwall |
| Putnam, Donald S. | Wethersfield |
| Rainville, Richard | Salem |
| Turecek, Jim | Ansonia |
| Vitale, Mace | Guilford |
| Zembko III, John | Berlin |

## DE

| | |
|---|---|
| Antonio Jr., William J. | Newark |
| Daland, B. Macgregor | Harbeson |
| Schneider, Karl A. | Newark |
| Willey, W.G. | Greenwood |

## FL

| | |
|---|---|
| Adams, Les | Hialeah |
| Amor Jr., Miguel | Miami |
| Angell, Jon | Hawthorne |
| Atkinson, Dick | Wausau |
| Bacon, David R. | Bradenton |
| Barry III, James J. | West Palm Beach |
| Bartrug, Hugh E. | St. Petersburg |
| Beckett, Norman L. | Satsuma |
| Beers, Ray | Lake Wales |
| Benjamin Jr., George | Kissimmee |
| Birnbaum, Edwin | Miami |
| Blackton, Andrew E. | Bayonet Point |
| Blackwood, Neil | Lakeland |
| Bosworth, Dean | Key Largo |
| Bradley, John | Pomona Park |
| Bray Jr., W. Lowell | New Port Richey |
| Brown, Harold E. | Arcadia |
| Burris, Patrick R. | Jacksonville |
| Butler, John | Havana |
| Chase, Alex | DeLand |
| Cole, Dave | Satellite Beach |
| D'Andrea, John | Citrus Springs |
| Davenport, Jack | Dade City |
| Davis Jr., Jim | Zephyrhills |
| Dietzel, Bill | Middleburg |
| Doggett, Bob | Brandon |
| Dotson, Tracy | Baker |
| Ellerbe, W.B. | Geneva |
| Ellis, Willy B. | Palm Harbor |
| Enos III, Thomas M. | Orlando |
| Fagan, James A. | Lake Worth |
| Ferrara, Thomas | Naples |
| Ferris, Bill | Palm Beach Garden |
| Fowler, Charles R. | Ft. McCoy |
| Gamble, Roger | St. Petersburg |
| Gardner, Rob | Loxahatchee |
| Garner Jr., William O. | Pensacola |
| Gibson Sr., James Hoot | Bunnell |

| Goers, Bruce | Lakeland |
|---|---|
| Griffin Jr., Howard A. | Davie |
| Grospitch, Ernie | Orlando |
| Harris, Ralph Dewey | Brandon |
| Heitler, Henry | Tampa |
| Hodge III, John | Palatka |
| Holland, John H. | Titusville |
| Hughes, Dan | West Palm Beach |
| Humphreys, Joel | Bowling Green |
| Hunter, Richard D. | Alachua |
| Hytovick, Joe "Hy" | Dunnellon |
| Jernigan, Steve | Milton |
| Johanning Custom Knives, Tom | Sarasota |
| Johnson, Durrell Carmon | Sparr |
| Johnson, John R. | Plant City |
| Kelly, Lance | Edgewater |
| King, Bill | Tampa |
| Krapp, Denny | Apopka |
| Levengood, Bill | Tampa |
| Leverett, Ken | Lithia |
| Lewis, Mike | DeBary |
| Long, Glenn A. | Dunnellon |
| Lovestrand, Schuyler | Vero Beach |
| Lozier, Don | Ocklawaha |
| Lunn, Gail | St. Petersburg |
| Lunn, Larry A. | St. Petersburg |
| Lyle III, Ernest L. | Chiefland |
| McDonald, Robert J. | Loxahatchee |
| Miller, Ronald T. | Largo |
| Mink, Dan | Crystal Beach |
| Newton, Larry | Jacksonville |
| Ochs, Charles F. | Largo |
| Owens, Donald | Melbourne |
| Parker, Cliff | Zephyrhills |
| Pendray, Alfred H. | Williston |
| Piergallini, Daniel E. | Plant City |
| Randall Made Knives, | Orlando |
| Reed, John M. | Oak Hill |
| Roberts, E. Ray | Monticello |
| Robinson III, Rex R. | Leesburg |
| Rodkey, Dan | Hudson |
| Rogers, Rodney | Wildwood |
| Ross, Gregg | Lake Worth |
| Russ, Ron | Williston |
| Schlomer, James E. | Kissimmee |
| Schwarzer, Stephen | Pomona Park |
| Simons, Bill | Lakeland |
| Smart, Steaten | Tavares |
| Smith, Michael J. | Brandon |
| Stapleton, William E. | Merritt Island |
| Steck, Van R. | Orange City |
| Stephan, Daniel | Valrico |
| Stipes, Dwight | Palm City |
| Straight, Kenneth J. | Largo |
| Sweder, Joram | Ocala |
| Turnbull, Ralph A. | Spring Hill |
| Vogt, Donald J. | Tampa |
| Waldrop, Mark | Summerfield |
| Wallace, Roger L. | Tampa |
| Watson, Tom | Panama City |
| Weiland Jr., J. Reese | Riverview |
| Wicker, Donnie R. | Panama City |
| Wyman, Marc L. | Ft. Lauderdale |
| Zaccagnino Jr., Don | Pahokee |
| Zahm, Kurt | Indialantic |
| Zinker, Brad | Homestead |

## GA

| Arrowood, Dale | Sharpsburg |
|---|---|
| Ashworth, Boyd | Powder Springs |
| Barker, Robert G. | Bishop |
| Bentley, C.L. | Albany |
| Bish, Hal | Jonesboro |
| Black, Scott | Covington |
| Bradley, Dennis | Blairsville |
| Buckner, Jimmie H. | Putney |
| Carey Jr., Charles W. | Griffin |
| Chamblin, Joel | Concord |
| Cofer, Ron | Loganville |
| Cole, Welborn I. | Atlanta |
| Coughlin, Michael M. | Winder |
| Crockford, Jack | Chamblee |
| Davis, Steve | Powder Springs |
| Dempsey, David | Macon |
| Dunn, Charles K. | Shiloh |
| Feigin, B. | Marietta |
| Frost, Dewayne | Barnesville |
| Gaines, Buddy | Commerce |
| Glover, Warren D. | Cleveland |
| Granger, Paul J. | Kennesaw |
| Greene, David | Covington |
| Halligan, Ed | Sharpsburg |
| Hardy, Douglas E. | Franklin |
| Harmon, Jay | Woodstock |
| Hawkins, Rade | Fayetteville |
| Haynie, Charles | Toccoa |
| Hensley, Wayne | Conyers |
| Hinson and Son, R. | Columbus |
| Hoffman, Kevin L. | Savannah |
| Hossom, Jerry | Duluth |
| Hyde, Jimmy | Ellenwood |
| Jones, Franklin (Frank) W. | Columbus |
| Kimsey, Kevin | Cartersville |
| King, Fred | Cartersville |
| Knott, Steve | Guyton |
| Landers, John | Newnan |
| Lonewolf, J. Aguirre | Demorest |
| Mathews, Charlie and Harry | Statesboro |
| McGill, John | Blairsville |
| McLendon, Hubert W. | Waco |
| Mitchell, James A. | Columbus |
| Moncus, Michael Steven | Smithville |
| Parks, John | Jefferson |
| Poole, Marvin O. | Commerce |
| Powell, Robert Clark | Smarr |
| Prater, Mike | Flintstone |
| Price, Timmy | Blairsville |
| Ragsdale, James D. | Lithonia |
| Rogers Jr., Robert P. | Acworth |
| Roghmans, Mark | LaGrange |
| Rosenfeld, Bob | Hoschton |
| Scofield, Everett | Chickamauga |
| Sculley, Peter E. | Rising Fawn |
| Smith Jr., James B. "Red" | Morven |
| Snell, Jerry L. | Fortson |
| Snow, Bill | Columbus |
| Sowell, Bill | Macon |
| Stafford, Richard | Warner Robins |
| Thompson, Kenneth | Duluth |
| Tomey, Kathleen | Macon |
| Walters, A.F. | TyTy |
| Washburn Jr., Robert Lee | Adrian |
| Werner Jr., William A. | Marietta |
| Whetsell, Alex | Sharpsburg |
| White, Lou | Ranger |

## HI

| Bucholz, Mark A. | Holualoa |
|---|---|
| Dolan, Robert L. | Kula |
| Fujisaka, Stanley | Kaneohe |
| Gibo, George | Hilo |
| Lui, Ronald M. | Honolulu |
| Mann, Tim | Honokaa |
| Matsuoka, Scot | Mililani |
| Mayo Jr., Tom | Waialua |
| Mitsuyuki, Ross | Waipahu |
| Onion, Kenneth J. | Kaneohe |
| Zakabi, Carl S. | Mililani Town |

## IA

| Brooker, Dennis | Derb |
|---|---|
| Brower, Max | Boor |
| Clark, Howard F. | Runne |
| Cockerham, Lloyd | Denham Spring |
| Helscher, John W. | Washingto |
| Lainson, Tony | Council Bluf |
| Lewis, Bill | Riversic |
| Miller, James P. | Fairbar |
| Thie, Brian | Burlingto |
| Trindle, Barry | Earlha |
| Westberg, Larry | Algor |
| Zscherny, Michael | E |

## ID

| Alderman, Robert | Sag |
|---|---|
| Alverson, Tim (R.V.) | Pe |
| Burke, Bill | Boi |
| Eddy, Hugh E. | Caldw |
| Hawk, Grant and Gavin | Idaho C |
| Hogan, Thomas R. | Boi |
| Horton, Scot | Bu |
| Howe, Tori | Ath |
| Mann, Michael L. | Spirit La |
| Metz, Greg T. | Casca |
| Mullin, Steve | Sandpoi |
| Nealey, Ivan F. (Frank) | Mt. Hor |
| Patton, Dick and Rob | Nam |
| Quarton, Barr | McC |
| Reeve, Chris | Boi |
| Rohn, Fred | Coeur d'Ale |
| Sawby, Scott | Sandpo |
| Schultz, Robert W. | Cocola |
| Selent, Chuck | Bonners Fe |
| Sparks, Bernard | Din |
| Steiger, Monte L. | Genes |
| Tippetts, Colten | Ketchu |
| Towell, Dwight L. | Midva |

## IL

| Abbott, William M. | Chandlervi |
|---|---|
| Bloomer, Alan T. | Maqu |
| Camerer, Craig | Chesterfi |
| Cook, Louise | Oza |
| Cook, Mike | Oza |
| Detmer, Phillip | Bree |
| Dicristofano, Anthony P. | Northla |
| Eaker, Allen L. | Pa |
| Hawes, Chuck | Weld |
| Heath, William | Bondv |
| Hill, Rick | Maryv |
| Knuth, Joseph E. | Rockfo |
| Kovar, Eugene | Evergreen Pa |
| Lang, Kurt | McHe |
| Leone, Nick | Pontoon Bea |
| Markley, Ken | Spa |
| Meier, Daryl | Carbond |
| Myers, Paul | Wood Ri |
| Nevling, Mark | Hu |
| Nowland, Rick | Waltonv |
| Potocki, Roger | Gorev |
| Pritchard, Ron | Dix |
| Rados, Jerry F. | Grant Pa |
| Rossdeutscher, Robert N. | Arlington Heig |
| Rzewnicki, Gerald | Elizab |
| Schneider, Craig M. | Clarem |
| Smale, Charles J. | Waukeg |
| Smith, John M. | Centra |
| Steinbrecher, Mark W. | Glenvi |
| Thomas, Bob G. | Thel |
| Todd, Richard C. | Chambersb |
| Tompkins, Dan | Peoto |
| Veit, Michael | LaSa |

| | |
|---|---|
| Voss, Ben | Galesburg |
| Werth, George W. | Poplar Grove |
| West, Charles A. | Centralia |
| Wheeler, Robert | Bradley |
| White, Robert J. | Gilson |
| White Jr., Robert J. Butch | Gilson |
| Young, Errol | Alton |

## IN

| | |
|---|---|
| Ball, Ken | Mooresville |
| Barrett, Rick L. (Toshi Hisa) | Goshen |
| Bose, Reese | Shelburn |
| Bose, Tony | Shelburn |
| Chaffee, Jeff L. | Morris |
| Claiborne, Jeff | Franklin |
| Damlovac, Sava | Indianapolis |
| Darby, Jed | Greensburg |
| Fitzgerald, Dennis M. | Fort Wayne |
| Fraps, John R. | Indianpolis |
| Hunt, Maurice | Brownsburg |
| Imel, Billy Mace | New Castle |
| Johnson, C.E. Gene | Portage |
| Kain, Charles | Indianapolis |
| Keeslar, Steven C. | Hamilton |
| Keeton, William L. | Laconia |
| Kinker, Mike | Greensburg |
| Largin, | Metamora |
| Mayville, Oscar L. | Marengo |
| Minnick, Jim | Middletown |
| Oliver, Todd D. | Spencer |
| Parsons, Michael R. | Indianapolis |
| Quakenbush, Thomas C. | Ft. Wayne |
| Robertson, Leo D. | Indianapolis |
| Shostle, Ben | Muncie |
| Smock, Timothy E. | Marion |
| Snyder, Michael Tom | Zionsville |
| Stover, Terry "Lee" | Kokomo |
| Thayer, Danny O. | Romney |
| Young, George | Kokomo |

## KS

| | |
|---|---|
| Bradburn, Gary | Wichita |
| Chard, Gordon R. | Iola |
| Courtney, Eldon | Wichita |
| Craig, Roger L. | Topeka |
| Culver, Steve | Meriden |
| Darpinian, Dave | Olathe |
| Dawkins, Dudley L. | Topeka |
| Dugger, Dave | Westwood |
| George, Les | Wichita |
| Greene, Steve | Rossville |
| Hegwald, J.L. | Humboldt |
| Herman, Tim | Overland Park |
| King, Jason M. | St. George |
| King Jr., Harvey G. | Alta Vista |
| Kraft, Steve | Abilene |
| Lamb, Curtis J. | Ottawa |
| Magee, Jim | Salina |
| Petersen, Dan L. | Auburn |

## KY

| | |
|---|---|
| ddison, Kyle A. | Murray |
| arr, A.T. | Nicholasville |
| askett, Lee Gene | Eastview |
| aumgardner, Ed | Glendale |
| odner, Gerald "Jerry" | Louisville |
| ybee, Barry J. | Cadiz |
| arson, Harold J. "Kit" | Vine Grove |
| lay, J.D. | Greenup |
| oil, Jimmie J. | Owensboro |
| owning, Larry | Bremen |
| unn, Steve | Smiths Grove |
| dwards, Mitch | Glasgow |
| Finch, Ricky D. | West Liberty |
| Fister, Jim | Simpsonville |
| France, Dan | Cawood |
| Frederick, Aaron | West Liberty |
| Gevedon, Hanners (Hank) | Crab Orchard |
| Greco, John | Greensburg |
| Hibben, Daryl | LaGrange |
| Hibben, Gil | LaGrange |
| Hibben, Joleen | LaGrange |
| Hoke, Thomas M. | LaGrange |
| Holbrook, H.L. | Sandy Hook |
| Howser, John C. | Frankfort |
| Keeslar, Joseph F. | Almo |
| Lott-Sinclair, Sherry | Greensburg |
| Miller, Don | Lexington |
| Mize, Richard | Lawrenceburg |
| Pease, W.D. | Ewing |
| Pierce, Harold L. | Louisville |
| Pulliam, Morris C. | Shelbyville |
| Rigney Jr., Willie | Bronston |
| Smith, Gregory H. | Louisville |
| Smith, John W. | West Liberty |
| Vowell, Donald J. | Mayfield |
| Walker III, John Wade | Paintlick |
| Wallingford Jr., Charles W. | Union |

## LA

| | |
|---|---|
| Barker, Reggie | Springhill |
| Blaum, Roy | Covington |
| Caldwell, Bill | West Monroe |
| Calvert Jr., Robert W. (Bob) | Rayville |
| Capdepon, Randy | Carencro |
| Capdepon, Robert | Carencro |
| Chauvin, John | Scott |
| Culpepper, John | Monroe |
| Dake, C.M. | New Orleans |
| Dake, Mary H. | New Orleans |
| Diebel, Chuck | Broussard |
| Durio, Fred | Opelousas |
| Elkins, R. Van | Bonita |
| Faucheaux, Howard J. | Loreauville |
| Fontenot, Gerald J. | Mamou |
| Forstall, Al | Pearl River |
| Gorenflo, Gabe | Baton Rouge |
| Gorenflo, James T. (JT) | Baton Rouge |
| Graffeo, Anthony I. | Chalmette |
| Holmes, Robert | Baton Rouge |
| Ki, Shiva | Baton Rouge |
| Laurent, Kermit | LaPlace |
| Leonard, Randy Joe | Sarepta |
| Mitchell, Max, Dean and Ben | Leesville |
| Phillips, Dennis | Independence |
| Potier, Timothy F. | Oberlin |
| Primos, Terry | Shreveport |
| Provenzano, Joseph D. | Chalmette |
| Randall Jr., James W. | Keithville |
| Randow, Ralph | Pineville |
| Reggio Jr., Sidney J. | Sun |
| Roath, Dean | Baton Rouge |
| Sanders, Michael M. | Ponchatoula |
| Tilton, John | Iowa |
| Trisler, Kenneth W. | Rayville |
| Wiggins, Horace | Mansfield |

## MA

| | |
|---|---|
| Aoun, Charles | Wakefield |
| Dailey, G.E. | Seekonk |
| Entin, Robert | Boston |
| Frankl, John M. | Cambridge |
| Gaudette, Linden L. | Wilbraham |
| Gedraitis, Charles J. | Holden |
| Grossman, Stewart | Clinton |
| Hinman, Ted | Watertown |
| Jarvis, Paul M. | Cambridge |
| Khalsa, Jot Singh | Millis |
| Kubasek, John A. | Easthampton |
| Lapen, Charles | W. Brookfield |
| Laramie, Mark | Fitchburg |
| Little, Larry | Spencer |
| Martin, Randall J. | Bridgewater |
| McLuin, Tom | Dracut |
| Moore, Michael Robert | Lowell |
| Olofson, Chris | Cambridge |
| Rebello, Indian George | New Bedford |
| Reed, Dave | Brimfield |
| Richter, Scott | S. Boston |
| Rizzi, Russell J. | Ashfield |
| Siska, Jim | Westfield |
| Smith, J.D. | Roxbury |
| Stoddard's, Inc., Copley Place | Boston |
| Szarek, Mark G. | Revere |

## MD

| | |
|---|---|
| Bagley, R. Keith | White Plains |
| Barnes, Aubrey G. | Hagerstown |
| Barnes, Gary L. | New Windsor |
| Beers, Ray | Monkton |
| Bouse, D. Michael | Waldorf |
| Cohen, N.J. (Norm) | Baltimore |
| Dement, Larry | Prince Fredrick |
| Freiling, Albert J. | Finksburg |
| Fuller, Jack A. | New Market |
| Gossman, Scott | Forest Hill |
| Hart, Bill | Pasadena |
| Hendrickson, E. Jay | Frederick |
| Hendrickson, Shawn | Knoxville |
| Hudson, C. Robbin | Rock Hall |
| Hurt, William R. | Frederick |
| Kreh, Lefty | "Cockeysville" |
| Kretsinger Jr., Philip W. | Boonsboro |
| McCarley, John | Taneytown |
| McGowan, Frank E. | Sykesville |
| Merchant, Ted | White Hall |
| Mills, Michael | Lanham |
| Moran Jr., Wm. F. | Braddock Heights |
| Nicholson, R. Kent | Phoenix |
| Rhodes, James D. | |
| Sentz, Mark C. | Taneytown |
| Smit, Glenn | Aberdeen |
| Sontheimer, G. Douglas | Potomac |
| Spickler, Gregory Noble | Sharpsburg |
| St. Clair, Thomas K. | Monrovia |
| Walker, Bill | Stevensville |

## ME

| | |
|---|---|
| Coombs Jr., Lamont | Bucksport |
| Corrigan, David P. | Bingham |
| Courtois, Bryan | Saco |
| Gray, Daniel | Brownville |
| Hillman, Charles | Friendship |
| Leavitt Jr., Earl F. | E. Boothbay |
| Oyster, Lowell R. | Corinth |
| Sharrigan, Mudd | Wiscasset |

## MI

| | |
|---|---|
| Ackerson, Robin E. | Buchanan |
| Andrews, Eric | Grand Ledge |
| Behnke, William | Kingsley |
| Bethke, Lora Sue | Grand Haven |
| Booth, Philip W. | Ithaca |
| Buckbee, Donald M. | Grayling |
| Canoy, Andrew B. | Hubbard Lake |
| Carlisle, Frank | Detroit |
| Carr, Tim | Muskegon |
| Carroll, Chad | Grant |
| Cashen, Kevin R. | Hubbardston |
| Cook, Mike A. | Portland |

| | |
|---|---|
| Cousino, George | Onsted |
| Cowles, Don | Royal Oak |
| Dilluvio, Frank J. | Warren |
| Ealy, Delbert | Indian River |
| Erickson, Walter E. | Atlanta |
| Gordon, Larry B. | Farmington Hills |
| Gottage, Dante | Clinton Twp. |
| Gottage, Judy | Clinton Twp. |
| Harm, Paul W. | Attica |
| Hartman, Arlan (Lanny) | N. Muskegon |
| Hughes, Daryle | Nunica |
| Krause, Roy W. | St. Clair Shores |
| Lankton, Scott | Ann Arbor |
| Leach, Mike J. | Swartz Creek |
| Lucie, James R. | Fruitport |
| Mankel, Kenneth | Cannonsburg |
| Mills, Louis G. | Ann Arbor |
| Nix, Robert T. | Wayne |
| Noren, Douglas E. | Springlake |
| Parker, Robert Nelson | Rapid City |
| Repke, Mike | Bay City |
| Sakmar, Mike | Rochester |
| Sandberg, Ronald B. | Browntown |
| Serven, Jim | Fostoria |
| Sigman, James P. | North Adams |
| Tally, Grant | Flat Rock |
| Van Eizenga, Jerry W. | Nunica |
| Vasquez, Johnny David | Wyandotte |
| Viste, James | Detroit |
| White, Richard T. | Grosse Pointe Farms |
| Whittaker, Wayne | Metamore |
| Whitworth, Ken J. | Sterling Heights |
| Wood, Webster | Atlanta |
| Zowada, Tim | Boyne Falls |

## MN

| | |
|---|---|
| Davis, Joel | Albert Lea |
| Goltz, Warren L. | Ada |
| Griffin, Thomas J. | Windom |
| Hagen, Philip L. | Pelican Rapids |
| Hansen, Robert W. | Cambridge |
| Johnson, R.B. | Clearwater |
| Knipschield, Terry | Rochester |
| Maines, Jay | Wyoming |
| Mickley, Tracy | North Mankato |
| Rydbom, Jeff | Annandale |
| Shadley, Eugene W. | Bovey |
| Steffen, Chuck | St. Michael |
| Voorhies, Les | Faribault |

## MO

| | |
|---|---|
| Bolton, Charles B. | Jonesburg |
| Burrows, Stephen R. | Kansas City |
| Buxton, Bill | Kaiser |
| Conner, Allen L. | Fulton |
| Cover, Raymond A. | Mineral Point |
| Cox, Colin J. | Raymore |
| Davis, W.C. | Raymore |
| Dippold, Al | Perryville |
| Driskill, Beryl | Braggadocio |
| Ehrenberger, Daniel Robert | Shelbyville |
| Engle, William | Boonville |
| Hanson III, Don L. | Success |
| Harris, Jeffery A. | St. Louis |
| Harrison, Jim (Seamus) | St. Louis |
| Jones, John A. | Holden |
| Kinnikin, Todd | House Springs |
| Knickmeyer, Hank | Cedar Hill |
| Knickmeyer, Kurt | Cedar Hill |
| Martin, Tony | Arcadia |
| Mason, Bill | Excelsior Springs |
| McCrackin, Kevin | House Springs |
| McCrackin and Son, V.J. | House Springs |
| McDermott, Michael | Defiance |
| McKiernan, Stan | Vandalia |
| Miller, Bob | Oakville |
| Muller, Jody | Pittsburg |
| Newcomb, Corbin | Moberly |
| Pryor, Stephen L. | Boss |
| Ramsey, Richard A. | Neosho |
| Rardon, A.D. | Polo |
| Rardon, Archie F. | Polo |
| Riepe, Richard A. | Harrisonville |
| Scroggs, James A. | Warrensburg |
| Sonntag, Douglas W. | Nixa |
| Steketee, Craig A. | Billings |
| Stewart, Edward L. | Mexico |
| Stormer, Bob | St. Peters |
| Warden, Roy A. | Union |
| Weddle Jr., Del | St. Joseph |
| Willis, Bill | Ava |

## MS

| | |
|---|---|
| Black, Scott | Picayune |
| Boleware, David | Carson |
| Davis, Jesse W. | Sarah |
| Evans, Bruce A. | Booneville |
| Lamey, Robert M. | Biloxi |
| Lebatard, Paul M. | Vancleave |
| Roberts, Michael | Clinton |
| Roberts, Mike | Clinton |
| Robinson, Chuck | Picayune |
| Shiffer, Steve | Leakesville |
| Skow, H. A. "Tex" | Senatobia |
| Taylor, Billy | Petal |
| Vandeventer, Terry L. | Terry |
| Wehner, Rudy | Collins |
| Wingo, Perry | Gulfport |
| Winston, David | Starkville |

## MT

| | |
|---|---|
| Barnes, Jack | Whitefish |
| Barnes, Wendell | Clinton |
| Barth, J.D. | Alberton |
| Beam, John R. | Kalispell |
| Beaty, Robert B. | Missoula |
| Becker, Steve | Conrad |
| Bizzell, Robert | Butte |
| Boxer, Bo | Whitefish |
| Brooks, Steve R. | Walkerville |
| Caffrey, Edward J. | Great Falls |
| Carlisle, Jeff | Simms |
| Christensen, Jon P. | Shepherd |
| Colter, Wade | Colstrip |
| Conklin, George L. | Ft. Benton |
| Crowder, Robert | Thompson Falls |
| Dunkerley, Rick | Seeley Lake |
| Eaton, Rick | Shepherd |
| Ellefson, Joel | Manhattan |
| Fassio, Melvin G. | Lolo |
| Forthofer, Pete | Whitefish |
| Gallagher, Barry | Lewistown |
| Harkins, J.A. | Conner |
| Hill, Howard E. | Polson |
| Hintz, Gerald M. | Helena |
| Hollar, Bob | Great Falls |
| Hulett, Steve | West Yellowstone |
| Kajin, Al | Forsyth |
| Kauffman, Dave | Montana City |
| Kraft, Elmer | Big Arm |
| Luman, James R. | Anaconda |
| McGuane Iv, Thomas F. | Bozeman |
| Mortenson, Ed | Darby |
| Moyer, Russ | Havre |
| Munroe, Deryk C. | Bozeman |
| Nedved, Dan | Kalispell |
| Patrick, Willard C. | Helena |
| Peele, Bryan | Thompson Falls |
| Peterson, Eldon G. | Whitefi |
| Piorek, James S. | Rexfc |
| Pursley, Aaron | Big San |
| Robinson, Robert W. | Pols |
| Rodewald, Gary | Hamilt |
| Ruana Knife Works, | Bonr |
| Smallwood, Wayne | Kalisp |
| Smith, Josh | Frenchto |
| Sweeney, Coltin D. | Missou |
| Taylor, Shane | Miles C |
| Thill, Jim | Missou |
| Weinand, Gerome M. | Misso |
| Woodiwiss, Dorren | Thompson Fa |
| Yashinski, John L. | Red Lod |

## NC

| | |
|---|---|
| Baker, Herb | Ed |
| Bauchop, Peter | Ca |
| Britton, Tim | Winston-Sal |
| Busfield, John | Roanoke Rap |
| Chastain, Wade | Horse Sh |
| Coltrain, Larry D. | Bux |
| Daniel, Travis E. | Chocowir |
| Drew, Gerald | Ashev |
| Edwards, Fain E. | Top |
| Fox, Paul | Clarem |
| Gaddy, Gary Lee | Washing |
| Goguen, Scott | Newp |
| Goode, Brian | She |
| Greene, Chris | She |
| Gross, W.W. | Archd |
| Gurganus, Carol | Coler |
| Gurganus, Melvin H. | Coler |
| Guthrie, George B. | Bassemer C |
| Hazen, Mark | Charlo |
| Kearney, Jarod | Brown Sum |
| Livingston, Robert C. | Mur |
| Maynard, William N. | Fayettev |
| McDonald, Robin J. | Fayettev |
| McLurkin, Andrew | Rale |
| McNabb, Tommy | Winston-Sal |
| McRae, J. Michael | Mint |
| Parrish, Robert | Weaverv |
| Patrick, Chuck | Brassto |
| Patrick, Peggy | Brassto |
| Scholl, Tim | An |
| Simmons, H.R. | Au |
| Snody, Mike | Lib |
| Sprouse, Terry | Ashev |
| Sterling, Murray | Mount |
| Summers, Arthur L. | Conc |
| Sutton, S. Russell | New B |
| Vail, Dave | Hampst |
| Wagaman, John K. | Se |
| Walker, Don | Burns |
| Warren, Daniel | Car |
| Whitley, L. Wayne | Chocowi |
| Williamson, Tony | Siler |
| Wilson, Mike | Hayes |
| Winkler, Daniel | Blowing R |
| Young, Paul A. | Bo |

## ND

| | |
|---|---|
| Keidel, Gene W. and Scott J. | Dickin |
| Pitman, David | Willis |

## NE

| | |
|---|---|
| Jensen Jr., Carl A. | B |
| Jokerst, Charles | Om |
| Marlowe, Charles | Om |
| Mosier, Joshua J. | Des |
| Robbins, Howard P. | Elk |
| Schepers, George B. | She |

| | |
|---|---|
| Suedmeier, Harlan | Nebraska City |
| Syslo, Chuck | Omaha |
| Tiensvold, Alan L. | Rushville |
| Tiensvold, Jason | Rushville |
| Till, Calvin E. and Ruth | Chadron |

## NH

| | |
|---|---|
| Carlson, Kelly | Antrim |
| Gunn, Nelson L. | Epping |
| Hill, Steve E. | Goshen |
| Hitchmough, Howard | Peterborough |
| MacDonald, John | Raymond |
| Philippe, D. A. | Cornish |
| Saindon, R. Bill | Goshen |

## NJ

| | |
|---|---|
| Eden, Thomas | Cranbury |
| Grussenmeyer, Paul G. | Cherry Hill |
| Licata, Steven | Garfield |
| Little, Guy A. | Oakhurst |
| McCallen Jr., Howard H. | So. Seaside Park |
| Nelson, Bob | Sparta |
| Phillips, Jim | Williamstown |
| Polkowski, Al | Chester |
| Pressburger, Ramon | Howell |
| Quick, Mike | Kearny |
| Schilling, Ellen | Hamilton Square |
| Sheets, Steven William | Mendham |
| Slee, Fred | Morganville |
| iele, H.J. | Westwood |
| eskoo, Richard C. | Summit |

## NM

| | |
|---|---|
| lack, Tom | Albuquerque |
| herry, Frank J. | Albuquerque |
| oleman, Keith E. | Albuquerque |
| ordova, Joseph G. | Peralta |
| umming, Bob | Cedar Crest |
| igangi, Joseph M. | Santa Cruz |
| uran, Jerry T. | Albuquerque |
| yess, Eddie | Roswell |
| isher, Jay | Clovis |
| oode, Bear | Navajo Dam |
| unter, Brad | Tijeras |
| ethcoat, Don | Clovis |
| ume, Don | Albuquerque |
| ones, Bob | Albuquerque |
| imberley, Richard L. | Santa Fe |
| ewis, Tom R. | Carlsbad |
| acdonald, David | Los Lunas |
| ogers, Richard | Magdalena |
| challer, Anthony Brett | Albuquerque |
| alcup, Eddie | Gallup |
| erzuola, Robert | Santa Fe |
| ujillo, Albert M.B. | Bosque Farms |
| alker, Michael L. | Rancho de Taos |
| are, Tommy | Datil |
| escott, Cody | Las Cruces |

## NV

| | |
|---|---|
| arnett, Van | Reno |
| easley, Geneo | Wadsworth |
| ameron, Ron G. | Logandale |
| efeo, Robert A. | Henderson |
| ellana | Reno |
| uff, Bill | Reno |
| eorge, Tom | Henderson |
| isoulas, Jim | Las Vegas |
| eibich, Donald L. | Reno |
| ount, Don | Las Vegas |
| shiuchi, Melvin S. | Las Vegas |
| omas, Devin | Panaca |
| Tracy, Bud | Reno |
| Washburn, Arthur D. | Pioche |

## NY

| | |
|---|---|
| Baker, Wild Bill | Boiceville |
| Champagne, Paul | Mechanicville |
| Cute, Thomas | Cortland |
| Davis, Barry L. | Castleton |
| Farr, Dan | Rochester |
| Faust, Dick | Rochester |
| Hobart, Gene | Windsor |
| Isgro, Jeffery | West Babylon |
| Johnson, Mike | Orient |
| Johnston, Dr. Robt. | Rochester |
| Levin, Jack | Brooklyn |
| Loos, Henry C. | New Hyde Park |
| Ludwig, Richard O. | Maspeth |
| Lupole, Jamie G. | Kirkwood |
| Maragni, Dan | Georgetown |
| McCornock, Craig | Willow |
| Meerdink, Kurt | Barryville |
| Meshejian, Mardi | E. Northport |
| Page, Reginald | Groveland |
| Palazzo, Tom | Bayside |
| Pattay, Rudy | Long Beach |
| Peterson, Karen | Brooklyn |
| Phillips, Scott C. | Gouverneur |
| Rachlin, Leslie S. | Elmira |
| Rappazzo, Richard | Cohoes |
| Rotella, Richard A. | Niagara Falls |
| Scheid, Maggie | Rochester |
| Schippnick, Jim | Sanborn |
| Schlueter, David | Syracuse |
| Serafen, Steven E. | New Berlin |
| Skiff, Steven | Broadalbin |
| Smith, Lenard C. | Valley Cottage |
| Smith, Raymond L. | Erin |
| Summers, Dan | Whitney Pt. |
| Szilaski, Joseph | Wappingers Falls |
| Turner, Kevin | Montrose |

## OH

| | |
|---|---|
| Babcock, Raymond G. | Vincent |
| Bailey, Ryan | Galena |
| Bendik, John | Olmsted Falls |
| Busse, Jerry | Wauseon |
| Collins, Harold | West Union |
| Collins, Lynn M. | Elyria |
| Coppins, Daniel | Cambridge |
| Cottrill, James I. | Columbus |
| Downing, Tom | Cuyahoga Falls |
| Downs, James F. | Londonderry |
| Etzler, John | Grafton |
| Foster, R.L. (Bob) | Mansfield |
| Francis, John D. | Ft. Loramie |
| Franklin, Mike | Aberdeen |
| Geisler, Gary R. | Clarksville |
| Gittinger, Raymond | Tiffin |
| Glover, Ron | Mason |
| Greiner, Richard | Green Springs |
| Guess, Raymond L. | Mechanicstown |
| Hinderer, Rick | Wooster |
| Hudson, Anthony B. | Amanda |
| Imboden II, Howard L. | Dayton |
| Jones, Roger Mudbone | Waverly |
| Kiefer, Tony | Pataskala |
| Kubaiko, Hank | Beach City |
| Longworth, Dave | Hamersville |
| Loro, Gene | Crooksville |
| Maienknecht, Stanley | Sardis |
| McDonald, Rich | Columbiana |
| McGroder, Patrick J. | Madison |
| Mercer, Mike | Lebanon |
| Messer, David T. | Dayton |
| Morgan, Tom | Beloit |
| Panak, Paul S. | Kinsman |
| Potter, Billy | Nashport |
| Ralph, Darrel | Galena |
| Rose, Derek W. | Gallipolis |
| Rowe, Fred | Amesville |
| Salley, John D. | Tipp City |
| Schuchmann, Rick | New Richmond |
| Shinosky, Andy | Canfield |
| Shoemaker, Carroll | Northup |
| Shoemaker, Scott | Miamisburg |
| Spinale, Richard | Lorain |
| Stoddart, W.B. Bill | Forest Park |
| Strong, Scott | Beavercreek |
| Summers, Dennis K. | Springfield |
| Thomas, Kim | Seville |
| Thourot, Michael W. | Napoleon |
| Tindera, George | Brunswick |
| Votaw, David P. | Pioneer |
| Ward, J.J. | Waverly |
| Ward, Ron | Loveland |
| Warther, Dale | Dover |
| Witsaman, Earl | Stow |
| Wood, Larry B. | Huber Heights |
| Wright, L.T. | Steubenville |
| Yurco, Mike | Canfield |

## OK

| | |
|---|---|
| Baker, Ray | Sapulpa |
| Barngrover, Jerry | Afton |
| Brown, Troy L. | Park Hill |
| Burke, Dan | Edmond |
| Carillo, Dwaine | Moore |
| Crenshaw, Al | Eufaula |
| Darby, David T. | Cookson |
| Dill, Dave | Bethany |
| Englebretson, George | Oklahoma City |
| Gepner, Don | Norman |
| Griffith, Lynn | Tulsa |
| Johns, Rob | Enid |
| Kennedy Jr., Bill | Yukon |
| Kirk, Ray | Tahlequah |
| Lairson Sr., Jerry | Ringold |
| Martin, John Alexander | Okmulgee |
| Miller, Michael E. | El Reno |
| Sanders, A.A. | Norman |
| Spivey, Jefferson | Yukon |
| Tomberlin, Brion R. | Norman |
| Williams, Michael L. | Broken Bow |
| Wingo, Gary | Ramona |

## OR

| | |
|---|---|
| Bell, Michael | Coquille |
| Bochman, Bruce | Grants Pass |
| Brandt, Martin W. | Springfield |
| Buchman, Bill | Bend |
| Buchner, Bill | Idleyld Park |
| Cameron House, | Salem |
| Carter, Murray M. | Vernonia |
| Clark, Nate | Yoncalla |
| Coon, Raymond C. | Gresham |
| Davis, Terry | Sumpter |
| Dowell, T.M. | Bend |
| Ferdinand, Don | Shady Cove |
| Fox, Wendell | Springfield |
| Frank, Heinrich H. | Seal Rock |
| Goddard, Wayne | Eugene |
| Harsey, William H. | Creswell |
| Hilker, Thomas N. | Williams |
| Horn, Jess | Eugene |
| Kelley, Gary | Aloha |
| Lake, Ron | Eugene |
| Little, Gary M. | Broadbent |
| Lockett, Lowell C. | North Bend |

| | |
|---|---|
| Lum, Robert W. | Eugene |
| Martin, Gene | Williams |
| Martin, Walter E. | Williams |
| Miller, Michael K. | Sweet Home |
| Olson, Darrold E. | Springfield |
| Rider, David M. | Eugene |
| Schoeningh, Mike | North Powder |
| Schrader, Robert | Bend |
| Sevey Custom Knife, | Gold Beach |
| Sheehy, Thomas J. | Portland |
| Shoger, Mark O. | Beaverton |
| Smith, Rick | Rogue River |
| Thompson, Leon | Gaston |
| Thompson, Tommy | Portland |
| Vallotton, Butch and Arey | Oakland |
| Vallotton, Rainy D. | Umpqua |
| Vallotton, Shawn | Oakland |
| Vallotton, Thomas | Oakland |
| Veatch, Richard | Springfield |

## PA

| | |
|---|---|
| Anderson, Gary D. | Spring Grove |
| Anderson, Tom | Manchester |
| Appleby, Robert | Shickshinny |
| Besedick, Frank E. | Ruffsdale |
| Candrella, Joe | Warminster |
| Chavar, Edward V. | Bethlehem |
| Clark, D.E. (Lucky) | Mineral Point |
| Corkum, Steve | Littlestown |
| Darby, Rick | Levittown |
| Evans, Ronald B. | Middleton |
| Frey Jr., W. Frederick | Milton |
| Goldberg, David | Blue Bell |
| Goodling, Rodney W. | York Springs |
| Gottschalk, Gregory J. | Carnegie |
| Heinz, John | Upper Black Eddy |
| Hudson, Rob | Northumberland |
| Janiga, Matthew A. | Hummelstown |
| Malloy, Joe | Freeland |
| Marlowe, Donald | Dover |
| Mensch, Larry C. | Milton |
| Milford, Brian A. | Knox |
| Miller, Rick | Rockwood |
| Moore, Ted | Elizabethtown |
| Morett, Donald | Lancaster |
| Navagato, Angelo | Camp Hill |
| Nealy, Bud | Stroudsburg |
| Neilson, J. | Wyalusing |
| Nott, Ron P. | Summerdale |
| Ogden, Bill | Avis |
| Ortega, Ben M. | Wyoming |
| Parker, J.E. | Clarion |
| Root, Gary | Erie |
| Rupert, Bob | Clinton |
| Sass, Gary N. | Sharpsville |
| Scimio, Bill | Spruce Creek |
| Sinclair, J.E. | Pittsburgh |
| Steigerwalt, Ken | Orangeville |
| Stroyan, Eric | Dalton |
| Valois, A. Daniel | Lehighton |
| Vaughan, Ian | Manheim |
| Whittaker, Robert E. | Mill Creek |
| Wilson, Jon J. | Johnstown |

## RI

| | |
|---|---|
| Bardsley, Norman P. | Pawtucket |
| Burak, Chet | E. Providence |
| Dickison, Scott S. | Portsmouth |
| McHenry, William James | Wyoming |
| Olszewski, Stephen | Coventry |
| Williams, Jason L. | Wyoming |
| Wright, Richard S. | Carolina |

## SC

| | |
|---|---|
| Barefoot, Joe W. | Liberty |
| Beatty, Gordon H. | Seneca |
| Branton, Robert | Awendaw |
| Campbell, Courtnay M. | Columbia |
| Cannady, Daniel L. | Allendale |
| Cox, Sam | Gaffney |
| Defreest, William G. | Barnwell |
| Denning, Geno | Gaston |
| Easler Jr., Russell O. | Woodruff |
| Fecas, Stephen J. | Anderson |
| Gainey, Hal | Greenwood |
| George, Harry | Aiken |
| Gregory, Michael | Belton |
| Hendrix, Jerry | Clinton |
| Hendrix, Wayne | Allendale |
| Herron, George | Springfield |
| Hucks, Jerry | Moncks Corner |
| Kaufman, Scott | Anderson |
| Kay, J. Wallace | Liberty |
| Kessler, Ralph A. | Fountain Inn |
| Knight, Jason | Harleyville |
| Langley, Gene H. | Florence |
| Lewis, K.J. | Lugoff |
| Lutz, Greg | Greenwood |
| Majer, Mike | Hilton Head |
| Manley, David W. | Central |
| McManus, Danny | Taylors |
| Montjoy, Claude | Clinton |
| Odom Jr, Victor L. | North |
| Page, Larry | Aiken |
| Parler, Thomas O. | Charleston |
| Peagler, Russ | Moncks Corner |
| Perry, Johnny | Spartanburg |
| Sears, Mick | Sumter |
| Thomas, Rocky | Moncks Corner |
| Tyser, Ross | Spartanburg |
| Whitmire, Earl T. | Rock Hill |

## SD

| | |
|---|---|
| Boysen, Raymond A. | Rapid City |
| Ferrier, Gregory K. | Rapid City |
| Sarvis, Randall J. | Fort Pierre |
| Thomsen, Loyd W. | Oelrichs |

## TN

| | |
|---|---|
| Bailey, Joseph D. | Nashville |
| Baker, Vance | Riceville |
| Blanchard, G.R. (Gary) | Pigeon Forge |
| Breed, Kim | Clarksville |
| Byrd, Wesley L. | Evensville |
| Canter, Ronald E. | Jackson |
| Casteel, Dianna | Monteagle |
| Casteel, Douglas | Monteagle |
| Centofante, Frank | Madisonville |
| Claiborne, Ron | Knox |
| Clay, Wayne | Pelham |
| Conley, Bob | Jonesboro |
| Coogan, Robert | Smithville |
| Copeland, George Steve | Alpine |
| Corby, Harold | Johnson City |
| Dickerson, Gordon S. | Hohenwald |
| Elder Jr., Perry B. | Clarksville |
| Ewing, John H. | Clinton |
| Harley, Larry W. | Bristol |
| Harley, Richard | Bristol |
| Heflin, Christopher M. | Nashville |
| Hurst, Jeff | Rutledge |
| Hutcheson, John | Chattanooga |
| Johnson, David A. | Pleasant Shade |
| Johnson, Ryan M. | Hixson |
| King, Herman | Millington |
| Levine, Bob | Tullahoma |
| Marshall, Stephen R. | Mt. Juli |
| McCarty, Harry | Blai |
| McDonald, W.J. "Jerry" | Germantov |
| McNeil, Jimmy | Memph |
| Moulton, Dusty | Loud |
| Raley, R. Wayne | Colliervi |
| Ramey, Larry | Chapmansbo |
| Rollick, Walter D. | Maryvi |
| Ryder, Ben M. | Copper |
| Sampson, Lynn | Jonesborou |
| Smith, Newman L. | Gatlinbu |
| Taylor, C. Gray | Fall Bran |
| Vanderford, Carl G. | Columb |
| Walker, John W. | Bon Aq |
| Ward, W.C. | Clint |
| Wheeler, Gary | Clarksv |
| Williams Jr., Richard | Morristo |
| Winter, George | Union C |

## TX

| | |
|---|---|
| Adams, William D. | Burt |
| Alexander, Eugene | Gana |
| Allen, Mike "Whiskers" | Malak |
| Ashby, Douglas | Dal |
| Bailey, Kirby C. | Ly |
| Barnes, Marlen R. | Atla |
| Barr, Judson C. | Irv |
| Batts, Keith | Hoc |
| Blasingame, Robert | Kilg |
| Blum, Kenneth | Brenh |
| Boatright, Basel | New Braunf |
| Bradshaw, Bailey | Dia |
| Bratcher, Brett | Plantersv |
| Brightwell, Mark | Lean |
| Broadwell, David | Wichita F |
| Brooks, Michael | Lubb |
| Bullard, Randall | Cany |
| Burden, James | Burkburr |
| Cairnes Jr., Carroll B. | Palac |
| Callahan, F. Terry | Boe |
| Cannon, Dan | Da |
| Carpenter, Ronald W. | Jas |
| Carter, Fred | Wichita F |
| Champion, Robert | Ama |
| Chase, John E. | Al |
| Chew, Larry | Granb |
| Churchman, T.W. (Tim) | Band |
| Cole, James M. | Bartonv |
| Connor, John W. | Ode |
| Connor, Michael | Wint |
| Cosgrove, Charles G. | Arling |
| Costa, Scott | Spicew |
| Crain, Jack W. | Granb |
| Darcey, Chester L. | College Sta |
| Davidson, Larry | Cedar |
| Davis, Vernon M. | W |
| Dean, Harvey J. | Rock |
| Dietz, Howard | New Braun |
| Dominy, Chuck | Colley |
| Dyer, David | Granb |
| Eldridge, Allan | Ft. W |
| Elishewitz, Allen | Canyon L |
| Epting, Richard | College Sta |
| Eriksen, James Thorlief | Garl |
| Evans, Carlton | Al |
| Fant Jr., George | Atla |
| Ferguson, Jim | San An |
| Fortune Products, Inc., | Marble F |
| Foster, Al | Magn |
| Foster, Norvell C. | San Ant |
| Fowler, Jerry | H |
| Fritz, Jesse | Sl |
| Fuller, Bruce A. | Bayt |
| Garner, Larry W. | T |
| Gault, Clay | Lexin |

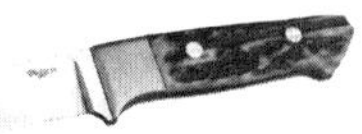

| | |
|---|---|
| Goytia, Enrique | El Paso |
| Graham, Gordon | New Boston |
| Green, Bill | Garland |
| Griffin, Rendon and Mark | Houston |
| Halfrich, Jerry | San Marcos |
| Hamlet Jr., Johnny | Clute |
| Hand, Bill | Spearman |
| Hawkins, Buddy | Texarkana |
| Hayes, Scotty | Tesarkana |
| Haynes, Jerry | San Antonio |
| Hays, Mark | Austin |
| Hearn, Terry L. | Lufkin |
| Hemperley, Glen | Willis |
| Hesser, David | Dripping Springs |
| House, Lawrence | Canyon Lake |
| Howell, Jason G. | Lake Jackson |
| Howell, Robert L. | Kilgore |
| Hudson, Robert | Humble |
| Hughes, Bill | Texarkana |
| Hughes, Lawrence | Plainview |
| Jackson, Charlton R. | San Antonio |
| Jaksik Jr., Michael | Fredericksburg |
| Johnson, Gorden W. | Houston |
| Johnson, Ruffin | Houston |
| Kern, R. W. | San Antonio |
| Kious, Joe | Kerrville |
| Knipstein, R.C. (Joe) | Arlington |
| Ladd, Jim S. | Deer Park |
| Ladd, Jimmie Lee | Deer Park |
| Lambert, Jarrell D. | Granado |
| Laplante, Brett | McKinney |
| Lay, L.J. | Burkburnett |
| Lemcke, Jim L. | Houston |
| Lister Jr., Weldon E. | Boerne |
| Lively, Tim and Marian | Marble Falls |
| Locke, Keith | Watauga |
| Love, Ed | San Antonio |
| Luchak, Bob | Channelview |
| Luckett, Bill | Weatherford |
| Marshall, Glenn | Mason |
| Martin, Michael W. | Beckville |
| McConnell Jr., Loyd A. | Odessa |
| Mellard, J. R. | Houston |
| Merz III, Robert L. | Katy |
| Miller, R.D. | Dallas |
| Mitchell, Wm. Dean | Warren |
| Moore, James B. | Ft. Stockton |
| Neely, Greg | Bellaire |
| Nelson, Dr. Carl | Texarkana |
| Nolen, R.D. and Steve | Pottsboro |
| Obrien, George | Katy |
| Odgen, Randy W. | Houston |
| Ogletree Jr., Ben R. | Livingston |
| Osborne, Warren | Waxahachie |
| Overeynder, T.R. | Arlington |
| Ownby, John C. | Plano |
| Pardue, Joe | Spurger |
| Patterson, Pat | Barksdale |
| Pierce, Randall | Arlington |
| Pollock, Wallace J. | Cedar Park |
| Polzien, Don | Lubbock |
| Powell, James | Texarkana |
| Pugh, Jim | Azle |
| Ray, Alan W. | Lovelady |
| Roberts, Jack | Houston |
| Robinson, Charles (Dickie) | Vega |
| Rogers, Charles W. | Douglas |
| Ruple, William H. | Charlotte |
| Ruth, Michael G | Texarkana |
| Scott, Al | Harper |
| Self, Ernie | Dripping Springs |
| Shipley, Steven A. | Richardson |
| Sims, Bob | Meridian |
| Sloan, Shane | Newcastle |
| Smart, Steve | McKinney |
| Stokes, Ed | Hockley |
| Stone, Jerry | Lytle |
| Stout, Johnny | New Braunfels |
| Theis, Terry | Harper |
| Thuesen, Ed | Damon |
| Treiber, Leon | Ingram |
| Turcotte, Larry | Pampa |
| Watson, Daniel | Driftwood |
| Watt III, Freddie | Big Spring |
| Watts, Johnathan | Gatesville |
| Watts, Wally | Gatesville |
| West, Pat | Charlotte |
| White, Dale | Sweetwater |
| Whitley, Weldon G. | Odessa |
| Wilcher, Wendell L. | Palestine |
| Wilkins, Mitchell | Montgomery |
| Wolf Jr., William Lynn | Lagrange |
| Wood, William W. | Seymour |
| Woodard, Wiley | Colleyville |
| Yeates, Joe A. | Spring |
| Zboril, Terry | Caldwell |

## UT

| | |
|---|---|
| Allred, Bruce F. | Layton |
| Baum, Rick | Lehi |
| Black, Earl | Salt Lake City |
| Ence, Jim | Richfield |
| Ennis, Ray | Ogden |
| Erickson, L.M. | Liberty |
| Hunter, Hyrum | Aurora |
| Johnson, Steven R. | Manti |
| Maxfield, Lynn | Layton |
| Nielson, Jeff V. | Monroe |
| Nunn, Gregory | Castle Valley |
| Palmer, Taylor | Blanding |
| Peterson, Chris | Salina |
| Rapp, Steven J. | Midvale |
| Strickland, Dale | Monroe |
| Velarde, Ricardo | Park City |
| Warenski, Buster | Richfield |
| Winn, Travis A. | Salt Lake City |

## VA

| | |
|---|---|
| Apelt, Stacy E. | Norfolk |
| Arbuckle, James M. | Yorktown |
| Ballew, Dale | Bowling Green |
| Batley, Mark S. | Wake |
| Batson, Richard G. | Rixeyville |
| Beverly II, Larry H. | Spotsylvania |
| Callahan, Errett | Lynchburg |
| Catoe, David R. | Norfolk |
| Chamberlain, Charles R. | Barren Springs |
| Compton, William E. | Sterling |
| Conkey, Tom | Nokesville |
| Davidson, Edmund | Goshen |
| Douglas, John J. | Lynch Station |
| Foster, Burt | Bristol |
| Frazier, Ron | Powhatan |
| Harris, Cass | Bluemont |
| Hawk, Jack L. | Ceres |
| Hawk, Joey K. | Ceres |
| Hedrick, Don | Newport News |
| Hendricks, Samuel J. | Maurertown |
| Holloway, Paul | Norfolk |
| Jones, Barry M. and Phillip G. | Danville |
| Jones, Enoch | Warrenton |
| Kellogg, Brian R. | New Market |
| McCoun, Mark | DeWitt |
| Metheny, H.A. "Whitey" | Spotsylvania |
| Murski, Ray | Reston |
| Norfleet, Ross W. | Richmond |
| Parks, Blane C. | Woodbridge |
| Pawlowski, John R. | Newport News |
| Richter, John C. | Chesapeake |
| Tomes, P.J. | Shipman |
| Vanhoy, Ed and Tanya | Abingdon |
| White, Gene E. | Alexandria |

## VT

| | |
|---|---|
| Haggerty, George S. | Jacksonville |
| Kelso, Jim | Worcester |

## WA

| | |
|---|---|
| Amoureux, A.W. | Northport |
| Baldwin, Phillip | Snohomish |
| Begg, Todd M. | Spanaway |
| Ber, Dave | San Juan Island |
| Berglin, Bruce D. | Mount Vernon |
| Bloomquist, R. Gordon | Olympia |
| Boguszewski, Phil | Lakewood |
| Boyer, Mark | Bothell |
| Bromley, Peter | Spokane |
| Brothers, Robert L. | Colville |
| Brown, Dennis G. | Shoreline |
| Brunckhorst, Lyle | Bothell |
| Bump, Bruce D. | Walla Walla |
| Butler, John R. | Shoreline |
| Campbell, Dick | Colville |
| Chamberlain, John B. | Wenatchee |
| Chamberlain, Jon A. | E. Wenatchee |
| Conti, Jeffrey D. | Bonney Lake |
| Crain, Frank | Spokane |
| Crossman, Daniel C. | Blakely Island |
| Crowthers, Mark F. | Rolling Bay |
| D'Angelo, Laurence | Vancouver |
| Davis, John | Selah |
| Diskin, Matt | Freeland |
| Dole, Roger | Buckley |
| Evans, Vincent K. and Grace | Cathlamet |
| Ferry, Tom | Auburn |
| Frey, Steve | Snohomish |
| Gallagher, Sean | Monroe |
| Goertz, Paul S. | Renton |
| Gray, Bob | Spokane |
| Greenfield, G.O. | Everett |
| Hansen, Lonnie | Spanaway |
| Higgins, J.P. Dr. | Coupeville |
| House, Gary | Ephrata |
| Hurst, Cole | E. Wenatchee |
| Mosser, Gary E. | Kirkland |
| Norton, Don | Port Townsend |
| O'Malley, Daniel | Seattle |
| Rogers, Ray | Wauconda |
| Sanderson, Ray | Yakima |
| Schempp, Ed | Ephrata |
| Schempp, Martin | Ephrata |
| Schirmer, Mike | Rosalia |
| Smith, D. Noel | Poulsbo |
| Stegner, Wilbur G. | Rochester |
| Swyhart, Art | Klickitat |
| Wright, Kevin | Quilcene |

## WI

| | |
|---|---|
| Bostwick, Chris T. | Burlington |
| Brandsey, Edward P. | Milton |
| Bruner Jr., Fred, Bruner Blades | Fall Creek |
| Delarosa, Jim | Whitewater |
| Fiorini, Bill | DeSoto |
| Genske, Jay | Fond du Lac |
| Haines, Jeff, Haines Custom Knives | Wauzeka |
| Hembrook, Ron | Neosho |
| Johnson, Richard | Germantown |
| Kanter, Michael | New Berlin |
| Kohls, Jerry | Princeton |
| Kolitz, Robert | Beaver Dam |
| Lary, Ed | Mosinee |
| Lerch, Matthew | Sussex |
| Maestri, Peter A. | Spring Green |

| | |
|---|---|
| Martin, Peter | Waterford |
| Millard, Fred G. | Richland Center |
| Nelson, Ken | Pittsville |
| Niemuth, Troy | Sheboygan |
| Ponzio, Doug | Pleasant Prairie |
| R. Boyes Knives | Menomonee Falls |
| Revishvili, Zaza | Madison |
| Ricke, Dave | West Bend |
| Rochford, Michael R. | Dresser |
| Schrap, Robert G. | Wauwatosa |
| Wattelet, Michael A. | Minocqua |

## WV

| | |
|---|---|
| Bowen, Tilton | Baker |
| Carnahan, Charles A. | Green Spring |
| Dent, Douglas M. | S. Charleston |
| Derr, Herbert | St. Albans |
| Drost, Jason D. | French Creek |
| Drost, Michael B. | French Creek |
| Elliott, Jerry | Charleston |
| Jeffries, Robert W. | Red House |
| Liegey, Kenneth R. | Millwood |
| Maynard, Larry Joe | Crab Orchard |
| McConnell, Charles R. | Wellsburg |
| Morris, Eric | Beckley |
| Pickens, Selbert | Liberty |
| Reynolds, Dave | Harrisville |
| Shaver II, James R. | Parkersburg |
| Sigman, Corbet R. | Liberty |
| Small, Ed | Keyser |
| Straight, Don | Points |
| Tokar, Daniel | Shepherdstown |
| Wilson, R.W. | Weirton |
| Wyatt, William R. | Rainelle |

## WY

| | |
|---|---|
| Alexander, Darrel | Ten Sleep |
| Ankrom, W.E. | Cody |
| Archer, Ray and Terri | Medicine Bow |
| Banks, David L. | Riverton |
| Bartlow, John | Sheridan |
| Bennett, Brett C. | Cheyenne |
| Draper, Audra | Riverton |
| Draper, Mike | Riverton |
| Fowler, Ed A. | Riverton |
| Friedly, Dennis E. | Cody |
| Justice, Shane | Sheridan |
| Kilby, Keith | Cody |
| Kinkade, Jacob | Carpenter |
| Rexroat, Kirk | Wright |
| Reynolds, John C. | Gillette |
| Ross, Stephen | Evanston |
| Spragg, Wayne E. | Lovell |
| Walker, George A. | Alpine |

## ARGENTINA

| | |
|---|---|
| Ayarragaray, Cristian L. | (3100) Parana-Entre Rios |
| Bertolami, Juan Carlos | Neuquen |
| Gibert, Pedro | San Rafael Mendoza |
| Kehiayan, Alfredo | CP B1623GXU Buenos Aires |
| Rho, Nestor Lorenzo | Buenos Aires |

## AUSTRALIA

| | |
|---|---|
| Bennett, Peter | Engadine N.S.W. 2233 |
| Brodziak, David | Albany |
| Crawley, Bruce R. | Croydon 3136 Victoria |
| Cross, Robert | Tamworth 2340 |
| Del Raso, Peter | Mt. Waverly, Victoria, 3149 |
| Gerus, Gerry | Qld. 4870 |
| Giljevic, Branko | N.S.W. |
| Green, William (Bill) | View Bank Vic. |
| Harvey, Max | Perth 6155 |
| Husiak, Myron | Victoria |
| Jones, John | Manly West, QLD 4179 |
| K B S, Knives | Vic 3450 |
| Maisey, Alan | Vincentia 2540 |
| Spencer, Keith | Chidlow WA |
| Tasman, Kerley | Western Australia |
| Zemitis, Joe | 2285 Newcastle |

## AUSTRIA

| | |
|---|---|
| Poskocil, Helmut | A-3340 Waidhofen/Ybbs |

## BELGIUM

| | |
|---|---|
| Dox, Jan | B 2900 Schoten |
| Monteiro, Victor | 1360 Maleves Ste Marie |

## BRAZIL

| | |
|---|---|
| Bodolay, Antal | Belo Horizonte MG-31730-700 |
| Bossaerts, Carl | 14051-110, Ribeirao Preto |
| Campos, Ivan | Tatui, SP |
| Dorneles, Luciano Oliverira | Nova Petropolis, RS |
| Gaeta, Angelo | SP-17201-310 |
| Gaeta, Roberto | Sao Paulo |
| Garcia, Mario Eiras | Sao Paulo SP-05516-070 |
| Ikoma, Flavio Yuji, R. Manoel, R. Teixeira | 108 SP-19031-220 |
| Lala, Paulo Ricardo P. and Lala, Roberto P. | SP-19031-260 |
| Neto Jr., Nelson and De Carvalho, Henrique M. | SP-12900-000 |
| Paulo, Fernandes R. | Sao Paulo |
| Petean, Francisco and Mauricio | SP-16200-000 |
| Ricardo Romano, Bernardes | Itajuba MG |
| Rosa, Pedro Gullherme Teles | SP-19065-410 |
| Sfreddo, Rodrito Menezes | Nova Petropolis, RS |
| Villa, Luiz | Sao Paulo, SP-04537-081 |
| Vilar, Ricardo Augusto Ferreira | Mairipora Sao Paulo 07600-000 |
| Zakharov, Gladiston | Jacaret SP |

## CANADA

| | |
|---|---|
| Arnold, Joe | London, ON |
| Beauchamp, Gaetan | Stoneham, PQ |
| Beets, Marty | Williams Lake, BC |
| Bell, Donald | Bedford, Nova Scotia |
| Berg, Lothar | Kitchener, ON |
| Beshara, Brent | Stayner, ON |
| Bold, Stu | Sarnia, ON |
| Boos, Ralph | Edmonton, Alberta |
| Bourbeau, Jean Yves | Ile Perrot, Quebec |
| Bradford, Garrick | Kitchener, ON |
| Dallyn, Kelly | Calgary, AB |
| Debraga, Jose C. | Aux Lievres, Quebec |
| Debraga, Jovan | Quebec |
| Deringer, Christoph | Cookshire, Quebec |
| Diotte, Jeff | LaSalle, ON |
| Doiron, Donald | Messines, PQ |
| Doucette, R | Brantford, ON |
| Doussot, Laurent | Montreal, Quebec |
| Downie, James T. | Port Franks, ON |
| Dublin, Dennis | Enderby, BC |
| Freeman, John | Cambridge, ON |
| Frigault, Rick | Niagara Falls, ON |
| Garvock, Mark W. | Balderson, ON |
| Gilbert, Chantal | Quebec City, Quebec |
| Haslinger, Thomas | Calgary, AB |
| Hayes, Wally | Orleans, ON |
| Hofer, Louis | Rose Prairie, BC |
| Hoffmann, Uwe H. | Vancouver, B |
| Jobin, Jacques | Levis, Queb |
| Kaczor, Tom | Upper London, C |
| Langley, Mick | Crescent Qualicum Beach, B |
| Lay, R.J. (Bob) | Falkland, B |
| Leber, Heinz | Hudson's Hope, B |
| Lightfoot, Greg | Kitscoty, A |
| Linklater, Steve | Aurora, C |
| Loerchner, Wolfgang | Bayfield, C |
| Lyttle, Brian | High River, A |
| Maneker, Kenneth | Galiano Island, B |
| Martin, Robb | Elmira, C |
| Marzitelli, Peter | Langley, B |
| Massey, Al | Mount Uniacke, Nova Sco |
| McKenzie, David Brian | Campbell River, B |
| Miville-Deschenes, Alain | Queb |
| O'Hare, Sean | Fort Simpson, N |
| Olson, Rod | High River, A |
| Painter, Tony | Whitehorse, Yuk |
| Patrick, Bob | S. Surrey, B |
| Pepiot, Stephan | Winnipeg, Ma |
| Piesner, Dean | Conestogo, C |
| Roberts, George A. | Whitehorse, |
| Ross, Tim | Thunder Bay, O |
| Schoenfeld, Matthew A. | Galiano Island, |
| St. Amour, Murray | Pembroke, C |
| Stancer, Chuck | Calgary, |
| Storch, Ed | Alberta T0B 2W |
| Stuart, Steve | Gores Landing, C |
| Tichbourne, George | Mississauga, |
| Tighe, Brian | St. Catharines C |
| Toner, Roger | Pickering, |
| Treml, Glenn | Thunder Bay, |
| Trudel, Paul | Ottawa, |
| Whitenect, Jody | Nova Sco |
| Wile, Peter | Bridgewater, Nova Sco |
| Young, Bud | Port Hardy, |

## DENMARK

| | |
|---|---|
| Andersen, Henrik Lefolii | 3480, Fredensb |
| Anso, Jens | 116, 8472 Spo |
| Dyrnoe, Per | DK 3400 Hillero |
| Henriksen, Hans J. | DK 3200 Helsin |
| Strande, Poul | Dastrup 4130 Viby |
| Vensild, Henrik | DK-8963 Aur |

## ENGLAND

| | |
|---|---|
| Boden, Harry | Derbyshire DE4 |
| Hague, Geoff | Wilton Marlborough, Wilts |
| Harrington, Roger | East Sus |
| Jackson, Jim | Chapel Row Buckleb RG7 6 |
| Jones, Charles Anthony | No. Devon E31 |
| Mehr, Farid R. | K |
| Morris, Darrell Price | De |
| Penfold, Mick | Tremar, Cornwall PL14 |
| Wardell, Mick | N Devon EX39 |
| Wise, Donald | East Sussex, TN3 |
| Wood, Alan | Brampton CA8 7 |

## EUROPE

| | |
|---|---|
| Sprokholt (Gatherwood), Rob | Neder |

## FRANCE

| | |
|---|---|
| Bennica, Charles | 34190 Moules et Bau |
| Bertholus, Bernard | Ant |
| Chauzy, Alain | 21140 Seur-en-Au |
| Doursin, Gerard | Pernes les Fonta |
| Ganster, Jean-Pierre | F-67000 Strasbo |
| Graveline, Pascal and Isabelle | 29350 Moelan-sur- |

| | |
|---|---|
| Headrick, Gary | Juane Les Pins |
| Madrulli, Mme Joelle | Salon De Provence |
| Reverdy, Pierre | |
| Thevenot, Jean-Paul | Dijon |
| Viallon, Henri | |

## GERMANY

| | |
|---|---|
| Balbach, Markus | 35789 Weilmunster-Laubuse Schbach/Ts. |
| Becker, Franz | 84533, Marktl/Inn |
| Boehlke, Guenter | 56412 Grossholbach |
| Borger, Wolf | 76676 Graben-Neudorf |
| Dell, Wolfgang | D-73277 Owen-Teck |
| Faust, Joachim | 95497 Goldkronach |
| Fruhmann, Ludwig | 84489 Burghausen |
| Greiss, Jockl | D 77773 Schenkenzell |
| Hehn, Richard Karl | 55444 Dorrebach |
| Hennicke, Metallgestaltung | 55578 Wallertheim |
| Herbst, Peter | 91207 Lauf a.d. Pegn. |
| Joehnk, Bernd | 24148 Kiel |
| Kressler, D.F. | Odetzhausen |
| Neuhaeusler, Erwin | 86179 Augsburg |
| Rankl, Christian | 81476 Munchen |
| Rinkes, Siegfried | Markterlbach |
| Selzam, Frank | Bad Koenigshofen |
| Steinau, Jurgen | Berlin 0-1162 |
| Tritz, Jean Jose | 20255 Hamburg |
| Wimpff, Christian | 70574 Stuttgart 70 |
| Wirtz, Achim | D -52146 |
| Zirbes, Richard | D-54526 Niederkail |

## GREAT BRITAIN

| | |
|---|---|
| Elliott, Marcus | Llandudno Gwynedd |

## GREECE

| | |
|---|---|
| Filippou, Ioannis-Minas | Athens 17122 |

## HOLLAND

| | |
|---|---|
| Van De Manakker, Thijs | 5759 px Helenaveen |

## ISRAEL

| | |
|---|---|
| Shadmot, Boaz | Arava |

## ITALY

| | |
|---|---|
| lbericci, Emilio | 24100, Bergamo |
| meri, Mauro | 16010 Genova |
| allestra, Santino | 18039 Ventimiglia (IM) |
| ertuzzi, Ettore | 24068 Seriate (Bergamo) |
| onassi, Franco | Pordenone 33170 |
| ogarizzu, Boiteddu | 07016 Pattada |
| iagu, Salvatore and Deroma Maria Rosaria | 07016 Pattada (SS) |
| achi, Francesco | 17046 Sassello (SV) |
| uddu, Salvatore | Quartu s Elena (CA) |
| iboni, Claudio | Truccazzano (MI) |
| cordia, Paolo | Roma |
| imonella, Gianluigi | 33085 Maniago |
| oich, Nevio | Vincenza |
| schager, Reinhard | I-39100 Bolzano |

## JAPAN

| | |
|---|---|
| da, Yoshihito | Itabashi-ku, Tokyo 175-0094 |
| oisu, Hidesaku | Hiroshima City |
| ujikawa, Shun | Osaka 597 0062 |
| ukuta, Tak | Seki-City, Gifu-Pref |
| ara, Kouji | Gifu-Prof. 501-32 |
| rayama, Harumi | Saitama Pref. 335-0001 |
| roto, Fujihara | Hiroshima |
| ao, Ohbuchi | Fukuoka |
| Ishihara, Hank | Chiba Pref. |
| Kagawa, Koichi | Kanagawa |
| Kanda, Michio | Yamaguchi 7460033 |
| Kanki, Iwao | Hydugo |
| Kansei, Matsuno | Gitu-City |
| Kato, Kiyoshi | Tokyo 152 |
| Kato, Shinichi | Moriyama-ku Nagoya |
| Katsumaro, Shishido | Hiroshima |
| Kawasaki, Akihisa | Kobe |
| Keisuke, Gotoh | Ohita |
| Koyama, Captain Bunshichi | Nagoya City 453-0817 |
| Mae, Takao | Toyonaka, Osaka |
| Makoto, Kunitomo | Hiroshima |
| Matsusaki, Takeshi | Nagasaki |
| Michinaka, Toshiaki | Tottori 680-0947 |
| Micho, Kanda | Yamaguchi |
| Ryuichi, Kuki | Saitama |
| Sakakibara, Masaki | Tokyo 156-0054 |
| Shikayama, Toshiaki | Saitama 342-0057 |
| Sugihara, Keidoh | Osaka, F596-0042 |
| Sugiyama, Eddy K. | Ohita |
| Takahashi, Kaoru | Kamoto Kumamoto |
| Takahashi, Masao | Gunma 371 0047 |
| Terauchi, Toshiyuki | Fujita-Cho Gobo-Shi |
| Toshifumi, Kuramoto | Fukuoka |
| Uchida, Chimata | Kumamoto |
| Uekama, Nobuyuki | Tokyo |
| Wada, Yasutaka | Nara Prefect 631-0044 |
| Waters, Glenn | Hirosaki City 036-8183 |
| Yoshihara, Yoshindo | Tokyo |
| Yoshikazu, Kamada | Tokushima |
| Yoshio, Maeda | Okayama |

## MEXICO

| | |
|---|---|
| Scheurer, Alfredo E. Faes | C.P. 16010 |
| Sunderland, Richard | Puerto Escondido Oaxaca |
| Young, Cliff | San Miguel De Allende, GTO. |

## NETHERLANDS

| | |
|---|---|
| Van Den Elsen, Gert | 5012 AJ Tilburg |
| Van Eldik, Frans | 3632BT Loenen |
| Van Rijswijk, Aad | 3132 AA Vlaardingen |

## NEW ZEALAND

| | |
|---|---|
| Gerner, Thomas | Oxford |
| Pennington, C.A. | Kainga Christchurch 8009 |
| Reddiex, Bill | Palmerston North |
| Ross, D.L. | Dunedin |
| Sandow, Norman E | Howick, Auckland |
| Sands, Scott | Christchurch 9 |
| Van Dijk, Richard | Harwood Dunedin |

## NORWAY

| | |
|---|---|
| Bache-Wiig, Tom | Eivindvik |
| Momcilovic, Gunnar | Waipahu |
| Sellevold, Harald | N5835 Bergen |
| Vistnes, Tor | |

## RUSSIA

| | |
|---|---|
| Kharlamov, Yuri | 300007 |

## SAUDI ARABIA

| | |
|---|---|
| Kadasah, Ahmed Bin | Jeddah 21441 |

## SINGAPORE

| | |
|---|---|
| Tay, Larry C-G. | Singapore 9145 |

## SLOVAKIA

| | |
|---|---|
| Bojtos, Arpa D. | 98403 Lucenec |
| Kovacik, Robert | Tomasovce |
| Laoislav, Santa-Lasky | Bystrica |
| Mojzis, Julius | |
| Pulis, Vladimir | 96 701 Kremnica |
| Steffan, Albert | Filakovo 98604 |

## SOUTH AFRICA

| | |
|---|---|
| Arm-Ko Knives, | |
| Baartman, George | Limpopo |
| Bauchop, Robert | Kwazulu-Natal 4278 |
| Beukes, Tinus | Vereeniging 1939 |
| Bezuidenhout, Buzz | Malvern, Queensburgh, Natal 4093 |
| Boardman, Guy | New Germany 3619 |
| Brown, Rob E. | Port Elizabeth |
| Burger, Fred | Kwa-Zulu Natal |
| De Villiers, Andre and Kirsten | Cascades 3202 |
| Dickerson, Gavin | Petit 1512 |
| Fellows, Mike | Velddrie 7365 |
| Grey, Piet | Naboomspruit 0560 |
| Harvey, Heather | Belfast 1100 |
| Harvey, Kevin | Belfast 1100 |
| Horn, Des | 7700 Cape Town |
| Kojetin, W. | Germiston 1401 |
| Lagrange, Fanie | Table View 7441 |
| Lancaster, C.G. | Free State |
| Liebenberg, Andre | Bordeauxrandburg 2196 |
| Mackrill, Stephen | Johannesburg |
| Mahomedy, A. R. | Marble Ray KZN, 4035 |
| Nelson, Tom | Gauteng |
| Pienaar, Conrad | Bloemfontein 9300 |
| Prinsloo, Theuns | Bethlehem 9700 |
| Rietveld, Bertie | Magaliesburg 1791 |
| Russell, Mick | Port Elizabeth 6070 |
| Schoeman, Corrie | Danhof 9310 |
| Watson, Peter | La Hoff 2570 |

## SWEDEN

| | |
|---|---|
| Bergh, Roger | 91598 Bygdea |
| Billgren, Per | |
| Eklund, Maihkel | S-820 41 Farila |
| Embretsen, Kaj | S-82821 Edsbyn |
| Hogstrom, Anders T. | |
| Johansson, Anders | S-772 40 Grangesberg |
| Lundstrom, Jan-Ake | 66010 Dals-Langed |
| Nilsson, Johnny Walker | |
| Nordell, Ingemar | 82041 Färila |
| Persson, Conny | 820 50 Loos |
| Ryberg, Gote | S-562 00 Norrahammar |
| Styrefors, Mattias | |
| Vogt, Patrik | S-30270 Halmstad |

## SWITZERLAND

| | |
|---|---|
| Gagstaetter, Peter | 9306 Freidorf Tg |
| Roulin, Charles | 1233 Geneva |
| Soppera, Arthur | CH-9631 Ulisbach |

## UNITED KINGDOM

| | |
|---|---|
| Heasman, H.G. | Llandudno |
| Horne, Grace | Sheffield Britian |
| Maxen, Mick | "Hatfield, Herts" |

## URUGUAY

| | |
|---|---|
| Gonzalez, Leonardo Williams | CP 20000 |
| Symonds, Alberto E. | Montevideo 11300 |

## ZIMBABWE

| | |
|---|---|
| Burger, Pon | Bulawayo |

Not all knifemakers are organization-types, but those listed here are in good standing with these organizations.

# the knifemakers' guild

## 2005 voting membership

**a** Les Adams, Yoshihito Aida, Mike "Whiskers" Allen, Tom Anderson, W. E. Ankrom, Boyd Ashworth, Dick Atkinson

**b** Santino Ballestra, Norman Bardsley, Van Barnett, A.T. Barr, James J. III Barry, John Bartlow, Gene Baskett, Gaetan Beauchamp, Norman L. Beckett, Raymond Beers, Donald Bell, Tom Black, Andrew Blackton, Gary Blanchard, Arpad Bojtos, Philip Booth, Tony Bose, Dennis Bradley, Edward Brandsey, W. Lowell Jr. Bray, Clint Breshears, Tim Britton, David Brown, Harold Brown, Rick Browne, Fred Jr. Bruner, Jimmie Buckner, R.D. "Dan" Burke, Patrick Burris, John Busfield

**c** Bill Caldwell, Errett Callahan, Ron Cameron, Daniel Cannady, Ron Canter, Robert Capdepon, Harold J. "Kit" Carson, Fred Carter, Dianna Casteel, Douglas Casteel, Frank Centofante, Jeffrey Chaffee, Joel Chamblin, William Chapo, Alex Chase, Edward Chavar, William Cheatham, Howard F. Clark, Wayne Clay, Vernon Coleman, Blackie Collins, Bob Conley, Gerald Corbit, Harold Corby, George Cousino, Colin Cox, Pat & Wes Crawford, Dan Cruze, Roy D. Cutchin

**d** George E. Dailey, Charles M. Dake, Alex Daniels, Jack Davenport, Edmund Davidson, Barry Davis, Terry A. Davis, Vernon M. Davis, W. C. Davis, Ralph Jr. D'Elia, Harvey Dean, Dellana, Dan Dennehy, Herbert Derr, Howard Dietz, William Dietzel, Robert Dill, Frank Dilluvio, Al Dippold, David Dodds, Bob Doggett, Tracy Dotson, T. M. Dowell, Larry Downing, Tom Downing, James Downs, Bill Duff, Steve Dunn, Jerry Duran, Fred Durio

**e** Russell & Paula Easler, Rick Eaton, Allen Elishewitz, Jim Elliott, David Ellis, William B. Ellis, Kaj Embretsen, Jim Ence, Virgil England, William Engle, James T. Eriksen

**f** Howard Faucheaux, Stephen Fecas, Lee Ferguson, Bill Fiorini, Jay Fisher, Jerry Fisk, Joe Flournoy, Derek Fraley, Michael H. Franklin, John R. Fraps, Ron Frazier, Aaron Frederick, Ralph Freer, Dennis Friedly, Larry Fuegen, Shun Fujikawa, Stanley Fujisaka, Tak Fukuta, Bruce Fuller, Shiro Furukawa

**g** Frank Gamble, Roger Gamble, William O. Jr. Garner, Ron Gaston, Clay Gault, James "Hoot" Sr. Gibson, Warren Glover, Stefan Gobec, Bruce Goers, David Goldberg, Warren Goltz, Greg Gottschalk, Roger M. Green, Jockl Greiss, Carol Gurganus, Melvin Gurganus, Kenneth Guth

**h** Philip L. Hagen, Geoffrey Hague, Jeff Hall, Ed Halligan & Son, Tomonori Hamada, Jim Hammond, Koji Hara, J.A. Harkins, Larry Harley, Ralph D. Harris, Rade Hawkins, Richard Hehn, Henry Heitler, Glenn Hemperley, Earl Jay Hendrickson, Wayne Hendrix, Wayne G. Hensley, Peter Herbst, Tim Herman, George Herron, Don Hethcoat, Gil Hibben, Steve E. Hill, R. Hinson & Son, Harumi Hirayama, Howard Hitchmough, Steve Hoel, Kevin Hoffman, D'Alton Holder, J. L. Hollett, Jerry Hossom, Durvyn Howard, Daryle Hughes, Roy Humenick, Joel Humphreys, Joseph Hytovick

**i** Billy Mace Imel, Michael Irie

**j** Jim Jacks, Paul Jarvis, John Jensen, Steve Jernigan, Brad Johnson, Ronald Johnson, Ruffin Johnson, Steven R. Johnson, Wm.C. "Bill" Johnson, Enoch D. Jones, Robert Jones

**k** Edward N. Kalfayan, William Keeton, Bill Keller, Bill Jr. Kennedy, Jot Singh Khalsa, Bill King, Joe Kious, Terry Knipschield, Roy W. Krause, D. F. Kressler, John Kubasek

**l** Kermit Laurent, Bob Lay, Mike Leach, Matthew J. Lerch, William Letcher, Bill Levengood, Yakov Levin, Bob Levine, Tom Lewis, Steve Linklater, Wolfgang Loerchner, Juan A. Lonewolf, R.W. Loveless, Schuyler Lovestrand, Don Lozier, Robert W. Lum, Larry Lunn, Ernest Lyle

**m** Stephen Mackrill, Joe Malloy, Dan Maragni, Peter Martin, Randall J. Martin, Kansei Matsuno, Jerry McClure, Charles McConnell, Loyd McConnell, Richard McDonald, Robert J. McDonald, W.J. McDonald, Ken McFall, Frank McGowan, Thomas McGuane, McHenry & Williams, Tommy McNabb, Kurt Meerdink, Mike Mercer, Ted Merchant, Robert L. III Merz, Toshiaki Michinaka, James P. Miller, Steve Miller, Louis Mills, Dan Mink, Jim Minnick, Gunnar Momcilovic, Sidney "Pete" Moon, James B. Moore, Jeff Morgan, C.H. Morris, Dusty Moulton

**n** Bud Nealy, Corbin Newcomb, Larry Newton, Ron Newton, R.D. & Steve Nolen, Ingemar Nordell, Ross Norfleet, Rick Nowland

**o** Charles F. Ochs, Ben R. Jr. Ogletree, Warren Osborne, T.R. Overeynder, John Owens

**p** Francesco Pachi, Larry Page, Robert Papp, Joseph Pardue, Melvin Pardue, Cliff Parker, W. D. Pease, Alfred Pendray, John L. Perry, Eldon Peterson, Kenneth Pfeiffer, Daniel Piergallini, David Pitt, Leon & Tracy Pittman, Al Polkowski, Joe Prince, Jim Pugh, Morris Pulliam

**r** Jerry Rados, James D. Ragsdale, Steven Rapp, Chris Reeve, John Reynolds, Ron Richard, Dave Ricke, Bertie Rietveld, Willie Rigney, Rex III Robinson, Fred Roe, Richard Rogers, Charles Roulin, Ron Russ, A. G. Russell

**s** Masaki Sakakibara, Mike Sakmar, Hiroyuki Sakurai, John Salley, Scott Sawby, Maurice & Alan Schrock, Steve Schwarzer, Mark C. Sentz, Yoshinori Seto, Eugene W. Shadley, John I. Shore, Bill Simons, R.J. Sims, James E. Sinclair, Cleston Sinyard, Jim Siska, Fred Slee, Scott Slobodian, J.D. Smith, John W. Smith, Michael J. Smith, Ralph Smith, Jerry Snell, Marvin Solomon, Arthur Soppera, Jim Sornberger, Bill Sowell, Ken Steigerwalt, Jurgen Steinau, Daniel Stephan, Murray Sterling, Barry B. Stevens, Johnny Stout, Keidoh Sugihara, Russ Sutton, Charles Syslo, Joseph Szilaski

**t** Grant Tally, Robert Terzuola, Leon Thompson, Brian Tighe, Dan Tompkins, John E. Toner, Bobby L. Toole, Dwight Towell, Leon Treiber, Barry Trindle, Reinhard Tschager, Jim Turecek, Ralph Turnbull, Arthur Tycer

**v** Frans Van Eldik, Edward T. VanHoy, Aad Van Rijswijk, Michael Veit, Ricardo Velarde, Howard Viele, Donald Vogt

**w** George Walker, James Walker, John W. Walker, Charles B. Ward, Tommy Ware, Daniel Warren, Dale Warther, Charles Weeber, John S. Weever, J. Reese Weiland, Robert Weinstock, Charles L. Weiss, Weldon Whitley, Wayne Whittaker, Donnie R. Wicker, R. W. Wilson, Daniel Winkler, Earl Witsaman, William Wolf, Frank Wojtinowski, Owen Wood, Tim Wright

**y** Joe Yeates, Yoshindo Yoshihara, George Young, Mike Yurco

**z** Brad Zinker, Michael Zscherny

## american bladesmith society

**a** Robin E. Ackerson, Lonnie Adams, Kyle A. Addison, Charles L. Adkins, Anthony "Tony" Aiken, Yoichiro Akahori, Douglas A. Alcorn, David Alexander, Mike Alexander, Eugene Alexander, Daniel Allison, Chris Amos, David Anders, Jerome Anders, Gary D. Anderson, Ronnie A. Andress Sr, E. R. (Russ) Andrews II, James M. Arbuckle, Doug Asay, Boyd Ashworth, Ron Austin

**b** David R. Bacon, Robert Keith Bagley, Marion Bagwell, Brent Bailey, Larry Bailey, Bruce Baker, David Baker, Stephen A. Baker, Randall Baltimore, Dwayne Bandy, Mark D. Banfield, David L. Banks, Robert G. Barker, Reggie Barker, Aubrey G. Barnes Sr., Cecil C. Barnes Jr., Gary Barnes, Marlen R. Barnes, Van Barnett Barnett International, Judson C. Barr, Nyla Barrett, Rick L. Barrett, Michael Barton, Hugh E. Bartrug, Paul C. Basch, Nat Bassett, James L. Batson, R. Keith Batts, Michael R. Bauer, Rick Baum, Dale Baxter, Geneo Beasley, Jim Beaty, Robert B. Beaty, Steve Becker, Bill Behnke, Don Bell, John Bendik, Robert O. Benfield Jr., George Benjamin Jr., Brett Bennett, Rae Bennett, Bruce D. Berglin, Brent Beshara, Chris Bethke, Lora Sue Bethke, Gary Biggers, Ira Lee Birdwell, Hal Bish, William M. Bisher, Jason Bivens, Robert Bizzell, Scott Black, Randy Blair, Dennis Blankenheim, Robert Blasingame, R. Gordon Bloomquist, Josh Blount, Otto Bluntzer, David Bolton, David Boone, Roger E. Bost, Raymond A. Boysen, Bailey Bradshaw, Sanford (Sandy) Bragman, Martin W. Brandt, Robert Branton, Brett Bratcher, W. Lowell Bray Jr., Steven Brazeale, Charles D. Breme, Arthur Britton, Peter Bromley, Charles E. Brooks, Christopher Brown, Dennis G. Brown, Mark D. Brown, Rusty Brown, Troy L. Brown, Steven W. Browning, C. Lyle Brunckhorst, Aldo Bruno, Jimmie H. Buckner, Nick Bugliarello-Wondrich, Bruce D. Bump, Larry Bundrick, Bill Burke, Paul A. Burke, Stephen R. Burrows, John Butler, John R. Butler, Wesley L. Byrd

**c** Jerry (Buddy) Cabe, Sergio B. Cabrera, Ed Caffrey, Larry Cain, F. Terry Callahan, Robt W. Calvert Jr., Craig Camerer, Ron Cameron, Courtnay M. Campbell, Dan Cannon, Andrew B. Canoy, Jeff Carlisle, Chris Carlson, Eric R. Carlson, William Carnahan, Ronald W. Carpenter, James V. Carriger, Chad Carroll, George Carter, Murray M. Carter, Shayne Carter, Terry Cash, Kevin R. Cashen, P. Richard Chastain, Milton Choate, Jon Christensen, Howard F. Clark, Jim Clary, Joe Click, Russell Coats, Charles Cole, Frank Coleman, Wade Colter, Larry D. Coltrain, Roger N. Comar, Roger Combs, Wm. E. (Bill) Compton, Larry Connelley, John W. Connor, Michael Connor, Charles W. Cook, III, James R. Cook, Robert Cook, James Roscoe Cooper, Jr., Ted Cooper, Joseph G. Cordova, David P. Corrigan, Dr. Timothy L. Costello, William Courtney, Collin Cousino, Gregory G. Covington, Monty L. Crain, Dawnavan M. Crawford, George Crews, Jim Crowell, Peter J. Crowl, Steve Culver, George Cummings, Kelly C. Cupples, John A. Czekala

**d** George E. Dailey, Mary H. Dake, B. MacGregor Daland, Kelly Dallyn, Sava Damlovac, Alex Daniels, David T. Darby, Chester L. Darcey, David Darpinian, Jim Davidson, Richard T. Davies, Barry Davis, John Davis, Patricia D. Davis, Dudley L. Dawkins, Michael de Gruchy, Angelo De Maria Jr., Harvey J. Dean, Anthony Del Giorno, Josse Delage, Clark B. DeLong, William Derby, Christoph Deringer, Dennis E. Des Jardins, Chuck Diebel, Bill Dietzel, Eric Dincauze, Jason Dingledine, Al Dippold, Matt Diskin, Michael Distin, Luciano Dorneles, Patrick J. Downey, Audra L. Draper, Mike Draper, Joseph D. Drouin, Paul Dubro, Ron Duncan, Calvin Duniphan, Rick Dunkerley, Steve Dunn, Eric Durbin, Kenneth Durham, Fred Durio, David Dyer

**e** Rick Eaton, Roger Echols, Mike Edelman, Thomas Eden, Gregory K. Edmonson, Randel Edmonson, Mitch Edwards, Lynn Edwards, Joe E. Eggleston, Daniel Robert Ehrenberger, Fred Eisen, Perry B. Elder Jr., Allen Elishewitz, R. Van Elkins, Rickie Ellington, Gordon Elliott, Carroll Ellis, Darren Ellis, Dave Ellis, Roger R. Elrod, Kaj Embretsen, Edward Engarto, Al Engelsman, Richard Epting, David Etchieson, Bruce E. Evans, Greg Evans, Ronald B. Evans, Vincent K. Evans, Wyman Ewing

**f** John E. Faltay, George Fant Jr., Daniel Farr, Alexander Felix, Gregory K. Ferrier, Robert Thomas Ferry III, Michael J. Filarski, Steve Filicietti, Ioannis-Minas Filippou, Jack Fincher, John Fincher, Ray Fincher, Perry Fink, Sean W. Finlayson, William Fiorini, Jerry Fisk, James O. Fister, John S. Fitch, Dawn Fitch, Mike Fletcher, Joe Flournoy, Charles Fogarty, Don Fogg, Stanley Fortenberry, Burt Foster, Edward K. Foster, Norvell C. Foster, Ronnie E. Foster, Timothy L. Foster, C. Ronnie Fowler, Ed Fowler, Jerry Fowler, Kevin Fox, Walter P. Framski, John M. Frankl, John R. Fraps, Aaron Frederick, Steve Freund, Steve Frey, Rolf Friberg, Rob Fritchen, Daniel Fronefield, Dewayne Frost, Larry D. Fuegen, Bruce A. Fuller, Jack A. Fuller, Richard Furrer

**g** Barry Gallagher, Jacques Gallant, Jesse Gambee, Tommy Gann, Tommy Gann, Rodney Gappelberg, Jim L. Gardner, Robert J. Gardner, Larry W. Garner, Mike Garner, Timothy P. Garrity, Mark W. Garvock, Bert Gaston, Brett Gatlin, Darrell Geisler, Thomas Gerner, James Gibson, Fabio Giordani, Joel Gist, Kevin Gitlin, Gary Gloden, Wayne Goddard, Jim Gofourth, Scott K. Goguen, David Goldberg, Rodney W. Goodling, Tim Gordon, Thomas L. Gore, Gabe Gorenflo, James T. Gorenflo, Greg Gottschalk, Rayne Gough, Edward Graham, Paul J. Granger, Daniel Gray, Don Greenaway, Jerry Louis Grice, Michael S. Griffin, Larry Groth, Anthony R. Guarnera, Bruce Guidry, Christian Guier, Tom & Gwen Guinn, Garry Gunderson, Johan Gustafsson

**h** Cyrus Haghjoo, Ed Halligan, N. Pete Hamilton, Timothy J. Hancock, Bill Hand, Don L. Hanson III, Douglas E. Hardy, Larry Harley, Sewell C. Harlin, Paul W. Harm, Brent Harper-Murray, Cass Harris, Jeffrey A. Harris, Tedd Harris, Bill Hart, Sammy Harthman, Heather Harvey, Kevin Harvey, Robert Hatcher, Buddy Hawkins, Rade Hawkins, Rodney Hawkins, Wally Hayes, Charlie E. Haynes, Gary Headrick, Kelly Healy, Chad Heddin, Dion Hedges, Win Heger, Daniel Heiner, John Heinz, E. Jay Hendrickson, Bill Herndon, Harold Herron, Don Hethcoat, Jim B. Hill, John M. Hill, Amy Hinchman, Vance W. Hinds, Donald R. Hinton, Dan Hockensmith, Dr. Georg Hoellwarth, William G. Hoffman, Thomas R. Hogan, Troy Holland, Michael Honey, Un Pyo Hong, John F. Hood, John Horrigan, Robert M. Horrigan, Lawrence House, Gary House, Michael Houston, Jason G. Howell, F. Charles Hubbard, Dale Huckabee, Gov. Mike Huckabee, C. Robbin Hudson, Anthony B. Hudson, Bill Hughes, Daryle Hughes, Tony Hughes, Brad Humelsine, Maurice Hunt, Raymon E. Hunt, Richard D. Hunter, K. Scott Hurst, William R. Hurt, David H. Hwang, Joe Hytovick

**i** Gary Iames, Hisayuki Ishida

**j** David Jackson, Jim L. Jackson, Chuck Jahnke, Jr., Karl H. Jakubik, Melvin Jennings Jr., John Lewis Jensen, Mel "Buz" Johns, David A. Johnson, John R. Johnson, Ray Johnson, Thomas Johnson, Clayton W. Johnston, Dr. Robt. Johnston, William Johnston, Chris E. Jones, Enoch Jones, Franklin W. Jones, John Jones, Roger W. Jones, William Burton Jones, Terry J. Jordan, Shane Justice

**k** Charles Kain, Al J. Kajin, Gus Kalanzis, Barry Kane, David Kazsuk, Jarod Kearney, Robert Keeler, Joseph F. Keeslar, Steven C. Keeslar, Jerry Keesling, Dale Kempf, Larry Kempf, R. W. Kern, Joe Kertzman, Lawrence Keyes, Charles M. Kilbourn, Jr., Keith Kilby, Nicholas Kimball, Richard L. Kimberley, Herman King, David R. King, Fred J. King, Harvey G. King Jr., Kenneth King, Frederick D. Kingery, Donald E. Kinkade, Ray Kirk, Todd Kirk, John Kish, Brad Kliensmid, Russell K. Klingbeil, Hank Knickmeyer, Kurt Knickmeyer, Jason Knight, Steven C. Koster, Bob Kramer, Lefty Kreh, Phil Kretsinger

**l** Simon Labonti, Jerry Lairson Sr., Curtis J. Lamb, J. D. Lambert, Robert M. Lamey, Leonard D. Landrum, Warren H. Lange, Paul Lansingh, Rodney Lappe, Kermit J. Laurent, Alton Lawrence, Randell Ledbetter, Denis H. LeFranc, Jim L. Lemcke, Jack H. Leverett Jr., Wayne Levin, Bernard Levine, Steve Lewis, Tom Lewis, John J. Lima, Lindy Lippert, Guy A. Little, Tim Lively, Keith Locke, Lowell C. Lockett, Anthony P. Lombardo, Phillip Long, Jonathan A. Loose, Eugene Loro, Jim Lott, Sherry Lott, Jim Lovelace, Ryan Lovell, Steven Lubecki, Bob Luchini, James R. Lucie, James R. Luman, William R. Lyons

**m** John Mackie, Madame Joelle Madrulli, Takao Mae, Mike Majer, Raymond J. Malaby, John Mallett, Bob Mancuso, Kenneth Mankel, Matt Manley, James Maples, Dan Maragni, Ken Markley, J. Chris Marks, Stephen R. Marshall, Tony Martin, John Alexander Martin, Hal W. Martin, Alan R. Massey, Roger D. Massey, Mick Maxen, Lynn McBee, Daniel McBrearty, Howard H. McCallen Jr., Michael McClure, Sandy McClure, Frederick L. McCoy, Kevin McCrackin, Victor J. McCrackin, Richard McDonald, Robert J. McDonald, Robin J. McDonald, Frank McGowan, Donald McGrath, Patrick T. McGrath, Eric McHugh, Don McIntosh, Neil H. McKee, Tim McKeen, David Brian McKenzie, Hubert W. McLendon, Tommy McNabb, J. Michael McRae, David L. Meacham, Maxie Mehaffey, J. R. Mellard, Walter Merrin, Mardi Meshejian, Ged Messinger, D. Gregg Metheny, Dan Michaelis, Tracy Mickley, Gary Middleton, Bob Miller, Hanford J. Miller, Michael Mills, David Mirabile, Wm. Dean Mitchell, Jim Molinare, Michael Steven Moncus, Charlie Monroe, Keith Montgomery, Lynn Paul Moore, Marve Moore, Michael Robert Moore, Shawn Robert Moore, William F. Moran Jr., Jim Moyer, Russell A. Moyer, James W. Mueller, Jody Muller, Deryk C. Munroe, Jim Mutchler, Ron Myers

**n** Ryuji Nagoaka, Evan Nappen, Maj. Kendall Nash, Angelo Navagato, Bob Neal, Darby Neaves, Gregory T. Neely, Thomas Conor Neely, James Neilson, Bill Nelson, Lars Nelson, Mark Nevling, Corbin Newcomb, Ron Newton, Tania Nezrick, John Nicoll, Marshall Noble, Douglas E. Noren, H.B. Norris, Paul T. Norris, William North, Vic Nowlan

**o** Charles F. Ochs III, Julia O'Day, Clyde O'Dell, Vic Odom, Michael O'Herron, Hiroaki Ohta, Michael E. Olive, Todd D. Oliver, Joe Olson, Kent Olson, Richard O'Neill, Robert J. O'Neill, Rich Orton, Philip D. Osattin, Donald H. Osborne, Warren Osborne, Fred Ott, Mac Overton, Donald Owens

**p** Anthony P. Palermo, Rik Palm, Paul Papich, Ralph Pardington, Cliff Parker, Earl Parker, John Parks, Jimmy D. Passmore, Rob Patton, Jerome Paul, Gary Payton, Michael Peck, Alfred Pendray, Christopher A. Pennington, Johnny Perry, John L. Perry, Conny Persson, Dan L. Petersen, Lloyd Pete C. Peterson, Dan Pfanenstiel, Jim Phillips, Benjamin P. Piccola, Ray Pieper III, Diane Pierce, Dean Piesner, Dietrich Podmajersky, Dietmar Pohl, Clifton Polk, Rusty Polk, Jon R. "Pop" Poplawski, Timothy Potier, Dwight Povistak, James Powell, Robert Clark Powell, Jake Powning, Houston Price, Terry Primos, Jeff Prough, Gerald Puckett, Martin Pullen

**q** Thomas C. Quakenbush

**r** Michael Rader, John R. Radford Jr., R. Wayne Raley, Darrel Ralph, Richard A. Ramsey, Gary Randall, James W. Randall Jr., David L. Randolph, Ralph Randow, Mike Reagan, George R. Rebello, Lee Reeves, Roland R. "Rollie" Remmel, Zaza Revishvili, Kirk Rexroat, Scott Reyburn, John Reynolds, Linden W. Rhea, Jim Rice, Stephen E. Rice, Alvin C. Richards Jr., James Richardson, David M. Rider, Richard A. Riepe, Dennis Riley, E. Ray Roberts, Jim Roberts, Don Robertson, Leo D. Robertson, Charles R. Robinson, Michael Rochford, James L. Rodebaugh, James R. Rodebaugh, Gary Rodewald, Charles W. Rogers, Richard Rogers, Willis "Joe" Romero, Frederick Rommel, Troy Ronning, N. Jack Ronzio, Steven Roos, Doun T. Rose, Robert Rosenfeld, Robert N. Rossdeutscher, George R. Roth, Charles Roulin, Kenny Rowe, Clark D. Rozas, Ronald S. Russ, Michael G. Ruth, Michael G. Ruth Jr., Brad Rutherford, Tim Ryan, Wm. Mike Ryan, Raymond B. Rybar Jr., Gerald Rzewnicki

**s** David Sacks, William Sahli, Ken Sands, Paul Sarganis, Charles R. Sauer, James P. Saviano, Ed Schempp, Ellen Schilling, Tim Scholl, Robert Schrader, Stephen C. Schwarzer, James A. Scroggs, Bert Seale, Turner C. Seale, Jr., David D. Seaton, Steve Seib, Mark C. Sentz, Jimmy Seymour, Rodrigo Menezes Sfreddo, Steve Shackleford, Gary Shaw, James F. Shull, Robert Shyan-Norwalt, Ken Simmons, Brad Singley, Cleston S. Sinyard, Charles Russel Sisemore, Charles J. Smale, Charles Moran Smale, Carel Smith, Clifford Lee Smith, Corey Smith, J.D. Smith, Joshua J. Smith, Lenard C. Smith, Raymond L. Smith, Timothy E. Smock, Michael Tom Snyder, Max Soaper, John E. Soares, Arthur Soppera, Bill Sowell, Randy Spanjer Sr., David R. Sparling, H. Red St. Cyr, Chuck Stancer, Craig Steketee, Daniel Stephan, Tim Stevens, Edward L. Stewart, Rhett & Janie Stidham, Jason M. Stimps, Walter Stockwell, J.B. Stoner, Bob Stormer, Mike Stott, Charles Stout, John K. Stout Jr., Johnny L. Stout, Howard Stover, John Strohecker, Robert E. Stumphy Jr., Harlan Suedmeier, Wayne Suhrbier, Alan L. Sullivan, Fred Suran, Tony Swatton, John Switzer, John D. Switzer, Arthur Swyhart, Mark G. Szarek, Joseph Szilaski

**t** Scott Taylor, Shane Taylor, Danny O. Thayer, Jean-Paul Thevenot, Brian Thie, David E. Thomas, Devin Thomas, Guy Thomas, Scott Thomas, Hubert Thomason, Robert Thomason, Kinzea L. Thompson, Alan L. Tiensvold, Jason Tiensvold, John Tilton, George Tindera, Dennis Tingle, Dennis P. Tingle, Brion Tomberlin, P. J. Tomes, Kathleen C. Tomey, Mark Torvinen, Lincoln Tracy, Joe E. Travieso III, James J. Treacy, Craig Triplett, Kenneth W. Trisler, James Turpin, Ross Tyser

**v** Michael V. Vagnino, Jr,, Butch Vallotton, Steve Van Cleve, Jerry W. Van Eizenga, Terry L. Vandeventer, Robert Vardaman, Chris Vidito, Michael Viehman, Gustavo

Colodetti Vilal, Ricardo Vilar, Mace Vitale, Patrik Vogt, Bruce Voyles

**W** Steve "Doc" Wacholz, Lawrence M. Wadler, Adam Waldon, Bill Walker, Don Walker, James L. Walker, Carl D. Ward, Jr., Ken Warner, Robert Lee Washburn Jr., Herman Harold Waters, Lu Waters, Robert Weber, Charles G. Weeber, Fred Weisenborn, Ronald Welling, Eddie Wells, Gary Wendell, Elsie Westlake, Jim Weyer, Nick Wheeler, Wesley Whipple, John Paul White, Lou White, Richard T. White, L. Wayne Whitley, Randy Whittaker, Timothy L. Wiggins, William Burton Wiggins, Jr., Scott Wiley, Dave Wilkes, Craig Wilkins, A. L. Williams, Charles E. Williams, Linda Williams, Michael L. Williams, Edward Wilson, George H. Wilson III, Jeff Wilson, Daniel Winkler, Randy Winsor, George Winter, Ronald E. Woodruff, Steve Woods, Bill Worthen, Terry Wright, Derrick Wulf

**Z** Mark D. Zalesky, Kenneth Zarifes, Matthew Zboray, Terry Zboril, Karl Zimmerman

## miniature knifemaker's society

Paul Abernathy, Joel Axenroth, Blade Magazine, Dennis Blaine, Gerald Bodner, Gary Bradburn, Brock Custom Knives, Ivan Campos, Mitzi Cater, Don Cowles, Creations Yvon Vachon, Dennis Cutburth, David Davis, Robert Davis, Gary Denms, Dennis Des Jardins, Eisenberg Jay Publishers, Allen Eldridge, Peter Flores, David Fusco, Eric Gillard, Wayne Goddard, Larah Gray, Gary Greyraven, Tom & Gwen Guinn, Karl Hallberg, Ralph Harris, Richard Heise, Laura Hessler, Wayne Hensley, Tom Hetmanski, Howard Hosick, Albert Izuka, Garry Kelley, Knife World Publishers, R. F. Koebbeman, Terry Kranning, Gary Lack, John LeBlanc, Mike Lee, Les Levinson, Jack Lewis, Mike Ley, Ken Liegey, Henry Loos, Jim Martin, Howard Maxwell, McMullen & Yee Publishing, Ken McFall, Mal Mele, Paul Meyers, Toshiaki Michinaka, Allen G. Miller, Wayne & June Morrison, Mullinnix & Co, National Knife Collectors Assoc., Allen Olsen, Charles Ostendorf, Mike Pazos, Jim Pear, Gordon Pivonka, Jim Pivonka, Prof. Knifemakers Assoc, Jim Pugh, Roy Quincy, John Rakusan, A. D. Rardon, Dawin Richards, Stephen Ricketts, Mark Rogers, Alex Rose, Hank Rummell, Helen Rummell, Sheffield Knifemakers Supply, Sporting Blades, Harry Stalter, Udo Stegemann, Mike Tamboli, Hank Rummell, Paul Wardian, Ken Warner, Michael Wattelet, Ken Wichard Jr. Charles Weiss, Jim Whitehead, Steve Witham, Shirley Whitt, G. T. Williams, Ron Wilson, Dennis Windmiller, Carol Winold, Earl Witsaman, James Woods

## professional knifemaker's association

Mike "Whiskers" Allen, John Anthon, Ray Archer, Eddie Baca, Cecil Barret, John Bartlow, Paul Basch, Brett Bennett, Nico Bernard, Phillip Booth, Kenneth Brock, Craig Camerer, Tim Cameron, Rod Carter, Jeff Chaffee, Roger Craig, Bob Cumming, Dave Darpinian, Michael Donato, Mike Draper, Audra Draper, Ray Ennis, Jim Eriksen, Jack Feder, John Fraps, Bob Glassman, Sal Glesser, John Greco, Jim Griksen, John Harbuck, Marge Hartman, Mike Henry, Gary Hicks, Guy Hielscher, Howard Hitchmough, Terrill Hoffman, Robert Hunter, Mike Irie, Donald Jones, Jot Singh Khalsa, Harvey King, Jason King, Steve Kraft, Jim Largent, Jim Lemcke (Texas Knifemakers Supply), WSSI (Mike Ludeman), Jim Magee, Daniel May, Jerry McClure, Mac McLaughlin, Larry McLaughlin, Clayton Miller, Mark Molnar, Ty Montell, Mike Mooney, NC Tool Company, Bill Noehren, Steve Nolen, Rick Nowland, Fred Ott, Dick Patton, Rob Patton, PKA, Pop Knives, Dennis Riley, Rocky Mountain Blade Collectors, Steve Rollert, Clint Sampson, Charles Sauer, Jerry Schroeder, Craig Steketee, Joe Stetter, Big Mike Taylor, Bob Terzuola, Loyd Thomsen, James Thrash, Ed Thuesen, Chuck Trice, Louis Vallet, Louis Vinquist, Bill Waldrup, Tommy Ware, David Wattenberg, Joe Wheeler, Dan Wittman, Owen Wood, Mike Zima, Daniel Zvonek

## state/regional associations

### alaska knifemakers association

A.W. Amoureux, John Arnold, Bud Aufdermauer, Robert Ball, J.D. Biggs, Lonnie Breuer, Tom Broome, Mark Bucholz, Irvin Campbell, Virgil Campbell, Raymond Cannon, Christopher Cawthorne, John Chamberlin, Bill Chatwood, George Cubic, Bob Cunningham, Gordon S. Dempsey, J.L. Devoll, James Dick, Art Dufour, Alan Eaker, Norm Grant, Gordon Grebe, Dave Highers, Alex Hunt, Dwight Jenkins, Hank Kubaiko, Bill Lance, Bob Levine, Michael Miller, John Palowski, Gordon Parrish, Mark W. Phillips, Frank Pratt, Guy Recknagle, Ron Robertson, Steve Robertson, Red Rowell, Dave Smith, Roger E. Smith, Gary R. Stafford, Keith Stegall, Wilbur Stegner, Norm Story, Robert D. Shaw, Thomas Trujillo, Ulys Whalen, Jim Whitman, Bob Willis

### arizona knifemakers association

D. "Butch" Beaver, Bill Cheatham, Dan Dagget, Tom Edwards, Anthony Goddard, Steve Hoel, Ken McFall, Milford Oliver, Jerry Poletis, Merle Poteet, Mike Quinn, Elmer Sams, Jim Sornberger, Glen Stockton, Bruce Thompson, Sandy Tudor, Charles Weiss

### arkansas knifemakers association

David Anders, Auston Baggs, Don Bailey, Reggie Barker, Marlen R. Barnes, Paul Charles Basch, Lora Sue Bethke, James Black, R.P. Black, Joel Bradford, Gary Braswell, Paul Brown, Shawn Brown, Troy L. Brown, Jim Butler, Buddy Cabe, Allen Conner, James Cook, Thom Copeland, Gary L. Crowder, Jim Crowell, David T. Darby, Fred Duvall, Rodger Echols, David Etchieson, Lee Ferguson, Jerry Fisk, John Fitch, Joe & Gwen Flournoy, Dewayne Forrester, John Fortenbury, Ronnie Foster, Tim Foster, Emmet Gadberry, Larry Garner, Ed Gentis, Paul

Giller, James T. Gilmore, Terry Glassco, D.R. (Rick) Gregg, Lynn Griffith, Arthur J. Gunn, Jr., David Gunnell, Morris Herring, Don "Possum" Hicks, Jim Howington, B. R. Hughes, Ray Kirk, Douglas Knight, Lile Handmade Knives, Jerry Lairson Sr., Claude Lambert, Alton Lawrence, Jim Lemcke, Michael H. Lewis, Willard Long, Dr. Jim Lucie, Hal W. Martin, Tony Martin, Roger D. Massey, Douglas Mays, Howard McCallen Jr., Jerry McClure, John McKeehan, Joe McVay, Bart Messina, Thomas V. Militano, Jim Moore, Jody Muller, Greg Neely, Ron Newton, Douglas Noren, Keith Page, Jimmy Passmore, John Perry, Lloyd "Pete" Peterson, Cliff Polk, Terry Primos, Paul E. Pyle Jr., Ted Quandt, Vernon Red, Tim Richardson, Dennis Riley, Terry Roberts, Charles R. Robinson, Kenny Rowe, Ken Sharp, Terry Shurtleff, Roy Slaughter, Joe D. Smith, Marvin Solomon, Hoy Spear, Charles Stout, Arthur Tycer, Ross Tyser, James Walker, Chuck Ward, Herman Waters, Bryce White, Tillmon T. Whitley III, Mike Williams, Rick Wilson, Terry Wright, Ray Young

**australian knifemakers guild inc.**

Peter Bald, Wayne Barrett, Peter Bennett, Wayne Bennett, Wally Bidgood, David Brodziak, Neil Charity, Terry Cox, Bruce Crawley, Mark Crowley, Steve Dawson, Malcolm Day, Peter Del Raso, John Dennis, Michael Fechner, Steve Filicietti, Barry Gardner, Thomas Gerner, Branko Giljevic, Eric Gillard, Peter Gordon, Stephen Gregory-Jones, Ben Hall, Mal Hannan, Lloyd Harding, Rod Harris, Glen Henke, Michael Hunt, Robert Hunt, Myron Husiak, John Jones, Simeon Jurkijevic, Wolf Kahrau, Peter Kandavnieks, Peter Kenny, Tasman Kerley, John Kilby, Murrary Lanthois, Anthony Leroy, Greg Lyell, Paul Maffi, Maurice McCarthy, Shawn McIntyre, Ray Mende, Dave Myhill, Adam Parker, John Pattison, Mike Petersen, Murray Shanaughan, Kurt Simmonds, Jim Steele, Rod Stines, David Strickland, Kelvin Thomas, Doug Timbs, Hardy Wangemann, Brendon Ware, Glen Waters, Bob Wilhelm, Joe Zemitis

**california knifemakers association**

Arnie Abegg, George J. Antinarelli, Elmer Art, Gregory Barnes, Mary Michael Barnes, Hunter Baskins, Gary Biggers, Roger Bost, Clint Breshears, Buzz Brooks, Steven E. Bunyea, Peter Carey, Joe Caswell, Frank Clay, Richard Clow, T.C. Collins, Richard Corbaley, Stephanie Engnath, Alex Felix, Jim Ferguson, Dave Flowers, Logwood Gion, Peter Gion, Joseph Girtner, Tony Gonzales, Russ Green, Tony Guarnera, Bruce Guidry, Dolores Hayes, Bill Herndon, Neal A. Hodges, Richard Hull, Jim Jacks, Lawrence Johnson, David Kazsuk, James P. Kelley, Richard D. Keyes, Michael P. Klein, Steven Koster, John Kray, Bud Lang, Tomas N. Lewis, R.W. Loveless, John Mackie, Thomas Markey, James K. Mattis, Toni S. Mattis, Patrick T. McGrath, Larry McLean, Jim Merritt, Greg Miller, Walt Modest, Russ Moody, Emil Morgan, Gerald Morgan, Mike Murphy, Thomas Orth, Tom Paar, Daniel Pearlman, Mel Peters, Barry Evan Posner, John Radovich, James L. Rodebaugh, Clark D. Rozas, Ron Ruppe, Brian Saffran, Red St. Cyr, James Stankovich, Bill Stroman, Tony Swatton, Gary Tamms, James P. Tarozon, Scott Taylor, Tru-Grit Inc., Tommy Voss, Jessie C. Ward, Wayne Watanabe, Charles Weiss, Steven A. Williams, Harlan M. Willson, Steve Wolf, Barry B. Wood

**canadian knifemakers guild**

Gaetan Beauchamp, Shawn Belanger, Don Bell, Brent Beshara, Dave Bolton, Conrad Bondu, Darren Chard, Garry Churchill, Guillaume J. Cote, Christoph Deringer, Jeff Diotte, Randy Doucette, Jim Downie, John Dorrell, Eric Elson, Lloyd Fairbairn, Paul-Aime Fortier, Rick Frigault, John Freeman, Mark Garvock, Brian Gilbert, Murray Haday, Tom Hart, Thomas Haslinger, Ian Hubel, Paul Johnston (London, Ont.), Paul Johnston (Smith Falls, Ont.), Jason Kilcup, Kirby Lambert, Greg Lightfoot, Jodi Link, Wolfgang Loerchner, Mel Long, Brian Lyttle, David Macdonald, Michael Mason, Alan Massey, Leigh Maulson, James McGowan, Edward McRae, Mike Mossington, Sean O'Hare, Rod Olson, Neil Ostroff, Ron Post, George Roberts, Brian Russell, Murray St. Armour, Michael Sheppard, Corey Smith, David Smith, Jerry Smith, Walt Stockdale, Matt Stocker, Ed Storch, Steve Stuart, George Tichbourne, Brian Tighe, Robert Tremblay, Glenn Treml, Steve Vanderkloff, James Wade, Bud Weston, Peter Wile

**florida knifemaker's association**

Dick Atkinson, Albert F. "Barney" Barnett, James J. Barry III, Howard Bishop, Andy Blackton, Stephen A. Bloom, Dean Bosworth, John Boyce, W. Lowell Bray Jr., Harold Brown, Douglas Buck, Dave Burns, Patrick Burris, Norman J. Caesar, Peter Channell, Mark Clark, Lowell Cobb, David Cole, Mark Condron, William (Bill) Corker, Ralph L. D'Elia, Jack Davenport, Kevin Davey, J.D. Davis, Kenny Davis, Bill Dietzel, Bob Doggett, William B. Douglas, John B. Durham, Jim Elliot, Tom M. Enos, Bob Ferring, Todd Fischer, Mike Fisher, Ricky Fowler, Mark Frank, Roger Gamble, Tony Garcia, John Gawrowski, James "Hoot" Gibson, Pedro Gonzalez, Ernie Grospitch, Pete Hamilton, Dewey Harris, Henry Heitler, David Helton, Phillip Holstein, John Hodge, Kevin Hoffman, Edward O. Holloway, Joel Humphreys, Joe Hytovick, Tom Johanning, Raymond C. Johnson II, Paul S. Kent, Bill King, F.D. Kingery, Russ Klingbeil, John E. Klingensmith, William S. Letcher, Bill Levengood, Tim Logan, Glenn A. Long, Gail Lunn, Larry Lunn, Ernie Lyle, Bob Mancuso, Randy Mason, R.J. McDonald, Faustina Mead, Maxie Mehaffey, Dennis G. Meredith, Steve Miller, Dan Mink, Steven Morefield, Martin L. "Les" Murphy, Toby Nipper, Cliff Parker, L.D. (Larry) Patterson, James Perry, Dan Piergallini, Martin Prudente, Carlo Raineri, Ron Russ, Rusty Sauls, Dennis J. Savage, David Semones, Ann Sheffield, Brad Shepherd, Bill Simons, Stephen J. Smith, Kent Swicegood, Louis M. Vallet, Donald Vogt, Roger L. Wallace, Tom Watson, Andrew M. Wilson, Stan Wilson, Hugh E. Wright III, Brad Zinker

**knifemakers' guild of southern africa**

Jeff Angelo, George Baartman, Francois Basson, Rob Bauchop, George Beechey, Arno Bernard, Buzz Bezuidenhout, Chris Booysen, Ian Bottomley, Peet Bronkhorst, Rob Brown, Fred Burger, Sharon Burger, William Burger, Larry Connelly, Z. Andre de Beer, Andre de Villiers, Melodie de Witt, Gavin Dickerson, Roy H. Dunseith, Leigh Fogarty, Andrew Frankland, Ettore Gianferrari, Stan Gordon, Nick Grabe, John Grey, Piet Grey, Heather Harvey, Kevin Harvey, Dries Hattingh, Gawie Herbst, Thinus Herbst, Greg Hesslewood, Des Horn, Billy Kojetin, Mark Kretschmer, Fanie La Grange, Steven Lewis, Garry Lombard, Steve Lombard, Ken Madden, Edward Mitchell, Gunther Muller, Tom Nelson, Jan Olivier, Christo Ooosthuizen, Cedric Pannell, Willie Paulsen, Nico Pelzer, Conrad Pienaar, David Pienaar, Jan Potgieter, Lourens Prinsloo, Theuns Prinsloo, Hilton Purvis, Derek Rausch, Chris Reeve, Bertie Rietveld, Dean Riley, John Robertson, Corrie Schoeman, Eddie Scott, Mike Skellern, Toi Skellern, Carel Smith, Ken Smythe, Graham Sparks, Andre E. Thorburn, Fanie Van Der Linde, Johan van der Merwe, Van van der Merwe, Marius Van der Vyver, Louis Van der Walt, Cor Van Ellinkhuijzen,

Danie Van Wyk, Ben Venter, Willie Venter, Gert Vermaak, Rene Vermeulen, Erich Vosloo, Desmond Waldeck, John Wilmot, Wollie Wolfaardt, Owen Wood

### midwest knifemakers association

E.R. Andrews III, Frank Berlin, Charles Bolton, Tony Cates, Mike Chesterman, Ron Duncan, Larry Duvall, Bobby Eades, Jackie Emanuel, James Haynes, John Jones, Mickey Koval, Ron Lichlyter, George Martoncik, Gene Millard, William Miller, Corbin Newcomb, Chris Owen, A.D. Rardon, Archie Rardon, Max Smith, Ed Stewart, Charles Syslo, Melvin Williams

### montana knifemaker's association

Bill Amoureux, Wendell Barnes, James Barth, Bob Beaty, Brett C. Bennett, Arno & Zine Bernard, Robert Bizzell, Peter Bromley, Bruce Bump, Ed Caffrey, C. Camper, John Christensen, Roger Clark, Jack Cory, Bob Crowder, Roger Dole, Rick Dunkerley, Mel Fassio, Tom Ferry, Gary Flohr, Vern Ford, Barry Gallagher, Doc Hagen, Ted Harris, Thomas Haslinger, Sam & Joy Henson, Gerald Hintz, Tori Howe, Al Inman, Dan Kendrick, Doug Klaudt, Mel Long, James Luman, Mike Mann, Jody Martin, Neil McKee, Larry McLaughlin, Mac & Nancy McLaughlin, Gerald Morgan, Ed Mortenson, Deryk Munroe, Dan Nedved, Joe Olson, Daniel O'Malley, Patton Knives, Eldon Peterson, Jim Raymond, Lori Ristinen, James Rodebaugh, Gary Rodewald, Gordon St. Clair, Andy Sarcinella, Charles Sauer, Dean Schroeder, Art Swyhart, Shane Taylor, Jim Thill, Frank Towsley, Bill Waldrup, Michael Wattelet, Darlene & Gerome Weinand, Daniel Westlind, Nick Wheeler, Michael Young, Fred Zaloudek

### new england bladesmiths guild

Phillip Baldwin, Gary Barnes, Paul Champagne, Jimmy Fikes, Don Fogg, Larry Fuegen, Rob Hudson, Midk Langley, Louis Mills, Dan Maragni, Jim Schmidt, Wayne Valachovic and Tim Zowada

### north carolina custom knifemakers' guild

Dana C. Acker, Robert E. Barber, Dr. James Batson, Wayne Bernauer, William M. Bisher, Dave Breme, Tim Britton, John (Jack) H. Busfield, E. Gene Calloway, R.C. Chopra, Joe Corbin, Robert (Bob) J.Cumming, Travis Daniel, Rob Davis, Geno Denning, Dexter Ewing, Brent Fisher, Charles F. Fogarty, Don Fogg, Alan Folts, Phillip L. Gaddy, Jim L. Gardner, Norman A. Gervais, Marge Gervais, Nelson Gimbert, Scott Goguen, Mark Gottesman, Ed Halligan, Robert R. Ham, Koji Hara, George Herron, Terrill Hoffman, Stacey Holt, Jesse Houser, Jr., B. R. Hughes, Jack Hyer, Dan Johnson, Tommy Johnson, Barry & Phillip Jones, Barry Jones, Jacob Kelly, Tony Kelly, Robert Knight, Dr. Jim Lucie, Laura Marshall, Dave McKeithan, Andrew McLurkin, Tommy McNabb, Charlie Monroe, Bill Moran, Ron Newton, Victor L. Odom, Jr., Charles Ostendorf, Bill Pate, Howard Peacock, James Poplin, Harry Powell, John W. Poythress, Joan Poythress, Darrel Ralph, Bob Rosenfeld, Bruce M. Ryan, Tim Scholl, Danks Seel, Rodney N. Shelton, J. Wayne Short, Harland & Karen Simmons, Ken & Nancy Simmons, Johnnie Sorrell, Chuck Staples, Murray Sterling, Russ Sutton, Kathleen Tomey, Bruce Turner, Kaiji & Miki Uchida, Dave Vail, Wayne Whitley, James A. Williams, Daniel Winkler, Rob Wotzak

### ohio knifemakers association

Raymond Babcock, Van Barnett, Harold A. Collins, Larry Detty, Tom Downing, Jim Downs, Patty Ferrier, Jeff Flannery, James Fray, Bob Foster, Raymond Guess, Scott Hamrie, Rick Hinderer, Curtis Hurley, Ed Kalfayan, Michael Koval, Judy Koval, Larry Lunn, Stanley Maienknecht, Dave Marlott, Mike Mercer, David Morton, Patrick McGroder, Charles Pratt, Darrel Ralph, Roy Roddy, Carroll Shoemaker, John Smith, Clifton Smith, Art Summers, Jan Summers, Donald Tess, Dale Warther, John Wallingford, Earl Witsaman, Joanne Yurco, Mike Yurco

### saskatchewan knifemakers guild

Marty Beets, Art Benson, Doug Binns, Darren Breitkrenz, Clarence Broeksma, Irv Brunas, Emil Bucharsky, Ernie Cardinal, Raymond Caron, Faron Comaniuk, Murray Cook, Sanford Crickett, Jim Dahlin, Herb Davison, Kevin Donald, Brian Drayton, Dallas Dreger, Roger Eagles, Brian Easton, Marvin Engel, Ray Fehler, Rob Fehler, Ken Friedrick, Calvin Granshorn, Vernon Ganshorn, Dale Garling, Alan Goode, Dave Goertz, Darren Greenfield, Gary Greer, Jay Hale, Wayne Hamilton, Phil Haughian, Robert Hazell, Bryan Hebb, Daug Heuer, Garth Hindmarch, John R. Hopkins, Lavern Ilg, Clifford Kaufmann, Meryl Klassen, Bob Kowalke, Todd Kreics, Donald Krueger, Paul Laronge, Patricia Leahy, Ron Lockhart, Pat Macnamara, Bengamin Manton, Ed Mcrac, Len Meeres, Randy Merkley, Arnold Miller, Robert Minnes, Ron Nelson, Brian Obrigewitsch, Bryan Olafson, Blaine Parrry, Doug Peltier, Darryl Perlett, Dean Pickrell, Barry Popick, Jim Quickfall, Bob Robson, Gerry Rush, Geoff Rutledge, Carl Sali, Kim Senft, Eugene Schreiner, Curtis Silzer, Christopher Silzer, David Silzer, Kent Silzer, Don Spasoff, Bob Stewart, Dan Stinnen, Lorne Stadyk, Eugene R. Thompson, Ron Wall, Ken Watt, Trevor, Whitfield, David Wilkes, Merle Williams, Gerry Wozencroft, Ed Zelter, Al Zerr, Brian Zerr, Ronald Zinkhan

### south carolina association of knifemakers

Bobby Branton, Gordo Brooks, Daniel L. Cannady, Thomas H. Clegg, John Conn, Geno Denning, Charlie Douan, Jerry G. Hendrix, Wayne Hendrix, George H. Herron, T.J. Hucks, Johnny Johnson, Lonnie Jones, Jason Knight, Col. Thomas D. Kreger, Gene Langley, Eddie Lee, David Manley, William (Bill) Massey, David McFalls, Claude Montjoy, Larry Page, Ricky Rankin, John (Mickey) Reed, Gene Scaffe, Mick Sears, Ralph Smith, S. David Stroud, Robert Stuckey, Rocky Thomas, Woodrow W. Walker, Charlie Webb, Thomas H. Westwood

### tennessee knifemakers association

John Bartlow, Doug Casteel, Harold Crisp, Larry Harley, John W. Walker, Harold Woodward, Harold Wright

# photo index

## etchers/carvers



## engravers



## knifemakers

## leatherworkers/ sheathmakers



## scrimshanders

The firms listed here are special in the sense that they make or market special kinds of knives made in facilities they own or control either in the U.S. or overseas. Or they are special because they make knives of unique design or function. The second phone number listed is the fax number.

# sporting cutlers

**A.G. RUSSELL KNIVES INC**
1920 North 26th St
Lowell, AR 72745-8489
479-631-0130 800-255-9034; 749-631-8493
ag@agrussell.com; www.agrussell.com
*The oldest knife mail-order company, highest quality. Free catalog available. In these catalogs you will find the newest and the best. If you like knives, this catalog is a must.*

**AL MAR KNIVES**
PO Box 2295
Tualatin, OR 97062-2295
503-670-9080; 503-639-4789
www.almarknives.com
*Featuring our ultrahight ™ series of knives. Sere 2000 ™ Shrike, Sere ™, Operator ™, Nomad ™ and Ultraligh series ™.*

**ALCAS CORPORATION**
1116 E State St
Olean, NY 14760
716-372-3111; 716-373-6155
www.cutco.com
*Household cutlery / sport knives*

**ANZA KNIVES**
C Davis
Dept BL 12 PO Box 710806
Santee, CA 92072
619-561-9445; 619-390-6283
sales@anzaknives.com; www.anzaknives.com

**B&D TRADING CO.**
3935 Fair Hill Rd
Fair Oaks, CA 95628

**BARTEAUX MACHETES, INC.**
1916 SE 50th St
Portland, OR 97215
503-233-5880
barteaux@machete.com; www.machete.com
*Manufacture of machetes, saws, garden tools*

**BEAR MGC CUTLERY**
1111 Bear Blvd. SW
Jacksonville, AL 36265
256-435-2227; 256-435-9348
*Lockback, commemorative, multi tools, high tech & hunting knives*

**BECK'S CUTLERY & SPECIALTIES**
Mcgregor Village Center
107 Edinburgh South Dr
Cary, NC 27511
919-460-0203; 919-460-7772
beckscutlery@mindspring.com;
www.beckscutlery.com

**BENCHMADE KNIFE CO. INC.**
300 Beaver Creek Rd
Oregon City, OR 97045
503-655-6004; 503-655-6223
info@benchmade.com; www.benchmade.com
*Sports, utility, law enforcement, military, gift and semi custom*

**BERETTA U.S.A. CORP.**
17601 Beretta Dr
Accokeek, MD 20607
800-528-7453
www.berettausa.com
*Full range of hunting & specialty knives*

**BLACKJACK KNIVES**
PO Box 3
Greenville, WV 24945
304-832-6878
www.knifeware.com

**BLUE GRASS CUTLERY CORP**
20 E Seventh St PO Box 156
Manchester, OH 45144
937-549-2602; 937-549-2709 or 2603
sales @bluegrasscutlery.com
www.bluegrasscutlery.com
*Manufacturer of Winchester Knives, John Primble Knives and many contract lines*

**BOB'S TRADING POST**
308 N Main St
Hutchinson, KS 67501
620-669-9441 or 620-474-6466
*Tad custom knives with Reichert custom sheaths one at a time one of a kind*

**BOKER USA INC**
1550 Balsam St
Lakewood, CO 80214-5917
303-462-0662;303-462-0668
sales@bokerusa.com;www.bokerusa.com
*Wide range of fixed blade and folding knives for hunting, military, tactical and general use*

**BROWNING**
One Browning Pl
Morgan, UT 84050
801-876-2711; 801-876-3331
www.browning.com
*Outdoor hunting & shooting products*

**BUCK KNIVES INC**
660 S Lochsa St
Post Falls, ID 83854
800-735-2825
www.buckknives.com
*Sports cutlery*

**BULLDOG BRAND KNIVES**
PO Box 23852
Chattanooga, TN 37422
423-894-5102; 423-892-9165
*Fixed blade and folding knives for hunting and general use*

**BUSSE COMBAT KNIFE CO.**
11651 CO Rd 12
Wauseon, OH 43567
419-923-6471; 419-923-2337
*Simple & very strong straight knife designs for tactical & expedition use*
www.bussecombat.com

**CAMILLUS CUTLERY CO.**
54 Main St.
Camillus, NY 13031
315-672-8111; 315-672-8832
customerservice@camillusknives.com
www.camillusknives.com

**CAS IBERIA INC**
650 Industrial Blvd.
Sale Creek, TN 37373
423-332-4700; 423-332-7248
www.casiberia.com
*Extensive variety of fixed-blade and folding knives for hunting, diving, camping, military and general use.*

**CASE CUTLERY**
W R & Sons
Owens Way
Bradford, PA 16701
800-523-6350; 814-368-1736
consumer-relations@wrcase.com
www.wrcase.com
*Folding pocket knives*

**CHICAGO CUTLERY CO.**
5500 Pearl St Ste 400
Rosemont, IL 60018
847-678-8600
www.chicagocutlery.com
*Sport & utility knives.*

**CHRIS REEVE KNIVES**
11624 W President Dr. No. B
Boise, ID 83713
208-375-0367; 208-375-0368
crknifo@chrisreeve.com; www.chrisreeve.com
*Makers of the award winning Yarborough/ Green Beret Knife; the One Piece Range; and the Sebenza and Mnandi folding knives*

**COAST CUTLERY CO**
2045 SE Ankeny St
Portland, OR 97214
800-426-5858 or 503-234-4545; 503-234-4422
www.coastcutlery.com
*Variety of fixed-blade and folding knives and multi-tools for hunting, camping and general use*

**COLD STEEL INC**
3036 Seaborg Ave. Suite A
Ventura, CA 93003
800-255-4716 or 805-650-8481; 805-642-9727
ric@coldsteel.com; www.coldsteel.com
*Wide variety of folding lockbacks and fixed-blade hunting, fishing and neck knives, as well as bowies, kukris, tantos, throwing knives, kitchen knives and swords*

**COLONIAL KNIFE COMPANY DIVISION OF COLONIAL CUTLERY INTERNATIONAL**
K.M. Paolantonio
PO Box 960
North Scituate, RI 02857
866-421-6500; 401-421-6555
colonialcutlery@aol.com;
www.colonialcutlery@aol.com or
www.colonialknifecompany.com
*Collectors edition specialty knives. Special promotions. Old cutler, barion, trappers, military knives. Industrial knives-electrician etc.*

**COLUMBIA RIVER KNIFE & TOOL**
9720 SW Hillman Ct. Ste 805
Wilsonville, OR 97070
800-891-3100; 503-682-9680
info@crkt.com; www.crkt.com
*Complete line of sport, work and tactical knives*

**CRAWFORD KNIVES**
205 N Center
West Memphis, AR 72301
870-732-2452
*Folding knives for tactical and general use*

**DAVID BOYE KNIVES**
PO Box 1238
Dolan Springs, AZ 86441
800-853-1617 or 928-767-4273; 928-767-3030
boye@ctaz.com; www.boyeknives.com
*Boye Dendritic Cobalt boat knives*

**DUNN KNIVES**
Steve Greene
PO Box 204
Rosville KS 66533
785-584-6856; 785-584-6856
sigreene@earthlink.net; www.dunnknives.com
*Custom knives*

**EMERSON KNIVES, INC.**
PO Box 4180
Torrance, CA 90510-4180
310-212-7455; 310-212-7289
www.emersonknives.com
*Hard use tactical knives; folding & fixed blades*

**EXTREMA RATIO SAS**
Mauro Chiostri/Maurizio Castrati
Via Tourcoing 40/P
59100 Prato ITALY
0039 0574 58 4639; 0039 0574 58 1312
info@extremaratio.com
*Tactical/military knives and sheaths, blades and sheaths to customers specs*

**FALLKNIVEN AB**
Havrevagen 10
S-96142 Boden
SWEDEN
46-92154422; 46-92154433
info@fallkniven.se; www.fallkniven.com
*High quality stainless knives*

**FROG TOOL CO**
PO Box 600
Getzville, NY 14068-0600
716-877-2200; 716-877-2591
gatco@buffnet.net; www.frogtool.net
*Precision multi tools*

**FROST CUTLERY CO**
PO Box 22636
Chattanooga, Tn 37422
800-251-7768 or423-894-6079; 423-894-9576
www.frostcutleryco.com
*Wide range of fixed-blade and folding knives with a multitude of handle materials*

**GATCO SHARPENERS**
PO Box 600
Getzville, Ny 14068
716-877-2200; 716-877-2591
gatco@buffnet.net; www.gatcosharpeners.com
*Precision sharpening systems, diamond sharpening systems, ceramic sharpening systems, carbide sharpening systems, natural Arkansas stones*

**GENUINE ISSUE INC.**
949 Middle Country Rd
Selden, NY 11784
631-696-3802; 631-696-3803
gicutlery@aol.com
*Antique knives, swords*

**GERBER LEGENDARY BLADES**
14200 SW 72nd Ave
Portland, OR 97223
503-639-6161
www.gerberblades.com
*Knives, multi-tools, axes, saws, outdoor products*

**GROHMANN KNIVES LTD.**
PO Box 40
Pictou Nova Scotia B0K 1H0
CANADA
888-756-4837 or 902-485-4224; 902-485-5872
*Fixed-blade belt knives for hunting and fishing, folding pocketknives for hunting and general use*

**GT KNIVES**
7734 Arjons Dr
San Diego, CA 92126
858-530-8766; 858-530-8798
gtknives@gtknives.com; www.gtknives.com
*Law enforcement & military automatic knives*

**H&B FORGE CO.**
235 Geisinger Rd
Shiloh, OH 44878
419-895-1856
hbforge@direcway.com; www.hbforge.com
*Special order hawks, camp stoves, fireplace accessories, muzzleloading accroutements*

**HISTORIC EDGED WEAPONRY**
1021 Saddlebrook Dr
Hendersonville, NC 28739
828-692-0323; 828-692-0600
histwpn@bellsouth.net
*Antique knives from around the world; importer of puukko and other knives from Norway, Sweden, Finland and Lapland; also edged weaponry book "Travels for Daggers" by Eiler R. Cook*

**HONEYCUTT MARKETING, INC., DAN**
3165 C-4 S Campbell
Springfield MO 65807
417-887-2635
danhoneycutt@sbcglobal.net
*All kinds of cutlery, military, Randalls. 28 years young in the cutlery business*

**IMPERIAL SCHRADE CORP.**
7 Schrade Ct
Ellenville, NY 12428
800-2-Schrade
www.schradeknives.com

**JOY ENTERPRISES-FURY CUTLERY**
1862 M.L. King Blvd
Riviera Beach, FL 33404
800-500-3879 or 561-863-3205; 561-863-3277
mail@joyenterprises.com;
www.joyenterprises.com; www.furycutlery.com
*Fury ™ Mustang™ extensive variety of fixed-blade and folding knives for hunting, fishing, diving, camping, military and general use; novelty key-ring knives. Muela Sporting Knives*

**KA-BAR KNIVES INC**
200 Homer St
Olean, NY 14760
800-282-0130
info@ka-bar.com; www.ka-bar.com

**KATZ KNIVES, INC.**
PO Box 730
Chandler, AZ 85224-0730
480-786-9334; 480-786-9338
katzkn@aol.com; www.katzknives.com

**KELLAM KNIVES CO.**
902 S Dixie Hwy
Lantana, FL 33462
800-390-6918; 561-588-3185; 561-588-3186
info@kellamknives.com; www.kellamknives.com
*Largest selection of Finnish knives; handmade & production*

**KERSHAW/KAI CUTLERY CO.**
25300 SW Parkway
Wilsonville, OR 97070

**MESSEV KLOTZLI**
Hohengasse E Ch 3400
Burgdorf
SWITZERLAND
(34) 422-2378; (34) 422-7693
info@klotzli.com; www.klotzli.com
*High-tech folding knives for tactical and general use*

**KNIFEWARE INC**
PO Box 3
Greenville, WV 24945
304-832-6878
www.knifeware.com
*Blackjack and Big Country Cross reference Big Country Knives see Knifeware Inc.*

**KNIGHTS EDGE LTD.**
5696 N Northwest Highway
Chicago, IL 60646-6136
773-775-3888; 773-775-3339
sales@knightsedge.com;
www.knightsedge.com
*Medieval weaponry, swords, suits of armor, katanas, daggers*

**KNIVES OF ALASKA, INC.**
Charles or Jody Allen
3100 Airport Dr
Denison, TX 75020 8623
903-786-7366, 800-572-0980; 903-786-7371
info@knivesofalaska.com;
www.knivesofalaska.com
*High quality hunting & outdoorsmen's knives*

**KUTMASTER KNIVES**
Div of Utica Cutlery Co
820 Noyes St
Utica, NY 13502
315-733-4663; 315-733-6602
www.kutmaster.com
*Manufacturer and importer of pocket, lockback, tool knives and multi-purpose tools*

**LAKOTA**
620 E Monroe
Riverton, WY 24945
307-856-6559; 307-856-1840
*AUS 8-A high-carbon stainless steel blades*

**LEATHERMAN TOOL GROUP, INC.**
PO Box 20595
Portland, OR 97294
503-253-7826; 503-253-7830
mktg@leatherman.com; www.leatherman.com
*Multi-tools*

**LONE WOLF KNIVES**
Doug Hutchens
17400 SW Upper Boones Ferry Rd Suite 240
Portland OR 97224
503-431-6777

**MARBLE'S OUTDOORS**
420 Industrial Park
Gladstone, Mi 49837
906-428-3710; 906-428-3711
marble@up.net; www.marblesoutdoors.com

**MASTER CUTLERY INC**
701 Penhorn Ave
Secaucus, NJ 07094
201-271-7600; 201-271-7666
www.mastercutlery.com
*Largest variety in the knife industry*

**MASTERS OF DEFENSE KNIFE CO**
4850 Brookside Court
Norfolk, VA 23502
800-694-5263; 888-830-2013
cs@blackhawk.com; www.modknives.com
*Fixed-blade and folding knives for tactical and general use*

**MEYERCO MANUFACTURING**
4481 Exchange Service Dr
Dallas, TX 75236
214-467-8949; 214-467-9241
www.meyercousa.com
*Folding tactical,rescue and speed-assisted pocketknives; fixed-blade hunting and fishing designs; multi-function camping tools and machetes*

**MCCANN INDUSTRIES**
132 S 162nd PO Box 641
Spanaway, WA 98387
253-537-6919; 253-537-6993
McCann.machine@worldnet.att.net;
www.mccannindustries.com

**MICRO TECHNOLOGY**
932 36th Ct. Sw
Vero Beach, FL 32968
772-569-3058; 772-569-7632
sales@microtechknives.com;
www.microtechknives.com
*Manufacturers of the highest quality production knives*

**MORTY THE KNIFE MAN, INC.**
4 Manorhaven Blvd
Pt Washington, NY 11050
516-767-2357; 516-767-7058

**MUSEUM REPLICAS LTD.**
2147 Gees Mill Rd
Conyers, GA 30012
800-883-8838
www.museumreplicas.com
*Historically accurate & battle-ready swords & daggers*

**MYERCHIN MARINE CLASSICS**
14765 Nova Scotia Dr
Fontana, CA 92336
909-463-6741; 909-463-6751
myerchin@myerchin.com; www.myerchin.com
*Rigging/ Police knives*

**NATIONAL KNIFE DISTRIBUTORS**
125 Depot St
Forest City, NC 28043
800-447-4342 or 828-245-4321; 828-245-5121
nkdi@nkdi.com
*Benchmark pocketknives from Solingen Germany*

**NORMARK CORP**
10395 Yellow Circle Dr
Minnetonka, MN 55343
800-874-4451; 612-933-0046
*Hunting knives, game shears and skinning ax*

**ONTARIO KNIFE CO.**
26 Empire St
Franklinville, NY 14737
800-222-5233; 800-299-2618
sales@ontarioknife.com; www.ontarioknife.com
*Fixed blades, tactical folders, military & hunting knives, machetes*

**OUTDOOR EDGE CUTLERY CORP.**
4699 Nautilus Ct. S #503
Boulder, CO 80301
800-447-EDGE; 303-530-7020
info@outdooredge.com; www.outdooredge.com

**PILTDOWN PRODUCTIONS**
Errett Callahan
2 Fredonia Ave
Lynchburg, VA 24503
434-528-3444

**QUEEN CUTLERY COMPANY**
PO Box 500
Franklinville, NY 14737
800-222-5233; 800-299-2618
sales@ontarioknife.com;
www.queencutlery.com
*Pocket knives, collectibles, Schatt & Morgan, Robeson, club knives*

**QUIKUT**
PO Box 29
Airport Industrial Park
Walnut Ridge, AR 72476
870-886-6774; 870-886-9162

**RANDALL MADE KNIVES**
PO Box 1988
Orlando, FL 32802-1988
407-855-8075; 407-855-9054
grandall@randallknives.com;
www.randallknives.com
*Handmade fixed-blade knives for hunting, fishing, diving, military and general use*

**REMINGTON ARMS CO., INC.**
870 Remington Drive
PO Box 700
Madison, NC 27025-0700
800-243-9700
www.remigton.com

**SANTA FE STONEWORKS**
3790 Cerrillos Rd.
Santa Fe, NM 87507
800-257-7625; 505-471-5953; 505-471-0036
knives@rt66.com; www.santafestoneworks.com
*Gem stone handles*

**SARCO CUTLERY LLC**
449 Lane Dr
Florence AL 35630
256-766-8099; 256-766-7246
sarcoknives@earthlink.net;
www.sarcoknives.com
*Etching and engraving services, club knives. etc. New knives, antique-collectible knives*

**SOG SPECIALTY KNIVES & TOOLS, INC.**
6521 212th St. S.W.
Lynwood, WA 98036
425-771-6230; 425-771-7689
info@sogknives.com; www.sogknives.com
*SOG assisted technology, Arc-Lock, folding knives, specialized fixed blades, multi-tools*

**SPYDERCO, INC.**
820 Spyderco Way
Golden, CO 80403
800-525-7770; 303-278-2229
sales@spyderco.com
www.spyderco.com
*Knives and sharpeners*

**SWISS ARMY BRANDS INC.**
PO Box 874
One Research Dr
Shelton, CT 06484-0874
800-243-4045; 800-243-4006
www.swissarmy.com
*Folding multi-blade designs and multi-tools for hunting, fishing, camping, hiking, golfing and general use. One of the original brands (Victorinox) of Swiss Army Knives*

**TAYLOR CUTLERY**
1736 N Eastman Rd
PO Box 1638
Kingsport, TN 37662-1638
800-251-0254 or 423-247-2406; 423-247-5371
taylor@preferred.com; www.taylorcutlery.com
*Fixed-blade and folding knives for tactical, rescue, hunting and general use*

**TIGERSHARP TECHNOLOGIES**
1002 N Central Expwy Suite 499
Richardson TX 75080
469-916-2861; 972-907-0716
chead@tigersharp.com; www.tigersharp.com

**TIMBERLINE KNIVES**
PO Box 600
Getzville, NY 14068-0600
716-877-2200; 716-877-2591
gatco@buffnet.net; timberlineknives.com;
www.timberlineknives.com
*High Technology production knives for professionals, sporting, tradesmen & kitchen use*

**TINIVES**
1725 Smith Rd
Fortson, GA 31808
888-537-9991; 706-322-9892
info@tinives.com; www.tinives.com
*High-tech folding knives for tactical, law enforcement and general use*

**TRU-BALANCE KNIFE CO.**
PO Box 140555
Grand Rapids, MI 49514

**TURNER, P.J., KNIFE MFG., INC.**
PO Box 1549
Afton, WY 83110
307-885-0611
pjtkm@silverstar.com; www.eknife.net

**UTICA CUTLERY CO**
820 Noyes St
Utica, NY 13503-1537
800-888-4223; 315-733-6602
sales@kutmaster.com
*Wide range of folding and fixed-blade designs, multi-tools and steak knives*

**WARNER, KEN**
PO Box 3
Greenville, WV 24945
304-832-6878; 304-832-6550
www.knifeware.com

**WENGER NORTH AMERICA**
15 Corporate Dr
Orangeburg, NY 10962
800-431-2996 or 845-365-3500; 845-365-3558
www.wengerna.com
*One of the official makers of folding multi-blade Swiss Army knives*

**WILD BOAR BLADES**
1701 Broadway PMB 282
Vancouver, WA 98663
888-476-4400 or 360-735-0570; 360-735-0390
wildboarblades@aol.com;
www.wildboarblade.com
*Wild Boar Blades is pleased to carry a full line of Kopormed knives and kitchenware imported from Poland*

**WILLIAM HENRY FINE KNIVES**
3200 NE Rivergate
McMinnville, OR 97128
888-563-4500 or 503-434-9700; 503-434-9704
www.williamhenryknives.com
*Semi-custom folding knives for hunting and general use; some limited editions*

**WORLD SURVIVAL INSTITUTE**
C Janowsky
Dept BL 12 Box 394
Tok, AK 99780
907-883-4243

**WUU JAU CO INC**
2600 S Kelly Ave
Edmond, OK 73013
800-722-5760 or 405-359-5031l 877-256-4337 or 405-340-5965
mail@wuujau.com; www.wuujau.com
*Wide variety of imported fixed-blade and folding knives for hunting, fishing, camping, and general use. Wholesale to knife dealers only*

**WYOMING KNIFE CORP.**
101 Commerce Dr.
Ft. Collins, CO 80524

**XIKAR INC**
PO Box 025757
Kansas City MO 64102
888-266-1193; 816-421-3530
info@xikar.com; www.xikar.com
*Gentlemen's cutlery and accessories*

# importers

**A. G. RUSSELL KNIVES INC**
1920 North 26th St
Lowell, AR 72745-8489
479-631-0130; 800-255-9034; 479-631-8493
ag@agrussell.com; www.agrussell.com
*The oldest knife mail-order company, highest quality. Free catalog available. In these catalogs you will find the newest and the best. If you like knives, this catalog is a must. Celebrating 40 years in the industry*

**ADAMS INTERNATIONAL KNIFEWORKS**
8710 Rosewood Hills
Edwardsville, IL 62025
*Importers & foreign cutlers*

**AITOR-BERRIZARGO S.L.**
P.I. Eitua PO Box 26
48240 Berriz Vizcaya
SPAIN
946826599; 94602250226
info@aitor.com; www.aitor.com
*Sporting knives*

**ATLANTA CUTLERY CORP.**
2147 Gees Mill Rd
Box 839FD
Conyers, GA 30207
770-922-3700; 770-388-0246
www.atlantacutlery.com
*Exotic knives from around the world*

**BAILEY'S**
PO Box 550
Laytonville, CA 95454
800-322-4539; 707-984-8115
www.baileys-online.com

**BELTRAME, FRANCESCO**
Via Molini 27
33085 Maniago PN
ITALY
39 0427 701859
www.italianstiletto.com

**BOKER USA, INC.**
1550 Balsam St
Lakewood, CO 80214-5917
303-462-0662; 303-462-0668
sales@bokerusa.com; www.bokerusa.com
*Ceramic blades*

**CAMPOS, IVAN DE ALMEIDA**
R. Stelio M. Loureiro, 205
Centro, Tatui
BRAZIL
00-55-15-33056867
www.ivancampos.com

**C.A.S. IBERIA, INC.**
650 Industrial Blvd
Sale Creek, TN 37373
423-332-4700; 423-332-7248
info@casiberia.com; www.casiberia.com

**CAS/HANWEI, MUELA**
Catoctin Cutlery
PO Box 188
Smithsburg, MD 21783

**CLASSIC INDUSTRIES**
1325 Howard Ave, Suite 408
Burlingame, CA 94010

**COAST CUTLERY CO.**
2045 Se Ankeny St
Portland, OR 97214

**COLUMBIA PRODUCTS CO.**
PO Box 1333
Sialkot 51310
PAKISTAN

**COLUMBIA PRODUCTS INT'L**
PO Box 8243
New York, NY 10116-8243
201-854-3054 or 201-854-8504; 201-854-7058
nycolumbia@aol.com; http://columbiaproducts.homestead.com/cat.html
*Pocket, hunting knives and swords of all kinds*

**COMPASS INDUSTRIES, INC.**
104 E. 25th St
New York, NY 10010
800-221-9904; 212-353-0826
jeff@compassindustries.com; www.compassindustries.com
*Imported pocket knives*

**CONAZ COLTELLERIE**
Dei F.Lli Consigli-Scarperia
Via G. Giordani, 20
50038 Scarperia (Firenze)
ITALY
36 55 846187; 39 55 846603
conaz@dada.it; www.consigliscarpeia.com
*Handicraft workmanship of knives of the ancient Italian tradition. Historical and collection knives*

**CONSOLIDATED CUTLERY CO., INC.**
696 NW Sharpe St
Port St. Lucie, FL 34983

**CRAZY CROW TRADING POST**
Po Box 847 Dept 96
Pottsboro, TX 75020
903-786-2287; 903-786-9059
info@crazycrow.com; www.crazycrow.com
*Solingen blades, knife making parts & supplies*

**DER FLEISSIGEN BEAVER**
(The Busy Beaver)
Harvey Silk
PO Box 1166
64343 Griesheim
GERMANY
49 61552231; 49 6155 2433
Der.Biber@t-online.de
*Retail custom knives. Knife shows in Germany & UK*

**EMPIRE CUTLERY CORP.**
12 Kruger Ct
Clifton, NJ 07013

**EXTREMA RATIO SAS**
Mauro Chiostri
Mavrizio Castrati
Via Tourcoing 40/p
59100 Prato (PO)
ITALY
0039 0574 58 4639; 0039 0574 581312
info@extremarazio.com; www.extremaratio.com
*Tactical & military knives manufacturing*

**FALLKNIVEN AB**
Havrevagen 10
S-96142 Boden
SWEDEN
46 92154422; 46 92154433
info@fallkniven.se
www.fallkniven.com
*High quality knives*

**FREDIANI COLTELLI FINLANDESI**
Via Lago Maggiore 41
I-21038 Leggiuno
ITALY

**GIESSER MESSERFABRIK GMBH, JOHANNES**
Raiffeisenstr 15
D-71349 Winnenden
GERMANY
49-7195-18080; 49-7195-64466
info@giesser.de; www.giesser.de
*Professional butchers and chef's knives*

**HIMALAYAN IMPORTS**
3495 Lake Side Dr
Reno, NV 89509
775-825-2279
himimp@aol.com; httpillmembers.aol.com/himinp/index.html

**IVAN DE ALMEIDA CAMPOS-KNIFE DEALER**
R. Xi De Agosto
107, Centro, Tatui, Sp 18270
BRAZIL
55-15-251-8092; 55-15-251-4896
campos@bitweb.com.br
*Custom knives from all Brazilian knifemakers*

**JOY ENTERPRISES**
1862 M.L. King Blvd
Riviera Beach, FL 33404
561-863-3205/800-500-3879; 561-863-3277
mail@joyenterprises.com; www.joyenterprises.com
*Fury™, Mustang™, Hawg Knives, Muela*

**KELLAM KNIVES CO.**
902 S Dixie Hwy
Lantana, FL 33462
561-588-3185; 800-390-6918; 561-588-3186
info@kellamknives.com; www.kellamknives.com
*Knives from Finland; own line of knives*

**KNIFE IMPORTERS, INC.**
PO Box 1000
Manchaca, TX 78652
800-531-5301; 800-266-2373
*Wholesale only*

**KNIGHTS EDGE**
5696 N Northwest Hwy
Chicago, IL 60646
773-775-3888; 773-775-3339
www.knightsedge.com
*Exclusive designers of our Rittersteel, Stagesteel and Valiant Arms and knightedge lines of weapon*

**LEISURE PRODUCTS CORP.**
PO Box 1171
Sialkot-51310
PAKISTAN

**L. C. RISTINEN**
Suomi Shop
17533 Co Hwy 38
Frazee MN 56544
218-538-6633; 218-538-6633
icrist@wcta.net
*Scandinavian cutlery custom antique, books and reindeer antler*

**LINDER, CARL NACHF.**
Erholungstr. 10
42699 Solingen
GERMANY
212 330856; 212 337104
info@linder.de; www.linder.de

**MARTTIINI KNIVES**
PO Box 44 (Marttiinintie 3)
96101 Rovaniemi
FINLAND

**MATTHEWS CUTLERY**
4401 Sentry Dr., Suite K
Tucker, GA 30084

**MESSER KLÖTZLI**
PO Box 104
Hohengasse 3, Ch-3402 Burgdorf
SWITZERLAND
034 422 2378; 034 422 7693
info@klotzli.com; www.klotzli.com

**MURAKAMI, ICHIRO**
Knife Collectors Assn. Japan
Tokuda Nishi 4 Chome, 76 Banchi, Ginancho
Hashimagun, Gifu
JAPAN
81 58 274 1960; 81 58 273 7369
www.gix.orjp/~n-resin/

**MUSEUM REPLICAS LIMITED**
2147 Gees Mill Rd
Conyers, GA 30012
800-883-8838
www.museumreplicas.com

**NICHOLS CO.**
PO Box 473, #5 The Green
Woodstock, VT 05091
802-457-3970; 802-457-2051
janjesse@sover.net
*Import & distribute knives from EKA (Sweden), Helle (Norway), Brusletto (Norway), Roselli (Finland). Also market Zippo products, Snow, Nealley axes and hatchets and snow & Neally axes*

**NORMARK CORP.**
Craig Weber
10395 Yellow Circle Dr
Minnetonka, MN 55343

**PRO CUT**
9718 Washburn Rd
Downey, CA 90241
562-803-8778; 562-803-4261
sales@procutdist.com
*Wholesale only. Full service distributor of domestic & imported brand name cutlery. Exclusive U.S. importer for both Marto Swords and Battle Ready Valiant Armory edged weapons*

**PRODUCTORS AITOR, S.A.**
Izelaieta 17
48260 Ermua
SPAIN
943-170850; 943-170001
info@aitor.com
*Sporting knives*

**SCANDIA INTERNATIONAL INC.**
5475 W Inscription Canyon Dr
Prescott, AZ 86305
928-442-0140; 928-442-0342
frosts@cableone.net; www.frosts-scandia.com
*Frosts Knives of Sweden*

**STAR SALES CO., INC.**
1803 N. Central St., PO Box 1503
Knoxville, TN 37901

**SVORD KNIVES**
Smith Rd., Rd 2
Waiuku, South Auckland
NEW ZEALAND

**SWISS ARMY BRANDS LTD.**
The Forschner Group, Inc.
One Research Drive
Shelton, CT 06484
203-929-6391; 203-929-3786
www.swissarmy.com

**TAYLOR CUTLERY**
PO Box 1638
1736 N. Eastman Rd
Kingsport, TN 37662
*Colman Knives along with Smith & Wesson, Cuttin Horse, John Deere, Zoland knives*

**UNITED CUTLERY CORP.**
1425 United Blvd
Sevierville, TN 37876
865-428-2532; 865-428-2267
order@unitedcutlery.com; www.unitedcutlery.com
*Harley-Davidson ® Colt ®, Stanley ®, U21 ®, Rigid Knives ®, Outdoor Life ®, Ford ®, hunting, camping, fishing, collectible & fantasy knives*

**UNIVERSAL AGENCIES INC**
4690 S Old Peachtree Rd, Ste C
Norcross, GA 30071-1517
678-969-9147; 678-969-9148; 678-969-9169
info@uai.org; www.knifesupplies.com; www.thunderforged.com; www.uai.org
*Serving the cutlery industry with the finest selection of India Stag, Buffalo Horn, Thurnderforged ™ Damascus. Mother of Pearl, Knife Kits and more*

**VALOR CORP.**
1001 Sawgrass Corp Pkwy
Sunrise, FL 33323-2811
954-377-4925; 954-377-4941
www.valorcorp.com
*Wide variety of imported & domestic knives*

**WENGER N. A.**
15 Corporate Dr
Orangeburg, NY 10962
800-431-2996
www.wengerna.com
*Swiss Army ™ Knives*

**WILD BOAR BLADES**
1701 Broadway, Suite 282
Vancouver, WA 98663
888-476-4400; 360-735-0570; 360-735-0390
usakopro@aol.com; www.wildboarblades.com
*Wild Boar Blades is pleased to carry a full line of Kopromed knives and kitchenware imported from Poland*

**ZWILLING J.A.**
Henckels Inc
171 Saw Mill River Rd
Hawthorne, NY 10532
914-749-0300; 914-747-9850
info@jahenckels.com; www.jahenckels.com
*Kitchen cutlery, scissors, gadgets, flatware and cookware*

# knife making supplies

**AFRICAN IMPORT CO.**
Alan Zanotti
22 Goodwin Rd
Plymouth, MA 02360
508-746-8552; 508-746-0404
africanimport@aol.com
*Ivory*

**AMERICAN SIEPMANN CORP.**
65 Pixley Industrial Parkway
Rochester, NY 14624
585-247-1640; 585-247-1883
www.siepmann.com
*CNC blade grinding equipment, grinding wheels, production blade grinding services. Sharpening stones and sharpening equipment*

**ANCHORAGE CUTLER**
Greg Gritten
801 Airport Hts #351
Anchorage, AK 99508
907-277-5843
cutlery@artic.net; www.anchoragecutlery.com
*Custom knife making supplies; ivory, gemstones, antler, horn, bone*

**ART JEWEL ENTERPRISES, LTD.**
460 Randy Rd
Carol Stream, IL 60188

**ATLANTA CUTLERY CORP.**
2147 Gees Mill Rd, Box 839XE
Conyers, GA 30012
800-883-0300

**BATAVIA ENGINEERING**
PO Box 53
Magaliesburg, 1791
SOUTH AFRICA
27-14-5771294
bertie@batavia.co.za; www.batavia.co.za
*Contact wheels for belt grinders and surface grinders; damascus and mokume*

**BLADEMAKER, THE**
Gary Kelley
17485 SW Phesant Ln
Beaverton, OR 97006
503-649-7867
garykelly@theblademaker.com;
www.theblademaker.com
*Period knife and hawk blades for hobbyists & re-enactors and in dendritic D2 steel. "Ferroulithic" steel-stone spear point, blades and arrowheads*

**BOONE TRADING CO., INC.**
PO Box 669
Brinnon, WA 98320
800-423-1945
www.boonetrading.com
*Ivory of all types, bone, horns*

**BORGER, WOLF**
Benzstrasse 8
76676 Graben-Neudorf
GERMANY
wolf@messerschmied.de;
www.messerschmied.de

**BOYE KNIVES**
PO Box 1238
Dolan Springs, AZ 86441
800-853-1617; 928-767-3030
boye@ctaz.com; www.boyeknives.com
*Dendritic steel and Dendritic cobalt*

**BRONK'S KNIFEWORKS**
C. Lyle Brunckhorst
23706 7th Ave SE, Country Village, Suite B
Bothell, WA 98021; 425-402-3484
bronks@net-tech.com;
www.bronksknifeworks.com
*Damascus steel*

**CRAZY CROW TRADING POST**
PO Box 847, Dept 96
Pottsboro, TX 75076
903-786-2287; 903-786-9059
info@crazycrow.com; www.crazycrow.com
*Solingen blades, knifemaking parts & supples*

**CUSTOM FURNACES**
PO Box 353
Randvaal, 1873
SOUTH AFRICA
27 16 365-5723; 27 16 365-5738
johnlee@custom.co.za
*Furnaces for hardening & tempering of knives*

**CUSTOM KRAFT**
PO Box 2337
Riverview, FL 33568
813-671-0661; 727-595-0378
RWPHIL413@earthlink.net;
www.rwcustomknives.com
*Specializes in precision screws and hardware for folders. Also carrys gemstones and cabochons for inlay work. Catalog available*

**DAMASCUS-USA CHARLTON LTD.**
149 Deans Farm Rd
Tyner, NC 27980-9718
252-221-2010
damascususa@intelifort.com;
www.damascususa.com

**DAN'S WHETSTONE CO., INC.**
418 Hilltop Rd
Pearcy, AR 71964
501-767-1616; 501-767-9598
questions@danswhetstone.com;
www.danswhetstone.com
*Natural abrasive Arkansas stone products*

**DIAMOND MACHINING TECHNOLOGY, INC. DMT**
85 Hayes Memorial Dr
Marlborough, MA 01752
800-481-5944; 508-485-3924
dmtsharp@dmtsharp.com; www.dmtsharp.com
*Knife and tool sharpeners - diamond, ceramic and easy edge guided sharpening kits*

**DIXIE GUN WORKS, INC.**
PO Box 130
Union City, TN 38281
731-885-0700; 731-885-0440 or 800-238-6785
info@dixiegunworks.com;
www.dixiegunworks.com
*Knife and knifemaking supplies*

**E CHRISTOPHER MFG.**
PO Box 685
Union City, TN 38281
731-885-0374; 731-885-0440
*Solingen blades from Germany (ground and polished)*

**EZE-LAP DIAMOND PRODUCTS**
3572 Arrowhead Dr
Carson City, NV 89706
775-888-9500; 775-888-9555
sales@eze-lap.com; www.eze-lap.com
*Diamond coated sharpening tools*

**FLITZ INTERNATIONAL, LTD.**
821 Mohr Ave
Waterford, WI 53185
800-558-8611; 262-534-2991
info@flitz.com; www.flitz.com
*Metal polish, buffing pads, wax*

**FORTUNE PRODUCTS, INC.**
205 Hickory Creek Rd
Marble Falls, TX 78654
830-693-6111; 830-693-6394
www.accusharp.com
*AccuSharp knife sharpeners*

**GILMER WOOD CO.**
2211 NW St Helens Rd
Portland, OR 97210
503-274-1271
www.gilmerwood.com

**GOLDEN AGE ARMS CO.**
PO Box 366, 115 E High St
Ashley, OH 43003

**GRS CORP.**
D.J. Glaser
PO Box 1153, 900 Overlander St
Emporia, KS 66801
620-343-1084 or 800-835-3519; 620-343-9640
glendo@glendo.com; www.glendo.com
*Engraving, equipment, tool sharpener, books/ videos*

**HALPERN TITANIUM INC.**
Les and Marianne Halpern
PO Box 214
Three Rivers, MA 01080
413-283-8627; 413-289-2372
info@halperntitanium.com
*Titanium, carbon fiber, G-10, fasteners; CNC milling*

**HARMON, JOE T.**
8014 Fisher Dr
Jonesboro, GA 30236

**HAWKINS CUSTOM KNIVES & SUPPLIES**
110 Buckeye Rd
Fayetteville, GA 30214
770-964-1177; 770-306-2877
radeh@bellsouth.net
www.radehawkinscustomknives.com
*All styles*

**HILTARY DIAMOND INDUSTRIES**
7303 E Earll Dr
Scottsdale, AZ 85251
480-945-0700 or 480-994-5752; 480-945-3333
usgrc@qwest.net; www.bigbrainsdont.com

**HOUSE OF TOOLS LTD.**
#136, 8228 Maclead Tr SE
Calgary, AB
CANADA T2H 2B8

**HOV KNIVES & SUPPLIES**
Box 8005
S-700 08 Arebro
SWEDEN

**INDIAN JEWELERS SUPPLY CO.**
Mail Order PO Box 1774, 601 E Coal Ave
Gallup NM 87301
2105 San Mateo Blvd
Albuquerque, NM 87110
505-722-4451; 505-722-4172
orders@ijsinc.com; www.ijsinc.com
*Handle materials, tools, metals*

**INTERAMCO INC.**
5210 Exchange Dr
Flint, MI 48507
810-732-8181; 810-732-6116
solutions@interamco.com
*Knife grinding and polishing*

**JANTZ SUPPLY**
PO Box 584-K4
Davis, OK 73030-0584

800-351-8900; 580-369-3082
jantz@brightok.net; www.knifemaking.com
*Pre shaped blades, kit knives, complete knifemaking supply line*

**JOHNSON, R.B.**
I.B.S. Int'l. Folder Supplies
Box 11
Clearwater, MN 55320
320-558-6128; 320-558-6128
www.customknives.com/r.b.johnson
*Threaded pivot pins, screws, taps, etc.*

**JOHNSON WOOD PRODUCTS**
34968 Crystal Rd
Strawberry Point, IA 52076

**K&G FINISHING SUPPLIES**
PO Box 458
Lakeside, AZ 85929
928-537-8877; 928-537-8066
cs@knifeandgun.com; www.knifeandgun.com
*Full service supplies*

**KOVAL KNIVES, INC.**
5819 Zarley St
New Albany, OH 43054
614-855-0777; 614-855-0945
koval@kovalknives.com; www.kovalknives.com
*Knifemaking supplies & equipment*

**KOWAK IVORY**
Roland and Kathy Quimby
PO Box 350
Ester, AK 99725
520-723-5827
rlqiv@yahoo.com
*Fossil ivories*

**LITTLE GIANT POWER HAMMER**
420 4th Corso
Nebraska City, NE 68410

**LIVESAY NEWT**
3306 S Dogwood St
Siloam Springs, AR 72761
479-549-3356; 479-549-3357
newt@newtlivesay.com; www.newtlivesay.com
*Combat utility knives, titanium knives, sportsmen knives, custom made orders taken on knives and after market Kydex© sheaths for commercial or custom cutlery*

**LOHMAN CO., FRED**
3405 NE Broadway
Portland, OR 97232

**M MILLER ORIGINALS**
Michael Miller
2960 E Carver Ave
Kingman AZ 86401
928-757-1359
mike@milleroriginals.com
*Supplies stabilized juniper burl blocks and scales*

**MARKING METHODS, INC.**
Sales
301 S. Raymond Ave
Alhambra, CA 91803-1531
626-282-8823; 626-576-7564
sales@markingmethods.com;
www.markingmethods.com
*Knife etching equipment & service*

**MASECRAFT SUPPLY CO.**
254 Amity St
Meriden, CT 06450
203-238-3049; 203-238-2373
masecraft@masecraftsupply.necoxmail.com;
www.masecraftsupply.com
*Natural & specialty synthetic handle materials & more*

**MEIER STEEL**
Daryl Meier
75 Forge Rd
Carbondale, IL 62903
www.meiersteel.com

**MOTHER OF PEARL CO.**
Joe Culpepper
PO Box 445, 293 Belden Cir
Franklin, NC 28734
828-524-6842; 828-369-7809
mopco@earthlink.net; www.knifehandles.com;
www.stingrayproducts.com
*Mother of pearl, bone, abalone, stingray, dyed stag, black clip, ram's horn, mammoth ivory, coral, scrimshaw*

**NICHOLAS EQUIPMENT CO.**
730 E Washington St
Sandusky, OH 44870

**NICO BERNARD**
PO Box 5151
Nelspruit 1200
SOUTH AFRICA
011-2713-7440099; 011-2713-7440099
bernardn@iafrica.com

**NORRIS MIKE**
Rt 2 Box 242A
Vanceburg, KY 41179
606-798-1217
*Damascus steel*

**OREGON ABRASIVE & MFG. CO.**
12345 NE Sliderberg Rd
Brush Prairie, WA 98606
360-892-1142; 360-892-3025
*Tripel grit 3 stone sharpening system*

**OSO FAMOSO**
Box 654
Ben Lomond, CA 95005
831-336-2343
oso@osofamoso.com; www.osofamoso.com
*Mammoth ivory bark*

**OZARK KNIFE & GUN**
3165 C-4 S Campbell
Springfield, MO 65807
417-886-CUTT; 417-887-2635
danhoneycutt@sbcglobal.net
*28 years in the cutlery business, Missouri's oldest cutlery firm*

**PAPAI, ABE**
5013 N 800 E
New Carlisle, IN 46552

**PARAGON INDUSTRIES, INC. L. P.**
2011 South Town East Blvd
Mesquite, TX 75149-1122
972-288-7557; 800-876-4328
paragonind@att.net; www.paragonweb.com
*Heat treating furnaces for knife makers*

**POPLIN, JAMES/POP KNIVES & SUPPLIES**
103 Oak St
Washington, GA 30673

**PUGH, JIM**
PO Box 711
Azle, TX 76098
817-444-2679; 817-444-5455
*Rosewood and ebony Micarta blocks,rivets for Kydex sheaths, 0-80 screws for folders*

**RADOS, JERRY**
PO Box 531, 7523E 5000 N. Rd
Grant Park, IL 60940
815-405-5061
jerryr@favoravi.com
*Damascus steel*

**REACTIVE METALS STUDIO, INC.**
PO Box 890
Clarksdale, AZ 86324
928-634-3434; 928-634-6734
info@reactivemetals.com;
www.reactivemetals.com

**R. FIELDS ANCIENT IVORY**
Donald Fields
790 Tamerlane St
Deltona, FL 32725
386-532-9070
donaldfields@aol.com
*Selling ancient ivories; Mammoth, fossil & walrus*

**RICK FRIGAULT CUSTOM KNIVES**
3584 Rapidsview Dr
Niagara Falls, Ontario
CANADA L2G 6C4
905-295-6695
zipcases@zipcases.com; www.zipcases.com
*Selling padded zippered knife pouches with an option to personalize the outside with the marker, purveyor, stores - address, phone number, email web-site or any other information needed. Available in black cordura, mossy oak camo in sizes 4"x2" to 20"x4.5"*

**RIVERSIDE MACHINE**
201M W Stillwell
Dequeen, AR 71832
870-642-7643; 870-642-4023
uncleal@ipa.net; www.riversidemachine.net

**ROCKY MOUNTAIN KNIVES**
George L. Conklin
PO Box 902, 615 Franklin
Ft. Benton, MT 59442
406-622-3410
bbgrus@ttc-cmc.net
*Working knives*

**RUMMELL, HANK**
10 Paradise Lane
Warwick, NY 10990

**SAKMAR, MIKE**
1451 Clovelly Ave
Rochester, MI 48307
248-852-6775; 248-852-8544
mikesakmar@yahoo.com
*Mokume bar stock. Retail & wholesale*

**SANDPAPER, INC. OF ILLINOIS**
270 Eisenhower Ln N, Unit 5B
Lombard, IL 60148
630-629-3320; 630-629-3324
sandinc@aol.com; www.sandpaperinc.com
*Abrasive belts, rolls, sheets & discs*

**SCHEP'S FORGE**
PO Box 395
Shelton, NE 68876-0395

**SENTRY SOLUTIONS LTD.**
33 S Commercial St #401
Manchester, NH 03101-2626
603-626-8888/800-546-8049; 603-626-8889
knives2002@sentrysolutions.com;
www.sentrysolutions.com
*Knife care products*

**SHEFFIELD KNIFEMAKERS SUPPLY, INC.**
PO Box 741107
Orange City, FL 32774-1107
386-775-6453; 386-774-5754
www.sheffieldsupply.com

**SHINING WAVE METALS**
PO Box 563
Snohomish, WA 98291-0563
425-334-5569; 425-334-5569
phb@shiningwave.com; www.shiningwave.com
*A full line of Mokune-Gane in precious and non-precious metals for knifemakers, jewelers and other artists*

**SMITH ABRASIVES, INC.**
1700 Sleepy Valley Rd
Hot Springs, AR 71901

**SMITH WHETSTONE, INC.**
1700 Sleepy Valley Rd
Hot Springs, AR 71901

**SMOLEN FORGE, INC.**
Nick Smolen
S1735 Vang Rd
Westby, WA 54667
608-634-3569; 608-634-3869
www.smolenforge.com
*Damascus billets & blanks, Mokume gane billets*

**SOSTER SVENSTRUP BYVEJ 16**
Dastrup 4130 VIBY SJ
DENMARK
45 46 19 4305; 45 46 19 5319
www.poulstrande.com

**STAMASCUS KNIFEWORKS INC.**
Ed Van Hoy
24255 N. Fork River
Abingdon, VA 24210
276-944-4885
*Blade steels*

**STOVER, JEFF**
PO Box 43
Torrance, CA 90507
310-532-2166
edgedealer@aol.com
*Fine custom knives, top makers*

**TEXAS KNIFEMAKERS SUPPLY**
Kevin Thuesen
10649 Haddington Suite 180
Houston TX 77043
713-461-8632
*Working straight knives. Hunters including upswept skinners and custom walking sticks*

**TRU-GRIT, INC.**
760 E Francis St #N
Ontario, CA 91761
909-923-4116 or 800-532-3336; 909-923-9932
trugrit1@aol.com; www.trugrit.com
*The latest in Norton and 3/M ceramic grinding belts. Also Super Flex, Trizact, Norax and Micron belts to 3000 grit. All of the popular belt grinders. Buffers and variable speed motors. ATS-34, 440C, BG-42, CPM S-30V, 416 and Damascus steel*

**UNIVERSAL AGENCIES, INC.**
4690 S Old Peachtree Rd Ste C
Norcross, GA 30071-1517
678-969-9147 or 678-969-9148; 678-969-9169
info@uai.org; www.knifesupplies.com, www.thunderforged.com; www.uai.org
*Serving the cutlery industry with the finest selection of India Stag, Buffalo Horn, Thurnderforged ™ Damascus. Mother of Pearl, Knife Kits and more*

**WASHITA MOUNTAIN WHETSTONE CO.**
PO Box 20378
Hot Springs, AR 71903
501-525-3914; 501-525-0816
wmw@hsnp

**WEILAND, J. REESE**
PO Box 2337
Riverview, FL 33568
813-671-0661; 727-595-0378
rwphil413@earthlink.net;
www.rwcustomknives.com
*Folders, straight knives etc.*

**WILD WOODS**
Jim Fray
PO Box 104
Monclova, OH 43542
419-866-0435

**WILSON, R.W.**
113 Kent Way
Weirton, WV 26062

**WOOD CARVERS SUPPLY, INC.**
PO Box 7500-K
Englewood, FL 34295-7500
800-284-6229; 941-698-0329
www.woocarverssupply.com
*Over 2,000 unique wood carving tools*

**WOOD STABILIZING SPECIALISTS INT'L.**
Mike & Cara Ludemann
2940 Fayette Ave
Ionia, IA 50645
641-435-4746; 641-435-4759
Mike@Stabilizedwood.com;
www.stabilizedwood.com
*Processor of acrylic impregnated materials*

**ZOWADA CUSTOM KNIVES**
Tim Zowada
4509 E. Bear River Rd
Boyne Falls, MI 49713
231-348-5416
knifeguy@nmo.net; www.tzknives.com
*Damascus, pocket knives, swords, Lower case gothic tz logo*

# mail order sales

**A. G. RUSSELL KNIVES INC**
1920 North 26th St
Lowell, AR 72745-8489
479-631-0130; 479-631-8493
ag@agrussell.com; www.agrussell.com
*The oldest knife mail-order company, highest quality. Free catalog available. In these catalogs you will find the newest and the best. If you like knives, this catalog is a must*

**ARIZONA CUSTOM KNIVES**
Julie Hyman
5099 Medoras Ave
Saint Augustine, FL 32080
904-460-9579
sharptalk@bellsouth.net;
www.arizonacustomknives.com
*Color catalog $5 U.S. / $7 Foreign*

**ARTISAN KNIVES**
Ty Young
575 Targhee Twn Rd
Alta, WY 83414
304-353-8111
tyfoto@yahoo.com; www.artisanknives.com
*Feature master artisan knives and makers in a unique "coffee table book" style format*

**ATLANTA CUTLERY CORP.**
2147 Gees Mill Rd
Conyers, GA 30012
800-883-0300
www.atlantacutlery.com
*Special knives & cutting tools*

**ATLANTIC BLADESMITHS/PETER STEBBINS**
50 Mill Rd
Littleton, MA 01460
978-952-6448
j.galt1100@verizon.ent;
www.atlanticbladesmiths.com
*Sell, trade, buy; carefully selected handcrafted, benchmade and factory knives*

**BALLARD CUTLERY**
1495 Brummel Ave.
Elk Grove Village, IL 60007

**BECK'S CUTLERY SPECIALTIES**
Macgregor Village #109
107 Edinburgh S
Cary, NC 27511
919-460-0203
www.beckscutlery.com
*Knives*

**BLADEGALLERY.COM**
107 Central Way
Kirkland WA 98033
877-56-blade
www.bladegallery.com
*Bladegallery.com specializes in hand-made one-of-a-kind knives from around the world. We have an emphasis on forged knives and high-end gentlemen's folders*

**BLUE RIDGE KNIVES**
166 Adwolfe Rd
Marion, VA 24354-6664
276-783-6143; 276-783-9298
www.blueridgeknives.com
*Wholesale distributor of knives*

**BOB NEAL CUSTOM KNIVES**
PO Box 20923
Atlanta, GA 30320
770-914-7794; 770-914-7796
bob@bobnealcustomknives.com;
www.bobnealcustomknives.com
*Exclusive limited edition custom knives-sets & single*

**BOB'S TRADING POST**
308 N Main St
Hutchinson, KS 67501
620-669-9441
bobstradingpost@cox.net
*Tad custom knives with reichert custom sheaths one at a time, one of a kind*

**BOONE TRADING CO., INC.**
PO Box 669
Brinnon, WA 98320
800-423-1945
www.boonetrading.com
*Ivory scrimshaw horns*

**CARMEL CUTLERY**
Dolores & 6th; PO Box 1346
Carmel, CA 93921
831-624-6699; 831-624-6780
ccutlery@ix.netcom.com;
www.carmelcutlery.com
*Quality custom and a variety of production pocket knives, swords; kitchen cutlery; personal grooming items*

**CLASSIC CUTLERY**
5 Logan Rd
Nashua, NH 03063
603-881-3776
yesdragonfly@earthlink.net
*Custom knives, gemstones, high quality factory knives*

**CREATIVE SALES & MFG.**
Box 111
Whitefish, MT 59937
406-849-5174; 406-849-5130
www.creativesales.com

**CUTLERY SHOPPE**
3956 E Vantage Pointe Ln
Meridian, ID 83642
800-231-1272; 208-884-4433
order@cutleryshoppe.com;
www.cutleryshoppe.com
*Discount pricing on top quality brands*

**CUTTING EDGE, THE**
1920 North 26th St
Lowell, AR 72745-8489
479-631-0055; 479-636-4618
ce_cuttingedge.com; www.cuttingedge.com
*After-market knives since 1968. We offer about 1,000 individual knives for sale each month. Subscription by first class mail, in U.S. $20 per year, Canada or Mexico by air mail, $25 per year. All overseas by air mail, $40 per year. The oldest and the most experienced in the business of buying and selling knives. We buy collections of any size, take knives on consignment. Every month there are 4-8 pages in color featuring the work of top makers*

**DENTON, J.W.**
102 N. Main St, Box 429
Hiawassee, GA 30546
706-896-2292; 706-896-1212
jwdenton@alltel.net
*Loveless knives*

**DUNN KNIVES INC.**
PO Box 204
Rossville, KS 66533
785-584-6856; 785-584-6856

**EPICUREAN EDGE, THE**
107 Central Way
Kirkland, WA 98033
425-889-5980
www.epicureanedge.com
*The Epicurean Edge specializes in high-end chef's knives from around the world. We have an empasis on handmade and hard to find knives*

**FAZALARE, ROY**
PO Box 1335
Agoura Hills, CA 91376
818-879-6161 after 7pm
ourfaz@aol.com
*Handmade multiblades; older case; Fight'n Rooster; Bulldog brand & Cripple Creek*

**FROST CUTLERY CO.**
PO Box 22636
Chattanooga, TN 37422

**GENUINE ISSUE, INC.**
949 Middle Country Rd.
Selden, NY 11784
516-696-3802; 516-696-3803
g.I._cutlery.com
*All knives*

**GEORGE TICHBOURNE CUSTOM KNIVES**
7035 Maxwell Rd #5
Mississauga Ontario L5S 1R5
CANADA
905-670-0200
sales@tichbourneknives.com;
www.tichbourneknives.com
*Canadian custom knifemaker has full retail knife store*

**GODWIN, INC. G. GEDNEY**
2139 Welsh Valley Rd
Valley Forge, PA 19481
610-783-0670; 610-783-6083
www.gggodwin.com
*18th century reproductions*

**GUILD KNIVES**
320 Paani Place 1A
Paia, HI 96779
808-877-3109; 808-877-3524
donguild1@aol.com; www.guildkives.com
*Purveyor of custom art knives*

**HAWTHORN GALLERIES, INC.**
214 E Walnut St
Springfield, MO 65806
417-866-6688; 417-866-6693
hginc@sbcglobal.net
*Heritage Antique Knives*

**BRUCE VOYLES**
PO Box 22171
Chattanooga, TN 37422
423-238-6753; 423-238-6711
bruce@jbrucevoyles.com;
www.jbrucevoyles.com
*Knives, knife auctions*

**HOUSE OF TOOLS LTD.**
#136, 8228 Macleod Tr. SE
Calgary, Alberta, Canada
T2H 2B8

**HUNTER SERVICES**
Fred Hunter
PO Box 14241
Parkville, MD 64152

**JENCO SALES, INC.**
PO Box 1000
Manchaca, TX 78652
800-531-5301; 800-266-2373
jencosales@sbcglobal.net
*Wholesale only*

**KELLAM KNIVES CO.**
902 S Dixie Hwy
Lantana, FL 33462
561-588-3185; 800-390-6918; 561-588-3186
info@kellamknives.com; www.kellamknives.com
*Largest selection of Finnish knives; own line of folders and fixed blades*

**KNIFEART.COM**
13301 Pompano Dr
Little Rock AR 72211
501-221-1010; 501-221-2695
www.knifeart.com
*Large internet seller of custom knives & upscale production knives*

**KNIFE IMPORTERS, INC.**
PO Box 1000
Manchaca, TX 78652

**KNIFEMASTERS CUSTOM KNIVES/J&S FEDER**
PO Box 208
Westport, CT 06881
(203) 226-5211; (203) 226-5312
*Investment grade custom knives*

**KNIVES PLUS**
2467 I 40 West
Amarillo, TX 79109
800-687-6202
*Retail cutlery and cutlery accessories since 1987*

**KRIS CUTLERY**
PO Box 133 KN
Pinole, CA 94564
510-223-8968
kriscutlery@attbl.com; www.kriscutlery.com
*Japanese, medieval, Chinese & Philippine*

**CUSTOM KNIFE CONSIGNMENT**
PO Box 20923
Atlanta, GA 30320
770-914-7794; 770-914-7796
bob@customknifeconsignment.com;
www.customknifeconsignment.com
*We sell your knives*

**LES COUTEAUX CHOISSIS DE ROBERTS**
Ron Roberts
PO Box 273
Mifflin, PA 17058

**LONE STAR WHOLESALE**
PO Box 587
Amarillo, TX 79105
806-356-9540; 806-359-1603
*Wholesale only; major brands and accessories*

**MATTHEWS CUTLERY**
4401 Sentry Dr., Suite K
Tucker, GA 30084

**MOORE CUTLERY**
PO Box 633
Lockport, IL 60441-0633
708-301-4201; 708-301-4222
gary@knives.cx; www.knives.cx
*Owned & operated by Gary Moore since 1991. (A full-time dealer) Purveyor of high quality custom & production knives*

**MORTY THE KNIFE MAN, INC.**
4 Manorhaven Blvd
Port Washington, NY 11050

**MUSEUM REPLICAS LTD.**
2143 Gees Mill Rd
Conyers, GA 30207
800-883-8838
www.museumreplicas.com
*Historically accurate and battle ready swords & daggers*

**NORDIC KNIVES**
1634 CZ Copenhagen Dr.
Solvang, CA 93463
805-688-3612
info@nordicknives.com; www.nordicknives.com
*Custom and Randall knives*

**OAKES WINSTON**
431 Deauville Dr
Dayton, OH 45429
937-434-3112
*Dealer in Bose JessHorn, Michael Walker & other quality knives. Some tactical folders. $100-$7,000*

**PARKER'S KNIFE COLLECTOR SERVICE**
6715 Heritage Business Court
Chattanooga, TN 37422
423-892-0448; 423-892-0448
bbknife@bellsouth.net

**PEN AND THE SWORD LTD., THE**
Po Box 290741
Brooklyn, NY 11229 0741
(718) 382-4847; (718) 376-5745
info@pensword.com
*Custom folding knives, engraving, scrimshaw, Case knives, English fruit knives, antique pocket knives*

**PLAZA CUTLERY, INC.**
3333 S. Bristol St., Suite 2060
South Coast Plaza
Costa Mesa, CA 92626
714-549-3932
dan@plazacutlery.com; www.plazacutlery.com
*Largest selection of knives on the west coast. Custom makers from beginners to the best. All customs, William Henry, Strider, Reeves, Randalls & others available online by phone*

**ROBERTSON'S CUSTOM CUTLERY**
PO Box 1367
Evans, GA 30809-1367
706-650-0252; 706-860-1623
customknives@comcast.net;
www.robertsoncustomcutlery.com
*World class custom knives, Vanguard knives - Limited exclusive design*

**ROBINSON, ROBERT W.**
1569 N. Finley Pt
Polson, MT 59860

**SHADOW JAY & KAREN**
9719 N Hayden Rd
Scottsdale, AZ 85258
480-947-2136; 480-481-2977
jaykar@cox.net; www.jaykar.com
*Diamonds imported direct from Belgium*

**SMOKY MOUNTAIN KNIFE WORKS**
2320 Winfield Dunn Pkwy
Sevierville, TN 37876
865-453-5871; 800-251-9306
info@smkw.com; www.eknifeworks.com
*The world's largest knife showplace, catalog and website*

**STIDHAM'S KNIVES/DBA MEADOWS' EDGE KNIFE SHOP**
PO Box 160
Meadows of Dan, VA 24120
276-952-2500; 276-952-6245
rstidham@gate.net;
www.randallknifesociety.com
*Randall, Loveless, Scagel, moran, antique pocket knives*

**STODDARD'S, INC.**
Copley Place 25
100 Huntington Ave
Boston, MA 02116
617-536-8688; 617-536-8689
*Cutlery (kitchen, pocket knives, Randall-made knives, custom knives, scissors & manicure tools) binoculars, Iwo vision aids, personal care items (hair brushes, manicure sets mirrors)*

# knife services

## appraisers

Levine, Bernard, P.O. Box 2404, Eugene, OR, 97402, 541-484-0294, brlevine@ix.netcom.com

Russell, A.G., Knives Inc, 1920 North 26th St, Lowell, AR, 72745-8489, 479-631-0055, 479-636-4618, ag@agrussell.com, www.agrussell.com

Vallini, Massimo, Via G. Bruno 7, 20154 Milano, ITALY, 02-33614751, massimo_vallini@yahoo.it, Knife expert

## custom grinders

Beauchamp, Gaetan, 125 de la Riviere, Stoneham, PQ, G0A 4P0, CANADA, 418-848-1914, (418) 848-6859, knives@gbeauchamp.ca, www.beauchamp.cjb.net

McGowan Manufacturing Company, 4854 N Shamrock Pl #100, Tucson, AZ, 85705, 800-342-4810, 520-219-0884, info@mcgowanmfg.com, www.mcgowanmfg.com, Knife sharpeners, hunting axes

McLuin, Tom, 36 Fourth St., Dracut, MA, 01826, 978-957-4899, tmcluin@attbi.com, www.people.ne.mediaone.net/tmcluin

Peele, Bryan, The Elk Rack, 215 Ferry St. P.O. Box 1363, Thompson Falls, MT, 59873

Schlott, Harald, Zingster Str. 26, 13051 Berlin, GERMANY, 049 030 9293346, harald.schlott@T-online.de, Custom grinder, custom handle artisan, display case/box maker, etcher, scrimshander

Wilson, R.W., P.O. Box 2012, Weirton, WV, 26062

## custom handles

Cooper, Jim, 1221 Cook St, Ramona, CA, 92065-3214, 760-789-1097, (760) 788-7992, jamcooper@aol.com

Burrows, Chuck, dba Wild Rose Trading Co, 289 Laposta Canyon Rd, Durango, CO, 81303, 970-259-8396, chuck@wrtcleather.com, www.wrtcleather.com

Fields, Donald, 790 Tamerlane St, Deltona, FL, 32725, 386-532-9070, donaldfields@aol.com, Selling ancient ivories; mammoth & fossil walrus

Grussenmeyer, Paul G., 310 Kresson Rd, Cherry Hill, NJ, 08034, 856-428-1088, 856-428-8997, pgrussentne@comcast.net, www.pgcarvings.com

Holland, Dennis K., 4908-17th Pl., Lubbock, TX, 79416

Imboden II, Howard L., hi II Originals, 620 Deauville Dr., Dayton, OH, 45429

Kelso, Jim, 577 Collar Hill Rd, Worcester, VT, 05682, 802-229-4254, (802) 223-0595

Knack, Gary, 309 Wightman, Ashland, OR, 97520

Marlatt, David, 67622 Oldham Rd., Cambridge, OH, 43725, 740-432-7549

Mead, Dennis, 2250 E. Mercury St., Inverness, FL, 34453-0514

Myers, Ron, 6202 Marglenn Ave., Baltimore, MD, 21206, 410-866-6914

Saggio, Joe, 1450 Broadview Ave. #12, Columbus, OH, 43212, jvsag@webtv.net, www.j.v.saggio@worldnet.att.net, Handle Carver

Schlott, Harald, Zingster Str. 26, 13051 Berlin, GERMANY, 049 030 9293346, harald.schlott@T-online.de, Custom grinder, custom handle artisan, display case/box maker, etcher, scrimshander

Snell, Barry A., 4801 96th St. N., St. Petersburg, FL, 33708-3740

Vallotton, A., 621 Fawn Ridge Dr., Oakland, OR, 97462

Watson, Silvia, 350 Jennifer Lane, Driftwood, TX, 78619

Wilderness Forge, 315 North 100 East, Kanab, UT, 84741, 435-644-3674, bhatting@xpressweb.com

Williams, Gary, (GARBO), PO Box 210, Glendale, KY, 42740-2010

## display cases and boxes

Bill's Custom Cases, P O Box 603, Montague, CA, 96064, 530-459-5968, billscustomcases@earthlink.net

Brooker, Dennis, Rt. 1, Box 12A, Derby, IA, 50068

Chas Clements' Custom Leathercraft, Chas, 1741 Dallas St., Aurora, CO, 80010-2018, 303-364-0403, GRYPHONS@HOME.NET, Display case/box maker, Leatherworker, Knife appraiser

Freund, Steve, Tomway LLC, 1646 Tichenor Court, Atlanta, GA, 30338, 770-393-8349, steve@tomway.com, www.tomway.com

Gimbert, Nelson, P.O. Box 787, Clemmons, NC, 27012

McLean, Lawrence, 12344 Meritage Ct, Rancho Cucamonga, CA, 91739, 714-848-5779, lmclean@charter.net

Miller, Michael K., M&M Kustom Krafts, 28510 Santiam Highway, Sweet Home, OR, 97386

Miller, Robert, P.O. Box 2722, Ormond Beach, FL, 32176

Retichek, Joseph L., W9377 Co. TK. D, Beaver Dam, WI, 53916

Robbins, Wayne, 11520 Inverway, Belvidere, IL, 61008

S&D Enterprises, 20 East Seventh St, Manchester, OH, 45144, 937-549-2602, 937-549-2602, sales@s-denterprises.com, www.s-denterprises.com, Display case/box maker. Manufacturer of aluminum display, chipboard type displays, wood displays. Silk screening or acid etching for logos on product.

Schlott, Harald, Zingster Str. 26, 13051 Berlin, GERMANY, 049 030 9293346, harald.schlott@T-online.de, Custom grinder, custom handle artisan, display case/box maker, etcher, scrimshander

## engravers

Adlam, Tim, 1705 Witzel Ave., Oshkosh, WI, 54902, 920-235-4589, www.adlamngraving.com

Alfano, Sam, 36180 Henry Gaines Rd., Pearl River, LA, 70452

Allard, Gary, 2395 Battlefield Rd., Fishers Hill, VA, 22626

Alpen, Ralph, 7 Bentley Rd., West Grove, PA, 19390, 610-869-7141

Baron, David, Baron Technology Inc., 62 Spring Hill Rd., Trumbull, CT, 06611, 203-452-0515, bti@baronengraving.com, www.baronengraving.com, Polishing, plating, inlays, artwork

Bates, Billy, 2302 Winthrop Dr. SW, Decatur, AL, 35603, bbrn@aol.com, www.angelfire.com/al/billybates

Bettenhausen, Merle L., 17358 Ottawa, Tinley Park, IL, 60477
Blair, Jim, PO Box 64, 59 Mesa Verde, Glenrock, WY, 82637, 307-436-8115, jblairengrav@msn.com
Bonshire, Benita, 1121 Burlington, Muncie, IN, 47302
Boster, A.D., 3000 Clarks Bridge Rd Lot 42, Gainesville, GA, 30501, 770-532-0958
Brooker, Dennis B., Rt. 1 Box 12A, Derby, IA, 50068
Churchill, Winston G., RFD Box 29B, Proctorsville, VT, 05153
Collins, Michael, Rt. 3075, Batesville Rd., Woodstock, GA, 30188
Cupp, Alana, PO Box 207, Annabella, UT, 84711
Dashwood, Jim, 255 Barkham Rd., Wokingham, Berkshire RG11 4BY, ENGLAND
Dean, Bruce, 13 Tressider Ave., Haberfield, N.S.W. 2045, Sydney, AUSTRALIA, 02 97977608
DeLorge, Ed, 6734 W Main St, Houma, LA, 70360, 504-223-0206
Dickson, John W., PO Box 49914, Sarasota, FL, 34230
Dolbare, Elizabeth, PO Box 502, Dubois, WY, 82513-0502
Downing, Jim, PO Box 4224, Springfield, MO, 65808, 417-865-5953, www.thegunengraver.com, Scrimshander
Duarte, Carlos, 108 Church St., Rossville, CA, 95678
Dubben, Michael, 414 S. Fares Ave., Evansville, IN, 47714
Dubber, Michael W., 8205 Heather Pl, Evansville, IN, 47710-4919
Eklund, Maihkel, Föne 1111, S-82041 Färila, SWEDEN, www.art-knives.com
Eldridge, Allan, 1424 Kansas Lane, Gallatin, TN, 37066
Ellis, Willy B, Willy B's Customs by William B Ellis, 4941 Cardinal Trail, Palm Harbor, FL, 34683, 727-942-6420, www.willyb.com
Engel, Terry (Flowers), PO Box 96, Midland, OR, 97634
Flannery Engraving Co., Jeff, 11034 Riddles Run Rd., Union, KY, 41091, engraving@fuse.net, http://home.fuse.net/engraving/
Foster, Norvell, Foster Enterprises, PO Box 200343, San Antonio, TX, 78220
Fountain Products, 492 Prospect Ave., West Springfield, MA, 01089
Gipe, Sandi, Rt. 2, Box 1090A, Kendrick, ID, 83537
Glimm, Jerome C., 19 S. Maryland, Conrad, MT, 59425
Gournet, Geoffroy, 820 Paxinosa Ave., Easton, PA, 18042, 610-559-0710, www.geoffroygournet.com
Harrington, Fred A., Winter: 3725 Citrus, Summer: 2107 W Frances Rd Mt Morris MI 48458-8215, St. James City, FL, 33956, Winter: 239-283-0721 Summer: 810-686-3008
Henderson, Fred D., 569 Santa Barbara Dr., Forest Park, GA, 30297, 770-968-4866
Hendricks, Frank, 396 Bluff Trail, Dripping Springs, TX, 78620, 512-858-7828
Holder, Pat, 7148 W. Country Gables Dr., Peoria, AZ, 85381
Hudson, Tommy, 1181 E 22nd St. Suite #18, Marysville, CA, 95901, 530-681-6531, twhunson@attbi.com, www.picturetrail.com/tommyhudson
Ingle, Ralph W., 151 Callan Dr., Rossville, GA, 30741, 706-858-0641, riengraver@aol.com, Photographer
Johns, Bill, 1716 8th St, Cody, WY, 82414, 307-587-5090
Kelly, Lance, 1723 Willow Oak Dr., Edgewater, FL, 32132
Kelso, Jim, 577 Coller Hill Rd, Worcester, VT, 05682
Koevenig, Eugene and Eve, Koevenig's Engraving Service, Rabbit Gulch, Box 55, Hill City, SD, 57745-0055
Kostelnik, Joe and Patty, RD #4, Box 323, Greensburg, PA, 15601
Kudlas, John M., 55280 Silverwolf Dr, Barnes, WI, 54873, 715-795-2031, jkudlas@cheqnet.net, Engraver, scrimshander
Limings Jr., Harry, 959 County Rd. 170, Marengo, OH, 43334-9625
Lindsay, Steve, 3714 West Cedar Hills Drive, Kearney, NE, 68847
Lyttle, Brian, Box 5697, High River AB CANADA, T1V 1M7
Lytton, Simon M., 19 Pinewood Gardens, Hemel Hempstead, Herts. HP1 1TN, ENGLAND
Mason, Joe, 146 Value Rd, Brandon, MS, 39042, 601-824-9867, www.joemasonengraving.com
McCombs, Leo, 1862 White Cemetery Rd., Patriot, OH, 45658
McDonald, Dennis, 8359 Brady St., Peosta, IA, 52068
McKenzie, Lynton, 6940 N Alvernon Way, Tucson, AZ, 85718
McLean, Lawrence, 12344 Meritage Ct, Rancho Cucamonga, CA, 91739, 714-848-5779, lmclean@charter.net
Meyer, Chris, 39 Bergen Ave., Wantage, NJ, 07461, 973-875-6299
Minnick, Joyce, 144 N. 7th St., Middletown, IN, 47356
Morgan, Tandie, P.O. Box 693, 30700 Hwy. 97, Nucla, CO, 81424
Morton, David A., 1110 W. 21st St., Lorain, OH, 44052
Moulton, Dusty, 135 Hillview Ln, Loudon, TN, 37774, 865-408-9779
Muller, Jody & Pat, PO Box 35, Pittsburg, MO, 65724, 417-852-4306/417-752-3260, mullerforge@hotmail.com, www.mullerforge.com
Nelida, Toniutti, via G. Pasconi 29/c, Maniago 33085 (PN), ITALY
Nott, Ron, Box 281, Summerdale, PA, 17093
Parsons, Michael R., McKee Knives, 7042 McFarland Rd, Indianapolis, IN, 46227, 317-784-7943
Patterson, W.H., P.O. Drawer DK, College Station, TX, 77841
Peri, Valerio, Via Meucci 12, Gardone V.T. 25063, ITALY
Pilkington Jr., Scott, P.O. Box 97, Monteagle, TN, 37356, 931-924-3400, scott@pilkguns.com, www.pilkguns.com
Poag, James, RR1, Box 212A, Grayville, IL, 62844
Potts, Wayne, 1580 Meade St Apt A, Denver, CO, 80204
Rabeno, Martin, Spook Hollow Trading Co, 530 Eagle Pass, Durango, CO, 81301
Raftis, Andrew, 2743 N. Sheffield, Chicago, IL, 60614
Roberts, J.J., 7808 Lake Dr., Manassas, VA, 20111, 703-330-0448, jjrengraver@aol.com, www.angelfire.com/va2/engraver
Robidoux, Roland J., DMR Fine Engraving, 25 N. Federal Hwy. Studio 5, Dania, FL, 33004
Rosser, Bob, Hand Engraving, 2809 Crescent Ave Ste 20, Homewood, AL, 35209-2526, www.hand-engravers.com
Rudolph, Gil, 20922 Oak Pass Ave, Tehachapi, CA, 93561, 661-822-4949, www.gtraks@csurfers.net
Rundell, Joe, 6198 W. Frances Rd., Clio, MI, 48420
Schickl, L., Ottingweg 497, A-5580 Tamsweg, AUSTRIA, 0043 6474 8583, Scrimshander
Schlott, Harald, Zingster Str. 26, 13051 Berlin, GERMANY, 049 030 9293346, 049 030 9293346, harald.schlott@T-online.de, www.gravur-kunst-atelier.de.vu, Custom grinder, custom handle artisan, display case/box maker, etcher, scrimshander
Schönert, Elke, 18 Lansdowne Pl., Central, Port Elizabeth, SOUTH AFRICA
Shaw, Bruce, P.O. Box 545, Pacific Grove, CA, 93950, 831-646-1937, 831-644-0941
Shostle, Ben, 1121 Burlington, Muncie, IN, 47302

Sinclair, W.P., The Roost Mill Lade, Blyth Bridge, Peeblesshire EH46 7HY, SCOTLAND, 44 0 1721 752787, songdog@clara.net

Smith, Ron, 5869 Straley, Ft. Worth, TX, 76114

Smitty's Engraving, 21320 Pioneer Circle, Hurrah, OK, 73045, 405-454-6968, smittys.engraving@prodigy.net, www.smittys-engraving.us

Spode, Peter, Tresaith Newland, Malvern, Worcestershire WR13 5AY, ENGLAND

Swartley, Robert D., 2800 Pine St., Napa, CA, 94558

Takeuchi, Shigetoshi, 21-14-1-Chome kamimuneoka Shiki shi, 353 Saitama, JAPAN

Theis, Terry, 21452 FM 2093, Harper, TX, 78631, 830-864-4438

Valade, Robert B., 931 3rd Ave., Seaside, OR, 97138, 503-738-7672, (503) 738-7672

Waldrop, Mark, 14562 SE 1st Ave. Rd., Summerfield, FL, 34491

Warenski, Julie, 590 East 500 N., Richfield, UT, 84701, 435-896-5319, julie@warenskiknives.com, www.warenskiknives.com

Warren, Kenneth W., P.O. Box 2842, Wenatchee, WA, 98807-2842, 509-663-6123, (509) 663-6123

Whitehead, James D., 204 Cappucino Way, Sacramento, CA, 95838

Whitmore, Jerry, 1740 Churchill Dr., Oakland, OR, 97462

Winn, Travis A., 558 E. 3065 S., Salt Lake City, UT, 84106

Wood, Mel, P.O. Box 1255, Sierra Vista, AZ, 85636

Zietz, Dennis, 5906 40th Ave., Kenosha, WI, 53144

## etchers

Baron Technology Inc., David Baron, 62 Spring Hill Rd., Trumbull, CT, 06611

Fountain Products, 492 Prospect Ave., West Springfield, MA, 01089

Hayes, Dolores, P.O. Box 41405, Los Angeles, CA, 90041

Holland, Dennis, 4908 17th Pl., Lubbock, TX, 79416

Kelso, Jim, 577 Collar Hill Rd, Worcester, VT, 05682

Larstein, Francine, FRANCINE ETCHINGS & ETCHED KNIVES, 368 White Rd, Watsonville, CA, 95076, 800-557-1525/831-426-6046, 831-684-1949, francine@francinetchings.com, www.francineetchings.com

Lefaucheux, Jean-Victor, Saint-Denis-Le-Ferment, 27140 Gisors, FRANCE

Mead, Faustina L., 2550 E. Mercury St., Inverness, FL, 34453-0514, 352-344-4751, scrimsha@infionline.net, www.scrimshaw-by-faustina.com

Myers, Ron, 6202 Marglenn Ave., Baltimore, MD, 21206, (acid) etcher

Schlott, Harald, Zingster Str. 26, 13051 Berlin, GERMANY, 049 030 9293346, harald.schlott@T-online.de, Custom grinder, custom handle artisan, display case/box maker, etcher, scrimshander

Vallotton, A., Northwest Knife Supply, 621 Fawn Ridge Dr., Oakland, OR, 97462

Watson, Silvia, 350 Jennifer Lane, Driftwood, TX, 78619

## heat treaters

Bay State Metal Treating Co., 6 Jefferson Ave., Woburn, MA, 01801

Bos Heat Treating, Paul, Shop: 1900 Weld Blvd., El Cajon, CA, 92020, 619-562-2370 / 619-445-4740 Home, PaulBos@BuckKnives.com

Holt, B.R., 1238 Birchwood Drive, Sunnyvale, CA, 94089

Kazou, Okaysu, 12-2 1 Chome Higashi, Ueno, Taito-Ku, Tokyo, JAPAN, 81-33834-2323, 81-33831-3012

Metal Treating Bodycote Inc., 710 Burns St., Cincinnati, OH, 45204

O&W Heat Treat Inc., One Bidwell Rd., South Windsor, CT, 06074, 860-528-9239, (860) 291-9939, owht1@aol.com

Progressive Heat Treating Co., 2802 Charles City Rd, Richmond, VA, 23231, 804-545-0010, 804-545-0012

Texas Heat Treating Inc., 303 Texas Ave., Round Rock, TX, 78664

Texas Knifemakers Supply, 10649 Haddington, Suite 180, Houston, TX, 77043

Tinker Shop, The, 1120 Helen, Deer Park, TX, 77536

Valley Metal Treating Inc., 355 S. East End Ave., Pomona, CA, 91766

Wilderness Forge, 315 North 100 East, Kanab, UT, 84741, 435-644-3674, bhatting@xpressweb.com

Wilson, R.W., P.O. Box 2012, Weirton, WV, 26062

## leather workers

Abramson, David, 116 Baker Ave, Wharton, NJ, 07885, lifter4him1@aol.com, www.liftersleather.com

Bruner, Rick, 7756 Aster Lane, Jenison, MI, 49428, 616-457-0403

Burrows, Chuck, dba Wild Rose Trading Co, 289 Laposta Canyon Rd, Durango, CO, 81303, 970-259-8396, chuck@wrtcleather.com

Clements' Custom Leathercraft, Chas, 1741 Dallas St., Aurora, CO, 80010-2018

Cooper, Harold, 136 Winding Way, Frankfort, KY, 40601

Cooper, Jim, 1221 Cook St, Ramona, CA, 92065-3214, 760-789-1097, 760-788-7992, jamcooper@aol.com

Cow Catcher Leatherworks, 3006 Industrial Dr, Raleigh, NC, 27609

Cubic, George, GC Custom Leather Co., 10561 E. Deerfield Pl., Tucson, AZ, 85749, 520-760-0695, gcubic@aol.com

Dawkins, Dudley, 221 N. Broadmoor Ave, Topeka, KS, 66606-1254, 785-235-3871, dawkind@sbcglobal.net, ABS member/knifemaker forges straight knives

Evans, Scott V, Edge Works Mfg, 1171 Halltown Rd, Jacksonville, NC, 28546, 910-455-9834, (910) 346-5660, edgeworks@coastalnet.com, www.tacticalholsters.com

Genske, Jay, 283 Doty St, Fond du Lac, WI, 54935, 920-921-8019/Cell Phone 920-579-0144, jaygenske@hotmail.com, Custom Grinder, Custom Handle Artisan

Hawk, Ken, Rt. 1, Box 770, Ceres, VA, 24318-9630

Homyk, David N., 8047 Carriage Ln., Wichita Falls, TX, 76306

John's Custom Leather, John R. Stumpf, 523 S. Liberty St, Blairsville, PA, 15717, 724-459-6802, 724-459-5996

Kravitt, Chris, HC 31 Box 6484, Rt 200, Ellsworth, ME, 04605-9805, 207-584-3000, 207-584-3000, sheathmkr@aol.com, www.treestumpleather.com, Reference: Tree Stump Leather

Larson, Richard, 549 E. Hawkeye, Turlock, CA, 95380

Layton, Jim, 2710 Gilbert Avenue, Portsmouth, OH, 45662

Lee, Randy, P.O. Box 1873, 270 N 9th West, St. Johns, AZ, 85936, 928-337-2594, 928-337-5002, randylee@randyleeknives.com, info@randyleeknives.com, Custom knifemaker

Long, Paul, 108 Briarwood Ln W, Kerrville, TX, 78028, 830-367-5536, kgebauer@classicnet.net

Mason, Arne, 258 Wimer St., Ashland, OR, 97520, 541-482-2260, (541) 482-7785, www.arnemason.com

McGowan, Liz, 12629 Howard Lodge Dr., Winter Add-2023 Robin Ct Sebring FL 33870, Sykesville, MD, 21784, 410-489-4323

Metheny, H.A. "Whitey", 7750 Waterford Dr., Spotsylvania, VA, 22553, 540-582-3228 Cell 540-542-1440, 540-582-3095, nametheny@aol.com, www.methenyknives.com

Miller, Michael K., 28510 Santiam Highway, Sweet Home, OR, 97386

Mobley, Martha, 240 Alapaha River Road, Chula, GA, 31733

Morrissey, Martin, 4578 Stephens Rd., Blairsville, GA, 30512

Niedenthal, John Andre, Beadwork & Buckskin, Studio 3955 NW 103 Dr., Coral Springs, FL, 33065-1551, 954-345-0447, a_niedenthal@hotmail.com

Neilson, Tess, RR2 Box 16, Wyalusing, PA, 18853, 570-746-4944, www.mountainhollow.net, Doing business as Neilson's Mountain Hollow

Parsons, Michael R., McKee Knives, 7042 McFarland Rd, Indianapolis, IN, 46227, 317-784-7943

Poag, James H., RR #1 Box 212A, Grayville, IL, 62844

Red's Custom Leather, Ed Todd, 9 Woodlawn Rd., Putnam Valley, NY, 10579, 845-528-3783

Rowe, Kenny, 3219 Hwy 29 South, Hope, AR, 71801, 870-777-8216, 870-777-0935, rowesleather@yahoo.com, www.knifeart.com or www.theedgeequipment.com

Schrap, Robert G., 7024 W. Wells St., Wauwatosa, WI, 53213-3717, 414-771-6472, (414) 479-9765, knifesheaths@aol.com, www.customsheaths.com

Strahin, Robert, 401 Center St., Elkins, WV, 26241, *Custom Knife Sheaths

Tierney, Mike, 447 Rivercrest Dr., Woodstock ON CANADA, N4S 5W5

Turner, Kevin, 17 Hunt Ave., Montrose, NY, 10548

Velasquez, Gil, 7120 Madera Dr., Goleta, CA, 93117

Walker, John, 17 Laber Circle, Little Rock, AR, 72210, 501-455-0239, john.walker@afbic.com

Watson, Bill, #1 Presidio, Wimberly, TX, 78676

Whinnery, Walt, 1947 Meadow Creek Dr., Louisville, KY, 40218

Williams, Sherman A., 1709 Wallace St., Simi Valley, CA, 93065

## miscellaneous

Hendryx Design, Scott, 5997 Smokey Way, Boise, ID, 83714, 208-377-8044, www.shdsheaths@msn.com

Kydex Sheath Maker

Robertson, Kathy, Impress by Design, PO Box 1367, Evans, GA, 30809-1367, 706-650-0982, (706) 860-1623, impressbydesign@comcast.net, Advertising/graphic designer

Strahin, Robert, 401 Center St., Elkins, WV, 26241, 304-636-0128, rstrahin@copper.net, *Custom Knife Sheaths

## photographers

Alfano, Sam, 36180 Henery Gaines Rd., Pearl River, LA, 70452

Allen, John, Studio One, 3823 Pleasant Valley Blvd., Rockford, IL, 61114

Bilal, Mustafa, Turk's Head Productions, 908 NW 50th St., Seattle, WA, 98107-3634, 206-782-4164, (206) 783-5677, mustafa@turkshead.com, www.turkshead.com, Graphic design, marketing & advertising

Bogaerts, Jan, Regenweg 14, 5757 Pl., Liessel, HOLLAND

Box Photography, Doug, 1804 W Main St, Brenham, TX, 77833-3420

Brown, Tom, 6048 Grants Ferry Rd., Brandon, MS, 39042-8136

Butman, Steve, P.O. Box 5106, Abilene, TX, 79608

Calidonna, Greg, 205 Helmwood Dr., Elizabethtown, KY, 42701

Campbell, Jim, 7935 Ranch Rd., Port Richey, FL, 34668

Cooper, Jim, Sharpbycoop.com photography, 9 Mathew Court, Norwalk, CT, 06851, jcooper@sharpbycoop.com, www.sharpbycoop.com

Courtice, Bill, P.O. Box 1776, Duarte, CA, 91010-4776

Crosby, Doug, RFD 1, Box 1111, Stockton Springs, ME, 04981

Danko, Michael, 3030 Jane Street, Pittsburgh, PA, 15203

Davis, Marshall B., P.O. Box 3048, Austin, TX, 78764

Earley, Don, 1241 Ft. Bragg Rd., Fayetteville, NC, 28305

Ehrlich, Linn M., 1850 N Clark St #1008, Chicago, IL, 60614, 312-209-2107

Etzler, John, 11200 N. Island Rd., Grafton, OH, 44044

Fahrner, Dave, 1623 Arnold St., Pittsburgh, PA, 15205

Faul, Jan W., 903 Girard St. NE, Rr. Washington, DC, 20017

Fedorak, Allan, 28 W. Nicola St., Amloops BC CANADA, V2C 1J6

Forster, Jenny, 534 Nantucket Way, Island Lake, IL, 60042, www.thesilkca.msn.com

Fox, Daniel, Lumina Studios, 6773 Industrial Parkway, Cleveland, OH, 44070, 440-734-2118, (440) 734-3542, lumina@en.com

Freiberg, Charley, PO Box 42, Elkins, NH, 03233, 603-526-2767, charleyfreiberg@tos.net

Gardner, Chuck, 116 Quincy Ave., Oak Ridge, TN, 37830

Gawryla, Don, 1105 Greenlawn Dr., Pittsburgh, PA, 15220

Goffe Photographic Associates, 3108 Monte Vista Blvd., NE, Albuquerque, NM, 87106

Graham, James, 7434 E Northwest Hwy, Dallas, TX, 75231, 214-341-5138, jamie@jamiephoto.com, www.jamiephoto.com, Product photographer

Graley, Gary W., RR2 Box 556, Gillett, PA, 16925

Griggs, Dennis, 118 Pleasant Pt Rd, Topsham, ME, 04086, 207-725-5689

Hanusin, John, Reames-Hanusin Studio, PO Box 931, Northbrook, IL, 60065 0931

Hardy, Scott, 639 Myrtle Ave., Placerville, CA, 95667

Hodge, Tom, 7175 S US Hwy 1 Lot 36, Titusville, FL, 32780-8172, 321-267-7989, egdoht@hotmail.com

Holter, Wayne V., 125 Lakin Ave., Boonsboro, MD, 21713, 301-416-2855, mackwayne@hotmail.com

Hopkins, David W, Hopkins Photography inc, 201 S Jefferson, Iola, KS, 66749, 620-365-7443, nhoppy@netks.net

Kerns, Bob, 18723 Birdseye Dr., Germantown, MD, 20874

LaFleur, Gordon, 111 Hirst, Box 1209, Parksville BC CANADA, V0R 270
Lear, Dale, 6544 Cora Mill Rd, Gallipolis, OH, 45631, 740-245-5482, dalelear@yahoo.com, Ebay Sales
LeBlanc, Paul, No. 3 Meadowbrook Cir., Melissa, TX, 75454
Lester, Dean, 2801 Junipero Ave Suite 212, Long Beach, CA, 90806-2140
Leviton, David A., A Studio on the Move, P.O. Box 2871, Silverdale, WA, 98383, 360-697-3452
Long, Gary W., 3556 Miller's Crossroad Rd., Hillsboro, TN, 37342
Long, Jerry, 402 E. Gladden Dr., Farmington, NM, 87401
Lum, Billy, 16307 Evening Star Ct., Crosby, TX, 77532
McCollum, Tom, P.O. Box 933, Lilburn, GA, 30226
Mitch Lum Website and Photography, 4616 25th Ave NE #563, Seattle, WA, 98105, mitch@mitchlum.com, www.mitchlum.com
Moake, Jim, 18 Council Ave., Aurora, IL, 60504
Moya Inc., 4212 S. Dixie Hwy., West Palm Beach, FL, 33405
Norman's Studio, 322 S. 2nd St., Vivian, LA, 71082
Owens, William T., Box 99, Williamsburg, WV, 24991
Palmer Studio, 2008 Airport Blvd., Mobile, AL, 36606
Payne, Robert G., P.O. Box 141471, Austin, TX, 78714
Peterson Photography, Kent, 230 Polk St., Eugene, OR, 97402, kdp@pond.net, www.pond.net/kdp
Pigott, John, 9095 Woodprint LN, Mason, OH, 45040
Point Seven, 810 Seneca St., Toledo, OH, 43608, 519-243-8880, www.pointsevenstudios.com
Rasmussen, Eric L., 1121 Eliason, Brigham City, UT, 84302
Rhoades, Cynthia J., Box 195, Clearmont, WY, 82835
Rice, Tim, PO Box 663, Whitefish, MT, 59937
Richardson, Kerry, 2520 Mimosa St., Santa Rosa, CA, 95405, 707-575-1875, kerry@sonic.net, www.sonic.net/~kerry
Ross, Bill, 28364 S. Western Ave. Suite 464, Rancho Palos Verdes, CA, 90275
Rubicam, Stephen, 14 Atlantic Ave., Boothbay Harbor, ME, 04538-1202
Rush, John D., 2313 Maysel, Bloomington, IL, 61701
Schreiber, Roger, 429 Boren Ave. N., Seattle, WA, 98109
Semmer, Charles, 7885 Cyd Dr., Denver, CO, 80221
Silver Images Photography, 2412 N Keystone, Flagstaff, AZ, 86004
Slobodian, Scott, 4101 River Ridge Dr., P.O. Box 1498, San Andreas, CA, 95249, 209-286-1980, (209) 286-1982, www.slobodianswords.com
Smith, Earl W., 5121 Southminster Rd., Columbus, OH, 43221
Smith, Randall, 1720 Oneco Ave., Winter Park, FL, 32789
Storm Photo, 334 Wall St., Kingston, NY, 12401
Surles, Mark, P.O. Box 147, Falcon, NC, 28342
Third Eye Photos, 140 E. Sixth Ave., Helena, MT, 59601
Thurber, David, P.O. Box 1006, Visalia, CA, 93279
Tighe, Brian, RR 1, Ridgeville ON CANADA, L0S 1M0, 905-892-2734, www.tigheknives.com
Towell, Steven L., 3720 N.W. 32nd Ave., Camas, WA, 98607, 360-834-9049, sltowell@netscape.net
Valley Photo, 2100 Arizona Ave., Yuma, AZ, 85364
Verno Studio, Jay, 3030 Jane Street, Pittsburgh, PA, 15203
Ward, Chuck, 1010 E North St, PO Box 2272, Benton, AR, 72018, 501-778-4329, chuckbop@aol.com
Weyer International, 2740 Nebraska Ave., Toledo, OH, 43607, 800-448-8424, (419) 534-2697, law-weyerinternational@msn.com, Books
Wise, Harriet, 242 Dill Ave., Frederick, MD, 21701
Worley, Holly, Worley Photography, 6360 W David Dr, Littleton, CO, 80128-5708, 303-257-8091, 720-981-2800, hsworley@aol.com, Products, Digital & Film

## scrimshanders

Adlam, Tim, 1705 Witzel Ave., Oshkosh, WI, 54902, 920-235-4589, www.adlamngraving.com
Alpen, Ralph, 7 Bentley Rd., West Grove, PA, 19390, 610-869-7141
Anderson, Terry Jack, 10076 Birnamwoods Way, Riverton, UT, 84065-9073
Bailey, Mary W., 3213 Jonesboro Dr., Nashville, TN, 37214, mbscrim@aol.com, www.members.aol.com/mbscrim/scrim.html
Baker, Duane, 2145 Alum Creek Dr., Cambridge Park Apt. #10, Columbus, OH, 43207
Barrows, Miles, 524 Parsons Ave., Chillicothe, OH, 45601
Brady, Sandra, P.O. Box 104, Monclova, OH, 43542, 419-866-0435, (419) 867-0656, sandyscrim@hotmail.com, www.knifeshows.com
Beauchamp, Gaetan, 125 de la Riviere, Stoneham, PQ, G0A 4P0, CANADA, 418-848-1914, (418) 848-6859, knives@gbeauchamp.ca, www.beauchamp.cjb.net
Bellet, Connie, PO Box 151, Palermo, ME, 04354 0151, 207-993-2327, phwhitehawk@gwl.net
Benade, Lynn, 2610 Buckhurst Dr, Beachwood, OH, 44122, 216-464-0777, llbnc17@aol.com
Bonshire, Benita, 1121 Burlington Dr., Muncie, IN, 47302
Boone Trading Co. Inc., P.O. Box 669, Brinnon, WA, 98320, 800-423-1945, ww.boonetrading.com
Bryan, Bob, 1120 Oak Hill Rd., Carthage, MO, 64836
Byrne, Mary Gregg, 1018 15th St., Bellingham, WA, 98225-6604
Cable, Jerry, 332 Main St., Mt. Pleasant, PA, 15666
Caudill, Lyle, 7626 Lyons Rd., Georgetown, OH, 45121
Cole, Gary, PO Box 668, Naalehu, HI, 96772, 808-929-9775, 808-929-7371, www.community.webshots.com/album/11836830uqyeejirsz
Collins, Michael, Rt. 3075, Batesville Rd., Woodstock, GA, 30188
Conover, Juanita Rae, P.O. Box 70442, Eugene, OR, 97401, 541-747-1726 or 543-4851, juanitaraeconover@yahoo.com
Courtnage, Elaine, Box 473, Big Sandy, MT, 59520
Cover Jr., Raymond A., Rt. 1, Box 194, Mineral Point, MO, 63660
Cox, J. Andy, 116 Robin Hood Lane, Gaffney, SC, 29340
Dietrich, Roni, Wild Horse Studio, 1257 Cottage Dr, Harrisburg, PA, 17112, 717-469-0587, ronimd@aol
DiMarzo, Richard, 2357 Center Place, Birmingham, AL, 35205
Dolbare, Elizabeth, PO Box 502, Dubois, WY, 82513-0502
Eklund, Maihkel, Föne 1111, S-82041 Färila, SWEDEN, +46 6512 4192, maihkel.eklund@swipnet.se, www.art-knives.com
Eldridge, Allan, 1424 Kansas Lane, Gallatin, TN, 37066
Ellis, Willy b, Willy B's Customs by William B Ellis, 4941 Cardinal Trail, Palm Harbor, FL, 34683, 727-942-6420, www.willyb.com
Fisk, Dale, Box 252, Council, ID, 83612, dafisk@ctcweb.net
Foster Enterprises, Norvell Foster, P.O. Box 200343, San Antonio, TX, 78220

Fountain Products, 492 Prospect Ave., West Springfield, MA, 01089

Gill, Scott, 925 N. Armstrong St., Kokomo, IN, 46901

Halligan, Ed, 14 Meadow Way, Sharpsburg, GA, 30277, ehkiss@bellsouth.net

Hands, Barry Lee, 26192 East Shore Route, Bigfork, MT, 59911

Hargraves Sr., Charles, RR 3 Bancroft, Ontario CANADA, K0L 1C0

Harless, Star, c/o Arrow Forge, P.O. Box 845, Stoneville, NC, 27048-0845

Harrington, Fred A., Summer: 2107 W Frances Rd, Mt Morris MI 48458 8215, Winter: 3725 Citrus, St. James City, FL, 33956, Winter 239-283-0721, Summer 810-686-3008

Hergert, Bob, 12 Geer Circle, Port Orford, OR, 97465, 541-332-3010, hergert@harborside.com, www.scrimshander.com

Hielscher, Vickie, 6550 Otoe Rd, P.O. Box 992, Alliance, NE, 69301, 308-762-4318, hielscher@premaonline.com

High, Tom, 5474 S. 112.8 Rd., Alamosa, CO, 81101, 719-589-2108, scrimshaw@vanion.com, www.rockymountainscrimshaw.com, Wildlife Artist

Himmelheber, David R., 11289 40th St. N., Royal Palm Beach, FL, 33411

Holland, Dennis K., 4908-17th Place, Lubbock, TX, 79416

Hutchings, Rick "Hutch", 3007 Coffe Tree Ct, Crestwood, KY, 40014, 502-241-2871, baron1@bellsouth.net

Imboden II, Howard L., 620 Deauville Dr., Dayton, OH, 45429, 937-439-1536, Guards by the "Last Wax Technic"

Johnson, Corinne, W3565 Lockington, Mindora, WI, 54644

Johnston, Kathy, W. 1134 Providence, Spokane, WA, 99205

Karst Stone, Linda, 903 Tanglewood Ln, Kerrville, TX, 78028-2945, 830-896-4678, 830-257-6117, karstone@ktc.com

Kelso, Jim, 577 Coller Hill Rd, Worcester, VT, 05682

Kirk, Susan B., 1340 Freeland Rd., Merrill, MI, 48637

Koevenig, Eugene and Eve, Koevenig's Engraving Service, Rabbit Gulch, Box 55, Hill City, SD, 57745-0055

Kostelnik, Joe and Patty, RD #4, Box 323, Greensburg, PA, 15601

Lemen, Pam, 3434 N. Iroquois Ave., Tucson, AZ, 85705

Martin, Diane, 28220 N. Lake Dr., Waterford, WI, 53185

McDonald, René Cosimini-, 14730 61 Court N., Loxahatchee, FL, 33470

McFadden, Berni, 2547 E Dalton Ave, Dalton Gardens, ID, 83815-9631

McGowan, Frank, 12629 Howard Lodge Dr., Winter Add-2023 Robin Ct Sebring FL 33870, Sykesville, MD, 21784, 863-385-1296

McGrath, Gayle, PMB 232 15201 N Cleveland Ave, N Ft Myers, FL, 33903

McLaran, Lou, 603 Powers St., Waco, TX, 76705

McWilliams, Carole, P.O. Box 693, Bayfield, CO, 81122

Mead, Faustina L., 2550 E. Mercury St., Inverness, FL, 34453-0514, 352-344-4751, scrimsha@infionline.net, www.scrimshaw-by-faustina.com

Mitchell, James, 1026 7th Ave., Columbus, GA, 31901

Moore, James B., 1707 N. Gillis, Stockton, TX, 79735

Ochonicky, Michelle "Mike", Stone Hollow Studio, 31 High Trail, Eureka, MO, 63025, 636-938-9570, www.bestofmissourihands.com

Ochs, Belle, 124 Emerald Lane, Largo, FL, 33771, 727-530-3826, chuckandbelle@juno.com, www.oxforge.com

Pachi, Mirella, Via Pometta 1, 17046 Sassello (SV), ITALY, 019 720086, WWW.PACHI-KNIVES.COM

Parish, Vaughn, 103 Cross St., Monaca, PA, 15061

Peterson, Lou, 514 S. Jackson St., Gardner, IL, 60424

Poag, James H., RR #1 Box 212A, Grayville, IL, 62844

Polk, Trena, 4625 Webber Creek Rd., Van Buren, AR, 72956

Purvis, Hilton, P.O. Box 371, Noordhoek, 7979, SOUTH AFFRIC, 27 21 789 1114, hiltonp@telkomsa.net, www.kgsa.co.za/member/hiltonpurvis

Ramsey, Richard, 8525 Trout Farm Rd, Neosho, MO, 64850

Ristinen, Lori, 14256 County Hwy 45, Menahga, MN, 56464, 218-538-6608, lori@loriristinen.com, www.loriristinen.com

Roberts, J.J., 7808 Lake Dr., Manassas, VA, 22111, 703-330-0448, jjrengraver@aol.com, www.angelfire.com/va2/engraver

Rudolph, Gil, 20922 Oak Pass Ave, Tehachapi, CA, 93561, 661-822-4949, www.gtraks@csurfers.net

Rundell, Joe, 6198 W. Frances Rd., Clio, MI, 48420

Saggio, Joe, 1450 Broadview Ave. #12, Columbus, OH, 43212, 614-481-1967, jvsaggio@earthlink.net, www.j.v.saggio@worldnet.att.net

Sahlin, Viveca, Konstvaktarevagem 9, S-772 40 Grangesberg, SWEDEN, 46 240 23204, www.scrimart.use

Satre, Robert, 518 3rd Ave. NW, Weyburn SK CANADA, S4H 1R1

Schlott, Harald, Zingster Str. 26, 13051 Berlin, 929 33 46, GERMANY, 049 030 9293346, 049 030 9293346, harald.schlott@t-online.de, www.gravur-kunst-atelier.de.vu

Schulenburg, E.W., 25 North Hill St., Carrollton, GA, 30117

Schwallie, Patricia, 4614 Old Spartanburg Rd. Apt. 47, Taylors, SC, 29687

Selent, Chuck, P.O. Box 1207, Bonners Ferry, ID, 83805

Semich, Alice, 10037 Roanoke Dr., Murfreesboro, TN, 37129

Shostle, Ben, 1121 Burlington, Muncie, IN, 47302

Sinclair, W.P., 3, The Pippins, Warminster, Wiltshire BA12 8TH, ENGLAND

Smith, Peggy, 676 Glades Rd., #3, Gatlinburg, TN, 37738

Smith, Ron, 5869 Straley, Ft. Worth, TX, 76114

Stahl, John, Images In Ivory, 2049 Windsor Rd., Baldwin, NY, 11510, 516-223-5007, imivory@msn.com, www.imagesinivory.org

Steigerwalt, Jim, RD#3, Sunbury, PA, 17801

Stuart, Stephen, 15815 Acorn Circle, Tavares, FL, 32778, 352-343-8423, (352) 343-8916, inkscratch@aol.com

Talley, Mary Austin, 2499 Countrywood Parkway, Memphis, TN, 38016, matalley@midsouth.rr.com

Thompson, Larry D., 23040 Ave. 197, Strathmore, CA, 93267

Toniutti, Nelida, Via G. Pascoli, 33085 Maniago-PN, ITALY

Tucker, Steve, 3518 W. Linwood, Turlock, CA, 95380

Tyser, Ross, 1015 Hardee Court, Spartanburg, SC, 29303

Velasquez, Gil, Art of Scrimshaw, 7120 Madera Dr., Goleta, CA, 93117

Wilderness Forge, 475 NE Smith Rock Way, Terrebonne, OR, 97760, bhatting@xpressweb.com

Williams, Gary, PO Box 210, Glendale, KY, 42740, 270-369-6752, garywilliam@alltel.net

Winn, Travis A., 558 E. 3065 S., Salt Lake City, UT, 84106

Young, Mary, 4826 Storeyland Dr., Alton, IL, 62002

## organizations

**AMERICAN BLADESMITH SOCIETY**
c/o Jan DuBois; PO Box 1481; Cypress, TX 77410-1481; 281-225-9159; Web: www.americangladesmith.com

**AMERICAN KNIFE & TOOL INSTITUTE*****
David Kowalski, Comm. Coordinator, AKTI; DEPT BL2, PO Box 432, Iola, WI 54945-0432;715-445-3781; communications@akti.org; www. akti.org

**AMERICAN KNIFE THROWERS ALLIANCE**
c/o Bobby Branton; 4976 Seewee Rd; Awendaw, SC 29429

**ART KNIFE COLLECTOR'S ASSOCIATION**
c/o Mitch Weiss, Pres.; 2211 Lee Road, Suite 104; Winter Park, FL 32789

**CALIFORNIA KNIFEMAKERS ASSOCIATION**
c/o Clint Breshears, Membership Chairman; 1261 Keats St; Manhattan Beach CA 90266; 310-372-0739; breshears@mindspring.com
*Dedicated to teaching and improving knifemaking*

**CANADIAN KNIFEMAKERS GUILD**
c/o Peter Wile; RR # 3; Bridgewater N.S. CANADA B4V 2W2; 902-543-1373; www.ckg.org

**CUTTING EDGE, THE**
1920 N 26th St; Lowell AR 72745; 479-631-0055; 479-636-4618; ce-info@cuttingedge.com
*After-market knives since 1968. We offer about 1,000 individual knives each month. The oldest and the most experienced in the business of buying and selling knives. We buy collections of any size, take knives on consignment or we will trade. Web: www.cuttingedge.com*

**JAPANESE SWORD SOCIETY OF THE U.S.**
PO Box 712; Breckenridge, TX 76424

**KNIFE COLLECTORS CLUB INC, THE**
1920 N 26th St; Lowell AR 72745; 479-631-0130; 479-631-8493; ag@agrussell.com Web:www.club@k-c-c.com
*The oldest and largest association of knife collectors. Issues limited edition knives, both handmade and highest quality production, in very limited numbers. The very earliest was the CM-1, Kentucky Rifle*

**KNIFE WORLD**
PO Box 3395; Knoxville, TN 37927; 800-828-7751; 865-397-1955; 865-397-1969; knifepub@knifeworld.com
*Publisher of monthly magazine for knife enthusiasts and world's largest knife/cutlery bookseller. Web: www.knifeworld.com*

**KNIFEMAKERS GUILD**
c/o Eugene W. Shadley, President; 26315 Norway De; Bovey, MN 55709; 218-245-1639; 218-245-1639

**KNIFEMAKERS GUILD OF SOUTHERN AFRICA, THE**
c/o Carel Smith; PO Box 1744; Delmars 2210; SOUTH AFRICA; carelsmith@therugby.co.za Web:www.kgsa.co.za

**KNIVES ILLUSTRATED**
265 S. Anita Dr., Ste. 120; Orange, CA 92868; 714-939-9991; 714-939-9909; knivesillustrated@yahoo.com; Web:www.knivesillustrated.com
*All encompassing publication focusing on factory knives, new handmades, shows and industry news, plus knifemaker features, new products, and travel pieces*

**MONTANA KNIFEMAKERS' ASSOCIATION, THE**
14440 Harpers Bridge Rd; Missoula, MT 59808; 406-543-0845
*Annual book of custom knife makers' works and directory of knife making supplies; $19.99*

**NATIONAL KNIFE COLLECTORS ASSOCIATION**
PO Box 21070; Chattanooga, TN 37424; 423-892-5007; 423-899-9456; info@nationalknife.org; Web: www.nationalknife.org

**NEO-TRIBAL METALSMITHS**
PO Box 44095; Tucson, AZ 85773-4095

**NEW ENGLAND CUSTOM KNIFE ASSOCIATION**
George R. Rebello, President; 686 Main Rd; Brownville, ME 04414; Web: www.knivesby.com/necka.html

**NORTH CAROLINA CUSTOM KNIFEMAKERS GUILD**
c/o Tommy McNabb, Pres.; 4015 Brownsboro Rd; Winston-Salem, NC 27106; tommy@tmcnabb.com; Web:www.ncknifeguild.org

**PROFESSIONAL KNIFEMAKERS ASSOCIATION**
2905 N. Montana Ave., Ste. 30027; Helena, MT 59601

**RESOURCE GUIDE AND NEWSLETTER / AUTOMATIC KNIVES**
2269 Chestnut St., Suite 212; San Francisco, CA 94123; 415-731-0210; Web: www.thenewsletter.com

**TACTICAL KNIVES**
Harris Publications; 1115 Broadway; New York, NY 10010

**TRIBAL NOW!**
Neo-Tribal Metalsmiths; PO Box 44095; Tucson, AZ 85733-4095

**WEYER INTERNATIONAL BOOK DIVISION**
2740 Nebraska Ave; Toledo, OH 43607-3245

## publications

**BLADE**
700 E. State St., Iola, WI 54990-0001; 715-445-2214; www.blademag.com
*The world's No. 1 knife magazine.*

**KNIFE WORLD**
PO Box 3395, Knoxville, TN 37927

**KNIVES ILLUSTRATED**
265 S. Anita Dr., Ste. 120, Orange, CA 92868; 714-939-9991; knivesillustrated@yahoo.com Web:www.knivesillustrated.com
*All encompassing publication focusing on factory knives, new handmades, shows and industry news*

**RESOURCE GUIDE AND NEWSLETTER / AUTOMATIC KNIVES**
2269 Chestnut St., Suite 212, San Francisco, CA 94123; 415-731-0210; Web:www.thenewsletter.com

**TACTICAL KNIVES**
Harris Publications, 1115 Broadway, New York, NY 10010

**WEYER INTERNATIONAL BOOK DIVISION**
2740 Nebraska Ave., Toledo, OH 43607-3245